textbook*plus*

Equipping Instructors and Students with
FREE RESOURCES for Core Zondervan Textbooks

Available Resources for Four Portraits, One Jesus

Teaching Resources

- Instructor's manual
- Presentation slides
- Chapter quizzes
- Image/map library
- Midterm & final exams
- Sample syllabus

Study Resources

- Chapter videos
- Quizzes
- Flashcards

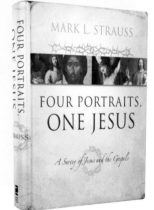

*How To Access Resources

- Go to www.ZondervanAcademic.com
- Click "Sign Up" button and complete registration process
- Find books using search field or categories navigation feature
- Click "Teaching Resources" or "Study Resources" tab once you get to book page to access resources

www.ZondervanAcademic.com

MARK L. STRAUSS

Four Portraits, One Jesus

A Survey of Jesus and the Gospels

ZONDERVAN®

ZONDERVAN

Four Portraits, One Jesus
Copyright © 2007 by Mark L. Strauss

Requests for information should be addressed to:
Zondervan, 3900 Sparks Dr. SE, Grand Rapids, Michigan 49546

Library of Congress Cataloging-in-Publication Data

Strauss, Mark L.
    Four portraits, one Jesus : a survey of Jesus and the Gospels / Mark L. Strauss.
        p. cm.
    Includes bibliographical references and index.
    ISBN 978-0-310-22697-0
    1. Bible N.T. Gospels—Criticism, interpretations, etc. 2. Jesus Christ—Person and offices.
    I. Title.
    BS2555.52.S86 2007
    266'.061—dc22
                                        2005034280

Interior design: Tracey Walker
Composition: Tracey Walker and Sherri Hoffman
Maps by International Mapping. Copyright © 2010 by Zondervan. All rights reserved.

Printed in Hong Kong

---

18 19 20 21 22 23 24 25 /PEH/ 30 29 28 27 26 25 24 23 22 21 20 19 18 17 16

Contents

List of Abbreviations 17
Introduction 19

PART ONE: INTRODUCTION TO THE FOUR GOSPELS

1. What Are the Gospels? 23
2. Exploring the Origin and Nature of the Gospels: Historical-Critical Methods of Gospel Research . . . 43
3. Reading and Hearing the Gospel Stories: Literary-Critical Methods of Gospel Research 67

PART TWO: THE SETTING OF THE GOSPELS

4. The Historical Setting of the Gospels 93
5. The Religious Setting: First-Century Judaism. 123
6. The Social and Cultural Setting of the Gospels 149

PART THREE: THE FOUR GOSPELS

7. Mark: The Gospel of the Suffering Son of God 171
8. Matthew: The Gospel of the Messiah 213
9. Luke: The Gospel of the Savior for All People. 259
10. John: The Gospel of the Son Who Reveals the Father 297

PART FOUR: THE HISTORICAL JESUS

11. Searching for the Real Jesus 347
12. The Historical Reliability of the Gospels 383
13. The Contours and Chronology of Jesus' Ministry. 399
14. Jesus' Birth and Childhood. 411
15. The Beginning of Jesus' Ministry 425
16. The Message of Jesus. 435
17. The Miracles of Jesus 455
18. The Messianic Words and Actions of Jesus 469
19. The Death of Jesus 493
20. The Resurrection of Jesus 511

Conclusion 525
Glossary 526
Index. 541

Contents

List of Abbreviations 17
Introduction 19

PART ONE: INTRODUCTION TO THE FOUR GOSPELS

1. What Are the Gospels? **23**

Four Gospels, One Jesus 24
The Synoptic Gospels and the Gospel of John 25
The Gospel Genre 25
    The Gospels Are Historical Literature 27
    The Gospels Are Narrative Literature 28
    The Gospels Are Theological Literature 29
Why Were the Gospels Written? 30
The Gospel Audiences: To Whom Were the Gospels Written? 31
Why *Four* Gospels? 32
Why *Only* Four Gospels? 32
Reading the Gospels Today 32
    Reading "Vertically": Following the Storyline 32
    Reading "Horizontally": Comparing Their Accounts 34
    When Is a Harmony Legitimate? 35
    Conclusion 35
Addendum: Sources for Information about Jesus outside of the Gospels 38
    The Letters of Paul 38
    Greco-Roman Sources 38
    Flavius Josephus 39
    Later Jewish Sources 40
    Apocryphal Gospels 40
    Conclusion 42

2. Exploring the Origin and Nature of the Gospels:
   Historical-Critical Methods of Gospel Research **43**

How the Gospels Came to Be: The Development of the Gospel Tradition 44
Source Criticism and the Synoptic Problem 46
    Why Are the Three Synoptic Gospels So Similar? 46
    Traditional Solutions to the Synoptic Problem 47
    Markan Priority and the Two- and Four-Source Theories 48
    Matthean Priority: The Griesbach or Two-Gospel Hypothesis 53
    Conclusion: Some Observations and Cautions on the Synoptic Problem 54

Form Criticism: Seeking the Spoken Word behind the Written Word 55
    Method of Form Criticism 55
    Assessment of Form Criticism 58
Redaction Criticism: Studying the Evangelists as Purposeful Editors 60
    The Method of Redaction Criticism 61
    Assessment of Redaction Criticism 62

3. Reading and Hearing the Gospel Stories:
    Literary-Critical Methods of Gospel Research **67**

Narrative Criticism: The Gospels as Story 68
    The Storyteller 69
    Narrative World and Evaluative Point of View 69
    The Story Receiver 70
    Plot: The Progress of the Narrative 71
    Characters 73
    Setting 74
    Rhetoric: Narrative Patterns and Literary Devices 76
    Assessment of Narrative Criticism 78
Other Literary Methods 79
    Rhetorical Criticism 79
    Canon Criticism 80
    Structuralism 81
    Reader-Response Criticism 82
    Liberationist and Feminist Approaches 83
    Deconstruction 83
The Approach of This Text 84

PART TWO: THE SETTING OF THE GOSPELS

4. The Historical Setting of the Gospels **93**

The Persian Period (539 – 334 BC) 94
The Greek Period (334 – 166 BC) 95
    Alexander the Great and the Hellenization of Palestine 95
    Ptolemaic Domination of Israel (323 – 198 BC) 98
    Seleucid Domination of Palestine (198 – 166 BC) 100
The Maccabees and Jewish Independence (166 – 63 BC) 101
    The Maccabean Revolt (166 – 135 BC) 101
    The Hasmonean Dynasty (135 – 63 BC) 102
The Roman Period (63 BC – AD 135) 104
    Herod the Great 105
    The Herodian Dynasty 108

Roman Rule and the Pax Romana 110
The Jewish Revolt of AD 66 – 73 114
After the War 116

5. The Religious Setting: First-Century Judaism **123**

Core Jewish Beliefs 124
Monotheism 124
The Covenant: Israel as God's Chosen People 124
The Law (Torah): Standards for Covenant Faithfulness 124
Temple, Priesthood, and Sacrifices 125
One Temple for the One True God 125
Levites and Priests 128
The High Priest 128
The Sanhedrin 128
Synagogues, Scribes, and the Study of Torah 129
Synagogue Worship 129
Scribes 130
Groups within Judaism 131
Sadducees 131
Pharisees 132
Essenes 135
Zealots, Social Bandits, and Other Revolutionaries 136
Herodians 138
People of the Land (Am-ha-Eretz) 138
Trends in First-Century Judaism 138
Apocalypticism 138
Messianic Expectation 139
Literary Sources for First-Century Jewish Life 140
Josephus 140
Philo 140
The Dead Sea Scrolls 140
The Apocrypha 141
The Pseudepigrapha 143
Rabbinic Writings 143

6. The Social and Cultural Setting of the Gospels **149**

Daily Life in New Testament Times 150
The Family 150
Food and Meals 152
Clothing and Style 154
Villages, Towns, and Cities 155
Work, Trades, and Professions 157

Commerce, Transportation, and Communication. 159
Entertainment and Leisure 160
Social Values 161
Group Rather Than Individual Mentality. 161
Honor and Shame 161
Family and Kinship 163
Hospitality 163
Social Status and Position in Life 164
Patronage. 164

PART THREE: THE FOUR GOSPELS

7. Mark: The Gospel of the Suffering Son of God **171**

Literary Features 173
Literary Style 173
Topical Ordering of Events 174
Intercalation or "Sandwiching". 174
Triads or Sets of Threes 177
Irony 177
The Plot of Mark's Gospel 178
The Beginning of the Gospel: The Preparation of the Son of God (1:1 – 13) 178
The Authoritative Ministry of the Son of God (1:14 – 8:26). 179
The Suffering of the Son of God as Servant of the LORD (8:27 – 16:8) 183
Mark's Portrait of Jesus: The Suffering Son of God 193
Other Characters in Mark's Gospel 196
The Antagonists: Satan's Forces and the Religious Leaders. 196
The Disciples: Antagonists or Protagonists? 197
"Minor" Characters 198
Theological Themes. 199
The Kingdom of God 199
Jesus the Servant-Messiah 200
Discipleship: Following the Servant's Suffering Path. 200
Narrative Purpose 201
The Historical Setting of Mark's Gospel: Author and Life Setting 201
Authorship 201
Setting and Occasion 202
Reading Mark Today 205

8. Matthew: The Gospel of the Messiah **213**

Literary Features 215
Concise Style 216
Fulfillment Formulas and Old Testament Quotations 216

    Topical Arrangement 218
    Structural Signals and Matthew's "Outline" 219
The Plot of Matthew's Gospel 220
    Prologue: The Genealogy and Birth Narrative (Chaps. 1–2) 220
    The Appearance of the Messiah (3:1–4:11) 225
    The Ministry of the Messiah to Israel (4:12–11:1) 227
    The Responses to the Messiah: Rejection by Israel, Acceptance by the Disciples (11:2–20:34) 230
    The Messiah Confronts Jerusalem (21:1–26:1). 232
    The Messiah Is Rejected: Arrest, Trial, and Crucifixion (Chaps. 26–27) 235
    The Messiah Is Vindicated: The Resurrection and the Great Commission (Chap. 28). 238
Matthew's Portrait of Jesus: The Messiah. 239
    Jesus the Messiah. 239
    Immanuel: The Presence and Wisdom of God 240
    Jesus the Son of God 241
Other Characters in Matthew's Gospel 242
    The Disciples 242
    Peter among the Disciples 243
    The Religious Leaders 245
    The Crowds 245
Theological Themes. 245
    Promise-Fulfillment and the Climax of Salvation History 245
    The Kingdom of Heaven 246
    Jesus and the Law. 247
Narrative and Theological Purpose 248
The Historical Setting of Matthew's Gospel: Author and Life Setting. 249
    Audience and Occasion. 249
    Place and Date. 251
    Authorship 252
Reading Matthew Today 253

9. Luke: The Gospel of the Savior for All People **259**

Literary Features 261
    The Unity of Luke and Acts 261
    Luke's Sources. 262
    Literary Style 262
    Historiography 262
    The Travel Narrative or Journey to Jerusalem 262
The Plot of Luke's Gospel 263
    The Prologue (1:1–4). 263
    The Birth of the Savior (1:5–2:52) 264
    The Preparation of the Savior (3:1–4:13) 267
    The Galilean Ministry of the Savior (4:14–9:50). 269
    The Mission of the Savior: The Journey to Jerusalem (9:51–19:27). 273

    The Savior in Jerusalem: Conflict and Controversy (19:28–21:38) 275
    The Passion of the Savior in Jerusalem (22:1–23:56) 277
    The Resurrection and Ascension of the Savior (24:1–53) 279
Luke's Portrait of Jesus: The Savior for All People 281
    Prophet Like Moses, Mighty in Word and Deed 281
    Christ the Lord 282
Other Characters in Luke's Gospel 282
    Apostles in Training 282
    The Religious Leaders 283
Theological Themes 284
    Promise-Fulfillment: The Salvation of God 284
    The Dawn of Salvation and the Coming of the Spirit 285
    Divine Sovereignty and the Purpose of God 286
    Salvation for Outsiders: A New Age of Reversals 286
    Jerusalem and the Temple: Settings of Rejection and Salvation 287
    Joy, Praise, and Celebration 288
    Prayer and Intimate Fellowship with the Father 289
The Historical Setting of Luke's Gospel: Author and Life Setting 289
    Authorship 289
    Date 290
    Occasion and Narrative Purpose 290
Reading Luke Today 291

10. John: The Gospel of the Son Who Reveals the Father **297**

Literary Features 298
    Unique Content 298
    Unique Literary Style 299
    The Relationship of John to the Synoptics 301
    Two Historical Settings, Two Levels of Meaning 301
    Structure 301
    Teaching Types: Personal Interviews, Public Debate, and Private Teaching 302
    The "Signs" of the Gospel 303
    Metaphor and Symbol 303
    Irony 304
The Plot of John's Gospel 305
    The Prologue (1:1–18) 305
    The Book of Signs (1:19–12:50) 307
    The Book of Glory (13:1–20:31) 322
    Epilogue (21:1–25) 327
John's Portrait of Jesus: The Son Who Reveals the Father 328
Other Characters in John's Gospel 329
    The Disciples 329

The Antagonists: The Religious Leaders, "the World," and Satan 329

Minor Characters 330

Theological Themes 330

The Revelation of the Father through the Son 330

Salvation as Knowing God, Eternal Life in the Present 331

The Paraclete 331

Narrative Purpose 332

The Historical Setting of John's Gospel: Author and Life Setting 332

Authorship 332

The Composition of the Gospel: A Johannine Community? 334

Place, Occasion, and Date 335

Reading John Today 337

PART FOUR: THE HISTORICAL JESUS

11. Searching for the Real Jesus 347

The Historical Quests for Jesus 348

The First Quest: The Nineteenth-Century Quest for the Historical Jesus 348

No Quest: Rudolf Bultmann and the End of the First Quest 350

The New (Second) Quest and the Post-Bultmannians (1953 – 1970s) 356

The Contemporary Scene: A Third Quest? 358

Questions of Method and Context 359

The Results: Contemporary Portraits of Jesus 365

Conclusion 378

12. The Historical Reliability of the Gospels 383

The Role of Presuppositions in Historical Research 384

Were the Gospel Writers Biased? 385

The Burden of Proof 385

Luke-Acts and Ancient History Writing 385

A Generally Reliable Gospel Tradition 386

The Testimony of the Eyewitnesses 387

The Faithful Transmission of the Gospel Tradition 387

The Church's Willingness to Preserve Difficult Sayings 387

The Distinction between the Words of Jesus and of Christian Prophets 387

The Absence of Discussion on Key Issues in the Later Church 387

The Ethical Argument: Were the Disciples Deceivers? 388

Contradictions between the Gospels? 388

Paraphrasing and Interpretation 388

Abbreviation and Omission 389

Reordering of Events and Sayings 390

Reporting Similar Events and Sayings 391
The Historical Reliability of John 392
The Author as Eyewitness 392
Alleged Contradictions with the Synoptics 393
John's Style and the Words of Jesus 394
The Christology of John. 395
Conclusion: The Gospels as History *and* Theology 395

13. The Contours and Chronology of Jesus' Ministry **399**

Basic Contours of Jesus' Ministry 400
A Portrait of Jesus from Afar 400
The General Progress of Jesus' Ministry 404
A Chronology of Jesus' Life 405
The Date of Jesus' Birth 405
The Date of Jesus' Ministry 406
The Date of Jesus' Crucifixion 408

14. Jesus' Birth and Childhood **411**

The Genre of the Birth Narratives: History or Fiction? 412
The Ancestry of Jesus. 412
The Virginal Conception 415
Bethlehem Birthplace. 416
The Census 416
The Birth of Jesus 417
Jesus' Family Life. 419

15. The Beginning of Jesus' Ministry **425**

John the Baptist, Herald of Messianic Salvation 426
The Baptism of Jesus 429
The Temptation of Jesus 430

16. The Message of Jesus **435**

Jesus the Teacher 436
Jesus' Central Message: The Kingdom of God. 438
The Jewish Background 438
Jesus and the Kingdom 438
Jesus and the Law: The Ethics of the Kingdom 441
The True Essence of the Law 441
Jesus as Fulfillment of the Law 442
The Greatest Commandment and the Character of God. 444
Grace and Works: The Free Gift and the Cost of Discipleship. 445

List of Abbreviations

1QS	*Rule of the Community* (Qumran scroll)
1QSa	*Rule of the Congregation* (Qumran scroll; 1Q28)
4QFlor	*Florilegium* (Qumran scroll; 4Q174)
4QpsDan⁹ar	*Pseudo-Daniel ar* (Qumran scroll; 4Q243)
ABD	*The Anchor Bible Dictionary.* Edited by David Noel Freedman. 6 vols. New York: Doubleday, 1992.
ABRL	Anchor Bible Reference Library
ANRW	*Aufstieg und Niedergang der römischen Welt: Geschichte und Kultur Roms im Spiegel der neueren Forschung.* Edited by H. Temporini and W. Haase. Berlin: Walter de Gruyter, 1972–.
Ant.	Josephus, *Jewish Antiquities*
b. B. Bat.	Babylonian Talmud *Baba Batra*
b. Ber.	Babylonian Talmud *Berakot*
b. Sanh.	Babylonian Talmud *Sanhedrin*
b. Sukkah	Babylonian Talmud *Sukkah*
c.	*circa,* "about"
CD	Cairo Genizah copy of the *Damascus Document*
chap.	chapter
ConBNT	Coniectanea neotestamentica or Coniectanea biblica: New Testament Series
DJG	*Dictionary of Jesus and the Gospels*, eds. Joel B. Green, Scot McKnight, and I. Howard Marshall (Downers Grove, IL: InterVarsity, 1992).
DNTB	*Dictionary of New Testament Background*, Craig A. Evans and Stanley E. Porter, eds. (Downers Grove, IL: InterVarsity, 2000).
ed.	editor
GBS	Guides to Biblical Scholarship
JAAR	*Journal of the American Academy of Religion*
JBL	*Journal of Biblical Literature*
JSOT	*Journal for the Study of the Old Testament*
JSNTSup	Journal for the Study of the New Testament: Supplement Series
J.W.	Josephus, *Jewish War*
m. ʾAbot	Mishnah *ʾAbot*
m. Demai	Mishnah *Demai*
m. Giṭ.	Mishnah *Gittin*
m. Ḥag.	Mishnah *Ḥagiga*

m. Ned.	Mishnah *Nedarim*
m. Sanh.	Mishnah *Sanhedrin*
m. Šabb.	Mishnah *Šabbat*
m. Šeqal.	Mishnah *Šeqalim*
m. Sukk.	Mishnah *Sukka*
m. Taʿan.	Mishnah *Taʿanit*
NIDNTT	*New International Dictionary of New Testament Theology.* Edited by C. Brown. 4 vols. Grand Rapids: Zondervan, 1975–1985.
NovTSup	Novum Testamentum Supplements
NTS	*New Testament Studies*
p.	page
par.	parallel passage
Pss. Sol.	*Psalms of Solomon*
SBL	Society of Biblical Literature
Sir.	Sirach
SNT	Studien zum Neuen Testament
SNTSMS	Society for New Testament Studies Monograph Series
Tob.	Tobit
tr.	translator
T. Sol.	*Testament of Solomon*
TynBul	*Tyndale Bulletin*
v.	verse
WUNT	Wissenschaftliche Untersuchungen zum Neuen Testament
y. Sanh.	Jerusalem Talmud *Sanhedrin*
y. Taʿan.	Jerusalem Talmud *Taʿanit*

   Pilate and the Romans 494
   Jewish Opposition 497
Jesus' Perspective on His Coming Death 503
   Did Jesus Foresee His Death? 503
   The Significance of Jesus' Death 504

20. The Resurrection of Jesus **511**

Rationalistic Explanations for the Resurrection 512
   The Swoon Theory 512
   The Wrong Tomb Theory 514
   The Theft Theory 515
   Visionary and Legendary Development Theories. 516
Historical Evidence for the Resurrection 518
   Jesus Was Crucified by the Romans around AD 30 518
   Jesus Was Buried in the Tomb of Joseph of Arimathea. 518
   The Tomb Was Discovered Empty on the Third Day 518
   Many Credible Witnesses Saw Jesus Alive. 520
   The Transformed Lives of the Disciples 521
The Significance of the Resurrection 521
   The Jewish Background 521
   The Significance of the Resurrection for Jesus and the Church. 522

   Conclusion 525
   Glossary 526
   Index 541

Social Justice: The Rich and the Poor 446
The Parables of the Kingdom. 447
    The Nature of Parables. 447
    The Purpose of the Parables: To Reveal and to Conceal. 448
    Interpreting the Parables. 449

17. The Miracles of Jesus **455**

The Question of Miracles 456
    Philosophical Objections to Miracles 456
    Miracles and the Historical Method. 457
Did Jesus Perform Miracles? 458
Ancient Parallels to Jesus' Miracles 459
The Significance of Jesus' Miracles: The Power and Presence of the Kingdom 461
    Exorcisms. 461
    Healings. 462
    Raising the Dead 463
    Nature Miracles 464
Conclusion. 466

18. The Messianic Words and Actions of Jesus **469**

The Authority of Jesus. 470
    Announcing and Inaugurating the Kingdom 470
    Authority over Demons and Disease. 470
    Authority to Speak for God: Jesus' Use of Amēn ("Truly" I Say to You). 471
    Authority over the Law and the Sabbath 471
    Authority to Forgive Sins 472
    Authority at the Final Judgment 473
The Aims of Jesus 473
    Calling Disciples: A New Community of Faith. 474
    Dining with Sinners: The Universal Offer of the Kingdom 477
    Jesus and the Gentiles: Salvation for All Humanity 478
    The "Triumphal Entry" 479
    Cleansing the Temple 480
The Messianic Titles 481
    Christ (Messiah). 481
    Son of Man 483
    Son of God. 485
    Lord. 487
    Jesus as God? 488

19. The Death of Jesus **493**

Historical Circumstances of the Death of Jesus. 494

Introduction

Congratulations! You are about to embark on a study of the most important person in human history. To Christian believers, the Gospels record the "greatest story ever told," the events of the life, death, and resurrection of Jesus, the Messiah. They narrate the climax and turning point of human history, when God acted decisively to achieve salvation for people everywhere. To study the Gospels is to study the foundation of Christianity.

Even to those who do not follow Jesus as their Lord, the Gospels serve as the primary source documents for information about the most influential life ever lived. Jesus of Nazareth has been the topic of more books, movies, discussions, and debates than any person in history. Even our calendar is dated from the beginning of this man's life. Millions have dedicated their lives to serving him. Countless thousands have died as martyrs for his cause. Great good has been done in his name, from feeding the poor, to educating children, to providing medical aid and developmental assistance to impoverished nations. Great evil has also been done, from crusades of conquest, to the slaughter of innocent people, to the torture of those labeled heretics.

But who was this man Jesus, and how did his movement begin? In this textbook, we will examine the nature and content of the four Gospels, the primary source documents on the life and ministry of Jesus of Nazareth. Where did these books come from? What was their purpose? What can they tell us about Jesus? These are the questions we will seek to answer.

This book is an introductory survey. Part 1 (chaps. 1–3) provides information concerning the nature of the Gospels and methods which have been developed for their study. Part 2 (chaps. 4–6) is concerned with the historical, religious, and cultural background to the Gospels—their first-century setting. Part 3 (chaps. 7–10) is a study of the four Gospels as narrative literature—their content, themes, and theology. Finally, part 4 (chaps. 11–20) turns to the question of the historical Jesus, examining the Jesus quests of the last three centuries, the historical reliability of the Gospels, and the life and teachings of Jesus of Nazareth. Because this is an introductory survey, I have avoided cluttering the text with excessive footnotes. Instead, bibliographies at the end of each chapter direct the student to resources for further study.

No one approaches history as an unbiased observer, and it would be naive to assume that this textbook could be written without presuppositions or a point of view. It is appropriate, therefore, to state my own. My goal is to produce a text which is both methodologically critical and confessionally evangelical. The text is critical in that it seeks to utilize the best literary and historical tools and resources available today. I have also tried to present the data in a fair and balanced manner, without glossing over problems or selectively manipulating results. The text is evangelical in that it is written from the perspective of one who confesses Jesus as Lord, and who believes that these Gospels are not merely human documents but the inspired and authoritative Word of God. While I will seek not to let these assumptions bias a critical analysis, it is unnecessary and even inappropriate to deny them. Indeed, adopting the same evangelical mindset of the Evangelists (the Gospel writers) will allow us to more fully enter their world, and to hear the gospel story as it was intended to be heard—as the good news of salvation achieved through the life, death, and resurrection of Jesus the Messiah.

I am most grateful to the scholars and friends who have read through parts or all of this text and have offered many insights and suggestions, especially Frank Thielman, Gary Burge, Jeannine Brown, and Donald Verseput. Don's untimely death in 2004 was a great loss to family, friends, and New Testament scholarship in general. I am also grateful to the hundreds of students who have used the work in draft form and have served as my informal editors. Particularly noteworthy in this regard were Marci Ford, Bill Zettinger, Janice Raymond, and Mike Anderson. Finally, I want to thank those at Zondervan who labored with me to bring this work to fruition, especially Stan Gundry (who first approached me about its writing), Jack Kuhatschek, Katya Covrett, and Brian Phipps.

PART ONE

Introduction to the Four Gospels

CHAPTER 1

What Are the Gospels?

» **CHAPTER OVERVIEW** «

1. Four Gospels, One Jesus
2. The Synoptic Gospels and the Gospel of John
3. The Gospel Genre
4. Why Were the Gospels Written?
5. The Gospel Audiences: To Whom Were the Gospels Written?
6. Why *Four* Gospels?
7. Why *Only* Four Gospels?
8. Reading the Gospels Today
   Addendum: Sources for Information about Jesus outside of the Gospels

» **OBJECTIVES** «

After reading this chapter, you should be able to:

- Describe the genre of the Gospels as history, narrative, and theology.
- Explain why there are four Gospels.
- Explain what it means to read "vertically" and "horizontally" through the Gospels.
- Discuss the benefits and potential liabilities of harmonizing the Gospels.

FOUR GOSPELS, ONE JESUS

When my oldest son was two years old, we took him to a portrait studio to have his picture taken. Two-year-olds are a bundle of emotions, and getting them to sit still through a photo shoot is a real challenge. During that short session, my son went through a range of moods, from contentment, to laughter, to pouting, to anger, to tears. I remember getting the proofs afterward. The first showed him serenely content, smiling at the camera. In the second, he was laughing delightedly as the photographer waved a stuffed animal in his face. In the next, he was beginning to get bored and had put on a cute little pout. The fourth showed him downright angry, with a defiant "just try to make me smile" look on his face. By the last shot, he had dissolved into tears. The poor little guy had had enough. Which of these pictures captured my son's personality? The answer, of course, is all of them! Each one caught a different side of his multifaceted personality. Together they give us an insightful glimpse into who he is.

> The four unique Gospels testify to the one gospel — the good news of salvation available through Jesus the Messiah.

This little story is a good analogy for the New Testament Gospels. Each of the four Gospels—**Matthew, Mark, Luke,** and **John**—paints a unique portrait of Jesus Christ. Each provides special insight into who he is and what he accomplished. The Gospels exhibit both **unity and diversity**, bearing witness to the same Jesus (unity) but viewing him from unique perspectives (diversity). What are these four unique portraits? At the risk of oversimplifying, we may say that Matthew presents Jesus as the *Jewish* **Messiah**, the fulfillment of Old Testament hopes; Mark portrays him as the *suffering* **Son of God**, who offers himself as a sacrifice for sins; Luke's Jesus is the *Savior for all people*, who brings salvation to all nations and people groups; and in John, Jesus is the *eternal Son of God*, the self-revelation of God the Father. These are not contradictory portraits but complementary ones. Having four Gospels gives us a deeper, more profound understanding of **Christology**—the nature of Jesus' person and work.

Figure 1.1—Four Portraits of the One Jesus			
Matthew	**Mark**	**Luke**	**John**
The Gospel of the Messiah	The Gospel of the suffering Son of God	The Gospel of the Savior for all people	The Gospel of the divine Son who reveals the Father
Most structured	Most dramatic	Most thematic	Most theological

Not only are the Gospels unique in their portraits of Jesus, they are also unique in their presentations. Mark is the most *dramatic* of the four, a powerful and vivid story which grips the reader from beginning to end. Matthew is the most *structured* of the Gospels, crafted around five carefully ordered teaching sections. Luke is the most *thematic*, with themes like God's love for the lost, the role of the Spirit, and Jerusalem's role in God's plan resurfacing again and again. John's is the most *theological* of the four, with more explicit statements concerning Jesus' identity and purpose. We should add that all of the Gospels are all of these things—dramatic, structured, thematic, and theological—but there are important differences in emphasis.

THE SYNOPTIC GOSPELS AND THE GOSPEL OF JOHN

There are also degrees of diversity among the Gospels. The first three—Matthew, Mark, and Luke—are known as the **Synoptic Gospels** (from the Greek *synopsis*, meaning "viewed together") because they view the life and ministry of Jesus from a similar perspective, follow the same general outline, and record a great deal of common material. The Gospel of John presents a strikingly different perspective. The author of the Fourth Gospel omits much material found in the Synoptics and includes much unique material. John also writes with a different style and dwells more on the theological significance of Jesus' words and deeds. Scholars debate whether the author knew the Synoptic Gospels and supplemented them or was writing independently of them. We will discuss this issue in more detail in our introduction to the Fourth Gospel.

Figure 1.2—The Synoptics and John	
Synoptic Gospels (Matthew, Mark, Luke)	**Gospel of John**
1. Emphasize the Galilean setting of the first part of Jesus' ministry	1. Considerable movement between Galilee and Judea
2. Little information given to determine the length of Jesus' ministry; material could fit into a single year	2. Mentions at least three different Passover feasts (2:13; 6:4; 13:1), and so a ministry of 2½ to 3½ years
3. Jesus teaches mostly in parables, short sayings, and epigrams	3. Relates long speeches by Jesus, dialogues with his opponents, and interviews with individuals
4. Teaching focuses on the kingdom of God; healings and exorcisms demonstrate the power of the kingdom and the dawn of eschatological salvation	4. Teaching focuses on Jesus himself and the Son's revelation of the Father. Signs or miracles reveal Jesus' identity and glorify the Father; no exorcisms

THE GOSPEL GENRE

The first question readers must ask when approaching any literature is, What am I reading? This is the question of **genre**, or type of literature. If I pick up a newspaper and read, "The President prepares to address Congress," I recognize this as a news report and expect to read factual information. On the other hand, if I pick up a book and read, "Once upon a time,

Figure 1.3—The Background to the Term *Gospel*

The English term *gospel* comes from the Old English *godspell*, a translation of the Greek noun *euangelion*, meaning "good tidings" or "good news." *Euangelion* was used in the Greek world for the announcement of good news, such as victory in battle, or for the enthronement of a Roman ruler. An inscription for the birthday of the Roman emperor Augustus reads, "Good news [*euangelia*] to the world!"

In the Old Testament, the announcement of God's end-time deliverance of his people is sometimes referred to as "good news." Isaiah 52:7 reads, "How beautiful on the mountains are the feet of those who bring good news … who proclaim salvation, who say to Zion, 'Your God reigns!'" (cf. Isa. 40:9; 61:1; Ps. 96:2). Jesus probably drew from this Old Testament background when he began preaching that God's day of salvation had arrived: "The time has come…. The kingdom of God is near. Repent and believe the good news!" (Mark 1:15; cf. Luke 4:18).

Though Jesus was probably speaking Aramaic, the early church translated his words into Greek and *euangelion* soon became a technical term for the good news about Jesus Christ. In 1 Thessalonians, one of the earliest New Testament letters (c. AD 50 – 51), Paul writes that "our *gospel* came to you not simply with words, but also with power, with the Holy Spirit and with deep conviction" (1 Thess. 1:5, emphasis added). Here Paul uses *euangelion* of the spoken word, the oral proclamation of the good news about Jesus Christ.

In time, *euangelion* came to be applied not only to the oral preaching but also to the written versions of the good news about Jesus Christ. Mark introduces his work with the words, "The beginning of *the gospel* about Jesus Christ, the Son of God" (Mark 1:1, emphasis added), and the church soon came to call these works Gospels. This tells us something about the way they viewed them. These were not dry historical accounts of the life of Christ but written versions of the oral proclamation. The Gospels have a living and dynamic quality, calling people to faith in Jesus. The Gospels were meant to be proclaimed … and to be believed.

Different kinds of literature (genres) require different reading strategies.

there were three bears," I know I am reading a fairy tale. I am not concerned about whether these bears actually existed, what country they were from, or whether they were grizzlies or brown bears. I read to be entertained and, perhaps, to look for moral lessons. In cases like these, we identify genre easily. But identification is not always so easy, and it is possible to misidentify literary genres. One person standing in a grocery-store checkout line may read the *National Enquirer* headline "Aliens Invade Los Angeles" and fear that they are in mortal danger. Another identifies the genre as entertainment tabloid and chuckles. Identifying genre is essential for both interpretation and application.

To understand the Gospels, we must first ask, *What are we reading?* What kind of documents are these and what sort of information are they meant to convey? Are they historical accounts meant to pass on factual information, or are they theological documents meant to teach spiritual truths? Or are they both? The identification of genre enables us to answer these questions. The genre of the Gospels may be examined under three headings: *history*, *narrative*, and *theology*.

The Gospels Are Historical Literature

The Gospels are historical in at least three ways. First, *they have a history of composition.* The authors drew on traditions and sources available to them to compile their works. The methods used to determine how the Gospels came to be are collectively known as *historical criticism*, or the *historical-critical method*. In the next chapter, we will examine types of historical criticism: source criticism, form criticism, and redaction criticism.

Second, the Gospels are historical in that *they are set in a specific historical context.* This setting is first-century **Palestine** during the period of Roman occupation. To understand the Gospels, we must enter into the world in which they were written, a world very different than our own. In part 2 (chaps. 4–6), we will examine the historical, religious, and cultural settings of the Gospels.

Third, the Gospels are historical in that *they are meant to convey accurate historical information.* This is implicit in all four Gospels and is explicitly stated by John (21:24) and Luke. Luke leaves no doubt that he intends to write history:

> Many have undertaken to draw up an account of the things that have been fulfilled among us, just as they were handed down to us by those who from the first were eyewitnesses and servants of the word. Therefore, since I myself have carefully investigated everything from the beginning, it seemed good also to me to write an orderly account for you, most excellent Theophilus, so that you may know the certainty of the things you have been taught.
>
> —Luke 1:1–4

Notice the author's piling up of terms of historical veracity. Luke certainly claimed to be writing accurate history. Of course, one could question whether Luke was a reliable historian or whether his sources were reliable. We will examine these questions in part 4. The point here is that Luke's intentions were historical.

The fact that the Gospels are historical in this third sense has profound implications for Christianity as a religion. The faith of the Gospel writers is based not on the esoteric teachings of a first-century philosopher nor on religious myths with symbolic meaning. It is based on the historical person and work of Jesus Christ. The Gospels claim to be the record of God's actions in human history, his entrance into human history in the person of his Son. As an essentially historical religion, Christianity rises or falls on the historicity of core Gospel events: (1) Jesus' words and deeds, (2) his death on the cross, and (3) his resurrection, the vindication of his claims. As the apostle Paul wrote with reference to Jesus' resurrection, "If Christ has not been raised, our preaching is useless and so is your faith" (1 Cor. 15:14). For Paul, as for the Gospel writers, the historicity of these events confirms the truth of Christianity.

The Gospels Are Narrative Literature

Although historical in nature, the Gospels are not merely collections of reports or sayings of the historical Jesus. They are also narratives with features typical of stories, including plot, characters, and setting. While all four Gospels are concerned with the same historical events—the life, death, and resurrection of Jesus Christ—they present different versions of these events. They present characters from different perspectives. They develop plot in different ways. They emphasize different settings. Viewing the Gospels as narratives provides important insights into their literary and theological distinctions. In chapter 3, we will examine narrative criticism and other literary approaches to the Gospels.

Figure 1.4—The Gospel Genre
Ancient Biographies?

A vigorous debate has taken place over the last century concerning the Gospel genre and its relationship to other ancient literature. Some scholars have held that the Gospels are unique in the ancient world, a genre created by the early Christians. This view was particularly popular among the form critics (we will discuss them in the next chapter), who considered the Gospels to be nonliterary collections of oral traditions, or folk literature. The Gospels were treated as products of the Christian community rather than of individual authors.

The last quarter century has seen much greater emphasis on the Gospels as literary works. It is recognized that the Gospel writers were not merely collectors of traditions but literary artists crafting their narratives. This has generated renewed interest in the literary features of the Gospels and their relationship to other ancient genres.

There is a consensus growing among scholars today that while the Gospels have many unique features, they also have much in common with Greco-Roman works, especially the broad category of writings known as "biographies" (*bioi*), or "lives." These writings were written to preserve the memory and celebrate the virtues, teachings, or exploits of famous philosophers, statesmen, or rulers. Examples of this category are Plutarch's *Parallel Lives*, Suetonius's *Lives of the Caesars*, and Jewish philosopher Philo's *Life of Moses*. Since the Gospels arose in the Greco-Roman world of the first century, it is profitable to compare them with other writings of this era, identifying common literary features and narrative techniques.

At the same time, the uniqueness of the Gospels must be kept in mind. They arose in the context of the needs and concerns of the early Christian communities, and in the preaching and teaching of the good news. The Gospels were not meant simply to preserve the memory or pass on the teachings of a great leader. They were written to proclaim the good news of salvation and to call people to faith in Jesus Christ, the risen Lord and Savior.

For more details, see Richard A. Burridge, *What Are the Gospels? A Comparison with Graeco-Roman Biography,* 2nd ed. (Grand Rapids: Eerdmans, 2004).

The Gospels Are Theological Literature

While the Gospels are meant to be historical, they are more than unbiased news reports. They are theological documents written to instruct and encourage believers and to convince unbelievers of the truth of their message. This is evident in that they focus especially on the saving work accomplished through the life, death, and resurrection of Jesus Christ. This is why we call the Gospel writers **Evangelists** (from *euangelizō*, "to announce good news"). They are proclaimers of the good news about Jesus Christ and the coming of the **kingdom of God**.

Notice John's statement of intent in John 20:30–31:

> Jesus did many other miraculous signs in the presence of his disciples, which are not recorded in this book. But these are written that you may believe that Jesus is the Christ, the Son of God, and that by believing you may have life in his name.

The recognition that the Gospel writers are theologians in their own right is one of the most important contributions of recent Gospel research. Each Evangelist has a story to tell and a perspective to emphasize. Each brings out certain aspects of Jesus' identity. Notice the unique way each introduces his work:

Matthew 1:1	Mark 1:1	Luke 1:3	John 1:1
"A record of the genealogy of Jesus Christ the son of David, the son of Abraham."	"The beginning of the gospel about Jesus Christ, the Son of God."	"Since I myself have carefully investigated everything from the beginning, it seemed good also to me to write an orderly account."	"In the beginning was the Word, and the Word was with God, and the Word was God."

Mark introduces his story as the "gospel" and emphasizes Jesus as the Christ and Son of God, two important titles in his work. Matthew shows an immediate interest in Jesus' Jewish ancestry, especially his lineage through Abraham and David. This indicates his interest in Jesus' fulfillment of the promises made to Israel. Luke brings out his interest in producing an accurate historical account. John introduces Jesus as the pre-existent divine Word, the self-revelation of God.

The identification of the Gospel writers as theologians has important implications for the way we read the Gospels. We ought to read each Gospel seeking to discern these theological themes.

In summary, we can classify the Gospels as *historical narrative motivated by theological concerns*. Their intention is not only to convey accurate historical material about Jesus but also to explain and interpret these salvation-bringing events. The Gospels were written not by detached, uninterested observers but by Evangelists, "proclaimers of good news," announcing the good news of Jesus Christ and calling people to faith in him.

> The Gospels are historical narrative motivated by theological concerns.

WHY WERE THE GOSPELS WRITTEN?

We have already touched on the question of why the Gospels were written. The simple answer is that each Gospel writer had a story to tell. Each wished to paint a particular portrait of Jesus, to emphasize certain theological themes, and to address specific concerns within the church. The following are some suggested further motivations.

Historical: The need for a faithful and authoritative record of the words and deeds of Jesus. The apostles would not live forever, and the Gospel writers wanted to preserve the traditions that had been entrusted to them.

Catechetical: The need to instruct converts in the Christian faith. New believers coming into the church needed to be instructed concerning the words and deeds of Jesus. Like a

© istockphoto

The Gospels served a teaching and worship purpose in the early church, much as Scripture is read in worship services today.

"new believers class" offered by a church today, the Gospels provided summaries of Jesus' life and teaching. Scholars sometimes distinguish between the ***kerygma***—the essential "preaching" of the message of salvation—and the ***didache***—the "teaching" of the Gospel traditions about Jesus.

Liturgical: The need for worship material in the church. The Hebrew Scriptures (the Old Testament) were read in the synagogues, but for Christians, this was only half the story. The promise had to be supplemented with the fulfillment. Some scholars have argued that the Gospels were written to provide a Christian liturgy.

Exhortatory: To encourage and assure believers in their faith. As a small and persecuted minority, the early believers needed reassurance of the truth and reliability of the story of Jesus.

Theological: The need to settle internal disputes. From time to time, false teaching arose in the church. The Gospels may have been written in part to counter false teaching about Jesus or to combat an alternate religious worldview like **Gnosticism**.

Apologetic: The need to respond to external attacks on the church. The church was under attack from its enemies, and the Gospels may have been written in part to respond to these attacks. Matthew's Gospel appears to be responding to accusations made by the Jewish community against Jesus' messiahship and against the Jewish-Christian church.

Evangelistic: The need to call people to faith in Jesus. While the Gospels were written primarily to believers, all of them contain an implicit call to faith in Jesus Christ. John's Gospel cites this as one of its purposes (20:31).

These factors are not mutually exclusive, of course, and various needs and concerns may have motivated each Gospel writer. We will discuss various proposals made by scholars as we examine the purpose and theme of each Gospel in part 3.

THE GOSPEL AUDIENCES: TO WHOM WERE THE GOSPELS WRITTEN?

There is almost universal agreement that the Gospels were written primarily to believers rather than to unbelievers. But who were the specific audiences? None of the Gospels identify their recipients except Luke, who addresses his work to a certain Theophilus (Luke 1:3). Yet even Theophilus is probably the patron who sponsored Luke's Gospel, rather than the primary or exclusive recipient. Luke surely expected his work to be read by others.

Over the last century, there has been a tendency to view each of the Gospels as written to a specific Christian church to address the needs of that community. For example, Mark's Gospel is often associated with the church in Rome, written to encourage that church to endure the persecutions instigated by the emperor Nero. Within this framework, scholars seek to "read between the lines" of individual Gospel stories to reconstruct the community situation in which the Gospel arose. In its extreme form, this perspective claims that the Gospels tell us more about the concerns of later Christian communities than about the life and ministry of the historical Jesus.

This perspective has been challenged in recent years, with some scholars arguing that the Gospels were written not to isolated Christian churches but to a broader Christian audience.[1] Evidence for this is the significant communication and travel among Christian communities seen in the letters of Paul and other early church writings. First-century churches were not isolated islands of belief but networks of interrelated communities scattered throughout the Mediterranean region. In this environment, an author is unlikely to have written and addressed his Gospel to a single church. A more general audience is also suggested by the literary interdependence of the Gospels. The likelihood that both Matthew and Luke used Mark as one of their sources (an issue we will discuss in chap. 2) suggests that Mark's Gospel was widely circulated among first-century churches.

While this debate over audience is far from resolved, the truth probably lies somewhere between two extremes. The Gospel writers were certainly members of individual churches and would naturally have written with the needs and concerns of their church (or groups of churches) in mind. For example, Matthew appears to be writing to Jewish-Christian communities struggling with their relationship to Judaism. He stresses the fulfillment of Old Testament prophecies to show that Jesus is the Jewish Messiah. It is not unlikely that Mark's Gospel was written in the context of Roman Christianity suffering under the Neronian persecutions. The author stresses Jesus' role as **suffering Servant** to call the church to cross-bearing discipleship. At the same time, it is unlikely that these communities were isolated from the larger network of first-century churches, or that they practiced idiosyncratic versions of Christianity. Even if the Gospel writers wrote especially with regard to the needs of their particular communities, they would certainly have kept a broader Christian audience in mind, expecting their Gospels to be copied and distributed among various churches.

In any case, since it is nearly impossible to identify the precise community situation in which each Gospel arose, as evidenced by the multitude of diverse and contradictory

---

1. See Richard Bauckham, ed., *The Gospels for All Christians: Rethinking the Gospel Audiences* (Grand Rapids: Eerdmans, 1998).

theories, it is more profitable to discuss the general kinds of readers—what we call the *implied audience*—to whom the Gospels are addressed, rather than insisting on a specific situation.

WHY *FOUR* GOSPELS?

We have already begun to answer the question of why there are four Gospels. Each of the four Gospels was written to provide a unique perspective on the person and work of Jesus Christ. Each also probably arose in a different community within the early church. But why did the church retain all four in the **canon of Scripture**? The most famous early attempt to synthesize the four Gospels into one is the ***Diatessaron*** ("through four"), compiled by the church father Tatian around AD 170. Tatian brought portions of all four Gospels together into one story. Since then there have been many attempts to produce a **harmony of the Gospels**, or to synthesize the Gospels into a single story. Yet in the end, the church chose to preserve the four distinct Gospels, recognizing each as a unique literary account and as an inspired and authoritative work of the Holy Spirit.

The *Gospel of Thomas* is an apocryphal gospel which was part of the Nag Hammadi library of Gnostic literature, discovered in Egypt in 1945.

WHY *ONLY* FOUR GOSPELS?

There are more than four ancient documents which claim to be Gospels, or which contain stories of Jesus, including works like the *Gospel of Thomas*, the *Gospel of Peter*, and a number of **infancy gospels**, fanciful accounts of Jesus' birth and childhood. The value and historicity of these so-called **apocryphal gospels** continues to be debated. Some scholars claim, for example, that the *Gospel of Thomas* may contain some independent traditions about Jesus. Yet while these writings might preserve an occasional authentic saying or story about Jesus, they are for the most part unreliable late compositions, **pseudepigraphic** (falsely written under an assumed name), and dependent on the canonical Gospels. Their greater value is in providing data concerning the first three centuries of church history, especially the second-century movement known as Gnosticism (see fig. 1.5). The sensational claim that the apocryphal gospels depict the "real Jesus" but were suppressed and silenced by the orthodox church does not hold up under critical scrutiny. In the end, the church rejected these later writings because they failed the test of historical veracity and because they lacked the spiritual power and authority that indicated the inspiration of the Holy Spirit. The addendum at the end of this chapter lists the more important apocryphal gospels.

READING THE GOSPELS TODAY

Reading "Vertically": Following the Storyline

The conclusions we have reached concerning the nature of the Gospels teach us much about how to read the Gospels. If each author has a unique story to tell, and if the Holy Spirit inspired four Gospels instead of one, then we should respect the integrity of each story. It is

Figure 1.5—Gnosticism

Gnosticism is the name given to a diverse religious movement which arose in the late-first and early second centuries AD. Gnostics were syncretistic in their beliefs, drawing together components of **paganism**, Judaism, and Christianity. In general, Gnostics taught that a person gained salvation through secret knowledge (*gnōsis*) of their true spiritual identity and heavenly origin. Gnosticism was characterized by a dualistic worldview which contrasted the pure spiritual realm and the evil material world. Most Gnostics rejected the incarnation of Christ (that God became a human being) and the saving significance of his death on the cross.

In the second century, Gnosticism became the greatest internal threat to the early church. A number of early church writers, including Justin Martyr, Irenaeus, Clement of Alexandria, Tertullian, and Origen, wrote against the heresy.

The Nag Hammadi Codices, discovered in 1945 in Egypt, was a Gnostic collection which included apocryphal gospels like the *Gospel of Thomas*, the *Apocryphon of James*, the *Gospel of Philip*, and the *Gospel of Truth*.

important to read the Gospels on their own terms, following the progress of each narrative from introduction, to conflict, to climax, to resolution. Reading this way has been called **reading vertically**, following the story from top to bottom—that is, from beginning to end. The alternative to such a vertical reading is a harmonistic approach, which brings the four Gospels together as one story. The danger of a harmony is that it risks distorting or obscuring each Gospel's inspired and unique presentation.

Figure 1.6—Reading the Gospel's Vertically
Following Each Storyline

| Matt's Story | Mark's Story | Luke's Story | John's Story |

We may illustrate this danger with an example. The four Gospels record seven sayings of Jesus from the cross. Many sermons have been preached on these seven "words" of Jesus. While insight can be gained from this approach, the danger is that we will miss each writer's unique contribution. No Gospel records more than three of these sayings, and each has its own perspective on the crucifixion (see fig. 1.7). In Mark, for example, Jesus says only one thing from the cross: "My God, my God, why have you forsaken me?" The crucifixion is a dark and foreboding scene. The narrator intentionally draws the reader into Jesus' experience of isolation and despair. Introducing Luke's reassuring "Father, into your hands I commit my spirit" or John's triumphant "It is finished" misses Mark's point. Similarly, throughout Luke's Gospel, Jesus offers God's love and forgiveness to sinners. Jesus' prayer life and intimacy with the Father is also a frequent theme. It is a fitting climax, therefore, that in Luke, Jesus continues to offer forgiveness to sinners from the cross ("Father, forgive them, for they do not know what they are doing"; "I tell you the truth, today you will be with me in paradise") and expresses his trust in and dependence on the Father ("Father, into your hands I commit my spirit"). To introduce Mark's statement of isolation and despair risks distorting Luke's portrait of Jesus. Each Gospel has a story to tell. By reading vertically, we hear that story on its own terms.

Figure 1.7—The Seven Sayings of Jesus from the Cross		
Luke	**John**	**Matthew/Mark**
1. "Father, forgive them, for they do not know what they are doing."	2. *To Mary*: "Dear woman, here is your son." *To John*: "Here is your mother."	
3. "I tell you the truth, today you will be with me in paradise."	4. "I am thirsty."	5. "My God, my God, why have you forsaken me?"
6. "Father, into your hands I commit my spirit."	7. "It is finished."	

Reading "Horizontally": Comparing Their Accounts

While there is a danger in harmonistically reading one Gospel's presentation into another, there are also benefits in comparing their accounts using a "synopsis,"[2] which places the Gospels in parallel columns. By comparing the Gospels, we can identify each writer's themes and theology. For example, by comparing Luke with Matthew and Mark, we see that Luke often introduces statements about Jesus' prayer life, revealing his interest in Jesus' intimacy with the Father. We may call this **reading horizontally**—comparing the Gospels to discern each Evangelist's unique theological perspective.

2. See K. Aland, ed., *Synopsis of the Four Gospels*, Greek-English Edition, 10th ed. (Stuttgart: United Bible Societies, 1994).

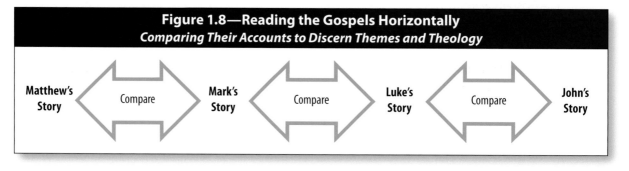

Figure 1.8—Reading the Gospels Horizontally
Comparing Their Accounts to Discern Themes and Theology

Matthew's Story — Compare — Mark's Story — Compare — Luke's Story — Compare — John's Story

When Is a Harmony Legitimate?

While harmonistically reading the Gospels risks missing each Gospel's narrative and theological themes, a harmony is beneficial when asking historical questions. The Gospels claim to be historical narratives, and so it is legitimate to investigate them from the perspective of what actually happened.

Jesus' trial scene, for example, takes on different contours in each of the four Gospels. While a narrative theologian may ask about the themes of each Gospel writer, the historian asks basic historical questions: What role did the Jewish and Roman authorities play in the arrest of Jesus? Before whom was he tried? What accusations were made against him? Why was he crucified? The historian's task is to examine and critique all of the available evidence in order to piece together a credible historical account. Here a harmonistic study is necessary and helpful in order to glean as much information as possible from the available sources.

> The Gospels present four accounts of the life and ministry of Jesus. Merging them as a single, harmonized "life of Christ" risks distorting the integrity of each story and the Spirit-inspired message.

Conclusion

Though the Gospels were written at a specific time, in a specific place, and with specific purposes, they are of timeless benefit for the church. The unique unity and diversity of the four Gospels provide the church of all ages with an authoritative and inspired portrait of Jesus Christ.

» CHAPTER SUMMARY «

1. The four Gospels were written to provide four unique portraits of Jesus Christ.

2. The Synoptic Gospels — Matthew, Mark, and Luke — have many stories in common and share similar language. The Gospel of John is written in a different style and provides unique material and a more theological presentation.

3. The Gospel genre may be identified as "historical narrative motivated by theological concerns." Each Gospel writer had a particular purpose in mind and particular themes to develop.

4. The Gospels were written with reference to the needs and concerns of particular communities within the church, but also with an eye toward their wider distribution among all the first-century churches.

5. The Gospels are best read "vertically," following the plot of each narrative from beginning to end. The Holy Spirit inspired four distinct Gospels with unique themes and purposes.

6. Reading the Gospels "horizontally" — comparing their accounts with one another — enables the reader to see more clearly each Gospel's particular themes and theology.

7. Harmonizing the Gospels into a single story risks distorting each Gospel writer's unique contribution. Harmonizing is helpful, however, when seeking to answer historical questions about the life of Jesus.

» KEY TERMS «

Matthew, Mark, Luke, John	Palestine	infancy gospels
unity and diversity	Evangelists	apocryphal gospels
Messiah, Christ	kingdom of God	pseudepigraphic
Son of God	Gnosticism, Gnostic	paganism
Christology	suffering Servant	reading vertically
Synoptic Gospels	canon, canonical	reading horizontally
genre	harmony of the Gospels	

» DISCUSSION AND STUDY QUESTIONS «

1. Why do we have four Gospels instead of one?

2. What are the Synoptic Gospels?

3. Describe the Gospel genre.

4. Why were the Gospels written? What suggestions have been made?

5. To whom were the Gospels written? What are the two main options?

6. What does it mean to read the Gospels "vertically"?

7. What does it mean to read the Gospels "horizontally"?

8. When is a harmonistic approach to the Gospels legitimate?

Digging Deeper

Gospel Surveys and Introductions

Blomberg, Craig L. *Jesus and the Gospels.* Nashville: Broadman, 1997.

Bridge, Steven. *Getting the Gospels: Understanding the New Testament Accounts of Jesus' Life.* Peabody, MA: Hendrikson, 2004.

Burridge, Richard A. *Four Gospels, One Jesus?* Grand Rapids: Eerdmans, 1994.

Griffith-Jones, Robin. *The Four Witnesses: The Rebel, the Rabbi, the Chronicler, and the Mystic.* San Francisco: HarperSanFrancisco, 2000.

Martin, Ralph P. *New Testament Foundations: A Guide for Christian Students.* Vol. 1, *The Four Gospels.* Grand Rapids: Eerdmans, 1975.

Powell, Mark Allan. *Fortress Introduction to the Gospels.* Minneapolis: Fortress, 1998.

Reddish, Mitchell G. *An Introduction to the Gospels.* Nashville: Abingdon, 1997.

Sanders, E. P., and Margaret Davies. *Studying the Synoptic Gospels.* Philadelphia: Trinity Press International, 1989.

Stanton, Graham. *The Gospels and Jesus.* 2nd ed. Oxford: Oxford Univ. Press, 2002.

The Genre of the Gospels

Aune, David E. *The New Testament in Its Literary Environment.* Philadelphia: Westminster, 1987.

Bauckham, Richard, ed. *The Gospels for all Christians: Rethinking the Gospel Audiences.* Grand Rapids: Eerdmans, 1998.

Burridge, Richard A. *What Are the Gospels? A Comparison with Graeco-Roman Biography.* 2nd ed. Grand Rapids: Eerdmans, 2004.

Guelich, Robert. "The Gospel Genre." In *The Gospel and the Gospels*, edited by P. Stuhlmacher. Grand Rapids: Eerdmans, 1991, 173–208.

Gundry, Robert N. "Recent Investigations into the Literary Genre 'Gospel.'" In *New Dimensions in New Testament Study*, edited by R. N. Longenecker and M. C. Tenney. Grand Rapids: Zondervan, 1974, 97–114.

Shuler, P. L. *A Genre for the Gospels.* Philadelphia: Fortress, 1982.

Talbert, Charles. *What Is a Gospel?* Philadelphia: Fortress, 1977.

Apocryphal Gospels

Bauckham, R. J. "Apocryphal Gospels." In *DJG*, 186–291.

Elliott, J. K., ed. *The Apocryphal New Testament.* Oxford: Clarendon, 1993.

France, R. T. *The Evidence for Jesus.* London: SCM, 1986.

Schneemelcher, Wilhelm, and Robert McLachlan Wilson, eds. *New Testament Apocrypha.* Rev. ed. 2 vols. Cambridge: James Clark; Louisville, KY: Westminster/John Knox, 1991.

Bibliography on Jesus and the Gospels

Aune, David E. *Jesus and the Synoptic Gospels: A Bibliographic Study Guide.* Theological Students Fellowship — Institute for Biblical Research Study Guides. Madison: Theological Students Fellowship, 1980.

Evans, Craig A. *Jesus.* Institute for Biblical Research Biographies No. 5. Grand Rapids: Baker, 1992.

———. *Life of Jesus Research: An Annotated Bibliography.* New Testament Tools and Studies 13. Leiden: Brill, 1989.

McKnight, Scot, and Matthew C. Williams. *The Synoptic Gospels: An Annotated Bibliography.* Institute for Biblical Research Bibliographies No. 6. Grand Rapids: Baker, 2000.

Addendum: Sources for Information about Jesus outside of the Gospels

What can be known about the historical Jesus apart from the four Gospels? Surprisingly little. The following are the main sources of data outside of the Gospels.

The Letters of Paul

The letters of the apostle Paul—the earliest Christian sources we have—actually give us little information about the historical Jesus. Paul rarely quotes Jesus directly and almost never refers to events in Jesus' life. Some have argued from this that Paul cared little about the historical Jesus, being interested only in the Christ of faith, exalted at the right hand of God.[3] We must remember, however, that Paul's letters are occasional in nature. By this we mean that they were written to address specific issues in the churches to which he wrote. More systematic teaching about Jesus' life and teachings would have occurred in other contexts in the early church, such as the catechism of new believers. When Paul does refer to the teaching of Jesus, it is in the context of practical ministry concerns within his churches.

Yet Paul actually gives more information about Jesus than appears at first sight. He notes that Jesus was descended from David (Rom. 1:3), lived under the law (Gal. 4:4), had a brother named James (Gal. 1:19), lived in relative poverty (2 Cor. 8:9), chose twelve special **disciples** (1 Cor. 15:5), taught on such issues as marriage and divorce (1 Cor. 7:10), instituted the Lord's Supper (1 Cor. 11:23ff.), was crucified, buried, and rose again the third day (1 Cor. 15:4). Paul also alludes to Jesus' habit of addressing God intimately with the Aramaic term *Abba* ("Father"; Gal. 4:6; Rom. 8:15).

Greco-Roman Sources

Greco-Roman sources of the first and second centuries also provide little information concerning the life of Jesus. This is not surprising when we consider how insignificant the crucifixion of a Jewish peasant in the distant province of Judea would have appeared to Roman historians. It was only when the Christians were accused of causing disturbances in Rome and the provinces that Roman writers began to take notice.

Writing in the early second century, the Roman historian Tacitus (AD 56–117) describes the persecution of Christians by the emperor Nero and identifies their founder as a certain Christus, who "suffered the extreme penalty during the reign of Tiberius at the hands of one of our procurators, Pontius Pilatus" (*Annales* 15.44).[4] Tacitus's only purpose is to describe Nero's torture and execution of Christians, whose beliefs he describes as a "mischievous superstition." Nothing else is said about Jesus or the beliefs of Christians.

Writing shortly after Tacitus (c. AD 120), the Roman historian Suetonius speaks about the expulsion of Jews from Rome by the emperor Claudius (an event also referred to in Acts 18:1–2): "Because the Jews at Rome caused continuous disturbances at the instigation of Chrestus, he expelled them from the city" (*Twelve Caesars, Claudius* 25.4).[5] Most scholars consider "Chrestus" to be a misspelling of the word "Christ." Suetonius probably

---

3. See chapter 11 for a discussion of this distinction between the historical Jesus and the Christ of faith.
4. Moses Hadas, ed., and A. J. Church and W. J. Brodribb, trans., *The Complete Works of Tacitus* (New York: Random House, 1942), 380–81.
5. Robert Graves, trans., *Suetonius: The Twelve Caesars* (Baltimore: Penguin, 1957), 197.

misunderstood the conflict between Jews and Jewish Christians, assuming that Chrestus was a ringleader of one of the factions.

Around AD 112, Pliny the Younger, governor of Bithynia in Asia Minor, wrote a letter to the emperor Trajan requesting advice on how to deal with Christians who would not worship the image of Caesar. Describing the Christians, he writes "that on an appointed day they had been accustomed to meet before daybreak, and to recite a hymn to Christ as to a god" (*Letter to Trajan* 10.96).[6]

In the late second century, Lucian of Samosata (AD 115–200) wrote a satire in which Peregrinus pretends to be a prophet and tricks Christians into worshiping him in the same way as they worship their founder, "who was crucified in Palestine because he introduced this new cult into the world" (Lucian, *Passing of Peregrinus*, 11, 13).[7]

In summary, Greco-Roman writers of the late first and early second centuries are aware that Jesus was a Judean who was crucified by **Pontius Pilate** during the reign of **Tiberius**, and that his followers now venerated him as a god.

Flavius Josephus

The most important extrabiblical references to Jesus come from the Jewish historian Flavius Josephus, who mentions Jesus in two passages. (For more on Josephus, see fig. 4.11.) One is a passing reference, as he describes how the high priest Ananus was deposed for orchestrating the execution of Jesus' half brother, James. Josephus writes that, during the period between the Roman governors Festus and Albinus, the high priest Ananus "convened the judges of the Sanhedrin and brought before them a man named James, the brother of Jesus who was called the Christ, and certain others. He accused them of having transgressed the law and delivered them up to be stoned" (*Ant.* 20.9.1 §§200–203).[8]

The most famous passage in Josephus, known as the *Testimonium Flavianum* ("testimony of Flavius [Josephus]"), describes Jesus as a wise teacher who did extraordinary deeds. There are doubts, however, about the passage's authenticity, since Josephus is made to sound like a Christian rather than a Jew, although he never converted to Christianity. Most scholars consider the passage to be authentic but to have been edited by later Christians. The text reads:

> About this time there lived Jesus, a wise man, if indeed one ought to call him a man. For he was one who wrought surprising feats and was a teacher of such people as accept the truth gladly. He won over many Jews and many of the Greeks. He was the Messiah. When Pilate, upon hearing him accused by men of the highest standing amongst us, had condemned him to be crucified, those who had in the first place come to love him did not give up their affection for him. On the third day alive he appeared to them restored to life, for the prophets of God had prophesied these and countless other marvelous things about him. And the tribe of Christians, so called after him, has still to this day not disappeared.
>
> —*Jewish Antiquities* 18.3.3 §§63–64[9]

---

6. Henry Bettenson, *Documents of the Christian Church* (London: Oxford Univ. Press, 1947), 5–7.

7. A. M. Harmon, K. Kilburn, and H. D. Macleod, trans., *Lucian*, 8 vols., Loeb Classical Library (Cambridge, MA: Harvard Univ. Press, 1913–67), 5:13.

8. L. H. Feldman, trans., *Josephus*, 9 vols., Loeb Classical Library (Cambridge, MA: Harvard Univ. Press, 1965), 9:497.

9. Ibid., 9:48–51.

A recently discovered Arabic version of the *Testimonium* is likely closer to Josephus's original, since it maintains a more neutral perspective:

> At this time there was a wise man who was called Jesus. And his conduct was good, and [he] was known to be virtuous. And many people from among the Jews and other nations became his disciples. Pilate condemned him to be crucified and to die. And those who had become his disciples did not abandon his discipleship. They reported that he had appeared to them three days after his crucifixion and that he was alive; accordingly, he was perhaps the Messiah concerning whom the prophets have recounted wonders.[10]

Josephus identifies Jesus as a renowned teacher and miracle worker who gained a large following, provoked opposition from the Jewish religious leaders, and was crucified by the Romans under Pontius Pilate. He also affirms that Jesus' disciples reported that he had risen and that the movement they started continued to grow.

Later Jewish Sources

Apart from Josephus, we have no early or reliable references to Jesus in the literature of Judaism. The few references we have are from centuries later and are highly polemical in nature. The Palestinian Talmud, Jewish traditions put in writing in the fourth century AD, condemns anyone who says he is a god or the son of man, a probable reference to Jesus (*y. Taʿan.* 65b). The Babylonian Talmud (c. fifth century AD) says that Jesus was accused of distorting the law and refers to him as a magician (*b. Sanh.* 103a; 107b). Jesus is said to have been hanged on the eve of Sabbath, after going around for forty days with a herald announcing his punishment, because he practiced sorcery and led Israel into apostasy. Jesus is said to have had five disciples, named Mattai, Maqai, Metser, Buni, and Todah (*b. Sanh.* 43a). This odd tradition may be a distortion of the four Gospels, since the first two names sound a little like Matthew and Mark.

A replica of an ancient Torah scroll

The early church father Origen (c. AD 185–254) cites a Jewish source which claimed Jesus came from an adulterous relationship with a Roman soldier named Panthera (*Contra Celsum* 1.32). This may be a corruption of the Greek word for "virgin," *parthenos* (cf. John 8:41, where illegitimacy is implied by Jesus' opponents).

Apocryphal Gospels

Browsing a local bookstore, you may come across books with sensational titles like *The Lost Books of the Bible* or *The Unknown Gospels*. In fact, these gospels are neither lost nor unknown. They are later Christian writings which scholars have known and studied for years, but which the church rejected as inauthentic or otherwise unworthy to be included in Scripture. Some of the apocryphal gospels are stories about Jesus' birth and childhood (infancy gospels); others are collections of sayings or events from Jesus' life; still others are not gospels *per se* but various kinds of writings attributed to Jesus' followers. The following are a few of the more important apocryphal gospels.

---

10. Shlomo Pines, *An Arabic Version of the Testimonium Flavianum and Its Implications* (Jerusalem: Israel Academy of Sciences and Humanities, 1971), 16.

The Gospel of Thomas (AD 100–200?)

This collection of 114 sayings of Jesus is the most important of the noncanonical gospels. It is part of the **Nag Hammadi library**, a collection of mostly Gnostic literature discovered in Egypt in 1945 (on Gnosticism, see fig. 1.5, p. 33). Because *The Gospel of Thomas* is a collection of sayings rather than a narrative, it has been compared to the hypothetical "Q" source, which we will discuss in the next chapter. The work claims to have been written by Thomas, one of the twelve apostles, but is pseudepigraphic, written in the mid-second century. The gospel begins, "These are the secret words which the living Jesus spoke, and which Didymus Judas Thomas wrote." Many of the sayings have parallels in the New Testament Gospels, but often with a Gnostic slant in their theology. It is hotly debated whether Thomas may contain some authentic sayings of Jesus independent of the four canonical Gospels. The copy of Thomas found at Nag Hammadi was written in Coptic, an ancient language of Egypt, but fragments of an earlier Greek text were discovered at the ancient Egyptian city of Oxyrynchus (*Oxyrynchus Papyri 1*, 654–55).

The Gospel of Peter (Early Second Century AD?)

Only part of this work has survived, narrating events from the end of the trial of Jesus to his appearances after the resurrection. The author speaks in the first person, eventually identifying himself as Simon Peter, the brother of Andrew (14:60). The work appears to be dependent on the four canonical Gospels and perhaps some other sources. It is characterized by an anti-Jewish bias, stress on the fulfillment of Scripture, and an apologetic interest in the resurrection. Several early Christian writers make reference to it, rejecting its authenticity and treating it as docetic. Docetists believed that Jesus was fully divine but only appeared to be a human being.

The Secret Gospel of Mark

In 1958 at the monastery of Mar Saba in the Judean desert, Morton Smith claimed to have discovered a previously unknown letter of the early church father Clement of Alexandria (mid-second century AD– c. 216), which contained references to a "Secret Gospel of Mark." In this letter, Clement says Mark left out some "secret" matters from his original Gospel but then added them to his Gospel when he went to Alexandria, Egypt. Clement quotes two stories from the Gospel, one of which recounts how Jesus raised a young man from the dead in Bethany. The story is closely related to John's account of the raising of Lazarus. Some scholars doubt Smith's claim, since Clement's letter has since disappeared and only copies are available for study. Others accept the authenticity of the letter but doubt Clement's assertions that the gospel is from Mark, since the story seems to be the kind of expansion typical of the Gnostic writings.

Other Gospel Fragments

There are various papyrus fragments containing a few sayings or stories of Jesus. Sometimes these have parallels to the canonical Gospels; other times they present apparently independent traditions. The most important fragment is *Papyrus Egerton 2*, dating from about AD 150 and containing four short passages: a dialogue between Jesus and Jewish leaders similar to several passages in John, the cleansing of a leper, a question about paying taxes, and a miracle story about Jesus causing seed to produce fruit. There are also several gospels known to us only through quotations in the early church fathers. Among these are several purported to have come from Jewish Christian groups: the *Gospel of the Hebrews*, the *Gospel of the Ebionites*, and the *Gospel of the Nazarenes*. Unfortunately, apart from a few sparse quotations, little is known about these documents.

> Almost all the information we have about the historical Jesus must be gleaned from the New Testament Gospels. The relative obscurity of his life resulted in other ancient sources providing little additional information.

Infancy Gospels

From the second century onward, curiosity about Jesus' early life resulted in the composition of a number of fanciful accounts about his birth and childhood. Scholars universally reject the historicity of these stories.

Protevangelium of James. *Protevangelium* means "before the gospel," and this work begins with the birth of Mary to a previously barren woman. Mary's parents are identified as Anna and Joachim. The story then expands on the birth narratives in Matthew and Luke. The perpetuity of Mary's virginity is taught, and imaginative details are added to the narrative. Animals and rivers become motionless at Jesus' birth.

The Infancy Gospel of Thomas. Not to be confused with the Gnostic *Gospel of Thomas*, this fanciful work deals with Jesus' childhood, presenting him as a divine child with miraculous powers. The story begins with Jesus making clay pigeons on the Sabbath and then, when he is criticized, clapping his hands to make them fly away. Jesus raises a boy from the dead who had fallen from the roof, and miraculously lengthens a beam which Joseph had accidently cut short in his carpentry shop. Yet Jesus turns out to be a capricious and dangerous playmate, cursing a child who is pestering him so that the boy withers like a barren tree (cf. Mark 11:14, but with different motives!). Another child who bumps into Jesus dies on the spot. Jesus also displays extraordinary wisdom, explaining the allegorical meaning of the Greek letter *alpha*, to the amazement of his teachers.

Conclusion

In summary, Greco-Roman sources outside the New Testament provide very little additional information concerning the historical Jesus. The few comments made by Josephus agree with the general portrait found in the canonical Gospels. While the apocryphal gospel writings may contain an occasional authentic saying or event from Jesus' life, they are for the most part late, legendary, and dependent on the four canonical Gospels. They provide us with little help in understanding Jesus.

While certain basic facts about Jesus may be verified from other biblical and extrabiblical sources, the great majority of information about the historical Jesus must be gleaned from the four New Testament Gospels. Whether this data is generally reliable, and what we can learn about Jesus from it, will be the topic of chapters 11–20.

CHAPTER 2

Exploring the Origin and Nature of the Gospels

HISTORICAL-CRITICAL METHODS OF GOSPEL RESEARCH

1. How the Gospels Came to Be: The Development of the Gospel Tradition
2. Source Criticism and the Synoptic Problem
3. Form Criticism: Seeking the Spoken Word behind the Written Word
4. Redaction Criticism: Studying the Evangelists as Purposeful Editors

After reading this chapter, you should be able to:

- Summarize the four stages by which the Gospels came to be written.
- Define the "synoptic problem" and describe the main proposed solutions, including their strengths and weaknesses.
- State the basic goals, methods, strengths, and weaknesses of form criticism.
- State the basic goals, methods, strengths, and weaknesses of redaction criticism.

The Gospels did not simply fall from heaven. They were written by real authors to real churches within a variety of historical and cultural contexts in the first century. Examining the process by which the Gospels came to be provides a better understanding of their nature and how they ought to be read and applied in the church today.

HOW THE GOSPELS CAME TO BE: THE DEVELOPMENT OF THE GOSPEL TRADITION

The Gospel tradition begins, of course, with the life of the historical Jesus. It is beyond dispute that Jesus of Nazareth was a historical figure who lived in Palestine during the period of Roman domination and was crucified by the Roman governor Pontius Pilate sometime around AD 30–33. Nor is there any doubt that a short time after his death, his disciples began proclaiming that he had risen from the dead. They proclaimed that his death and resurrection not only were God's vindication of Jesus as the Messiah but also brought salvation from their sins.

As the message of Jesus began to spread from Palestine throughout the Roman Empire, stories about Jesus were told and retold, passed down from one person to the next by word of mouth. In time, these stories were put into written form. The writers of the Gospels took these written and oral sources and produced their works.

From this brief overview, we can discern four main stages in the development of the Gospels:

Stage 1: The life, death, and resurrection of the historical Jesus (the events themselves)

Stage 2: The period of oral tradition, when the sayings and stories of Jesus were passed down primarily through the spoken word

Stage 3: The period of written sources, when collections of sayings and other material began to be written down and collected

Stage 4: The writing of the Gospels themselves

Luke refers to these four stages in his prologue:

> Many have undertaken to draw up an account of the things that have been fulfilled among us, just as they were handed down to us by those who from the first were eyewitnesses and servants of the word. Therefore, since I myself have carefully investigated everything from the beginning, it seemed good also to me to write an orderly account for you, most excellent Theophilus.
>
> —Luke 1:1–3

Notice that Luke speaks of the "things that have been fulfilled among us" (stage 1), the preaching of the "eyewitnesses and servants of the word" (stage 2), the "many" written accounts which had already been produced (stage 3), and his writing of his own Gospel (stage 4).

These periods probably overlapped. It is likely, for example, that written material was produced during the oral period and perhaps even during Jesus' ministry. Such overlaps, however, do not negate the general movement from the spoken to the written word. Since the earliest likely date for any of the Gospels is the mid-50s of the first century, there must have been a period of twenty years or more which was primarily oral.

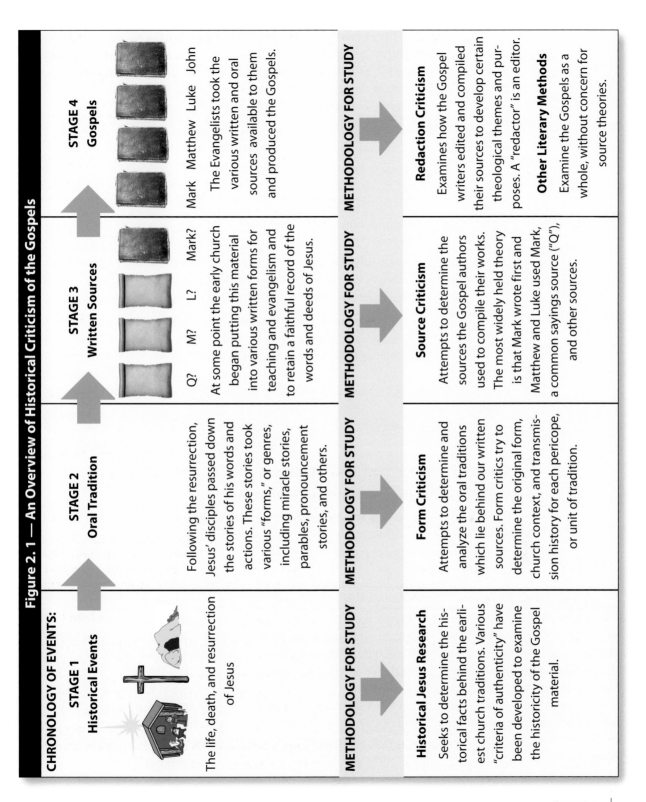

Figure 2. 1 — An Overview of Historical Criticism of the Gospels

CHRONOLOGY OF EVENTS:

STAGE 1
Historical Events

The life, death, and resurrection of Jesus

STAGE 2
Oral Tradition

Following the resurrection, Jesus' disciples passed down the stories of his words and actions. These stories took various "forms," or genres, including miracle stories, parables, pronouncement stories, and others.

STAGE 3
Written Sources

Q?   M?   L?   Mark?

At some point the early church began putting this material into various written forms for teaching and evangelism and to retain a faithful record of the words and deeds of Jesus.

STAGE 4
Gospels

Mark   Matthew   Luke   John

The Evangelists took the various written and oral sources available to them and produced the Gospels.

METHODOLOGY FOR STUDY

Historical Jesus Research

Seeks to determine the historical facts behind the earliest church traditions. Various "criteria of authenticity" have been developed to examine the historicity of the Gospel material.

METHODOLOGY FOR STUDY

Form Criticism

Attempts to determine and analyze the oral traditions which lie behind our written sources. Form critics try to determine the original form, church context, and transmission history for each pericope, or unit of tradition.

METHODOLOGY FOR STUDY

Source Criticism

Attempts to determine the sources the Gospel authors used to compile their works. The most widely held theory is that Mark wrote first and Matthew and Luke used Mark, a common sayings source ("Q"), and other sources.

METHODOLOGY FOR STUDY

Redaction Criticism

Examines how the Gospel writers edited and compiled their sources to develop certain theological themes and purposes. A "redactor" is an editor.

Other Literary Methods

Examine the Gospels as a whole, without concern for source theories.

Throughout the history of Gospel research, tools have been developed to examine each stage in this transmission process. These tools are collectively known as **historical criticism**, since they trace the history of the Jesus traditions through its various stages. The term *criticism* is used not in the sense of a negative assessment ("He's so critical!") but in the sense of analysis or critique, as we might speak of a literary or film critic. The tools are:

Stage 1: Historical Jesus research examines the nature and historicity of the traditions about Jesus. We will examine methods related to the historical Jesus in chapter 11.

Historical criticism seeks to trace the traditions about Jesus from the earliest preaching of the apostles to the completion of the written Gospels.

Stage 2: **Form criticism** attempts to analyze the oral "forms," or units of tradition, which were passed down and used by the early church in their preaching and teaching.

Stage 3: **Source criticism** tries to identify the written sources which lie behind the Gospels and their relationship to one another.

Stage 4: **Redaction criticism** seeks to determine the emphases and purposes of the Gospel writers by analyzing how they "redacted," or edited, their sources to produce our present Gospels.

Other more recent methodologies, known broadly as *literary criticism*, have tended to examine the Gospels in their final form, without reference to the process by which they came to be. These include narrative criticism, structuralism, canon criticism, and reader-response criticism. These methodologies will be discussed together with other approaches in the next chapter.

Study the chart in figure 2.1 carefully and refer to it frequently as you read through the rest of this chapter. In this chapter, we will examine form, source, and redaction criticism.

SOURCE CRITICISM AND THE SYNOPTIC PROBLEM

Why Are the Three Synoptic Gospels So Similar?

One of the first things any reader notices when reading through Matthew, Mark, and Luke is their striking similarity, especially in contrast to the Gospel of John. At the same time, they are far from mere copies of one another. Compare the following parallel passages in the three Synoptics.

Matthew 19:13 – 14	Mark 10:13 – 14	Luke 18:15 – 16
"Then little children were brought to Jesus for him to place his hands on them and pray for them. But the disciples rebuked those who brought them. Jesus said, 'Let the little children come to me, and do not hinder them, for the kingdom of heaven belongs to such as these.'"	"People were bringing little children to Jesus to have him touch them, but the disciples rebuked them. When Jesus saw this, he was indignant. He said to them, 'Let the little children come to me, and do not hinder them, for the kingdom of God belongs to such as these.'"	"People were also bringing babies to Jesus to have him touch them. When the disciples saw this, they rebuked them. But Jesus called the children to him and said, 'Let the little children come to me, and do not hinder them, for the kingdom of God belongs to such as these.'"

Notice that at times the Gospel writers use exactly the same words. At other times, they say essentially the same thing, but using different words. Sometimes one writer gives additional details. There are dozens of such passages. The question is the relationship between these three Gospels. Why do they so closely resemble each other? Why do they differ at so many points? Did they borrow material from each other? Which was written first and which borrowed from the others? The question of these relationships has been termed the *synoptic problem*.

Two key questions to answer: (1) Are the Gospels dependent on one another? (2) If so, which was written first and which depended on the others?

Traditional Solutions to the Synoptic Problem

Prior to the time of the early church father **Augustine** (AD 354–430), there is little evidence of discussion on the relationship of the Synoptic Gospels. Certain statements in the early church fathers suggest that the relative independence of the Gospels was assumed. Church historian Eusebius quotes Papias (early second century) as saying that Mark became Peter's interpreter and wrote his version of the Gospel, and that Matthew produced a collection of "the oracles" (Greek: *ta logia*) of Jesus.[1] The latter may be a reference to the Gospel of Matthew or perhaps to a collection of Jesus' sayings. These statements seem to indicate early belief in the literary independence of the Synoptics.

Augustine appears to have been the first to discuss their potential literary relationship.[2] He suggested that Matthew wrote first and that Mark used and abbreviated Matthew. Luke wrote next, apparently using both Matthew and Mark. Augustine's conclusion appears to have been based more on the canonical order of the Gospels than on a scholarly comparison, but it set the stage for later discussion.

The chief problem with viewing the Gospels as literarily independent is the frequent exact verbal agreement between the Synoptics. Even when two historians faithfully record the same event, they seldom use exactly the same words. This problem is especially striking when we consider that the sayings of Jesus were first passed down in the Aramaic language. Yet our Gospels are written in Greek. It is unlikely that Matthew and Mark would have independently trans-

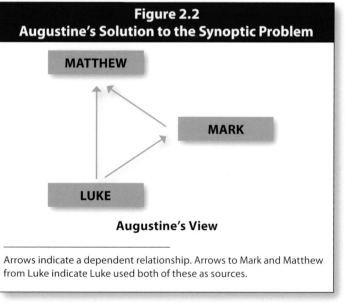

St. Augustine in his study. Fresco by Botticelli (1445 – 1510). The early church father Augustine of Hippo (AD 354 – 430) was one of the first to discuss the likely relationships between the three Synoptic Gospels.

Figure 2.2
Augustine's Solution to the Synoptic Problem

MATTHEW

MARK

LUKE

Augustine's View

Arrows indicate a dependent relationship. Arrows to Mark and Matthew from Luke indicate Luke used both of these as sources.

---

1. Eusebius, *Ecclesiastical History* 3.39.15 – 16.
2. Augustine, *De consensu evangelistarum*.

lated from Aramaic to Greek with so much identical language. Two independent translators of a written document seldom use identical words. It seems likely, therefore, that there is some literary relationship between the Synoptics (see fig. 2.3). While a few scholars continue to affirm the independence of the Synoptics,[3] the great majority see some interdependence.

The recognition that some written sources probably lie behind the Gospels resulted in the discipline known as *source criticism*. The goal of source criticism is to identify the sources behind the Synoptic Gospels and to determine the relationship between these sources. Many source theories have been proposed, with each of the three Synoptics suggested as the first written. The most widely held view today places Mark first.

Markan Priority and the Two- and Four-Source Theories

Markan priority is the view that Mark is the oldest Gospel and is the prototype for the other Gospels. Mark wrote first, then Matthew and Luke composed their Gospels by

---

3. See, for example, E. Linnemann, *Is There a Synoptic Problem? Rethinking the Literary Dependence of the First Three Gospels* (Grand Rapids: Baker, 1992).

Figure 2.3—Did the Gospel Writers Use Each Other As Sources?

MATTHEW　　　　**MARK**　　　　**LUKE**

While a few scholars hold to the literary independence of the Synoptics, most see at least some literary relationship between them. The following are some key reasons.

1. So Much Common Material

One need only look to the Gospel of John to see what another Gospel *could* have looked like. While over 90 percent of the material in John is unique to that Gospel, over 90 percent of Mark's material appears in either Matthew or Luke. This suggests some relationship between these three.

2. So Much Verbal Agreement

While there are many differences in wording in the Synoptics, there are also an extraordinary number of exact parallels, including not only words and phrases but even full sentences. What is striking is that these parallels, while closest in the sayings of Jesus (which might well have been memorized by the disciples), also frequently occur in narrative material.

Figure 2.3— CONTINUED
Did the Gospel Writers Use Each Other As Sources?

3. So Much Agreement in Order

Even when the Gospel writers do not seem to be following a chronological order, they often present episodes in the same order. For example, all three Synoptics present a series of controversy stories in the same order near the beginning of Jesus' ministry (Matt. 9:1 – 17; 12:1 – 14; Mark 2:1 – 3:6; Luke 5:17 – 6:11. Cf. Matt. 22:15 – 23:36; Mark 12:13 – 40; Luke 20:20 – 47).

4. Agreement in Parenthetic Comments and Narrative Asides

Matthew 9:6	Mark 2:10 – 11	Luke 5:24
" 'But so that you may know that the Son of Man has authority on earth to forgive sins….' *Then he said to the paralytic*, 'Get up, take your mat and go home.' "	" 'But that you may know that the Son of Man has authority on earth to forgive sins….' *He said to the paralytic*, 'I tell you, get up, take your mat and go home.' "	" 'But that you may know that the Son of Man has authority on earth to forgive sins….' *He said to the paralyzed man*, 'I tell you, get up, take your mat and go home.' "

Notice that each of the three Synoptics introduces a narrative comment at exactly the same point in Jesus' statement. Identical parenthetical statements or narrative asides are unlikely to be coincidental, pointing instead to literary dependence. For other examples, see Matthew 24:15 and Mark 13:14; Mark 5:8 and Luke 8:29; Matthew 27:18 and Mark 15:10.

5. Identical Alterations of Old Testament Quotes

Matthew 3:3	Mark 1:2 – 3	Luke 3:4
"This is he who was spoken of through the prophet Isaiah: 'A voice of one calling in the desert, "Prepare the way for the Lord, *make straight paths for him*." ' "	"It is written in Isaiah the prophet: '… a voice of one calling in the desert, "Prepare the way for the Lord, *make straight paths for him*." ' "	"As is written in the book of the words of Isaiah the prophet: 'A voice of one calling in the desert, "Prepare the way for the Lord, *make straight paths for him*." ' "

The Synoptics all quote Isaiah 40:3 with reference to John the Baptist. Not only do all three follow the Septuagint (LXX), but they also make exactly the same alteration to that text. The LXX reads "make straight paths for our God" rather than "make straight paths for him." If made independently, such alterations would represent an extraordinary coincidence.

adding to the framework of Mark. There is significant evidence that Mark is the original Gospel:

1. Though Matthew and Luke differ considerably from one another, most of Mark (approximately 93 percent) is found in one or the other. This suggests either that Mark abbreviated both Matthew and Luke, or that Matthew and Luke both used Mark. Under close scrutiny, Mark does not look like an abridgement of Matthew and Luke. Mark's individual stories tend to be fuller in detail than theirs, suggesting that they have abridged Mark's accounts rather than vice versa. Compare, for example, the story of the Gerasene demoniac, which in Mark has 325 words (in Greek) but in Matthew only 135 words (Mark 5:1–20; Matt. 8:28–34).

The Goals of Source Criticism

- To identify the written sources for the Gospels (especially the Synoptic Gospels)
- To determine their relationship to one another, including the order in which they were written and how they borrowed from each other

2. It is also difficult to explain why Mark, if he is borrowing from both Matthew and Luke, would leave out so much seemingly important material. For example, although Mark frequently refers to Jesus as a great teacher, he recounts very little of the teaching material found in Matthew and Luke. Why would Mark ignore a masterpiece like Matthew's Sermon on the Mount?

3. In the "triple tradition" (stories included in all three Synoptics), readings in Matthew and Luke do not generally agree with each other when one or the other differs from Mark. This suggests that Matthew and Luke are using not each other but rather another common source, Mark.

4. Similarly, the order of events in Mark seems to be original, since wherever Matthew departs from Mark, Luke supports Mark's order, and wherever Luke departs from Mark, Matthew agrees with Mark's order. This also suggests that both are following Mark.

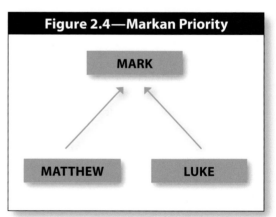

Figure 2.4—Markan Priority

MARK

MATTHEW   LUKE

5. Mark tends to have a rougher, less-polished Greek style, which Matthew and Luke frequently smooth over.

6. Matthew and Luke tend to alter readings in Mark that could be taken as offensive or theologically questionable. For example, Mark seems to limit Jesus' power in Nazareth when he writes that Jesus "could do no mighty works there" (Mark 6:5).

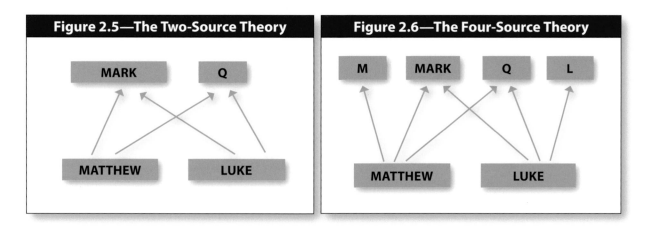

Figure 2.5—The Two-Source Theory

MARK   Q

MATTHEW   LUKE

Figure 2.6—The Four-Source Theory

M   MARK   Q   L

MATTHEW   LUKE

While the context indicates that this was because of the people's unbelief, Matthew avoids any misunderstanding by writing, "And he did not do many mighty works there" (Matt. 13:58). Matthew and Luke also tend to drop statements from Mark in which Jesus seems to manifest negative emotions, such as anger (Mark 3:5) or indignation (Mark 10:14). It seems unlikely that Mark would have changed Matthew's and Luke's easier readings into harder ones.

7. Mark occasionally preserves the original Aramaic words which Jesus used, such as *talitha koum* (5:41), *corban* (7:11), *ephphatha* (7:34), and *Abba* (14:36). Matthew and Luke consistently replace these with a Greek translation. One would expect Mark's Aramaic words to be original.

> Most New Testament scholars hold to Markan priority—the view that Mark was the first of the Synoptics written and that it served as a source for Matthew and Luke.

These arguments have convinced the majority of New Testament scholars that Mark was the first Gospel written. Mark alone, however, cannot account for all of the Synoptic material, so additional sources had to be proposed. The main expansions on Markan priority are known as the **two-source theory** and the **four-source theory**.

The Two-Source Theory: Mark + Q. The priority of Mark does not account for the so-called "double tradition," material which appears in both Matthew and Luke but not in Mark. Another source was therefore proposed, known as the **Synoptic Sayings Source** or "**Q**," which Matthew and Luke are said to have used independently. This material is mostly sayings of Jesus, with a few narratives. The origin of the designation Q is uncertain, but it was probably derived from the German word *Quelle*, meaning "source."

The Four-Source Theory: Mark + Q + M and L. The two-source theory was further clarified in 1924 by B. H. Streeter in his classic text *The Four Gospels: A Study of Origins.*[4] Streeter suggested two additional sources to account for the material unique to Matthew and Luke. He designated these "M" (Matthew's unique material) and "L" (Luke's unique

---

4. B. H. Streeter, *The Four Gospels: A Study of Origins* (London: Macmillan, 1924).

material). The four-source theory is the same as the two-source theory except that it adds two more sources to explain the unique material in Matthew and Luke not accounted for by Mark and Q.

Many other theories, some simple and some complex, have been proposed which build on the foundation of Markan priority. Some of these propose an earlier version of Mark (Ur-Markus) or an earlier version of Luke (Proto-Luke), as well as other hypothetical

---

Figure 2.7—What Is Q?

A key component of the two- and four-source theories is the Q hypothesis. Q, or the Synoptic Sayings Source, refers to the material common to Matthew and Luke. Yet there is considerable debate as to what exactly Q was and even whether it existed.

There are four views:

1. *A Figment of Scholarly Imagination.* For those who reject Markan priority, Q is an unnecessary scholarly construct, without a trace of historical or archeological evidence to support it. For those who believe Matthew wrote first, the so-called Q material is simply the material Luke borrowed from Matthew's Gospel.

2. *A Variety of Sources, Written and Oral.* For some scholars who accept Markan priority, Q is simply a convenient designation for the material common to Matthew and Luke. It has no special homogeneity and may have been a variety of sources, both written and oral.

3. *A Single Written Source.* Many other scholars consider Q to be a single written source of sayings of Jesus. It may have been produced quite early and could be identified with the *logia* of Matthew to which Papias refers. Arguments for a single written source include frequent exact verbal agreements, common order of material between Matthew and Luke, and the existence of "doublets," sayings that appear both in the triple tradition (Mark, Matthew, and Luke) and again in the double tradition (Matthew and Luke).

4. *Evidence for a Heterodox Community of Christianity.* For other scholars, Q is not only a single written source but also the core teachings of a distinct community within early Christianity. These scholars speak of "the theology of Q" and even of the nature of the "Q community." Some even claim that the Q community represented a distinct form of Christianity which developed over time and differed considerably from the later orthodox communities of the Gospels. Since the Q material does not contain a passion narrative, it has been suggested that the earliest Q community did not have a theology of the cross—the belief in the atoning significance of Jesus' death. Later and earlier editions of Q are even hypothesized. Such speculation would appear to go well beyond the available evidence.

sources. Though the nature and existence of Q (see fig. 2.7) and especially M and L are much disputed, the majority of New Testament scholars today hold the view that Matthew and Luke both used (1) The Gospel of Mark, (2) a source or sources which Matthew and Luke had in common, conveniently referred to as Q, and (3) unique material which each had in hand, conveniently designated as M (Matthew's unique material) and L (Luke's unique material).

Matthean Priority: The Griesbach or Two-Gospel Hypothesis

The most serious challenge to Markan priority and the two- and four-source theories is the **Griesbach hypothesis**, so called because of the support it received from the influential New Testament scholar J. J. Griesbach in the late eighteenth century. This is the view that Matthew wrote first, Luke used Matthew as a source, and Mark combined and abridged their two accounts. This solution to the synoptic problem has been revived and defended in recent years by William R. Farmer[5] and has since gained a significant following. It is also known as the *two-gospel hypothesis*, since Matthew and Luke are considered the sources for Mark.

Key evidence for Matthean priority includes the following:

1. *Church tradition points most strongly toward Matthean priority.* Until the nineteenth century, it was generally assumed that Matthew was the first Gospel written.
2. *The Matthew-Luke agreements against Mark.* The strongest argument in favor of Matthean priority are the agreements of Matthew and Luke against Mark in the triple tradition. If Matthew and Luke independently used Mark and did not use each other (as the two-source theory claims), how could they agree against Mark at times?

    Supporters of Markan priority respond that there are relatively few of these agreements and that many can be explained as coincidental, where Matthew and Luke happen to smooth over rough sections of Mark in the same way. For other agreements, however, no such explanation is possible and an overlap of Q or another source with Mark must be proposed.

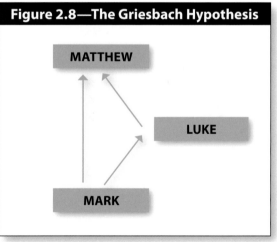

Figure 2.8—The Griesbach Hypothesis

3. *Lack of physical evidence for Q.* Proponents of the Griesbach hypothesis also point to the lack of physical evidence of Q. Archeology and history have discovered no trace of any Q document. Did such a document even exist?

    Supporters of Markan priority respond that it is not necessary to the theory of Markan priority that the material common to

---

5. William R. Farmer, *The Synoptic Problem: A Critical Analysis* (New York: Macmillan, 1964; repr. Dillsboro, NC: Western North Carolina Press, 1976).

Matthew and Luke existed in a single document. Q may have been a body of oral and written traditions. Furthermore, the vast majority of written material from the ancient world has been lost. It is not surprising that a source wholly contained in Matthew and Luke would no longer be copied and so would disappear from history.

Conclusion: Some Observations and Cautions on the Synoptic Problem

1. *Source theories remain theories.* All source theories have some difficulties and so remain theories. A complete explanation of all the agreements and disagreements is impossible with the evidence available to us. These difficulties, together with the probability that sources existed which we no longer possess, should warn us against an overly simplistic approach to the synoptic problem.

2. *For most scholars, Markan priority best explains the available evidence.* Despite some unanswered questions, the nature of the triple tradition appears to favor Markan priority. Perhaps the strongest evidence for this comes from those who write commentaries, working passage-by-passage through the Synoptics. In most cases, Matthew and Luke are quite easily explained as expansions on Mark. Yet Mark often seems inexplicable as an abbreviation of Matthew and Luke.

3. *The nature of other sources, like Q, M, and L, remains uncertain.* While it is possible that Q was a single written source, this is far from certain. Exact verbal agreements suggest that at least part of Q was a written source or sources, but the differences in wording and order raise questions about the unity of Q. It seems certain that there were many oral and written reports circulating at the time of the Evangelists (Luke 1:1–4), so it is unnecessary to suppose that Q was a single written source. It would

---

Figure 2.9—What About the Inspiration by the Holy Spirit?

After slogging through the technical details of the synoptic problem, students often ask in exasperation, "But what about the Holy Spirit? If these documents are inspired by God, couldn't that account for the agreements?" While for believing Christians the inspiration by the Holy Spirit must play a key role when interpreting the Word of God, it alone does not resolve the synoptic problem.

On the one hand, the use of sources in no way compromises the authority and inspiration of the Bible. Luke explicitly speaks of sources for his writings (Luke 1:1–4). The writer of Chronicles used a variety of sources, both canonical (Samuel and Kings) and noncanonical (e.g., the *History of Nathan the Prophet*, the *Words of Gad the Seer*, the *Prophecy of Ahijah the Shilonite*, the *Visions of Iddo the Seer*; see 1 Chron. 29:29; 2 Chron. 9:29). While the Holy Spirit inspired authors as they wrote, he did not dictate Scripture to them. Rather, the human authors wrote from their own experiences and situations, using the source materials available to them, whether that was their own memory, oral reports, or written sources. Like Jesus the living Word, the written Word of God is both fully human and fully divine.

Furthermore, we have to ask why, if the Holy Spirit produced the exact agreements in wording, he allowed so many differences! Claiming that exact parallels between the Synoptics prove the divine origin of Scripture creates the dilemma that differences in wording would compromise that divine origin. It is better to conclude that both the agreements and differences resulted when human authors edited their sources, guided and inspired by the Holy Spirit.

---

seem to go beyond the evidence to talk about the nature of the Q community or to develop detailed theologies of Q. Even more caution must be exercised with reference to the hypothetical sources M and L.

4. *The importance of eyewitness testimony and a strong oral tradition must be taken into account.* Ancient peoples tended to have better memories than we have today, and the authority of oral tradition was considered to be as high as, and sometimes higher than, the authority of written sources. The early church father Papias said, "For I did not suppose that information from books would help me so much as the word of a living and surviving voice."[6] Many of the agreements in the Synoptics may be attributed to the strong oral tradition within the church.[7]

5. *Church tradition about authorship should be taken seriously, but it is not infallible.* The claim by Papias that Mark followed the tradition of Peter seems likely, since church tradition tells us that Mark was written from Rome and that Peter was in Rome later in his life (cf. 1 Peter 5:13). This could explain why Matthew, a disciple of Jesus, would be willing to follow Mark, who was not a disciple. If Matthew recognized Peter's authority behind Mark, he would have had no problem using Mark as a source. As to the tradition that Matthew wrote first, it is possible that Matthew first wrote a collection of Jesus' sayings (Q?) and then revised these sayings into a Gospel after Mark was written. The discovery of the *Gospel of Thomas* (see fig. 1.5) has demonstrated that groups within Christianity made such collections of Jesus' sayings.

FORM CRITICISM: SEEKING THE SPOKEN WORD BEHIND THE WRITTEN WORD

Form criticism (from the German *Formgeschichte*, "history of form") of the Gospels was developed in Germany in the early decades of the twentieth century. Its goal was to go behind the written sources and identify the earlier oral forms of the Gospel tradition.

Method of Form Criticism

Form critics operate from the assumption that between the time of Jesus and the writing of the Gospels, there was an oral period when the sayings and stories of Jesus were passed along by word of mouth. The technical term **pericope** (pronounced *pĕríkopē*) is used to identify each story, or unit of tradition. These pericopae (plural form) were preserved and passed down by the church because of their practical value for preaching and teaching. In this way, they assumed particular "forms" according to the function they performed in the Christian community. A form is a mini-genre, or a particular type of story, like a parable, a miracle story, or a wisdom saying.

---

6. Quoted by Eusebius, *Ecclesiastical History*, trans. Kirsopp Lake, Loeb Classical Library (New York: G. P. Putman, 1926), 3.39.4.

7. Two Scandanavian scholars, B. Gerhardsson (*Memory and Manuscript: Oral Tradition and Written Transmission in Rabbinic Judaism and Early Christianity* [Uppsala: Gleerup, 1961]) and H. Riesenfeld (*The Gospel Tradition and Its Beginnings* [London: Mowbray, 1957]), have argued that Jesus followed the pattern of the rabbis of his day and had the disciples memorize his sayings.

Figure 2.10— Form-Critical Categories		
Form	**Description**	**Examples**
Pronouncement Stories Apophthegms (Bultmann) Paradigms (Dibelius)	A story which culminates in an authoritative statement by Jesus or, sometimes, in a statement about the reaction of onlookers	Mark 2:1 – 12, 15 – 17, 18 – 22, 23 – 28; 3:1 – 6, 20 – 30, 31 – 35; 10:13 – 16; 12:13 – 17; 14:3 – 9
Miracle Stories Novellen (Dibelius)	A story which demonstrates Jesus' supernatural power and authority	Exorcisms: Mark 5:1 – 20; 9:14 – 29 Healings: Mark 1:40 – 45; 5:21 – 43 Nature Miracles: Mark 4:35 – 41; 6:35 – 44, 45 – 52
Sayings and Parables Paränesis (Dibelius)	A general category for all the teaching of Jesus outside of the pronouncement stories	Much of the Sermon on the Mount (Matthew 5 – 7) Parables in Mark 4, etc.
Stories about Jesus Dibelius called these *legends* and *myths*. Bultmann called them *historical stories* and *legends*.	A narrative which reveals something about the identity of Jesus Categories like "myths" and "legends" are intended to denote activities in the divine sphere rather than (necessarily) nonhistoricity. According to Dibelius, a legend is a story which shows the works and fate of a holy man. A myth is a story about the supernatural breaking upon the human scene.	Baptism (Mark 1:9 – 11) Temptation (Matt. 4:1 – 11) Transfiguration (Mark 9:2 – 8)
Passion Narrative	Taylor identified the passion narratives — the accounts of the Last Supper and the arrest, trial, and crucifixion — as a distinct genre.	Mark 14:12 – 15:47

Descriptions in bold print are those of Vincent Taylor, *The Formation of the Gospel Tradition,* 2nd ed. (London: Macmillan, 1935).

Figure 2.11—A Pronouncement Story
Mark 2:15 – 17

The Story	"While Jesus was having dinner at Levi's house, many tax collectors and 'sinners' were eating with him and his disciples, for there were many who followed him. When the teachers of the law who were Pharisees saw him eating with the 'sinners' and tax collectors, they asked his disciples: 'Why does he eat with tax collectors and "sinners"?'"
The Pronouncement	"On hearing this, Jesus said to them, 'It is not the healthy who need a doctor, but the sick. I have not come to call the righteous, but sinners.'"

Figure 2.12—A Miracle Story
Mark 1:23 – 28

The Problem	"Just then a man in their synagogue who was possessed by an evil spirit cried out, 'What do you want with us, Jesus of Nazareth? Have you come to destroy us? I know who you are — the Holy One of God!'"
The Solution	"'Be quiet!' said Jesus sternly. 'Come out of him!' The evil spirit shook the man violently and came out of him with a shriek."
The Response	"The people were all so amazed that they asked each other, 'What is this? A new teaching — and with authority! He even gives orders to evil spirits and they obey him.' News about him spread quickly over the whole region of Galilee."

Form critics classify these forms differently. The most commonly used categories are those developed by Rudolf Bultmann, Martin Dibelius, and Vincent Taylor.[8] Taylor's categories are summarized in figure 2.10, with alternate titles utilized by Bultmann and Dibelius.

Form critics identify patterns that each of these forms took. For example, a **pronouncement story** is a short episode which introduces an authoritative pronouncement by Jesus. The purpose of the story is to set up the pronouncement. Similarly, **miracle stories** are said to take certain, stereotypical forms, with a statement of the problem, followed by the healing, followed by a reaction from onlookers.

The early-church setting in which each form was used is called its *Sitz im Leben* (a German phrase meaning "setting in life"). Miracle stories may have been used in apologetic contexts, when Christians were defending the truth of Jesus' claims. Pronouncement stories

---

8. Martin Dibelius, *From Tradition to Gospel* (New York: Scribner's Sons, 1965); Rudolf Bultmann, *The History of the Synoptic Tradition* (New York: Harper, 1963); Vincent Taylor, *The Formation of the Gospel Tradition* (London: Macmillan, 1933).

may have been used as examples or illustrations in the preaching of the early church. The **passion narrative**—the account of the Last Supper and Jesus' arrest, trial, and crucifixion—was likely told again and again when the church celebrated the Lord's Supper.

The goals of form criticism are (1) to classify and analyze forms, (2) to determine the church context in which that form originated and was used, and (3) to trace the history of its transmission in the church, that is, how it developed and was modified over time. Sometimes this third task is kept distinct from form criticism and is labeled *tradition criticism*.

The Goals of Form Criticism

- To classify forms (mini-genres)
- To determine the church context (*Sitz im Leben*) in which that form originated and was used
- To trace the history of its development and transmission in the church

Assessment of Form Criticism

Form criticism was developed primarily as a historical tool to determine which sayings and stories could be traced to Jesus and which were developed and modified by the early church. Most early form critics assumed that the majority of the Gospel material had its origin in the preaching and teaching of the early church, rather than in the life of the historical Jesus. More moderate scholars, like Vincent Taylor, have utilized form criticism with more positive results, affirming the general historicity of the Gospel tradition. Because form criticism's results concerning the historical Jesus have been mostly negative, some conservative scholars have rejected its use altogether.

Are there insights to be gained from form criticism? The answer is a qualified yes. The basic assumptions of form criticism would seem to be sound. Most of the Jesus tradition almost certainly first circulated orally in small independent units (*pericopae*), and these units were passed on in the context of the preaching and teaching of the church. When certain unwarranted presuppositions are eliminated, the fundamental principles are true and can shed light on the Gospels. The following are positive contributions of form criticism:

1. *The Importance of Preaching the Gospel in the Early Church.* Form criticism rightly emphasizes the oral proclamation of the gospel in the period between the resurrection of Jesus and the writing of the Gospels. The church did not pass on information about Jesus merely out of academic or biographical interest. Rather, their primary concern was to spread the good news concerning the life, death, and resurrection of Jesus Christ. The good news was meant to be preached.

2. *The Importance of Genre Identification.* By classifying forms, form criticism takes account of the fact that the Gospels contain different kinds of material which communicate truth differently. A parable, for example, must be interpreted for what it is—a story from common life meant to teach a particular lesson. Not all of the individual elements should be allegorized, nor should the interpreter seek historical data in a literary form that was never meant to be historical. The parable of the rich man and Lazarus (Luke 16:19–31), for example, should not be used to develop a detailed theology of the afterlife, complete with Abraham's bosom, a chasm between the righteous and the wicked, and conversation taking place be-

tween the two. This is a parable meant to teach the danger of love for riches, not a description of the intermediate state of the wicked.

Similarly, a pronouncement story builds to the final pronouncement, and it is that point which should be stressed. The central message of Mark 3:31–35 is not that Jesus rejects his own family but that the kingdom of God establishes spiritual relationships that supersede physical ones. Jesus' true family are those who do God's will. Form criticism reminds us to take seriously the genre of each Gospel story.

3. *The Importance of Individual Pericopae.* Form criticism confirms that much of the Gospel material was originally passed down in individual units. This shows the legitimacy of teaching or preaching an individual Gospel passage without necessarily following the structural progression of the Gospel in which it occurs. Each unit of tradition may be viewed as a "little gospel" — the gospel within a Gospel — and preached and taught as it stands. The parable of the prodigal son, for example, may be preached either apart from or within its narrative context in Luke.

While the principles behind form criticism are sound, the methodology has frequently been used to draw unwarranted conclusions. The following are some important weaknesses and dangers of form criticism:

1. *Presuppositions of Nonhistoricity and an Antisupernatural Bias.* Perhaps the greatest problem with form criticism is the common presupposition of nonhistoricity. Many form critics suppose that the early church had little interest in the historical Jesus and created most of the Gospel tradition. This arises in part from an antisupernatural bias, the assumption that miracles simply do not occur. Any supernatural elements in the Gospel tradition are immediately viewed with suspicion. Yet the historian's role is not to assume *a priori* what can and cannot happen but to draw reasonable conclusions from the evidence. Much more will be said about this in chapter 12, when we examine the historicity of the Gospel tradition.

2. *An Exclusively Oral Period?* Though the earliest period of the church was almost certainly primarily oral, it is doubtful whether it was exclusively oral. It is likely that some stories were written down at an early stage.

3. *Problems of Classification.* The "forms" of the Gospel material are not as clear-cut as some form critics have supposed. Some pericopae do not fit well in any category, and others contain characteristics of more than one form. For example, the healing of the paralytic in Mark 2:1–12 contains features of both a miracle story and a pronouncement story. Some form critics attribute less historical value to such "mixed" or "impure" forms. But this is unwarranted. Could not Jesus have healed a man and then made an authoritative pronouncement? So-called mixed forms tell us nothing one way or the other about the historicity of the material. The problem rather is with oversimplified categories.

4. *Subjectivity in Identifying the Setting in Life and Tracing a Transmission History.* Suggestions of the original *Sitz im Leben* tend to be highly subjective and speculative, and form critics seldom agree on specifics. Furthermore, form critics

talk about the "laws of transmission" as though oral traditions develop in standard ways. Generally, they say that oral stories developed from the simple to the more complex. But more recent study has shown that these laws are not so standard and that oral traditions sometimes become simpler over time.[9] This makes it doubtful that the transmission history of a particular pericope can be traced with any accuracy.

In summary, while the first goal of form criticism—identifying the form or genre of individual Gospel stories—can provide illumination to the Gospel interpreter, the second two goals—identifying the setting and tracing the transmission—can be fraught with difficulty. Conclusions here tend to be highly subjective and speculative, providing little insight into the historical Jesus or the early Christian communities. Form criticism, while potentially helpful, should be used with caution.

REDACTION CRITICISM: STUDYING THE EVANGELISTS AS PURPOSEFUL EDITORS

Redaction criticism (*Redaktionsgeschichte*) arose in the middle of the twentieth century as a reaction against form criticism and its treatment of the Gospel writers as mere compilers of traditions ("scissors-and-paste men"). It is recognized today that each Gospel writer is an author and a theologian in his own right. Each has particular emphases and writes with a distinct purpose. Redaction criticism looks at the work of these "redactors," or editors, and tries to determine why they collected, edited, and ordered the material the way they did. The first major works of redaction criticism came from German scholars Günther Bornkamm (Matthew), Willi Marxsen (Mark), and Hans Conzelmann (Luke).[10]

The key point of redaction criticism—that the purpose and emphasis of the Gospel writer is important—is not new. It has long been recognized that the Gospel writers wrote for a purpose and that they were selective in what they chose to report about Jesus (see John 21:25). What is new about redaction criticism is that it builds on the foundations of source criticism and form criticism, and so focuses more strongly on the community situation, use of sources, and purpose for which each writer wrote.

The Goals of Redaction Criticism

- To analyze how the Gospel writers "redacted" or edited their sources

- To discern from this redaction the theological emphases of each writer

- To determine each author's purpose in writing

- To identify their *Sitz im Leben* ("setting in life")

---

9. See, for example, E. P. Sanders, *The Tendencies of the Synoptic Tradition*, SNTSMS 9 (Cambridge, MA: Cambridge Univ. Press, 1969).

10. G. Bornkamm, G. Barth, and H. J. Held, *Tradition and Interpretation in Matthew* (London: SCM; Philadelphia: Westminster, 1963); Willi Marxsen, *Mark the Evangelist: Studies on the Redaction History of the Gospel* (Nashville: Abingdon, 1969); Hans Conzelmann, *The Theology of St. Luke* (New York: Harper and Row, 1960).

The Method of Redaction Criticism

The goals of redaction criticism are (1) to analyze how the Gospel writers "redacted" or edited their sources, (2) to discern from this redaction the theological emphases of each writer, (3) to determine each author's purpose in writing, and (4) to identify the community situation, or setting in life (*Sitz im Leben*), within which the author wrote.

The Evangelists' emphases, purpose, and theology can be determined by examining their various kinds of editorial work. The following examples from Luke's Gospel will highlight the process of redaction criticism.

Individual Comments and Editorial Links. Sometimes a Gospel writer will add an editorial comment to bring out the significance of an episode. Notice Luke's addition below.

Matthew 3:11	Mark 1:7–8	Luke 3:15–16
" 'I baptize you with water for repentance. But after me will come one who is more powerful than I.' "	"And this was his message: 'After me will come one more powerful than I.' . . . 'I baptize with water . . .'"	"The people were waiting expectantly and were all wondering in their hearts if John might possibly be the Christ. John answered them all, 'I baptize you with water. But one more powerful than I will come.'"

While all three Synoptics describe John the Baptist's preaching about the "more powerful" one coming after him, Luke alone adds a comment about the expectation of the people that John might be the Christ. This serves to emphasize John's disclaimer: John denies that he is the Christ and points instead to Jesus. This contrast between John, who is the forerunner, and Jesus, who is the Messiah, is a special emphasis of Luke's throughout his Gospel and Acts (see Luke 1–2; Acts 13:25).

Summaries. A good indicator of an Evangelist's emphasis is the way he summarizes Jesus' activity. In Mark 1:45, the author describes how after healing a man with leprosy, Jesus' popularity was so great he had to withdraw to the countryside. In his parallel account, Luke makes a similar statement but gives an additional reason for Jesus' withdrawal: "But Jesus often withdrew to lonely places and prayed" (Luke 5:16). Jesus' prayer life and his close communion with his Father are themes found frequently in Luke (Luke 3:21; 5:16; 6:12; 9:18, 28f.; 10:21f.; 11:1; 22:31f., 41ff.; 23:46). By comparing Luke's redaction with Mark, this theme is highlighted.

Additions and Omissions of Material. Additions and omissions made to material can indicate an Evangelist's interests and purpose. Notice Luke's addition below.

In both his Gospel and Acts, Luke places great emphasis on the role of the Holy Spirit in the life of Jesus and in the early church. It is

Jesus' prayer life is a theme which Luke emphasizes in his redaction of his sources. Detail from Dore's "Agony of Christ."

Matthew 4:1	Mark 1:12 – 13	Luke 4:1 – 2
"Then Jesus was led by the Spirit into the desert to be tempted by the devil."	"At once the Spirit sent him out into the desert, and he was in the desert forty days, being tempted by Satan."	"Jesus, *full of the Holy Spirit*, returned from the Jordan and was led by the Spirit in the desert, where for forty days he was tempted by the devil."

not surprising, therefore, that after the account of the descent of the Spirit on Jesus at his baptism, Luke adds that Jesus was "full of the Spirit" when he was tempted by Satan in the wilderness.

Arrangement of Material. Where an Evangelist places an episode may demonstrate his purpose and emphasis. For example, many scholars believe that the synagogue sermon in Luke 4:16 – 30 is the same sermon recorded in Mark 6:1 – 6. If so, Luke has brought this episode forward to serve as an introduction to Jesus' whole ministry. The rejection of Jesus in his hometown prepares the reader for the coming rejection by his own people.

Use of Additional Source Material. Luke includes many parables and stories, which emphasize Jesus' special care for people of low estate, for sinners, and for society's outcasts, that are not found in the other Gospels (Luke 13:10 – 17; 14:7 – 14, 15 – 24; 15:7 – 10, 11 – 32; 16:19 – 31; 17:11 – 19; 18:9 – 14; 19:1 – 10). Though these stories probably came to Luke from tradition, his decision to include them shows his special interest in this theme.

Since most redaction critics have adopted Markan priority, the majority of redaction criticism has focused on how Matthew and Luke used Mark, Q, and their special material. Redaction criticism of Mark is more difficult since the sources he used are no longer available to us. Nevertheless, Mark's emphases can be determined by examining his individual comments, summaries, transitions, and overall arrangement of material.

Assessment of Redaction Criticism

Like form criticism, the basic assumptions behind redaction criticism are sound. It is certain that the Evangelists used sources in writing their Gospels, and it is legitimate to ask how and why they used these sources the way they did. The following are some positive contributions of redaction criticism:

1. Redaction criticism affirms that the Evangelists were purposeful writers and not mere compilers of material.
2. Redaction criticism treats the Gospels as wholes and so corrects the approach of form criticism, which looks only at individual units of tradition.
3. By comparing the Gospels, redaction criticism affirms the unique theological contribution of each Evangelist. It was for a purpose that the Holy Spirit inspired four Gospels, rather than one, and each has a role to play in the life of the church.

Though the method as a whole is sound, redaction critics sometimes draw unwarranted conclusions. The following are potential weaknesses of redaction criticism:

1. Many redaction critics too quickly assume that a saying or story found in only one Gospel was created by that writer. For example, if Matthew's style is detected in a pericope, it is often assumed to be unhistorical and his own creation. But *redaction* does not necessarily mean *creation*. It only means that the Gospel writer has edited that source to make it his own. Historical conclusions must be made on broader historical-critical grounds, not merely stylistic ones.

2. Redaction critics tend to find theological significance in every alteration made by the Evangelists. For example, the change of a verb form or a preposition may be seen to carry great theological importance. But such changes could be due to stylistic preference or to differences in sources. The theology of a Gospel writer must be discerned from his total presentation, not from minor alterations alone. Redaction critics sometimes miss the forest for the trees.

3. Perhaps the greatest problem of redaction criticism is its high degree of subjectivity. Redaction critics often come to radically different conclusions from the same data. This raises questions about the viability of a method which seeks to discern authorial motivations behind sometimes minor editorial changes.

   A good corrective to this subjectivity is to keep an eye on the whole of the Gospel story, rather than only on its editorial alterations. This has led scholars to develop new methods which examine the Gospels as literary wholes. These will be discussed in the following chapter.

» CHAPTER SUMMARY «

1. The message of Jesus was originally passed down primarily by word of mouth, gradually being written down to produce our Gospels. Historical criticism examines this process with methods such as form, source, and redaction criticism.

2. Source criticism seeks to identify and evaluate the written sources used by the Gospel writers.

3. The synoptic problem is the question of the literary relationship between Matthew, Mark, and Luke, the Synoptic Gospels. The most widely held view is that Mark wrote first (Markan priority) and that Matthew and Luke used Mark and other sources.

4. The designation "Q" is used for the "double tradition," the common source or sources used by Matthew and Luke in addition to Mark. The designations "M" (Matthew's special source) and "L" (Luke's special source) are used for the unique material each utilized.

5. A minority of scholars hold to the priority of Matthew (the Griesbach hypothesis). A few claim the Gospel writers wrote independently, using only common oral traditions.

6. Form criticism seeks to identify and evaluate the oral forms of the stories about Jesus which lie behind our written sources. Form critics in general have rejected much of the historicity of the Jesus tradition, attributing its creation to the early church.

7. Redaction criticism seeks to evaluate the process by which the Evangelists redacted, or edited, their sources to produce the Gospels. Redaction critics try to discern the main themes and theology of each Gospel writer and to establish the *Sitz im Leben* ("setting in life"), the community situation in which the Gospel arose.

» KEY TERMS «

historical criticism

form criticism

source criticism

redaction criticism

Augustine

Markan priority

two (or four) source theory

Synoptic Sayings Source "Q"

Griesbach, or two-gospel, hypothesis

pericope (*pĕríkopē*)

pronouncement stories

miracle stories

Sitz im Leben

passion narrative

» DISCUSSION AND STUDY QUESTIONS «

1. Summarize the four stages which led to the production of the Gospels.

2. What is the synoptic problem?

3. What is source criticism? What are its goals?

4. What is the most widely held solution to the synoptic problem? What are its main strengths and weaknesses?

5. What is form criticism? What are its goals? What are its main strengths and weaknesses?

6. Identify the main "forms" of the Gospel tradition.

7. What is redaction criticism? What are its goals? What are its main strengths and weaknesses?

Digging Deeper

The Synoptic Problem and Source Criticism

Black, David Alan, and David R. Beck, eds. *Rethinking the Synoptic Problem.* Grand Rapids: Baker, 2001.

Farmer, William R. *The Synoptic Problem: A Critical Analysi*s. Dillsboro, NC: Western North Carolina Press, 1976.

Gerhardsson, B. *The Origins of the Gospel Traditions.* Philadelphia: Fortress, 1979.

Kloppenborg, John S. *The Formation of Q: Trajectories in Ancient Wisdom Collections.* Philadelphia: Fortress, 1987.

Richmond, Thomas, Willis Longstaff, and Page A. Thomas. *The Synoptic Problem: A Bibliography, 1716–1988.* Macon, GA: Mercer Univ. Press, 1988.

Stein, Robert H. *The Synoptic Problem: An Introduction.* Grand Rapids: Baker, 1987.

Streeter, B. H. *The Four Gospels: A Study of Origins.* London: Macmillan, 1924.

Form Criticism

Blomberg, C. L. "Form Criticism." In *DJG*, 243–50.

Bock, Darrell. "Form Criticism." In *Interpreting the New Testament: Essays on Methods and Issues*, edited by David Alan Black and David S. Dockery. Nashville: Broadman, 2001, 105–27.

Bultmann, R. *The History of the Synoptic Tradition.* New York: Harper, 1963.

Dibelius, Martin. *From Tradition to Gospel.* New York: Scribner's Sons, 1965.

McKnight, E. V. *What Is Form Criticism?* Philadelphia: Fortress, 1969.

Taylor, Vincent. *The Formation of the Gospel Tradition.* 2nd ed. London: Macmillan, 1935.

Redaction Criticism

Carson, D. A. "Redaction Criticism: On the Legitimacy and Illegitimacy of a Literary Tool." In *Scripture and Truth*, edited by D. A. Carson and J. Woodbridge. Grand Rapids: Zondervan, 1983, 119–42.

Osborne, Grant R. "Redaction Criticism." In *Interpreting the New Testament: Essays on Methods and Issues*, edited by David Alan Black and David S. Dockery. Nashville: Broadman, 2001, 128–49.

Perrin, Norman. *What Is Redaction Criticism?* Philadelphia: Fortress, 1969.

Rhode, J. *Rediscovering the Teaching of the Evangelists.* London: SCM, 1968.

Stein, R. H. "What Is *Redaktionsgeschichte*?" *JBL* 88 (1969): 45–56.

CHAPTER 3

Reading and Hearing the Gospel Stories

LITERARY-CRITICAL METHODS OF GOSPEL RESEARCH

» CHAPTER OVERVIEW «

1. Narrative Criticism: The Gospels as Story
2. Other Literary Methods

   Rhetorical Criticism

   Canon Criticism

   Structuralism

   Reader-Response Criticism

   Liberationist and Feminist Approaches

   Deconstruction

3. The Approach of This Text

» OBJECTIVES «

After reading this chapter, you should be able to:

- Distinguish literary criticism from historical criticism in overall purpose and goals.
- Describe the goals, methods, and main categories of narrative criticism, as well as its strengths and potential weaknesses.
- Summarize the nature, strengths, and weaknesses of other literary methods, including rhetorical criticism, canon criticism, structuralism, reader-response criticism, liberationist and feminist approaches, and deconstruction.

Literary criticism refers to methods of studying the Gospels as unified literary works, rather than dissecting them into hypothetical sources and oral traditions.

We tend to buy a lot of children's videos at our home. This is because my kids love to watch the same movie over and over again. As they watch the latest release, I find myself passing through the room, catching a bit of the story here, a snippet there. After many trips, I gradually figure out the contours of the plot until I have a pretty good idea what the movie is about. When my wife and I watch a movie, we do it very differently. We get out the popcorn and watch from beginning to end, engrossed in the story from the opening scene through the twists and turns of the plot to the climactic ending. I read novels the same way, consuming them into the wee hours of the night until I reach the end.

The historical-critical methods examined in the last chapter (form, source, and redaction criticism) have been criticized for treating the Gospels as bits and pieces rather than as unified narratives. Narratives are stories, and stories are meant to be read and experienced from beginning to end. By dissecting the Gospels into oral traditions and hypothetical sources, the student can miss the forest for the trees—the powerful effect the story was meant to have on the reader.

While New Testament scholarship continues to benefit from historical-critical methods, Gospel studies have decidedly turned from the *historical process* by which the Gospels arose, to their *present unity as literary works*. These approaches, though diverse, may be categorized as **literary criticism**. We will focus primarily on narrative criticism, and then turn briefly to other literary methods: rhetorical criticism, canon criticism, structuralism, reader-response criticism, feminist and liberationist approaches, and deconstruction.

NARRATIVE CRITICISM: THE GOSPELS AS STORY

Narrative criticism arose as a correction to the tendency of form and redaction critics to focus on the components of the text at the expense of its narrative unity. While redaction criticism also focuses on the final form of the Gospel, its concern is with the history of the text, examining how the Evangelists edited their sources to pursue certain theological goals. Narrative criticism is interested not in this editorial process but in the literary nature of the text itself, how it functions to produce the desired effect on the reader.

Narrative critics have taken categories from modern literary criticism, especially those related to the novel, and applied them to the biblical text. The call for a more literary approach was made by scholars like William Beardslee, Hans Frei, and Norman R. Peterson.[1] Groundbreaking narrative-critical works on the Gospels were produced by David Rhoads and Donald Michie (Mark), R. Alan Culpepper (John), Jack Dean Kingsbury (Matthew), and Robert Tannehill (Luke-Acts).[2]

---

1. William Beardslee, *Literary Criticism of the New Testament*, GBS (Philadelphia: Fortress, 1969); Hans W. Frei, *The Eclipse of Biblical Narrative: A Study in Eighteenth and Nineteenth Century Hermeneutics* (New Haven, CT: Yale Univ. Press 1974); Norman R. Peterson, *Literary Criticism for New Testament Critics*, GBS (Philadelphia: Fortress, 1978).

2. David Rhoads and Donald Michie, *Mark as Story: An Introduction to the Narrative of a Gospel* (Philadelphia: Fortress, 1982); R. Alan Culpepper, *The Anatomy of the Fourth Gospel: A Study in Literary Design* (Philadelphia: Fortress, 1983); Jack Dean Kingsbury, *Matthew as Story* (Philadelphia: Fortress, 1986); Robert Tannehill, *The Narrative Unity of Luke-Acts: A Literary Interpretation,* 2 vols. (Philadelphia: Fortress, 1986–90).

As we have seen in chapter 1, the Gospels may be described as *historical narrative motivated by theological concerns*. They show similarities to the first-century genre "biography" (*bioi*), an interpretive narrative of the life and significance of a great leader (see fig. 1.4). The authors seek to present reliable accounts of Jesus' life, as well as the interpretive framework to understand that life.

The Storyteller

Narrative critics distinguish between the **real author**, the **implied author**, and the **narrator**. The real author is the historical person who wrote the Gospel. Though we can assume this person existed, the reader has no direct access to him. We may therefore speak of an implied author, *the literary version of the author as discerned in the text*. Though I cannot ask the writer of Mark's Gospel questions about the meaning of the text, I form an impression of the author's beliefs and worldview by following his narrative strategy. The distinction between real and implied authors is important, since the Gospels, like most other biblical narratives, are, strictly speaking, anonymous documents. Although we do not know for certain the identity of the real author, we can speak with some authority of that person's beliefs and purpose in writing.

A third category, the narrator, refers to *the voice we hear telling the story*. The narrator is not the real author or the implied author but a literary device which the implied author uses to tell the story. Different narratives have different kinds of narrators. The narrator may be outside the story, using the third person ("he," "she," "they"), or may be a character in the story, speaking in the first person ("I," "we"). In Mark Twain's classic *Huckleberry Finn*, Huck narrates the story in the first person, using the accent, grammar, and slang of a backwoods boy. With the exception of a few first-person passages in Acts (16:10–17; 20:5–15; 21:1–18; 27:1–28:16), the New Testament narratives always have third-person narrators. Narrators who are story characters are usually limited in their knowledge and experience. Huckleberry Finn does not know people's thoughts or what they are doing when he is not present. Third-person narrators, on the other hand, may be omniscient and omnipresent, describing thoughts and events which no finite person could know. The Gospel writers reveal a measure of omniscience and omnipresence. The narrator of Mark, for example, describes what the scribes are thinking (2:6–7) and recounts secret meetings behind closed doors (14:10–11).

Narrators can also be reliable or unreliable. The narrator in Edgar Allan Poe's short story *A Tell-Tale Heart* is insane and commits murder. This does not mean the real author (or the implied author) is insane or murderous, but only that he has used this literary device to tell his macabre story. The Gospel narrators are always reliable. Readers are expected to accept what they say as true and reliable.

Narrative World and Evaluative Point of View

Closely related to the perspective of the narrator and implied author are the **narrative world** and the **evaluative point of view** of the narrative. The narrative world is the universe created by the implied author within which the story takes place. *Created* does not mean that the setting has no counterpart in the real world. The Gospels are set in first-century Palestine—a real place and time. It means that in telling the story, the implied author "sets the stage" upon which the characters interact and the plot develops. The narrative world of the Gospels is a narrative portrait of first-century Palestine, a landscape painted by the implied author to provide the setting for the plot. Of course, the narrative world of the Gospels is not just first-century Palestine but also a supernatural universe inhabited by God, angels, Satan, and demons. Whether or not the reader believes in God, it is impossible to comprehend the story without entering—at least for the sake of the story—this narrative world.

Evaluative point of view refers to the values, beliefs, and worldview which the reader is expected to adopt in order to judge the events and characters of the narrative. The narrator assumes that certain actions and attitudes are right and good, and others are wrong and bad. The Gospel narrators always affirm the evaluative point of view of God, who is righteous and just and loving. By contrast, Satan and his demons are deceitful, evil, and destructive. Characters in the story are viewed as good if they follow God's way and evil if they reject him and follow Satan. For readers to comprehend the plot and track its narrative strategy, they must adopt the implied author's evaluative point of view.

The Story Receiver

Just as narrative critics distinguish between the real author, implied author, and narrator, so they distinguish between **real readers**, **implied readers**, and **narratees**. A real reader is any actual reader of the text, whether ancient or modern. The implied reader represents an imaginary person who responds appropriately to the narrative strategy. While an actual reader may respond to a text in a variety of ways depending on their background and circumstances (with misunderstanding, indifference, etc.), the implied reader's response is

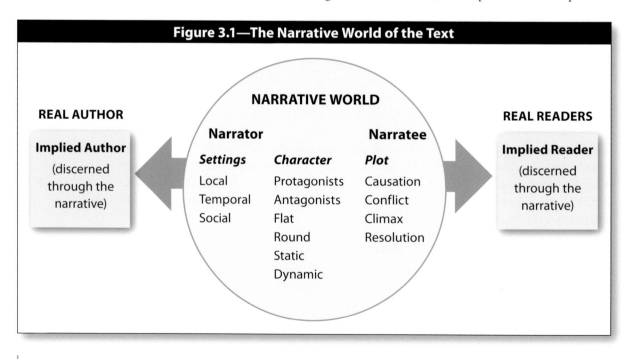

Figure 3.1—The Narrative World of the Text

NARRATIVE WORLD

REAL AUTHOR

Implied Author
(discerned through the narrative)

Narrator

Settings
Local
Temporal
Social

Character
Protagonists
Antagonists
Flat
Round
Static
Dynamic

Narratee

Plot
Causation
Conflict
Climax
Resolution

REAL READERS

Implied Reader
(discerned through the narrative)

predictable and dependent on the narrative strategy. When Judas betrays Jesus, the implied reader responds with dismay at this act of treachery. Yet in his classic missionary account *Peace Child*, Don Richardson describes a tribe in Papua New Guinea which considered deceit to be a virtue and so viewed Judas as the hero. In this case, real readers (or hearers) did not adopt the evaluative point of view of the narrative and so responded inappropriately to the narrator's strategy. The imaginary implied reader, by contrast, always responds appropriately so that the intention of the narrative is fulfilled.

Just as the narrator is the voice telling the story, so the narratee is the hearer of the story. Like the narrator, the narratee is a literary device used by the implied author to accomplish his or her purpose. While the narrator's voice is a constant feature of the Gospel narratives, only rarely is attention drawn to the narratee, as when the narrator in Luke addresses Theophilus (Luke 1:1–4) or when Mark's narrator pauses in the midst of Jesus' Olivet Discourse to comment, "Let the reader understand" (Mark 13:14).[3]

Plot: The Progress of the Narrative

All stories have three fundamental components: **plot**, *setting*, and *characters*. Plot refers to the progress of the narrative, the sequence of **events** which move the story from introduction, to conflict, to climax, to conclusion. Events (also called *incidents* or *scene parts*) refer to any actions or sayings by a character. The narrator in Mark describes an event with the words "Jesus went into Galilee, proclaiming the good news of God" (1:14). A group of related events make up a **scene** (also called an *episode*). When Jesus walks beside the sea of Galilee and calls two pairs of brothers who were fishermen, and they drop their nets and follow him (Mark 1:16–20), this sequence of events makes up a scene. A group of related scenes constitutes an **act**. Though this is not a category often used by New Testament critics, the sequence of controversy stories in Mark 11–12 could be identified together as an act.

Two fundamental features of plot are **causation** and **conflict**. Causation concerns the relationship of one scene to another. A plot progresses as one event leads to another, moving toward a climax and resolution. Sometimes causes are implied; other times they are explicitly stated. Jesus' growing popularity in Mark is causally linked to the reports of his healing powers (Mark 1:45). The narrator in John makes the raising of Lazarus the decisive turning point which leads to Jesus' crucifixion (John 11:45–57).

Conflict is common to all narrative. Characters face opposition of some kind, which they must work through to resolution. Conflict comes early in Mark's Gospel as Jesus is tempted by Satan in the desert (1:12). The narrator signals by this that the story is not a merely human struggle but a spiritual conflict of cosmic proportions, with Jesus representing the evaluative point of view of God. This is confirmed as Jesus immediately comes in conflict with a demon-possessed man in the synagogue at Capernaum (1:21–25). These spiritual encounters set the stage for his conflicts with the religious leaders (2:1–3:34). By juxtaposing these episodes, the narrator portrays the religious leaders as allies of Satan in opposition to God.

---

3. Some commentators, by contrast, consider this to be a statement of Jesus rather than the narrator, especially in Matthew's version (Matt. 24:15), referring to the reader of the Daniel passage just quoted.

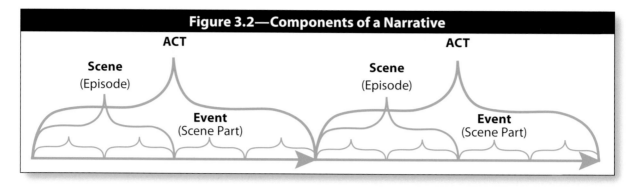

Figure 3.2—Components of a Narrative

ACT

ACT

Scene
(Episode)

Scene
(Episode)

Event
(Scene Part)

Event
(Scene Part)

While this basic conflict is common to all four Gospels, it develops in different ways and to different degrees. Matthew paints an extremely negative portrait of the religious leaders as evil and unredeemable opponents of Jesus. Luke provides a more mixed view. Jesus socializes with Pharisees (Luke 7:36; 11:37; 14:1) and is even warned by them of Herod's schemes (13:31). This sets the stage for Acts, where the religious leaders are given a second chance to respond (Acts 3:17–19), and where the Pharisees show some affinity with the Christian movement (5:33–39; 15:5; 23:7–9). Other conflicts also differ among the Gospels. Mark provides the most negative picture of the disciples. They fail to understand Jesus' words or comprehend his mission, creating an air of tension and conflict. The implied reader is left wondering whether they will stand or fall. In Luke, the disciples fare much better. Although at times they are slow to understand and succeed, their role as future leaders in the church seems assured.

Just as conflict is treated somewhat differently in each of the four Gospels, so the climax and resolution work out differently. While all four Gospels climax and resolve in crucifixion and resurrection, a close examination reveals a more complex picture. For Luke, the resolution is not only the resurrection but also Jesus' ascension to heaven, an event not narrated in the other Gospels. Even this is not the final resolution, since Luke provides a second volume in which the Gospel goes forth from Jerusalem to Rome, and from its Jewish roots to the **Gentile** world. The resolution is tied not only to the events of Jesus' life but also to the worldwide outreach of the church. In Matthew, the resolution is not only the resurrection but also the Great Commission, promising Jesus' continued presence and power for the disciples (Matt. 28:18–20). Mark has a much darker ending. It reports no resurrection appearances and only announces that Jesus is risen. The Gospel ends with the fear and bewilderment of the women at the tomb. We will discuss the possible reasons for this ending later. For now it is sufficient to say that while the four Gospels tell the same basic story, their narrative presentations—plot, characters, and settings—are sometimes very different.

Another important feature of plot relates to time and sequence. Narrative critics speak of **story time** and **narrative time** (or discourse time). Story time concerns the passage of time in the narrative world of the text. Jesus' ministry in John covers approximately three years (John 2:13; 6:4; 11:55). Jesus' crucifixion in Mark covers six hours (Mark 15:25–33). This is story time. The concept of narrative time often confuses students and should be understood not as a different kind of time but rather as the manner in which story time is narrated, in terms of order, speed, and duration. Story time may move quickly, as when the narrator summarizes Jesus' activity. Matthew 9:35 says, "Jesus went through all the towns and villages, teaching in their synagogues, preaching the good news of the kingdom and healing every disease and sickness." Here a single sentence in the narrative summarizes weeks or even months of story time. Story time may stop, as the narrator provides an explanation or makes an aside comment (Mark 7:3–4). It may jump forward days, months, or years (twenty years between Luke 2:51 and 3:1), or back to a previous time. Mark 6:14–29 is a flashback referring to Herod's execution of John the Baptist. The speed with which story time is narrated may indicate an author's emphasis. In Matthew's Gospel, Jesus often teaches in long discourses in which the narration runs at approximately the same speed as story time (e.g., Matthew 5–7). This slowing emphasizes Jesus' role in Matthew as a great Moses-like teacher. In all four Gospels, story time slows considerably during the last week of Jesus' life and particularly through the passion narrative. This reveals the importance of Jesus' death for the Evangelists.

Characters

Closely related to the plot are its **characters**, whose actions and interactions carry the narrative forward. Characters can either be individuals—like Peter, Nicodemus, Judas—or groups, like the disciples, the Pharisees, or the crowds. Groups function as characters when they share similar traits and act together in the narrative. When the crowd cries for Jesus' death, "Crucify him!" (Mark 15:13), they are functioning as a single character.

Characterization is the manner in which characters are portrayed for the reader. Characters are understood from their *traits*, qualities attributed to them in the narrative. These traits may emerge in two ways, through "telling" or "showing." Telling is when the narrator explicitly ascribes a trait to the character. Jesus' father Joseph is identified as a "righteous man" (Matt. 1:19), and Zechariah and Elizabeth are "upright in the sight of God, observing all the Lord's commandments and regulations blamelessly" (Luke 1:6). Showing is when a character's traits emerge indirectly through their words and actions, their interaction with other characters, or their assessment by others. John the Baptist's righteous character is revealed in Matthew through his preaching and baptizing ministry (3:1–17), Jesus' testimony to his greatness (11:7–19), and the events surrounding his martyrdom (14:1–12).

Literary critics distinguish various types of characters. **Round characters** are complex and often unpredictable, with multiple traits. **Flat characters** are simple, one-dimensional, and predictable. Peter is a classic round character, with his contradictory traits of impetuous zeal, extreme loyalty, and wavering faith. The religious leaders are generally flat, predictably self-righteous, envious, and hypocritical. Characters can also be static or dynamic. **Dynamic characters** develop and change in the course of the narrative, while **static characters** remain the same. The disciples in Mark do not experience significant change, though they do have their ups and downs. In Luke-Acts, on the other hand, we see the disciples moving from immaturity to leadership in the church.

Jesus does not fit easily into these categories. He is certainly round rather than flat, a multifaceted and complex figure. Yet he is also in some sense static and predictable, since he always represents God's evaluative point of view. There is never a time the implied reader doubts that Jesus will act according to God's will.

This brings up the relationship of characterization to evaluative point of view. Characters are either good or bad, right or wrong, depending on their relationship to the story's evaluative point of view. Jesus is the main character and protagonist because he reflects perfectly the evaluative point of view of God. The chief antagonists—Satan, demons, and the religious leaders—oppose Jesus and so run counter to God's purpose and plan.

Setting

Setting refers to all facets of the narrative world in which characters act and events occur. There are three kinds of setting: local, temporal, and social.

Local setting refers to any spatial orientation, whether geography (mountains, lakes, etc.), political-cultural locales (Galilee, Judea, Jerusalem), or any other object or place (a room, a boat, a chair). The Synoptic Gospels locate Jesus' early ministry in Galilee, and especially in the towns and villages around the Sea of Galilee. Jesus' movement from Galilee to Jerusalem leads to the climax of the narrative. In John, by contrast, Jesus moves back and forth between Galilee and Judea, attending several Jewish festivals in Jerusalem.

Settings often carry symbolic as well as historical significance. Mountains are places of revelation, especially in Matthew's Gospel, in which Jesus is presented as a kind of new Moses giving God's law on the mountain (Matt. 5:1). The desert is a place of testing and revelation. Just as Israel was tested for forty years in the wilderness, so Jesus spends forty days in the desert tempted by Satan (Mark 1:13, par.). Jerusalem plays an important symbolic role in Luke's Gospel. It is the place where God's salvation is accomplished and from where the message of salvation goes forth in Acts. But it also represents Israel's stubborn rejection of God's purpose and her coming judgment.

Temporal settings also appear throughout the Gospels. Many of these are general ("one day as he was teaching," Luke 5:17); others are more specific. Jesus' transfiguration occurs

Sunrise over the Sea of Galilee

Richard Strauss

"after six days" (Mark 9:2); he dies at the "ninth hour" (Mark 15:34) and rises "on the first day of the week" (Luke 24:1). Temporal indicators may be chronological, related to sequence, or may be descriptive, related to type or kind of time. After a late night of ministry, Jesus rises "very early in the morning, while it was still dark," to pray (Mark 1:35). The point is the priority of prayer in Jesus' life. When Jesus says "pray that your flight will not take place in winter" (Matt. 24:20), he is referring not to the time of year *per se* but to the harsh conditions of the season. Jesus' healing on the Sabbath provokes outrage from the religious leaders because of the Old Testament law against Sabbath work. Jesus redefines the Sabbath as a day created for the benefit, not the burden, of people (Mark 2:27). Temporal settings, like physical ones, can carry symbolic significance. As noted above, the forty days of Jesus' testing in the wilderness are analogous to Israel's forty years of wandering. In John, Jesus' teaching during various Jewish festivals often carries symbolic links to those festivals. Jesus identifies himself as the "light of the world" and offers "living water" to the thirsty while teaching at the Feast of Tabernacles, a festival marked by water-pouring and lamp-lighting ceremonies (John 7:2, 37 – 39; 8:12).

Social-cultural setting refers to the world of human relationships in which the narrative occurs. These settings may be po-

Top: Sunrise from the top of Jebel Musa ("mountain of Moses"), looking west at the granite scenery and St. Catherine peak. *Bottom:* The Judean wilderness.

Settings like mountains, lakes, and deserts have theological as well as physical significance in the Gospels. The mountain is a place of revelation for Matthew, as it was for Moses and the nation Israel. The desert is a place of testing and danger.

litical, social, cultural, or economic. The Gospel narratives take place during the Roman occupation of Palestine in the first century AD. Jesus' statement "Give back to Caesar what is Caesar's" (Mark 12:17 TNIV, par.) makes little sense without an awareness of Roman hegemony and the Jewish revolutionary movements which arose from it. Jesus' parable of the tenant farmers (Mark 12:1 – 12, par.) comes to life when we recognize, first, that it is an adaptation of Isaiah's parable of the vineyard (Isa. 5:1 – 7) and, second, that it has as its backdrop the economic realities of poor peasant farmers and wealthy absentee landlords in the Galilean countryside. Jesus' call to invite the crippled, the lame, and the blind to one's

Jerusalem and the temple are important settings in Luke's Gospel. A view of Jerusalem from the southwest, from the model of first-century Jerusalem at the Holy Land Hotel. The temple and the Fortress of Antonia are at the top of the photo.

Richard Strauss

The settings of a narrative can include place, time, or social circumstances.

banquets (Luke 14:13–14) is perceived very differently today than in the first century, when meals were important rituals of social status.

To understand the narrative world of the Gospels, the reader must enter into their historical and cultural contexts. This aspect of setting is so important that the next three chapters will be devoted to the historical, religious, and social backgrounds of the Gospels.

Rhetoric: Narrative Patterns and Literary Devices

Rhetoric refers to the way in which a story is told to achieve the desired response from the reader. The Gospel narratives utilize a variety of narrative patterns and rhetorical devices. The recognition of these literary forms is not new to narrative criticism. Scholars have always recognized that the Gospels utilize many literary techniques. The following represent a small sampling.

Repetition is one of the simplest ways of stressing a theme. Repetition may be of words, phrases, or any number of narrative patterns. Matthew's narrator repeatedly says, "This was to fulfill what was spoken by the prophet, saying . . ." in order to emphasize that the Jesus story is the fulfillment of the Old Testament Scriptures. Mark is fond of series of threes. Three boat scenes illustrate the disciples' lack of faith (4:35–41; 6:45–52; 8:14–21); three times Jesus predicts his death (8:31–38; 9:31–37; 10:32–45); three times Peter denies him (14:68, 70, 71). Repetition indicates an author's concerns and emphases.

Chiasm refers to inverse parallelism, a concentric pattern in which a series repeats itself in reverse order. While this may be a simple pattern of four (ABBA), it can also be more complex, with six or more items (ABCDCBA). The item or items in the middle (here D) is often the point of emphasis. The narrative builds to this point and then descends from it. The prologue of John's Gospel is often treated as a chiasm (see fig. 10.4). While scholars sometimes go overboard in finding a chiasm under every biblical rock and tree, it is a fairly common literary device in ancient literature and an effective means of structuring a discourse.

Inclusio is a "bookend" structure in which the narrator identifies the boundaries of a section by placing a similar statement or episode at the beginning and end. A good example of inclusio is the two statements of Jesus' growth in "wisdom" (Luke 2:40, 52) on either side of the story of the boy Jesus' extraordinary wisdom (Luke 2:41–51). The two bookends provide an explanatory summary of the middle episode.

Intercalation, or "sandwiching," is similar to inclusio, except that one episode is inserted (intercalated) into the middle of another. The two episodes are generally related to a common theme. This is one of Mark's favorite literary devices, occurring numerous times throughout his Gospel. One of the most important examples is the author's sandwiching of Jesus' cleansing of the temple between the cursing of a fig tree and its discovery as withered (11:12–25). The intercalation suggests that the withering, like the temple clearing, represents God's judgment against Israel.

Symbolism is a general term for one thing standing for something else. As we have seen, settings of various kinds can carry symbolic significance (mountains, deserts, Jerusalem). Teaching methods like *metaphors* and *similes* are symbolic, making their points through comparison. Similes do this indirectly (the crowds are "*like* sheep without a shepherd," Matt. 9:36), while metaphors directly ("You *are* the light of the world," Matt. 5:14). A *similitude* is an extended simile. Jesus compares the kingdom of God to leaven, which works its way through the entire dough (Matt. 13:33). A *parable* is a short story with symbolic significance.

While in symbolism, the literal or apparent meaning points to a deeper meaning, in **irony** the apparent meaning is contrary to the real meaning. *Situational irony* is when events themselves are ironic. In a sense, the whole Gospel story is situational irony, since salvation is accomplished through the apparent defeat of the Messiah. John's Gospel is full of situational irony, as characters inadvertently make statements or raise questions that are ironically true. Nathanael doubts if anything good can come from Nazareth (1:46), and the Samaritan woman asks if Jesus is greater than her father Jacob (4:12). In the episode of the man born blind, the Pharisees ask sarcastically, "What? Are we blind too?" (9:40). The episode implies that, spiritually speaking, they are! *Verbal irony* is when a character intentionally uses irony. Jesus "congratulates" the religious leaders for setting aside the commandments of God in favor of their own traditions (Mark 7:9). He accuses the religious leaders of knowing how to interpret the changing weather, yet not recognizing the signs of the times (Matt. 16:2–3). In the parable of the rich fool, Jesus points to the irony of a man who has stored up great wealth for retirement but will die and lose it that very night (Luke 12:16–20).

Irony is a powerful rhetorical device because it creates a sense of community between the author and the readers. By recognizing the irony, readers become "insiders" to meaning which the story's characters miss. Symbolism plays a similar role. Readers who "get" the symbols identify with the author and the narrative's evaluative point of view.

Assessment of Narrative Criticism

Narrative criticism is a useful tool which provides important correctives to the abuses of historical-critical methods. Here are some of its strengths:

1. *Narrative criticism reads the text according to its literary form, as narrative or story.* The Gospel writers intentionally chose narrative as their medium, utilizing plot, characters, and settings to pass on the significance of Jesus. A method is needed which takes this genre seriously. Many students, after wading through the technical and subjective analyses of historical criticism, find narrative analysis refreshingly clear and relevant. This is partly because story is common to all human experience. We intuitively recognize the elements of narrative because we hear stories all our lives and live them out every day.

2. *Narrative criticism respects the unity and integrity of the text*, focusing on its present form rather than on the oral traditions or hypothetical sources which stand behind it. Protestant hermeneutics has traditionally considered the canonical text to be the authoritative Word of God. It is the biblical authors, not their sources, which were inspired by the Holy Spirit.

3. *By respecting the integrity of the text, narrative criticism allows a more objective analysis.* The subjectivity of reconstructing sources and determining editorial purposes is eliminated when the object of study is the text as it stands. While there are always some uncertainties concerning narrative purpose and strategy, these are considerably lessened because of the transparent nature of the story.

4. *Narrative criticism allows the determination of meaning without certainty concerning the life situation of the authors and their communities.* The narrative strategy and theological themes of the Second Gospel, for example, are discernible whether or not the author was John Mark, the companion of Paul and Peter, and whether or not he wrote while living in Rome in the late 60s.

5. *Narrative critics identify artistic and literary features of the Gospels*, which have received insufficient attention in the past. Narrative analysis has confirmed that the Evangelists are indeed authors and literary artists, not just compilers of traditions. Gospel studies have been enriched through an expanded vocabulary related to plot, character, and setting.

What are the weaknesses of narrative criticism? Most weaknesses are not fundamental to the method but relate to tendencies among some narrative critics:

1. *Narrative critics sometimes assume the nonhistoricity of the text, treating "story" as synonymous with "fiction."* This assumption is not necessary, however, since historical narrative means "history told as story," using narrative to depict real events which occurred in space and time. *Historical narrative* must here be distinguished from *historical novel*, in which the historical setting is real but the characters are fictitious.

2. *Narrative critics sometimes ignore or avoid historical and cultural background.* Since authors create narrative worlds, it is sometimes suggested that historical and cultural background are of little significance. Stories have lives of their own. But this wrongly assumes that narrative worlds have no relationship to the real world. While some stories may be told with little historical context (for example, I could tell a story about a boy and his dog without identifying the place, period of time, or cultural context), in historical narrative (and historical novel) the setting is a key part of the narrative world. The more readers know about this background, the better they will understand the story. Just as our understanding of Charles Dickens' historical novel *A Tale of Two Cities* is enriched if we know the history of eighteenth-century France, so our understanding of the Gospel narratives is deepened by learning their historical, cultural, and social backgrounds.

3. *Narrative critics sometimes impose modern literary categories on ancient literature.* Since narrative criticism borrows categories from contemporary literary theory, there is a danger of artificially imposing modern literary categories onto very different ancient forms. This is less of a danger than it may first appear, since all stories have certain common features, like plot, characters, and settings. Yet the caution is a good one, and narrative critics should look first to first-century rather than twenty-first-century literary models when analyzing the Gospels. As noted in chapter 1, recent research on ancient biography has enriched our understanding of the Gospel genre.[4]

> Narrative criticism is a valuable tool because it studies the Gospels according to their primary literary category: narrative or story.

4. *Narrative critics sometimes reject historical-critical approaches.* Narrative critics often treat the Gospels as independent works, rejecting any comparison between them. Yet while source and redaction analyses go beyond the scope of narrative criticism, they are not incompatible with it, and the methods can be used together. The likelihood that the Gospel writers used each other as sources means we can gain insights through their comparison.

OTHER LITERARY METHODS

Narrative criticism is not the only method which examines the text as a literary unity. Indeed, there are a variety of new methods being used in Gospel research today. Each has its own history, goals, and vocabulary. They have in common the study of the text in its final form, rather than its history of composition.

Rhetorical Criticism

Rhetoric refers to the skillful use of language to produce a desired effect in an audience. It is an ancient art which became the foundation of the educational system of the Greco-

---

4. See fig. 1.4; Richard A. Burridge, *What Are the Gospels? A Comparison with Graeco-Roman Biography* 2nd ed. (Grand Rapids: Eerdmans, 2004); David E. Aune, *The New Testament in Its Literary Environment* (Philadelphia: Westminster, 1987).

Roman world. The Greek philosopher Aristotle and the Roman orator Cicero both wrote major works on rhetoric.[5] Aristotle distinguished three types of rhetoric. *Judicial* rhetoric was meant to accuse or defend, as a lawyer would do in a court of law. *Deliberative* rhetoric was used to persuade or dissuade, as a politician trying to convince an audience at a political rally. *Epideictic* rhetoric was used to praise or blame another's actions, as a friend might eulogize another at a memorial service. Aristotle also categorized three kinds of appeal: *logos* (logic; sound reasoning of the mind), *pathos* (stirring the emotions of the heart), and *ethos* (character; appealing to what is morally right or noble). Cicero identified three purposes of rhetoric: to *instruct*, *delight*, and *persuade*.

Rhetorical criticism uses these and other categories to analyze the means of persuasion and rhetorical strategy of authors. Key pioneers in biblical rhetorical criticism have been James Muilenburg (Old Testament), and Amos Wilder and George A. Kennedy (New Testament).[6] Rhetorical criticism has proven especially useful in analyzing epistolary literature like the letters of Paul, and discourses found in narrative, like the speeches in Acts and the sermons of Jesus.

Rhetorical criticism is similar in some ways to narrative criticism in that both analyze the strategies used to produce a desired effect on the reader. One strength of rhetorical criticism is that it uses ancient categories to analyze ancient literature. While neither Paul nor the Gospel writers are likely to have had formal training in Greco-Roman rhetoric, they would have been familiar with the patterns of speech and methods of argumentation used by the philosophers and teachers of their day.

While helpful for analyzing letters and individual speeches, rhetorical criticism is less effective when studying the Gospel narratives as wholes. This is because the conclusions of rhetorical criticism are more dependent on the specific life situation (the *Sitz im Leben*) of the author and readers. While these settings are quite clear for a letter like 1 Corinthians (Paul is in Ephesus on his third missionary journey writing to the church in Corinth), they are less certain for our Gospels. We can make a good guess that Matthew is writing to a mixed church of Jews and Gentiles in Antioch, or that Mark is writing to persecuted believers in Rome, but it is precarious to base our narrative analysis on these hypotheses. It seems better to draw conclusions first and foremost from what we can see directly—the literary features of the text—than from a hypothetical reconstruction of the Gospel writer's setting in life.

Canon Criticism

As noted in chapter 1, the *canon* refers to the collection of books considered by the church to be authoritative Scripture. For Protestants, the canon is made up of the sixty-six books of the Old and New Testaments. Roman Catholics include the books of the Apocrypha. **Canon criticism** refers to a variety of methods which focus on the relationship of the books of the Bible to one another and the role they play in the life of the church. The goal of canon criticism is *to study the biblical text as the church's Scripture*, not merely as historical writings.

---

5. Aristotle, *The "Art" of Rhetoric* (mid-fourth century BC); Cicero, *Partitions of Oratory* (c. 87 BC).

6. James Muilenburg, "Form Criticism and Beyond," *JBL* 88: 1–18; Amos Wilder, *Early Christian Rhetoric: The Language of the Gospel* (Cambridge: Harvard, 1964); George A. Kennedy, *New Testament Interpretation through Rhetorical Criticism* (Chapel Hill: Univ. of North Carolina, 1984).

Key pioneers of canon criticism are Brevard Childs and James A. Sanders.[7] While canon critics of the Gospels do not reject historical-critical methods, they are more interested in the Gospels as literary wholes. Yet they go beyond narrative and rhetorical criticism to the broader question of how these texts were collected, preserved, and interpreted in faith communities. Some canon critics focus on the history of interpretation, others on the interplay of textual meaning between the Testaments and in the later church, still others on the hermeneutics of canon, that is, how it functions as authoritative Scripture.

While redaction critics might analyze the process by which Matthew edited Mark, and narrative critics the narrative strategy of the implied author, a canon critic is more interested in how the Gospels have been read and interpreted in church settings. Though each Gospel arose under unique circumstances, the church has traditionally viewed them as an inspired collection. This canonical approach is evident in the writings of a church father like Irenaeus, who insisted on the divine necessity of four Gospels and compared them to the four winds, the four points of the compass, the four covenants (Adam, Noah, Moses, Christ), and the four living creatures of Revelation 4:7 and Ezekiel 1:10 (man, lion, ox, eagle).[8]

For canon critics, it is not enough to seek a book's historical origin or the author's intention. While historical critics often deny Paul's authorship of the Pastoral Epistles (1–2 Timothy, Titus), the church has historically viewed them as part of the Pauline corpus, and so inspired Scripture. From a canon-critical perspective, historical authorship is secondary to canonical status, which confirms that the Pastorals are inspired Scripture and authoritative for the church's faith and practice. One explicit goal of canon critics is to take the Bible out of the ivory towers of critical scholarship and give it back to the church, for whom it was written.

Canon criticism can be seen as a positive contribution in that it focuses on the unity of the Gospels and their role as inspired Scripture. The same Holy Spirit who inspired the writing also guided the church's collection, preservation, and interpretation of the Gospels. On the other hand, there is a danger in shifting the locus of meaning from authors and texts to reading communities. Truth is unduly relativized when authority is seen to reside primarily in inspired communities rather than in an inspired text. There is also a danger in treating historical questions of origin and authorship as irrelevant. As we have noted before, the Bible's claim to truth is inextricably linked to its historical reliability.

Structuralism

Structuralism is not just a literary method but a variety of philosophical approaches which have their roots in the linguistic theories of Ferdinand de Saussure, the anthropological studies of Claude Lévi-Strauss, and the structural analysis of Russian folklore by Vladimir Propp.[9]

---

7. Brevard Childs, *The New Testament as Canon* (London: SCM, 1984; Philadelphia: Fortress, 1985); James A. Sanders, *Canon and Community: A Guide to Canonical Criticism* (Philadelphia: Fortress, 1984). Also see Robert W. Wall and Eugene E. Lemcio, *The New Testament as Canon: A Reader in Canonical Criticism*, JSNTSup 76 (Sheffield: JSOT, 1992).

8. Irenaeus, *Against Heresies* 3.11.8–9.

9. F. de Saussure, *Course in General Linguistics* (New York: McGraw-Hill, 1974); Claude Lévi-Strauss, *Structural Anthropology* (Garden City, NY: Basic Books, 1963); Vladimir Propp, *Morphology of the Folktale*, trans. L. Scott, 2nd ed. (Austin: Univ. of Texas, 1968; Russian ed. 1928).

The application of structuralism to biblical studies has been particularly championed by Daniel Patte and his colleagues at Vanderbilt University.[10]

Structuralists claim that literature, like language, functions in conventional patterns. Just as there are rules of grammar which govern the way we speak, so there is a "grammar" of literature which determines the way stories operate. While each story may have a different plot, setting, and characters, below this surface structure is a "deep structure" which follows certain stereotypical patterns. Certain plot movements, character types, and kinds of action are common to all stories. By identifying and categorizing these structures, stories can be objectively analyzed.

Structuralism is fundamentally *formalist* and *text-centered*. It is the underlying form or pattern—the deep structure—which determines the meaning of the story. Since an author may not even be conscious of this structure, meaning resides not in the author's intention but in the text itself.

While structuralism holds some promise of a more objective analysis of a narrative, it has not made deep inroads into Gospel studies and is not widely practiced today. This is probably because its technical vocabulary and complex methods are difficult to master and seldom seem to provide greater insights than a straightforward reading of the text.

Reader-Response Criticism

The next three methodologies may all be called *post-structuralist*, since they represent reactions against the claims of objective analysis found in structuralism. They all move the locus of meaning from the text to the reader.

Reader-response criticism represents a variety of approaches which find meaning not in the author's intention or in the text alone but in the response of readers. Within this broad category there are many variations. For some reader-response critics, there is no objective meaning in the text, since every reader creates his or her own meaning. No one reading is better than any other. Readers use the text to pursue their own interests and agendas. Others reject this "anything goes" approach and claim that there are legitimate and illegitimate readings but that these are determined not by the author's intention but by "reading communities."[11] A community's worldview, background, and context determine the correct meaning of the text. Still others consider meaning to reside neither in readers nor in texts but in some kind of dynamic interchange between the two. Readers produce meaning, but they do so within certain boundaries or limits established by the text.[12] More conservative reader-response practitioners study the way various readers respond to the text. This approach, sometimes called *audience criticism*, is usually more historical and text-centered than the others.

Reader-response criticism correctly recognizes that meaning is never perceived apart from a reader, and that readers always bring their worldviews, interests, and biases to the

---

10. Daniel Patte, *What Is Structural Exegesis?* (Philadelphia: Fortress, 1976); Daniel Patte, *Structural Exegesis for New Testament Critics* (Valley Forge, PA: Trinity Press International, 1990).

11. See Stanley Fish, *Is There a Text in This Class? The Authority of Interpretive Communities* (Cambridge, MA: Harvard Univ. Press, 1980).

12. See, for example, Wolfgang Iser, *The Act of Reading: A Theory of Aesthetic Response* (Baltimore: Johns Hopkins Univ., 1978).

text. Nobody reads without presuppositions. It is also important to recognize how much the reader's community determines his or her approach to the text. Readers from the industrialized West would do well to recognize that their reading is not the only one and that they can learn much through the eyes of others, particularly those whose cultures are closer to the first-century Mediterranean world in which the Gospels arose.

At the same time, identifying meaning with readers can open a Pandora's box of subjectivity and short-circuit the communication process. Though meaning is never perceived apart from a receiver, all true communication begins with a sender, whose intention or speech act provides the foundation for meaning. A methodology which takes into account the important role of readers in the interpretive process also needs to respect the integrity of the text as a means of communication and the author as the instigator of this speech act.

Liberationist and Feminist Approaches

Feminist and liberationist criticism may be viewed as subcategories of reader-response criticism, since they read the text from a particular viewpoint, whether from the view of women, ethnic minorities, the poor, or the politically oppressed.

Within this broad framework are a wide variety of approaches, from conservative to liberal. Feminist and liberationist approaches may also utilize other methods, such as redaction, narrative, or rhetorical criticism. What is common to these approaches is the goal of viewing the text through the eyes of the oppressed, the outsider, or the minority.

The strengths and weaknesses of these approaches are similar to reader-response methods. Our understanding of Scripture is enriched as we seek to read it through the eyes of others. On the other hand, forcing liberationist concerns onto the text risks losing both its historical meaning and its Spirit-inspired significance for today.

Deconstruction

Deconstruction may be treated as an extreme form of reader-response criticism, but in fact it is beyond its pale since it views all literature as having no inherent meaning. Initially developed in the works of Jacques Derrida, deconstruction began as a reaction against structuralism, claiming that the key to language is not structure but lack of structure and meaning.[13] Like structuralism, deconstruction is not just a literary theory but a whole philosophical system which can be applied to history, literature, and the arts.

Deconstruction begins with the premise that language is inherently unstable and imprecise. Since words can mean many different things, all communication, and hence all meaning, is constantly shifting and relative. Any piece of literature can be "deconstructed" to reveal its ambiguity and hence its meaninglessness. Since there are as many meanings as readers for any text, meaning is imposed on texts rather than inherent in them. When used by those in power, language is not a means of communication but a vehicle of oppression, a weapon which defines, limits, and controls rather than sets free. The goal of deconstruction is to free readers from the oppression of language and consequently from other types of oppression.

---

13. J. Derrida, *Writing and Difference*, trans. Alan Bass (Chicago: Univ. of Chicago Press, 1978); *A Derrida Reader: Behind the Blinds*, ed. Peggy Kamuf (New York: Columbia Univ. Press, 1991).

On the positive side, deconstructionists have correctly pointed out that all communication has a measure of imprecision and ambiguity. This should encourage humility and caution in all biblical interpretation. But what deconstructionists fail to acknowledge is that while any sentence can be deconstructed to show its ambiguities, incomplete knowledge does not mean zero knowledge. Something can be true without being 100 percent verifiable. Indeed little on this side of eternity is 100 percent certain. The apostle Paul confirms that while we live in this body, our knowledge is incomplete, a dim reflection of eternity (1 Cor. 13:12). Yet this partial knowledge is still meaningful and true. Even deconstructionists must admit that language has some ability to communicate, since they insist that what they are saying about their theory is true, and therefore meaningful. While deconstruction is treated with great seriousness in philosophical and literary circles, it has little value for any meaningful interpretation of the Gospels.

THE APPROACH OF THIS TEXT

Our approach to the four Gospels will be an eclectic one, taking into account their historical, social, literary, and theological features. First, we will assume that the Gospels are historical documents, written to Christian communities in a first-century Mediterranean context. Historical, social, and cultural backgrounds are therefore essential to understanding the text.

Second, we assume that these works have a composition history. It is beyond dispute that the authors used sources and that to a greater or lesser extent, we can discern these sources. While Markan priority is favored, most of our conclusions will be based on general Gospel comparison rather than a specific source theory.

> The present text seeks to take into account the historical, social, literary, and theological nature of the Gospels.

Third, Gospel comparisons (horizontal reading) will be done in the service of a narrative and theological analysis of the text (vertical reading). Though the Gospel writers used sources, each has a story to tell, and that story should be read as a literary and theological unity. Primary attention will be given to how the writers narrated their plots, portrayed their characters, developed their theological themes, and employed rhetorical devices.

Finally, from this narrative and theological analysis, we will seek to answer questions concerning the historical context of the authors and original audiences. While we assume the Gospels were written by historical authors to real audiences, our access to these specific contexts is limited and our conclusions are necessarily tentative. In our study of them, we will move from what is most certain to what is least. From a literary analysis, we can draw likely conclusions concerning the author's evaluative point of view and theological perspective. Tentative suggestions can then be made concerning authorship, audience, date, and life situation. Not only is this the most objective approach to the Gospels, but since inspiration by the Holy Spirit has traditionally been associated with the Gospels in their canonical form, it also represents a reverent and devotional approach.

Because the Gospel narrators are always reliable, and because we are assuming a real author behind the implied one, we will not always adhere to strict distinctions between real authors, implied authors, and narrators. Furthermore, when we use the designations "Matthew," "Mark," "Luke," and "John," we mean the implied author (the author as perceived in the narrative) behind whom lies a real author.

» CHAPTER SUMMARY «

1. Literary criticism refers to various methods of studying the Gospels as unified wholes, rather than from the perspective of sources and composition history.

2. Narrative criticism examines the Gospels as story, analyzing features such as plot, character, and setting.

   a. The evaluative point of view is the worldview, beliefs, and values which the implied reader is expected to adopt. The Gospels affirm the evaluative point of view of God, and of his agent Jesus Christ.

   b. The plot of a narrative is the progress of the story. It is made up of events, scenes, and acts, which move forward through causation and conflict to climax and resolution.

   c. Story time refers to the passage of time in the world of the text. Narrative time is the manner in which story time is presented. Story time can be narrated slowly or quickly. It can stop, move forward, or move backward (flashback).

   d. Characters can be individuals or groups. Characterization refers to the manner in which their traits are revealed in the story, either by telling or by showing. Characters can be round (complex) or flat (one dimensional); they can also be static (unchanging) or dynamic (progressing).

   e. Setting is all the features of the narrative world of the text. These settings can be local, temporal, or social-cultural.

   f. Rhetoric refers to the narrative patterns and literary devices used by the author to achieve a response. Some of the more common rhetorical features in the Gospels are repetition, chiasm, *inclusio*, and intercalation. Metaphors, similes, similitudes, and parables carry symbolic significance. Irony is also used with great effect throughout the Gospels.

   g. The primary strength of narrative criticism is that it analyzes the Gospels according to their basic genre: narrative. The main weakness is that narrative critics sometimes ignore the historical nature of these texts: their composition history (sources and redaction), their historical life setting, and the historicity of the events portrayed.

3. Other literary methods have also been applied to the Gospels:

   a. Rhetorical criticism uses categories developed in the ancient world to evaluate the rhetorical methods used to produce a desired effect on readers.

   b. Canon criticism seeks to read the Bible with reference to its role as inspired Scripture within the life of the church.

c. Structuralism seeks to identify conventional patterns — a "deep structure" — which lies behind the surface structure of the Gospel narratives. Structuralists seek an objective analysis of the text through the identification of universal and stereotypical features of plot, character, and setting.

d. Reader-response criticism is post-structuralist in that it claims the meaning of the text is to be found not in its formal structure but in the response of its readers. Reader-focused approaches are diverse, from those who claim texts have no inherent meaning and that the reader alone creates the meaning, to those who accept an original authorial meaning but seek to discern how certain readers would hear the text.

e. Liberationist and feminist approaches seek to read the text from the perspective of those who are less empowered or are oppressed.

f. Deconstruction rejects any inherent meaning in the text, considering all language to be a means of power and oppression.

4. The perspective of this text is eclectic, utilizing narrative and redaction criticism, with a constant eye on the historical, social, literary, and theological nature of the Gospels.

» KEY TERMS «

literary criticism

narrative criticism

real author, implied author, narrator

narrative world

evaluative point of view

real readers, implied readers, narratees

plot: events, scenes, acts

causation

conflict

Gentile

story time

narrative time

characters, characterization: round, flat, dynamic, static

settings: local, temporal, social-cultural

rhetoric: repetition, chiasm, inclusio, intercalation, symbolism, irony

rhetorical criticism

canon criticism

structuralism

reader-response criticism

feminist and liberationist criticism

deconstruction

1. What is the difference between historical and literary criticism, as defined in the text?

2. What is the goal of narrative criticism?

3. What is the difference between a real author, an implied author, and a narrator?

4. What does *evaluative point of view* mean? What is the evaluative point of view of the Gospels?

5. Describe the main features of plot, characterization, and setting.

6. Summarize the main goal of each of these other literary methods: rhetorical criticism, canon criticism, structuralism, reader-response criticism, liberation and feminist criticism, deconstruction.

7. Identify one strength and one weakness of each of these methods.

Digging Deeper

General Works on Literary Criticism

Beardslee, William. *Literary Criticism of the New Testament.* GBS. Philadelphia: Fortress, 1969.

Frei, Hans W. *The Eclipse of Biblical Narrative: A Study in Eighteenth and Nineteenth Century Hermeneutics.* New Haven, CT: Yale Univ. Press, 1974.

Green, Joel B., ed. *Hearing the New Testament: Strategies for Interpretation.* Grand Rapids: Eerdmans, 1995.

Moore, Stephen D. *Literary Criticism and the Gospels.* New Haven: Yale, 1989.

Peterson, Norman R. *Literary Criticism for New Testament Critics.* GBS. Philadelphia: Fortress, 1978.

Narrative Criticism

Culpepper, R. Alan. *The Anatomy of the Fourth Gospel: A Study in Literary Design.* Philadelphia: Fortress, 1983.

Kingsbury, Jack Dean. *Matthew as Story.* Philadelphia: Fortress, 1986.

Kingsbury, Jack Dean, ed. *Gospel Interpretation: Narrative-Critical and Social-Scientific Approaches.* Harrisburg, PA: Trinity Press International, 1997.

Powell, Mark Allen. *What Is Narrative Criticism?* GBS. Minneapolis: Fortress, 1990.

Resseguie, James L. *Narrative Criticism of the New Testament: An Introduction.* Rev. ed. Grand Rapids: Baker, 2005.

Rhoads, David, and Donald Michie. *Mark as Story: An Introduction to the Narrative of a Gospel.* 2nd ed. Philadelphia: Fortress, 1999.

Tannehill, Robert. *The Narrative Unity of Luke-Acts: A Literary Interpretation.* 2 vols. Philadelphia: Fortress, 1986–90.

Rhetorical Criticism

Kennedy, George A. *New Testament Interpretation through Rhetorical Criticism.* Chapel Hill: Univ. of North Carolina, 1984.

Mack, Burton. *Rhetoric and the New Testament.* Edited by Dan O. Via. GBS. Minneapolis: Fortress, 1990.

Porter, Stanley E., and Dennis L. Stamps, eds. *Rhetorical Criticism and the Bible.* JSNTSup 195. Sheffield: Sheffield Academic Press, 2002.

Canon Criticism

Childs, Brevard. *The New Testament as Canon.* London: SCM, 1984; Philadelphia: Fortress, 1985.

Sanders, James A. *Canon and Community: A Guide to Canonical Criticism.* Edited by Gene M. Tucker. GBS. Philadelphia: Fortress, 1984.

Wall, Robert W., and Eugene E. Lemcio. *The New Testament as Canon: A Reader in Canonical Criticism.* JSNTSup 76. Sheffield: JSOT, 1992.

Structuralism

Collins, Raymond. "Structural Analysis." In *Introduction to the New Testament.* Garden City, NY: Doubleday, 1983.

Patte, Daniel. *Structural Exegesis for New Testament Critics.* Valley Forge, PA: Trinity Press International, 1990.

———. *What Is Structural Exegesis?* Philadelphia: Fortress, 1976.

Reader-Response Criticism

Fish, Stanley. *Is There a Text in This Class? The Authority of Interpretive Communities.* Cambridge, MA: Harvard Univ. Press, 1980.

Iser, Wolfgang. *The Act of Reading: A Theory of Aesthetic Response.* Baltimore: Johns Hopkins Univ., 1978.

McKnight, Edgar V. *Postmodern Use of the Bible: The Emergence of Reader-Oriented Criticism.* Nashville: Abingdon, 1988.

Resseguie, J. "Reader-Response Criticism and the Synoptic Gospels." *JAAR* 52 (1984): 307–24.

Liberationist and Feminist Approaches

Bailey, Randall C. *Yet with a Steady Beat: Contemporary U.S. Afrocentric Biblical Interpretation.* Atlanta: SBL, 2003.

Brenner, Athalya, and Carole Fontaine, eds. *A Feminist Companion to Reading the Bible: Approaches, Methods and Strategies.* Sheffield: Sheffield Academic Press, 1997.

Fiorenza, Elisabeth Schussler. *Bread Not Stone: The Challenge of Feminist Biblical Interpretation.* Boston: Beacon, 1995.

Riggs, John W. *Postmodern Christianity.* Harrisburg, PA: Trinity Press International, 2003.

Schottroff, Luise, Silvia Schroer, and Marie-Theres Wacker. *Feminist Interpretation: The Bible in Women's Perspective.* Translated by Martin and Barbara Rumscheidt. Minneapolis: Fortress, 1998.

Schroer, Silvia, and Sophia Bietenhard, eds. *Feminist Interpretation of the Bible and the Hermeneutics of Liberation.* London: Sheffield Academic Press, 2003.

Tolbert, Mary Ann, ed. *The Bible and Feminist Hermeneutics. Semeia* 28. Atlanta: Scholars Press, 1983.

Deconstruction

Adam, K. M. *What Is Postmodern Biblical Criticism?* Edited by Dan O. Via. GBS. Minneapolis: Fortress, 1995.

Norris, Christopher. *Deconstruction: Theory and Practice.* New York: Methuen, 1982.

PART TWO

The Setting of the Gospels

Four score and seven years ago our fathers brought forth on this continent, a new nation, conceived in liberty, and dedicated to the proposition that all men are created equal. Now we are engaged in a great civil war, testing whether that nation, or any nation so conceived and so dedicated, can long endure. We are met here on a great battlefield of that war.

These words, the opening lines of the "Gettysburg Address" delivered by Abraham Lincoln on November 19, 1863, are among the most famous in American history. While the words are deeply moving in their own right, the address can be properly understood only in its historical context, the bloody Civil War which divided a nation, pitted brother against brother on the battlefield, and took more lives than any war in United States history. The more we know of the historical, political, and social world in which the speech was delivered, the more its words, images, and allusions come to life for the reader.

It is the same with the Gospels. While the stories of Jesus are profoundly significant in their own right, they can be fully understood only in light of the historical, social, and cultural context of Jesus' day. On the positive side, understanding factors like the importance of covenant and Torah (the law of Moses) in Israel's history, the history of Roman oppression in Palestine, and the background to the Pharisees and Sadducees will provide insight into the Gospel narratives. On the negative side, the reader who does not enter the world of the first century risks imposing twenty-first century ideas, attitudes, and worldviews on first-century texts and the Herodian dynasty.

CHAPTER 4

The Historical Setting of the Gospels

» CHAPTER OVERVIEW «

1. The Persian Period (539 – 334 BC)
2. The Greek Period (334 – 166 BC)
3. The Maccabees and Jewish Independence (166 – 63 BC)
4. The Roman Period (63 BC – AD 135)

» OBJECTIVES «

After reading this chapter, you should be able to:
- Summarize the main events of Israel's history from the close of the Old Testament canon to the destruction of Jerusalem by the Romans in AD 70.
- Identify and summarize the significance of key historical figures for this period, including Alexander the Great, Antiochus IV Epiphanes, Judas Maccabeus, Caesar Augustus, Herod the Great, Pontius Pilate, and Herod Antipas.
- Explain the significance of hellenization for the period of Jesus and the Gospels, including the nature of Ptolemaic and Seleucid rule in Palestine.
- Discuss the events leading up to the Maccabean Revolt and the period of Jewish independence under the Hasmonean dynasty.
- Summarize the nature of Roman rule in Palestine, first under Herod the Great and then under Roman governors.

At the end of the Old Testament period, the dominant power in the ancient Near East was the Medo-Persian Empire. When the reader opens the New Testament, four hundred years have passed, and the Roman Empire is now in control of the whole of the Mediterranean region. A survey of the political, religious, and cultural changes that took place during this period is essential for understanding the world in which Jesus lived and the birth of the New Testament.

THE PERSIAN PERIOD (539–334 BC)

The last major historical event in the Old Testament is the return of the Babylonian exiles to Israel under the Persian ruler Cyrus the Great. Unlike the Babylonians, who had destroyed the temple in Jerusalem and sent the Jews into exile, Cyrus had an enlightened policy of allowing exiled peoples to return to their homelands and worship their gods as they pleased. After conquering Babylon in 539 BC, Cyrus issued decrees allowing the Jews to return and

---

Figure 4.1—What's in a Name?
Naming and Dating the Period between the Testaments

"Second Temple" or "Intertestamental" Period?

Many scholars prefer the designation "Second Temple" to "intertestamental" for the period leading up to the New Testament era. The first temple, completed by Solomon around 960 BC, was destroyed by the Babylonians in 587 BC. The second temple, completed by Zerubbabel in 516 BC (and expanded later by Herod the Great), was eventually destroyed by the Romans in AD 70. *Intertestamental period* refers to approximately the same time frame, running from the writing of the last Old Testament book (Malachi; about 430 BC) to the birth of Jesus (about 4 BC). Second Temple is the more precise designation since it is unclear whether "intertestamental" culminates in the birth of Jesus, the writing of the New Testament (late first century), or its official recognition as canon (fourth century?). Second Temple is also more acceptable to Jewish scholars, who do not recognize the divine inspiration of the second (New) Testament.

The Intertestamental Period or "Four Hundred Silent Years"

c. 430 BC (BCE)	c. 4 BC (BCE)
Malachi Written	Birth of Jesus

The Second Temple Period

516 BC (BCE)	AD 70 (CE)
Second Temple Completed	Second Temple Destroyed by Romans

AD or CE?

For similar ecumenical reasons, the designations AD (*Anno Domini*, "the year of our Lord") and BC (Before Christ) are sometimes replaced with CE (Common Era) and BCE (Before the Common Era). The Common Era refers to the period in which Christianity and Judaism have existed together.

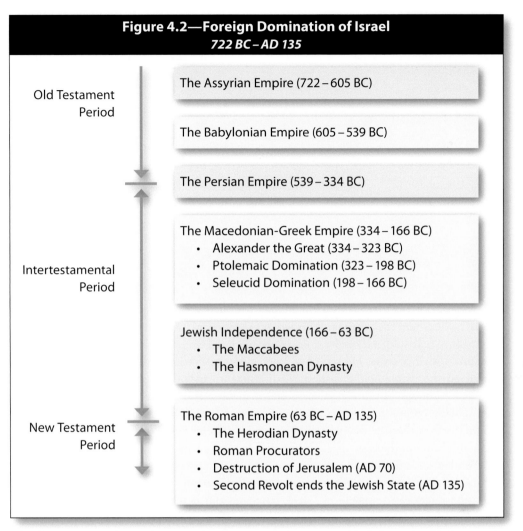

Figure 4.2—Foreign Domination of Israel
722 BC – AD 135

Old Testament Period

The Assyrian Empire (722 – 605 BC)

The Babylonian Empire (605 – 539 BC)

The Persian Empire (539 – 334 BC)

Intertestamental Period

The Macedonian-Greek Empire (334 – 166 BC)
- Alexander the Great (334 – 323 BC)
- Ptolemaic Domination (323 – 198 BC)
- Seleucid Domination (198 – 166 BC)

Jewish Independence (166 – 63 BC)
- The Maccabees
- The Hasmonean Dynasty

New Testament Period

The Roman Empire (63 BC – AD 135)
- The Herodian Dynasty
- Roman Procurators
- Destruction of Jerusalem (AD 70)
- Second Revolt ends the Jewish State (AD 135)

rebuild the city and temple. Over 42,000 returned with Zerubbabel to rebuild the temple (Ezra 1 – 6). More followed with Ezra (Ezra 7 – 10), and Nehemiah later returned to rebuild the walls of Jerusalem (Nehemiah 1 – 6; c. 445 BC). The last of the Old Testament books, Malachi, was written about this time (c. 430 BC).

Old Testament history ends with this return and restoration of Israel in the land. The period which followed is called the **Second Temple period**, or the intertestamental period (see fig. 4.1).

THE GREEK PERIOD (334 – 166 BC)

Alexander the Great and the Hellenization of Palestine

One of the most remarkable leaders of the ancient world was **Alexander the Great**, the son of Philip II of Macedon. Philip was an ambitious ruler who had succeeded in unifying the Greek city-states and developing the Macedonians into a mobile and effective army.

Alexander the Great's Conquests

When Philip's plans to overthrow the Persian Empire were cut short by his assassination in 336 BC, Alexander took over both his father's throne and his passion for conquest. Though only twenty years old, Alexander quickly consolidated his power in Greece and then swept eastward with his army. He repeatedly defeated the Persians and, in a very short time, conquered the whole of the eastern Mediterranean, including Syria, Egypt, Persia, and Babylon. Although Alexander died suddenly at only thirty-three years of age (probably from malaria complicated by drunkenness—though poison has also been suggested!), in a mere thirteen years he established a vast empire stretching from Greece to Egypt in the south and India in the east.

While Alexander's swift conquest proved his military genius, his most influential role in history is his promotion of the process of **hellenization**. *Hellas* means Greece, and hellenization refers to the spread of Greek language and culture. Alexander, who had been trained by the philosopher Aristotle, had a deep affection for all things Greek and sought to introduce Greek ways throughout the territories he conquered. He founded Greek-style cities with theaters, public baths, and gymnasiums and encouraged the introduction of Greek customs and manners. Alexander also settled Greek colonists throughout his empire and encouraged his soldiers to marry local women. Although the Romans would later conquer the Greeks, in many ways the Greeks conquered the Romans, as the latter adopted Greek models of art, literature, philosophy, and religion.

> Alexander's most enduring legacy for New Testament background is his promotion of the process of hellenization.

Because the Jews did not resist Alexander's conquest, they were allowed a degree of independence, and temple worship continued unhindered. Nevertheless, hellenization had a profound impact on Jewish society.[1] Virtually every inhabit-

---

1. See Martin Hengel, *Judaism and Hellenism: Studies in Their Encounter in Palestine during the Early Hellenistic Period*, trans. J. Bowden, 2 vols. (Philadelphia: Fortress, 1974).

ant of Israel came into contact with Greek culture, whether through soldiers, government officials, merchants, or landowners. While all of Judaism became hellenized to one degree or another, this clash of cultures inevitably produced conflict. Many Jews—particularly those of the upper classes—willingly embraced Greek customs and philosophy as superior to their own. Others opposed what they viewed as the paganization of Judaism. The stage was being set for crisis and conflict.

One of the most important results of hellenization for the background to the New Testament was the emergence of **koinē** ("common") **Greek** as the *lingua franca*, or trade and diplomatic language, of the eastern Mediterranean. Throughout the "civilized" (Roman) world, anyone who could not speak Greek was considered a barbarian. Though Latin was the official language of the Roman Empire, it was spoken mainly in the west, and Greek remained the *lingua franca* throughout the empire. The Israel of Jesus' day was trilingual. Hebrew was still read and spoken in religious contexts; Aramaic—the *lingua franca* prior to Alexander's conquests—was the language of the common people; and Greek was the language of trade and government. (Latin would have also been spoken by Roman officials.) Jesus probably conversed in all three languages, though most of his teaching was in Aramaic. The New Testament books are all written in *koinē* Greek, though the style and

> The Israel of Jesus' day was trilingual; Greek, Aramaic, and Hebrew were spoken in various contexts.

Figure 4.3—The Language Milieu of First-Century Palestine

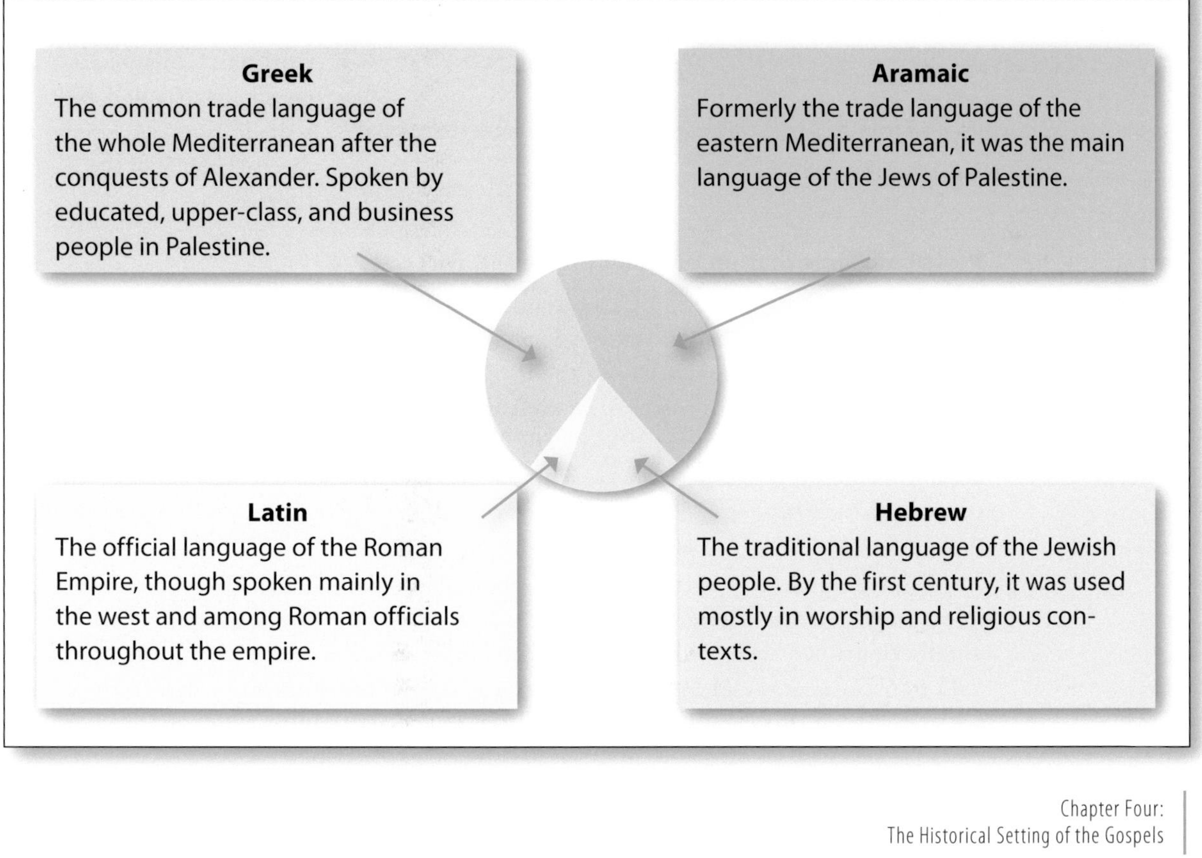

Greek
The common trade language of the whole Mediterranean after the conquests of Alexander. Spoken by educated, upper-class, and business people in Palestine.

Aramaic
Formerly the trade language of the eastern Mediterranean, it was the main language of the Jews of Palestine.

Latin
The official language of the Roman Empire, though spoken mainly in the west and among Roman officials throughout the empire.

Hebrew
The traditional language of the Jewish people. By the first century, it was used mostly in worship and religious contexts.

Seleucid and Ptolemaic Kingdoms in 323 – 166 BC

literary quality differs among the various authors. Occasional Aramaic, Hebrew, and Latin words appear, transliterated with Greek letters.

It has sometimes been claimed that God divinely prepared *koinē* Greek as the perfect language for divine revelation, with its precise grammatical nuance and exact definitions of words. This linguistic argument is flawed, since no human language—including Greek—is free from ambiguities. Yet divine providence can be seen in the conquests of Alexander and the dissemination of the Greek language throughout the Mediterranean region. This linguistic homogeneity enabled the Christian missionaries to preach, teach, and write in a single language among the diverse peoples of the Roman Empire.

Ptolemaic Domination of Israel (323 – 198 BC)

When Alexander died in 323 BC, a power struggle ensued for control of his empire. War and conflict between his four leading generals eventually resulted in the establishment of two great dynasties. The dynasty of the **Ptolemies** was centered in Egypt, with Alexandria as its capital. The dynasty of the **Seleucids** was centered in Syria, with Antioch as its capital. Because Israel was strategically located between Syria and Egypt, the nation became caught in a tug-of-war between these two rivals. The Ptolemies gained control of Israel and ruled her for 125 years. The Jews lived in relative peace and prosperity under Ptolemaic rule.

During this time, Alexandria, Egypt, the capital of the Ptolemaic Empire, developed into a major center of scholarship and learning. A vibrant Greek-speaking Jewish community flourished there. Since most Jews no longer spoke or read Hebrew, the need arose for a translation of the Hebrew Scriptures into Greek. One of the most significant literary achievements of this period was the translation of the **Septuagint** (abbreviated **LXX**), the

Figure 4.4—The Septuagint

The Septuagint was the most widely used Greek translation of the Old Testament. The term is derived from the legend about its origin found in the *Letter of Aristeas*, written about the end of the second century BC. According to this letter, during the reign of Ptolemy II Philadelphus (284 – 247 BC), Ptolemy's librarian Demetrius found that he was lacking a Greek translation of the Law of the Jews. Ptolemy sent a request to Eleazar, the Jewish high priest in Jerusalem, who sent 72 scholars, six from each of the twelve tribes, to undertake the task. The translation was reportedly completed in 72 days and was read to the assembled Jewish community, which rejoiced at its accuracy.

A later version of the story claims that by divine inspiration, all the scholars working independently produced an identical Greek text! The name Septuagint comes from the Latin word for seventy (*septuaginta*), a rounded-off reference to the 72 scholars who supposedly completed the work. The Roman numeral for seventy, LXX, is used as an abbreviation for the translation.

Though the details of the story are doubtful, it is likely that a Greek version of the Pentateuch arose in Alexandria in the third century BC. Because Hebrew was no longer widely spoken, Jews of the Diaspora ("dispersion," Jews living outside of Israel) needed a Greek translation of the Scriptures. The Law was probably translated first, and the rest of the Hebrew Bible (the Prophets and the Writings) gradually followed. The LXX is a rather uneven translation, sometimes more literal, sometimes more free. Like the Hebrew Scriptures and the Greek New Testament, it also has its own textual history of transmission and recension.

Though far from a perfect translation, the Septuagint had a profound effect on the Judaism of the Diaspora and on the origins of Christianity:

1. The LXX became the Bible of Diaspora Jews, most of whom no longer spoke Hebrew. The translation was widely used in the synagogues throughout the Mediterranean.
2. The LXX provided Hebrew senses to many Greek words. For example, in classical Greek, the term *doxa* generally carried the sense of "opinion." Its use in the LXX to translate the Hebrew *kābôd* helped define its sense as "glory." The LXX thus aided in the translation of Old Testament concepts for a Greek audience and gave the Christians a ready-made Greek vocabulary for preaching a gospel whose background lay in the Old Testament.
3. The LXX clarified Hebrew ideas that could have been misunderstood in the Gentile world. For example, in Joshua 4:24 in the LXX, the Hebrew phrase "*hand* of the LORD" is translated as "*power* of the LORD," perhaps to avoid the anthropomorphism, which a Gentile might interpret literally.
4. The LXX provided the early Christians with a Bible that was understandable throughout the Mediterranean world. Christians could use it when preaching to both Jews and Gentiles. In this way, the LXX became a powerful apologetic tool for the early church. Most Old Testament quotations in the New Testament are taken from the LXX. An example of this apologetic value may be seen in Isaiah 7:4, where the Hebrew term ʿ*almāh* ("young woman") is translated in the LXX with *parthenos*, a Greek term with strong connotations of virginity (cf. Matt. 1:23). Using the LXX, Christians could point to this Old Testament text as evidence for the virgin birth of Christ.

Codex Sinaiticus, a fourth-century manuscript containing the Septuagint (Greek Old Testament) and the New Testament

Ronald Youngblood

Greek version of the Old Testament. The Septuagint became the primary Bible of both Jews of the **Diaspora** and the early Christians (see fig. 4.4). *Diaspora* means "dispersion" and refers to Jews who were not living in Israel but were dispersed throughout the rest of the Mediterranean world.

Seleucid Domination of Palestine (198 – 166 BC)

There was constant war and strife between the Ptolemies of Egypt and the Seleucids of Syria. The Syrians failed repeatedly to gain control of Israel until 198 BC, when the Seleucid ruler Antiochus III (known as Antiochus the Great) defeated Egypt at the battle of Paneion and occupied Israel. Antiochus's aspirations for dominance were dampened, however, as he faced a new and growing threat from the west, the rising power of Rome. When he invaded Greece, Rome intervened, forcing him to withdraw and requiring him to pay a huge annual tribute. The Romans also took his son to Rome as a hostage.

Antiochus IV "Epiphanes." When Antiochus III's son was released from Rome fourteen years later, he returned to Syria and succeeded his brother Seleucus IV as ruler of the Seleucid Empire. Under **Antiochus IV** (175 – 163 BC), Israel would face perhaps its greatest threat to survival ever. Antiochus called himself **Epiphanes**, "manifest one"—a claim to be a god. His erratic behavior, however, earned him the nickname "Epimanes," meaning "madman."[2] Antiochus was not satisfied with the gradual assimilation of Hellenistic ideas which had taken place under the Ptolemies. He sought to bring Israel fully into his empire by turning it into a Hellenistic state. Facing crushing tribute to Rome, he increased taxation and repeatedly looted the treasures of the Jerusalem temple. He sold the office of high priest to the highest bidder, first to Jason, the brother of the high priest Onias III, and later to a man named Menelaus, who did not even have priestly ancestry. Jason, an ardent Hellenist,

---

2. Polybius, *Histories* 26.1 – 14

Figure 4.5—Antiochus IV "Epiphanes"
Prototype of Antichrist

The calculated and ruthless attempts by Antiochus IV Epiphanes to eradicate Judaism were not quickly forgotten by the Jews, setting a standard of evil which later generations recalled when evil rulers set themselves up in opposition to God's people (see Dan. 7:7 – 8; 8:9 – 14; 11:21 – 35; *Testament of Moses* 6 – 10; Mark 13:14, par.). New Testament writers echo these passages from Daniel, identifying the coming world ruler variously as "antichrist" (1 John 2:18, 22; 4:3; 2 John 7), "man of lawlessness" (2 Thess. 2:1 – 12), and the "beast" (Rev. 11:7; 13:1 – 18).

> And the king [Antiochus] sent letters by messengers to Jerusalem and the towns of Judah; he directed them to follow customs strange to the land, to forbid burnt offerings and sacrifices and drink offerings in the sanctuary, to profane sabbaths and festivals, to defile the sanctuary and the priests, to build altars and sacred precincts and shrines for idols, to sacrifice swine and other unclean animals, and to leave their sons uncircumcised. They were to make themselves abominable by everything unclean and profane, so that they would forget the law and change all the ordinances.
>
> He added, "And whoever does not obey the command of the king shall die."
>
> — 1 Maccabees 1:44–50 NRSV

began to turn Jerusalem into a Greek city, building a gymnasium below the sacred temple site. Greek-style games were held, in which Jewish youths competed nude in Greek style. Operations were even performed to reverse the effects of circumcision. While many Jews were enamored with Hellenism and so were receptive to such changes, others were outraged. Increasing division arose between reforming **Hellenists**, who favored the adoption of Greek ideas, and conservative **Hasidim** (meaning "holy ones"), who opposed them.

Coin with the bust of Antiochus IV "Epiphanes," whose policy of forced hellenization provoked the Maccabean revolt.

The "Abomination of Desolation." The situation went from bad to worse after one of Antiochus's military campaigns against Egypt. Outside of Alexandria, a Roman diplomat met him and ordered him to turn back or face the wrath of Rome. Knowing firsthand the power of Rome from his years as a hostage, Antiochus withdrew in humiliation. Aware that many in Jerusalem were still loyal to the Egyptian Ptolemies, Antiochus vented his anger against the city by looting the temple, destroying the city walls, and killing thousands of citizens. In the dark days that followed, he moved to suppress Judaism. Sabbath observance, circumcision, and keeping the law were banned. Copies of Scripture were confiscated and burned. On the 25th day of Chislev (December), 167 BC, an altar dedicated to Zeus Olympius was set up in the Jerusalem temple, and pigs and other unclean animals were offered as sacrifices. This idolatrous desecration of the temple is referred to in Daniel as the "**abomination of desolation**" — the sacrilege which brings destruction (Dan. 11:31; 12:11). Jesus would later draw on this powerful imagery to predict the horrors of the siege and destruction of Jerusalem in AD 70 (Mark 13:14, par.).

THE MACCABEES AND JEWISH INDEPENDENCE (166–63 BC)

Though the desecration of the temple by Antiochus Epiphanes was one of the darkest times in Jewish history, out of this came one of the most exciting times, the Maccabean Revolt and a period of Jewish independence.

The Maccabean Revolt (166–135 BC)

Pious Israelites realized that Antiochus's actions threatened their national and religious existence. Rebellion broke out in the Judean village of Modein, where an old priest named Mattathias was ordered by a Syrian official to offer a pagan sacrifice. Mattathias refused, and another Jew stepped forward to perform the rite. Infuriated, Mattathias rushed forward

On Hanukkah, the celebration of the victory of the Maccabees, lamps are lit to show that darkness will give way to light.

and killed both the man and the Syrian official. He destroyed the pagan altar and fled with his five sons into the hills. There they gathered an army of rebels to fight the Syrians. They were joined by the Hasidim, the pious separatists who desired to purge Judaism of pagan influence.

Mattathias died in 166 BC, leaving his son **Judas** to lead the revolt (166–160 BC). Judas's prowess in battle earned him the nickname "Maccabeus," from the Aramaic word meaning "hammer." From this name, the rebellion came to be called the Maccabean Revolt, and its leaders **the Maccabees**. Judas developed the Jews into an effective guerrilla army and repeatedly defeated the Syrians in battle. After some setbacks, he eventually succeeded in liberating the temple in Jerusalem. On Chislev (December) 25, 164 BC, exactly three years after the desecration by Antiochus Epiphanes, Judas reinitiated Jewish sacrifices. This victory became commemorated in the Jewish festival of **Hanukkah**, meaning "dedication" (also called the Festival of Lights). The story of the victory of Judas and his brothers is told in the apocryphal books of 1 and 2 Maccabees (see chap. 5, pp. 141–42).

The Hasmonean Dynasty (135–63 BC)

After Judas was killed in battle in 160 BC, leadership passed to his brothers, first Jonathan (160–143 BC) and then Simon (143–135 BC). Simon eventually gained political independence from the Syrians, taking the title "leader and high priest." He thus established the **Hasmonean dynasty** (named after Hasmon, an ancestor of Mattathias), a line of priest-kings which would rule Israel until the Roman occupation in 63 BC.

Modein burial site of the Maccabees. This area is where the Jewish revolt of 166 BC against Antiochus Epiphanes began. The burial chambers are topped by heavy blocks.

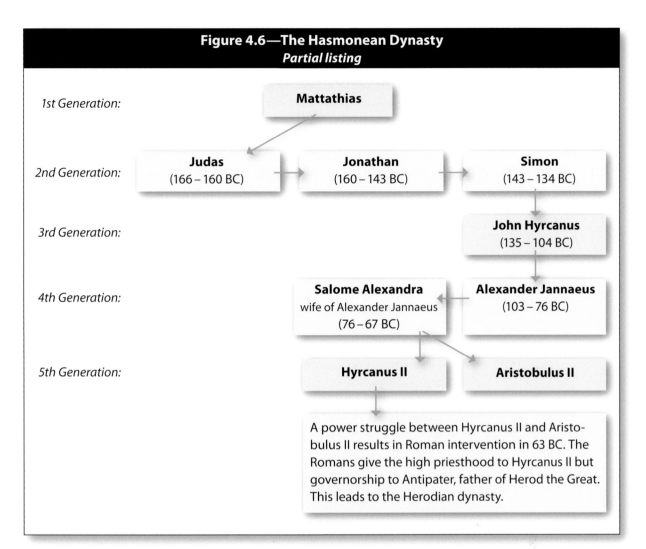

Figure 4.6—The Hasmonean Dynasty
Partial listing

1st Generation: **Mattathias**

2nd Generation: **Judas** (166–160 BC) → **Jonathan** (160–143 BC) → **Simon** (143–134 BC)

3rd Generation: **John Hyrcanus** (135–104 BC)

4th Generation: **Salome Alexandra** wife of Alexander Jannaeus (76–67 BC) ← **Alexander Jannaeus** (103–76 BC)

5th Generation: **Hyrcanus II** **Aristobulus II**

A power struggle between Hyrcanus II and Aristobulus II results in Roman intervention in 63 BC. The Romans give the high priesthood to Hyrcanus II but governorship to Antipater, father of Herod the Great. This leads to the Herodian dynasty.

While the Maccabean Revolt ended Seleucid domination of Israel, the subsequent history of the Hasmonean dynasty is one of power struggles and political intrigue. Simon and two of his sons were assassinated in 135 BC by Ptolemy, Simon's son-in-law. His only surviving son, John Hyrcanus (135–104 BC), took the throne and began an expansionist policy. He defeated the Idumeans in the south (the ancient Edomites, descendants of Jacob's brother Esau; Idumea is Latin for Edom) and forced Judaism upon them. He also conquered the Samaritans, burning their temple on Mount Gerizim. Such actions increased the animosity between Jews and Samaritans that had begun in the Old Testament era. Evidence of this antagonism appears repeatedly in the Gospels (Luke 9:51–56; 10:25–37; John 4:9). Alexander Jannaeus (103–76 BC), the son of John Hyrcanus, continued this expansionist policy, gaining territories as extensive as the kingdoms of David and Solomon.

Ironically, these later Hasmoneans openly adopted Hellenistic ways and became involved in the political machinations common to Hellenistic kings. Out of a growing alienation, the religious-minded Hasidim began to separate themselves from the Hasmonean leadership and from political life in general. Two groups which emerged from this separation were the Pharisees and the Essenes. Both groups opposed not only the corruption and hellenization of the Hasmonean priest-kings but also the elimination of the traditional balance of power between the king from the line of David and the high priest descended from Levi. In their eyes, the Hasmoneans illegitimately combined both offices. In opposition to the Pharisees, the party of the Sadducees arose from the supporters of the Hasmonean priesthood. They were aligned with the Jerusalem aristocracy and the temple priesthood. We will discuss the beliefs and practices of these groups in the next chapter.

THE ROMAN PERIOD (63 BC–AD 135)

Roman domination of Palestine began in 63 BC, when the Roman general Pompey captured a Jerusalem weakened by a power struggle between two Hasmoneans, Hyrcanus II and Aristobulus II, both sons of Alexander Jannaeus. The conquering Romans made Hyrcanus II high priest and ethnarch ("ruler of a people"—a title for a minor ruler). The real power behind the throne, however, lay with Hyrcanus's advisor, a man named Antipater who had gained the favor of the Roman authorities (see fig. 4.7). The Romans made Antipater governor of Judea, and he appointed his sons Phasael and Herod as military governors of Jerusalem and Galilee. Although Antipater was an **Idumean** (or Edomite) rather than a Jew, the Romans made little distinction since the Jews had ruled Idumea under the Hasmoneans.

When Antipater was killed in 43 BC, a power struggle ensued between Antigonus, the son of Aristobulus II, and Antipater's two sons, Herod and Phasael. Phasael was captured and committed suicide, but Herod fled to Rome. There he appealed to the Romans for help and was appointed king of Judea. Returning to Israel with a Roman army, he defeated

The Roman Empire

and executed Antigonus, the last of the Hasmonean rulers. The Hasmonean dynasty was over. The Herodian dynasty had begun.

Herod the Great

Herod "the Great" ruled as king of the Jews under Roman authority for thirty-three years, from 37 – 4 BC. It is this Herod who appears in the account of Jesus' birth (Matt. 2:1 – 19; Luke 1:5). From the start, Herod proved to be an extraordinary political survivor. When civil war broke out in Rome between Mark Antony and Octavian, Herod first sided with Antony and his ally Cleopatra VII, queen of Egypt. When Octavian defeated Antony and Cleopatra at Actium in 31 BC, Herod immediately switched sides, convincing Octavian of his loyalty. Following his victory, Octavian returned to Rome, where the Roman Senate made him *imperator*, or supreme military leader, and gave him the honorary title "Augustus" ("exalted one"). Historians mark this event as the end of the Roman Republic and the beginning of the Roman Empire, the transfer from rule by the Senate to rule by a supreme emperor. Under the patronage of Octavian — now **Caesar Augustus** — Herod's position as king of the Jews was secure. For his part, Herod would prove to be a loyal subject to his Roman overlords, maintaining order in Israel and protecting the western flank of the Roman Empire.

Roman soldier

Z. Radovan, Jerusalem

Herod was a strange mix of a clever and efficient ruler and a cruel tyrant. On the one hand, he was distrustful, jealous, and brutal, ruthlessly crushing any potential opposition. Because he was an Idumean, the Jews never accepted him as their legitimate king, a rejection which infuriated him. Having usurped the Hasmonean rulers, he constantly feared conspiracy. To legitimize his claim to the throne, he divorced his wife Doris and married the Hasmonean princess Miriamne, later executing her when he suspected she was plotting against him. Three of his sons, another wife, and his mother-in-law met the same fate when they too were suspected of conspiracy. The Roman emperor Augustus once said he would rather be Herod's pig than his son, a play on words in Greek, since the two words sound alike (*hus* and *huios*).[3] Herod, trying to be a legitimate Jew, would not eat pork, but he freely murdered his sons! Matthew's account of Herod's slaughter of the infants in Bethlehem fits well with what we know of the king's ambition, paranoia, and cruelty (Matt. 2:1 – 18).

> Herod the Great was a strange mix of a clever and efficient ruler and a cruel tyrant.

At the same time, Herod presented himself as the protector of Judaism and sought to gain the favor of the Jews. He encouraged the development of the synagogue communities and in time of calamity remitted taxes and supplied the people with free grain. He was also a great builder, a role which earned him the title "the Great." His greatest project was the rebuilding and beautification of the temple in Jerusalem, restoring it to even greater splendor than in the time of Solomon.

---

3. Macrobius, *Saturnalia* 2.4.11

Above and below left: One of the many building projects of Herod the Great, the Herodium is located 3.5 miles southeast of Bethlehem. According to Josephus, it served as a palace and a fortress for Herod, and he was buried here in 4 BC. The Herodium later served as a base for Jewish rebels during the first and second revolts against the Romans.

Above: A reproduction of Herod's palace in Jerusalem. From the model of Jerusalem at the Holy Land Hotel.

Right: An aqueduct built by Herod the Great in Caesarea Maritima

Judea prospered economically during Herod's reign. He extended Israel's territory through conquest and built fortifications to defend the Roman frontiers. A committed Hellenist and an admirer of Roman culture, Herod built Greek-style theaters, amphitheaters, and hippodromes (outdoor stadiums for horse and chariot racing) throughout the land. While this earned him the favor of many upper-class Jews, it brought disdain from the more conservative Pharisees and the common people. The Herodians mentioned in the Gospels (Mark 3:6; 12:13) were Hellenistic Jewish supporters of the Herodian dynasty, who favored the stability and status quo brought by Roman authority.

Herod died in 4 BC (cf. Matt. 2:19), probably from intestinal cancer. As a final act of vengeance against his contemptuous subjects, he rounded up leading Jews and commanded that at his death they should be executed. His reasoning was that if there was no mourning *for* his death, at least there would be mourning *at* his death! (At Herod's death, the order was overruled and the prisoners were released.)

The Kingdom of Herod the Great.

Below: Caesarea Maritima, built by Herod the Great, was the center of Roman administration for Palestine during the time of Christ.

The Herodian Dynasty

Herod had changed his will several times during his life, and after his death it was contested by three of his sons. They appealed to Caesar Augustus, who divided the kingdom among them.

Archelaus (4 BC–AD 6) became ethnarch of Judea, Samaria, and Idumea, with the promise that if he ruled well, he would be made king. Instead, he proved to be oppressive and erratic, and Augustus removed him from office in AD 6. Matthew notes that Joseph and Mary moved to Galilee to avoid Archelaus's rule (Matt. 2:21–23). When Archelaus was removed from office, Judea and Samaria were transferred to the control of Roman governors, known as prefects and, later, procurators. The most important of these for the study of the New Testament is **Pontius Pilate** (AD 26–36), under whose administration Jesus was crucified. Other governors who appear in the New Testament are Felix (AD 52–59) and Festus (AD 59–62), before whom Paul stood trial (Acts 23–26).

Herod Antipas became tetrarch of Galilee and Perea from his father's death in 4 BC until he was deposed by the emperor Caligula in AD 39. The title tetrarch originally meant ruler of a fourth part of a region but came to be used of any minor ruler. This is the Herod of Jesus' public ministry. He imprisoned and eventually executed John the Baptist when John spoke out against

The Herodian Kingdoms. After AD 6, the territory formerly allotted to Archelaus was ruled by successive Roman governors.

his marriage to Herodias, his brother Philip's ex-wife (Luke 3:19–20; Mark 6:17–29). He also wondered about Jesus' identity when people speculated that John had risen from the dead (Mark 6:14–16, par.). When warned by some Pharisees that Herod was seeking his life, Jesus derisively called him "that fox," probably a reference to his cunning and deceit (Luke 13:31–32). Eventually, Antipas got his wish to see Jesus when Pilate sent Jesus to stand before him at his trial (Luke 23:7–12; cf. Acts 4:27).

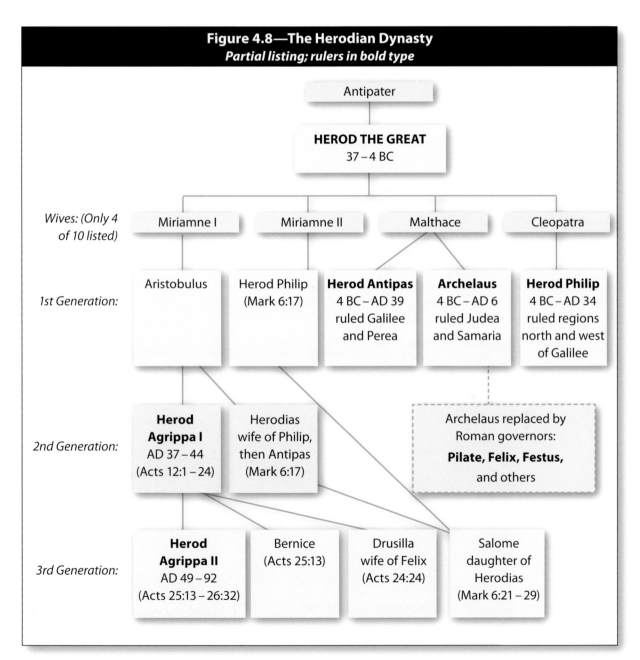

Figure 4.8—The Herodian Dynasty
Partial listing; rulers in bold type

Herod Philip became tetrarch of Iturea, Trachonitis, Gaulanitis, Auranitis, and Batanea, regions north and east of Galilee. He died without an heir, and his territory became part of the Roman province of Syria. He is mentioned in the New Testament only in Luke 3:1 (the Philip of Mark 6:17 [cf. Matt. 14:3] is a different son of Herod the Great).

Only two other members of the Herodian dynasty appear in the New Testament, both in Acts. Herod Agrippa I was the son of Aristobulus and the grandson of Herod the Great. He executed James, the brother of John, and arrested Peter (Acts 12). His death at Caesarea as judgment by God is recorded both by Luke and by the Jewish historian Josephus (Acts 12:19–23; Josephus, *Ant.* 19.8.2 §§343–52). Herod Agrippa II was the son of Agrippa I. It was this Herod, together with his sister Bernice, who was invited by the Roman governor Festus to hear Paul's defense at Caesarea (Acts 25–26). Another sister, Drusilla, was married to the Roman governor Felix (Acts 24:24).

A bust of Caesar Augustus, first emperor of the Roman Empire (30 BC – AD 14)

Roman Rule and the *Pax Romana*

When Augustus became emperor in 31 BC, the Roman Empire entered a period of relative peace known as the ***Pax Romana*** ("Roman Peace"). Never before had the whole Mediterranean region had the kind of political stability that Rome brought. The Mediterranean Sea became a "Roman Lake."

The stability brought by Roman occupation allowed relative freedom of travel and a large degree of order throughout the empire, a situation ideal for the spread of Christianity. The Romans built roads, which greatly aided the traveling missionaries and Roman forces, and the Roman system of law and order gave Christians a measure of protection as they went from town to town preaching the gospel.

Caesar Augustus built the "Altar of Peace" in Rome to celebrate his inauguration of the *Pax Romana*.

Of course, peace is a relative term, and the Romans enforced this "peace" through the ruthless suppression of revolt. The Roman historian Tacitus quotes the Scottish leader Calgacus on the eve of a battle with the Roman legions: *"solitudinem faciunt, pacem appellant"*: "they create a desert and call it peace."[4]

Roman Government. As emperor, Augustus reorganized the Roman provinces, dividing them into two types, senatorial and imperial. The senatorial provinces were governed by **proconsuls** appointed by the Roman Senate for one-year terms. These were usually the more loyal and peaceful Roman territories, with little need for a large military presence. Two proconsuls are named in the book

> Robbery, butchery and rapine they call government; they create a desert and call it peace.
>
> —Tacitus, quoting the Scottish leader Calgacus's assessment of the *Pax Romana* (*Life of Cnaeus Julius Agricola*, 30)

---

4. Tacitus, *Life of Cnaeus Julius Agricola*, 30.

Figure 4.9—Rulers of Judea in the New Testament Period
Names in bold appear in the New Testament

Roman Client Kingdom	**Herod the Great** (37–4 BC)
	Archelaus (4 BC–6 AD)
Roman Imperial Province (governed by *prefects*)	Coponius (AD 6–9)
	Marcus Ambivius (AD 9–12)
	Annius Rufus (AD 12–15)
	Valerius Gratus (AD 15–26)
	Pontius Pilate (AD 26–36)
	Marcellus (AD 36–37)
	Marullus (AD 37–41)
Roman Client Kingdom	**Herod Agrippa I** (AD 41–44)
Roman Imperial Province (governed by *procurators*)	Cuspius Fadus (AD 44–46)
	Tiberius Alexander (AD 46–48)
	Ventidius Cumanus (AD 48–52)
	Marcus Antonius Felix (AD 52–59)
	Porcius Festus (AD 59–62)
	Albinus (AD 62–64)
	Gessius Florus (AD 64–66)
	Jewish War and Destruction of Jerusalem (AD 66–73)

of Acts, Sergius Paulus of Cyprus (13:7–8) and Gallio of Achaia (18:12). The imperial provinces were governed by **legates** appointed by the emperor himself. These provinces were generally near the frontiers of the empire, where most of the Roman legions were based. Quirinius, mentioned in Luke 2:2, was legate of Syria from AD 6–9. Proconsuls and legates both were from the senatorial ranks, the highest aristocratic class in Roman society.

A third class of governors known as **prefects** and, later, **procurators** were from the lower "equestrian" ranks of the Roman aristocracy and governed smaller, newer, or more rebellious imperial provinces. Judea became such a province in AD 6 when Archelaus, the son of Herod the Great, was deposed. All of these governors (proconsuls, legates, prefects, procurators) exercised *imperium*, the authority to act semi-autonomously under the terms of an original provincial charter. As long as taxes were collected and rebellions put down, they were given a relatively free hand.

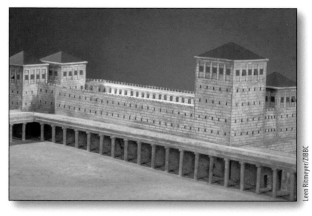

A model of the Fortress of Antonia, which overlooked the temple. Pilate would garrison troops from Caesarea there during the Jewish festivals.

Some outlying Roman territories, like Judea under Herod the Great, functioned not as provinces but as client kingdoms ruled by local vassal kings. Such kings were approved and installed by the emperor. These kingdoms tended to function as "buffer states" between Rome and the enemies on her frontiers.

Judea under Roman Governors. When Herod's son Archelaus was removed and exiled by Augustus in AD 6, Judea converted from a client state to an imperial province, governed by prefects and procurators. It would return to rule by king for a brief time under Herod's grandson Agrippa I (AD 41–44).

While the seat of Roman government in Judea was at Caesarea on the Mediterranean coast, the governor would come to Jerusalem

A reproduction of a plaque containing a reference to Pontius Pilate, discovered in the Roman theatre in Caesarea Maritima, which was used by the Roman governors as headquarters. The plaque reads, "Tiberius [Po]ntius Pilate, [Pref]ect of Judea."

to maintain order during the various festivals. This is why the prefect Pontius Pilate was present in Jerusalem during Jesus' trial. While the Roman governors had a mixed history of tolerance and oppression, most exhibited a general insensitivity toward the Jews. Pilate, who governed Judea from AD 26–36, was no exception. When he first arrived in AD 26, he provoked protests by secretly bringing army standards bearing the images of Roman emperors—idols in Jewish eyes—into Jerusalem. On another occasion, demonstrations broke out when Pilate used money from the temple treasury to build an aqueduct for Jerusalem. Pilate sent soldiers to surround and attack the protestors, killing many. Luke 13:1 refers to a similar episode near the Temple Mount, where Pilate massacred some Galileans, "mixing their blood with their sacrifices." Typical of the Romans, Pilate met protest with ruthless and overwhelming force.

Roman Taxation. The cost of maintaining the vast Roman Empire was enormous, and Rome imposed a variety of taxes on its citizens, from direct poll and land taxes to indirect

---

Figure 4.10—Main Roman Emperors of the New Testament Period

Caesar Augustus or **Octavian** (30 BC–AD 14) was the emperor associated with the census at Jesus' birth (Luke 2:1). Demonstrating extraordinary skills as leader and administrator, Augustus inaugurated the *Pax Romana* ("Roman Peace"), an unprecedented period of peace and stability throughout the Mediterranean region. The freedom and relative safety of travel afforded by this peace would prove to be major factors for the rapid expansion of Christianity.

Tiberius (AD 14–37) was the emperor during Jesus' public ministry (Luke 3:1). It was to him Jesus referred when he said, "Give to Caesar what is Caesar's and to God what is God's" (Mark 12:17, par.).

Caligula (AD 37–41) provoked a crisis among the Jews by demanding that his image be set up in the Jerusalem temple. Agrippa I eventually convinced Caligula to cancel the order, and the emperor was assassinated before it was carried out. Paul may be alluding to this event as a type of the antichrist when he speaks of the "man of lawlessness" who "sets himself up in God's temple, proclaiming himself to be God" (2 Thess. 2:4).

Claudius (AD 41–54) expelled the Jews from Rome in AD 49, probably because of conflicts with Jewish Christians (Suetonius, *Life of Claudius* 25.4). Priscilla and Aquila came from Rome to Corinth at this time (Acts 18:2; cf. 11:28).

Nero (AD 54–68) was the Caesar to whom Paul appealed during his trial (Acts 25:10; 28:19). Later, in AD 64, Nero began the first major persecution against Christians, blaming them for a fire he was rumored to have set in Rome (Tacitus, *Annals* 15.44). Both Paul and Peter were probably martyred under Nero.

Vespasian (AD 69–79) was declared emperor while in Israel putting down the Jewish Revolt of AD 66–73. He returned to Rome, leaving his son Titus to complete the destruction of Jerusalem and the temple.

Domitian (AD 81–96) was the second emperor (after Nero) to persecute the church. This persecution is likely the background to the book of Revelation.

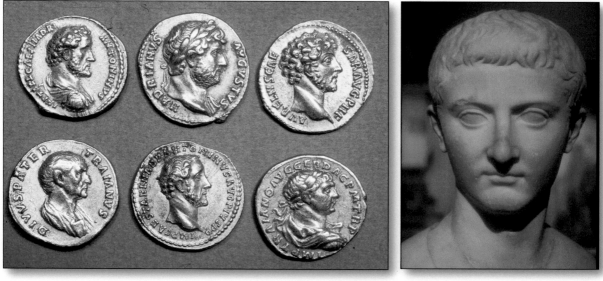

Above left: Roman coins with busts of various Roman emperors. *Right:* Bust of Tiberius, emperor of Rome during Jesus' ministry.

tolls or customs on goods in transit. During the time of Jesus, direct taxes were collected by officials of the emperor, but the right to collect indirect taxes was generally leased to the highest bidder. These were often members of the Roman equestrian class who would then use publicans, or "tax farmers," to oversee the collection. This system was open to great abuse and corruption, since Rome did not generally control the surcharges imposed by their agents. Zacchaeus is identified in Luke as a "chief tax collector," probably a tax farmer with authority over other collectors (Luke 19:2). Levi may be a subordinate to a tax farmer (Mark 2:14, par.). Since he is sitting in his "tax booth" on the road when Jesus encounters him, he may have been collecting customs on goods in transit, either for the Romans or for the local administration of Herod Antipas.

The weight of this taxation could be devastating to a poor craftsman or farmer in Israel. Tax collectors were despised, not only because of their reputation for extortion but also because they worked for the hated Romans. A later rabbinic saying goes so far as to say it is permissible to lie to tax collectors to protect one's property (*m. Ned.* 3:4)! Jesus' association with tax collectors was an important part of his identification with the sinners and outcasts in Israel.

In addition to government taxes, Jews both in Israel and throughout the empire paid a half-shekel temple tax to pay for the completion and maintenance of the Jerusalem temple. After the destruction of the temple in AD 70, this tax was changed to a poll tax and was used to maintain the temple of Jupiter which the Romans built on the Temple Mount.

The Jewish Revolt of AD 66–73

Various factors converged to make Palestine a hotbed of dissent and political insurrection:

1. Traditional conflict between hellenizers and conservatives
2. Widespread corruption of and oppression by wealthy aristocrats and landowners

Left: The Arch of Titus, constructed by his brother Domitian (later an emperor) to honor the destruction of Jerusalem in AD 70. *Right:* A detail on the Arch of Titus showing Roman soldiers carrying away the treasures of the temple, including the golden Menorah.

3. Severe Roman taxation
4. Heavy-handed Roman suppression of opposition
5. At times incompetent and insensitive Roman administration

These factors, together with the history of successful revolt under the Maccabees, set the stage for the **Jewish Revolt of AD 66 – 73**.

Various protests and minor revolts had occurred throughout the first century, but all had been quickly suppressed by the Romans. Full-scale rebellion erupted in AD 66, when Gessius Florus was procurator of Judea. The emperor Nero sent his general Vespasian to put down the revolt. Vespasian began conquering the cities of Galilee and Judea, but the siege of Jerusalem was delayed when Nero died and a struggle ensued over his succession. Vespasian was proclaimed emperor by his troops and returned to Rome to defeat his rivals, leaving his son Titus to complete the battle for Jerusalem. In AD 70, after a horrific three-year siege, Jerusalem was taken and the temple destroyed. Josephus, who was present at the destruction, por-

Top: Remnants of the Roman camp at Masada have been excavated. *Bottom:* Excavations on Masada.

Left: The fortress of Masada, where Jewish Zealots held out for several years against the Romans. The Roman siege ramp is still visible in this aerial view.
Right: Replicas of Roman siege machines built for a movie about Masada.

Judea Capta Coin celebrating Titus's defeat of Jerusalem. Caesar Vespasian is on one side, and on the obverse is a Roman soldier, foot on a skull, with a weeping Judean woman and the inscription "Judea Conquered." S.C. means that the Senate was consulted to mint the coin.

trays it in gruesome detail. Many died from a terrible famine; others were killed by Jewish infighting and by desperate bandits in the city; many thousands more were slaughtered by the Romans when they breached the walls.

Though pockets of Jewish resistance held out for several years after Jerusalem's collapse, defeat was inevitable. The last citadel to fall was the mountaintop fortress at Masada in AD 73. To reach it, the Romans built a massive earthen ramp (still visible today). According to Josephus, when the Romans finally breached the walls, they found that the 900 Jewish defenders had committed suicide rather than surrender.

The early church historian Eusebius claims that prior to the destruction of Jerusalem, the Jewish Christians there received an oracle telling them to flee the city and go to the town of Pella in the Decapolis. In this way, many escaped the destruction.[5]

After the War

After the war, Judea was reorganized as a Roman province, overseen by a legate with a permanent Roman legion stationed at Caesarea. The war had a profound and transforming effect on Judaism. With the destruction of the temple, the priestly hierarchy lost its influence and eventually disappeared from history. Study of Torah and worship in the

---

5. Eusebius, *Ecclesiastical History* 3.5. Eusebius's statements have been doubted by some scholars.

The name of the Jewish historian Josephus occurs frequently in this chapter as our most important primary source for first-century Jewish history. Josephus was not only an important historian but also one of the more fascinating, colorful, and controversial figures of the first century. Josephus can be given many paradoxical labels: Pharisee, priest, aristocrat, Jewish patriot, freedom fighter, traitor, Roman collaborator, scholar, author, historian, apologist, and propagandist.

Josephus was born around AD 37 to a Jewish aristocratic family with priestly and Hasmonean ancestry. He describes himself as a precocious child whose wisdom was sought after by his own Jewish teachers. As a young man, he examined the various sects of Judaism, choosing to become a Pharisee.

Knowing the overwhelming might of Rome, Josephus tried unsuccessfully to dissuade his people from revolution. When hostilities broke out in AD 66, he felt compelled to side with his countrymen, becoming a military general in Galilee. The Romans subjugated Galilee until Josephus's forces were besieged in the town of Jotapata. The Romans captured the city, but Josephus and forty companions hid in a cave. When Josephus proposed surrendering, the others threatened to kill him, pledging themselves to a suicide pact. Josephus shrewdly suggested that they draw lots, each man killing his companion and the last two committing suicide. When only Josephus and another man were left, Josephus convinced his companion to surrender. When he was brought before the Roman general Vespasian, Josephus accurately "prophesied" that Vespasian would be the next emperor of Rome. The general was impressed and took Josephus under his protection, eventually sending him to the siege of Jerusalem to serve as a translator and negotiator for Vespasian's son Titus. There Josephus witnessed firsthand the horrors of the destruction of the city and temple.

After the war, Josephus was taken to Rome, where Vespasian and Titus became his patrons. He took on Vespasian's family name, Flavius, and was given a villa and a stipend. He spent much of the rest of his life writing. Four of Josephus's works have survived: *The History of the Jewish War*, a seven-volume account of the Jewish revolution; *The Antiquities of the Jews*, a twenty-volume work tracing the history of the Jewish people from creation to Josephus's own day; *The Life of Josephus*, which is both autobiography and apologetic for his role in the war; and *Against Apion*, a defense of the beliefs of Judaism against Apion, a pagan opponent.

While providing a wealth of information concerning first-century Judaism, Josephus is anything but an unbiased observer. His collusion with the Romans makes him at the same time pro-Roman and pro-Jewish. He blames not the Romans but undesirable elements among his people for the disaster that befell them. The Zealots and other rebels were not freedom fighters but rogues and bandits bent on the destruction of the Jewish state. At the same time, he seeks to convince his Roman readers of the antiquity and nobility of the Jewish religion.

Though generally a good historian, Josephus exhibits many shortcomings. Events are sometimes distorted and numbers exaggerated. Yet despite these faults, our knowledge of first-century history would be much poorer if not for the prolific pen of Flavius Josephus.

synagogue replaced the sacrificial system as the heart of Jewish religious life. Particularly significant in this regard was the work of Rabbi **Johanan ben Zakkai**, who in the years after the Jewish War established an academy for the study of the law at **Jamnia** (or Jabneh) on the Mediterranean coast. The discussions of this school and others like it unified Judaism into a relatively homogenous religious movement centered on the study of the law. This marks the beginning of rabbinic Judaism, the antecedent of orthodox Judaism of today.

> The Jewish Revolt of AD 66–73 dramatically changed the face of Judaism, shifting the focus of religious devotion from temple to Torah (study of the law).

The destruction of Jerusalem also had a major impact on the young and growing Christian movement. Jesus had predicted the destruction of Jerusalem,[6] and Christians saw her collapse and the cessation of the temple ritual and sacrifices as God's judgment on Israel for rejecting the Messiah and as divine vindication that a new era of salvation had begun. This new era was based not on animal sacrifices but on Jesus' once-for-all sacrifice on the cross. The geographic and ethnic center of Christianity also shifted after the war. While before, Christians saw Jerusalem as the mother church, afterward Jewish Christianity decreased

---

6. Mark 13:1–20; Matt. 23:37–39; 24:1–22; Luke 13:34–35; 19:43–44; 21:5–24.

The Western, or "Wailing," Wall. This wall was part of the western retaining wall of the temple platform on top of which Herod refurbished the actual temple building. The plaza in front of the wall was cleared in 1967 and then paved. Above it the Moslem shrine called the "Dome of the Rock" sits on the site of the Jerusalem temple.

in influence. The split with Judaism which had begun throughout the Christian communities gained momentum.

A second Jewish rebellion, known as the **Bar Kokhba Revolt**, broke out in AD 132 when the emperor Hadrian banned circumcision and ordered the building of a temple of Jupiter on the Temple Mount. The Jewish revolutionaries were led this time by Simon bar Koseba, a charismatic leader who was hailed by the famous rabbi Akiba as the Messiah. Simon was nicknamed "Bar Kokhba" ("son of the star"), a reference to the messianic "star" prophecy of Numbers 24:17. Again the mighty Roman legions moved in, and by AD 135, the rebellion had been crushed. After his defeat and humiliation, Bar Koseba was derisively called Bar Koziba, "son of a lie." The Romans made Jerusalem a pagan city and forbade Jews from entering it on pain of death. Circumcision, observance of the Sabbath, and study of the law were banned. Not until 1948 would Israel emerge again as a political state.

Coins minted during the Bar Kokhba Revolt (AD 134), depicting the front facade of the temple in Jerusalem.

Z. Radovan, Jerusalem

» CHAPTER SUMMARY «

1. The Second Temple (or intertestamental) period of Israel's history — running from approximately the fifth century BC to the end of the first century AD — provides the historical background for Jesus and the Gospels.

2. The conquests of Alexander the Great in the fourth century BC resulted in the spread of Greek language and culture (hellenization) throughout the Mediterranean region.

3. The Egyptian dynasty of the Ptolemies dominated Palestine for one hundred years following the division of Alexander's empire. The Jews fared well during this time.

4. Antiochus IV Epiphanes, ruler of the Syrian dynasty of the Seleucids, persecuted the Jews and tried to force hellenization on them.

5. Led by Judas Maccabeus ("the hammer") and his brothers, the Maccabees defeated the Syrians and gained independence for the Jews. Hanukkah is the celebration of this victory.

6. The Hasmonean (Maccabean) dynasty ruled in Israel for the next seventy years, until the Roman conquest in 63 BC.

7. Caesar Augustus (Octavian) was the emperor at Jesus' birth. Tiberius Caesar was the emperor during his public ministry.

8. The Romans made Herod the Great, an Idumean, king of the Jews. Herod was a cruel but effective ruler and a great builder. He restored and expanded the Jerusalem temple into one of the great buildings of the ancient world. Herod died shortly after Jesus' birth.

9. When Herod's son Archelaus ruled Judea poorly, the emperor appointed Roman governors to succeed him. One of these governors was Pontius Pilate, who ordered Jesus' crucifixion.

10. Herod Antipas, another son of Herod the Great, ruled Galilee and Perea. Antipas executed John the Baptist and participated in Jesus' trial.

11. After years of unrest, the Jews revolted in AD 66. The Romans crushed the rebellion and in AD 70 destroyed Jerusalem and the temple.

12. Sixty-two years later, the Jews rebelled again under Simon bar Koseba. The so-called Bar Kokhba Revolt was again aggressively put down by the Romans, this time ending Israel's existence as a political state.

» KEY TERMS «

Second Temple period	Hellenists and Hasidim	Pontius Pilate
Alexander the Great	abomination of desolation	Herod Antipas
hellenization	Judas Maccabeus	*Pax Romana*
koinē Greek	the Maccabees	proconsul, legate
Ptolemies	Hanukkah	prefect, procurator
Seleucids	Hasmonean dynasty	Jewish Revolt of AD 66–73
Septuagint (LXX)	Idumean	Johanan ben Zakkai, Jamnia
Diaspora	Herod the Great	Bar Kokhba Revolt of
Antiochus IV "Epiphanes"	Caesar Augustus (Octavian)	AD 132–35

1. Summarize briefly the main events of the history of Israel from the close of the Old Testament to the destruction of the Jewish state in AD 135.

2. What is hellenization? How did the conquests of Alexander the Great result in widespread hellenization?

3. Where was the Ptolemaic Empire centered? How did the Jews fare under the Ptolemies?

4. What great Bible translation was produced during the period of the Ptolemies?

5. Where was the Seleucid Empire centered? What actions did Antiochus IV Epiphanes take against the Jews?

6. Who sparked the Maccabean Revolt? Who led it in the years that followed?

7. What Jewish feast celebrates the cleansing of the temple by the Maccabees?

8. Who were the Hasmoneans? Who were the main Hasmonean rulers?

9. From where did the Pharisees and Essenes emerge? The Sadducees?

10. Who was Antipater? Who was Herod the Great? What was the nature and significance of his rule?

11. Identify the main rulers of the Herodian dynasty who followed Herod the Great.

12. What Roman emperor ruled at the time of Jesus' birth? His public ministry? What prefect (governor) ruled over Judea during Jesus' public ministry?

13. How did the *Pax Romana* help the spread of Christianity?

14. Why did Roman governors rule Judea during the period of Jesus and the early church? What governors appear in the New Testament?

15. How did the Jewish Revolt of AD 66–73 change the face of Judaism? What effect did it have on Christianity?

16. Who was Johanan ben Zakkai? What happened at Jamnia?

17. Who was Josephus? What are the basic facts about his life?

Digging Deeper

Arnold, Clinton E., gen. ed. *Zondervan Illustrated Bible Backgrounds Commentary.* 4 vols. Grand Rapids: Zondervan, 2002.

Barrett, C. K. *The New Testament Background: Selected Documents.* 2nd ed. New York: Harper, 1987.

Bruce, F. F. *New Testament History.* Garden City, NY: Doubleday, 1969.

Cohen, S. J. D. *From the Maccabees to the Mishnah.* Library of Early Christianity. Philadelphia: Westminster, 1987.

Davies, W. D., and L. Finkelstein, eds. *The Cambridge History of Judaism.* Vol. 2, *The Hellenistic Age.* Cambridge: Cambridge Univ. Press, 1989.

Evans, Craig A., and Stanley E. Porter, eds. *Dictionary of New Testament Background: A Compendium of Contemporary Biblical Scholarship.* Downers Grove, IL: InterVarsity, 2000.

Ferguson, E. *Backgrounds of Early Christianity.* 3rd ed. Grand Rapids: Eerdmans, 2003.

Hengel, Martin. *Judaism and Hellenism: Studies in Their Encounter in Palestine during the Early Hellenistic Period.* Translated by J. Bowden. 2 vols. Philadelphia: Fortress, 1974.

Jeffers, James S. *The Greco-Roman World of the New Testament Era.* Downers Grove, IL: InterVarsity, 1999.

Millar, F. *The Roman Near East 31 BC–AD 337.* Cambridge, MA: Harvard Univ. Press, 1993.

Moore, G. F. *Judaism in the First Centuries of the Christian Era: The Age of the Tannaim.* 3 vols. Cambridge, MA: Harvard Univ. Press, 1927–30.

Reicke, Bo. *The New Testament Era: The World of the Bible from 500 BC to AD 100.* Translated by David E. Green. Philadelphia: Fortress, 1968.

Schürer, E. *The History of the Jewish People in the Time of Jesus Christ.* Translated, revised, and edited by G. Vermes, F. Millar, M. Goodman, and M. Black. 3 vols. Edinburgh: T. and T. Clark, 1973–87.

CHAPTER 5

The Religious Setting

FIRST-CENTURY JUDAISM

» CHAPTER OVERVIEW «

1. Core Jewish Beliefs
2. Temple, Priesthood, and Sacrifices
3. Synagogues, Scribes, and the Study of Torah
4. Groups within Judaism
5. Trends in First-Century Judaism
6. Literary Sources for First-Century Jewish Life

» OBJECTIVES «

After reading this chapter, you should be able to:

- Identify the core beliefs and main institutions of first-century Judaism.
- Describe the roles of priests, the high priest, Levites, and scribes.
- Summarize the origin and main beliefs of the Sadducees, Pharisees, and Essenes.
- Describe the nature of revolutionary movements in Judaism.
- Define apocalypticism and summarize the main types of messianic expectations in Israel.
- Identify the primary collections of Jewish literature which provide helpful background for a study of the Gospels.

As we have seen, the destruction of the temple and its sacrificial system in AD 70 eventually resulted in a relatively unified Judaism centered on the synagogue communities and the study of the law. The Judaism of Jesus' day, however, was a much more diverse collection of movements and belief systems. Some scholars even speak of the Judaisms (plural) of the first century. Before discussing this diversity, it is important to identify certain core beliefs which most all Jews shared.

CORE JEWISH BELIEFS

Monotheism

Fundamental to Judaism is belief in the one true God, **Yahweh**, who created the heavens and the earth (see fig. 5.1). All other gods are mere idols, unworthy of worship. This belief separated Judaism from the many polytheistic religions of the Greco-Roman world.

The Covenant: Israel as God's Chosen People

The one true God entered into a unique covenant relationship with the people of Israel. The **covenant** was originally given to Abraham, who was promised God's blessings, a great nation, and a land for his descendants (Gen. 12:1–3; 15:1–21).

Circumcision for all male children was the sign and seal of the covenant (Genesis 17). God confirmed his covenant by delivering Abraham's descendants, the children of Israel, from their slavery in Egypt. The exodus from Egypt became for later generations the model of God's merciful deliverance.

The Abrahamic covenant was applied to the nation of Israel in the Mosaic covenant, the law (**Torah**) given through Moses at Mount Sinai (Exodus 19, 24). If the people of Israel would obey God's law, he would bless them and give them the Promised Land.

The Law (Torah): Standards for Covenant Faithfulness

Israel's responsibility in this covenant relationship was to remain faithful to God's law, the body of commandments given to Israel through Moses. The term law (Hebrew: *torah*; Greek: *nomos*) could be used of the commandments themselves, or of the five books of Mo-

---

Figure 5.1—The Divine Name YHWH

God identified himself to Israel with the covenant name *YHWH* (Hebrew: יהוה; Exod. 3:15), known as the tetragrammaton, or "four letters." The name is related to the Hebrew verb meaning "I am" and refers to God's self-existence (Exod. 3:14). While sometimes mispronounced "Jehovah," the name was probably originally pronounced "Yahweh."

The Jews considered the divine name so sacred they would not utter it, saying instead *ha-Shem* ("the Name"), or *adonai* ("lord; master"). Writing in Greek, the New Testament writers followed the pattern of the Septuagint (the Greek Bible) by translating both Hebrew words *YHWH* and *adonai* with the Greek term *kyrios*. Depending on the context, *kyrios* can mean "Yahweh," "Lord," or even "sir."

Most English translations use "LORD" (small caps) for *YHWH* and "Lord" (lowercase) for *adonai* in the Old Testament. In the New Testament, *kyrios* is usually translated "Lord." We will follow this same procedure in this text, though sometimes referring to Yahweh in Old Testament contexts.

The Mosaic covenant was given to Israel through Moses at Mount Sinai following the Exodus from Egypt. St. Catherine's Monastery at the base of Mount Sinai, or Jebel Musa ("Mount of Moses"), the traditional site of the giving of the covenant.

ses (the Pentateuch: Genesis–Deuteronomy) in which these are recorded. The phrase "the law and the prophets" was a shorthand way of referring to the Hebrew Scriptures (the Old Testament for Christians). Faithfulness to the law, and hence the covenant, would bring blessings and prosperity in the land of Israel. Unfaithfulness would mean judgment and exile. The prophets, especially Isaiah and Jeremiah, maintained that the Babylonian exile was punishment for Israel's covenant unfaithfulness.

While the law of Moses contained many ethical standards common to other ancient cultures (such as prohibitions against murder and theft), certain beliefs and practices set Judaism apart. Especially important were (1) *worship of Yahweh* alone, (2) *circumcision* for all male children, (3) observance of a weekly *Sabbath* rest, and (4) *dietary laws* prohibiting the eating of certain "unclean" or ceremonially defiled foods. When Judaism came into conflict with the cultures around her, these were the fundamentals to which the Jews rallied.

TEMPLE, PRIESTHOOD, AND SACRIFICES

The landscape of Judaism may best be surveyed by distinguishing two important and parallel institutions: (1) the **Jerusalem temple** with its priesthood and sacrificial system, and (2) the local **synagogues** centered on worship and the study of Torah. By the first century, both were flourishing.

One Temple for the One True God

The Jerusalem temple was the center of Israel's religious life. The book of Deuteronomy identifies this central sanctuary as the only place where sacrifices may be made (Deut. 12:5–14)—the one temple for the one God. Before the temple, Israel had the portable **tabernacle**, which they carried around with them in the wilderness after the exodus from

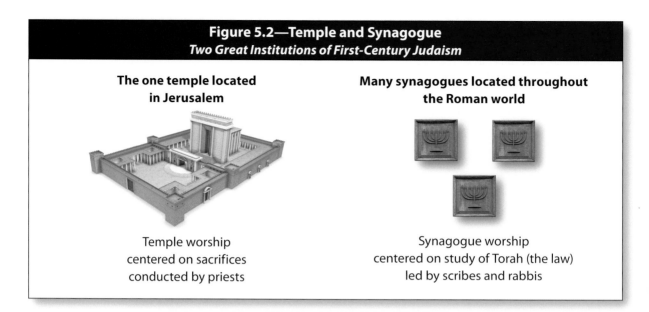

Figure 5.2—Temple and Synagogue
Two Great Institutions of First-Century Judaism

The one temple located in Jerusalem

Temple worship
centered on sacrifices
conducted by priests

Many synagogues located throughout the Roman world

Synagogue worship
centered on study of Torah (the law)
led by scribes and rabbis

Egypt (Exodus 25 – 30). The first Jerusalem temple was built by king Solomon but was subsequently destroyed by the Babylonians in 587 BC. The second Jerusalem temple, built by Zerubbabel after the exile, was greatly expanded by Herod the Great and transformed into one of the most magnificent buildings of the ancient world. Josephus gives a detailed description of the temple and remarks that the sun reflecting off the massive gold plates on the temple walls was so bright that people "had to avert their eyes as though looking at solar rays." Massive white stones, some forty- to sixty-feet long, were used in the construction so that to those approaching from a distance, the temple looked like snow-covered mountains.[1] In Mark 13:1, one of Jesus' disciples comments on the beauty of the temple: "Look, Teacher! What massive stones! What magnificent buildings!"

Not only the beauty but also the design of the temple was meant to reflect the holiness and majesty of God, with a series of concentric courtyards moving toward greater exclusivity. Non-Jews could go no farther than the outer Court of the Gentiles, where a plaque warned of death for any who transgressed. Moving inward, one came to the Court of Women (for all Israelites), the Court of Israel (for ritually pure males), and finally the Court of Priests, where the temple building proper stood. In this courtyard, priests offered daily burnt sacrifices upon the altar. The temple building

Model of Herod's temple from the Holy Land Hotel

---

1. Josephus, *J.W.* 5.5.6 §§222 – 24; and *Ant.* 15.11.3 – 7 §§391 – 425; cf. *m. Middot.*

was divided into two chambers, each protected by a large curtain. The first, the Holy Place, contained a golden lamp stand, the table of consecrated bread, and the altar of incense. A priest would enter here only twice a day to burn incense. The inner Holy of Holies, the most sacred place in Judaism, was entered only once a year by the high priest on the Day of Atonement. In the Old Testament period, the Holy of Holies contained the ark of the covenant, but no evidence of its presence is found in first-century literature. Instead there was a small rock upon which the high priest offered incense and sprinkled the blood of the atoning sacrifice.[2]

> He who has not seen the temple of Herod has never seen a beautiful building.
>
> —A rabbinic proverb
>
> (*b. B. Bat.* 4a; *b. Sukkah* 41b)

The temple compound was more than a place of sacrifices. It was also a center for judicial, religious, and community life. Worship was conducted here, with choirs of Levites

2. M. O. Wise, "Temple, Jewish," in *DNTB*, 1169.

Herod's temple in Jerusalem

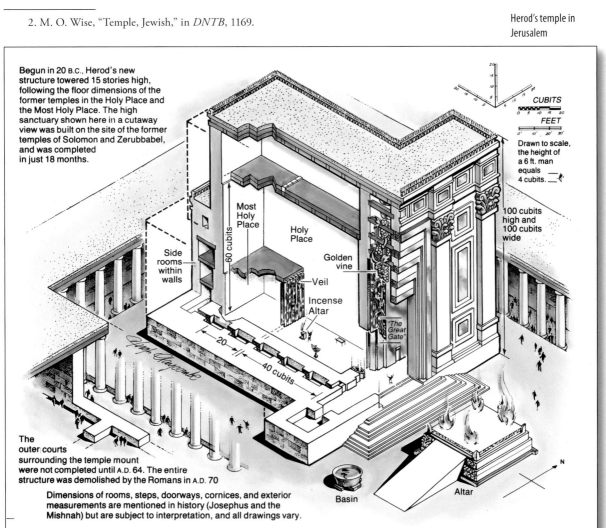

Begun in 20 B.C., Herod's new structure towered 15 stories high, following the floor dimensions of the former temples in the Holy Place and the Most Holy Place. The high sanctuary shown here in a cutaway view was built on the site of the former temples of Solomon and Zerubbabel, and was completed in just 18 months.

CUBITS

FEET

Drawn to scale, the height of a 6 ft. man equals 4 cubits.

Most Holy Place

Holy Place

60 cubits

Side rooms within walls

Golden vine

Veil

Incense Altar

"The Great Gate"

100 cubits high and 100 cubits wide

20

40 cubits

The outer courts surrounding the temple mount were not completed until A.D. 64. The entire structure was demolished by the Romans in A.D. 70

Dimensions of rooms, steps, doorways, cornices, and exterior measurements are mentioned in history (Josephus and the Mishnah) but are subject to interpretation, and all drawings vary.

Basin

Altar

N

Hugh Claycombe

singing, prayers offered (Luke 18:11; 24:53), tithes collected (Mark 12:41), and festivals celebrated. Rabbis taught here (Mark 14:49), and the Sanhedrin—the Jewish high court—held its sessions.

Levites and Priests

The **Levites** were descendants of Levi, one of the twelve sons of Jacob. Unlike the other tribes of Israel, they were not given a tribal allotment in the land but rather were consecrated as God's special tribe in place of the firstborn of all the Israelites (Num. 3:41, 45; 8:18; 35:2–3; Deut. 18:1; Josh. 14:3). Their role was to serve as assistants to the priests in the service of the tabernacle and, later, the temple (Num. 18:4). Levites are mentioned only three times in the New Testament (Luke 10:32; John 1:19; Acts 4:36).

The **priests** were also Levites but were more specifically descendants of Aaron, the brother of Moses and first high priest of Israel (Exod. 28:1–3). The functions of the priests were to offer daily sacrifices, maintain the temple grounds, collect tithes, pronounce blessings, and perform purification rites (Leviticus 13–14; cf. Mark 1:44).

Leen Ritmeyer/ZIBBC

An artist's conception of the high priest of Judaism

The High Priest

The priests were overseen by the **high priest**, the highest religious office in Judaism. The office was supposed to be hereditary and a lifelong appointment. The high priest oversaw the temple worship, collected taxes, and performed many administrative functions. As noted above, he had the once-a-year privilege of entering the Holy of Holies on the Day of Atonement to offer sacrifices for the entire nation (Lev. 16:1–34; Heb. 9:6–7).

After the Babylonian exile, the priesthood played a key role in reorganizing the people and in reestablishing corporate worship in Israel. With the absence of a Davidic king on the throne, the high priest took on many administrative as well as religious functions. Despite the abuses of the Hasmonean period, the high priest was well regarded among the people. **Caiaphas** was the high priest in Jesus' time, though his father-in-law, Annas, who had been deposed earlier by the Romans, also exercised a great deal of influence (Matt. 26:3, 57; John 18:13–14, 24; Acts 4:6).

The Sanhedrin

The high priest was also head of the **Sanhedrin**, the Jewish high court. Though later rabbis traced the origin of the Sanhedrin back to the appointment of seventy elders by Moses in Numbers 11:16 (*m. Sanh.* 1:6), there is little evidence of a formal council until the Persian period (Ezra 5:5, 9; Neh. 2:16). The Sanhedrin was originally made up of the Jerusalem nobility, both lay leaders and priests.

The power of the priesthood waxed and waned depending on the political situation. It reached its zenith under the later Hasmoneans, who took on the authority of both high priest and king. It diminished greatly under Herod the Great, who reserved the right to appoint the high priest and kept the priestly vestments in his own quarters. Josephus reports that Herod consolidated his reign by ordering the execution of the whole Sanhedrin (*Ant.*

The interior of a fourth- or fifth-century synagogue in Capernaum in Galilee. The black foundation walls that were excavated under the synagogue may have been part of the synagogue in which Jesus preached.

14.9.4 §175). During the period of Roman governors after Herod's death, the high priest and the Sanhedrin regained a powerful role. With the procurators ruling from Caesarea and concerned mainly with administrative affairs, the Jerusalem-based Sanhedrin exercised wide-ranging jurisdiction in judicial and religious matters.

The Gospels also speak of high priests in the plural (usually translated "chief priests"). These were probably the wealthy aristocratic priests of Jerusalem who served on the Sanhedrin. Not all priests, of course, were wealthy or influential. Many priests lived in the countryside (see Zechariah in Luke 1), practicing a secular trade to make ends meet. Though they were supposed to receive portions of sacrifices and temple tithes (1 Cor. 9:13; Heb. 7:5), these tithes were not always paid because of poverty or corruption.

SYNAGOGUES, SCRIBES, AND THE STUDY OF TORAH

While the temple in Jerusalem was the center of Jewish worship, Judaism was becoming more decentralized with the growth in synagogue communities throughout the Roman Empire. Synagogues were Jewish meeting places for worship, education, and community gatherings. The origin of the synagogue is uncertain but probably goes back to the Babylonian exile, after the temple of Solomon was destroyed and the sacrificial system ceased. During the Second Temple period, the synagogue and the temple both functioned as key institutions for Jewish worship. Wherever ten Jewish males were present, a synagogue could be formed.

Synagogue Worship

The oldest accounts of synagogue services appear in Luke 4:14–30 and Acts 13:14–48. Agreements with later rabbinic sources indicate a relatively fixed order of service. This

Figure 5.3—The Shema

Hear, O Israel: The LORD our God, the LORD is one. Love the LORD your God with all your heart and with all your soul and with all your strength....

The most important confession of faith in Judaism is the Shema, which consists of three Old Testament passages: Deuteronomy 6:4 – 9; 11:13 – 21; and Numbers 15:37 – 41. Every Jewish male was required to utter it twice a day, once in the morning and once in the evening. *Shema* is Hebrew for "hear," the word which begins the confession.

would include the recitation of the confession of faith known as the Shema (see fig. 5.3), prayers, readings from the Law and the Prophets, an oral Targum (an Aramaic paraphrase of the Scripture reading), a sermon on the text for the day, and a closing benediction. Any qualified male might be invited to read the Scripture and give instruction (as with Jesus in Luke 4:16 and Paul in Acts 13:15). The synagogue ruler (*archisynagōgos*) maintained the synagogue and organized the worship services (Mark 5:35; Luke 13:14). He was assisted by an attendant (*hazzan*), who took care of the Scripture scrolls (Luke 4:20) and blew the ram's horn to announce the beginning and end of the service.

Scribes

One of the most important developments in the postexilic Jewish communities was the establishment of the profession of **scribe**. Also called "teachers of the law" and "lawyers" in the New Testament, scribes were experts in the exposition and interpretation of the

law of Moses. The scribes traced their origin back to the priest Ezra, who established postexilic Judaism based on the law (Ezra 7:6 – 26; Neh. 8:1 – 9). Ezra 7:10 says, "Ezra had devoted himself to the study and observance of the Law of the LORD, and to teaching its decrees and laws in Israel."

As the teaching of Torah gained a more central place in the life of Judaism, the scribal office took on greater importance and influence. Later known as rabbis, scribes would be found throughout the cities and towns of Israel, providing exposition of the law for everyday life, training disciples, and educating children in rabbinic schools. Scribal instruction took place both in the temple (Luke 2:49; Mark 14:49) and in synagogues. Teaching was normally done by rote, and students were taught to repeat verbatim the traditions of the elders. In the Gospels, Jesus' dynamic teaching and personal authority are set in contrast to the scribes, who merely recited the traditions of the past (Mark 1:22).

A Torah being copied by hand on parchment (animal skin) by a professional scribe

Z. Radovan, Jerusalem

Many scribes were Pharisees (Mark 2:16; Acts 23:9), though there were also Sadducees and priests among them (cf. Matt. 2:4; 21:15). Unlike the priesthood, the scribal office was gained not through inheritance but through knowledge and ability. A group of students would gather around a teacher, seeking entrance into his "school." Those with promise would be examined and, if accepted, would accompany him, watching his lifestyle and learning from him. According to Acts 22:3, Paul was educated at the feet of Gamaliel, one of the leading rabbis of Jerusalem. The most famous rabbinic schools of the first century were those of Hillel and Shammai. The school of Shammai represented the more restrictive interpretation of the law.

Most New Testament references to scribes are negative, and scribes are condemned together with the Pharisees for their legalism and hypocrisy. Yet Jesus speaks of the validity of the office in Matthew 13:52: "Every teacher of the law who has been instructed about the kingdom of heaven is like the owner of a house who brings out of his storeroom new treasures as well as old" (cf. Matt. 23:1–2).

GROUPS WITHIN JUDAISM

While groups like the Pharisees and Sadducees are usually identified as religious parties, they were really both religious and political in purpose and beliefs. Since Israel's national identity was fundamentally religious, revolving around the foundations of monotheism, covenant, and Torah, the religious and political aspirations of these groups cannot be separated.

Sadducees

The origin of the **Sadducees** is uncertain, but they appear to have arisen from the priestly families of the Jerusalem aristocracy who supported the Hasmonean dynasty. Their name is probably derived from the priestly line of Zadok, who served as high priest during the reign of David. In Jesus' day, the Sadducees controlled the priesthood and most political affairs, dominating the Sanhedrin (Acts 5:17). Because of their political involvement, they were more open to Hellenistic influence than the Pharisees or Essenes.

The Sadducees were the party of the status quo, content with the order and stability brought by the Romans. This resulted in theological conservatism. They considered only the Pentateuch, the first five books of Moses, to be fully authoritative Scripture, denying the oral traditions of the Pharisees. This may be because the historical books of the Old Testament describe the establishment of the Davidic dynasty and the prophets predict its future restoration. The Sadducees were not looking for a messiah (king) from David's line who would threaten their political power! The Sadducees also differed from the Pharisees by rejecting belief in predestination (or determinism), the immortality of the soul, and the resurrection of the body. Evidently they saw these doctrines as going beyond the teaching of the Pentateuch (cf. Matt. 22:23; Mark 12:18; Luke 20:27). Luke also notes in Acts that the Sadducees did not believe in angels or spirits (Acts 23:8), which may mean the kinds of angelic orders and hierarchies characteristic of apocalyptic Judaism (see below).

Since the Sadducean power base was the priesthood and the temple, the destruction of Jerusalem in AD 70 ended their political influence and the group disappeared from history.

Figure 5.4—The Pharisees according to Josephus

"... the Pharisees have delivered to the people a great many observances by succession from their fathers, which are not written in the law of Moses; and for that reason it is that the Sadducees reject them and say that we are to esteem those observances to be obligatory which are in the written word, but are not to observe what are derived from the tradition of our forefathers; and concerning these things it is that great disputes and differences have arisen among them, while the Sadducees are able to persuade none but the rich, and have not the populace obsequious to them, but the Pharisees have the multitude on their side."

Josephus on the differences between the Pharisees and Sadducees concerning the oral law (*Ant.* 13.10.6 §297–98).

Pharisees

The **Pharisees** probably arose from the Hasidim, the pious Jews who had fought with the Maccabees against the oppression of Antiochus Epiphanes (175–163 BC). They then split off in opposition to the hellenizing tendency of the later Hasmoneans. Josephus claims they numbered about six thousand.[3] While the Sadducees were mostly upper-class aristocrats and priests, the Pharisees appear to have been primarily middle-class laypeople, perhaps craftsmen and merchants. The Sadducees had greater political power, but the Pharisees had broader support among the people. They were more involved in the synagogue communities and functioned as a mediating force between the poorer classes and the aristocracy.

The most distinctive characteristic of the Pharisees was their strict adherence to Torah, not only the written law but also the oral law, a body of traditions which expanded and elaborated on the Old Testament law (the "tradition of the elders," Mark 7:3). According to some rabbinic traditions, both the written and oral law had been given to Moses on Mount Sinai (*m. ʾAbot* 1:1–2). The Pharisees' goal was twofold: (1) to apply Torah's mandates to everyday life, and (2) to "build a fence" around Torah to guard against any possible infringement. Hands and utensils had to be properly washed. Food had to be properly grown, tithed, and prepared. Only certain clothing could be worn. Since ritual purity was so important, the Pharisees refused to share table fellowship with those who ignored these matters. The common "people of the land" were often shunned. Some scholars believe that the Pharisees' goal was to apply to themselves the Old Testament purity laws originally intended for priests and Levites.[4]

The term Pharisee is probably derived from a Hebrew word for "separatists" (*perushim*) and was applied because of the dietary and purity laws which restricted table fellowship with the common people and with non-Jews. Others have suggested that the term was

---

3. Important references to the Pharisees in Josephus include *J.W.* 1.5.2 §110; 2.8.14 §§162–65; *Ant.* 13.5.9 §§171–72; 13.10.6 §§297–8; 17.2.4 §§41–45; 18.1.4 §16.

4. See Jacob Neusner, *Rabbinic Traditions about the Pharisees*, 3 vols. (Leiden: E. J. Brill, 1971) and the discussion in E. P. Sanders, *Judaism: Practice and Belief, 63 BCE–66 CE* (Philadelphia: Trinity Press International, 1992), 438–40.

originally derogatory, meaning "persianizer." If this is the case, when the Pharisees accused the Sadducees of being hellenizers (adopters of pagan Greek culture), the Sadducees countered that the Pharisees were persianizers, drawing their religious ideas from Persian and other Eastern religions.

In contrast to the Sadducees, the Pharisees believed in the resurrection of the dead (Acts 23:8) and steered a middle road between the Sadducees' belief in free will and the predestination (determinism) of the Essenes. They also cultivated a strong hope in the coming of the Messiah, the **Son of David**, who would deliver them from foreign oppression. This made them anti-Roman but with less inclination to active resistance than Zealots and other revolutionaries.

According to the Gospels, Jesus came into frequent conflict with the Pharisees. He condemned them for raising their traditions to the level of Scripture and for focusing on the outward requirements of the law, while ignoring matters of the heart (Luke 11:39–44; Matt. 23:23–26). For their part, the separatist Pharisees attacked Jesus' association with tax collectors and sinners (Mark 2:13–17, par.; Luke 15:1–2; etc.) and the way he placed himself above Sabbath regulations (Mark 2:23–28, par.). Despite these differences, Jesus was much closer theologically to the Pharisees than to the Sadducees, sharing beliefs in the authority of Scripture, the resurrection, and the coming of the Messiah. His frequent conflicts arose because he challenged them on their own turf and because he was viewed as a threat to their leadership and influence over the people.

Figure 5.5—Were the Pharisees So Bad after All?

Today the term Pharisee is often equated with hypocrisy and a legalistic spirit, but this would not have been the view of most people in first-century Israel, who generally respected the Pharisees for their piety and devotion to the law. Indeed, the Pharisees' fundamental goal was a noble one: to maintain a life of purity and obedience to God's law.

Since the Old Testament law did not provide specific guidelines for every situation in life, the Pharisees sought to fill in the details, or "build a fence" around the Torah. The rabbinic dialogues in the Mishnah, many of which go back to Pharisaic traditions, contain detailed descriptions of and debates about what is and what is not lawful. For example, while the Old Testament law forbids work on the Sabbath, it gives few details (Exod. 20:8–11; Deut. 5:12–15). The rabbis therefore specify and discuss thirty-nine forbidden activities (m. Šabb. 7:2). While knot-tying is unlawful, certain knots, like those which can be untied with one hand, are allowed. A bucket may be tied over a well on the Sabbath, but only with a belt, not with a rope (m. Šabb. 15:1–2)! While such minutiae may seem odd and arbitrary to us, the Pharisee's goal was not to be legalistic but to please God through obedience to his law.

Jesus criticized the Pharisees not for their goals of purity and obedience but for their hypocrisy. He accused them of saying one thing but doing another, of raising their interpretations (mere "traditions of men") to the level of God's commandments (Mark 7:8), and of becoming obsessed with externals while neglecting the more important things: justice, mercy, and faithfulness. They "strain out a gnat but swallow a camel" (Matt. 23:23–24).

Of course such hypocrisy is not unique to the Pharisees but is common in all religious traditions. It is easy to follow the form of religion and miss its substance.

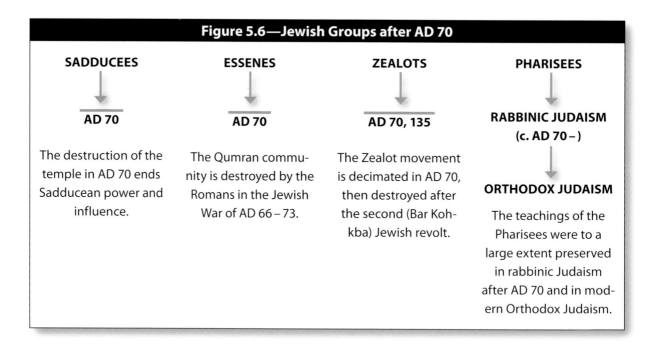

Figure 5.6—Jewish Groups after AD 70

SADDUCEES	ESSENES	ZEALOTS	PHARISEES
↓	↓	↓	↓
AD 70	**AD 70**	**AD 70, 135**	**RABBINIC JUDAISM (c. AD 70 –)**
The destruction of the temple in AD 70 ends Sadducean power and influence.	The Qumran community is destroyed by the Romans in the Jewish War of AD 66 – 73.	The Zealot movement is decimated in AD 70, then destroyed after the second (Bar Kohkba) Jewish revolt.	↓
			ORTHODOX JUDAISM
			The teachings of the Pharisees were to a large extent preserved in rabbinic Judaism after AD 70 and in modern Orthodox Judaism.

There is significant debate today as to just how influential the Pharisees were during Jesus' day, particularly in Galilee. The traditional view is that they had enormous political clout and sway over the people. This is based especially on their prominence in the Gospel accounts and on Josephus's claims that they were the leading sect of Judaism. Recently this view has been challenged, with some arguing that the Pharisees of Jesus' day were a relatively obscure group which mostly withdrew from politics after the period of Herod the Great.[5] While the power and prestige of the Pharisees may have been overstated in the past, the traditional view still seems best. The evidence from Josephus and the Gospels confirms the Pharisees held significant influence, especially in the synagogue communities and among the common people.

As we have seen, after the destruction of Jerusalem, a group of rabbis under Rabbi Johanan ben Zakkai worked at Jamnia to renew Judaism as a religion centered on the study of Torah. Scholars debate how influential the Pharisees were in this movement. Some argue that only Pharisaic Judaism survived the destruction of Jerusalem and that rabbinic Judaism arose directly from Pharisaism. Others see Ben Zakkai's group as a broad coalition of leaders who survived the destruction, including priests, scribes, Pharisees, and Sadducees.[6] While it is true that the rabbis at Jamnia do not identify themselves as Pharisees, their beliefs and teachings are much closer to Pharisaic Judaism than to any other pre-AD 70 Jewish group. This suggests a *relatively* unbroken line of tradition from the teachings of Pharisaic Judaism, to rabbinic Judaism, to modern Orthodox Judaism (see fig. 5.6).

---

5. See J. Neusner, *From Politics to Piety* (Englewood Cliffs, NJ: Prentice-Hall, 1973).
6. See S. Mason, "Pharisees," in *DNTB*, 786.

Essenes

Like the Pharisees, the **Essenes** probably grew out of the Hasidim movement. They were similar to the Pharisees in their beliefs but were even more separatist. They rigorously kept the law, developing their own strict legal code. They refused to offer animal sacrifices in the Jerusalem temple because they regarded the temple as polluted by a corrupt priesthood. Some Essenes married and lived in villages throughout Israel, while others lived in celibacy in monastic settlements. According to Josephus, the monastic Essenes numbered about four thousand.[7]

Most scholars believe that the **Qumran** community, which produced the **Dead Sea Scrolls**, were Essenes. According to what can be pieced together from the scrolls, the community began when a group of priests descended from Zadok withdrew from the Jerusalem priesthood and moved to the Judean wilderness near the Dead Sea. This withdrawal resulted from opposition to the Hasmonean priest-kings, whom they viewed as illegitimate rulers. The Qumran sectarians were greatly influenced by a leader known as the Teacher of Righteousness, who was persecuted by a Jerusalem high priest identified in the scrolls as the "Wicked Priest" (perhaps John Hyrcanus, who ruled 135–104 BC).

The group was apocalyptic in its perspective (see discussion on apocalypticism below), viewing themselves as the righteous remnant, the "true Israel" facing the imminent end of the age. They interpreted Scripture accordingly, using what has been called a *pesher* method to apply biblical prophecies to their own situation. They expected that God would soon intervene to deliver his people and that they would join God's angels in a great war against the Romans. The group expected not a single messiah but two: a military messiah from the line of David and a priestly messiah from the line of Aaron. The Qumran community was eventually destroyed by the Romans in the Jewish Revolt of AD 66–73.

Top: Excavated ruins of the Qumran community of Essenes, which produced the Dead Sea Scrolls

Bottom: Cave IV, one of the caves in which the Qumran scrolls were discovered

---

7. Josephus, *Ant.* 18.1.5 §§18–22.

There are some interesting parallels between early Christianity and the Qumran sect. Both considered themselves God's righteous remnant, those few who had remained faithful to his covenant promises despite the apostasy of others (see Rom. 11:1–10). Both were **eschatologically** oriented, with expectations of an imminent end of the present age. Both interpreted the Old Testament with reference to events in their recent past and near future.

Yet there were also important differences. The Qumran sectarians were very legalistic, exclusive, and looked to the *future* coming of their messiahs. Christians, by contrast, claimed that with the coming of Jesus the Messiah, the end times had already begun. God's promises were now being fulfilled through Jesus' life, death, and resurrection and through the worldwide proclamation of the gospel. The salvation to be consummated in the future had already been achieved.

Because of his apocalyptic preaching and ascetic lifestyle in the Judean desert, some have suggested that John the Baptist may have had some connections with the Essenes and even the Qumran community itself. Unfortunately there is little evidence to support or refute this hypothesis.

Zealots, Social Bandits, and Other Revolutionaries

As we have seen, first-century Israel was a hotbed of revolutionary activity. The designation **Zealots** is often used to describe such revolutionaries, although as a political party, the Zealots seem to have arisen quite late, during the Jewish War of AD 66–73. Yet Zealot-like movements occurred throughout the period of Roman occupation, taking on a variety of forms. Some centered on *social banditry*, arising from the economic deprivation of the peasantry in Israel. Social bandits were the "Robin Hoods" of first-century Israel, attacking the elite and powerful upper class within Israel and the Roman troops who protected them. Such bandits often gained popular support from the poor and common people. Other movements might be called *messianic* in that they had political aims to overthrow the Roman rulers and establish an independent Jewish state. Still others were *prophetic*, centered around a charismatic leader who gained a popular following by claiming that God's deliverance was about to take place.

Jay King/ZIBBC

A Roman military dagger, similar to what the Sicarii may have used

Josephus describes many such revolutionaries and speaks of a "Fourth Philosophy" of Judaism (in addition to the Sadducees, Pharisees, and Essenes), tracing its origin to Judas the Galilean, who led a revolt against Roman taxation in AD 6 (Josephus, *J.W.* 2.8.1 §118; *Ant.* 18.1.6 §23; 18.1.1 §§5–7; cf. Acts 5:37). Josephus claims this Fourth Philosophy held beliefs similar to the Pharisees but would accept no one but God as their ruler, and so actively sought to overthrow the Romans.[8]

---

8. Richard A. Horsley and John S. Hanson, *Bandits, Prophets, and Messiahs* (San Francisco: Winston, 1988) argue that the so-called Fourth Philosophy engaged not in armed rebellion but rather in passive resistance against the Romans, inviting martyrdom. This, they believed, would cause God to act in vindication and judgment against the Romans.

The Romans and Roman sympathizers like Josephus considered all such insurrectionists to be thugs and bandits engaged in terrorist activities. But most common people considered them freedom fighters, seeking to rid Israel of foreign oppression. Unable to defeat the Romans in open battle, the rebels engaged in guerrilla warfare, raiding Roman garrisons and attacking Jews who collaborated with the enemy. Among the most vicious groups were the Sicarii, who would mingle with the crowds during the festivals and stab Roman sympathizers with small swords (*sicae*) hidden under their robes (Josephus, *J.W.* 2.13.3 §§254–56; *Ant.* 20.8.10 §185).

A number of figures involved in this kind of insurrection and social banditry are mentioned in the New Testament. In addition to Judas the Galilean, Acts 5:36 refers to a certain Theudas, who gathered four hundred men around him, and Acts 21:38 speaks of an Egyptian "who stirred up a revolt and led the four thousand men of the Assassins [Sicarii?] out into the wilderness." Barabbas, the prisoner released in place of Jesus, is described variously as a rebel who had committed murder in the insurrection (Mark 15:7; Luke 23:19; cf. Acts 3:14), "a notorious prisoner" (Matt. 27:16), and a "robber" (John 18:40 NASB). This same Greek term is used of the "robbers" crucified with Jesus in Mark 15:27, who were probably also Zealot-like revolutionaries.

One of Jesus' disciples, Simon, is identified as "the Zealot" (Mark 3:18, par.; Acts 1:13), but it is uncertain whether he was a former rebel or whether this is a description of his zeal for the law (see Acts 21:20; 22:3). A few scholars have even suggested that Jesus himself

> ... there sprang up another sort of robbers in Jerusalem, which were called Sicarii, who slew men in the daytime, and in the midst of the city; this they did chiefly at the festivals, when they mingled themselves among the multitude, and concealed daggers under their garments, with which they stabbed those that were their enemies.
>
> —Josephus, *Jewish War* 2.13.3 §§254–55

Figure 5.7—Political Tendencies of Jewish Groups

PRO-ROMAN ←————————————————→ **ANTI-ROMAN**

Herodians	**Sadducees**	**Pharisees**	**Essenes**	**Zealots**
Active supporters of pro-Roman Herodian dynasty	Supporters of status quo and favorable to Romans	Anti-Roman, though still involved in political affairs	Withdrew from society, waiting for God to overthrow the Romans	Violently anti-Roman, actively seeking to overthrow the government

had Zealot tendencies.[9] This is unlikely since Jesus affirmed the legitimacy of paying taxes to Caesar (Mark 12:17, par.) and preached that the kingdom of God would come through God's actions alone (Mark 4:26–29).

Herodians

The Herodians, mentioned only three times in the Gospels (Mark 3:6; 12:13; Matt. 22:16), may be viewed as the political opposites of social bandits and revolutionaries. They were supporters of the pro-Roman Herodian dynasty. During Jesus' ministry, they were based primarily in Galilee and Perea, where Herod Antipas ruled.

People of the Land (Am-ha-Eretz)

It must be noted that all of these groups made up only a small percentage of the Jewish population of Israel. Most people were not members of any group but were poor farmers, craftsmen, and merchants. In general, they hated Roman rule and taxation and respected the piety of the Pharisees and the scribes. Most were eagerly awaiting a political messiah who would overthrow the harsh Roman rule (see Luke 3:15).

In general, the higher a person's social and political status, the more Hellenistic and pro-Roman they would be. Wealthy landowners, the priestly aristocracy, and rich merchants would have been more content with the status quo than the destitute poor, who eked out a meager living under heavy-handed Roman taxation.

TRENDS IN FIRST-CENTURY JUDAISM

Apocalypticism

Apocalypticism (from the Greek *apokalypsis*, meaning "revelation") refers to a variety of eschatological ("end time") movements which arose in Israel from about 200 BC to AD 200 during periods of political instability and repeated foreign domination. Apocalyptic writings look to the imminent intervention of God in human history to establish his kingdom, deliver the righteous, judge sinners, and bring in the age to come. While arising in diverse settings and circumstances, apocalyptic literature is generally "crisis" literature, written to encourage God's people to persevere in the face of extreme adversity (such as the persecutions of Antiochus Epiphanes). In some apocalyptic works, God alone appears as deliverer. In others, a messiah or some other agent of God intervenes. Apocalyptic literature is usually pseudonymous—falsely attributed to an Old Testament figure like Enoch, Ezra, Baruch—and contains symbolic and often bizarre imagery describing the times and events leading up to the end. Angels and other heavenly figures often appear as God's agents, explaining God's mysteries to the recipient of the revelation.

Figure 5.8—Some Jewish Apocalyptic Works

1 Enoch
2 Enoch
4 Ezra
2 Baruch
3 Baruch
Apocalypse of Abraham

---

9. See S. G. F. Brandon, *Jesus and the Zealots: A Study of the Political Factor in Primitive Christianity* (New York: Charles Scribner's Sons, 1967).

Much of the imagery found in apocalyptic literature comes from the Old Testament prophetic eschatology of Isaiah (chaps. 24–27, 56–66), Ezekiel, Joel, Zechariah, and especially Daniel. In one sense, the early Christians may be called apocalyptic since they looked to the imminent return of Jesus to deliver the righteous and punish the wicked. Jesus' Olivet Discourse (Mark 13, par.) and the book of Revelation (the "Apocalypse") contain Old Testament apocalyptic imagery. An important difference between Christian and Jewish apocalypticism is that for Christians, salvation has past, present, and future dimensions. It is achieved in the past (Rom. 8:24), worked out in the present (Phil. 2:12), and consummated in the future (Rom. 5:9–10).

Messianic Expectation

The intense desire among Jews for God's intervention in human history increased hope for the coming of an "anointed one" or a "messiah" who would act on God's behalf to set up a just and righteous kingdom on earth. The most widespread messianic hope in the first century was for the **Davidic Messiah**, the coming king from David's line who would destroy Israel's oppressors, reestablish her independence, and reign forever on David's throne in justice and righteousness (see 2 Samuel 7; Isaiah 9, 11; Jer. 23:5–6; Psalms 2, 89, 110). The *Psalms of Solomon*, a pseudepigraphic work written in Pharisaic circles in the first century BC, reflects this expectation:

Z. Radovan, Jerusalem

> See, Lord, and raise up for them their king, the son of David,
>   to rule over your servant Israel. . . .
> Undergird him with the strength to destroy the unrighteous
>   rulers;
> to purge Jerusalem from Gentiles who trample her to
>   destruction;
> in wisdom and in righteousness to drive out the sinners from
>   the inheritance;
> to smash the arrogance of sinners like a potter's jar;
> to shatter all their substance with an iron rod;
> to destroy unlawful nations with the word of his mouth;
> at his warning the nations will flee from his presence;
> and he will condemn sinners by the thoughts of their hearts.
>
> —*Psalms of Solomon* 17:21–25[10]

House of David inscription. Hope for a Davidic Messiah in Israel centered around the restoration of the glories of the dynasty of King David. The earliest inscriptional evidence for David's dynasty, this Aramaic inscription found in Dan dates from the ninth century BC and refers to the "House of David" (1 Kings 15:20).

Similar hopes appear in Luke 1, where the old priest Zechariah praises God because "he has raised up a horn of salvation for us in the house of his servant David . . . salvation from our enemies and from the hand of all who hate us" (Luke 1:69–71).

---

10. R. B. Wright, "Psalms of Solomon: A New Translation and Introduction," in *The Old Testament Pseudepigrapha*, ed. J. H. Charlesworth (Garden City, NY: Doubleday, 1985), 2:667.

While the expectation of a messiah from David's line was widespread among first-century Jews, it was not universal. Groups like the Sadducees were not expecting a messiah at all but were content with the present rule by the priestly leadership. The Samaritans were expecting not a Davidic messiah but a Moses-like deliverer known as Taheb (the "restorer" or "returning one"). As noted before, the Qumran sectarians looked for two messiahs, a military-political one from the line of David and a priestly messiah from the line of Aaron. The characteristics of these messiahs also varied from group to group. In some texts, the Messiah seems little more than a powerful human king who accomplishes God's purpose (e.g., *Psalms of Solomon*). In others, he appears as a heavenly figure with superhuman powers (e.g., *4 Ezra*). In the pseudepigraphic apocalypse known as *1 Enoch*, a preexistent heavenly deliverer identified as the "Elect One" and the "Son of Man" (an image drawn from Daniel 7) provides deliverance for God's people. These examples illustrate that while Jewish hopes focused especially on the Davidic Messiah, there was significant diversity among various sects and movements.[11]

LITERARY SOURCES FOR FIRST-CENTURY JEWISH LIFE

Josephus

The writings of **Josephus** provide us with our most important source for first-century Jewish history. See figure 4.11 in chapter 4 for a summary of Josephus's life and works.

Philo

Philo was a Jewish scholar and philosopher who lived in Alexandria, Egypt, from about 20 BC to AD 50. He wrote more than seventy treatises, of which forty-nine have survived. These include commentaries on biblical books, philosophical writings, and apologetic works defending Judaism against pagan opponents. Philo's writings give us important insights into how certain Hellenistic Jews sought to integrate the philosophical traditions of the Greeks into a Jewish worldview. He is perhaps best known for his allegorical interpretations of the Hebrew Scriptures, discovering in them the teachings of Plato and other Greek philosophers.

The Dead Sea Scrolls

We have already discussed the Essenes and their likely identification with the community of Qumran, which produced the Dead Sea Scrolls (DSS). The scrolls themselves—probably the greatest archeological find of the twentieth century (see fig. 5.9)—were discovered in 1947 in caves near the ancient settlement of Qumran on the shores of the Dead Sea. They are important because of the insight they give us into the Jewish sect which produced them, and because they contain a wealth of information on the manuscript tradition of the Old Testament.

The scrolls comprise three types of literature:

1. *Sectarian Literature.* Material produced by the Qumran community itself, including rules and regulations for community life, commentaries on and interpreta-

---

11. See J. Neusner, W. C. Green, and E. S. Frerichs, et al., eds., *Judaisms and Their Messiahs at the Turn of the Christian Era* (Cambridge: Cambridge Univ., 1987).

tion of the biblical text, historical material, and a variety of liturgical sources like psalms, prayers, and hymns.

2. *Biblical Manuscripts.* Fragments from almost every book in the Old Testament. Since the oldest Old Testament manuscripts available prior to this discovery were from the Middle Ages, the DSS pushed back the textual history of the Old Testament almost a thousand years. The greatest find was a magnificent scroll containing almost the entire text of Isaiah.

Z. Radovan, Jerusalem

The temple scroll of the Dead Sea Scrolls Library

3. *Extrabiblical Literature.* In addition to canonical books, the DSS contained fragments of other Jewish literature, including apocryphal and pseudepigraphic works.

The Apocrypha

The **Apocrypha** (meaning "hidden") is a collection of Jewish writings that were produced during the Second Temple period and are included in the Old Testament of the Roman Catholic, Coptic, and Eastern Orthodox churches. Roman Catholicism identifies these books as deuterocanonical, meaning the "second canon," but attributes to them full authority as Scripture. Protestants reject the Apocrypha as authoritative because the Jews did not regard them as part of the Hebrew Scriptures and because they do not have the same character as the canonical books: (1) they contain historical errors, (2) they contain teachings at variance with Scripture, and (3) they lack the prophetic power of the biblical books (i.e., evidence of inspiration by the Holy Spirit). At the same time, these works are important for

Figure 5.9—The Dead Sea Scrolls

The Dead Sea Scrolls were discovered in 1947 near the archeological site of Khirbet Qumran, about fifteen miles southwest of Jerusalem. A shepherd boy looking for a lost goat tossed a rock into a cave. Hearing pottery breaking, he ran away, later returning to discover jars containing ancient manuscripts. In the years which followed, eleven caves were excavated, eventually yielding thousands of papyrus and parchment fragments.

www.HolyLandPhotos.org

View of one of the jars in which the Qumran scrolls were discovered

the study of the New Testament, providing insight into the historical, literary, cultural, and religious life of the Jews between the Old and New Testaments.

The number of apocryphal works ranges from seven to eighteen, depending on the church tradition and the manner of counting (some books are included as part of another; see fig. 5.10). The Apocrypha includes *religious novels* (Tobit, Judith), *wisdom literature* similar to the book of Proverbs (the Wisdom of Solomon, the Wisdom of Jesus ben Sirach, also called Ecclesiasticus), *historical narratives* (1 and 2 Maccabees, 1 Esdras), *prophetic and apocalyptic literature* (Baruch, the Letter of Jeremiah, 2 Esdras [4 Ezra]), *additions to biblical books* (Additions to Esther, Additions to Daniel [Susanna, the Prayer of Azariah, the Song of the Three Jews, and Bel and the Dragon]), and additional *psalms* and *prayers* (the Prayer of Manasseh, Psalm 151).

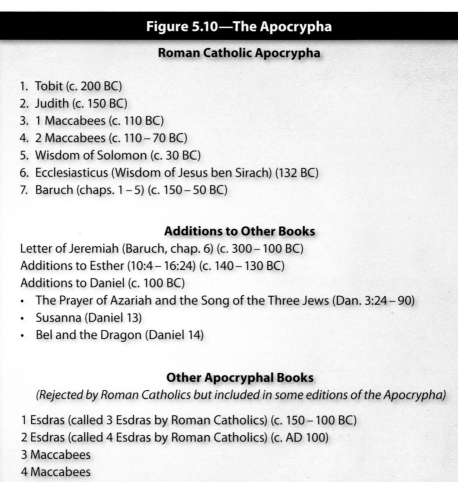

Figure 5.10—The Apocrypha

Roman Catholic Apocrypha

1. Tobit (c. 200 BC)
2. Judith (c. 150 BC)
3. 1 Maccabees (c. 110 BC)
4. 2 Maccabees (c. 110 – 70 BC)
5. Wisdom of Solomon (c. 30 BC)
6. Ecclesiasticus (Wisdom of Jesus ben Sirach) (132 BC)
7. Baruch (chaps. 1 – 5) (c. 150 – 50 BC)

Additions to Other Books

Letter of Jeremiah (Baruch, chap. 6) (c. 300 – 100 BC)
Additions to Esther (10:4 – 16:24) (c. 140 – 130 BC)
Additions to Daniel (c. 100 BC)
- The Prayer of Azariah and the Song of the Three Jews (Dan. 3:24 – 90)
- Susanna (Daniel 13)
- Bel and the Dragon (Daniel 14)

Other Apocryphal Books
(Rejected by Roman Catholics but included in some editions of the Apocrypha)

1 Esdras (called 3 Esdras by Roman Catholics) (c. 150 – 100 BC)
2 Esdras (called 4 Esdras by Roman Catholics) (c. AD 100)
3 Maccabees
4 Maccabees
Prayer of Manasseh (2nd or 1st century BC)
Psalm 151

The Pseudepigrapha

The **pseudepigrapha**, meaning "written under a false name," refers to a large body of Second Temple works which were not included in the Apocrypha. Most were written somewhat later than the Apocrypha. They include: apocalyptic literature; "testaments" (last words) of biblical figures; expansions on Old Testament narratives; wisdom literature (similar to the book of Proverbs); prayers, psalms, etc.

Like the Apocrypha, the pseudepigrapha provide us with a wealth of important background material for New Testament history, culture, and religion.

Rabbinic Writings

In Jesus' day, the teachings of the scribes were a body of oral traditions memorized and passed down from generation to generation. The rabbis claimed that this oral law, like the written law, was fully authoritative and had been delivered to Moses on Mount Sinai. After Judaism was reconstituted in the decades following the destruction of Jerusalem in AD 70, this body of oral tradition continued to grow and develop. It was eventually put into written form around AD 200 in the **Mishnah** (meaning "repetition"), under the direction of Rabbi Judah ha-Nasi ("the prince"). The Mishnah is about the length of the Bible and is composed of rabbinic rulings on a wide range of issues concerning the application of Torah to everyday life. The goal of the rabbis was to "build a fence" around the law to protect pious Jews from breaking its commandments.

> ## A Fence around the Torah
>
> Moses received the Law from Sinai and committed it to Joshua, and Joshua to the elders, and the elders to the Prophets; and the Prophets committed it to the men of the Great Synagogue. They said three things: Be deliberate in judgement, raise up many disciples, and make a fence around the Law.
>
> — *m. ʾAbot* 1:1

In the centuries that followed, other rabbinic writings were added to the Mishnah. The Tosefta (meaning "additions") are alternate interpretations and other material not included in the Mishnah. The Gemara (meaning "completion") are comments on the Mishnah by rabbis from the third through the fifth centuries. Together, the Mishnah and Gemara make up the **Talmud** (meaning "learning"), the complete body of Jewish oral law. There are two editions of the Talmud. The Palestinian edition is sometimes called the Jerusalem Talmud, though it was produced in northern Israel, not Jerusalem. It was completed in the late fourth or early fifth century AD. The Babylonian edition is much longer (thirty-five volumes) and dates to the late fifth century. It is considered the "standard" authoritative edition by the rabbis.

The Talmud contains two main types of material, *halakah*, which are legal rulings and interpretations, and *haggadah*, or nonlegal portions (stories, legends, explanatory narratives, illustrative material).

The greatest problem with using the Talmud to study the background to the New Testament is the difficulty in dating its material to the first century. Even when rabbis from the first century are quoted, it is not certain that material attributed to them is authentic. At

Figure 5.11—The Literature of Judaism
Arranged approximately by date

HEBREW SCRIPTURES "TaNaK" (Old Testament) traditionally dated from about 1400–400 BC	The Law (*Torah*) The Prophets (*Nevi'im*) The Writings (*Kethu'bim*)

SECOND TEMPLE (OR INTERTESTAMENTAL) LITERATURE
(Approximately 3rd century BC through 1st century AD)

Religious Literature

Translation

Dead Sea Scrolls, *c. 200 BC – AD 70*
Sectarian library of the Qumran community near the Dead Sea

Apocrypha, *c. 3rd to 1st centuries BC*
Collection of intertestamental Jewish works included in the Roman Catholic and Eastern Orthodox Bibles. *Apocrypha* means "hidden" and refers to the esoteric nature of these books.

Pseudepigrapha, *most dated from 2nd century BC to 2nd century AD*
Diverse collection of over 60 intertestamental works, most later than the Apocrypha. *Pseudepigrapha* means "written under an assumed name."

Septuagint (LXX)
c. 3rd century BC
Greek translation of Hebrew Scriptures

POSTBIBLICAL (RABBINIC) JEWISH LITERATURE

Rabbinic Discussion of Torah
Includes *halakah* (legal rulings) and *haggadah* (illustrative material)

Bible Versions and Commentaries

Talmud
Two editions:
- Palestinian (4th century AD)
- Babylonian (5th century AD)

Mishnah, c. AD 200
Oral traditions of the rabbis, codified in written form. Mostly *halakah*, or legal rulings

Tosefta, 3rd – 4th centuries AD
"Additions" to the Mishnah

Gemarah, 3rd – 5th centuries AD
Expansions on the Mishnah, both *halakah* and *haggadah*

Targums
Aramaic paraphrases of the Hebrew Scriptures

Midrashim
Rabbinic commentaries on Hebrew Scriptures

the same time, the many agreements between the New Testament Gospels and the Talmud with reference to Jewish culture, customs, and theology confirm that the Talmud, and especially the earliest part of the Mishnah, provides valuable information for first-century Jewish background.

In addition to the Talmud, other rabbinic writings include the **Targums** and the midrashim. The midrashim (meaning "interpretation" or "examination") are rabbinic commentaries on the biblical books. The Targums are Aramaic paraphrases of the Hebrew text. Since most first-century Jews no longer spoke Hebrew, readings of the Hebrew Scriptures in synagogue services were followed by a Targum ("interpretation") in Aramaic provided by an interpreter (*meturgeman*). Many of these interpretations were eventually standardized and written down. Because the Targums are generally loose and interpretive paraphrases rather than formal translations, they provide us with important information concerning how the rabbis interpreted the biblical text. For example, the Targums have a very strong messianic emphasis, identifying the Messiah even in passages that did not originally refer to a future deliverer. Unfortunately, the traditions found in the Targums, like those of the Talmud, are notoriously difficult to date.

» CHAPTER SUMMARY «

1. Core beliefs of Judaism included monotheism (Yahweh as the one true God), the covenant at Mount Sinai as the establishment of Israel's relationship with Yahweh, and obedience to the law as the means to maintain this covenant relationship.

2. The two main religious institutions of Judaism were the one temple in Jerusalem, with its system of priests offering sacrifices, and the many synagogues scattered throughout the empire. Synagogues were community meeting places centered on education and the study of the law (Torah).

3. Levites and priests, led by the high priest, oversaw the temple worship. The Sanhedrin, or Jewish high court, was the highest religious authority in Judaism.

4. Scribes were experts in the Mosaic law. As synagogue worship and the study of Torah became more central to Israel's religious life, the office of scribe increased in prominence.

5. The Sadducees appear to have arisen from the priestly and aristocratic families who supported the Hasmonean dynasty. They were the party of the status quo and were religiously conservative, viewing only the Pentateuch (Genesis through Deuteronomy) as fully authoritative.

6. The primary opponents to the Sadducees were the Pharisees, who probably arose from the Hasidim, who fought with the Maccabees for Jewish independence. The Pharisees viewed as authoritative not only the Hebrew Scriptures but also the oral traditions passed down from the fathers.

7. The Essenes shared many beliefs with the Pharisees but were even more legalistic and separatist, often living in monastic communities (like Qumran) and holding strong end-times expectations that God would soon come to judge the Romans and the wicked leaders of Israel.

8. Social bandits, Zealots, and other revolutionaries engaged in active resistance against the Romans.

9. Apocalypticism was a Jewish movement which looked to God's imminent intervention to destroy the wicked, deliver the righteous, and establish God's just rule in a new age of peace and security. Apocalyptic literature was normally written in times of national crisis, when God's people were severely persecuted.

10. Messianic expectations were diverse in first-century Judaism, although the most widespread hope was for a messiah from the line of David who would restore God's kingdom.

11. Jewish literature providing helpful and informative background for the Gospels includes the works of Josephus and Philo, the Apocrypha and the pseudepigrapha (writings of Second Temple Judaism), and the postbiblical rabbinic writings.

» KEY TERMS «

monotheism	Sanhedrin	Davidic Messiah
Yahweh ("the LORD")	scribes	Josephus
covenant	Sadducees	Philo
Torah (the law)	Pharisees	Apocrypha
Jerusalem temple	Son of David	pseudepigrapha
synagogues	Essenes	rabbinic writings
tabernacle	Qumran	Mishnah
Levites	Dead Sea Scrolls	Talmud
priests	eschatology, eschatological	Targums
high priest	Zealots	
Caiaphas	apocalypticism	

1. What core beliefs did most all Jews share?

2. What role did the temple play in Israel's national life?

3. Who were the Levites? The priests? The high priest? What was the Sanhedrin?

4. What role did the synagogue play? Who were the scribes?

5. What are the basic beliefs of the Pharisees and the Sadducees? Which group's beliefs continued to thrive after the destruction of Jerusalem and the temple?

6. Who were the Essenes? What is the relationship of the Dead Sea Scrolls to the Qumran community?

7. Who were the Zealots? What did they wish to achieve? Who were the Herodians?

8. What is apocalypticism? What are its main features?

9. What were the primary messianic expectations of first-century Israel?

10. Identify the main collections of Jewish literature, including the Apocrypha, the pseudepigrapha, the Mishnah, the Talmud, the Targums, and the Midrashim.

Digging Deeper

Judaism in the First Century

(See also bibliographies in chapters 4 and 6.)

Arnold, Clinton E., gen. ed. *Zondervan Illustrated Bible Backgrounds Commentary.* 4 vols. Grand Rapids: Zondervan, 2002.

Cohen, S. J. D. *From the Maccabees to the Mishnah.* Library of Early Christianity. Philadelphia: Westminster, 1987.

Evans, Craig A., and Stanley E. Porter, eds. *Dictionary of New Testament Background: A Compendium of Contemporary Biblical Scholarship.* Downers Grove, IL: InterVarsity, 2000.

Ferguson, E. *Backgrounds of Early Christianity.* 3rd ed. Grand Rapids: Eerdmans, 2003.

Förster, W. *Palestinian Judaism in New Testament Times.* Translated by G. E. Harris. Edinburgh: Oliver and Boyd, 1965.

Hengel, M. *Judaism and Hellenism: Studies in Their Encounter in Palestine during the Early Hellenistic Period.* Translated by J. Bowden. 2 vols. Philadelphia: Fortress, 1974.

Moore, G. F. *Judaism in the First Centuries of the Christian Era: The Age of the Tannaim.* 3 vols. Cambridge, MA: Harvard Univ. Press, 1927–30.

Saldarini, A. J. *Pharisees, Scribes and Sadducees in Palestinian Society: A Sociological Approach.* Wilmington, DE: Michael Glazier, 1988.

Sanders, E. P. *Judaism: Practice and Belief, 63 BCE–66 CE.* Philadelphia: Trinity Press International, 1992.

Schürer, E. *The History of the Jewish People in the Time of Jesus Christ.* Translated, revised, and edited by G. Vermes, F. Millar, M. Goodman, and M. Black. 3 vols. Edinburgh: T. and T. Clark, 1973–87.

Jewish Literature

Bowker, J. *The Targums and Rabbinic Literature: An Introduction to Jewish Interpretations of Scripture.* Cambridge: Cambridge Univ. Press, 1969.

Charlesworth, J. H., ed. *The Old Testament Pseudepigrapha.* 2 vols. Garden City, NY: Doubleday, 1983, 1985.

Charlesworth, J. H. *The Pseudepigrapha and Modern Research.* Rev. ed. Missoula, MT: Scholars Press, 1981.

Collins, J. J. *The Apocalyptic Imagination: An Introduction to the Jewish Matrix of Christianity.* New York: Crossroad, 1984.

Danby, H., trans. *The Mishnah.* Oxford: Clarendon, 1933.

Epstein, I., ed. *The Babylonian Talmud.* 35 vols. London: Soncino, 1935–48. Reprint in 18 vols.

Maccoby, H. *Early Rabbinic Writings.* Cambridge: Cambridge Univ. Press, 1988.

Martinez, F. G. *The Dead Sea Scrolls Translated: The Qumran Texts in English.* Leiden: Brill, 1994.

McNamara, M. *Targum and Testament: Aramaic Paraphrases of the Hebrew Bible—A Light on the New Testament.* Grand Rapids: Eerdmans, 1972.

Neusner, J. *Introduction to Rabbinic Literature.* Anchor Bible Reference Library. Garden City, NY: Doubleday, 1994.

Nickelsburg, G. W. E. *Jewish Literature between the Bible and the Mishnah: A Historical and Literary Introduction.* Philadelphia: Fortress, 1981.

Russell, D. S. *The Method and Message of Jewish Apocalyptic 200 BC–AD 100.* Philadelphia: Westminster, 1964.

Sperber, A., ed. *The Bible in Aramaic.* 4 vols. Leiden: Brill, 1959–68.

Strack, H. L., and G. Stemberger. *Introduction to the Talmud and Midrash.* Translated by M. Bockmuehl. Minneapolis: Fortress, 1992.

Thackeray, H. St. J. et al., ed. and trans. *Josephus.* 10 vols. Loeb Classical Library. Cambridge, MA: Harvard Univ. Press, 1926–65.

Vermes, G. *The Dead Sea Scrolls in English.* 3rd ed. Harmondsworth: Penguin; Sheffield: JSOT Press, 1987.

Messianic Expectations and Movements in Judaism

Charlesworth, James H., ed. *The Messiah: Developments in Earliest Judaism and Christianity.* Minneapolis: Fortress, 1992.

Collins, John J. *The Scepter and the Star: The Messiahs of the Dead Sea Scrolls and Other Ancient Literature.* ABRL. New York: Doubleday, 1995.

Horsley, Richard A., and John S. Hanson. *Bandits, Prophets, and Messiahs: Popular Movements in the Time of Jesus.* San Francisco: Harper and Row, 1988.

Neusner, J., W. C. Green, and E. S. Frerichs, et al., eds. *Judaisms and Their Messiahs at the Turn of the Christian Era.* Cambridge: Cambridge Univ. Press, 1987.

Oegema, Gerbern S. *The Anointed and His People: Messianic Expectations from the Maccabees to Bar Kochba.* Sheffield: Sheffield Academic Press, 1998.

Strauss, Mark L. *The Davidic Messiah in Luke-Acts: The Promise and Its Fulfillment in Lukan Christology.* Sheffield: Sheffield Academic Press, 1995.

CHAPTER 6

The Social and Cultural Setting of the Gospels

» **CHAPTER OVERVIEW** «

1. Daily Life in New Testament Times
2. Social Values

» **OBJECTIVES** «

After reading this chapter, you should be able to:

- Describe key features of the social and cultural life of the first-century Mediterranean world.
- Identify the main social values of the Middle East in the first century and contrast these with common Western values.

A story appeared in *Newsweek* in October 2002, as United States forces were seeking out terrorist cells after the war in Afghanistan. A team of U.S. Special Forces was going door to door, seeking insurgents. Trained to be sensitive to the culture, U.S. Special Forces worked behind the scenes making alliances with local people. The team knocked on one door in a half-ruined mud compound. An old farmer let them in, after allowing his female relatives to move to a back room out of the gaze of strange men. When the team asked if the man had any weapons, he proudly produced a century-old hunting rifle. They took time to admire it and then searched the house, carefully letting the women stay out of sight. The farmer then served tea. Afterward, the Americans thanked him and left. As they moved down the street, they looked back to see six soldiers from a different division, part of the same operation, preparing to break down the door of the same house. They yelled, but it was too late. The door crashed in and the terrified farmer panicked and ran. He was tackled by the helmeted troops, who rushed through the house, frisking the women for weapons. By the time the Special Forces captain could run back, the place was in chaos. The women were screaming and the family was in a state of shock. The captain said, "The guy was in tears. He had been completely dishonored." Following similar incidents, intelligence reports from local sources dried up, as the villagers grew increasingly distrustful of the American presence.[1]

The story vividly illustrates the importance of understanding and respecting the norms and values of a particular society. Issues like discreetness and modesty, hospitality to strangers, and honor and respect for a patriarchal head of the household may be relatively insignificant in the West but are core values in the Middle East, both ancient and modern. To understand the Gospels, we must seek to enter into the first-century social and cultural world in which the events of the Gospels took place.

DAILY LIFE IN NEW TESTAMENT TIMES

The Family

Families were patriarchal in both Greco-Roman and Jewish societies, with the father as the highest authority. Families usually lived together in extended family units, including parents, children, grandparents, and often even aunts and uncles. Parents were treated with esteem and honor, especially in Judaism, because of the fifth commandment to "honor your father and mother" (Exod. 20:12). To shame a parent, as when the Prodigal Son asked for his inheritance early, essentially saying to his father, "I wish you were dead" (Luke 15:12), was viewed as despicable. The Old Testament even mandated stoning a rebellious son (Deut. 21:18–21). Providing for aging parents was an essential responsibility of adult children.

In Judaism, a woman's honor came primarily through childbearing, and to be childless brought great shame. Children were viewed as gifts from God (Ps. 127:3–5), and large families were the norm in Palestinian society. Boys were especially favored, since a male would carry on the family name and provide greater earning power to the family. The firstborn son would usually receive the bulk of the inheritance. In pagan society, unwanted children, especially girls, were sometimes "exposed," or left to die. Baby girls left this way

---

1. Colin Soloway, "I Yelled at Them to Stop," *Newsweek*, October 7, 2002, 36–38.

would sometimes be taken and raised as slave prostitutes. Judaism had a far more favorable attitude toward girls, though male children were still preferred.

Jewish boys would be circumcised and named eight days after birth (Luke 1:59). The meaning of names had greater significance than today and could be related to the circumstances of the birth or the hopes and expectations of parents. John means "the Lord has shown favor," and the name was given to John because God provided Elizabeth with a son in her old age. Isaac means "laughter," and Isaac was so named because God brought laughter to Sarah for the same reason (Gen. 21:6). Because certain names in Judaism were common, the identity of individuals would be clarified with the name of their father ("John the son of Zebedee"), their hometown ("Joseph of Arimathea"), or their profession ("Simon the tanner"). Jewish boys were educated in the trade of their father and were taught Torah in the home and in the synagogue. In general, girls were not formally educated but were taught domestic tasks in the home, like cooking, weaving, and cleaning.

Marriage. Marriages were arranged by parents and were almost always within the same socioeconomic class. In Judaism, a girl would normally be betrothed early and married by age twelve to sixteen. It was a major social stigma for a woman to reach twenty unmarried. Men were commonly married between eighteen and twenty. Engagements lasted for a year or so and were officially contracted, requiring a "divorce" to break the contract. In Matthew 1:19–20, Joseph decides to divorce Mary quietly so as not to publicly shame her, suspecting she has been unfaithful during the engagement (a serious offense: Deut. 22:23–24).

Weddings were the most important social events in Jewish society, involving the entire village. The ceremony began with the groom going to the home of the bride's parents to bring her to his father's home. Friends and townspeople would accompany him on the way, singing and rejoicing (see the parable of the ten virgins in Matt. 25:1–13). He would bring the bride—veiled and adorned in lavish wedding clothes—and her attendants to the wedding banquet. Festivities would last a week or more and would be marked by feasting, dancing, and celebration. For food or wine to run out during such an event would bring shame to both families (John 2:3).

While polygamy existed, it was rare both in Jewish and Greco-Roman society. Monogamy was the norm. Yet moral values were generally low among the Greeks. In addition to having a wife to produce legitimate children, a man might have a mistress and also regularly visit temple prostitutes. Homosexual behavior and pederasty (sex with boys) were also common and were viewed as acceptable by some Greeks. Jews considered such behavior as abhorrent and contrary to God's law.

Statue of Aphrodite, Greek goddess of love

Divorce was common in the Greco-Roman world. Under first-century Roman law, either the man or the woman could initiate divorce. In Judaism, except in extreme circumstances, only men could initiate divorce. The Old Testament recognized the reality of divorce, even if it did not sanction it, and guidelines were given to protect both parties (Deut. 24:1–4). The rabbis debated the legitimate grounds for divorce. The conservative school of **Shammai** allowed a man to divorce his wife only for unfaithfulness, while the more liberal school of **Hillel** accepted almost any reason, including ruining a meal. Rabbi Akiba is cited as saying that divorce was allowed if the man "found another fairer than she" (*m. Giṭ.* 9:10). Easy divorce seemed to be the norm in first-century Judaism. Jesus reacted strongly against this casual attitude and pointed to the inviolable nature of marriage (Mark 10:11–12; Matt. 5:32; 19:9). To break a marriage vow and marry another constituted adultery.

Slaves. Slavery was common in the Roman Empire, and slaves made up as much as a third of the population. Slaves were considered part of the household, under the authority of the *paterfamilias*, the male head of the family. Though it was somewhat less common, Jews and Christians also kept slaves, and both the Old and New Testaments provided guidelines for their behavior and treatment (Leviticus 25; Deut. 23:15–16; Eph. 6:5–9; Col. 3:22–4:1; 1 Peter 2:18). The New Testament, however, provides evidence that slavery is contrary to God's will and that the new age begun in Christ should result in its abolition (1 Cor. 7:21; Gal. 3:28; Eph. 6:9; 1 Tim. 1:10; Rev. 18:13).

Unlike in America, Greco-Roman slavery had nothing to do with race. People became slaves in a variety of ways, most commonly as prisoners of war. Sometimes people would sell themselves into slavery because of extreme poverty. The Old Testament called for the freeing of indentured slaves after six years (Exod. 21:2; Deut. 15:12–18). Slaves also held a wide range of social positions. The lowest form of slavery was in mines or galley ships, where life was brutal and short. Runaway slaves were often branded or executed. At the opposite end of the spectrum were slaves who held high positions of authority as managers over wealthy households. Such slaves could own property, conduct business, and purchase their own freedom. Despite these widely divergent statuses, slaves were still considered property and functioned at the whim of their owners.

Food and Meals

Staples of Middle Eastern diet: dates, grapes, and olives

Romans normally ate four meals a day. Wealthy people had a wide-ranging diet, including fruits, vegetables, meats, poultry, and fish. Poor people lived mostly on bread and veg-

Date palm. A single palm tree can produce over 125 lbs. (55 kg.) of fruit each year. The fruit can be eaten fresh or dried.

An ancient olive press near Capernaum

etables. Jews normally ate two meals a day, one at noon and another in the evening. A common diet consisted of bread, vegetables (beans, lentils, cucumbers), fruit (especially grapes, olives, dates, figs, and pomegranates), fish, and milk products (milk, yogurt, and cheese). Meat was uncommon and usually eaten only during festivals. Bread made from wheat was considered superior to that made from barley. Sugar was unknown, but honey and dates were used for sweetening. Water was often unsafe, so it was commonly mixed with wine, usually three or four parts water to wine.

Most meals were consumed while sitting on mats. Bread would be dipped into a common bowl containing a sauce or soup (John 13:26–27). More formal banquets were eaten while reclining around a low table. Participants would lean on their left arms and use their right hands to eat. Meals of this kind were rituals of social status. The position assigned at the table confirmed one's social status in the community. Greco-Roman accounts even note that different qualities of food would be served to people of different statuses, which would be like serving filet mignon to your favored guests and hamburger to everyone else! The positions to the left and right of the host held the greatest honor. In Luke 14:7–14, Jesus warns against seeking the best seats at a banquet and risking the humiliation of being asked to move to a lower place. He also encourages his followers to invite all types of people — especially those below their social class — to these banquets. When the poor beggar Lazarus dies and goes to "Abraham's bosom" (Luke 16:23), he is pictured as reclining beside Abraham at the **messianic banquet**, an image of God's end-times salvation (see Isa. 25:6–8). In John 13:23, the "disciple whom Jesus loved" reclines in an honored position beside Jesus.

Clothing and Style

Men normally wore a tunic, a shirtlike knee-length garment made of linen or cotton and tied around the waist with a sash. On cooler days, a heavier cloak, perhaps of wool, would be worn over the tunic. Women wore a short tunic as an undergarment and an outer robe which extended to the feet.

Leather sandals or shoes were worn on the feet, though poorer people would walk barefoot. Because the roads were dusty, when guests arrived for a social occasion, a servant would remove their sandals and wash their feet. This task was viewed as too degrading for anyone other than a servant, and even the disciples of rabbis were not expected to do it. Jesus' washing the disciples' feet was particularly shocking and countercultural (John 13:1–17).

Greek and Roman men normally were clean shaven and wore their hair short (see 1 Cor. 11:14). Jewish men wore beards and somewhat longer hair. Both Greek and Jewish women typically wore their hair long, though prostitutes sometimes cropped it short. Wealthy Greco-Roman women wore cosmetics, jewelry, and elaborate hairstyles, often decorated with ornaments. In Judaism, unmarried girls went unveiled, but married women would cover their hair (but not their faces) with a shawl-like veil in public. A woman's covering symbolized modesty and respect for her husband, preventing sexual attention from other males. Uncovered hair was a sign of promiscuity or even prostitution. Jesus' actions in allowing an immoral woman to touch his feet and wipe them with her hair was viewed as scandalous by Simon the pious Pharisee (Luke 7:36–50). In general, the farther east you went in the Mediterranean world, the more women were expected to cover up. Persian women in the East were completely veiled in public, while Roman and Greek women more often had their heads and arms uncovered.

Sandals found at Masada

Left: A young Bedouin woman. *Right:* A marble statue of a woman with an elaborate Roman hairstyle.

The village of Yata, near Hebron, preserves the appearance of a typical ancient village in Judea.

Villages, Towns, and Cities

A village (*komē*) was a small rural settlement, while a city (*polis*) was a larger municipality protected by walls. We may also speak of a "town," larger than a village but smaller and less fortified than a city. But the New Testament normally uses the same word (*polis*) for both cities and towns. Cities often had small satellite villages clustered around them. In times of war, the villagers would come into the city for protection.

Along the city walls, fortified towers would be built for defense. Large wooden gates, sometimes covered with iron or bronze, would protect the main entrance to the city. These would be closed and sealed at night for protection from bandits. The city gate normally opened onto the marketplace, the center of commerce and public life. In the marketplace, merchants would sell their goods, day workers would find work (Matt. 20:3), city officials would meet to conduct business (Acts 16:19), friends would socialize, philosophers and preachers would find an audience for their teachings (Acts 17:17), and children would play (Luke 7:32). The marketplace was like the modern-day mall, the place to see and be seen.

Cities had narrow alleylike streets lined with homes and shops. Shop owners would normally live in quarters immediately behind or above the shop. Conditions in cities were often unsanitary, without running water and with sewage running freely through the streets. This was not always the case, however, and some Roman cities had elaborate plumbing and sewage systems. Aqueducts brought water over long distances to the city.

Homes. Wealthy people lived in large villas, usually a cluster of buildings around a central courtyard. Homes were made of brick, concrete, or hewn stone. In Palestine, wealthy merchants, priests, and government officials lived in a style similar to the rich elsewhere in the empire.

Typical flat-roofed homes in Judea during the Roman period. From the model of Jerusalem at the Holy Land Hotel.

A model of Roman-period table arrangement

The vast majority of people were poor and lived in small one- or two-room dwellings made of mud or dried brick. On the upper level would be the eating and sleeping quarters. An adjacent lower level would house animals. Windows were small for security reasons, and there would be a single front door, which would be bolted shut at night. Families would sleep beside one another on mats on the floor. An oil lamp in a stone alcove would be kept burning at night (Matt. 5:15). This is the situation envisioned in Jesus' parable in Luke 11:5–8, in which a man does not want to answer the door for a friend at night because of the inconvenience of stepping over children and unbolting the sealed door. On the side of the house, external stairs would lead to a flat roof made of beams covered with thatched reeds and dried mud or clay. The roof could be used for storage, drying fruit, and for sleeping on warm summer nights. This architecture helps to explain the account of the healing of the paralytic, in which four men dig through a roof to lower their friend to Jesus (Mark 2:1–12; Matt. 9:1–8; Luke 5:17–26). It would have been relatively easy (though still probably irritating to the homeowner!) to dig through the reeds and mud to reach Jesus.

Reconstruction of a typical rural house roof built of wattle and reed

Public Buildings. Greek and Roman cities contained many municipal facilities, including indoor theaters and outdoor amphitheaters, stadiums, public baths, gymnasiums, temples, and a large agora, or marketplace. Gymnasiums were for recreation, exercise, and fellowship, and also served as educational centers for boys. During the forced hellenization by the Syrians, Greek-style gymnasiums, stadiums, and amphitheaters were built throughout the land of Israel. Many more were constructed, rebuilt, or enlarged by Herod the Great. Most of the larger cities, especially those with large Gentile populations like Tiberius, Caesarea, and Sepphoris, contained many such facilities.

Synagogues. For the Jewish community, life centered around the synagogue, which served as a center for worship, administration, education, and community gatherings. There were large Jewish populations in most of the major cities in the empire, and synagogues could be found in most towns or cities. In Palestine, at least one existed in every village (wherever ten Jewish men could gather), and there were many more in the larger cities.

Work, Trades, and Professions

The Roman Empire had a small and wealthy upper class made up of royalty, politicians, military generals, and wealthy merchants. There was almost no middle class, and the vast majority of people eked out a living as poor farmers, shepherds, craftsmen, and merchants. The poorest workers (apart from slaves) were day workers, who would be hired from the marketplace to work in the fields (Matt. 20:1 – 16). A common wage for a day worker was one denarius for eight to ten hours work (Matt. 20:2). Most peasants lived at a subsistence level, buying food each day. The phrase in the Lord's Prayer, "Give us today our daily bread" (Matt. 6:11), was a reality for most people.

Craftsmen practiced trades such as tanning, weaving, dyeing, carpentry, metal work, tentmaking, masonry, and potterymaking. Most trades were passed down from father to son. In general, men practiced a trade while women performed domestic tasks in the home. Craftsmen would often form themselves into trade guilds, similar to the labor unions of today. The term *carpenter* used of Jesus and his father (*tektōn*, Matt. 13:55; Mark 6:3) referred generally to those who built with a variety of materials, like wood, stone, and metal. Dyeing secrets were carefully guarded within family businesses, and colored garments were viewed as luxuries. Lydia is a "dealer in purple cloth from the city of Thyatira" (Acts 16:14), probably meaning she owned a dyeing business in that city. Purple dye was often made from murex, a type of shellfish. The apostle Paul was not only a rabbi but also a tentmaker (*skēnopoios*, Acts 18:3). Tents were normally made of skins or leather, and so Paul might also have fashioned and repaired other leather products. While upper-class Greeks viewed manual labor as degrading, in Judaism such work was honorable, and most rabbis were expected to practice a trade.

Sheep and goats were kept for their wool, skin, milk, for food, and for temple sacrifices. Shepherding was usually a family affair, with the younger members of the family watching the flocks. Sometimes wealthy people would own large herds, hiring shepherds to watch them. Jesus allegorically contrasts himself as the true shepherd who knows and protects the sheep with the unreliable hired hand who runs away at the first sign of danger (John 10:1 – 18). There is debate today as to how shepherds were viewed in the Mediterranean world and in Judaism in particular. Later rabbinic writings describe them as dishonest and untrustworthy, similar to the way gypsies are viewed in Eastern Europe today. Yet the biblical portrait is almost always positive. David was a shepherd; the LORD is our shepherd (Ps. 23:1); Jesus is the good shepherd (John 10:11; 1 Peter 2:25; Heb. 13:20). God's people are often portrayed as sheep who need protection and care and who easily go astray (Isa. 53:6).

www.HolyLandPhotos.org

Sheep

Fishing on the Mediterranean coast

© Neal Bierling/Zondervan Image Archives

Fishing was common around the Sea of Galilee, and fish was a diet staple. A beautifully preserved first-century fishing boat was recently discovered in the mud banks of the Sea of Galilee. Different kinds of nets were used for fishing: long nets supported on floats and weighted at the bottom for night fishing in deep water (Luke 5:2, 5), round casting nets used for shallow-water day-fishing (Mark 1:16; Matt. 4:18), and dragnets towed along between two boats (Matt 13:47).

Farmers grew wheat and barley in the fields. They would normally sow first, carrying a bag of grain and scattering it by hand onto the soil. They would then plow the seed into the ground using a wooden plow and a team of oxen. This is the scenario of Jesus' parable of the sower (Mark 4:1 – 20, par.), in which seed that fell on the path or the rocky places would not get plowed into the soil and would be eaten by the birds or dry out in the sun.

The most important agricultural products of Israel were olives and grapes. Olive trees could live hundreds of years. The ancient trees in the Garden of Gethsemane today may have grown from the roots of those in Jesus' day, which the Romans cut down when they destroyed Jerusalem in AD 70. Olives were eaten as fruit and used for making olive oil. The olives would be crushed to pulp in a large stone press, and then the oil from the pulp would be squeezed through filters. Olive oil was used for cooking, for flavoring bread (i.e., like butter), and as an ingredient in many dishes. It was also used for making soap, as a skin moisturizer, and as fuel in lamps. To anoint someone's head with oil was a sign of honor and hospitality (Luke 7:46). Prophets, priests, and kings were anointed with olive oil as confirmation of their God-ordained role.

Z. Radovan, Jerusalem

First-century Galilean fishing boat discovered in 1986

© Neal Bierling/Zondervan Image Archives

A vineyard in Lachish

© Neal Bierling/Zondervan Image Archives

Gordon Franz/ZIBBC

Grapes were grown for eating, but especially for winemaking. Vineyards would often have a protective wall and a tower in the middle for a caretaker to guard the vines against animals or thieves. Isaiah compares the nation of Israel to an unproductive vineyard whose wall and tower will be broken down to allow enemies to overrun it (Isa. 5:1–7). Jesus draws from this analogy to portray Israel's religious leaders as corrupt tenant farmers who want to steal the vineyard for themselves (Mark 12:1–12, par.). Such a scenario fits the situation in Galilee, where wealthy landowners—often foreigners—would rent vineyards and fields to poor peasants, requiring a large portion of the harvest in return. As in all feudal systems, this arrangement was open to abuse and corruption, and created ill will between peasants and overlords. Such a climate was ripe for unrest and even revolution.

Top: A Palestinian farmer plowing his vineyard

Bottom: Working wheat

Commerce, Transportation, and Communication

The Romans were master builders, and roads were their most lasting legacy. Roman roads were as straight as possible, paved with stones, and wide enough for two chariots to pass each other. Many Roman roads are still visible today.

Traveling by ship was often the quickest and most efficient means of trade and transport. It could also be dangerous, particularly in winter when the seas were treacherous. Paul, a frequent traveler, reports being shipwrecked three times (2 Cor. 11:25). The Romans were not the ablest of sailors and tended to sail close to shore for safety. Sailing also depended on favorable winds. A trip which took three weeks in one direction could take three months in the other. A classic account of a first-century Mediterranean sea voyage is found in Luke's story of Paul's journey to Rome, with all the drama of storms, contrary winds, and shipwreck (Acts 27).

While the Roman peace allowed much freedom of movement, travel was still slow and sometimes dangerous. The wealthy rode horses or in horse-drawn carriages and chariots. Merchants of moderate means would have donkeys, camels, or other beasts of burden. Most

The remains of Roman roads can still be seen today. View of a portion of the Via Egnatia near the city of Philippi.

View of a milestone from the Roman period. The inscription on this stone has been worn away by the weather, but typically such a stone would state the name of the ruling Roman emperor, sometimes the name of the governor, and also the distances (in Roman miles) to and from major cities.

people walked. A healthy person could walk fifteen to twenty miles a day. The journey from Galilee to Jerusalem took about five days. There were roadside inns on major roads, but these had a reputation for poor conditions and seedy occupants. Most people would stay with relatives or friends.

There was no public postal system, but government couriers carried important documents. It took imperial riders about forty-five days to travel from Rome to Caesarea. Common people got their news mostly through letters carried by friends and acquaintances. Notice boards in the marketplace or agora were used for public announcements.

Entertainment and Leisure

The Greeks and Romans developed many recreational and entertainment activities. The most gruesome of these were the arena games, in which gladiators and wild beasts fought to the death. While gladiatorial games took place throughout the empire, the most spectacular were at the Colosseum in Rome. The games consisted of every kind of contest imaginable: man against man, man against beast, and beast against beast. Human participants were usually prisoners of war or criminals. Like modern sports stars, successful gladiators often became heroes and celebrities. Lions, tigers, bulls, elephants, alligators, and other animals fought and were slaughtered by gladiators or by one another. The apostle Paul may have faced wild animals in the arena, if 1 Corinthians 15:32 and 2 Timothy 4:17 are to be taken literally.

Other less barbaric recreational activities were also common. Public baths and gymnasiums provided for personal hygiene, exercise, and socializing. Plays were performed in indoor and outdoor amphitheaters. Some of these were bawdy and obscene, reflecting the low moral climate of society. Pagan temples served as banquet venues for celebrations like birthdays and anniversaries. Chariot races and athletic contests were conducted in stadiums or hippodromes. The most important athletic games were the Olympic Games and the Isthmian Games in Corinth, where athletes competed for a crown wreath (*stephanos*) made of foliage.

In Israel, the wealthy and aristocratic participated in many of these same activities, visiting baths and gymnasiums and attending theaters and athletic contests. But Jewish social and religious life centered to a much greater extent on family gatherings and participation in the annual festivals of the Jewish calendar. The highlight of the year for most would be attending the great pilgrim festivals in Jerusalem—Passover, Pentecost, and Tabernacles.

The Colosseum in Rome

SOCIAL VALUES

Cultural background concerns not only the way people lived but also what they thought—the values, beliefs, and worldview which motivated their behavior. Since these values were often quite different from those of today, they bear closer examination.

Group Rather Than Individual Mentality

One of the fundamental differences between Middle Eastern and Western values is that of **group mentality** versus individual mentality. People with group mentality find their identities not in themselves and their personal accomplishments but in relationship with others. This is sometimes called **dyadism**, meaning that essential identity comes from being a member of a family, a community, or a nation. Paul took pride in his status as a Pharisee, a Hebrew born of Hebrews, and a member of the tribe of Benjamin (Phil. 3:5). In John 8:39, the religious leaders defend themselves before Jesus by claiming that they are children of Abraham. The early believers are said to be one in heart and mind, sharing their possessions like a family (Acts 4:32). These are all dyadic associations.

If identity comes from the group, then actions should be for the good of the community. Individual interests and desires take second place to the common good. To sacrifice for family, friend, and community is the greatest of all actions (John 15:13).

Group mentality also relates to order and authority. The hierarchical structures of society are viewed as divinely ordained and provide stability to all institutions. Respect for and obedience to parents as authorities in the home (Exod. 20:12; Eph. 6:1), to kings as authorities over the state (Rom. 13:1–2), and to priests or elders as religious authorities (Heb. 13:7) are essential for the maintenance of the divinely ordained balance of life.

Honor and Shame

In a society in which identity comes from the group, the values of **honor and shame** are among the most important. Honor is gaining status and esteem from others; shame is losing those things. While wealth, fame, and power are the most prominent symbols of success in the Western world, in Mediterranean culture, the greatest achievement is to gain honor.

The Theater at Ephesus

Jesus' teachings and parables assume this core value. The man who takes an honored seat at a banquet and is then asked to move to a lower one is publicly shamed before his colleagues—a fate almost worse than death (Luke 14:8–9).

Honor and shame are group values, since shame given to an individual brings shame to the group. An unfinished tower is a monument of shame for the whole community (Luke 14:29). A rebellious son shames the whole family. The angry response of the older brother in the parable of the prodigal son is understandable in this context, and the free forgiveness of the father is extraordinary (Luke 15:11–32). Jesus' parable of the importune friend at night also illustrates this value. The man lying in bed *must* get up and provide bread for his neighbor's guest, lest the whole community be shamed for failing to show hospitality (Luke 11:5–8; see "Hospitality" below). Elizabeth's infertility brings shame not only to herself but to her husband, whose lineage will end. Her shame is turned to honor at the birth of John (Luke 1:58).

Jesus' debates with the religious leaders have honor and shame in the background. In Mediterranean culture, to silence one's opponents through argument brought honor to you and loss of face to them. Jesus repeatedly confounds the leaders with wise and clever words. After a series of controversies in Jerusalem, Matthew notes that "no one could say a word in reply, and from that day on no one dared ask him any more questions" (Matt. 22:46).

The paradox of the gospel is that Jesus' honor first turns to shame when he is crucified, the most shameful death imaginable. At Jesus' trial and on the cross, he is shamed and mocked by everyone: Pilate, Herod, the soldiers, the religious leaders, the crowds, and even the criminals beside him. Crucifixion not only was excruciating torture but also was meant to humiliate and degrade the victim. Ancient peoples considered the public "exposure" of a dead or dying body to be horribly shameful. Yet Jesus' shame is dramatically reversed at his resurrection. Vindicated by God as Messiah, Jesus is bestowed with all honor and authority (Matt. 28:18–20; cf. Phil. 2:5–11). The great paradox of the Christian life is that the foolish message of the gospel is the wisdom and power of salvation, and the shame of the cross brings glory to all who believe (Rom. 1:16–17; Gal. 6:14; 1 Cor. 1:18–31). In order to be great (to have honor), believers must take up their crosses and follow Jesus (Mark 8:34, par.).

Family and Kinship

In a context in which membership in a group is more important than individual identity, family relationships are the most important of all relationships. The father was the supreme authority, and parents were to be honored in every way. Respect for one's parents came from the fact that they gave one life and because they were the guardians of the sacred traditions. Parents taught their children the values which bound the community together and which gave structure and meaning to life. Through inheritance, parents also established one's connection to the land. This was of critical importance, since Israel's national identity was closely linked to her possession of the land (*ha-aretz*). God's blessing meant fruitfulness and peace in the land; his judgment meant destruction and exile.

The goal for children in such a culture was not to make a better life than their parents', as is often the case in the West, but to guard the traditions, status, and honor of the family and to keep family bonds strong. In the parable of the prodigal son, the older brother should have acted as a mediator between the father and the estranged son, instead of shaming his father by refusing to attend the feast (Luke 15:25–32). The greatest good is the family's good.

Christianity strongly affirmed family relations, particularly honor and respect for parents, but radically redefined the essence of true relationships. Kinship was no longer based on blood relations but on association with the new community of Jesus the Messiah. When Jesus called James and John to be his disciples, they immediately left their father and the family business to follow him (Mark 1:20; Matt. 4:22). Such an abandonment was shocking and would produce shame in the community. Elsewhere, Jesus said, "Do not call anyone on earth 'father,' for you have one Father, and he is in heaven" (Matt. 23:9). At one point, he refused to see his family, saying that his true mother and brothers were those who did God's will (Mark 3:31–35, par.). Jesus is not repudiating his family but rather is affirming deeper spiritual bonds. It is not surprising that the early believers referred to each other as "brothers and sisters" (*adelphoi*). As Jewish followers of Jesus were increasingly expelled from the synagogues and Jewish families were divided, this emphasis on spiritual kinship became extremely important.

Hospitality

Anyone who has visited the Middle East knows the fundamental value given to hospitality, or welcoming strangers. My brother and I were once walking through a field in Israel where an Arab family was tending crops. They had stopped for lunch and immediately invited us—complete strangers—to have tea with them. In a situation of hospitality, the host is expected to meet the needs of the guest, to offer the guest the best of food and lodging. The guest in turn is expected to graciously accept whatever is offered, to honor the host and his family, and to praise their hospitality to others, increasing their honor in the community.

Jesus refers to hospitable acts when he is anointed with perfume by a sinful woman. He points out that his host, Simon, did not offer him a kiss of greeting, nor wash his feet, nor anoint his head with oil. In contrast, the woman went beyond the norms of hospitality, washing his feet with her tears and hair, kissing him on the feet, and anointing his feet with costly perfume (Luke 7:36–50).

Hospitality was particularly important for the traveling preachers in the early church, since they would often enter communities where they had no friends or relatives (Rom. 16:23; 1 Tim. 5:10; 1 Peter 4:9; 3 John 1:8). Jesus provided guidelines for how disciples should receive such hospitality (Mark 6:8–11, par.; Luke 10:5–12).

Social Status and Position in Life

As we have several times alluded, social position in the ancient world was well established. Everyone knew their place in life—who was above them and who was below them. Democratic values of equality and equal rights were almost nonexistent. Though people certainly had ambition, the greatest goal in life was not to climb the socioeconomic ladder but to protect the status quo. This was done by serving those above you and exercising authority over those below.

Jesus often acted in a countercultural manner against these social distinctions. We see this in his association with tax collectors and other sinners (Mark 2:16, par.; Luke 7:34; 15:1–2; Matt. 11:19), his identification of Mary as a disciple who could learn from him (Luke 10:39, 42), his call to invite those of lower status to banquets (Luke 14:12–14), and his conversation with a Samaritan woman, who would have been viewed as his inferior by virtue of her ethnicity, gender, and low social status (John 4).

Patronage

Closely related to social status was the concept of **patronage**. If challenging the social structure is taboo, how does one get something that is beyond one's means? The answer is the patronage system, in which a *patron* or *benefactor* provides favors to a *client* of lower status. In return, the patron expects loyalty, obedience, and honor from the client. Such patron-client agreements formed the foundation of almost every relationship in the Middle East, whether economic, political, military, or religious. Indeed, everyone in society functioned in some way as a client or a patron, or both. Herod the Great served as a client-king for his patron Caesar Augustus, whose legions kept Herod in power. The leading priests of Jerusalem found a patron, though a sometimes dangerous and erratic one, in Herod himself, as he built their Jerusalem temple and provided resources for their synagogue communities. The Jewish elders of Capernaum found a patron in a certain centurion, who had provided resources to build their synagogue (Luke 7:4–5). Of course, God was Israel's ultimate patron, providing provision and protection and expecting loyalty, love, and obedience in return.

1. The extended family was the most important social unit in the ancient world. Families were generally patriarchal, with the male head of the house exercising most authority. A woman's honor in the family came primarily through childbearing and her domestic skills.

2. Marriages were generally arranged with families of similar social and cultural status. Weddings were among the most important social events in society.

3. Slavery was common in the Roman Empire, although the status and privilege of slaves varied enormously. While some first-century Christians kept slaves, the New Testament provides clear indications of the evil of slavery and the need for its abolition.

4. Banquets were not just meals or social events but rituals of social status which demonstrated one's position in the community.

5. Married women in Jewish society normally had their heads covered with a veil. Greco-Roman customs were more diverse in style and dress.

6. Cities were larger municipalities, typically surrounded by a wall. Cities were often surrounded by small agrarian villages, whose inhabitants would enter the city for protection in time of war.

7. Greco-Roman cities often had many municipal facilities, including theaters, stadiums, baths, gymnasiums, and temples. Synagogues, scattered throughout the Roman Empire, were the center of Jewish community life.

8. The vast majority of people were poor farmers and tradespeople. A small upper class wielded most of the power and controlled most of the wealth.

9. Upper-class Greeks and Romans considered manual labor degrading; Jews viewed it as more honorable, and most rabbis practiced a trade.

10. The most common agricultural activities of Israel and the Mediterranean region were raising livestock, fishing, and growing wheat, barley, olives, grapes, figs, and dates.

11. Roman roads provided much better conditions for travel than in previous centuries, but travel could still be difficult and dangerous.

12. Greco-Roman entertainment included arena games, theater plays, athletic contests, and public baths and gymnasiums. Jewish life centered more on family and the annual pilgrimage festivals in Jerusalem.

13. Social values in the first-century Middle East were sometimes very different from those of Western culture today:

    a. The well-being of the group — whether family, clan, or country — was more valued than the good of the individual.
    b. Honor in the community was most highly esteemed, and receiving shame was the greatest fear.
    c. People were expected to accept their status in society and to respect society's hierarchical structures.
    d. Hospitality — meeting the needs of visitors and strangers — was highly valued, bringing honor to the community.
    e. Most relationships were based on patronage, whereby a wealthy or powerful patron or benefactor would provide for the needs of a client of lower status, and in return would receive honor and loyalty.

» KEY TERMS «

Shammai	group mentality	honor and shame
Hillel	dyadism	patronage
messianic banquet		

» DISCUSSION AND STUDY QUESTIONS «

1. What was the nature of first-century family life? Of marriages and weddings?
2. What role did slavery play in the Roman Empire? Among Christian believers?
3. What function did banquets have in society?
4. Describe the various characteristics of cities in the first century.
5. Were most people in the Roman Empire from the upper, middle, or lower class?
6. What were the most common agricultural products in Israel?
7. What was the nature of travel and commerce in the Roman Empire?
8. Describe various Greco-Roman forms of entertainment and recreation.

9. What is the difference between group mentality and individual mentality? Which was most valued in first-century culture?

10. What do we mean by the first-century social values of honor and shame?

11. Describe the importance of hospitality in the Mediterranean world.

12. What is patronage? Who are clients?

Digging Deeper

General Works

Arnold, Clinton E., gen. ed. *Zondervan Illustrated Bible Backgrounds Commentary.* 4 vols. Grand Rapids: Zondervan, 2002.

Bell Jr., Albert A. *Exploring the New Testament World.* Nashville: Thomas Nelson, 1998.

Evans, Craig A., and Stanley E. Porter, eds. *Dictionary of New Testament Background: A Compendium of Contemporary Biblical Scholarship.* Downers Grove, IL: InterVarsity, 2000.

Ferguson, Everett. *Backgrounds of Early Christianity.* 3rd ed. Grand Rapids: Eerdmans, 2003.

Jeremias, J. *Jerusalem in the Time of Jesus: An Investigation into Economic and Social Conditions during the New Testament Period.* Translated by F. H. Cave and C. H. Cave. Philadelphia: Fortress, 1969.

Daily Life in the First-Century Mediterranean World

Bouquet, A. C. *Everyday Life in New Testament Times.* New York: Scribner's, 1954.

Casson, Lionel. *Travel in the Ancient World.* Rev. ed. Baltimore: Johns Hopkins, 1994.

Enns, Paul. *Manners and Customs of Bible Times: Shepherd's Notes.* Edited by David R. Shepherd. Nashville: Broadman and Holman, 2000.

Matthews, V. H. *Manners and Customs in the Bible.* 2nd ed. Peabody, MA: Hendrickson, 1991.

Thompson, J. A. *Handbook of Life in Bible Times.* Downers Grove, IL: InterVarsity, 1986.

Social and Cultural Values

Bailey, Kenneth E. *Poet and Peasant and Through Peasant Eyes.* Combined ed. Grand Rapids: Eerdmans, 1983.

Malina, Bruce J. *The New Testament World: Insights from Cultural Anthropology.* Louisville, KY: Westminster John Knox, 1993.

Malina, Bruce J., and Richard L. Rohrbaugh. *Social-Science Commentary on the Synoptic Gospels.* Minneapolis: Fortress, 1992.

Pilch, John J., and Bruce J. Malina. *Handbook of Biblical Social Values.* Peabody, MA: Hendrickson, 1993, 1998.

Stambaugh, John E., and David L. Balch. *The New Testament in Its Social Environment.* Philadelphia: Westminster, 1986.

PART THREE

The Four Gospels

PROCLAIMING AND INTERPRETING THE STORY OF JESUS

In chapter 1, we identified the genre of the Gospels as *historical narrative motivated by theological concerns*. In part 3, we turn to an analysis of these four Gospels. Since the Holy Spirit inspired four distinct accounts of Jesus' life and ministry, it is in line with their purpose and literary form to read and study them as distinct stories and to draw out the unique theological themes and emphases of each.

Our method will begin with a narrative and text-centered approach. We will first examine the story each Evangelist tells, focusing on their unique portrait of Jesus. From this narrative analysis we will then draw out the main theological themes of that author. Finally, drawing on the available evidence, we will propose specific life situations (place, date, occasion) for each Gospel and seek to identify the historical author. This method moves from what is most certain (the features of the story itself) to what is less certain (the specific life circumstances in which the Gospel arose). The *narrative* points to the implied author's *theological perspective*, which provides clues to the historical author's *specific life setting*.

Figure 7.0

The Narrative → **Theological Themes and Perspective** → **Specific Life Setting (author, place, time, occasion)**

CHAPTER 7

Mark

THE GOSPEL OF THE SUFFERING SON OF GOD

» CHAPTER OVERVIEW «

1. Literary Features
2. The Plot of Mark's Gospel
3. Mark's Portrait of Jesus: The Suffering Son of God
4. Other Characters in Mark's Gospel
5. Theological Themes
6. Narrative Purpose
7. The Historical Setting of Mark's Gospel: Author and Life Setting
8. Reading Mark Today

» OBJECTIVES «

After reading this chapter, you should be able to:

- Identify and define the main rhetorical devices of Mark's Gospel.
- Summarize the plot of Mark's Gospel, especially with reference to the key turning point in chapter 8.
- Describe the main features of Mark's portrait of Jesus, especially with reference to the titles Christ, Son of God, Son of Man, and Servant.
- Identify the role played by various characters, including demons, religious leaders, the disciples, and other minor characters.
- Summarize Mark's main theological themes, including the kingdom of God, discipleship, and the identity of Jesus.
- Explain what we know about John Mark, the likely author of this Gospel.
- Provide basic evidence for the likely historical setting and occasion of Mark's Gospel.

I remember vividly January 17, 1991. It was the night the first Gulf War began with the launching of an allied air assault against Iraq. From their hotel in downtown Baghdad, CNN reporters Bernard Shaw and Peter Arnett gave a moment-by-moment report, describing the sounds of planes overhead and the sky lighting up with anti-aircraft fire and the explosion of bombs. Those watching from around the world could not help but feel they were present in Baghdad, watching the war unfold before their eyes.

In many ways, Mark's Gospel has the same feel as an on-the-spot news report. The narrative is vivid, fast moving, and action packed. Jesus appears as the mighty **Messiah** and **Son of God**, moving through the Galilean countryside, exercising authority over friend and foe alike. He calls disciples, heals the sick, casts out demons, and teaches with great

» CENTRAL THEME «

Jesus the mighty Messiah and Son of God obediently suffers as the Servant of the Lord to pay the ransom price for sins, and as a model of suffering and sacrifice for his disciples to follow.

» KEY VERSE «

Mark 10:45

» BASIC OUTLINE OF MARK «

1. The Preparation of the Son of God (1:1 – 13)

2. The Authoritative Ministry of the Son of God in and around Galilee (1:14 – 8:26)
    A. The Kingdom-Authority of the Son of God (1:14 – 3:12)
    B. The "Disciple-Family" of the Son of God and Those "Outside" (3:13 – 6:6)
    C. The Mission of the Son of God (6:7 – 8:26)

3. The Suffering of the Son of God as Servant of the LORD (8:27 – 16:8)
    A. The Confession of Peter and Jesus' Role as Servant Messiah (8:27 – 10:52)
    B. The Son of God Confronts Jerusalem (10:46 – 13:37)
    C. Climax: The Death of the Son of God (14:1 – 15:47)
    D. Resolution: The Resurrection of the Son of God (16:1 – 8)

authority. There is a sense of awe and mystery about him, and amazement from those he encounters. Mark's lively story invites the reader to enter his narrative world and experience the coming of the Messiah, the arrival of God's promised salvation.

For centuries, the church paid little attention to the Gospel of Mark because it was considered to be merely an abbreviated version of Matthew, with little value of its own. This view changed in the nineteenth and twentieth centuries when Mark came to be viewed as the first Gospel written and so of significant historical value. In recent years, scholars have come to appreciate Mark's Gospel as a unique literary work with its own narrative structure, theological themes, and christological purpose. The Gospel reveals a fascinating and unique portrait of Jesus, an important contribution to the church's understanding of Jesus the Messiah.

LITERARY FEATURES

Literary Style

Mark's Gospel has a fast-moving narrative style. The narrator is fond of the Greek word *euthys*, an adverb often translated "immediately." It appears forty-two times, whereas in Matthew it appears five times, and in Luke, only once. While the word does not always mean "just then," its effect is to propel the narrative forward (see fig. 7.1, p. 175).

The narrator also uses present-tense verbs to describe past actions, a Greek idiom known as the *historical present* (151 times; Matthew 93 times; Luke 11 times). While characteristic of a rougher, less-refined Greek (the author probably spoke Greek as a second language), the historical present also gives the narrative a vivid and realistic feel, like a newscaster giving

» CHARACTERISTICS OF MARK'S GOSPEL «

Look for these while reading Mark:
- Fast-moving narrative; use of immediately (*euthys*) and Greek historical present tense.
- Vivid descriptions of persons and events.
- Prominence of Galilee as the locus of Jesus' early ministry.
- Strong emphasis on Jesus' authority in teaching and in miracles.
- Amazed reaction by others to Jesus' authority.
- Emphasis on challenges to Jesus by the forces of Satan and his defeat of them.
- Jesus portrayed as the authoritative Messiah and Son of God.
- Jesus portrayed as the suffering Son of Man, who will die as a sacrifice of atonement for the sins of his people.
- Outsiders become insiders by faith; hints of Gentile salvation.
- Negative portrait of the disciples; models of how not to follow Jesus.
- Lengthy passion narrative; emphasis on Jesus' death.
- Brief and enigmatic resurrection narrative.

Caesarea Philippi

an on-the-spot report. Translated literally, the account of Jesus' calming of the sea reads, "Leaving the crowd, they are taking him along with them in the boat.... There is arising a fierce gale of wind ... and they are waking him and saying to him ..." (Mark 4:36–38, my trans.).

Topical Ordering of Events

Mark groups events for rhetorical effect. For example, Jesus' ministry begins with a collection of healings and **exorcisms** which demonstrate his authority (1:21–28, 29–31, 32–39, 40–45). This is followed by a series of controversy stories, the beginning of conflict with the religious leaders (2:1–12, 13–17, 18–22, 23–27; 3:1–6). Jesus' parables are similarly brought together to teach about the nature of the kingdom (4:1–34). Chapter 12 presents a series of challenges and controversies brought by the religious leaders to trap Jesus. By grouping events, the narrator structures the story and highlights narrative themes.

Intercalation or "Sandwiching"

One of the most distinctive features of Mark's rhetoric is the literary device known as **intercalation**, the "sandwiching" of one event between the beginning and end of another (see p. 77 and fig. 7.2). The events are related to the same theme and serve to interpret one another. For example, Mark sandwiches Jesus' cleansing of the temple between his cursing of a fig tree and the disciples' later discovery of the withered tree (11:12–25). The intercalation suggests that the withering, like the temple clearing, represents God's judgment against Israel for her unbelief. Similarly, Mark intercalates the Beelzebub controversy in the middle of an episode relating to Jesus and his family (3:20–35). The rejection of Jesus by his own family mirrors the rejection of Jesus by his own people, the leaders of Israel. A third example is the raising of Jairus's daughter, which frames the healing of the woman with a blood disease. Both episodes stress the importance of faith (5:21–43). The execution of John the Baptist is framed by Jesus' commissioning of the Twelve and their later return (6:7–30). The point seems to be that John's death illustrates the willingness of a true disciple to lay down his life for the kingdom.

Sometimes intercalation is used to contrast episodes. Jesus' confession before the Sanhedrin is framed by Peter's denial (14:53–72) so that Jesus' faithfulness is set in contrast to Peter's unfaithfulness. Similarly, the plot against Jesus by the chief priests and scribes sandwiches the faithful devotion of the woman who anoints him with costly perfume (14:1–11).

Figure 7.1—Mark's Frequent Use of *Euthys* ("Immediately") and the Historical Present Tense
(Author's literal translation)

1:10 [Jesus has just been baptized.] And *immediately* coming up out of the water, he saw the heavens opening and the Spirit like a dove descending to him.

1:12 And *immediately* the Spirit drives him to go out into the wilderness.

1:18 And *immediately* leaving their nets, they followed him.

1:20 And *immediately* he called them and leaving their father Zebedee in the boat with the hired servants, they departed following him.

1:21 And they go to Capernaum; and *immediately* on the Sabbath entering the synagogue he began to teach.

1:23 And *immediately* there was in their synagogue a man with an unclean spirit; and he cried out.

1:28 And *immediately* the report about him went out everywhere into the whole region of Galilee.

1:29 And *immediately* after coming out of the synagogue, they came into the house of Simon and Andrew with James and John.

1:30 Now Simon's mother-in-law was lying sick with a fever; and *immediately* they are speaking to him about her.

1:42 And *immediately* the leprosy left him and he was cleansed.

1:43 And He sternly warned him and *immediately* sent him away.

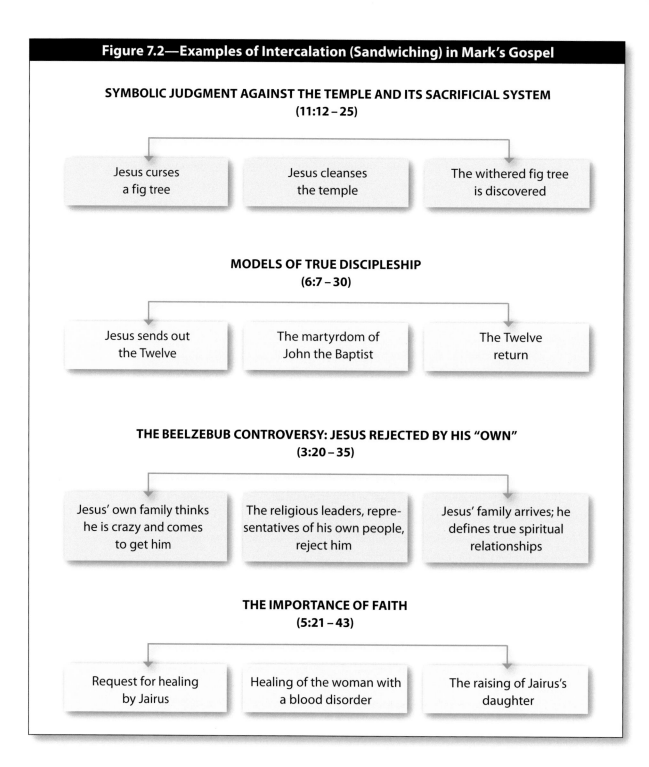

Figure 7.2—Examples of Intercalation (Sandwiching) in Mark's Gospel

SYMBOLIC JUDGMENT AGAINST THE TEMPLE AND ITS SACRIFICIAL SYSTEM
(11:12 – 25)

| Jesus curses a fig tree | Jesus cleanses the temple | The withered fig tree is discovered |

MODELS OF TRUE DISCIPLESHIP
(6:7 – 30)

| Jesus sends out the Twelve | The martyrdom of John the Baptist | The Twelve return |

THE BEELZEBUB CONTROVERSY: JESUS REJECTED BY HIS "OWN"
(3:20 – 35)

| Jesus' own family thinks he is crazy and comes to get him | The religious leaders, representatives of his own people, reject him | Jesus' family arrives; he defines true spiritual relationships |

THE IMPORTANCE OF FAITH
(5:21 – 43)

| Request for healing by Jairus | Healing of the woman with a blood disorder | The raising of Jairus's daughter |

While they wickedly plot his death, she reverently prepares his body for burial. Many of Mark's most distinctive themes are illuminated through this rhetorical device.

Triads or Sets of Threes

Mark is fond of patterns of three, or **triads**, using them especially in relation to the passion narrative. Three boat scenes illustrate the disciples' lack of faith and comprehension (4:35–41; 6:45–52; 8:14–21). In three cycles of events, Jesus predicts his death and then teaches his disciples about servant leadership (8:31–38; 9:31–37; 10:32–45; see fig. 7.5). In his eschatological sermon on the Mount of Olives, Jesus three times calls his disciples to alertness (13:33, 35, 37) and then three times finds them sleeping in Gethsemane (14:37, 40, 41). Peter denies Jesus three times (14:68, 70, 71), and three three-hour intervals are mentioned during the crucifixion (15:25, 33, 34). Like a good preacher, the narrator uses repetition to drive his point home.

Irony

Because Mark's central theological theme—the Messiah who suffers—is itself paradoxical, **irony** plays a major role in the narrative. Much of this is situational irony. Jesus' opponents inadvertently speak ironically. They accuse Jesus of being in league with Satan, when in fact *they* are opposing God's kingdom (3:22). Seeking to trap him through flattery, they call him a man of truth who teaches the true way of God (12:13–14). While they do not believe this, ironically the reader knows that it is true. These same leaders mock Jesus on the cross, saying, "He saved others ... but he can't save himself ... this Christ, this King of Israel" (15:31–32). Their sarcastic comments are in fact true. Jesus is both savior and king. Though the religious elite of Israel reject Jesus as the Son of God, a Gentile centurion recognizes it (15:39). Throughout the Gospel, the spiritual insiders of Israel—the religious leaders—become the outsiders in the kingdom of God, and the spiritual outsiders—sinners, tax collectors, Gentiles—become the insiders. Jesus' teaching in parables enforces this ironic reversal. Down-to-earth parables, stories from everyday life, actually conceal the message of the kingdom from the spiritually elite whose hearts are hard. It is ironic that blind Bartimaeus "sees" that Jesus is the Son of David, but his religious opponents are spiritually blind (10:46–52). It is ironic that while Jesus is standing before the Sanhedrin faithfully confessing that he is the Messiah, Peter is outside in the courtyard denying that he knows him (14:53–72).

There is also much verbal irony in the Gospel. Jesus quotes an ironic proverb that "only in his hometown ... is a prophet without honor" (6:4). Ironic sarcasm is evident as he congratulates the religious leaders for setting aside the commandments of God in favor of their own traditions (7:9). He nicknames Peter "the rock" (3:16), even though Peter turns out to be anything but stable.

These literary devices drive the powerful rhetoric of Mark's Gospel. Look for them as you follow his plot.

Yardenit, a traditional site for John's baptizing ministry

THE PLOT OF MARK'S GOSPEL

The Beginning of the Gospel: The Preparation of the Son of God (1:1 – 13)

Mark introduces his work as "the beginning of the gospel about Jesus Christ, the Son of God" (1:1).[1] The phrase probably does not just announce the start of the book but also serves as the title for the whole volume. Mark's Gospel will describe how the good news of salvation got its start with the coming of Jesus. The gospel here is the proclamation of the good news which began with John the Baptist and which continues in Mark's church.

While Matthew and Luke begin with extended birth stories, Mark wastes no time with such introductions. The reader is plunged "immediately" into the ministry of Jesus. Jesus appears on the scene abruptly, taking the Galilean countryside by storm. Short vignettes tumble one after another in quick succession. Within a few short paragraphs, Jesus is baptized by John, tempted by Satan, and embarks on a ministry of teaching, healing, and exorcism.

While appearing on the scene abruptly, Jesus' arrival is no accident of history. He is the "Christ, the Son of God," the long-awaited messianic king who will bring salvation to his people Israel. His coming is heralded by John the Baptist, who fulfills the role

---

1. There is a difficult textual question as to whether "Son of God" in 1:1 is an original part of Mark's text. The manuscript evidence seems to favor its inclusion. Even if it is not part of the original text, Jesus as Son of God is clearly an important title for Mark and is introduced very shortly in the baptism narrative which follows (1:11).

predicted by the prophets, to prepare the way for the Lord. The quotation which begins the Gospel draws from three Old Testament texts: (1) Exodus 23:20, which announces that God's "messenger" (angel) will lead Israel in exodus through the wilderness to the Promised Land; (2) Isaiah 40:3, which proclaims a glorious new exodus that God will accomplish; and (3) Malachi 3:1, which warns of the messenger who will prepare God's people for the Lord's coming and the day of judgment. Drawing together such an amalgamation of texts around a mutual theme was common in first-century Judaism. Mark does not err in identifying all three citations as from "Isaiah" but intentionally identifies Jesus' whole ministry as a fulfillment of Isaiah's vision of eschatological salvation. Jesus will accomplish God's new exodus by leading his people on the "way" to victory.[2]

Modern Nazareth

Richard Strauss

The Authoritative Ministry of the Son of God (1:14–8:26)

The purpose of Mark's high-speed narrative is to portray Jesus as the Messiah and Son of God of power and authority, a theme which dominates the first half of the Gospel. For centuries, Israel longed for God's great deliverance. Jesus proclaims that this salvation has now arrived: "The time has come ... the kingdom of God is near. Repent and believe the good news!" (1:15). Through his words and deeds, the reign of God is being actualized. Those who respond with faith and repentance receive salvation. When Jesus calls four fishermen to follow him—men immersed in lives, families, and livelihoods—they drop their nets and leave everything (1:16–20). Jesus teaches with great authority. In the first account of his teaching, the narrator twice notes that the people were amazed because Jesus taught "as one who had authority, not as the teachers of the law" (1:22, 27). While the scribes passed on traditions handed down to them, Jesus speaks with divine wisdom and authority.

> The first half of Mark's Gospel presents Jesus as the mighty Messiah and Son of God, who acts with authority and power.

Most profoundly, Jesus claims prerogatives normally attributed to God alone. He forgives sins (2:5), discerns the thoughts of his opponents (2:8), claims lordship over the Sabbath (2:28), and annuls Old Testament dietary laws (7:18–19).

The Miracle-Working Messiah. Contributing to this tone of action and authority is an emphasis on Jesus' miracles. For its length, Mark contains more miracles than the other Gospels. While repeatedly identifying Jesus as a teacher of great renown, the narrator provides few examples of teaching, focusing instead on his powerful deeds. Jesus exercises

---

2. See Joel Marcus, *The Way of the Lord: Christological Exegesis of the Old Testament in the Gospel of Mark* (Louisville: Westminster/John Knox, 1992); Rikki Watts, *Isaiah's New Exodus in Mark* (Grand Rapids: Baker, 2000).

Figure 7.3—The Messianic Secret in Mark

One of the first scholars to treat Mark's Gospel as a distinctly theological document was William Wrede, who in 1901 published a groundbreaking work called *The Messianic Secret*. Noting that in the earliest Gospel tradition there was little of messianic significance, Wrede concluded that the historical Jesus never claimed to be the Messiah. After the resurrection, when Jesus' followers came to believe that he was in fact the Messiah, the church had to deal with the problem that their stories said little about Jesus' messiahship.

According to Wrede, Mark solved this problem by creatively rewriting the gospel story, introducing a motif called the "messianic secret," in which Jesus intentionally keeps his identity a secret. Wrede claimed that Mark created those passages where Jesus commands silence in order to explain away Jesus' essentially unmessianic life.

Wrede's conclusion concerning Mark's purpose has been rejected by most scholars today. One major problem is that, though Jesus calls for silence, this silence is often broken. Those Jesus heals go out and proclaim freely what has happened to them, and his popularity grows and grows (1:45; 7:36). If Mark's purpose was to show that nobody knew about Jesus' messiahship during his life, he did a poor job of it!

The messianic secret is better understood as Jesus' attempt to define his messiahship on his own terms, which means in light of the cross. He does not wish demons to proclaim his identity since they will inevitably distort it. He calls those he heals to silence to temper the messianic fervor of the crowds, and he silences his disciples since they remain ignorant that his messiahship will involve suffering and sacrifice. It is also Mark's way to show that Jesus' deeds were so remarkable that no one could keep them a secret.

Though the details of Wrede's thesis have largely been rejected by scholars, his work has had a profound impact on New Testament scholarship because it introduced the idea that the Gospels were not primarily historical works but theological propaganda. We will deal again with this point in part 4, when we discuss issues related to the historical Jesus.

authority over natural and supernatural enemies alike, healing the sick, casting out demons, even raising the dead. He controls the forces of nature, calming the storm and feeding thousands with a few loaves and fishes. The purpose of these miracles is not to gain popularity but to demonstrate that he is acting and speaking with the authority of God.

The narrator enhances this sense of authority by noting the awed reactions of those who encounter Jesus. The people are amazed at his teaching (1:22, 27; 11:18) and astonished at his exorcisms and healing power (1:27; 2:12; 5:20; 6:2; 7:37). The disciples express awe when he raises the dead and calms the sea (5:42; 6:51). His popularity grows and grows (1:33, 37, 45; 2:2; 3:7 – 10; 5:24). The powerful words and deeds of Jesus demonstrate that he is the mighty Messiah and Son of God, the inaugurator of God's kingdom.

A profound sense of mystery pervades Jesus' life. This is enhanced by a *secrecy motif* which the narrator develops, as Jesus repeatedly commands silence from those around him.

He silences demons who try to announce his identity (1:24–25, 34; 3:11–12; 5:7); he insists that his miracles be kept quiet (1:44; 5:43; 7:36; 8:26); and he warns his disciples to tell no one that he is the Messiah (8:30; 9:9). While this "**messianic secret**" has sometimes been treated as Mark's creative attempt to explain Jesus' unmessianic life, it is better to see it as part of the mystery and awe which surrounds Jesus' identity (see fig. 7.3). Jesus' frequent commands to silence raise the tension of the narrative around the theme of the identity of Jesus.

Conflict Begins. Not everyone is happy with Jesus' authority, and conflict begins early in Mark. Jesus' first conflicts are spiritual ones, as he engages and does battle with the forces of evil. Immediately following his baptism, Jesus is tempted by Satan in the wilderness (1:13). Returning to Galilee to begin his ministry, he repeatedly encounters demonic opposition (1:23–27, 34; 3:11; 5:7). Evil spirits recognize and challenge him but shrink back in terror at his awesome authority. The narrator's purpose is to present Jesus' mission as one of profound spiritual significance. Jesus is engaged in not merely a human conflict but a spiritual one of cosmic proportions. In one conflict with the religious leaders — the Beelzebub incident (3:20–30) — Jesus explains the significance of these conflicts with a parable: the stronger man (Jesus) is invading the home of the strong man (Satan) and plundering his goods (people in Satan's possession). Through Jesus' exorcisms, the kingdom of God is breaking down and overwhelming the kingdom of Satan, freeing people from its power.

Jesus' other main conflicts are with the religious leaders, who repeatedly challenge his authority (2:1–12, 13–17, 18–22, 23–28; 3:1–6). By introducing their opposition to Jesus in the wake of his conflicts with demons, the narrator places them alongside Satan's forces as opponents of God's rule. Their opposition arises especially over Jesus' table fellowship with sinners and his apparent violations of the Sabbath command. Jesus responds by pointing out their hypocrisy and failure to grasp the true meaning of God's commands. The Sabbath command was made to benefit human beings, so how can good deeds on the Sabbath be contrary to God's will? (2:27–28). The religious leaders do not comprehend God's heart for the lost and so fail to rejoice when sinners receive forgiveness. Instead of recognizing Jesus as God's agent of salvation, they see him as a threat to their power. The climax to this first series of controversies occurs during a Sabbath synagogue service (3:1–6). A man with a deformed hand is present, and the Pharisees and scribes look for an opportunity to accuse Jesus of violating the Sabbath by healing the man. Jesus cuts to the heart of the Sabbath command by asking whether it is lawful to do good or to do harm, to save life or to destroy it. The implication is that doing nothing to help this man would be equivalent to doing evil. The passage is full of irony. The real Sabbath violation is not Jesus' healing but the hypocrisy of the leaders, who care more about the minutiae of the law than the welfare of a human being. It is further ironic that after Jesus heals the man, the Pharisees plot to take his life. While Jesus seeks to "do good" and to "save a life" on the Sabbath, the Pharisees seek to "do harm" and to "destroy" one. Who then is in violation? A final bit of irony is that the Pharisees plot with the Herodians to kill Jesus (3:6). These are strange bedfellows, since the pious Pharisees would normally be at odds with the supporters of the Herodian dynasty. Their willingness to enter into such an alliance shows their desperation to destroy Jesus. They stand in opposition to God's reign manifested in Jesus' ministry.

The origin of the name Beelzebul is uncertain, though it was probably originally a title for the Canaanite god Baal (or "lord") and meant "Baal, the Prince," or "Baal of the Heavenly Dwelling." The Israelites evidently mocked this name, changing it to Beelzebub, meaning "Lord of the Flies" (see Judg. 10:6; 2 Kings 1:2 – 3, 6). Beelzebub eventually came to be used in Judaism for the "Prince of Demons," the highest ranking angel in heaven prior to his fall (*T. Sol.* 3:2 – 5; 4:2; 6:1 – 3). The New Testament calls this archenemy of God by many names, including Satan, the Devil, Belial (2 Cor. 6:15), the evil one (Matt. 6:13; 13:19; etc.), the father of lies (John 8:44), the god of this world (2 Cor. 4:4), the prince of the power of the air (Eph. 2:2), the dragon (Rev. 12:9), and the ancient serpent (Rev. 12:9).

Their true heart is revealed in the **Beelzebub controversy** which follows, in which the scribes accuse Jesus of casting out demons by Beelzebub, the prince of demons (3:20 – 30). Jesus responds by refuting their claim ("How can Satan drive out Satan?") and then accusing them of blaspheming the Holy Spirit, an eternal sin which will not be forgiven. The narrator explains this blasphemy as their claim that Jesus is possessed by an evil spirit (3:30). They have seen the power of God and have attributed it to Satan. In the presence of light, they have turned to darkness.

It is important to note that Jesus begins teaching in parables immediately following the Beelzebub controversy and in the context of identifying his true family as "whoever does God's will" (3:35). The connection between these events becomes clear as Jesus explains to his disciples why he teaches in parables:

> The secret of the kingdom of God has been given to you. But to those on the outside everything is said in parables so that, "they may be ever seeing but never perceiving, and ever hearing but never understanding; otherwise they might turn and be forgiven!"
>
> —4:11 – 12, citing Isaiah 6:9 – 10

Jesus explains that he teaches in parables for two reasons: *to reveal* and *to conceal*. To his disciples, who are responding to his kingdom proclamation, the parables reveal the kingdom. But to those who are rejecting the message, the parables hide the truth. "Those on the outside" (4:11) who get the parable but not its interpretation are the religious leaders who are rejecting Jesus. Their fate is sealed and the truth is concealed.

Jesus teaches in parables both to reveal and to conceal.

Mark carefully sandwiches (intercalates) the Beelzebub controversy in the middle of a story in which Jesus' family fails to comprehend his mission. When Jesus' family hears he has no time even to eat, they come to take charge of him, thinking he is out of his mind (3:20 – 21). When they arrive (3:31), Jesus is informed that his family is "outside," wishing to see him. Jesus points to his disciples and identifies *them* as his true family. "Whoever does God's will is my brother and sister and mother" (3:31 – 35). In the context of the Beelzebub controversy, the point is clear: kinship in the kingdom of God is based not on ethnic identity or family background but on a relationship with God through Jesus. Israel's leaders — formerly the insiders—are now the outsiders blinded to the truth, while sinners and outcasts are receiving the message of salvation.

This same point is driven home as Jesus teaches in the synagogue in his hometown (6:1–6). While amazed at his teaching, the townspeople are offended by his presumptuous teaching. Jesus responds that "only in his hometown, among his relatives and in his own house, is a prophet without honor" (6:4). Again Jesus is rejected by his own. The stage is set for his rejection in Jerusalem.

The Suffering of the Son of God as Servant of the LORD (8:27–16:8)

The Turning Point: The Confession of Peter and the Servant Messiah (8:27–10:52). The question of Jesus' identity is raised implicitly throughout the first half of Mark's Gospel. It comes to center stage in the account of the calming of the storm, when the astonished disciples ask, "Who is this? Even the wind and the waves obey him!" (4:41). The answer, of course, has already been given: He is the Christ, the Son of God. The implied reader already knows this (1:1); the Father has announced it to the Son (1:11); Satan and his demonic forces know it (1:24, 34). Yet the narrative reaches its midpoint and initial climax when the first human character proclaims it. The **confession of Peter** at Caesarea Philippi marks a key turning point as the chief representative of the disciples recognizes Jesus to be "the Christ" (8:27–29). Jesus' authoritative words and deeds have confirmed that he is indeed the Messiah.

The Jordan River near Caesarea Philippi, where Peter confessed that Jesus is the Christ

© Neal Bierling/Zondervan Image Archives

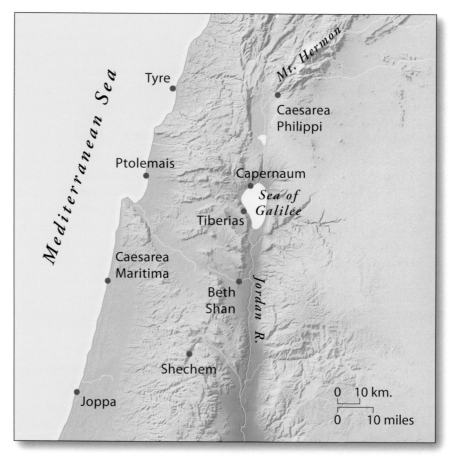

Location of Caesarea Philippi

The implied reader is shocked, however, when Jesus commands the disciples to silence and then teaches them that his role is to suffer and die (8:30–31). Peter reacts to this first **passion prediction** by rebuking Jesus for such defeatist talk. A Messiah who would suffer? Unthinkable! Jesus, in turn, rebukes Peter with the stinging indictment, "Get behind me, Satan! . . . You do not have in mind the things of God, but the things of men." Jesus is about to radically redefine the role of the Messiah and, by implication, the role of the Messiah's followers. Paradoxically, Peter's desire for Jesus to avoid suffering places him in league with Satan and the religious leaders—in opposition to God's reign.

While Jesus' rejection and death have been hinted at earlier in the narrative (2:20; 3:6; 6:4), from this point on, his suffering mission becomes the primary focus of the narrative. Indeed, so much of Mark's story is concerned with the cross that the Gospel has been called a passion narrative with an extended introduction.[3] Three times Jesus predicts his death (8:31; 9:31; 10:33–34). Each time the disciples fail to get it, responding with pride

---

3. This designation appears to have been first used by M. Kähler, *The So-Called Historical Jesus and the Historic Biblical Christ* (ET; Philadelphia: Fortress, 1964; orig. Ger. ed. 1896), 80.

and incomprehension (8:32; 9:33–34; 10:35–41). Three times Jesus must teach that the true path of discipleship is one of suffering and sacrifice (8:33–38; 9:35–37; 10:42–45). The third of these triads comes in chapter 10. Jesus begins his journey to Jerusalem and announces for a third time that he is going there to suffer and die. James and John demonstrate pride by asking for the chief seats in the kingdom; the other disciples respond with indignation (10:35–41). For a third time Jesus must teach a lesson in humble servanthood: those who wish to be great must become the servants of all (10:42–45). Mark 10:45 has rightly

> The key turning point in Mark's Gospel is Peter's confession, and the second half of the Gospel portrays Jesus as the Messiah of suffering and sacrifice.

been called a theme verse for the Gospel: "For even the Son of Man did not come to be served, but to serve, and to give his life as a ransom for many." The verse echoes the role of the **Servant of the LORD** of Isaiah, who suffers an atoning death for the sins of the nation (Isa. 52:13–53:12). As the narrative turns toward its climax, the reader is reminded that the Messiah must first pass through suffering and sacrifice on his way to glory (see fig. 7.5).

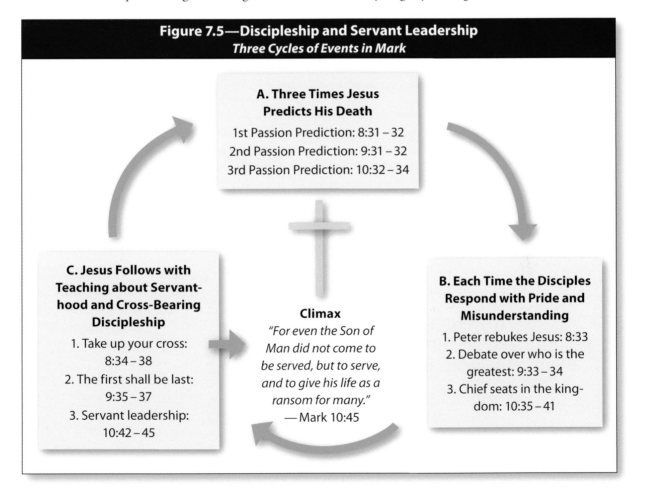

Figure 7.5—Discipleship and Servant Leadership
Three Cycles of Events in Mark

A. Three Times Jesus Predicts His Death

1st Passion Prediction: 8:31–32
2nd Passion Prediction: 9:31–32
3rd Passion Prediction: 10:32–34

C. Jesus Follows with Teaching about Servant-hood and Cross-Bearing Discipleship

1. Take up your cross: 8:34–38
2. The first shall be last: 9:35–37
3. Servant leadership: 10:42–45

Climax
"For even the Son of Man did not come to be served, but to serve, and to give his life as a ransom for many."
—Mark 10:45

B. Each Time the Disciples Respond with Pride and Misunderstanding

1. Peter rebukes Jesus: 8:33
2. Debate over who is the greatest: 9:33–34
3. Chief seats in the kingdom: 10:35–41

Map of Galilee showing Mt. Hermon and Mt. Tabor, two possible sites of the transfiguration

The theme of "glory to come" permeates the **transfiguration** narrative which follows Peter's confession and the first passion prediction (9:2 – 13). Jesus' transformed appearance before the three disciples confirms he is indeed the Messiah destined for glory. Like the witness of John the Baptist at the beginning of the Gospel, the appearance of Elijah and Moses confirms that the Old Testament promises are coming to fulfillment. The voice from heaven saying, "This is my Son …" similarly echoes the divine voice at Jesus' baptism. Just as the Father's announcement set the stage for the revelation of the miracle-working Son of God (chaps. 1 – 8), so this second one prepares the way for the revelation of the suffering **Son of Man** (chaps. 9 – 16).

The Son of God Confronts Jerusalem (10:46 – 13:37). Like the transfiguration, Jesus' approach to Jerusalem confirms his messiahship. Yet now, the messianic secret is about to end. In Jericho, on the road to Jerusalem, the blind beggar Bartimaeus cries out to Jesus as the "Son of David," a traditional messianic title (10:47 – 48). While in the past Jesus has silenced such acclamations, he now accepts it (only the crowd tries to silence the man). The blind man's acclamation prepares the reader for Jesus' **triumphal entry** into Jerusalem. Jesus acts intentionally, arranging for a colt to carry him into Jerusalem as a royal figure. Though Jesus' entry is not explicitly linked to Zechariah's prophecy of the peace-loving king riding on a colt (Zech. 9:9), the implied reader would certainly make the connection (cf.

Left: Mount Tabor, the traditional site of the transfiguration. *Right:* Snow-capped Mount Hermon, which some have suggested was the site of the transfiguration.

Richard Strauss

© Neal Bierling/Zondervan Image Archives

Left: A fig tree. *Right:* Early figs on a fig tree.

Matt. 21:4–5). The crowds pay royal homage by laying garments and branches in his path and crying out, "Blessed is the coming kingdom of our father David!" Expectations are high that God is about to establish the messianic kingdom promised to David. What the crowd does not comprehend is that Jesus' kingdom will be established not through conquest but through suffering. Like Peter, they are ignorant of the Messiah's true role.

This messianic theme plays out further on the following days. In one of Mark's famous sandwiching episodes, Jesus curses a fig tree, drives the merchants from the temple, and then returns the next day to find the fig tree withered (11:12–25). While at first sight Jesus' actions may seem like an arbitrary tantrum against an innocent tree (Mark notes that figs were not in season), the intercalation shows something far more significant. In the Old Testament, unfaithful Israel is sometimes portrayed as a barren vine or fig tree (Mic. 7:1; Hos. 9:16; Isa. 5:1–7). For Mark, then, both the cursing of the

> The intercalation of the cursing of the fig tree and the clearing of the temple reveal coming judgment against Israel for her unfaithfulness.

fig tree and the clearing of the temple represent Jesus' judgment of Israel. The Messiah symbolically acts against an unfaithful nation.

Such authoritative actions cannot go unchallenged, and the religious leaders begin plotting Jesus' death (11:18). They engage him in a series of challenges, seeking to trap him (11:27–12:40; see fig. 7.6). Yet Jesus always comes out ahead, confounding them with his superior wisdom and authority. Positively, these controversies confirm that Jesus is indeed the Messiah of wisdom and power (see Isa. 11:1–3). Negatively, they increase the resolve of Jesus' enemies to destroy him, and so provoke his arrest and crucifixion.

In the midst of these controversies, Jesus tells an allegorical parable—the **parable of the wicked tenant farmers**—which plays out in miniature the history of God's dealings with Israel, climaxing with the death of God's Son, Jesus (12:1–12). Imitating Isaiah's famous parable of the vineyard (Isa. 5:1–7), Jesus portrays the religious leaders as tenant farmers over God's vineyard, who refuse to return to God the fruit of his vineyard (see fig. 7.7).

Figure 7.6—Conflict and Controversy in Jerusalem	
The Challenge or Question	**Jesus' Response**
(1) Challenge to Jesus' authority Mark 11:27 – 33; Matthew 21:23 – 27; Luke 20:1 – 8 The priests, scribes, and elders question Jesus' authority in clearing the temple.	Jesus counters with a question of his own: "John's baptism — was it from heaven, or from men?" The leaders are afraid to answer because of John's popularity. Jesus follows with the parable of the wicked tenant farmers (Mark 12:1 – 12; Matt. 21:33 – 46; Luke 20:9 – 19), which uses Isaiah's parable of the vineyard (Isaiah 5) to allegorize their rejection and murder of the Son. In Matthew, Jesus also tells the parable of the two sons (Matt. 21:28 – 32) and the parable of the marriage feast (Matt. 22:1 – 14; cf. Luke 14:15 – 23).
(2) Paying taxes to Caesar Mark 12:13 – 17; Matthew 22:15 – 22; Luke 20:20 – 26 The Pharisees and Herodians ask whether tribute should be paid to Caesar, hoping to build a charge of sedition against Jesus.	Jesus responds, "Give to Caesar what is Caesar's and to God what is God's," thus confounding his critics.
(3) The resurrection Mark 12:18 – 27; Matthew 22:23 – 33; Luke 20:27 – 39 The Sadducees question Jesus about the resurrection in the context of levirate marriage (when a man married his dead brother's wife to carry on the family name). If a woman married seven times, whose wife would she be in the resurrection?	Jesus ridicules the Sadducees for understanding neither the Scriptures nor the power of God. The resurrection will not merely restore life but also change the mode of life; there will be no institution of marriage. Then he proves the resurrection from Exodus 3:6: "I *am* … the God of Abraham, the God of Isaac and the God of Jacob."
(4) The Greatest Commandment Mark 12:28 – 34; Matthew 22:34 – 40; cf. Luke 10:25 – 28 A Pharisaic scribe asks Jesus what is the greatest commandment.	Jesus answers with Deuteronomy 6:4 – 5, to which the scribe responds positively. Jesus says, "You are not far from the kingdom of God."

Figure 7.6—Conflict and Controversy in Jerusalem CONTINUED	
The Challenge or Question	**Jesus' Response**
Jesus' critics are silenced Mark 12:34; Matthew 22:46; Luke 20:40	**(5) David's son or David's Lord?** Mark 12:35–36; Matthew 22:41–46; Luke 20:41–44 Jesus takes the offensive and asks the Pharisees about the relationship of the Messiah to David. How can he be merely David's son if David himself calls him "Lord" in Psalm 110:1?
	(6) Warning against the scribes' hypocrisy Mark 12:38–40; Matthew 23:1–36; Luke 20:45–47 In Matthew, this becomes seven lengthy woes against the hypocrisy of the scribes and Pharisees.

After beating and killing the owner's messengers (the prophets), the tenants eventually seize and kill his own son (Jesus). The owner will respond, Jesus says, by coming and killing the tenants and giving the vineyard to others (citing Ps. 118:22–23). The narrator concludes the account by pointing out that after the parable, "They looked for a way to arrest him because they knew he had spoken the parable against them" (12:12). There is heavy irony here. While Jesus' past parables were intended to conceal the truth from these leaders, this last one is to reveal the truth and so provoke Jesus' arrest and crucifixion. The messianic secret is out. Though Jesus' antagonists appear to be guiding the plot toward his destruction, in fact the sovereign God is using them to carry forward his plan of salvation—the ransom for sins accomplished through Jesus' death.

The judgment against Israel symbolized by Jesus' clearing of the temple (11:15–17) and allegorized in the parable of the wicked tenant farmers (12:1–12) is now directly predicted by Jesus in the **Olivet Discourse** (chap. 13). When the disciples point out the magnificent beauty of the Jerusalem temple, Jesus predicts its destruction (13:1–2). Later, on the Mount of Olives, the disciples ask about the time of this event and the signs that will accompany it (13:3–4). Jesus first warns the disciples not to be alarmed by catastrophic events common to the present age, which may be misconstrued as signs of the end: false messiahs will arise and deceive many; there will be wars, earthquakes, and famines. These are merely precursor events, like the birth pains of a woman

> The parable of the wicked tenant farmers symbolizes a history of Israel's rejection of God's messengers, climaxing with the murder of God's Son, Jesus.

www.HolyLandPhotos.org

In the center of the image is a well-constructed and maintained watch tower. Note how fields have been cleared of stones (used as fencing) and trees and vines have been planted.

in labor (13:5 – 9). Jesus seems to envision a significant time gap before the end: the gospel will be preached to all nations; believers will suffer great persecution and even betrayal by friends and family. The climactic event will be the "abomination of desolation," a phrase originally used of the desecration of the temple by Antiochus IV "Epiphanes" (Dan. 11:31 – 32; see chap. 4, pp. 100–101). Jesus says a similar idolatrous sacrilege will climax this great period of persecution. When his followers see this horrific event, they should flee Jerusalem, for the greatest persecution of all time will follow (13:14 – 23). Yet out of this great trial will come their deliverance: the Son of Man will come on the clouds with great power and glory, and his angels will gather his chosen ones from around the world (13:24 – 27).

The interpretation of the discourse is complicated because of the close connection Jesus draws between the destruction of the temple and the return of the Son of Man (13:24 – 31; see fig. 7.8). Yet the central theme is clear: Jesus' disciples must be faithful to the end and always ready for his return. Jesus repeatedly tells them to be alert, keep watch, and be on their guard (13:5, 9, 23, 33, 34, 35, 37). The discourse thus continues two key themes in Mark's Gospel: Israel's rejection and its consequences, and the need for faithfulness and self-sacrificial discipleship. The suffering and trials which Jesus predicts for his disciples are those he is about to face. His faithfulness will serve as their example.

The Climax of the Narrative: The Death of the Son of God (14:1 – 15:47). Mark's passion narrative is one of betrayal, desertion, and rejection (chaps. 14 – 15). The section begins with the religious leaders plotting to kill Jesus. Jesus is fully aware of his coming fate. When a woman in Bethany anoints him with expensive perfume, he identifies this as the anointing of his body for burial. At the Last Supper, he predicts his betrayal, teaches about his coming death, and announces that all the disciples will desert him. While facing death with fear and dread, Jesus remains faithful to his calling. In Gethsemane, he is "deeply distressed and troubled" and "overwhelmed with sorrow to the point of death." In agony, he prays that this cup of suffering may be taken away, yet he remains submissive to the Father's will.

A coin with the head of Emperor Tiberius (AD 14–37)

In contrast to Jesus' faithfulness stands the failure of the disciples. When Jesus predicts that they will all fall away, Peter and the rest vehemently deny it. Yet in Gethsemane, they cannot stay awake and pray. When Judas arrives with a mob to arrest Jesus, everyone deserts him and flees. Peter shows some courage by following at a distance but then fails miserably by denying him three times. The narrator uses his sandwiching technique to contrast Jesus' confession before the Sanhedrin (14:55 – 65) with Peter's denial that he even knows Jesus (14:53 – 54, 66 – 72).

The rejection Jesus experiences from his disciples is magnified in the hatred and scorn heaped on him by his enemies. At his Jewish trial, false charges are brought against him.

Figure 7.8—The Olivet Discourse
Ancient History or End-Times Prophecy?

The most problematic part of the Olivet Discourse is the close connection Jesus seems to make between the destruction of the temple and the return of the Son of Man. Did Jesus err in claiming that the Son of Man would return at the time of the fall of Jerusalem? One solution — known as the preterist interpretation — is that the whole discourse concerns the events of AD 70. In this view, the coming of the Son of Man is viewed not as the return of Christ but rather as his symbolic coming in judgment against Jerusalem. This interpretation also fits well Jesus' statement that all these things will happen to "this generation" (13:30). The greatest problem with this view is that the gathering of the elect seems to point to final salvation (13:27), not merely the destruction of Jerusalem.

A better solution may be that the destruction of the temple in AD 70 served as a *typological preview* of the judgments associated with the coming of the Son of Man and the end of the age. As is so often the case with Old Testament prophecies, the two events are telescoped together because both are eschatological, relating to God's final salvation and judgment. Jesus' first coming accomplished salvation; his second will consummate it. The destruction of Jerusalem serves as temporal judgment in history, a preview of the final judgment. "This generation" could then be a double reference, both to the Jews of Jesus' generation and to the final generation which will see the coming of the Son of Man.

Mark's passion narrative is one of betrayal, desertion, and rejection.

When he admits that he is "the Christ, the Son of the Blessed One," the high priest accuses him of blasphemy and the Sanhedrin calls for his execution. They mock and spit upon him; the guards beat him. At the trial before Pilate, the crowds which thronged to him for healing and free bread now cry out for his crucifixion. Pilate, the supposed administrator of Roman justice, turns a blind eye to Jesus' innocence and orders his crucifixion. The soldiers mock his kingship, beat him, and spit on him.

In the crucifixion scene, everyone present hurls abuse at Jesus. Passersby ridicule his claims; the religious leaders belittle him; even the crucified criminals heap insults on him. The disciples are nowhere to be seen. (Only Jesus' female followers remain faithful, though still at a distance [15:40–41].) Just as "darkness came over the whole land" (15:33), so darkness descends over the Gospel narrative. Jesus' only words from the cross, a quote from Psalm 22:1, reiterate this theme of rejection and anguish: "My God, my God, why have you forsaken me?" Jesus dies in agony and despair, alone and forsaken by God and men alike. From all external appearances, Jesus' mission has ended in failure.

Yet the reader with eyes of faith knows this is not the end. These events are no unforeseen tragedy but God's purpose and plan. Jesus has moved intentionally toward this climax, predicting his death again and again and explaining its significance. This is the "ransom for many" (10:45), a payment for the sins of the world. Jesus' blood, "poured out for many," establishes the new covenant between God and humanity (14:24). His death is not a defeat but a sacrifice of atonement and victory over sin.

Two events at Jesus' death confirm this significance. First, the curtain of the temple, separating the Holy of Holies from the Holy Place, is torn in two from top to bottom (15:38). The informed reader recognizes that through Jesus' death, the way to God's presence has been opened up, allowing God's glory to be revealed. Second, and related to this, the Roman centurion overseeing the crucifixion now sees with eyes of faith and cries out, "Surely this man was the Son of God!" (15:39). While all of the other participants—the disciples, the crowds, the religious leaders—are blind to the significance of Jesus' death, the most unlikely of characters—a Gentile—recognizes it! As is the case elsewhere in Mark's Gospel, the insiders who should know better are blind to God's kingdom purpose, while outsiders receive it by faith. The cry of the centurion confirms again that Jesus' identity and mission are revealed not through power and conquest but through sacrificial death.

It is significant that at the beginning of Mark's narrative, heaven is "torn open" at Jesus' baptism and God announces that Jesus is his beloved Son (1:10–11). Now at the end, the temple curtain is "torn open" (same Greek word) and the centurion announces that Jesus is God's Son. The whole Gospel narrative may be viewed as an *inclusio*—the explanation of these two great acclamations.

Wooden cross

Z. Raodvan, Jerusalem

Resolution: The Resurrection Announced (16:1–8). Mark's resurrection account is one of the most puzzling parts of his Gospel. The problem is that the earliest and most reliable manuscripts do not contain verses 9–20, ending instead with verse 8. Yet this seems like an odd way to end the Gospel. The women visit the tomb, where a young man dressed in white reports that Jesus has risen from the dead. He tells them to report this to the disciples, who should go to Galilee where they will see Jesus. The final verse says that the women fled trembling and bewildered and said nothing to anyone. The reader is left wondering what this means. Did the women ever recover from their fear and tell the disciples? Did the disciples go to Galilee and see Jesus? Why are there no resurrection appearances reported?

If verses 9–20 are not part of the original Gospel, as seems likely (see fig. 7.9), there are two possibilities. Some scholars believe that the original ending was somehow lost in the transmission process. If this is the case, the last section may have looked something like Matthew 28:16–20, which includes Jesus' appearance to the disciples in Galilee. Other scholars, however, believe that the abrupt ending of the Gospel was no accident, but that the author intended to end the story this way. According to this view, the sense of mystery and awe which runs through the entire Gospel also characterizes the resurrection account. The women are left not with resurrection appearances but with the empty tomb and the announcement of the risen Lord. Like the characters in the narrative, the reader must decide how to respond to this proclamation—with faith or with rejection.

This is not to say that the author did not know about the resurrection appearances. He surely knew that Jesus' disciples saw him alive, recovered from their failure, and became the foundation of the apostolic church. The angel's command to go to Galilee would be inexplicable unless the disciples later saw Jesus there. But these historical events have no part in the narrative. The narrator rather leaves the readers with the proclamation of the resurrection and an implicit call to decision. Will they, like Jesus, face suffering and trials with faithfulness, or will they flee and deny him like the disciples? Will they respond to Jesus' suffering with recognition and faith, like the centurion, or with unbelief and rejection, like the religious leaders? The resolution (or perhaps irresolution) of the plot calls the reader to decision.

MARK'S PORTRAIT OF JESUS: THE SUFFERING SON OF GOD

Having examined Mark's plot, we turn next to the characters of his narrative. In Mark, as in all the Gospels, Jesus is the central figure and chief protagonist. One caution is especially important for the modern reader when approaching the characterization of Jesus in the Gospels. This is to recognize that the contemporary preoccupation with the deity of Christ was not the primary concern of the Gospel writers (especially not the Synoptics). Their primary purpose was to demonstrate that Jesus was the Christ, the promised Messiah. While some Old Testament prophecies about the Messiah have implications of divinity, the term Messiah is not synonymous with deity but rather refers to the end-times agent who accomplishes God's salvation. Nor was divinity an essential or universal component in predictions of the Messiah found in first-century Judaism. It is therefore important to read the Gospels without allowing the christological controversies of later centuries to distort their portraits of Jesus. The Jesus of Mark's Gospel certainly exhibits divine attributes, but these must be

Figure 7.9—The Ending of Mark

There are many reasons for doubting that Mark 16:9–20 was an original part of this Gospel:

1. The text does not appear in the oldest and most reliable manuscripts of the Gospel. (It does appear, however, in some early manuscripts.)
2. Many of the words in this section are non-Markan; that is, they are different from the vocabulary Mark uses throughout the rest of the Gospel.
3. The Greek style is different from that used elsewhere in the Gospel.
4. The transition between verses 8 and 9 is very awkward. The subject of verse 8 is the women, but verse 9 assumes that the subject is Jesus. (The word "Jesus" in verse 9 does not appear in the Greek, which reads "having risen early on the first day of the week.")
5. Mary Magdalene is identified in verse 9 as the one "out of whom he had cast seven demons," as though the reader does not know who she is. Yet she was just mentioned in Mark 15:40, 47.
6. Verses 9–20 look like a compilation of resurrection appearances from the other Gospels. Verses 12–13, for example, summarize Luke's account of the two disciples on the road to Emmaus (Luke 24:13–35).
7. There is a third, shorter ending given in some manuscripts, suggesting that different copyists knew of the missing text and tried to add an appropriate ending.*

The author of this textbook could add a personal testimony to this body of evidence. When I was learning Greek, I translated the Gospel of Mark. As I worked my way through the text, I began to learn the author's vocabulary and style, and the text became easier to translate. By the end, I was moving through chapters very quickly, until I reached 16:9. It was like hitting a brick wall. I found myself scrambling for lexicons and translation aids to work through the dramatic changes in vocabulary and style. The striking change confirmed for me that these verses were penned by a different author.

In summary, it seems likely that verses 9–20 were added by a later copyist in an attempt to "correct" the abrupt and unusual manner in which the Gospel ended. Such a correction was unnecessary, however, since the abrupt ending is well explained within the literary and theological purposes of the author.

---

* For details, see Bruce M. Metzger, *A Textual Commentary on the Greek New Testament*, 2nd ed. (Stuttgart: Deutsche Bibelgesellschaft and United Bible Societies, 1994). For a scholarly defense of the longer ending, see W. R. Farmer, *The Last Twelve Verses of Mark* (Cambridge: Cambridge Univ. Press, 1974).

read through the lenses of first-century Judaism and the testimony of the early church, rather than through that of twenty-first century Christian orthodoxy.

Of the four Gospels, Mark presents the most human and down-to-earth portrait of Jesus. Jesus expresses a range of human emotions, including compassion (1:41; 6:34), indignation (10:14), grief (3:5), amazement (6:6), anger (3:5), and love (10:21). At Gethsemane, he experiences extreme anxiety at the prospect of his coming death (14:33–34) but perseveres by trusting in God. Jesus' knowledge is also limited, as he expresses ignorance concerning the time of his return (13:32). His miracle-working powers are also limited and contingent on the faith of those healed (6:5; cf. 8:23–24). This is a person readers can relate to, a person who experiences the same emotions they do. He perseveres not because he calls on divine attributes to pull him through but because he lives a life of faith and dependence on God.

Hand in hand with this focus on Jesus' humanity is an equally strong emphasis on his awesome power and authority. By virtue of his Spirit-anointing, Jesus acts and speaks with the authority of God. He displays extraordinary authority in teaching, healing, exorcism, and **nature miracles**. He exercises divine attributes, forgiving sins and discerning thoughts. These twin themes of true humanity and divine authority raise the fundamental narrative question: Who is this? (4:41; 8:27). An aura of mystery and intrigue surrounds Jesus' person throughout the Gospel. In one sense, Jesus' identity is no secret. The book begins with the bold acclamation that he is "the Christ, the Son of God." Yet there is more here than meets the eye. Jesus doesn't fulfill the traditional expectations concerning the Messiah. He doesn't conquer Israel's enemies. He doesn't establish a messianic kingdom centered in Jerusalem. What, then, can it mean that Jesus is the Christ and Son of God? The narrative provides an answer which is both surprising and mysterious.

Jesus' identity is revealed progressively in the narrative. While the reader knows from the beginning that Jesus is the Messiah (1:1), the characters recognize this only gradually. At first, only the spirit world knows him. The Father announces at the baptism, "You are my Son" (1:11) and demons repeatedly recognize him as the "Holy One of God" and the "Son of God" (1:24, 34; 3:11; 5:7). Finally in Peter's confession we have the first human recognition. Yet Peter fails to comprehend the suffering role of the Christ. In the end, only the centurion at the cross gets it right, seeing that through suffering and death Jesus is revealed to be the Son of God (15:39).

The titles used for Jesus also develop this theme of the suffering Messiah. The titles Christ (Messiah) and Son of God are almost synonymous in Mark's Gospel, both identifying Jesus as God's agent of salvation (14:61). Yet the centurion's cry at the foot of the cross suggests that Son of God is the more complete and adequate title, encompassing both Jesus' messiahship and his suffering role. By submitting to the Father's will, Jesus reveals his intimate relationship as God's Son and accomplishes the messianic task.

While Christ and Son of God are key titles in Mark's narrative, Jesus most often identifies himself as the Son of Man. In the Old Testament, the Hebrew designation *ben adam* ("son of man") means "a human being" (see Ps. 8:4), and Jesus' use of the title points especially to his humanity. Yet there is further significance to the title. The Old Testament book of Daniel speaks of "one like a son of man," an exalted messianic figure who comes with the clouds of heaven and receives authority, glory, and sovereign power from God, setting up an eternal kingdom that will never be destroyed (Dan. 7:13–14). On several occasions in Mark, Jesus explicitly identifies himself with this messianic figure (Mark 8:38; 13:26–27; 14:62). Historically, Jesus probably preferred the title because it expressed his identity without the connotations of political and military insurrection which titles like Christ and Son of David carried in first-century Judaism. In Mark's narrative, the title serves double duty, demonstrating Jesus' true humanity and revealing his messianic authority and destiny.

OTHER CHARACTERS IN MARK'S GOSPEL

The Antagonists: Satan's Forces and the Religious Leaders

As noted above, Jesus' primary opponents are first Satan and his demons and second the religious leaders of Israel. Both stand in opposition to Jesus' proclamation of the reign of God. Jesus' repeated victories over the demons reveals his sovereign authority to announce and establish the kingdom of God. Jesus' first demonic encounter drives this point home (1:21–24). While teaching in the synagogue at Capernaum, Jesus is approached by a demon-possessed man. The demon cries out, "What do you want with us, Jesus of Nazareth? Have you come to destroy us? I know who you are—the Holy One of God!" Though only one demon is mentioned, he speaks for the whole demonic realm. ("What do you want with *us*.") The point is that the kingdom of Satan knows of Jesus' arrival and reacts with terror. This pattern is repeated again and again as demons recognize Jesus and shrink back in horror (1:34; 3:11). The Gerasene demoniac cries out, "What do you want with me, Jesus, Son of the Most High God? Swear to God that you won't torture me!" (5:7) The forces of Satan are powerless against God's agent of salvation.

Top: Kursi, or Gergesa, a possible site for the demoniac episode of Mark 5. Bottom: The region of Gerasa from the Sea of Galilee.

The religious leaders are Jesus' other main opponents. From their perspective, Jesus' status as a teacher and rabbi is rendered suspect by his association with sinners and his casual attitude toward the law. More significantly, his growing popularity among the people threatens their leadership and so their very way of life. The religious leaders are portrayed as flat characters, hypocritical and unbelieving figures who consistently oppose God's purpose as revealed through Jesus.

Their fate is revealed in the parable of the wicked tenant farmers. For what they have done to the prophets and what they will do to the Son, they will suffer destruction and the vineyard will be given to others. For Mark's readers, this prophecy probably points both to the destruction of Jerusalem, and God's salvation passing to the Gentiles.

The Disciples: Antagonists or Protagonists?

If Jesus is the clear protagonist and the religious leaders are flat antagonists, the disciples play a more ambiguous role in Mark's narrative. On the one hand, they hold a privileged position in Jesus' ministry. Jesus personally seeks them out and calls them to be his disciples. From among his many followers, he appoints twelve to be his special "apostles" (3:13–19; 6:30). The number twelve is surely significant, identifying these as leaders among the restored remnant of the twelve tribes of Israel. As his representatives, Jesus places great trust in them and sends them out with extraordinary authority to proclaim his message of the kingdom and to cast out demons (6:7–13, 30).

Yet despite this special status and responsibility, the Twelve are more often examples of failure than success. Of the four Gospels, Mark's portrait of the disciples is the most negative. They repeatedly fail to understand Jesus' teaching (4:13; 7:18) and to recognize his authoritative power (6:37, 52; 8:4). They cannot comprehend the true nature of his messiahship (8:32; 9:32). They act with pride and from self-interest (9:38; 10:13, 37, 41). Jesus repeatedly rebukes them for their failure to understand his teaching and for their lack of faith (4:13, 40; 7:18; 9:19).

> The disciples in Mark's Gospel represent a primarily negative model; it is Jesus himself who represents the correct role of a true disciple.

A critical juncture is reached in chapter 8, when Jesus warns the disciples against the "leaven" of the Pharisees and of Herod (8:15). The leaven in this case is the opposition to the kingdom by the Pharisees, who demand further signs (8:11–12), and by Herod, who executed John the Baptist (6:14–29). The disciples misunderstand Jesus, thinking he is speaking about their failure to bring bread. Jesus rebukes them for their lack of understanding: "Why are you talking about having no bread? Do you still not see or understand? Are your hearts hardened? Do you have eyes but fail to see, and ears but fail to hear?" (8:17–18).

Jesus' words, alluding to Jeremiah 5:21, sound eerily like his earlier teaching, when he quoted from Isaiah 6:9 to show that his parables concealed the truth from those whose hearts were hardened (4:11–12). In that context, the religious leaders were hardened, having blasphemed the Holy Spirit. They could no longer comprehend what their ears heard or their eyes saw. The similar language here suggests that the disciples are in danger of the same thing, going the way of the Pharisees and turning their backs on the kingdom of God. Their fate hangs in the balance.

Critical to the disciples' failure is their unwillingness to recognize the suffering role of the Messiah. As we have seen, the narrator drives this home with three cycles of failures, in which Jesus predicts his death, the disciples respond with pride and incomprehension, and Jesus teaches on servant leadership (8:31–38; 9:31–37; 10:32–45; see fig. 7.5).

Unlike the other Gospels, Mark does not describe the recovery of the disciples. When Jesus is arrested, they flee in terror. Judas betrays Jesus. Peter denies him three times. No one comes to his defense. No account is given of the disciples' restoration after the resurrection. The narrator's purpose seems to be to set the example of Jesus in contrast to the disciples. While he remains faithful, they are faithless. While he perseveres, they collapse and run. In this sense, Mark's disciples function almost as antidisciples, revealing to the reader how followers of Jesus should not behave. Jesus himself becomes the model of true discipleship, doing the Father's will even through suffering and death.

Another clarification should be added. While the implied author presents the disciples in a negative light, he is aware of their restoration and their future role in the church. The Gospel records Jesus' prediction that they will see him in Galilee following the resurrection (14:28; 16:7). Jesus also teaches that they will eventually proclaim him before governors and kings and will suffer for his sake (10:39; 13:9–13). It seems unlikely, therefore, that the Gospel is meant to be a repudiation of the Twelve or of the Christian communities which they established. Rather, Mark uses the failure of the disciples to highlight the faithfulness of Jesus, the agent of salvation and model for all discipleship.

"Minor" Characters

If the religious leaders actively oppose Jesus, and the disciples fail again and again, it is the small and insignificant characters who reveal the right response to Jesus. Levi, a despised tax collector, answers the call to discipleship (2:13–17). A woman with a blood disease has faith to touch Jesus' garment and be healed (5:25–34). Jairus, the synagogue ruler, has faith and so receives his daughter back from the dead (5:35–42). A father sees his demon-possessed son healed after crying out to Jesus, "I do believe; help me overcome my unbelief!" (9:24). Blind Bartimaeus calls out insistently for mercy from the Son of David and is healed because of his faith. There is irony here. While the religious leaders are imperceptive even though they have eyes to see (4:12), and the disciples are in danger of the same blindness (8:18), a blind man "sees" with eyes of faith (10:52; cf. 8:22–26).

The widow's "mite." Bronze lepta and the terra-cotta jar in which they were found.

Z. Radovan, Jerusalem

Actions performed by minor characters also receive commendation. A woman who anoints Jesus with expensive perfume is rebuked by others for the waste but commended by Jesus for anointing his body for burial (14:3–9). A widow's small but sacrificial offering for the temple is commended over the much larger offerings of the wealthy (12:41–44). The narrator places this incident in the context of Jesus' condemnation of the scribes for their hypocritical show of religiosity while exploiting the poor and widows.

Particularly striking are the examples of Gentile faith. A Syrophoenician woman perceives that God cares even for the Gentiles and so receives healing for her demon-possessed daughter (7:24–30). While Jesus' own people reject and desert him at the cross, a Roman centurion proclaims him to be the Son of God (15:39).

In summary, it is the outsiders—the sinners, the despised, the outcasts, and even Gentiles—who are examples of faith in Mark's narrative. These are the ones who respond with repentance, faith, and humility to God's reign and so receive salvation blessings.

THEOLOGICAL THEMES

From our narrative analysis, we can summarize some of the key theological themes of Mark's Gospel.

The Kingdom of God

Jesus' central message in Mark concerns the coming of the **kingdom of God** (1:15). But what is the nature of this kingdom? The Old Testament concept of God's kingdom was dynamic and multidimensional rather than static and one-dimensional. It could refer to God's sovereign authority over the cosmos *in the present*, or the consummation of that reign *in the future.* It could refer to a dynamic *reign*, God's spiritual authority in the lives of his people, or a static *realm*, a messianic kingdom centered in Jerusalem. In short, the kingdom could be conceived as present and future, a reign and a realm. The apocalyptic Judaism of Jesus' day acknowledged the present reality of God's sovereign authority but placed greatest emphasis on the future and eschatological dimensions of the kingdom. The persecuted people of God longed for the day when God would intervene in human history to actualize his reign and establish his kingdom on earth.

In Mark, Jesus' kingdom teaching contains both present and future elements. Jesus speaks of those who in the future will see the kingdom of God come with power (9:1) and refers to a future time when he will drink wine again in the kingdom of God (14:25). Joseph of Arimathea is longing for the kingdom of God (15:43), and at the triumphal entry, the people express their hope in "the coming kingdom of our father David!" (11:10). While this latter passage could reflect a misapprehension on the part of the people, the future establishment of the kingdom is implied in Jesus' teaching concerning the coming of the Son of Man "with great power and glory" to "gather his elect" (13:26 – 32; cf. 8:38; 13:33 – 34;

Mustard seed and plants. Jesus said that with faith the size of a mustard seed, you can move a mountain.

Gordon Franz/ZIBBC

Hanan Isachar/ZIBBC

14:62). This teaching of the future establishment of God's reign is in line with the expectations of apocalyptic Judaism.

The kingdom is realized not through conquest but through sacrifice.

At the same time, there are present dimensions to the kingdom. Jesus speaks of "receiving" the kingdom of God like a little child (10:15) and the difficulty of entering for those who are rich (10:23–25; cf. 9:47). The parable of the growing seed describes the kingdom as the slow growth from seed to plant until the day of harvest (4:26–29). Similarly, the parable of the mustard seed represents the kingdom as a tiny seed which grows into a great tree (4:30–32). In both parables, the kingdom is something which begins with Jesus' ministry and is consummated at his return. Jesus' central message, "the kingdom of God has come near," itself suggests this ambiguity between present and future aspects of the kingdom. The Greek verb *ēngiken* could be translated either "has arrived" or "has come near." It could denote either present or future and may be intentionally ambiguous.

This ambiguity is best explained by seeing the kingdom as intimately related to the person of Jesus. The kingdom has come near because the king is present. God's reign is evident in his healings, exorcisms, and nature miracles. His disciples experience the power of the kingdom—casting out demons and healing the sick—through his authority (5:7, 13). If the kingdom is directly related to the person of Jesus, then it is ultimately achieved through his death on the cross, the ransom for sins. The kingdom is inaugurated not through conquest but through sacrifice. It will be consummated when he returns in power and glory.

Jesus the Servant-Messiah

This close association of the kingdom with the person of Jesus leads us to the second major theme in Mark, the identity of Jesus. Though Jesus is the mighty Son of God and Messiah, his role is not to conquer but to suffer and die as the Servant of the LORD—an atoning sacrifice for sins. The anguish of death on the cross is in fact victory over the powers of Satan, sin, and death. The Gospel does not reject the traditional designations of Jesus as the Son of David and Messiah but rather redefines them. Jesus is the mighty Messiah who fulfills the role of the humble servant of Isaiah 53, the one who dies as a ransom for many (Mark 10:45).

Mark's Gospel presents Jesus as the mighty Messiah who surprisingly suffers as a ransom payment for the sins of his people.

Discipleship: Following the Servant's Suffering Path

The third major theme of Mark's Gospel is authentic **discipleship**. True followers of Jesus must be willing to take up their crosses and follow him, even to suffering and death. The disciples in Mark's Gospel serve primarily as negative models. They, like many of Jesus' would-be followers, are seeking power and position, yet shrink back in fear in the face of opposition. Jesus, in contrast, serves as the model disciple. He came to serve, not to be served, and to faithfully follow God's will. True disciples have in mind God's values, not human values (8:33).

NARRATIVE PURPOSE

From our examination of the Gospel's narrative progression and theological themes, we may suggest a threefold narrative purpose: (1) to confirm that Jesus is indeed the promised Messiah and Son of God, the inaugurator of God's kingdom and the fulfillment of Israel's promises; (2) to show that he fulfills these promises in a surprising way—not through conquest but through servanthood and suffering; and (3) on the basis of this revelation, to call believers to follow in the suffering path of their Messiah and Lord. The path to glory is through suffering and sacrifice.

While these main themes can be discerned through the narrative itself, specific conclusions concerning the historical situation of the Gospel must be more tentatively proposed.

THE HISTORICAL SETTING OF MARK'S GOSPEL: AUTHOR AND LIFE SETTING

Authorship

So who wrote this vivid and powerful account of the story of Jesus? Like the other three Gospels, this one is anonymous. By this we mean the author is not named in the body of the text (although the original readers would likely have known his identity). The title "According to Mark" (*kata Markon*) was probably added when the Gospels were brought together into a collection. Despite this anonymity, there is good reason to believe that the traditional identification of the author as John Mark, the companion of both Paul and Peter, is an accurate one.

The early church historian Eusebius, writing in the fourth century AD, quotes a church leader named Papias as affirming that "Mark became the interpreter of Peter" and wrote his version of the gospel. Papias, bishop of Hieropolis in Asia Minor till about AD 130, claims that he received this information from John "the Elder," probably a reference to the apostle John.[4] This would take the tradition back to the first generation of believers. Other early

---

4. Eusebius, *Ecclesiastical History* 3.39.15. Eusebius claims to be citing from the five books of Papias, titled *The Sayings of the Lord Interpreted*.

Figure 7.10—A Strange Story and an Intriguing Proposal

One of the most unusual stories in the Gospels appears in Mark's account of Jesus in Gethsemane. After describing Jesus' arrest and the desertion of the disciples, the narrator notes that "a young man, wearing nothing but a linen garment, was following Jesus. When they seized him, he fled naked, leaving his garment behind" (Mark 14:51–52).

This strange scene, unique to Mark's Gospel, seems to have no significant narrative or theological purpose. Some have suggested that Mark included it because he himself was this young man! The theory is sometimes expanded to suggest that the Last Supper took place in the home of Mark's mother, Mary (see Acts 12:12), and that the young man Mark quietly slipped out of the house to follow Jesus and the disciples to Gethsemane.

While this theory is fascinating, there is little evidence to confirm or refute it. It also would contradict Papias' claim that Mark had neither heard Jesus teach nor been one of his followers.

church writers, including Irenaeus, Tertullian, Clement of Alexandria, Origen, and Jerome affirm that Mark was the author of this Gospel and that he was dependent on the eyewitness accounts of Peter.

But who was this Mark? While Mark was a common name in the first century, only one figure in the New Testament appears as a likely candidate. John Mark was the son of a certain Mary, in whose house the Jerusalem church met (Acts 12:12). As a young man, Mark accompanied his cousin Barnabas and the apostle Paul on their first missionary journey (Acts 13:5). For unknown reasons, he left the missionary group at Perga in Pamphylia and returned to Jerusalem (Acts 13:13). Because of this desertion, Paul refused to take Mark on his second journey. A rift developed between Paul and Barnabas and the two separated, with Barnabas taking Mark and sailing to Cyprus, while Paul chose Silas and returned to Galatia (Acts 15:36–41). Despite this division, we know Mark and Paul were eventually reconciled, since Paul refers to him as his "fellow worker" in letters written ten years later (Col. 4:10; Philem. 24). Mark's value to Paul is also evident in 2 Timothy 4:11, where Paul tells Timothy to bring Mark with him to Rome because he is "helpful to me in my ministry."

While most closely associated with Paul in the New Testament, the early church tradition that Mark became Peter's companion finds support in 1 Peter 5:13, where Peter sends greetings from "my son Mark." While this could be a different Mark, its agreement with the early church tradition makes its identification with John Mark likely. What Papias means by saying that Mark became Peter's "interpreter" (*hermēneutēs*) is debated. Some believe that Peter normally preached in Aramaic and Mark served as his Greek interpreter. Others think that the term refers to the task of putting Peter's oral preaching into written form.

Although the value of the Second Gospel does not depend on its authorship by John Mark of Jerusalem, there seems no good reason to reject this tradition, and sufficient evidence to affirm it. No contrary opinion appeared in the early church. And we might ask why, if the early church ascribed false authorship to this Gospel, they chose a minor character like Mark, who was neither an apostle nor eyewitness to the ministry of Jesus.

> Many scholars believe Mark's Gospel was written in Rome to the persecuted church there.

Setting and Occasion

Place of Writing. Where was Mark's Gospel written? Early church tradition claims that Mark wrote from Rome to a Roman Christian audience.[5] This agrees with New Testament references which place Mark in Rome with both Paul (Col. 4:10; Philem. 24; cf. 2 Tim. 4:11) and Peter (1 Peter 5:13; where "Babylon" is probably a cryptic reference to Rome).

A Roman location also fits well with material found in the Gospel. Mark translates Aramaic expressions for a Greek-speaking audience (3:17; 5:41; 7:34; 14:36; 15:34) and

---

5. Clement of Alexandria (Eusebius, *Ecclesiastical History* 2.15; 6.14.6), and implied by Irenaeus, *Against Heresies* 3.1.1. The anti-Marcionite prologue speaks of the "regions of Italy." The only contrary claim comes from John Chrysostom (*Homilae in Matthaeum* 1:3), who identifies Egypt as the place of the Gospel's origin. Chrysostom has probably misunderstood Eusebius' reference to Mark's later ministry in Egypt (Eusebius, *Ecclesiastical History* 2:16).

explains Jewish customs for Gentile readers (7:2–4; 15:42). While these could point to any non-Palestinian context, Mark also explains Greek expressions by their Latin equivalents. For example, in 12:42 the widow's two *lepta*, Greek coins, are said to be equivalent to a *quadrans*, a Roman coin.[6] Although Greek was spoken throughout the empire, Latin was primarily used in Rome and Italy. Another bit of incidental evidence for Rome comes from 15:21, where Rufus and Alexander are named as the sons of Simon of Cyrene, presumably because they were known by Mark's church. This could be the same Rufus identified by Paul as a member of the Roman church (Rom. 16:13). Finally, the Gospel's special interest in persecution and martyrdom would fit well with a Roman audience, since the Roman church was a persecuted body.

While compelling, this evidence is not conclusive. The church traditions concerning Rome could have been surmised from the New Testament data itself, and Latin expressions were common throughout the Roman Empire. Rufus of Romans 16:13 could be a different individual than that of Mark 15:21, and the theme of persecution could fit a variety of New Testament churches. Despite these

Rome, the likely destination of Mark's Gospel. *Top:* Roman Colosseum. *Bottom:* Roman Forum.

uncertainties, Rome remains the most likely provenance (place of origin). Other proposals, including Galilee, Syria, and Egypt, have even less evidence to support them.

Date. The date of Mark is also uncertain. Some evidence points to a date in the AD 50s or 60s: (1) Clement of Alexandria claimed Mark wrote his Gospel while Peter was ministering in Rome.[7] Eusebius says that Peter came to Rome when Claudius was emperor, sometime between AD 41–54.[8] (2) Since Peter is in Jerusalem in Acts 15, around AD 49, then he must have come to Rome after this date, perhaps in the early 50s. Peter appears to have

6. For many more examples of loan words and expressions, see Ralph Martin, *Mark: Evangelist and Theologian* (Grand Rapids: Zondervan, 1972), 64; Robert H. Gundry, *Mark: A Commentary on His Apology for the Cross* (Grand Rapids: Eerdmans, 1993), 1044.

7. Cited by Eusebius, *Ecclesiastical History* 2.15; 6.14.6.

8. Ibid., 2.14.6.

been in Corinth before Paul wrote 1 Corinthians (c. AD 55; see 1 Cor. 1:12; 3:22; 9:5). (3) Church tradition tells us Peter was martyred during the persecutions of the emperor Nero, around AD 64–67. This would allow for a date anytime from the mid-50s to the early 60s. A 50s date would fit a solution of the synoptic problem, which sees Mark as the first Gospel. If Luke used Mark as a source for his Gospel, and if he completed Acts while Paul was still in prison in Rome (around AD 60–62; see Acts 28:30–31), then Mark's Gospel would have been written prior to this imprisonment, in the mid to late 50s.

Other scholars prefer a date in the late 60s. The church father Irenaeus differs from Clement by claiming that Mark wrote after the "departure" of Peter and Paul.[9] If departure here means death, Mark's Gospel must have been written in the late 60s or in the 70s. Evidence for this comes from the Gospel itself. In Jesus' Olivet Discourse in Mark 13, the author adds the cryptic narrative aside "let the reader understand" (13:14). This may indicate that at the time of writing, the Jewish War of AD 66–73 had already begun and the destruction of the temple was imminent.

Still other scholars use the allusion in Mark 13:14 to date the Gospel even later, after the destruction of Jerusalem in AD 70. This is less likely, however, since the description of the siege in Mark 13 is quite general and does not seem to have been composed after the fact.

Purpose and Occasion. What specific life situation prompted Mark to write? Scholars have tended toward three directions: (1) The first is *historical.* As the original apostles began to pass from the scene, Mark sought to record for posterity the apostolic witness concerning Jesus. As we have seen, the church fathers repeatedly stress Mark's intention to record Peter's teaching.

Top: Coin of Nero. *Bottom:* Bust of a youthful Nero (Corinth Museum).

(2) The second suggested purpose is *christological,* meaning that Mark wrote to correct a false or inadequate view of Jesus being promoted by some in the church. Some scholars have claimed that Mark wrote to combat a "divine man" Christology, which identified Jesus as a kind of first-century magician and miracle worker.[10] In response, Mark stresses Jesus' sacrificial death. Others have suggested that Mark's very human portrait of Jesus was intended to correct the heresy of **Docetism**, which denied Jesus' true humanity.[11]

(3) A third view is that Mark makes a *practical* call to cross-bearing discipleship. He wrote to challenge his readers that true discipleship means following the path of Jesus through suffering to glory. This view is often linked to the persecution of the church in

---

9. Irenaeus, *Against Heresies* 3.1.1.
10. See T. J. Weeden, *Mark: Traditions in Conflict* (Philadelphia: Fortress, 1971).
11. See E. Schweizer, *The Good News according to Mark* (ET; London: SPCK, 1971); Martin, *Mark.*

Rome instigated by the Roman emperor Nero. This began in AD 64 after a terrible fire destroyed more than half the city of Rome. When rumors began circulating that the emperor had ordered the fire as a means of "urban renewal," Nero shifted the blame to the Christians. Already viewed with suspicion, Christians were persecuted with terrible cruelty. The Roman historian Tacitus notes how some were crucified; others were sewn in animal skins and hunted by dogs; still others were covered with pitch and burned at night as torches.[12] Mark's emphasis on the need to suffer for Christ would fit this period of intense persecution. Another possibility is that the allusions to persecution reflect an earlier period and are linked to riots between Jews and Jewish Christians in AD 49–50. These disputes prompted the emperor Claudius to expel the Jewish population from Rome (Acts 18:2).[13] The theme of suffering could then fit either the earlier or later dates suggested for the Gospel.

Mark, of course, may have written for a variety of reasons, historical, christological, or practical. We must not neglect an *evangelistic* purpose as well, since all the Gospels call people to faith in Jesus.

Though conclusions concerning authorship, place, date, and circumstances must remain tentative, the scales tip in favor of John Mark writing in Rome in the mid-50s or late 60s. While a specific occasion remains uncertain, his general purpose was certainly to present Jesus as the mighty Messiah and Son of God, whose suffering and death provided atonement for sins. True disciples are called to follow him through suffering to glory.

READING MARK TODAY

One day not so long ago, I was flipping through a Christian magazine, reading articles on the kinds of things American Christians tend to fight over: the nature of church governance, issues of church and state, theological debates about eschatology and spiritual gifts. I casually turned a page, and there before me was a gruesome picture of two bodies, bloody and badly mutilated. In the context of my "light" reading, it startled me. I read the caption describing Christian martyrs in Indonesia. The picture showed their enemies beating their lifeless bodies. Later that day, an e-mail crossed my desk. It told of an Australian missionary and his two young sons who were burned alive in their car in India by an angry mob. These were sobering moments. Sitting in my comfortable office, in the safety of my middle-class community, in a nation of peace and prosperity, these images brought home the sobering reality that many Christians around the world do not live in such ease but are suffering and dying for their faith.

Mark's Gospel reminds us that the goal of the Christian life is not to find security or self-fulfillment. Following Jesus is responding to a radical call to commitment, taking up our crosses and following him. The gospel holds no promise for those who are seeking power and wealth and fame and prestige. To be first, Jesus says, you must be last. To be a leader, you must become a slave. To live, you must die.

The Gospel begins with the startling announcement that the reign of God, his sovereign authority, has arrived through the powerful words and deeds of Jesus, the mighty

---

12. Tacitus, *Annals* 15.44.
13. Suetonius, *Twelve Caesars, Claudius* 25.4.

Messiah and Son of God. The glories of God's kingdom are available to all who will receive it. Yet startlingly, the king does not conquer but rather dies. His followers are scattered and bewildered. Even the announcement of the resurrection brings puzzlement and fear. This is "good news"?

Comprehending Mark's Gospel requires a paradigm shift for the modern reader. It requires us to see beyond the present world, where tyrants still rule and oppressors still oppress. The good news of salvation is that Jesus' death, though seemingly a defeat, was a spiritual victory of cosmic proportions. Satan and sin and death are now defeated. The age to come has broken into human history and is now available to those who receive it.

Paradoxically, receiving the kingdom means dying to self and living for God. It means giving up efforts to earn God's favor, and receiving his free gift of grace. In our age, in which human accomplishment and personal fulfillment are considered the highest of life's goals, Mark's Gospel calls us to radical faith and self-denial. Relationships are now defined not through the bonds of family or culture or ethnicity but rather through spiritual identity: Our brothers and sisters are those who do the will of God (Mark 3:35). As the people of God living simultaneously in the present evil age and the age to come, believers are called to alertness and anticipation for the return of the Son of Man and willing submission to follow his path of suffering.

» CHAPTER SUMMARY «

1. Mark's Gospel has a vivid, fast-moving style which draws the reader into the events of the story.

2. Literary devices common in Mark include the topical ordering of events, intercalation, triads, and irony.

3. The first half of Mark's Gospel presents Jesus as the mighty and powerful Son of God, defeating the forces of Satan, healing the sick, and teaching with great authority. The people respond with amazement and awe.

4. Jesus' authority is also seen in spiritual conflicts, as he casts out demons and challenges the religious leaders for their hypocrisy, obsession with external rules, and failure to share God's heart for the lost.

5. The turning point of the narrative comes with Peter's confession that Jesus is the Christ, and Jesus' subsequent revelation that the Messiah must suffer and die.

6.   In three parallel episodes which follow, Jesus predicts his death, his disciples fail to get it, and Jesus teaches about true servant discipleship (8:31 – 38; 9:31 – 37; 10:32 – 45). The climax comes in Mark 10:45: "For even the Son of Man did not come to be served, but to serve, and to give his life as a ransom for many."

7.   Jesus' entrance into Jerusalem and his actions in the temple serve as a public announcement of his messiahship, ending the messianic secret and leading to a series of conflicts with the religious leaders. Jesus repeatedly confounds them with his superior wisdom, and they in turn plot his death.

8.   Jesus' arrest and crucifixion in Mark are scenes of betrayal, desertion, and rejection. The disciples flee at his arrest; his opponents mock and scorn him. He dies in agony on the cross, forsaken by all, even his Father in heaven.

9.   Yet the informed reader knows that Jesus' death is not in vain but is a messianic act of atonement, the ransom sacrifice for the sins of the world.

10.   The vindication of Jesus' claims is the resurrection. The earliest and best manuscripts conclude the Gospel at 16:8. The last part may have been lost, but more likely the ending emphasizes the announcement of Jesus' resurrection over narrated appearances. The reader is called to faith in the proclamation of salvation achieved through Jesus the Messiah.

11.   As the protagonist and main character, Jesus is portrayed in Mark's Gospel as the mighty Son of God, who suffers and dies as the Servant of the LORD — a ransom for sinners.

12.   The chief antagonists are Satan, his demons, and the religious leaders, who oppose Jesus and his kingdom purpose. The role of the disciples is more ambiguous but is primarily negative, demonstrating ignorance, pride, and wavering faith. Jesus instead provides the true model of discipleship for the reader to follow.

13.   Key theological themes of Mark's Gospel include the in-breaking power of the kingdom of God, the identity of Jesus as Son of God and Servant-Messiah, and the need for cross-bearing discipleship.

14.   Though issues of provenance are uncertain, the Gospel of Mark was likely written in Rome by John Mark, in the 50s or 60s of the first century.

15.   The book was likely written for a variety of reasons, but it was especially written to provide an authoritative written version of the oral proclamation of the Gospel, to clarify the identity of Jesus as the Servant-Messiah, and to call the persecuted church to faithfully follow him through suffering to glory.

» KEY TERMS «

Messiah	Beelzebub controversy	parable of the wicked
Son of God	confession of Peter	tenant farmers
exorcisms	passion prediction	Olivet Discourse
intercalation	Servant of the LORD	nature miracles
triad	transfiguration	kingdom of God
irony	Son of Man	discipleship
messianic secret	triumphal entry	Docetism

» DISCUSSION AND STUDY QUESTIONS «

1. Describe Mark's literary style. Identify and define his main rhetorical devices, including topical ordering, intercalation, triads, and irony.

2. How is Jesus presented in the first half of the Gospel? How does he demonstrate his authority?

3. What is the relationship between the Beelzebub controversy (3:22 – 30) and the two incidents relating to Jesus' family (3:20 – 21, 31 – 35)? What is the blasphemy of the Holy Spirit?

4. Why did Jesus teach in parables, according to Mark 4:10 – 12?

5. What is the key turning point in Mark's narrative?

6. What significance does the first passion prediction have coming immediately after Peter's confession?

7. Describe the three cycles of passion predictions and responses. What verse serves as a key theme verse for Mark's Gospel?

8. What is allegorized in the parable of the wicked tenant farmers? What does each character represent? To what Old Testament passage does this parable allude?

9. What impression of Jesus' crucifixion is given in Mark's narrative?

10. What key role does the centurion at the cross play?

11. Why is Mark's resurrection account so unusual? What textual problem occurs at the end of Mark's Gospel?

12. Summarize how Jesus' identity is gradually revealed in Mark's Gospel.

13. What title does Jesus most often use for himself in Mark's Gospel? What is its significance?

14. Mark places great emphasis on the disciples in his Gospel. What role do they play and how does this relate to Mark's theme of discipleship?

15. What role do the "minor characters" in Mark's Gospel play?

16. Summarize the main theological themes of Mark's Gospel. Describe the nature of the kingdom of God.

17. Summarize the threefold narrative purpose suggested in the text.

18. What do we know about John Mark from the New Testament? According to church tradition, whose version of the Gospel did Mark record?

19. From where and under what circumstances was Mark's Gospel likely written?

20. What are some possible reasons that Mark's Gospel was written?

Digging Deeper

Commentaries

Beginning and Intermediate

Anderson, Hugh. *The Gospel of Mark.* 2nd ed. Grand Rapids: Eerdmans, 1981.

Brooks, James A. *Mark.* New American Commentary. Nashville: Broadman, 1991.

Cole, Alan. *The Gospel according to Mark.* Tyndale New Testament Commentary. Grand Rapids: Eerdmans, 1989.

Edwards, James R. *The Gospel according to Mark.* The Pillar New Testament Commentary. Grand Rapids: Eerdmans, 2002.

Garland, David E. *Mark.* NIV Application Commentary. Grand Rapids: Zondervan, 1996.

Hooker, Morna D. *The Gospel according to St. Mark.* Black's New Testament Commentary. Peabody, MA: Hendrickson, 1992.

Hurtado, Larry. *Mark.* New International Biblical Commentary. Peabody, MA: Hendrickson, 1989.

Lane, William L. *The Gospel according to Mark.* New International Commentary. Grand Rapids: Eerdmans, 1974.

Maloney, Francis J. *The Gospel of Mark: A Commentary.* Peabody, MA: Hendrickson, 2002.

Mann, C. S. *Mark. A New Translation with Introduction and Commentary.* Anchor Bible Commentary. Garden City, NY: Doubleday, 1986.

Schweizer, E. *The Good News according to Mark.* Translated by D. H. Madvig. London: SPCK, 1971.

Wessel, Walter W. "Mark." In *The Expositors Bible Commentary*, vol. 8, edited by Frank E. Gaebelein. Grand Rapids: Zondervan, 1984.

Witherington, Ben, III. *The Gospel of Mark: A Socio-Rhetorical Commentary.* Grand Rapids: Eerdmans, 2001.

Advanced and Greek/Technical

Cranfield, C. E. B. *The Gospel according to St. Mark.* Cambridge Greek Testament. Rev. Ed. Cambridge: Cambridge Univ. Press, 1977.

Evans, Craig A. *Mark 8:27–16:20.* Word Biblical Commentary 34B. Nashville: Nelson, 2001.

France, R. T. *The Gospel of Mark.* The New International Greek Testament Commentary. Grand Rapids: Eerdmans, 2002.

Guelich, Robert A. *Mark 1–8:26.* Word Biblical Commentary 34A. Dallas: Word, 1989.

Gundry, Robert H. *Mark: A Commentary on His Apology for the Cross.* Grand Rapids: Eerdmans, 1993.

Marcus, Joel. *Mark 1–8: A New Translation with Introduction and Commentary.* Anchor Bible 27. New York: Doubleday, 2000.

Taylor, Vincent. *The Gospel according to St. Mark: The Greek Text with Introduction, Notes and Indexes.* 2nd ed. 1966. Reprint, Grand Rapids: Baker, 1981.

Themes and Theology of Mark

Best, Ernest. *Following Jesus: Discipleship in the Gospel of Mark.* JSNTSup 4. Sheffield: JSOT Press, 1988.

———. *The Temptation and the Passion: The Markan Soteriology.* Society for New Testament Monograph Series 2. Cambridge: Cambridge Univ. Press, 1965.

Camery-Hoggat, J. *Irony in Mark's Gospel: Text and Subtext.* SNTSMS 72. Cambridge: Cambridge Univ. Press, 1992.

Harrington, Daniel. *What Are They Saying about Mark?* Mahwah, NJ: Paulist, 2005.

Hengel, Martin. *Studies in the Gospel of Mark.* Philadelphia: Fortress, 1985.

Kee, Howard Clark. *Community of the New Age: Studies in Mark's Gospel.* Philadelphia: Westminster, 1977.

Kelber, W. H. *The Kingdom in Mark.* Philadelphia: Fortress, 1974.

Kingsbury, Jack Dean. *The Christology of Mark's Gospel.* Philadelphia: Fortress, 1983.

Mack, Burton L. *A Myth of Innocence.* Philadelphia: Fortress, 1988.

Marcus, Joel. *The Way of the Lord: Christological Exegesis of the Old Testament in the Gospel of Mark.* Louisville: Westminster/John Knox, 1992.

Martin, Ralph. *Mark: Evangelist and Theologian.* Grand Rapids: Zondervan, 1972.

Marxsen, W. *Mark the Evangelist.* Translated by James Boyce, et al. Nashville: Abingdon, 1969.

Matera, F. *What Are They Saying about Mark?* New York: Paulist, 1987.

Stock, Augustine. *The Method and Message of Mark.* Wilmington: Glazier, 1989.

Telford, W. R. *The Theology of the Gospel of Mark.* Cambridge: Cambridge Univ. Press, 1999.

Telford, W. R., ed. *The Interpretation of Mark.* Philadelphia: Fortress, 1985.

Trocmé, Etienne. *The Formation of the Gospel according to Mark.* Philadelphia: Fortress, 1975.

Via, S. O., Jr. *The Ethics of Mark's Gospel: In the Middle of Time.* Philadelphia: Fortress, 1985.

Watts, Rikki E. *Isaiah's New Exodus in Mark.* Grand Rapids: Baker, 2000.

Newer Methods and Approaches

Anderson, J. C., and S. D. Moore, eds. *Mark and Method: New Approaches in Biblical Studies.* Minneapolis: Fortress, 1992.

Best, Ernest. *Mark, the Gospel as Story.* Edinburgh: T and T Clark, 1983.

Fowler, Robert M. *Let the Reader Understand: Reader-Response Criticism and the Gospel of Mark.* Minneapolis: Fortress, 1991.

Heil, John Paul. *The Gospel of Mark as Model for Action: A Reader-Response Commentary.* New York: Paulist, 1992.

Van Iersel, B. M. F. *Mark: A Reader-Response Commentary.* Translated by W. H. Bisscheroux. Sheffield: Sheffield Academic, 1998.

Levine, Amy-Jill, ed. *A Feminist Companion to Mark.* With Marianne Blickenstaff. Sheffield: Sheffield Academic, 2001.

Malbon, E. S. *Narrative Space and Mythic Meaning in Mark.* Sheffield: JSOT Press, 1991.

Rhoads, David, and Donald Michie. *Mark as Story. An Introduction to the Narrative of a Gospel. 2nd ed.*Philadelphia: Fortress, 1999.

Smith, Stephen H. *A Lion with Wings: A Narrative-Critical Approach to Mark's Gospel.* Sheffield: Sheffield Academic, 1996.

Tolbert, Mary A. *Sowing the Gospel: Mark's World in Literary-Historical Perspective.* Minneapolis: Fortress, 1989.

Bibliography

Kealy, Séan P. *Mark's Gospel: A History of Its Interpretation from the Beginning until 1979.* New York: Paulist, 1982.

Neirynck, F. *The Gospel of Mark: A Cumulative Bibliography 1950–1990.* Leuven: University Press and Peeters, 1992.

CHAPTER 8

Matthew
THE GOSPEL OF THE MESSIAH

» CHAPTER OVERVIEW «

1. Literary Features
2. The Plot of Matthew's Gospel
3. Matthew's Portrait of Jesus
4. Other Characters in Matthew's Gospel
5. Theological Themes
6. Narrative and Theological Purpose
7. The Historical Setting of Matthew's Gospel: Author and Life Setting
8. Reading Matthew Today

» OBJECTIVES «

After reading this chapter you should be able to:

- Identify the main literary features of Matthew's Gospel, especially with reference to style and structural features.
- Summarize the themes of the five major discourses in Matthew.
- Describe the main features of Matthew's Christology, especially with reference to the titles Christ, Son of David, Son of God, and Immanuel.
- Compare and contrast the characterization of the religious leaders and the disciples with Mark's presentation.
- Summarize Matthew's main theological themes, especially with reference to Jesus' role in the climax of salvation history.
- Suggest the likely audience of Matthew's Gospel and his narrative purpose in writing.
- Provide basic evidence for the provenance, date, and authorship of Matthew's Gospel.

I glanced out my window when I heard the bicycles pull up. Two young men in white shirts and ties were getting off their bikes, each carrying several books and pamphlets. I immediately recognized them as Mormons. I had mixed feelings. On the one hand, I groaned at the thought of stopping my work and losing precious time preparing for my courses. On the other hand, I felt a measure of excitement at the opportunity to share my faith with two who held a very different perspective from my own. When they knocked on the door, I opened it and cheerfully invited them in. I could tell they were a bit taken aback by my friendliness and enthusiasm, and perhaps a little suspicious. Without thinking, I made the *faux pas* of offering them a Coke (Mormons avoid caffeine). We laughed and, the ice now broken, sat down for a discussion. Before long, the conversation turned to the nature

» CENTRAL THEME «

Jesus the Jewish Messiah brings salvation history to its climax, saving his people from their sins.

» KEY VERSES «

Matthew 1:21; 28:18–20

» BASIC OUTLINE OF MATTHEW «

1. Prologue: The Genealogy and Birth Narrative of the Messiah (chaps. 1–2)
2. The Appearance of the Messiah (3:1–4:11)
3. The Ministry of the Messiah to Israel (4:12–11:1)
4. The Responses to the Messiah: Rejection by Israel; Growing Acceptance by the Disciples (11:2–20:34)
5. The Messiah Confronts Jerusalem (21:1–26:1)
6. The Messiah Is Rejected Yet Victorious: The Passion and Resurrection (chaps. 26–28)

of authentic faith. "But we are Christians!" one of my new friends insisted. "The Book of Mormon is really the completion of the Christian faith, God's final revelation through Joseph Smith." From there, the conversation turned to the truth or falsity of the claims of Joseph Smith. Is Mormonism in fact the completion of God's plan of salvation? Or is it a dangerous sect distorting the authentic message of the gospel?

In many ways, Matthew's Gospel is just such a discussion and debate. It is an extended defense, in narrative form, of the claim that a new sect within Judaism, known originally as "the Way" and later as Christianity, in fact is authentic Judaism, the completion or fulfillment of God's purpose for Israel and the world. At the time of its writing, the debate has reached a fevered pitch, with strong words flying in both directions. The authentic people of God, the narrator emphatically affirms, are defined no longer by ancestry or ethnic identity but by allegiance to Jesus the Messiah. The risen Lord is now calling forth disciples from all nations, Jews and Gentiles alike, a new people of God.

LITERARY FEATURES

Among the four Gospels, Matthew shows the most evidence of careful structure and design. The author is clearly a skilled literary artist.

www.HolyLandPhotos.com

The Mount of Beatitudes, traditional site of the Sermon on the Mount

Concise Style

Whereas Mark has a lively expansive style with lots of details, Matthew is generally shorter and more concise. For example, the account of the raising of Jairus's daughter takes 345 words in Greek in Mark, but only 139 words in Matthew (see fig. 8.1). Mark writes more like a storyteller; Matthew more like a reporter (though still an interpreter).

Fulfillment Formulas and Old Testament Quotations

One of Matthew's most distinctive structural features is his use of **fulfillment formulas** to demonstrate that the events of Jesus' life fulfilled Old Testament prophecies. Ten times the narrator uses a similar formula: "*This was to fulfill what was spoken by the prophet, saying . . .*" followed by an Old Testament quotation.[1] In many other passages, the Old Testament is identified as fulfilled in Jesus' words and deeds[2] (see fig. 8.2).

The Old Testament text the narrator uses in these quotations is unique. Those quotations in common with the other Synoptics generally follow the Septuagint (LXX), the

---

1. Matt. 1:22–23; 2:15, 17–18, 23; 4:14–16; 8:17; 12:17–21; 13:35; 21:4–5; 27:9–10.
2. Matt. 2:5–6; 3:3; 10:34–35; 11:2–6, 10; 13:14–15; 15:7–9; 21:16, 42; 26:31.

Matthew's Account (139 words in Greek)	**Mark's Account** (345 words in Greek)
While he was saying this, a ruler came and knelt before him and said, "My daughter has just died. But come and put your hand on her, and she will live." Jesus got up and went with him, and so did his disciples. Just then a woman who had been subject to bleeding for twelve years came up behind him and touched the edge of his cloak. She said to herself, "If I only touch his cloak, I will be healed." Jesus turned and saw her. "Take heart, daughter," he said, "your faith has healed you." And the woman was healed from that moment. When Jesus entered the ruler's house and saw the flute players and the noisy crowd, he said, "Go away. The girl is not dead but asleep." But they laughed at him. After the crowd had been put outside, he went in and took the girl by the hand, and she got up. News of this spread through all that region.	When Jesus had again crossed over by boat to the other side of the lake, a large crowd gathered around him while he was by the lake. Then one of the synagogue rulers, named Jairus, came there. Seeing Jesus, he fell at his feet and pleaded earnestly with him, "My little daughter is dying. Please come and put your hands on her so that she will be healed and live." So Jesus went with him. A large crowd followed and pressed around him. And a woman was there who had been subject to bleeding for twelve years. She had suffered a great deal under the care of many doctors and had spent all she had, yet instead of getting better she grew worse. When she heard about Jesus, she came up behind him in the crowd and touched his cloak, because she thought, "If I just touch his clothes, I will be healed." Immediately her bleeding stopped and she felt in her body that she was freed from her suffering. At once Jesus realized that power had gone out from him. He turned around in the crowd and asked, "Who touched my clothes?" "You see the people crowding against you," his disciples answered, "and yet you can ask, 'Who touched me?'" But Jesus kept looking around to see who had done it. Then the woman, knowing what had happened to her, came and fell at his feet and, trembling with fear, told him the whole truth. He said to her, "Daughter, your faith has healed you. Go in peace and be freed from your suffering." While Jesus was still speaking, some men came from the house of Jairus, the synagogue ruler. "Your daughter is dead," they said. "Why bother the teacher any more?" Ignoring what they said, Jesus told the synagogue ruler, "Don't be afraid; just believe." He did not let anyone follow him except Peter, James and John the brother of James. When they came to the home of the synagogue ruler, Jesus saw a commotion, with people crying and wailing loudly. He went in and said to them, "Why all this commotion and wailing? The child is not dead but asleep." But they laughed at him. After he put them all out, he took the child's father and mother and the disciples who were with him, and went in where the child was. He took her by the hand and said to her, "*Talitha koum*!" (which means, "Little girl, I say to you, get up!"). Immediately the girl stood up and walked around (she was twelve years old). At this they were completely astonished. He gave strict orders not to let anyone know about this, and told them to give her something to eat.

Figure 8.2—Matthew's Fulfillment Quotations

Ten "Fulfillment Formulas": "This Was to Fulfill ..."

1:22 – 23	Jesus' virgin birth fulfills Isaiah 7:14.
2:15	The escape to and return from Egypt fulfills Hosea 11:1.
2:17 – 18	The murder of the infants of Bethlehem fulfills Jeremiah 31:15.
2:23	Jesus' childhood in Nazareth fulfills an unknown prophecy.*
4:14 – 16	Jesus establishes his ministry in Galilee, fulfilling Isaiah 9:2.
8:17	Jesus heals disease, fulfilling Isaiah 53:4.
12:17 – 21	Jesus fulfills the role of the Servant of Isaiah 42:2.
13:35	Jesus speaks in parables, fulfilling Psalm 78:2; 2 Chronicles 29:30.
21:4 – 5	Jesus enters Jerusalem as the humble king of Zechariah 9:9.
27:9 – 10	Jesus is betrayed for thirty pieces of silver, fulfilling Zechariah 11:12 – 13.

Other Fulfillment Citations

2:5 – 6	Jesus' Bethlehem birth fulfills Micah 5:2.
3:3	John the Baptist fulfills Isaiah 40:3.
5:17	Jesus fulfills the whole law and the prophets.
10:34 – 35	The division of families fulfills Micah 7:6.
11:2 – 6	Jesus performs messianic signs, fulfilling Isaiah 35:5; 61:1, etc.
11:10	John the Baptist fulfills Malachi 3:1.
13:14 – 15	Parables conceal the truth from the hard-hearted (Isa. 6:9).
15:7 – 9	Israel's disobedience fulfills Isaiah 29:13.
21:13	The temple is a den of robbers (Isa. 56:7; Jer. 7:11).
21:16	Praise from the lips of children is predicted in Psalm 8:2.
21:42	The rejected stone becomes the capstone (Ps. 118:22).
26:31	The shepherd is struck down and the sheep scattered (Zech. 13:7).

*"He will be called a Nazarene" may be a reference to the "branch" (*netser*) of Isaiah 11:1, or a general statement of the humble origins of the Messiah.

Greek Old Testament. But in others, he translates directly from the Hebrew text.[3] This suggests that the author was proficient in Hebrew as well as Greek and that his primary Bible was the Hebrew Scriptures. This is one more indication of the Jewishness of this Gospel.

Topical Arrangement

While all of the Gospels at times utilize a topical rather than chronological arrangement of events, this is especially true of Matthew, in which related material often appears together.

---

3. See Krister Stendahl, *The School of St. Matthew and Its Use of the Old Testament*, 2nd ed. (Philadelphia: Fortress, 1968); Robert Gundry, *The Use of the Old Testament in St. Matthew's Gospel, with Special Reference to the Messianic Hope*, SNT 18 (Leiden: Brill, 1967).

There are collections of teaching (chaps. 5–7), miracle stories (chaps. 8–9), mission instructions (chap. 10), parables (chap. 13), teachings about the church (chap.18), denunciations against the religious leaders (chap. 23), and eschatological teaching (chaps. 24–25). Scholars debate whether Matthew's famous Sermon on the Mount (chaps. 5–7) was a single sermon given by Jesus or whether the author has brought together a representative collection of Jesus' teaching (see fig. 8.8).

Structural Signals and Matthew's "Outline"

In addition to fulfillment formulas and topical collections, various **structural signals** mark key transitions in Matthew's narrative. These provide clues to the overall structure of the Gospel.

> Matthew structures his narrative around five major discourses, all of which end with the structural signal, "And it came about when Jesus finished these words …"

One such marker appears as a formula at the end of each of Jesus' five major discourses: *"And it came about when Jesus finished these words …"* (7:28; 11:1; 13:53; 19:1; 26:1; see fig. 8.3). Matthew groups his narrative sections around these five discourses, providing a pattern of alternating narrative and discourse throughout the Gospel. In a book published in 1930, Benjamin Bacon proposed that Matthew's five discourses were meant to parallel the five books of Moses (the Pentateuch) and so present the Gospel as a kind of "Christian Pentateuch," with Jesus as the new Moses.[4] Few scholars have accepted Bacon's idea of a pentateuchal structure, especially since it treats two key sections in Matthew, the birth narrative and the passion narrative, merely as prologue and epilogue respectively. Yet many investigators have picked up on the pattern of alternating discourses and narratives. Some have proposed a chiastic or concentric arrangement, with each of the narrative and discourse sections in the first half of the book related to those in the second half.[5]

A very different outline has been suggested by another structural signal, the phrase *"From that time Jesus began to …"* This formula appears twice, marking the beginning of Jesus' public ministry (4:17) and the beginning of his journey to Jerusalem to suffer and die (16:21). Jack Kingsbury points to this marker as the key to Matthew's structure.[6] The resulting outline is similar to Mark's, focusing first on the identity and ministry of the Messiah and then on his road to the cross.

Figure 8.3—The Five Major Discourses of Matthew's Gospel

1. Sermon on the Mount (chaps. 5–7)
2. Commissioning of the Twelve (chap. 10)
3. Parables of the Kingdom (chap. 13)
4. Church Life and Discipline (chap. 18)
5. Woes and Olivet Discourse (chaps. 23–25)

---

4. Benjamin W. Bacon, *Studies in Matthew* (London: Constable, 1930); cf. Dale C. Allison Jr., *The New Moses: A Matthean Typology* (Minneapolis: Fortress, 1993).

5. H. J. B. Combrink, "The Structure of the Gospel of Matthew as Narrative," *TynBul* 34 (1983), 61–90.

6. Jack Dean Kingsbury, *Matthew as Story*, 2nd ed. (Philadelphia: Fortress, 1988), 38; cf. Jack Dean Kingsbury, *Matthew: Structure, Christology, Kingdom* (Philadelphia: Fortress, 1975), 12–25.

So which represents Matthew's outline, the fivefold alternating discourses and narratives or the threefold progression of the narrative?[7] There is probably not an either-or solution, since both features appear to be part of the author's plan. Ancient writers were certainly not as concerned with a "table of contents" as writers are today, and Matthew may have used a variety of structural features simultaneously. Scot McKnight has suggested a mediating outline, whereby the alternating narratives and discourses are organized under an essentially biographical or chronological plot (see fig. 8.4).[8] It is this framework—noting the alternating discourses and narratives but seeking to follow the flow of the story—which we will follow:

1. Prologue: The Genealogy and Birth Narrative (chaps. 1–2)
2. The Appearance of the Messiah (3:1–4:11)
3. The Ministry of the Messiah to Israel (4:12–11:1)
4. The Responses to the Messiah: Rejection by Israel; Acceptance by the Disciples (11:2–20:34)
5. The Messiah Confronts Jerusalem (21:1–26:1)
6. The Messiah Is Rejected Yet Victorious: The Passion and Resurrection (chaps. 26–28)

THE PLOT OF MATTHEW'S GOSPEL

Prologue: The Genealogy and Birth Narrative (Chaps. 1–2)

The **birth narratives** of Matthew and Luke are not comprehensive accounts of Jesus' early life. They are selective introductions, preparing the reader for the narratives that follow. Like the overture of a symphony, they set the stage and summarize the themes. The two accounts differ significantly. Matthew's centers on Joseph, whose dreams and actions stitch the narrative together. Luke's centers on Mary and parallels the births of Jesus and John the Baptist. Both focus on the themes of promise and fulfillment and the arrival of messianic salvation. Jesus is the promised Messiah, the descendant of David born to be king. His coming is the fulfillment of Jewish hopes.

Matthew begins with a genealogy tracing the royal ancestry of Jesus (1:1–17). Modern readers often find genealogies strange, tedious, and even boring. The *Reader's Digest* condensation of the Bible eliminated most of them![9] But from Matthew's Jewish perspective, Jesus' genealogy is profoundly important, confirming his legitimacy as the promised savior and king who will bring Israel's history to its climax. The narrator identifies Jesus as the

---

7. The former has been criticized for glossing over the extended discourse in chapter 23, Jesus' "woes" against the religious leaders. To make the scheme work, chapter 23 must be treated together with the Olivet Discourse, even though the latter has its own narrative introduction (24:1–3). The threefold structure has been criticized because Matthew has taken it over from his source (Mark) and because these verses (4:17; 16:21) do not indicate critical turning points in Matthew's narrative. For a good discussion, see D. R. Bauer, *The Structure of Matthew's Gospel* (Sheffield: Almond, 1988).

8. Scot McKnight, "Matthew, Gospel of," in *DJG*, 531.

9. Bruce M. Metzger, gen. ed., *The Reader's Digest Bible* (Pleasantville, NY: Reader's Digest Association, 1982).

Figure 8.4—Various Suggestions for the Outline of Matthew's Gospel

A "CHRISTIAN PENTATEUCH"
B. W. Bacon

A Christian Pentateuch, with Jesus' five major discourses modeled after the five books of Moses; key transitional phrase, *"And it came about when Jesus finished these words …"*:

Preamble: The Birth Narrative (chaps. 1 – 2)
First Book: Discipleship (3 – 7)
    A. Introductory Narrative (3 – 4)
    B. First Discourse (5 – 7)
Second Book: Apostleship (8 – 10)
    A. Introductory Narrative (8 – 9)
    B. The Discourse (10)
Third Book: Hiding of the Revelation (11 – 13)
    A. Israel Is Stumbled (11 – 12)
    B. Teaching in Parables (13)
Fourth Book: Church Administration (14 – 18)
    A. Jesus and the Brotherhood (14 – 17)
    B. The Discourse (18)
Fifth Book: Judgment (19 – 25)
    A. Jesus in Judea (19 – 22)
    B. Discourse on Judgment to Come (23 – 25)
Epilogue: Passion and Resurrection (26 – 28)

NARRATIVE-DISCOURSE CHIASM (ABBA)
H. J. B. Combrink (and Others)

A chiasmic structure around the alternating discourses and narratives, with the parables of the kingdom as the centerpoint:

  A. 1:1 – 4:17 **Narrative**: The birth and preparation of Jesus.
    B. 4:18 – 7:29 Introductory material, *First Discourse*: Jesus teaches with authority.
      C. 8:1 – 9:35 **Narrative**: Jesus acts with authority — ten miracles.
        D. 9:36 – 11:1 *Second Discourse*: The Twelve commissioned with authority.
          E. 11:2 – 12:50 **Narrative**: The invitation of Jesus rejected by "this generation."
            F. 13:1 – 53 *Third Discourse*: The parables of the kingdom.
          E′. 13:54 – 16:20 **Narrative:** Jesus opposed and confessed, acts in compassion to Jews and Gentiles.
        D′. 16:21 – 20:34 *Fourth Discourse* within **Narrative**: the impending passion of Jesus; lack of understanding of the disciples.
      C′. 21:1 – 22:46 **Narrative**: Jesus' authority questioned in Jerusalem.
    B′. 23:1 – 25:46 *Fifth Discourse:* Judgment on Israel and false prophets.
  A′. 26:1 – 28:20 **Narrative**: The passion, death, and resurrection of Jesus.

continued on next page

NARRATIVE PROGRESSION
J. D. Kingsbury

Following the progress of Jesus' ministry and the transitional formula *"From this time on Jesus began to …"* (Matt. 4:17; 16:21):

I.   The Figure of Jesus Messiah (1:1 – 4:16)

II. The Ministry of Jesus Messiah to Israel and Israel's Repudiation of Jesus (4:17 – 16:20)

III. The Journey of Jesus Messiah to Jerusalem and His Suffering, Death, and Resurrection (16:21 – 28:20)

COMBINATION OUTLINE
Scot McKnight

Alternating discourses and narrative under a chronological and biographical outline focused to the Messiah's confrontation of Israel and her subsequent rejection:

Prologue (1:1 – 2:23)

Introduction (3:1 – 4:11)

1. The Messiah Confronts Israel in His Galilean Ministry (4:12 – 11:1)
    1.1 Narrative: Introduction (4:12 – 22)
        Summary (4:23 – 25)
    1.2 Discourse: The Messiah's Call to Righteousness (5:1 – 7:29)
    1.3 Narrative: The Messiah's Ministry (8:1 – 9:34)
        Summary (9:35; cf. 4:23 – 25)
    1.4 Discourse: The Messiah Extends His Ministry (9:36 – 11:1)

2. The Responses to the Messiah: Rejection and Acceptance from Galilee to Jerusalem (11:2 – 20:34)
    2.1 Narrative: The Messiah Is Rejected by Jewish Leaders but Accepted by Disciples (11:2 – 12:50)
    2.2 Discourse: The Messiah Teaches about the Kingdom (13:1 – 53)
    2.3 Narrative: The Messiah Is Rejected by Jewish Leaders but Accepted by the Disciples: Responses Intensify (13:54 – 17:27)
    2.4 Discourse: The Messiah Instructs on Community Life (18:1 – 19:1)
    2.5 Narrative: The Messiah Instructs on the Way to Jerusalem (19:2 – 20:34)

3. The Messiah Inaugurates the Kingdom of Heaven through Rejection and Vindication: Jesus the Messiah Confronts Jerusalem (21:1 – 28:20)
    3.1 Narrative: The Messiah Confronts Israel in Jerusalem (21:1 – 22:46)
    3.2 Discourse: The Messiah Predicts the Judgment of Unbelieving Israel (23:1 – 26:2)
    3.3 Narrative: The Messiah Is Rejected in Jerusalem but Vindicated by God through Resurrection (26:3 – 28:20)

Modern Bethlehem

"Christ, the son of David, the son of Abraham," and traces his ancestry from Abraham through David to Joseph and Mary. Abraham and David are figures of great importance both in Israel's history and in Matthew's narrative purpose. Abraham was not only the father of the Jewish nation but also the recipient of the promise that all nations would be blessed through him (Gen. 12:2–3). The mission to the Gentiles in Matthew's day thus finds justification in the Abrahamic covenant (Matt. 8:11; 28:18–20). David was Israel's greatest king and the prototype of the coming Messiah. In the Davidic covenant, God promised that through David's "seed" (descendants) the messianic king would come (2 Sam. 7:12–16; Isa. 9:2–7; 11:1–16).

The author's penchant for organization is evident as he structures the genealogy into three sections of fourteen names: Abraham to David, David to the Babylonian exile, the Babylonian exile to the Christ (1:17). The number fourteen may represent twice seven (the number of completion) or, more likely, draws on the numerical value of the Hebrew name David (see fig. 8.5). Since there are names known to be missing from Matthew's genealogy, it is clear that Matthew has intentionally shortened or telescoped the list. This was a common practice in Jewish genealogies and was intended to develop a memorable structure or to emphasize certain individuals.

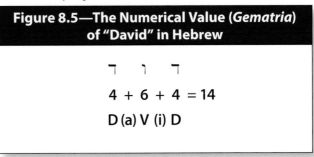

Figure 8.5—The Numerical Value (*Gematria*) of "David" in Hebrew

ד   ו   ד

4 + 6 + 4 = 14

D (a) V (i) D

The structuring of the genealogy around King David and the Babylonian exile is particularly significant. The exile was viewed by Israel's prophets as punishment for the nation's sin and rebellion against God. Since the exile, no Davidic king had reigned in Israel, and many Jews of Jesus' day considered Israel still to be in exile, oppressed by the Gentiles and under God's judgment, awaiting the restoration of the Davidic dynasty by the Messiah. With his genealogy, Matthew announces that Jesus' birth marks the coming of the "Christ," the Messiah who will "save his people from their sins" (1:17, 21) — the very sins which caused the exile.

> Matthew's birth narrative carries forward the theme that Jesus is the promised Messiah who will bring salvation to his people.

Matthew's genealogy is also unusual in its inclusion of five women — Tamar, Rahab, Ruth, the wife of Uriah (Bathsheba), and Mary the mother of Jesus — since women were not normally included in genealogies. Their significance is debated but is probably related to the fact that all were in some sense outsiders (sinners, outcasts, foreigners) whom God used to carry forward his saving purpose. They foreshadow the poor and lowly, the outcasts, and ultimately the Gentiles, who will respond to God's salvation. (On the historical question of the names in the genealogies of Matthew and Luke, see "The Ancestry of Jesus" in chap. 14).

The birth story (1:18 – 2:23) which follows carries forward the theme that Jesus is the promised Messiah who will bring salvation to his people. The narrator repeatedly notes that these events fulfill prophecy. Jesus is born to Joseph, a descendant of David (1:16, 20), in Bethlehem, David's hometown and the prophesied birthplace of the Davidic Messiah (1:23; Mic. 5:2). He will be called Jesus (Hebrew: *Yeshua*, or Joshua), meaning "Yahweh saves" (1:21). His birth to a virgin fulfills Isaiah 7:14 and confirms that he is "God with us" (Immanuel), the presence of God among his people (1:22 – 23).

Left: Modern Bethlehem, view looking east at the plaza and the entrance to the Church of the Nativity. *Right:* The Church of the Nativity in Bethlehem.

The narrative is permeated with the theme of divine purpose and providence. The four dreams of Joseph (and one of the Magi) carry the story forward, confirming that God is in charge, protecting his Anointed One and bringing his salvation plan to pass. Guided by a dream, Joseph risks scandal by marrying Mary (1:20). The first conflict in the story begins as Herod, the illegitimate king of the Jews, seeks to kill Jesus, the legitimate king. The Magi's dream allows them to thwart Herod's plan (2:12). Joseph's three more dreams guide him to escape to Egypt (2:13), to return to Israel after Herod's death (2:20), and to settle in Nazareth (2:22).

Traditional birthplace of Jesus in the Church of the Nativity in Bethlehem. The lower "cave area" is said to be the exact spot.

Through it all, God is orchestrating events, inaugurating his plan of salvation.

As in the genealogy, hints are given that this salvation will extend to the Gentiles. Magi from the East arrive in Jerusalem, seeking the king of the Jews. Their importance in the narrative is to provide confirmation of Jesus' identity through heavenly signs and to show that already Gentiles are seeking and worshiping the Messiah.

The Appearance of the Messiah (3:1 – 4:11)

Following the birth narrative, the narrator provides an introduction to Jesus' public ministry. Like the birth narrative, its main theme is the identity of Jesus. As in the other Gospels, Jesus' public ministry begins with John the Baptist, whose role is to prepare the way for the Messiah and to point people to him. Two events, the baptism and the temptation, set the stage for Jesus' ministry and establish his identity for the implied reader. As in Mark's Gospel, the voice from heaven at Jesus' baptism identifies him as the messianic Son of God (*"This is my beloved son …"*; Ps. 2:7) who will fulfill the role of the suffering Servant of

The Jordan River

Isaiah (" … *with him I am well pleased*"; Isa. 42:1). Matthew has a special interest in both of these titles. Son of God appears at climactic points in the narrative (3:17; 4:3, 6; 14:33; 16:16; 17:5; 27:54). The declaration of Jesus as "my Son" at both the baptism and the transfiguration confirms that this is *God's evaluative point of view of Jesus.* Matthew also shows particular interest in Jesus' role as the Servant of the LORD, the suffering figure who appears in the celebrated "Servant Songs" of Isaiah (Isaiah 42, 49, 50, 53). The extended summary of Jesus' ministry in 12:15 – 21 cites Isaiah 42:1 – 4: "Here

Left: Judean wilderness, where Jesus was tempted for forty days by Satan. *Right:* Mount of Temptation, just west of Jericho, showing the monastery up in the cliffs.

is my servant whom I have chosen, the one I love, in whom I delight; I will put my Spirit on him" (cf. Isa. 53:4 at Matt. 8:16 – 17).

Since righteousness and obedience are key qualities of the Messiah (*Psalms of Solomon* 17), Jesus' testing naturally follows the baptismal announcement. The temptation develops a theme related to his role as Servant and Son: *Jesus as the fulfillment of Israel's role and purpose.* Jesus' forty days of temptation in the wilderness are analogous to Israel's forty years, and the three Old Testament passages Jesus cites in response to Satan's temptations all relate to Israel's failures in the desert (Deut. 8:3; 6:16; 6:13). While God's "son" Israel (Exod. 4:22 – 23) failed when tested, Jesus the true Son remains obedient and emerges victorious.

The identification of Jesus as Son of God, Servant of the LORD, and true Israel are closely related when viewed from the context of Old Testament theology. Just as the nation Israel is sometimes called the son of God (Exod. 4:22 – 23; Hos. 11:1), so the anointed king from David's line is God's son (2 Sam. 7:14; Ps. 2:7; 89:26). This meant that the king had a special relationship with God, serving as his representative to the people and the people's

Figure 8.6—"Out of Egypt I Called My Son"
Does Matthew Play "Fast and Loose" with the Old Testament Text?

Matthew's Jesus-Israel analogy helps to explain his puzzling use of Hosea 11:1 (*"Out of Egypt I called my son"*) as a fulfillment formula in Matthew 2:15. Matthew has been criticized for taking this Old Testament passage out of context, applying it to Jesus' return from Egypt when it was originally about Israel's exodus from Egypt. In fact, the author is developing a sophisticated Israel-Jesus typology. Just as Israel emerged from Egypt in God's great act of salvation, so Jesus, the true Israel, emerges from Egypt to bring salvation to his people. Matthew is not saying that Hosea 11:1 originally referred to Jesus; rather he's saying that Jesus typologically fulfills the role of eschatological Israel. (For more on this, see fig. 8.11.)

representative before him. Similarly, the enigmatic figure of the Servant of the LORD, who repeatedly appears in Isaiah 40–55, is sometimes identified with the nation Israel (Isa. 44:1) and sometimes as an individual who brings salvation to the nation (Isaiah 42, 49, 50, 53). In other words, both the Servant and the Davidic king function as representatives of Israel, fulfilling her role and accomplishing her salvation. It is not surprising, therefore, that Matthew develops a **typology** relating Jesus to Israel as he fulfills the role of both the Servant and the messianic Son of God. (See figs. 8.6 and 8.11.)

> Matthew develops a typology relating Jesus to Israel as he fulfills the role of both the Servant and the messianic Son of God.

The Ministry of the Messiah to Israel (4:12–11:1)

Following Jesus' temptation, the narrator begins the account of Jesus' public ministry with a brief introduction summarizing what will be coming in the next six chapters (4:12–25). The essence of Jesus' preaching is identified (*"Repent, for the kingdom of heaven is near"*; v. 17), his call of disciples is narrated (vv. 18–22), and his preaching and healing ministries are summarized (vv. 23–25). The author's literary skill is on display in the summary of 4:23, which is repeated almost verbatim in 9:35. These two verses form an ***inclusio***, a literary device which bookends the beginning and end of a section. The first bookend (4:23) summarizes what Jesus *will be doing* in the next five chapters: preaching and teaching (chaps. 5–7; *First Discourse*) and healing (chaps. 8–9). The second bookend (9:35) closes out the section by repeating what Jesus *has been doing* (*"preaching the good news of the kingdom and healing every disease and sickness"*). Chapter 10 (*Second Discourse*) then concludes this larger section by describing Jesus' delegation of his mission and authority to the disciples. He instructs them and sends them out *to preach and to heal* (10:7–8); that is, to carry on the

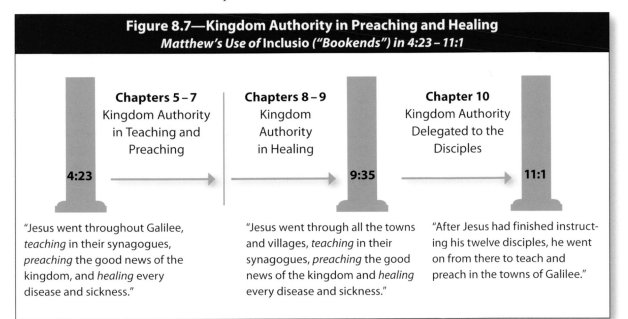

Figure 8.7—Kingdom Authority in Preaching and Healing
Matthew's Use of Inclusio ("Bookends") in 4:23–11:1

Chapters 5–7 Kingdom Authority in Teaching and Preaching	**Chapters 8–9** Kingdom Authority in Healing	**Chapter 10** Kingdom Authority Delegated to the Disciples
4:23	9:35	11:1
"Jesus went throughout Galilee, *teaching* in their synagogues, *preaching* the good news of the kingdom, and *healing* every disease and sickness."	"Jesus went through all the towns and villages, *teaching* in their synagogues, *preaching* the good news of the kingdom and *healing* every disease and sickness."	"After Jesus had finished instructing his twelve disciples, he went on from there to teach and preach in the towns of Galilee."

ministry he has been doing. This passage ends with another summary of Jesus' teaching and preaching (11:1). The large section from 4:12–11:1 thereby provides a well-organized package summarizing the nature of Jesus' ministry and the role his disciples will play in it. (See fig. 8.7.)

Zooming in for a closer look, the **Sermon on the Mount** (chapters 5–7) provides the example *par excellence* of Jesus' teaching: his inaugural kingdom address. In it Jesus identifies himself as the true interpreter of the Old Testament law and the one who fulfills its purpose. As Moses went up to Mount Sinai to receive the first law, so Jesus goes up to a mountain to set forth his new law. He has come not to abolish the law but to fulfill it; that is, to bring it to its prophesied completion in the age of salvation which he is inaugurating (5:17). The old law written on stone is now superseded by the new "law" written on people's hearts (see Jer. 31:33). Jesus repeatedly clarifies the law of Moses, identifying its true intent and raising its standards to a higher plane. Whereas the Mosaic law forbade murder, Jesus

> The Sermon on the Mount provides the example *par excellence* of Jesus' teaching: his inaugural kingdom address.

Figure 8.8—Matthew's Sermon on the Mount

Jesus' most famous sermon is the Sermon on the Mount, recorded in Matthew 5–7. It epitomizes many of Jesus' great teaching themes and serves as his inaugural address for the kingdom of God. Historically, the question arises whether Matthew's sermon is the same as that recorded by Luke in Luke 6:17–49. While there are many similarities, there are also many differences. Matthew's sermon is placed earlier in the Galilean ministry and is much longer than Luke's sermon. Much of its content appears elsewhere in Luke. For example, the Lord's Prayer of Matthew 6:9–13 appears in Luke 11:2–4, and Jesus' exhortation not to worry in Matthew 6:25–34 appears in Luke 12:22–31. At the same time, there are many agreements. Both sermons begin with Beatitudes and end with the account of the wise and foolish builders. Both include Jesus' teaching on love for enemies, judging others, and a tree's being known by its fruit.

The position of the sermon in Matthew's Gospel is not really a problem, since Matthew frequently follows a topical rather than a chronological order. He may have moved the sermon forward to serve as Jesus' inaugural address (just as Luke did with the Nazareth sermon in Luke 4:16–30). While some have contrasted the setting of the sermons, calling Matthew's the Sermon on the *Mount* and Luke's the Sermon on the *Plain*, such a distinction is unnecessary. Luke speaks not of a plain but rather of a "level place" to which Jesus descends after a night of prayer on the mountain (6:12, 17). The implication is that Jesus was seeking a level place or plateau on the mountain where he could teach.

It is probably best to conclude that these are two versions of the same sermon. The differences in content may be explained by some combination of the following: (1) Both Gospel writers may be abbreviating and editing a much longer address by Jesus. (2) Matthew may have brought together a synopsis of Jesus' kingdom preaching. (3) Under the inspiration of the Holy Spirit, both writers had the freedom to explain or interpret Jesus' sayings. For example, Matthew may well have interpreted Jesus' original Beatitude, "Blessed are the poor" (Luke 6:20) with the clarification "Blessed are the poor *in spirit*" (Matt. 5:3).

The Hill of Beatitudes, the traditional site of Jesus' Sermon on the Mount. The Sea of Galilee is in the background.

now forbids even anger, which is murder committed in one's heart. Whereas the Mosaic law forbade adultery, the law of the kingdom forbids lust—adultery of the heart. These are new standards for the new age of salvation. (See more on the law under "Theological Themes" later in this chapter.)

If the Sermon on the Mount demonstrates Jesus' kingdom-authority in teaching (see the summary in 7:28), chapters 8–9 reveal his kingdom-authority through healing and exorcism. The primary significance of these miracles is *to confirm the coming of the king-*

Mount Beatitudes Church

dom through Jesus' words and deeds. As in Mark's Gospel, this introductory section is also marked by the beginning of conflict with the religious leaders. They challenge Jesus' authority to forgive sins (9:3), despise him for associating with sinners (9:11), and accuse him of casting out demons by the prince of demons (9:34). Matthew delays recounting the more serious Sabbath controversies (12:1–13) until the next major section (11:2–19:1), which deals in-depth with the rejection of Jesus by Israel's leaders.

Chapter 10 (*Second Discourse*) forms the conclusion of this first section of Jesus' ministry.

The theme is discipleship, as Jesus commissions and sends out the Twelve to preach and to heal as he has been doing. Their mission at this time, like Jesus', is only to "the lost sheep of Israel." They are not (yet) to go to the Gentiles or Samaritans (10:5–6; cf. 15:24). Jesus repeatedly emphasizes the opposition and persecution they will encounter, both from the Jews, who will flog them in their synagogues, and from Gentile rulers (10:17–18). In line with his organizational tendencies, Matthew appears to have brought together a variety of material on the role of disciples. Material which occurs in various contexts in Mark and Luke (the mission of the Twelve, the mission of the Seventy, the Olivet Discourse, etc.) appears here in one great commissioning sermon. The purpose of this section is to set out the requirements of discipleship (chap. 10) in light of the nature and significance of Jesus' ministry (chaps. 4–9). The fact that the commission Jesus gives concerns only the mission to Israel sets the stage for the next major section (11:2–19:1), which appropriately records the response of Israel's religious leaders and Jesus' disciples to his ministry. Only after Israel has had her chance to receive or reject the gospel will Jesus give the **Great Commission** to go to all nations (28:18–20).

> The primary significance of Jesus' miracles is to confirm the coming of the kingdom through Jesus' words and deeds.

The Responses to the Messiah: Rejection by Israel, Acceptance by the Disciples (11:2–20:34)

The dual themes which hold this section together are the responses, positive and negative, to Jesus' ministry. On the one hand, there is increasing rejection by and animosity from the religious leaders. On the other, there is a degree of acceptance and understanding on the part of the disciples. The stage is set for these dual themes by the question of John the Baptist from prison: "Are you the one who was to come [the Messiah]?" Jesus responds by defining his ministry as the great end-times restoration promised in Isaiah (35:4–6; 61:1) and then pronounces a blessing on those who do not "fall away on account of me" (11:4–6). The time for decision is now. With the coming of John the forerunner and Jesus the Messiah, the age of promise is giving way to the age of fulfillment (11:12–15). Jesus denounces "this generation" for rejecting both John's somber call for repentance and his own joyful announcement of the kingdom (11:16–19).

The negative theme of rejection continues in a series of disputes, including Sabbath controversies (12:1–13), challenges over clean and unclean foods (15:1–10), and demands for a sign (12:38–45; 16:1–4). This growing conflict is epitomized in the Beelzebub controversy and its aftermath (12:22–50). By accusing Jesus of casting out demons by Satan's power, the religious leaders commit the blasphemy of the Holy Spirit, an unforgivable sin (12:24–32). Their fate is now sealed, and Jesus begins teaching in absolute terms of their rejection. They are "bad trees" which cannot bear any good fruit (12:33), a "brood of vipers" and "evil men" (12:34); they are a "wicked generation" (12:45), "hypocrites" (15:7), and "blind guides" (15:14). No more signs will be given to them, except the sign of Jonah (Jesus' death and resurrection; 12:39–41).

The **parables of the kingdom** appear in the middle of this section and serve as its structural and thematic climax (chap. 13; *Third Discourse*). When the disciples ask why Jesus speaks in parables, he responds that while the secrets of the kingdom of God have been given to them, they have been withheld from others. This is because "though seeing, they do not see; though hearing, they do not hear or understand." Quoting Isaiah 6:9–10, Jesus explains that those whose hearts are dull will continue to be blinded to the truth (13:13–15). There is a sense of finality here. As in Isaiah's day, only judgment awaits those who have rejected God's messenger.

In contrast to this rejection by Israel's leaders is a measure of acceptance by the disciples. They are the ones to whom the Son reveals the Father (11:27), his true spiritual family (12:49). While the parables conceal the message from those who are hard-hearted, they also reveal the secrets of the kingdom to those who respond positively to Jesus' kingdom preaching (13:11–12). When Jesus asks the disciples if they have understood the parables, they answer in the affirmative (13:51).

> While the parables conceal the message from those who are hard-hearted, they reveal the secrets of the kingdom to those who respond positively to Jesus' kingdom preaching.

It is true that Matthew's disciples, like Mark's, often show spiritual dullness, lack of faith, and pride.[10] Yet they also reveal some awareness of Jesus' identity. When Jesus walks on water and calms the storm, the disciples are not just amazed (as in Mark) but confess, "Truly you are the Son of God" (14:33). In Mark, Jesus does not respond to Peter's confession but immediately redirects the disciples toward his coming death (Mark 8:29–30). In Matthew, by way of contrast, Jesus commends Peter ("Blessed are you, Simon son of Jonah") and then predicts his authoritative role in the church ("I will give you the keys of the kingdom"; Matt. 16:16–20). Similarly, in the transfiguration account which follows, Matthew omits Mark's comment about Peter's fear and ignorance, which motivated his statement about building booths (Mark 9:6; Matt. 17:4–5). Together, these render Peter's confession more significant by showing that the disciples' evaluative point of view is, at least in part, in line with God's. They still falter, as Jesus' rebuke of Peter reveals (16:23), but they remain part of Israel's faithful remnant, who are responding positively to Jesus' kingdom announcement.

Matthew's two references to the still-future church also indicate a more positive attitude toward the disciples, since they will assume its authoritative leadership (16:18; 18:18). Matthew alone includes Jesus' extended discourse on church life and discipline (*Fourth Discourse*; chap. 18). While the disciples will fail miserably during Jesus' arrest and crucifixion,[11] they are clearly on Jesus' side and so stand in stark contrast to the religious leaders. Though they will fall, they will also be restored. Indeed, when the Son of Man sits on his glorious throne, they "will also sit on twelve thrones, judging the twelve tribes of Israel" (19:28).

---

10. Matt. 6:30; 8:26; 14:31; 15:16; 16:23; 17:20; 20:24; 26:8, 36–46, 56, 69–75.
11. Matt. 26:31, 36–46, 56, 69–75.

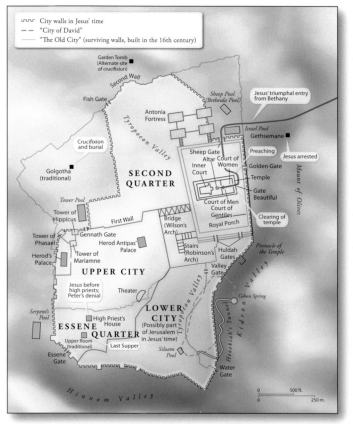

Map of the triumphal entry path into Jerusalem

The Messiah Confronts Jerusalem (21:1–26:1)

Jesus' arrival in Jerusalem is marked by (1) public acts which announce his messiahship and (2) direct confrontation of Israel's leaders. Three times on his way to Jerusalem Jesus has predicted that he is going there to suffer, die, and rise again (16:21; 17:9–11; 20:17–19), and now he takes decisive steps to bring this to pass.

As in Mark's Gospel, Jesus' approach to Jerusalem represents a public announcement of his messiahship. By arranging to enter Jerusalem riding a colt,[12] Jesus fulfills the messianic prophecy of Zechariah 9:9, which Matthew cites in a formula quotation (21:5). The crowd accompanying Jesus expresses the messianic significance of the event by crying out, "Hosanna to the Son of David!" and, "Blessed is he who comes in the name of the Lord" (21:9).[13] **Son of David** is one of Matthew's favorite titles for the Messiah, appearing nine times in the Gospel.[14] "Blessed is he who comes" is an allusion to Psalm 118:26, which Jesus will quote at 23:39 with reference to Jerusalem's rejection and coming judgment. While Jesus enters Jerusalem as the Messiah, Israel's leaders will acknowledge this only when he comes again in judgment.

Jesus' messianic actions continue as he clears the money changers from the temple (21:12–16). Since the temple represents the religious center of Israel and the power base for the religious leaders, Jesus here directly challenges their authority. He then uses the temple as a place of healing for the blind and the lame (his messianic mission as the Servant of the Lord;

---

12. The other Synoptics mention only the colt, while Matthew refers to a colt and a donkey (its mother) and says that Jesus approached the city riding on "them." Some interpreters claim that Matthew has misunderstood the poetic parallelism in Zechariah 9:9, thinking the donkey and the colt are two different animals and so presenting an almost comical image of Jesus riding two animals at once. But it hardly seems likely that a Jewish writer of Matthew's abilities would so blatantly misunderstand Hebrew poetry. A better explanation is that there were two animals (an unridden colt would naturally be accompanied by its mother), and Matthew's "them" is a general statement about the procession.

13. While this acclamation fulfills the narrator's purpose of presenting Jesus as the royal Messiah, it seems at cross-purposes with his presentation elsewhere, where the crowds appear ignorant of Jesus' identity. Yet even here the crowds are ambivalent. When the people of Jerusalem wonder, "Who is this?" the crowds acknowledge only that he is "the prophet from Nazareth in Galilee" (21:11). Though Jesus enters Jerusalem as the Messiah, the crowds recognize him as a prophet. These same fickle crowds will subsequently reject him and call for his crucifixion (27:20–25).

14. Matt. 1:1; 9:27; 12:23; 15:22; 20:30, 31; 21:9, 15; 22:42.

see 11:4–6). While the Jerusalem leaders have turned the temple into a "den of thieves," Jesus reestablishes it as a house of prayer and a place of healing. The messianic significance of these events is evident as children shout the same cry as the crowds entering Jerusalem: "Hosanna to the Son of David!" The religious leaders object, but Jesus points out that this too is a fulfillment of prophecy: "From the lips of children and infants you have ordained praise" (21:16, citing Ps. 8:2). While Israel's religious elite fail to recognize Jesus' identity, children—those with no social status in Israel—proclaim him as the Messiah. The passage not only reminds the reader of the positive response Jesus has been receiving from other outsiders (sinners, the poor, Gentiles) but also recalls Jesus' prayer in 11:25–30, in which he praises God for revealing the truth to "little children" but hiding it from "the wise and learned." Those who wish to enter the kingdom of heaven must become like little children, receiving it with faith and humility (18:2–4).

> While the Jerusalem leaders have turned the temple into a "den of thieves," Jesus reestablishes it as a house of prayer and a place of healing.

Jesus performs a third messianic action on the following morning, cursing a barren fig tree, which immediately withers (21:18–22).[15] Like the clearing of the temple, this is a symbolic act of judgment. Israel's rejection of her Messiah confirms that her religious life is barren and so she faces judgment (see Mic. 7:1, which similarly portrays Israel as a barren fig tree).

The rest of the week leading up to Jesus' arrest is marked by his conflict with the religious leaders. There are three stages of this conflict: (1) controversies and debates with the religious leaders (21:23–22:46), (2) Jesus' "woes" or denunciations against the religious leaders (chap. 23), and (3) the **Olivet Discourse** (chaps. 24–25).

In the first series of controversies, the religious leaders challenge Jesus concerning his authority (21:23–27) and repeatedly attempt to trap him in his words (22:15–22, 23–33, 34–40). Jesus, in response, tells three parables central to Matthew's narrative purpose. All three allegorically depict the religious leaders: the first as a *son* who claims he will work for the father but then fails to show up (21:28–32), the second as *tenant farmers* who reject the vineyard owner and murder his son (21:33–45), and the third as *guests* who reject the king's invitation to the wedding banquet of his son (22:1–14). All three have the same central theme: Israel's leaders, though spiritual insiders, are rejecting God's purpose revealed through Jesus and so will suffer judgment. Meanwhile, outsiders will receive God's salvation blessings.

Throughout this sequence, the narrator presents Jesus as defeating his opponents and shaming them with his superior wisdom (see fig. 7.6, pp. 188–89). Finally, Jesus confounds them with a question of his own concerning the identity of the Messiah as both Son of David and David's Lord (22:41–45). The sequence ends with the narrative conclusion that "no one could say a word in reply, and from that day on no one dared to ask him any more questions" (22:46). The implication is that if the religious leaders cannot defeat Jesus in debate, they will have to find other means to destroy him.

Chapter 23 presents Jesus' response to the previous challenges. He sets out a series of seven "woes," scathing denunciations against the Pharisees and the scribes for their blindness,

---

15. Matthew, as he often does, abbreviates the event by bringing together a story which Mark tells in two parts.

hypocrisy, and evil intentions. These "woes" are followed by Jesus' eschatological sermon, or Olivet Discourse (chaps. 24–25), so called because it is given on the Mount of Olives (24:3). In the "five discourses" outline of Matthew, chapter 23 is treated together with chapters 24–25 as the *Fifth Discourse.* In one sense, this is problematic, since the Olivet Discourse is clearly distinguished by its change in setting and narrative introduction (24:1–3). At the same time, it represents a natural sequel to chapter 23, since Jesus' prediction of Jerusalem's destruction (24:2) represents judgment against those he has denounced in chapter 23. This connection is made clear at the end of chapter 23. Jesus calls

> In chapter 23, Jesus sets out a series of seven "woes," scathing denunciations against the Pharisees and the scribes for their blindness, hypocrisy, and evil intentions.

the religious leaders a "brood of vipers" and predicts that just as they have persecuted God's messengers in the past, so they will persecute and kill the messengers he is sending to them in the future. The blood of God's righteous messengers that they have shed will return against them in their own judgment and destruction (23:33–36). Like a mother hen, Jesus has longed to gather Jerusalem's children under his protective wings, but they were unwilling. Consequently, their house will be left desolate (23:37–39, citing Ps. 118:26). Jesus' message here extends beyond his own ministry to the future persecution of his disciples and the coming judgment against Jerusalem. The Olivet Discourse which follows picks up these two themes: the destruction of Jerusalem and the responsibilities of Jesus' disciples till the end of the age.

Z. Radovan, Jerusalem

The Seat of Moses was the chair in the synagogue where the scribes sat teaching the Mosaic law. This particular chair was in a synagogue on the Island of Delos.

The Olivet Discourse is set in the context of Jesus' prediction of the temple's destruction (24:1) and the disciples' question, "When will this happen, and what will be the sign of your coming and of the end of the age?" (24:3). In Mark, the disciples ask two questions about one event: the time and signs related to the temple's destruction (Mark 13:4). In Matthew, two events are queried: (1) the time of the destruction of the temple and (2) the signs related to Jesus' return at the end of the age. As we noted in chapter 7, the interpretation of the discourse is problematic because it is difficult to tell which event Jesus is describing at any particular point. Is the discourse primarily about the destruction of Jerusalem, or the coming of the Son of Man? Or is it both? (See fig. 7.8 for possible solutions.) Jesus affirms that many things will take place before the end: the appearance of false messiahs, wars, earthquakes, famines, persecution, the empire-wide preaching of the gospel (24:4–14). The climax to these events will be the "abomination of desolation" spoken of by Daniel the prophet. When God's people see this, they should flee to the mountains, for it will be a time of great suffering and calamity (24:15–25). Yet from this great suffering will come their deliverance: the Son of Man will be seen coming in the clouds of heaven and sending his angels to gather the elect (24:30–31).

View from the top of the Mount of Olives looking northwest and down toward the eastern wall of the Old City of Jerusalem

While many signs will precede the end, no one knows the precise day or hour of Jesus' return, except the Father alone (24:36). In light of this uncertainty, Jesus' disciples are called to be constantly alert and prepared, exercising good stewardship of time and resources (24:36–51). The three parables which conclude the discourse all point to this theme of the responsibilities of disciples to readiness (25:1–13), faithful stewardship (25:14–30), and loving service to fellow believers (25:31–46).

The Messiah Is Rejected: Arrest, Trial, and Crucifixion (Chaps. 26–27)

Following the Olivet Discourse, events in the Gospel move rapidly toward Jesus' arrest and crucifixion. The narrator sets the stage with Jesus' fourth passion prediction (26:2) and with a description of the plot of the chief priests and elders (26:3–4). The irony is that both Jesus and the religious leaders are moving toward the same goal, but for vastly different reasons. From their evaluative point of view, the leaders are seeking to rid Israel of a deceiver and blasphemer, and to protect their authority to lead the people. Jesus, however, is in line with God's evaluative point of view. His sacrificial death will accomplish God's purpose to bring salvation to the world. Though seemingly the victim, he is fully in charge of his destiny. These two parallel purposes play themselves out in the following scenes. Judas Iscariot carries forward the purpose of the religious leaders by betraying Jesus to them (26:14–16). But Jesus is already aware of the plot, identifying Judas as betrayer at the Last Supper (26:20–25) and then interpreting his death as the sacrificial "blood of the covenant" which will bring forgiveness of sins (26:28–29). Jesus knows too that the disciples will all desert him, that Peter will deny him,

> The irony is that both Jesus and the religious leaders are moving toward the same goal, but for vastly different reasons.

but that they will be restored after the resurrection (26:31–35). In Gethsemane, the plot against Jesus is successfully hatched as Judas arrives with a crowd to seize him (26:47–49). Yet Jesus is in charge even here, commanding Judas to "do what you came for" and then ordering his disciples to stop resisting. If he wished, he could call on his Father to send twelve legions of angels to his rescue, "But how then would the Scriptures be fulfilled?" (26:50–54). He rebukes the crowd for coming deceitfully at night to arrest him, but then adds that even this occurred "that the writings of the prophets might be fulfilled" (26:55–56). Through apparent defeat, Jesus is controlling his fate, steadfastly carrying out the plan of God prophesied in Scripture.

> Through apparent defeat, Jesus is controlling his fate, steadfastly carrying out the plan of God prophesied in Scripture.

Throughout these scenes, the disciples stand by as impotent spectators, ignorant of God's purpose and faltering in their loyalty to Jesus. When Jesus is anointed with expensive perfume by a woman in Bethany, they complain about the waste, while Jesus praises her devotion in preparing his body for burial (26:6–13). When at the Last Supper Jesus predicts their desertion and Peter's denial, they all deny it (26:31–35). Yet in Gethsemane, they cannot even stay awake (26:36–46). The narrator ends the arrest narrative with the dismal conclusion, "Then all the disciples deserted him and fled" (26:56). During Jesus' trial, Peter fulfills Jesus' prophecy by denying him three times (26:69–75). As in Mark's Gospel, the disciples' failure stands in stark contrast to Jesus' faithfulness. It also stands in contrast to the women, who do not fear but remain physically loyal throughout the crucifixion (27:55–56, 61).

The duplicity of the religious leaders reaches its climax at Jesus' trial before the Sanhedrin (26:57–68). They seek "false evidence" and produce "false witnesses" against him. Jesus remains silent to their accusations until the high priest charges him under oath to answer whether he is "the Christ, the Son of God." Jesus' enigmatic response, "You have said it," must be seen as an affirmation, since the high priest subsequently accuses him of blasphemy. It is, however, a qualified affirmation, for the Sanhedrin's conception of the Messiah is very different from that of Jesus. Jesus therefore qualifies by saying, "But I say to all of you: In the future you will see the Son of Man sitting at the right hand of the Mighty One and coming on the clouds of heaven." The first half of this statement alludes to the enthronement of the Messiah in Psalm 110:1, the second to the coming of the Son of Man in Daniel 7:13. Together they indicate that the messianic Son of Man will be vindicated at his heavenly enthronement at God's right hand, from whence he will return to judge the wicked. Jesus claims not only to be the Messiah but also that he will one day judge those who are now judging him!

The high priest's question and the trial scene as a whole recall for the reader Jesus' parable of the wicked tenant farmers (21:33–46), in which the tenants kill the owner's son in order to inherit the vineyard for themselves. In the same way, the high priest now accuses Jesus of blasphemy, and the Sanhedrin condemns him as worthy of death. After mocking and abusing him, they deliver him over to Pilate.

An alabaster jar for perfume

© Neal Bierling/Zondervan Image Archives

Above: Gethsemane. View of old olive trees in the garden next to the Church of All Nations.
Right: Bottom of the Kidron Valley with its spring and olive trees, looking up at the East Gate (Golden Gate). Jesus and his disciples would have passed this way and viewed a similar scene.

Matthew's account of the trial before Pilate portrays the governor as a bit player molded by the evil will of the religious leaders. Though he recognizes Jesus' innocence both by his own judgment (27:23) and by his wife's dream (27:19), he nevertheless turns Jesus over to be crucified. His unwillingness to take responsibility for his actions, demonstrated symbolically by washing his hands (27:24), stands in stark contrast to the willingness of the people of Israel to accept culpability. Persuaded by the religious leaders, the crowds choose Barabbas over Jesus (27:20), repeatedly call for Jesus' crucifixion (27:22–23), and climactically cry out, "Let his blood be on us and on our children!" (27:25). This shocking line, which through the centuries has been tragically misunderstood to justify anti-Semitism, must be viewed in its narrative context and in the context of the Jewish-Christian community to which Matthew is writing. From a narrative perspective, the implied reader recognizes that the crowd and their children will receive God's judgment for their rejection of the Messiah in the coming destruction of Jerusalem (23:38; 24:2). From a historical perspective, Matthew's churches will view Jerusalem's destruction both as *judgment* against Israel for her rejection of God's messenger of salvation and as *vindication* that God's plan of salvation is moving forward through the church of the risen Messiah, Jesus Christ.

> Matthew's account of the trial before Pilate portrays the governor as a bit player molded by the evil will of the religious leaders.

The crucifixion of Jesus in Matthew is full of ironic tragedy. The soldiers dress Jesus regally and mock and abuse him as the "king of the Jews" (27:27–31, 37). Passersby, the religious leaders, and even the criminals crucified with Jesus mock him as the "king of Israel" and the "Son of God." "If he saved others, why can't he save himself!" "If he is the Son of God, why doesn't God rescue him!" (26:39–44). The heavy irony is that Jesus is everything they mock him as: the king of Israel, the Son of God, the savior. Yet by willingly submitting to death, he will bring salvation to others and reveal himself to be the king of Israel and the Son of God.

This point is dramatically brought home by four events which accompany Jesus' death. As in Mark, the curtain of the temple is torn, confirming that a new way to God's presence has been opened up through Jesus' death. Second, an earthquake occurs, splitting rocks and opening tombs. Earthquakes in Scripture demonstrate God's awesome power and judgment and often carry eschatological significance.[16] Here the earthquake probably signifies both God's judgment against sin and the cosmic disturbances associated with the arrival of the kingdom of God, the dawn of the age of salvation. This interpretation is reinforced by the third event, Matthew's unique and puzzling reference to the tombs being opened and the resurrection of many "holy ones."[17] While this passage raises many historical questions,[18] its theological significance in Matthew seems clear: the death and resurrection of Jesus represents the dawn of the new age and the beginning of the final resurrection.

The fourth event serves as the climax of the crucifixion scene. The centurion and those with him exclaim, "Surely he was the Son of God!" (27:54). While Jesus' opponents have mocked this claim, the centurion and his companions affirm it, recognizing in Jesus' death and its accompanying events God's approval of Jesus' mission. Their evaluative point of view now comes in line with God's, as expressed at the baptism and the transfiguration. While Peter and the other disciples had previously identified Jesus as the Son of God (14:33; 16:16), these Gentile soldiers are the first to acknowledge that this sonship is revealed not through conquest but through his sacrificial death.

The Messiah Is Vindicated: The Resurrection and the Great Commission (Chap. 28)

Matthew's resurrection narrative brings the plot to its resolution, vindicating Jesus' identity and mission and restoring the disciples to their position as Jesus' representatives for leadership over his church. The religious leaders, in contrast, continue to appear as evil and duplicitous, seeking to cover up the resurrection with lies about a stolen body even though they know the truth (28:11 – 15).

Matthew's account of the resurrection does not have the same ambiguity and mystery as Mark's, since two resurrection appearances are narrated. These provide a greater sense of resolution and vindication. The first resurrection appearance is to the two Marys. Following the angelic announcement of the resurrection at the tomb, they meet Jesus, who tells them to report the resurrection to his "brothers"—the disciples—and that he will meet them in Galilee (cf. 26:32). Jesus' use of the term "brothers" confirms the restoration of the

---

16. Isa. 2:19, 21; 13:13; 24:18; 29:5 – 6; Ezek. 38:19; Joel 2:10; Zech. 14:1 – 10; Heb. 12:25 – 29; Rev. 6:12; 8:5; 11:13, 19; 16:18.

17. The narrator appears to have condensed events here (as elsewhere in the Gospel), intending to communicate that while the earthquake opened the tombs, the saints rose and entered the city "after the resurrection" (27:53). This interpretation excludes the strange scene of people wandering for two days (prior to Jesus' resurrection) before entering Jerusalem, and also conforms with New Testament teaching that Jesus was the "firstfruits of the dead" (1 Cor. 15:20, 23; cf. Col. 1:18). His resurrection begins the end-times resurrection.

18. Questions such as, Is this event historical or symbolic? Did these saints rise in glorified bodies? If so, where did they go next? If not, did they die again?

disciples, since he has earlier identified his true family members as those who do the will of his father (12:50).

The second resurrection appearance is to the eleven disciples in Galilee and contains the Great Commission (28:18–20). This final commission may be viewed as a thematic summary of the Gospel, bringing the plot to its resolution and carrying forward important themes. First, Jesus' *authority* to speak and act on God's behalf is now made universal and complete by virtue of his vindication in resurrection. Second, as in chapter 10, Jesus *delegates this authority to the disciples* to make disciples, baptize, and teach all he has commanded them. They are his representatives in the present age. Third, while the first mission of the disciples was only to Israel, now it is expanded to the whole world, *to make disciples of all nations.* Finally, the success of this worldwide mission is assured because *his absolute authority and abiding presence will sustain the disciples.* The Gospel which began with the announcement that Jesus is Immanuel, "God with us" (1:23), ends with the promise that he will be with his disciples till the end of the age (28:20).

> While the first mission of the disciples was only to Israel, now it is expanded to the whole world, to make disciples of all nations.

MATTHEW'S PORTRAIT OF JESUS: THE MESSIAH

As in the other Gospels, Jesus is the leading character and the chief protagonist in Matthew. Everything Jesus says and does represents the evaluative point of view of God. Those who side with Jesus are on the side of God. Those who oppose him are opposing God's purpose and plan. Two main portraits control Matthew's Christology: (1) Jesus as *the Messiah, the fulfillment of God's promises* and (2) Jesus as *Immanuel, the presence and wisdom of God.* A third important theme, Jesus as *the Son of God*, appears to integrate these two.

Jesus the Messiah

The identity of Jesus is set out in the first sentence of the Gospel: he is "Jesus Christ, the son of David, the son of Abraham" (1:1). While in many New Testament contexts Christ (*christos*) functions almost as a last name for Jesus, here it clearly serves as a title, meaning the Messiah or the Anointed One (cf. 1:16–17; 2:4). Jesus is the promised king from David's line who will bring salvation to his people. This identification of Jesus as the royal or Davidic Messiah takes center stage throughout the birth narrative, functioning as Matthew's foundational category for Jesus (1:1, 16–17, 20; 2:2, 4–6).

This royal messianic theme is evident in the narrator's fondness for the title Son of David, which is applied to Jesus nine times in the Gospel (only three times each in Mark and Luke). In Judaism, this title often carried strong political connotations. Like the great warrior King David, the son of David would lead God's people in victory over their enemies (see, for example, *Psalms of Solomon* 17–18). Matthew does not shy away from this politically volatile title. Jesus is indeed the promised Messiah, the king from David's line, who will bring salvation and restoration. Yet Matthew links the title especially to Jesus' humble presence (21:1–11) and compassionate healing ministry (9:27; 12:22–23; 15:22; 20:30–31; 21:14–15). Those with physical needs cry out for mercy from the "son of David" and receive healing. When John the Baptist hears of the "deeds of the Christ" and questions whether he is indeed the coming one, Jesus points not to political ambitions but to his healings and exorcisms (11:2–6). Jesus' messiahship is revealed not first through conquest but through self-sacrificial love and service.

While the Davidic Messiah serves as Matthew's foundational category, it by no means exhausts his messianic portrait of Jesus. As we have seen, for Matthew, Jesus is also the son of Abraham, the Son of God, the Son of Man, the suffering Servant, the new Moses, and the true Israel. What do all of these titles and typologies have in common? All are intimately connected to the Old Testament and to the theme of promise and fulfillment. All point to the coming of the salvation available through Jesus. For Matthew, Jesus fulfills it all: all of God's promises and covenants, to Abraham, Moses, and David. He fulfills the eschatological role of Israel, of the Servant and of the Son of Man. He is the climax of salvation history, the inaugurator of God's reign. It is not quite right to say that Matthew subsumes these other titles and images under that of the Messiah. It is better to say that Matthew's conception of the Messiah broadens to include these Old Testament motifs. Jesus the Messiah does not fulfill just part of Scripture. He fulfills it all.

> Matthew presents Jesus as the promised Messiah, the king from David's line, who will bring salvation and restoration.

Immanuel: The Presence and Wisdom of God

While Matthew's portrait of Jesus may be called thoroughly messianic (relating to promise and fulfillment), there are also indications that Jesus' identity exceeds traditional messianic categories. In this regard, we may point to various "divine" or "transcendent" features of Matthew's Christology. From the start, the reader learns that Jesus is Immanuel—"God with us" (1:23). While this could refer generally to Jesus as God's representative, there are indications that it carries a deeper significance, that Jesus is the very presence of God. In the Sermon on the Mount, Jesus quotes the Old Testament law, *"It has been said . . ."* then provides a clarification *"but I say to you . . ."* The phrase echoes the authoritative Old Testament pronouncement "Thus says the LORD" and suggests that the words of Jesus are the words of God. Jesus also exercises functions and prerogatives traditionally associated with God. He forgives sins (9:2) and knows the thoughts of human beings (9:4; 12:25; 22:18). While affirming that people should worship God alone (4:10), he repeatedly receives and accepts worship from others (2:11; 8:2; 9:18; 14:33; 15:25; 20:20; 28:9, 17).

Similarly, Jesus speaks and acts in ways which recall Old Testament language related to God. He sends prophets and wise men and teachers to Israel (Matt. 23:34). As God is a protective mother bird for his people (Pss. 17:8–9; 91:4; Isa. 31:5), so Jesus longs to gather Jerusalem to himself like a mother hen (Matt. 23:37). When the Son of Man comes to establish "his kingdom" (the kingdom of God) he will send "his angels" (God's angels) to gather the elect (Matt. 13:41; 24:31; cf. 15:31; 16:21, 28). At the final judgment, he will determine the eternal destiny of all human beings (25:31–46; 7:21–23). Perhaps most significant, in language reminiscent of the omnipresent Spirit of God in the Old Testament, Jesus promises his presence with his disciples whenever they gather in his name (18:20), even to the end of the age (28:20). While Matthew never explicitly identifies Jesus as God, the baptismal formula in 28:19 comes close, placing him in relational equality with the Father and the Holy Spirit.

Closely related to this divine language is Matthew's portrait of Jesus as the wisdom of God. In the Old Testament book of Proverbs, wisdom is sometimes personified as a woman who brings God's truth to human beings (Proverbs 1–9). This wisdom tradition underwent significant development in later Jewish literature, in which the woman Wisdom is portrayed as being with God before the creation of the world and coming to earth to teach human beings.[19] Jesus' statement in 11:25–30 about the unique relationship between the Father and the Son and about taking up his yoke has striking parallels in this wisdom tradition (see fig.

> In addition to portraying Jesus as the mighty Messiah, in Matthew Jesus speaks and acts in ways which recall Old Testament language related to God.

8.9). Similarly, the "deeds" of wisdom Jesus refers to in 11:19 are no doubt the "deeds" of the Messiah described in 11:2–6. As God's wisdom, Jesus speaks the words of God.

Figure 8.9—Jesus as God's Wisdom in Matthew's Gospel	
Matthew	**Jewish Wisdom Tradition**
"Come to me, all you who are weary and burdened, and I will give you rest. Take my yoke upon you and learn from me, for I am gentle and humble in heart, and you will find rest for your souls. For my yoke is easy and my burden is light." —Matthew 11:28–30 (NIV)	"Draw near to me, you who are uneducated, and lodge in the house of instruction.… Acquire wisdom for yourselves without money. Put your neck under her yoke, and let your souls receive instruction … See with your own eyes that I have labored but little and found for myself much serenity." —Sirach 51:23, 25–27 (NRSV)

Jesus the Son of God

J. D. Kingsbury has argued in various articles and books that Son of God is Matthew's most important designation for Jesus.[20] There is much evidence to support this claim. The theme appears at critical points in Matthew's narrative, particularly those which relate to Jesus' essential identity. God himself, whose evaluative point of view is always determinative, declares Jesus to be his Son both at the baptism and the transfiguration (3:17; 17:5). Jesus' supernatural enemies, Satan and the demons, recognize him as such (8:29; 4:3, 6). Indeed, the whole temptation narrative revolves around the theme "If you are the Son of God …" (4:3, 6). Jesus' disciples come to this recognition at climactic points in the narrative. After the calming of the storm, they worship Jesus and declare him to be the Son of God. Peter confesses him to be not just "the Christ" (as in Mark) but "the Christ, the Son of the living

---

19. Sirach; Wisdom of Solomon 6:12–11:1; Baruch 3; 1 Enoch 42.
20. See, for example, Kingsbury, *Matthew: Structure, Christology, Kingdom*.

God" (16:16). At Jesus' trial, the high priest questions whether he is "the Christ, the Son of God," and Jesus responds affirmatively. On the cross, Jesus is repeatedly and ironically mocked as the Son of God (27:40, 43). As in Mark, the climax of the crucifixion scene is the centurion's cry, "Surely he was the Son of God." Finally, the Great Commission commands baptism in the name of the Father, *the Son*, and the Holy Spirit (28:19). When we add to these Jesus' self-identification as "the son" both in parable (21:37; 22:2) and in teaching (11:27; 24:36), and his many references to God as his Father, it is clear that this portrait is an important one for Matthew.

What, then, is its significance? A likely answer is that for Matthew, this designation brings together the messianic and transcendent features of Jesus' identity, epitomizing his person and mission. In some contexts, the title clearly carries messianic implications, referring to Jesus as the promised king from David's line (8:29; 16:16; 26:63; 27:40, 54). In other contexts, divine sonship carries a more transcendent sense, referring to the unique and intimate relationship between the Father and the Son (11:25–27; 26:39; 28:19). The Father commits all things to the Son, who alone knows and reveals the Father (11:27). Ultimately, the title identifies Jesus as the obedient Son, who reveals the Father's will, inaugurates the kingdom, and accomplishes God's salvation through his sacrificial death on the cross.[21]

OTHER CHARACTERS IN MATTHEW'S GOSPEL

The Disciples

We have already noted that the disciples in Matthew play a more positive role than in Mark. Though they struggle with their faith and often fail to understand Jesus' teaching, they are clearly on his side. Twice the narrator reports that the disciples understand Jesus' teaching (16:12; 17:13; cf. 13:51). Although they desert Jesus at his arrest and fail him in his time of need, in the end they are restored and commissioned to assume leadership over his church.

It is true that the lack of faith of the disciples is an important theme in Matthew, just as it is in Mark. Four times Jesus refers to the disciples as "you of little faith" (6:30; 8:26; 14:31; 16:8; cf. 17:20). While this is clearly criticism and a call for greater faith, Jesus also teaches that with the faith of a mustard seed, a person can move a mountain (17:20). While the disciples are weak and needy, Jesus remains faithful to them. While the disciples in Mark are said to have "no faith" (Mark 4:40), in Matthew they have "little faith" (Matt. 8:26) which has the potential of growing into greater faith.

> While Mark's disciples may be regarded almost as antidisciples, starkly contrasted with Jesus by their lack of faith and understanding, Matthew portrays them somewhat more positively.

While Mark's disciples may be regarded almost as *antidisciples*, starkly contrasted with Jesus by their lack of faith and understanding, Matthew's may better be called *disciples in process*. Though they struggle and fail, after the resurrection they will be restored to posi-

---

21. See Don Verseput, "The Role and Meaning of the 'Son of God' Title in Matthew's Gospel," *NTS* 33 (1987), 532–56.

tions of leadership. The Gospel ends not with mystery and bewilderment, as in Mark, but with the disciples worshiping Jesus and accepting his commission to go and make disciples of all nations. Yet even here there remains some measure of indecision and ambiguity, as "some doubt" Jesus' resurrection (28:17).

Peter among the Disciples

While Peter appears in all four Gospels as the leading disciple and spokesperson for the others, in Matthew he plays an especially prominent role. Several stories about him are unique to Matthew, including his finding a coin in a fish's mouth to pay the temple tax (17:24–27) and his question to Jesus about how many times he should forgive a fellow believer (18:21–22). While the account of Jesus' walking on the water also appears in Mark and John (Mark 6:47–52; John 6:15–21), only in Matthew does Peter get out of the boat and walk to Jesus (Matt. 14:28–31). Most significant, only in Matthew is Peter's confession followed by Jesus' commendation and prediction of the authoritative role he will play in the church (Matt. 16:17–20). This important passage confirms that Peter in particular, and the disciples in general, will be restored and will assume authoritative leadership in the church.

What, then, does Peter's role in Matthew signify? There are two main views.[22] (1) Some see Peter as a symbol of leadership. Only Peter is given the "keys" of the kingdom (16:19), indicating his authoritative role among the disciples. (2) Others argue that Peter functions not as the leader but as the representative of the disciples.[23] Evidence of this is that the same authority to "bind and loose" given to Peter in 16:19 is given to all of the disciples in 18:18. While these two views are not mutually exclusive, the greatest emphasis

22. See R. Brown, K. Donfried, J. Reumann, eds., *Peter in the New Testament: A Collaborative Assessment by Protestant and Roman Catholic Scholars* (Minneapolis: Augsburg; New York: Paulist, 1973).

23. See Michael J. Wilkins, *The Concept of Disciple in Matthew's Gospel: As Reflected in the Use of the Term Mathetes*, NovTSup 59 (Leiden: Brill, 1988); J. D. Kingsbury, "The Figure of Peter in Matthew's Gospel as a Theological Problem," *JBL* 98 (1979), 67–83.

Left: Keys to the kingdom. Door key to a house, found in Tiberias (late Roman era). *Right*: Remains of what may have been the home of Peter in Capernaum. The property was converted into a church during the second to the fourth centuries.

seems to be on the latter. Peter, like the other disciples, pledges strong allegiance to Jesus but still wavers. Successful leadership in the church comes to those who keep their eyes on Jesus (14:30), sustained by his power and presence (28:18 – 20).

Figure 8.10—Who Is "the Rock" in Matthew 16:18?

In Matthew's account of Peter's confession, Jesus responds by announcing the establishment of his church: "You are Peter and upon this rock I will build my church." Jesus' statement is a play on words, since the name Peter (*petros*, "rock" or "stone") is closely related to the word rock (*petra*, "rock" or "bedrock"). The question is, What is this rock upon which Jesus will build his church? There are three main interpretations. (1) The traditional Roman Catholic interpretation is that the rock is Peter himself. This is sometimes linked to the idea of papal succession, with Peter as the first pope passing on his authority to subsequent popes. There are two main Protestant views: (2) The rock is Jesus himself. He is the one who builds the church. (3) The rock is the confession of Peter. The church will be built upon the confession that Jesus is the Christ.

The first interpretation remains the most likely, though without any necessary link to papal succession. The following arguments support this view:

1. Some argue that Peter cannot be the rock since *petros* means a small stone or pebble, while *petra* means a bedrock or foundation stone. But this is a lexical fallacy. The two words are often used synonymously, and that seems to be the case here. Peter is named *petros* and not *petra* because the latter is a feminine noun. While appropriate for a foundation stone, it is inappropriate as a masculine proper name.
2. Jesus was probably speaking Aramaic, in which the Greek *petros-petra* distinction would not have been made. Jesus likely used the Aramaic *kepha* in both clauses: "You are a rock [*kepha*], and upon this rock [*kepha*] I will build my church." We know from John 1:42 that Jesus actually gave Simon this Aramaic name.
3. We must also ask why Jesus named Simon this in the first place. It was certainly not because of his stable character when Jesus met him! Peter was often wavering and unstable. This passage explains the reason, which is that Peter would grow and mature and eventually become a foundation stone for the church.
4. While it may be countered that Jesus is the foundation stone (1 Cor. 3:10ff.; 1 Peter 2:6 – 8), the apostles are also identified as foundational (Eph. 2:20; Rev. 21:14; cf. Gal. 2:9).
5. Finally, in the immediate context, Jesus clearly bestows high authority on Peter, giving him "the keys of the kingdom" (Matt. 16:19). This confirms that Jesus' intention was to give Peter, together with the other disciples, an important role in the establishment of his church.

In summary, Jesus likely designated Peter as the rock in the sense of a key foundation stone for the apostolic church. As the representative and spokesperson for the apostles, he would open the door of the gospel to Jews and Gentiles alike (Acts 2, 8, 10). On the other hand, the context says nothing about papal or apostolic succession. Peter fulfilled the promised role as a representative of the disciples and as a leader in the church in Acts.

The Religious Leaders

If the disciples play a more positive role in Matthew than in Mark, the religious leaders play a more negative one. In Mark, their primary character trait is that they *lack authority* and so are envious of Jesus' power and influence. For Matthew, however, they are *evil* through and through (Matt. 9:4; 12:34, 39, 45; 16:4; 22:18).[24] They are implacably opposed to Jesus and so are aligned with Satan, who himself is the "evil one" (5:37; 6:13; 13:19, 38). There is no hope for their redemption, since their hearts are thoroughly corrupt. This negative portrayal comes out in a variety of ways. Jesus and John the Baptist refer to them as a "brood of vipers" (3:7; 12:34; 23:33), and Jesus repeatedly calls them a "wicked and adulterous generation" (12:39; 16:4). The whole of chapter 23 concerns Jesus' woes, or denunciations against the scribes and Pharisees for their hypocrisy, spiritual blindness, and evil deeds. Their characterization is epitomized in the parable of the wheat and the tares, which appears only in Matthew (Matt. 13:24–30, 36–43). In that parable, the religious leaders are "children of the evil one," weeds sowed by the devil among the good seed in the kingdom of God. Though they presently grow together with the good wheat, the righteous "children of the kingdom," in the end they will be weeded out and destroyed.

> If the disciples play a more positive role in Matthew than in Mark, the religious leaders play a more negative one.

The Crowds

In Matthew's narrative, the crowds appear to represent the nation Israel as a whole and its response to Jesus. Though they are amazed at Jesus' miracles and come to him for healing and to be fed, they never fully grasp his identity, mistakenly referring to him as John the Baptist, Elijah, or one of the prophets (16:14; 21:11, 46). They are also fickle and easily manipulated. In the passion narrative, the "crowds" which first hailed him as the "Son of David" show up to arrest him (26:47, 55). At his trial before Pilate, they are persuaded by the religious leaders to call for Jesus' crucifixion (27:20, 23, 25). Their cry, "Let his blood be on us and on our children!" represents their final, and chilling, rejection of Jesus, a rejection which will bring God's judgment upon the nation and on Jerusalem. (On the question of anti-Semitism in Matthew, see "Reading Matthew Today" later in this chapter.)

THEOLOGICAL THEMES

Promise-Fulfillment and the Climax of Salvation History

The genealogy, the formula quotations, the titles of Jesus, the typologies—all of these point to a common theme: *in Jesus, God has acted decisively to save his people.* The promises and covenants of the Old Testament are coming to fulfillment in him. The term **salvation history** is used to describe the narration or schematization of God's actions in human history to accomplish his salvation. Matthew's central theological theme is that *salvation history reaches its goal and purpose in Jesus the Messiah.*

> Matthew's central theological theme is that salvation history reaches its goal and purpose in Jesus the Messiah.

---

24. See especially Kingsbury, *Matthew as Story*, 17–23.

Figure 8.11—Matthew and Prophetic Fulfillment

Matthew's frequent Old Testament citations have raised eyebrows for many scholars, since at times he seems to quote the Old Testament with little regard for its context or original meaning. Is Matthew playing fast and loose with the Old Testament text? A partial answer to this question is the recognition that Matthew uses the term *fulfilled* in a much broader sense than we generally use it today. At least three kinds of fulfillment must be distinguished in Matthew's Gospel.

1. *Direct, Single, or Literal Fulfillment.* At times, Old Testament prophecies are cited which are uniquely fulfilled by Jesus. This is the case, for example, in the prophecy of the Bethlehem birth of the Messiah from Micah 5:2 (Matt. 2:5–6). Jesus directly and uniquely fulfilled this prophecy.
2. *Typological Fulfillment.* Other fulfillment citations function typologically. This means that an Old Testament event or person serves as a type or model for an ultimate fulfillment in Jesus, the "antitype." This is probably the case with the virgin prophecy of Isaiah 7:14 cited in Matthew 1:23. While the context of this prophecy in Isaiah confirms that it was first fulfilled in Isaiah's time (see Isa. 7:16), the ultimate fulfillment comes in Christ, who is the consummate Immanuel, "God with us."
3. *Analogical Fulfillment.* In still other cases, the fulfillment seems not to be typology but merely analogy. In other words, the author is saying, "This event parallels, or is similar to, what happened in the Old Testament." Analogical fulfillments confirm God's sovereignty over human history and his consistent character in his dealings with his people. An example of an analogical fulfillment is the quote from Jeremiah 31:15 in Matthew 2:17. The weeping of Rachel for her "children" (the Babylonian exiles) in Jeremiah is analogous to the weeping of the mothers of Bethlehem for their children.

The Kingdom of Heaven

Matthew's presentation of salvation history is closely related to his perspective on the kingdom of God. In Jewish fashion, Matthew prefers the designation **kingdom of heaven** (thirty-two times) over the kingdom of God (four times), with the circumlocution "heaven" replacing the divine name out of reverence.[25] There seems to be no difference in meaning between the two expressions, and they often appear in identical contexts. As in Mark, God's kingdom in Matthew is both present and future. In the present, Jesus' miracles, exorcisms, and healings reveal the power of the kingdom breaking in on human history and defeating the forces of Satan. What distinguishes Matthew's presentation from Mark's is a stronger stress on Jesus as not just God's representative but also his actual presence — "God

---

25. Other possible reasons for Matthew's preference include (1) kingdom of heaven better encompasses the kingship of both Jesus and God, or (2) Matthew wants to distinguish the earthly human kingdoms from God's heavenly kingdom. The latter was suggested to me by Jonathan T. Pennington.

with us." The kingdom is present in the church because of the abiding presence of Jesus with his people (Matt. 18:20; 28:20). As kingdom people living in the new age of salvation, the church is called to live on a higher plane, so that their righteousness exceeds even that of the scribes and Pharisees. Inaugurated in the present, the kingdom will be consummated in the future when the Son of Man returns in glory to judge and reward.

Jesus and the Law

Jesus speaks more about the Old Testament law in Matthew than in the other Gospels. The issue of the nature of the law and its continuing validity for the church was clearly an important one for Matthew and his community. One problem we encounter is that two seemingly contradictory perspectives appear side by side in Jesus' teaching. On the one hand, Jesus seems to teach the continuing authority of the law. In his Sermon on the Mount, he says that not a single letter will disappear from the law until everything is accomplished. Anyone who breaks the least of its commandments will be called least in the kingdom of heaven (5:18–19). Not only this, but "unless your righteousness exceeds that of the Pharisees and the teachers of the law, you will certainly not enter the kingdom of heaven" (5:20). Later, he calls on his followers to "be perfect, therefore, as your heavenly Father is perfect" (5:48). On the other hand, Jesus makes statements which seem to abolish aspects of the law: "You have heard that it was said … But I tell you …" (Matt. 5:21–48). Some of these statements merely bring out the true intent of the law. Anger is equivalent to murder because it entails the same attitude of the heart (5:21–22). Lust equals adultery of the heart (5:27–28). In other cases, however, Jesus goes farther and seems to alter or abrogate the Old Testament commands. Divorce, permitted in the Old Testament, is now a cause of sin (Matt. 5:31–32; cf. Deut. 24:1). Oaths, which the Old Testament said must not be broken, are now forbidden (5:33–37; cf. Num. 30:2).

Torah scroll

How can Jesus' teaching concerning the eternal validity of the law be reconciled with these statements? Some scholars have suggested that Matthew is a moderate attempting to mediate between *antinomians*, those in the church who are rejecting the law altogether, and *legalists*, those who are preaching that believers are still under the Mosaic law. While there may be some truth here, a better solution is to be found in Matthew's view of salvation history and the kingdom of God. Jesus announced that in his own words and deeds, the kingdom of God was breaking in on humanity. The age of promise was giving way to the age of fulfillment. With the new age comes a new covenant (Jer. 31:31; Matt. 26:28) and hence a new law. Citizens of the kingdom of heaven are no longer under the old covenant but are under the new and greater covenant. As the inaugurator of the new covenant, Jesus claimed the prerogative to interpret, expand, and even overrule the law of Moses.

> As the inaugurator of the new covenant, Jesus claimed the prerogative to interpret, expand, and even overrule the law of Moses.

This perspective helps to explain much of Jesus' teaching. He has come not to abolish the law but to "fulfill it" (Matt. 5:17–18). As the inaugurator of the kingdom of God and the new era of salvation, Jesus completes the purpose of the Mosaic law. The purpose of the law was twofold: (1) to reveal God's righteous standards and (2) to provide the means to remain in covenant relationship with him. Both of these are fulfilled in Jesus himself, who through his righteous life and death on the cross establishes for his followers a permanent new covenant relationship with God.

New covenant believers, then, have not a lower standard of righteousness but a higher standard, since the law is now written on their hearts rather than on tablets of stone (Jer. 31:33). This is why Jesus says that their righteousness must surpass that of the scribes and Pharisees (Matt. 5:20). As citizens of the kingdom of heaven, their standards must reflect the character of their heavenly Father (5:48). This is also why Jesus defines the law as the attitude of the heart, not merely the external command (5:22, 28). The whole law can be summed up in the commandments to love God and to love your neighbor (22:40), because the righteous actions which proceed from these two commands exceed the written standards of the Mosaic law.

> The coming of the Messiah represents the climax of salvation history, the fulfillment of God's plan to bring salvation to his people Israel and to the Gentile nations.

How, then, do we explain Jesus' statements in Matthew which seem to affirm the continuing validity of the law of Moses (5:19; 23:3, 23), or which assume Jesus' followers are continuing to keep it (offering sacrifices, 5:23–24; giving alms, 6:1–4; fasting, 6:16–18)? A partial answer is the transitional nature of Jesus' ministry, which bridged the period of the old and new covenants. Jesus assumes that his disciples (who were, of course, Jewish) are continuing to keep the law of Moses during the period of his ministry. Beyond this, however, we must recognize that the law of Moses was "holy, righteous and good" (Rom. 7:12), reflecting God's character. Jesus never encourages his followers to break the law but encourages them to live to even higher standards. When Jesus says, "Anyone who breaks one of the least of these commandments . . ." (5:19), he is calling them not to the legalism and casuistry practiced by the Pharisees but to the heart-righteousness which comes through the inward transformation of the Spirit in the age of salvation.

NARRATIVE AND THEOLOGICAL PURPOSE

From our narrative analysis, we may conclude that the primary purpose of Matthew's Gospel is to demonstrate that Jesus is the fulfillment of Jewish hopes for the Messiah. The coming of the Messiah represents the climax of salvation history, the fulfillment of God's plan to bring salvation to his people Israel and to the Gentile nations. It is likely that this theme has, at least in part, an *apologetic* goal, providing the church with a response against those who are denying that Jesus is the Messiah and that the church, made up of Jews and Gentiles, is the authentic people of God in the present age.

A second narrative purpose is to call the church to greater faith and trust in their risen and ever-present Lord. This is suggested by Matthew's references to the still-future church (16:18; 18:17), his emphasis on the abiding presence of the risen Christ in the church (18:20; 28:20), and his frequent use of the exalted title "Lord" for Jesus.

This twofold purpose fits well with the dual portraits of Jesus—one messianic and the other transcendent—which we have suggested above. Jesus is the promised Messiah from the line of David, but he is also "God with us," the very presence of God among his people. It seems likely that Messiah, together with its related designations (son of David, Son of Man, Servant, new Moses, true Israel), functions as the primary category for Matthew's *apologetic* purpose. With these images, the narrator seeks to show that Jesus fulfills all the promises and covenants made to Israel. It follows that the people of the Messiah (Matthew's community) are the true people of God.

At the same time, the title Lord, together with its related concepts (Immanuel, the wisdom of God, the abiding presence of God), functions as Matthew's primary *confessional* designation for Jesus, reflecting the continuing relationship of Matthew's community to its risen Lord. The title Son of God may be seen as a bridge, carrying both apologetic and confessional significance. Jesus is the messianic Son of God, who accomplishes God's promised salvation through suffering (16:16; 27:54). He is also the transcendent Son, who reveals the Father to his disciples and remains with them as God's abiding presence even to the end of the age (Matt. 11:27; 28:18–20).

THE HISTORICAL SETTING OF MATTHEW'S GOSPEL: AUTHOR AND LIFE SETTING

Audience and Occasion

Matthew has long been recognized as the "Jewish Gospel" because of its Jewish features and orientation. That the author is writing to a predominantly Jewish or a mixed Jewish and Gentile audience is suggested by the many Jewish terms and customs presented without explanation (ceremonial washings, 15:2; the temple tax, 17:24–27; phylacteries and tassels, 23:5; whitewashed tombs, 23:27). At the same time, the Gospel is written in Greek, so we are probably to think of a Hellenistic-Jewish environment.

Concerning a specific life situation, the themes of the Gospel suggest that the author's community is in conflict and debate with the larger Jewish community. Notice, for example, the negative portrayal of the Jewish leaders (chap. 23, etc.), the culpability of the Jewish crowds at Jesus' trial (27:25), and Jewish reports "even to this day" that the disciples stole the body of Jesus (27:62–66; 28:11–15). In response to such accusations, the author seeks to show that the authentic people of God are those who have responded in faith to Jesus the Messiah.

A major scholarly debate continues concerning whether the church or churches to whom the author is writing still consider themselves to be a part of Judaism, or whether there has been a decisive break with (or expulsion from) the synagogue. Is this community still working within Judaism to reform it, or do they consider themselves the authentic people of God distinct from Judaism? A complete break is suggested by those scholars who consider the Gospel to be a Christian response to the "council" of Jamnia. As we have seen in chapter 5, following the destruction of Jerusalem in AD 70, Rabbi Johanan ben Zakkai

Phylactery in their original leather box, dating from the first century and found in one of the Qumran caves

established a "school" for the reorganization of Judaism in the town of Jamnia on the Mediterranean coast. Up to this time, Christianity was broadly viewed as a sect within Judaism. With the rabbinic discussions defining more precisely the beliefs and boundaries of Judaism, Christians and other groups were condemned as heretics. Christians were expelled from the synagogue. According to this theory, Matthew's Gospel is a response to Jamnia, defending Christianity as the authentic fulfillment of Judaism.[26] Other scholars do not necessarily appeal to Jamnia but still consider Matthew's community to have decisively broken with Judaism.[27] They point especially to references in the Gospel to "their" scribes (7:29) and "their" synagogues (4:23; 9:35; 10:17; 12:9; 13:54). The polemic against the Pharisees is particularly severe in Matthew (see 15:12–14; chap. 23).

> Matthew's mixed community of Jews and Gentiles is asserting itself as the authentic people of God over against the larger Jewish community.

Others see Matthew's community as still within Judaism but trying to assert itself as the authentic representation of the Jewish faith.[28] In the chaos that followed the destruction

---

26. This view was especially developed by W. D. Davies, *The Setting of the Sermon on the Mount* (Cambridge: Cambridge Univ. Press, 1964).

27. See G. Strecker, *Der Weg der Gerechtigkeit: Untersuchung zur Theologie des Matthäus*, 2nd ed. (Göttingen: Vandenhoeck and Ruprecht, 1966); David Garland, *The Intention of Matthew 23*, NovTSup 52 (Leiden: Brill, 1979); U. Luz, *Matthew 1–7: A Continental Commentary* (Minneapolis: Augsburg, 1989); D. R. A. Hare, *The Theme of Jewish Persecution of Christians in the Gospel according to St. Matthew*, SNTSMS 6 (Cambridge: Cambridge Univ. Press, 1967).

28. Variations of this view appear in R. Hummel, *Die Auseinandersetzung zwischen kirche und Judentum im Matthäusevangelium* (Munich: Kaiser Verlag, 1963); A. J. Saldarini, *Matthew's Christian-Jewish Community* (Chicago: Univ. of Chicago, 1994); Graham Stanton, *A Gospel for a New People: Studies in Matthew* (Edinburgh: T. and T. Clark, 1992); J. Andrew Overman, *Matthew's Gospel and Formative Judaism: The Social World of the Matthean Community* (Minneapolis: Fortress, 1990).

of Jerusalem, no one Judaism dominated. Matthew's community is trying to assert itself as the true Judaism, the locus of God's purposes and promises.

While the "us versus them" tone of the Gospel would seem to favor a more complete break with the synagogue, in the end these two positions are not very far apart. Both agree that Matthew's mixed community is asserting itself as the authentic people of God over against the larger Jewish community. Whether some or all of the members of Matthew's community have been formally excommunicated and expelled from the synagogue does not change the basic theme and purpose of the book.

Place and Date

Though the Gospel does not indicate its place of origin, a surprising number of scholars have proposed Antioch in Syria as a likely location. The earliest quotation from Matthew comes from Ignatius, bishop of Antioch, around AD 115. The Gospel also seems to have been used as a source for the *Didache*, a church manual probably produced in Syria around AD 100.

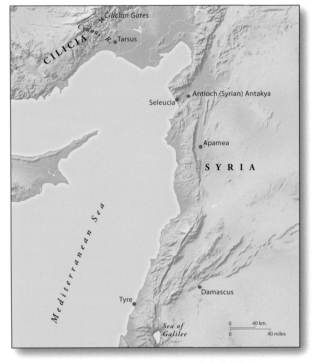

Antioch in Syria

The likelihood that the Gospel was written in Greek to Jewish Christians also fits Antioch, since the church was founded when Greek-speaking Jewish Christians fled there from Jerusalem (Acts 11:19–21). The debate over authentic Judaism and the author's concern for Gentiles is also appropriate to this location, since the city had large Jewish and Gentile populations, and since the church there was missions-minded, sending Paul and Barnabas on their first missionary journey (Acts 13:1–2).

The date of Matthew is disputed. A date in the 80s or 90s is claimed by those who view Matthew as a Christian response to Jamnia. A later date may also be suggested in Matthew's parable of the wedding banquet, which speaks of the king who "sent his army and destroyed those murderers and burned their city" (Matt. 22:7). Some see here an allusion to the Roman destruction of Jerusalem, interpreted as God's judgment for the crucifixion of Jesus.

Others favor an earlier date, in the 60s, claiming there is no indication in 24:1–28 that the destruction of Jerusalem

> Though the Gospel of Matthew does not indicate its place of origin, a surprising number of scholars have proposed Antioch in Syria as a likely location.

has already occurred. An early date is also suggested by church tradition. Irenaeus wrote around AD 175 that "Matthew also issued a written Gospel among the Hebrews in their own dialect while Peter and Paul were preaching at Rome and laying the foundations of the church" (Irenaeus, *Against Heresies* 3.1.1). Irenaeus's statement is suspect, however, since Matthew does not seem to have been originally written in Hebrew, and since neither Peter nor

Paul founded the church in Rome (it was already long established when Paul wrote Romans around AD 55). If Irenaeus is wrong on these basic facts, can he be trusted on the time of writing? A firm conclusion on the date of Matthew remains elusive.

Authorship

We come finally to the question of authorship, perhaps the most disputed historical question related to this Gospel. While the book does not name its author, church tradition ascribes it to Matthew, a tax collector who became a disciple of Jesus. All three Synoptics list Matthew as one of Jesus' twelve disciples (Matt. 10:3; Mark 3:18; Luke 6:15; Acts 1:13). The Gospel of Matthew explicitly identifies him as "a tax collector" (10:3) and narrates the story of his call by Jesus (9:9–13). Mark and Luke relate this same story but identify the tax collector as Levi (Mark 2:14–17; Luke 5:27–32), naming Matthew only in their lists of disciples (Mark 3:18; Luke 6:15; Acts 1:13). While some scholars claim that these were two separate individuals, it is more likely that Matthew had two names, Matthew and Levi, perhaps because he was a member of the tribe of Levi.

External Evidence. While early church tradition is unanimous in ascribing this book to Matthew, the nature of this ascription is somewhat garbled. As in the case of Mark, the earliest evidence comes from Papias, quoted by Eusebius:

> Matthew compiled (or "arranged," or "composed") the *logia* ("oracles," "sayings" or perhaps "gospel") in the Hebrew (or, "Aramaic") language (or, "style"?), and everyone interpreted (or, "translated") them as best they could.[29]

The problem, as indicated by the variants in parentheses, is that Papias's statement is open to various interpretations. Is Papias saying that Matthew wrote a Gospel? Or only that he collected sayings of Jesus? Was this Gospel written in Hebrew or Aramaic, or was it written in a Jewish or Hebrew style? Did others translate it, or did they interpret its meaning?

Many scholars doubt Matthean authorship for a variety of reasons: (1) Papias's statement cannot be trusted since the First Gospel reads like a Greek original. (2) Markan priority renders Matthean authorship unlikely. Why would an apostle and eyewitness borrow from the writings of a non-apostle? (3) The Gospel reflects the concerns of second-generation Christians, and so is unlikely to have come from an apostle.

None of these arguments is decisive. Perhaps Matthew wrote an original Gospel (or a collection of Jesus' sayings; Q?) in Aramaic or Hebrew. He could have later published a Greek edition of this Gospel (not a translation but a new edition). As a tax collector, Matthew no doubt would have been proficient in both Aramaic and Greek. Another possibility is that Papias's phrase "Hebrew language" means "Hebrew style" and refers to Matthew's Jewish emphasis. Perhaps Mark wrote first and Matthew followed by writing a Jewish-styled Gospel. Concerning Matthew's likely dependence on Mark, if Mark is in fact recording Peter's version of the Gospel, Matthew would certainly be willing to use him as a source. Finally, there is nothing in Matthew's Gospel that necessarily points to a second-generation situation. The conflict over whether the followers of Jesus were the authentic heirs of Judaism began with the earliest preaching of the gospel.

---

29. Eusebius, *Ecclesiastical History* 3.39.16.

Internal Evidence. Some have claimed that internal evidence points to Matthew as the author: (1) the skillful organization of the Gospel (a tax collector would have organizational skills), (2) the use of the name Matthew in 9:9, and (3) the prominence of money and tax-collecting themes (10:3; 17:24–27; 18:23–25; 20:1–16; 27:3–5; 28:11–15). On its own, this evidence carries little weight, suggesting only that someone like Matthew wrote the Gospel. A counterargument is that the Gospel's emphasis on Jewish ritual and the law would not fit a tax collector, who would be an outsider to religious affairs. Some have suggested that the author was a converted scribe or Pharisee. They point to Matthew 13:52 as a possible self-designation: "Every teacher of the law who has been instructed about the kingdom of heaven is like the owner of a house who brings out of his storeroom new treasures as well as old." Is Matthew this Jewish scribe, bringing his scholarly training in Jewish tradition (the old treasures) into the service of the kingdom of God (the new)?

The mixed data means a conclusion on authorship must be made with caution. In the absence of better evidence, the strong church tradition tips the scale in favor of Matthean authorship. As with Mark's Gospel, it seems unlikely that the early church would ascribe the work to a relatively obscure figure like Matthew unless they had good reason to do so. Uncertain authorship, of course, does not render questionable the authority or inspiration of the text. The authors of many Old and New Testament books are unknown.

READING MATTHEW TODAY

The modern reader often cringes when reading the strong language which Matthew uses against Jesus' Jewish opponents. The history of anti-Semitism, culminating with the Holocaust, makes these passages sound dangerously provocative. Indeed, through the centuries Matthew's Gospel, like other New Testament passages, has been used to justify persecution of the Jews.

Yet to read these passages as anti-Semitic is to read them anachronistically ("out of their proper time"), and so to misread them. The Gospel is not an indictment on the Jews as a people. After all, Matthew and the majority of his church were almost certainly Jews. The Gospel is rather an internal debate within Judaism, between those who believe that Jesus is the promised Messiah and those who reject this claim. Matthew seeks to show that Jesus is the culmination of salvation history. God's purpose to bring salvation to lost humanity finds its culmination in him. The prophecies have been fulfilled! If Jesus is indeed the promised Messiah, then the church, made up of both Jews and Gentiles, is the authentic people of God. God's plan of salvation for the world is now going forward, not through the synagogue but through the new people of God made up of people from all nations. This is the critical point at issue for Matthew and his community.

Seen in this light, the questions Matthew answers are just as profound and important today. What is God's purpose and goal for this world? What characterizes the true followers of God? What must people do to find salvation? The First Gospel rejects any claims to truth which do not find their center in the kingdom of heaven inaugurated through the life, death, and resurrection of Jesus the Messiah. All other worldviews, religions, and philosophies fall short.

1. Matthew's Gospel is the most Jewish of the four Gospels, presenting Jesus as the Jewish Messiah who brings God's people salvation from their sins. It is also the most systematically arranged, utilizing concise style, fulfillment formulas, topical arrangement, and structural signals to provide a carefully structured presentation.

2. Matthew includes five major discourses by Jesus and alternates between narrative and discourse, presenting Jesus as the great Moses-like bringer of the new covenant.

3. Only Matthew and Luke include birth narratives, which serve as prologues or introductions to their respective Gospels. Both birth narratives center on the theme of promise-fulfillment, with Jesus as the promised Messiah from David's line.

4. Matthew's genealogy presents Jesus as the fulfillment of the covenants made to Abraham and David, and as the legitimate king of Israel.

5. The preaching of John the Baptist, and the accounts of Jesus' baptism and temptation, initiate Jesus' ministry (3:1 – 4:11), confirming that he is indeed the Messiah, Son of God, Servant of the LORD, and true Israel — the fulfillment of Israel's hopes.

6. Jesus' healing and preaching ministry in Galilee demonstrates the power of the kingdom in his ministry to Israel and reveals the beginning of opposition from Israel's religious leaders (4:12 – 11:1). The Sermon on the Mount (*First Discourse*, chaps. 5 – 7) represents Jesus' inaugural kingdom address, presenting standards of righteousness for the new covenant age of salvation. The *Second Discourse* (chap. 10) is a commissioning sermon to Jesus' disciples to take the message of the kingdom to Israel.

7. Matthew 11:2 – 20:34 reveals the various responses to Jesus and his proclamation of the kingdom. The parables of the kingdom (*Third Discourse*, chap. 13) contrast those who are rejecting the message with those who are receiving it. Israel's leaders reject the message and so face judgment. Jesus' disciples repeatedly fail but acknowledge him as the Messiah and continue to follow him. The *Fourth Discourse* (chap. 18) instructs them on aspects of church life after Jesus' departure.

8. In Matthew 21:1 – 26:1, Jesus arrives in Jerusalem, publicly revealing his messiahship (Zech. 9:9) and symbolically judging Israel for her unbelief (clearing the temple, cursing the fig tree). He repeatedly debates the religious leaders and confounds them with his wisdom and with parables. They plot his death. In a series of "woes" and in the Olivet Discourse (*Fifth Discourse*, chaps. 23 – 25), Jesus denounces the leaders for their hypocrisy and predicts the destruction of Jerusalem as judgment against the nation of Israel for her unbelief.

9.	At Jesus' trial and crucifixion, the religious leaders continue to act treacherously against Jesus, the disciples desert him, Pilate fails to exercise justice, and the fickle crowds call for his crucifixion. Yet Jesus remains in control of his destiny, willingly taking the road to the cross.

10.	Jesus' resurrection vindicates his claim to be the Messiah. With all authority bestowed on him by the Father, he now commissions his followers to make disciples of all nations, baptizing them in the name of the Father, the Son, and the Holy Spirit.

11.	Matthew's Christology has two main foci: Jesus as the Jewish Messiah fulfilling the promises given to Israel, and as Immanuel, the presence and wisdom of God, and now authoritative Lord of the church. The title Son of God is a particularly important one for Matthew, integrating these two portraits.

12.	As narrative characters, the disciples play a somewhat more positive role in Matthew than in Mark. Though wavering in faith, they remain on Jesus' side. Peter plays an especially prominent role as the representative of the disciples.

13.	The religious leaders play a more negative role in Matthew than in Mark. They are wicked and hypocritical opponents of God's plan who will face judgment for their sins.

14.	Matthew's central theological theme is that salvation history finds its climax in the coming of Jesus the Messiah, inaugurator of the kingdom of heaven and the new age of salvation.

15.	By inaugurating the kingdom, Jesus does not abolish the law but rather fulfills it, bringing it to its destined completion. New covenant believers are no longer under the old covenant but are under the new, inaugurated through Jesus' life, death, and resurrection. Standards of righteousness are even higher because the law is now written on the hearts of believers, who are guided and empowered by the Spirit of God.

16.	Matthew's theological themes suggest that his primary narrative purpose is to confirm that Jesus is indeed the Messiah, and that the church, made up of Jews and Gentiles, are the people of God in the present age. He also writes to call God's people to experience and submit to the abiding presence and authority of Jesus in the church.

17.	Matthew's church, or churches, was probably a mixed Jewish and Gentile community struggling against challenges from the larger Jewish community. The exact provenance is unknown, though Antioch in Syria is a likely possibility. The date of writing is also unknown and could be anywhere from the 60s to the 90s of the first century.

18.	The identification of Matthew the tax collector as the author of this Gospel comes from church tradition rather than inspired Scripture, but fits well with both internal and external evidence.

» KEY TERMS «

fulfillment formulas	*inclusio*	Son of David
structural signals	Sermon on the Mount	Olivet Discourse
birth narratives	Great Commission	salvation history
typology/type/antitype	parables of the kingdom	kingdom of heaven

» DISCUSSION AND STUDY QUESTIONS «

1. What structural features are evident in Matthew's Gospel? What is a fulfillment formula? Know the two main structural signals that have been identified with Matthew's "outline."

2. How does Matthew's narrative style compare with Mark's?

3. What are the key themes of the five major discourses in Matthew's Gospel?

4. What is Matthew's purpose in his genealogy? Who are the main characters in Matthew's genealogy, and why?

5. What is the key theme of the temptation in Matthew?

6. What two portraits control Matthew's Christology?

7. What title for Jesus does J. D. Kingsbury claim is most important for Matthew? Why?

8. How are the disciples presented in Matthew compared with Mark? How is Peter presented?

9. How are the religious leaders presented in Matthew compared with Mark?

10. What role do the crowds play?

11. What is Matthew's central theological theme?

12. What apparent contradiction surrounds Jesus' teaching about the law? How would you resolve this difficulty?

13. What is Matthew's primary narrative purpose?

14. What is the likely makeup of his audience, and what are their circumstances?

15. From where was Matthew's Gospel likely written (according to many scholars)?

16. What is the evidence that Matthew the tax collector was the author of this Gospel?

Digging Deeper

Commentaries

Beginning and Intermediate

Blomberg, Craig L. *Matthew*. New American Commentary. Nashville: Broadman, 1992.

Carson, D. A. "Matthew." In *Expositor's Bible Commentary*. Vol. 8. Edited by Frank E. Gaebelein. Grand Rapids: Zondervan, 1984.

France, R. T. *The Gospel according to Matthew*. Tyndale New Testament Commentary. Rev. ed. Grand Rapids: Eerdmans, 1985.

Green, Michael. *Matthew for Today*. London: Hodder and Stoughton, 1988; Dallas: Word, 1989.

Hill, David. *The Gospel of Matthew*. New Century Bible. Grand Rapids: Eerdmans, 1981.

Keener, Craig S. *A Commentary on the Gospel of Matthew*. Grand Rapids: Eerdmans, 1999.

Morris, Leon. *The Gospel according to Matthew*. Pillar New Testament Commentary. Grand Rapids: Eerdmans, 1992.

Mounce, Robert H. *Matthew*. New International Biblical Commentary. Peabody, MA: Hendrickson, 1991.

Ridderbos, H. N. *Matthew*. Grand Rapids: Zondervan, 1987.

Senior, Donald. *Matthew*. Abingdon New Testament Commentary. Nashville: Abingdon, 1998.

Wilkins, Michael J. *Matthew*. The NIV Application Commentary. Grand Rapids: Zondervan, 2004.

Advanced and Greek/Technical

Davies, W. D., and Dale C. Allison Jr. *A Critical and Exegetical Commentary on the Gospel according to Saint Matthew*. 3 vols. Edinburgh: T. and T. Clark, 1988–2004.

Gundry, Robert H. *Matthew: A Commentary on His Handbook for a Mixed Church under Persecution*. 2nd ed. Grand Rapids: Eerdmans, 1994.

Hagner, Donald A. *Matthew*. 2 vols. Word Biblical Commentary. Dallas: Word, 1993–95.

Luz, Ulrich. *Matthew 1–7: A Commentary*. Philadelphia: Fortress, 1992.

———. *Matthew 8–20: A Commentary*. Minneapolis: Fortress, 2001.

Nolland, John. *Gospel of Matthew*. New International Greek Testament Commentary. Grand Rapids: Eerdmans, 2005.

Schnackenburg, Rudolf. *The Gospel of Matthew*. Translated by Robert R. Barr. Grand Rapids: Eerdmans, 2002.

Themes and Theology of Matthew

Aune, David E. *The Gospel of Matthew in Current Study*. Grand Rapids: Eerdmans, 2001.

Balch, David L., ed. *Social History of the Matthean Community*. Minneapolis: Fortress, 1991.

Bauer, David R. and Mark Allan Powell, eds. *Treasures New and Old: Recent Contributions to Matthean Studies*. Atlanta: Scholars Press, 1996.

Bornkamm, Günther, Gerhard Barth, and Heinz J. Held. *Tradition and Interpretation in Matthew*. Philadelphia: Westminster, 1963.

Brown, Jeannine. *Disciples in Narrative Perspective: The Portrayal and Function of the Matthean Disciples.* Society of Biblical Literature Academia Biblica. Atlanta: SBL, 2002.

France, R. T. *Matthew: Evangelist and Teacher.* Downers Grove, IL: Intervarsity, 1998.

Garland, David. *Reading Matthew.* Macon, GA: Smyth and Helwys, 1999.

Kingsbury, Jack Dean. *Matthew: Structure, Christology, Kingdom.* Philadelphia: Fortress, 1975.

———. *Matthew as Story.* 2nd ed. Philadelphia: Fortress, 1988.

Luz, Ulrich. *The Theology of the Gospel of Matthew.* Cambridge: Cambridge Univ. Press, 1995.

Meier, John P. *The Vision of Matthew: Christ, Church and Morality in the First Gospel.* New York: Paulist, 1979.

Powell, Mark A. *God with Us: A Pastoral Theology of Matthew's Gospel.* Minneapolis: Fortress, 1995.

Saldarini, Anthony J. *Matthew's Christian-Jewish Community.* Chicago: Univ. of Chicago Press, 1994.

Senior, Donald, *What Are They Saying about Matthew?* Rev. ed. New York: Paulist, 1996.

Stanton, Graham. *A Gospel for a New People: Studies in Matthew.* Edinburgh: T and T Clark, 1992.

Stanton, Graham N., ed. *The Interpretation of Matthew.* Rev. ed. Edinburgh: T. and T. Clark, 1995.

Stock, Augustine. *The Method and Message of Matthew.* Collegeville, MN: Liturgical Press, 1994.

Wilkins, Michael James. *The Concept of Disciple in Matthew's Gospel.* NovTSup 59. Leiden: Brill, 1988.

New Methods and Approaches

Edwards, R. *Matthew's Story of Jesus.* Philadelphia: Fortress, 1985.

Levine, Amy-Jill. *A Feminist Companion to Matthew.* With Marianne Blickenstaff. Sheffield: Sheffield Academic, 2001.

Neyrey, Jerome H. *Honor and Shame in the Gospel of Matthew.* Louisville: Westminster John Knox, 1998.

Overman, J. Andrew. *Matthew's Gospel and Formative Judaism: The Social World of the Matthean Community.* Minneapolis: Fortress, 1990.

Patte, Daniel. *The Gospel of Matthew: A Structural Commentary on Matthew's Faith.* Philadelphia: Fortress, 1987.

Powell, Mark Allan. *Chasing the Eastern Star: Adventures in Biblical Reader Response Criticism.* Louisville: Westminster John Knox, 2001.

Bibliography

Mills, Watson E. *The Gospel of Matthew.* Lewiston, NY: Mellen, 2002.

Neirynck, F., J. Verheyden, and R. Corstjens, eds. *The Gospel of Matthew and the Sayings Source Q: A Cumulative Bibliography, 1950–1995.* Leuven: Leuven Univ. Press/Peeters, 1998.

CHAPTER 9

Luke

THE GOSPEL OF THE SAVIOR FOR ALL PEOPLE

» CHAPTER OVERVIEW «

1. Literary Features
2. The Plot of Luke's Gospel
3. Luke's Portrait of Jesus: The Savior for All People
4. Other Characters in Luke's Gospel
5. Theological Themes
6. The Historical Setting of Luke's Gospel: Author and Life Setting
7. Reading Luke Today

» OBJECTIVES «

After reading this chapter, you should be able to:

- Identify the main literary features of Luke's Gospel, especially with reference to the unity of Luke-Acts, the fine literary style, and Luke's historiographic interest.
- Summarize the main themes and structural features of Luke's birth narrative.
- Explain the narrative and theological significance of the Nazareth sermon (Luke 4).
- Identify the narrative and theological function of Luke's "travel narrative," including the main theme of the stories and parables presented there.
- Describe the main features of Luke's portrait of Jesus, especially with reference to the titles prophet and Christ.
- Identify the central theme of Luke's Gospel and list the major subthemes which support it.
- Explain what we know about the author Luke and the likely identity of Theophilus, the recipient of Luke-Acts.
- Summarize the likely purpose and occasion of Luke-Acts.

In 1871 French archeologist Charles Clermont-Ganneau discovered a plaque which once stood at the entrance to the Jerusalem temple (see photo on p. 288). The plaque, written in Greek, reads, "No outsider shall enter the protective enclosure around the sanctuary. And whoever is caught will only have himself to blame for the ensuing death."[1] The inscription well illustrates the exclusive nature of first-century Judaism, when Gentiles were forbidden from entering the temple of God upon pain of death. Luke's Gospel and its companion volume, Acts, boldly announce that this time of exclusion is past. God's end-times salvation inaugurated through the life, death, resurrection, and ascension of Jesus Christ means that all people everywhere—whether Jew or Gentile, slave or free, male or female—now have access to God's salvation. By fulfilling the promises made to Israel, Jesus the Messiah has become the Savior for all people everywhere.

---

1. A portion of a second plaque with the same inscription was discovered in 1935. See P. Segal, "The Penalty of the Warning Inscription from the Temple in Jerusalem," *Israel Exploration Quarterly* 39 (1989), 89–94; cf. Josephus, *War* 5.5.2§193; *Ant.* 15.11.5 §418.

» CENTRAL THEME (OF LUKE-ACTS) «

God's end-times salvation predicted by the prophets has arrived through the coming of Jesus the Messiah, the Savior of the world, and this salvation is now going forth to the whole world.

» KEY VERSES «

Luke 2:11; 19:10

» BASIC OUTLINE OF LUKE «

1. The Prologue (1:1 – 4)
2. The Birth of the Savior (1:5 – 2:52)
3. The Preparation of the Savior (3:1 – 4:13)
4. The Galilean Ministry of the Savior (4:14 – 9:50)
5. The Mission of the Savior: The Journey to Jerusalem (9:51 – 19:27)
6. The Savior in Jerusalem: Conflict and Controversy (19:28 – 21:38)
7. The Passion of the Savior in Jerusalem (22:1 – 23:56)
8. The Resurrection and Ascension of the Savior (24:1 – 53)

» CHARACTERISTICS OF LUKE'S GOSPEL «

Look for these while reading Luke:

- Historical notes and dating with reference to secular and religious leaders.
- The universality of the Gospel message: it is for all people.
- References to Jesus as Savior, Christ, Lord, and Prophet.
- Old Testament allusions to Isaiah and the promise of salvation for all people.
- Emphasis on promise and fulfillment.
- The presence, or "today," of salvation in the words and deeds of Jesus.
- Jesus' special concern for outsiders: the poor, sinners, Samaritans (in Acts: Gentiles).
- The theme of reversal of fortunes: the rich become poor and vice versa.
- Special emphasis placed on women and their needs and concerns.
- The coming of the Holy Spirit as a sign of the new age.
- References to Jesus' prayer life and his teaching on prayer.
- References to praise, joy, and celebration at the arrival of God's salvation.
- The importance of Jerusalem and Jesus' extended journey there.
- Emphasis on the present reign of Christ following his ascension.

LITERARY FEATURES

The Gospel according to Luke is the longest book in the New Testament. Together with its companion volume, Acts, it comprises the largest amount of material by a New Testament author (even more than Paul). Luke also begins earlier (with the announcement of John's birth) and ends later (with Jesus' ascension) than the other Synoptics.

The Unity of Luke and Acts

Luke's Gospel is also unique in that it contains a sequel — the book of Acts — which narrates the events of the early church following Jesus' death and resurrection. It is widely recognized today that not only were Luke and Acts written by the same author but they are a literary unity — a single two-volume work. H. J. Cadbury, a pioneer in the study of the theology of Luke, wrote that Luke and Acts "are not merely two independent writings from the same pen; they are a single continuous work. Acts is neither an appendix nor an afterthought."[2] To fully understand the Gospel, we must read Acts. The hyphenated expression **Luke-Acts** is used to describe this two-volume work.

> Luke and Acts were not only written by the same author but are a single two-volume work, Luke-Acts.

2. Henry J. Cadbury, *The Making of Luke-Acts*, 2nd ed., with a new introduction by Paul N. Anderson (Peabody, MA: Hendrickson, 1999); 8–9. For a recent challenge to this unity, see Mikeal C. Parsons and Richard I. Pervo, *Rethinking the Unity of Luke and Acts* (Minneapolis: Fortress, 1993).

At the beginning of Acts, the author refers back to the Gospel: "In my former book, Theophilus, I wrote about all that Jesus began to do and to teach until the day he was taken up to heaven." If the Gospel is what Jesus *began to do and to teach*, then Acts is what he *continues to do* through the establishment and spread of his church in the power of the Holy Spirit, which he has poured out. The story which begins in the Gospel does not reach its conclusion until the end of Acts.

Evidence for this literary unity is seen in a number of remarkable parallels between the Gospel and Acts.[3] Many of Jesus' actions in Luke are echoed in the actions of Peter, Paul, and others in Acts.

Luke's Sources

Only Luke among the Gospels refers explicitly to written sources about Jesus, noting that "many have undertaken to draw up an account of the things that have been fulfilled among us" (1:1). Since Luke claims not to have been an eyewitness (1:2), he likely drew from these sources. As we noted in chapter 2, most scholars believe that Luke used at least three sources: Mark, Q (a source or sources used also by Matthew), and L (a source or sources used only by Luke).

> The most unique structural feature of Luke's Gospel is the extended journey to Jerusalem, or travel narrative, from 9:51 to 19:27.

Whereas Matthew contains almost all of Mark (about 90 percent), Luke uses only about half. He also integrates Mark less thoroughly with his other sources, alternating Markan and non-Markan material. Mark's material is grouped in three main sections: Luke 3:1–6:1, 8:4–9:50, and 18:15–24:11. Most surprising is the absence of any material from Mark 6:45–8:26, a large and seemingly significant section. This so-called great omission has puzzled scholars, raising further doubts about a simple solution to the synoptic problem.

Literary Style

Luke's two books present some of the finest Greek in the New Testament, as the author seamlessly crafts his sources into a literary masterpiece. The author is clearly a skilled literary artist, able to adapt style to fit the occasion. For example, while the **prologue of Luke** is written in a very fine literary Greek (1:1–4), the birth narrative which follows has a strong Semitic style befitting its Jewish context. The book of Acts returns to a more Greek style in line with the transition of the gospel message from a Jewish to a Gentile environment.

Historiography

Luke shows a strong interest in **historiography**, or history writing, claiming to be drawing from eyewitness accounts and to have carefully investigated these events himself (1:1–4). He dates the Gospel with reference to Roman history, identifying key rulers and religious leaders (cf. 1:5; 2:1–3; 3:1–2). This does not mean that he is obsessed with precise details

---

3. See especially Charles H. Talbert, *Literary Patterns, Theological Themes, and the Genre of Luke-Acts* (Missoula, MT: Scholars Press, 1974).

or chronological order (many events are not chronological). His interest, rather, is in showing the historical veracity and worldwide significance of these events. God's saving actions are coming to fulfillment in human history.

The Travel Narrative or Journey to Jerusalem

The most unique structural feature of Luke's Gospel is the extended journey to Jerusalem, or **travel narrative**, from 9:51 to 19:27. Luke takes ten chapters to treat a period which in Mark occupies a single chapter. Mark's brief transition to the passion narrative becomes in Luke an entire phase of Jesus' ministry. Many of the most famous Gospel parables and narratives (the prodigal son, the good Samaritan, Zacchaeus, Mary and Martha, etc.) appear during this period, as Luke develops important narrative themes. We will discuss the theological significance of the travel narrative when we examine the narrative progress of Luke's Gospel.

> Luke's prologue contains some of the finest literary Greek in the New Testament.

THE PLOT OF LUKE'S GOSPEL

The Prologue (1:1–4)

Luke's Gospel begins with a formal prologue similar in style to Hellenistic writers of the first century (see fig. 9.1). These verses contain some of the finest literary Greek in the New Testament. The author is obviously an educated and skilled writer. The prologue sets out the purpose of the work, which is to confirm for **Theophilus** the truth of the gospel. Luke stresses the historical reliability of his story, claiming to have received his information from eyewitnesses and to have carefully investigated these accounts to ensure their veracity.

Figure 9.1—The Prologues of Luke and Josephus

While many Greco-Roman works have introductions similar to Luke's, the Jewish historian Josephus's two-volume work *Against Apion* is the most striking. Josephus dedicates his work to a patron, "most excellent Epaphroditus," refers to previous works on the subject (his own in this case), and describes an apologetic purpose in writing:

> I suppose that, by my books of the Antiquities of the Jews, most excellent Epaphroditus, I have made it evident to those who peruse them, that our Jewish nation is of very great antiquity ... However, since I observe a considerable number of people giving ear to the reproaches that are laid against us, I therefore have thought myself under an obligation to write ... in order to convict those that reproach us of spite and voluntary falsehood, and to correct the ignorance of others, and withal to instruct all those who are desirous of knowing the truth of what great antiquity we really are.
> —*Against Apion* 1.1 § §1–3

Josephus' second volume, like Acts, refers back to the first:

> In the former book, most honored Epaphroditus, I have demonstrated our antiquity, and confirmed the truth of what I have said ... I shall now therefore begin a confutation of the remaining authors who have written anything against us.
> —*Against Apion* 2.1 § §1–2

The Birth of the Savior (1:5 – 2:52)

As the reader moves from Luke's formal introduction to the birth narrative, the writing style changes dramatically. The language suddenly takes on an archaic sound reminiscent of the Septuagint, the Greek Old Testament. For the modern reader, it would be something like beginning a story with "Once upon a time" or dropping into a King James style of English. Judging from the author's literary skills, this stylistic change is intentional and serves to transport the reader into the world of the Old Testament. Parallels and motifs from the Old Testament abound. The characters we encounter are models of Jewish piety, the faithful remnant of Israel awaiting their Messiah. Zechariah and Elizabeth are of priestly ancestry, righteous before God and faithful to his law. Mary and Joseph are willing servants of God, faithfully following the Old Testament laws of purification and dedication. The aged Simeon is righteous and devout, anxiously awaiting Israel's salvation and the coming Messiah. Anna is a model of Jewish piety, a widow devoting herself wholly to worship, fasting, and prayer. The narrator's purpose is to introduce the reader to the faithful remnant of the people of God, waiting expectantly for the fulfillment of the promises God has made to them.

> The central theme of Luke's birth narrative is the arrival of God's salvation and the fulfillment of his promises to Israel.

The central theme of the birth narrative *is the arrival of God's salvation and the fulfillment of his promises to Israel.* Related themes include Jesus as the Messiah from David's line, John the Baptist as the Elijah-like forerunner of the Messiah, the central role of the Holy Spirit in the age of salvation, the gospel as good news especially for the lowly, poor, and oppressed, and salvation for the Gentiles as well as the Jews. These themes confirm that Luke's birth narrative is not intended merely to provide the curious reader with details about Jesus' birth. It serves rather as an overture for the symphony which follows, setting the theological stage for the rest of the Gospel and for Acts.

Two structural features help to carry these themes forward. The first is the dual accounts of the births of Jesus and John. The two stories are intertwined, with parallel

A traditional home in the hill country of Judea

Left: Ein Kerem, the traditional home of John the Baptist. View of St. John's Church across the way at Ein Kerem. *Right*: Ein Kerem. View of Mary and Elizabeth greeting each other at the Church of the Visitation.

announcements by the angel Gabriel and similar accounts of their birth, circumcision, and naming. Mary's visit to her relative Elizabeth further connects the stories (1:39 – 56). The narrator's purpose is twofold, both to *link* Jesus and John as co-agents of God's salvation and especially to *distinguish* their status and roles. While John will be "a prophet of the Most High" (1:76), Jesus is the "Son of the Most High" (1:32). John's birth to a barren woman is miraculous, but Jesus' birth to a virgin is unique and unprecedented. John's role is to prepare the way for the Lord (1:17), but Jesus *is* that Lord—the Savior, who is Christ the Lord (2:11). Like others in the narrative, John prepares the way for Jesus and bears testimony that he is the Messiah and Savior of the world.

A second structural feature of the birth narrative is the series of **birth narrative hymns**, or songs of praise, offered up by Spirit-filled characters in the drama. These hymns, which

Song*	Singer	Theme
Figure 9.2—The Hymns of Luke's Birth Narrative		
The *Magnificat* 1:46 – 55	Mary	God's exaltation of the lowly and humiliation of the mighty
The *Benedictus* 1:68 – 79	Zechariah	God's salvation through the Davidic Messiah, prepared for by John the Baptist
Gloria in Excelsis 2:14	Angelic chorus	Glory to God; peace to the recipients of his grace
The *Nunc Dimittis* 2:29 – 32	Simeon	God's salvation as the glory of Israel and a light to the Gentiles

*Named for the first word in the Latin translation.

resemble Old Testament psalms, function much like the songs in a modern musical play. Just as the characters in *Oklahoma!* or *My Fair Lady* suddenly break into song, explaining or elaborating on the story, so Mary, Zechariah, Simeon, and the angelic chorus break into Spirit-inspired celebration of God's salvation. Mary glorifies the Lord for exalting the lowly and humbling the proud (1:46–55). Zechariah praises God for raising up the Savior from David's line (1:67–79). The old prophet Simeon predicts that this Messiah will bring salvation to the Gentiles as well as the Jews (2:29–32).

While the birth stories confirm that Jesus is the glorious Messiah, there are indications that his fulfillment of the promises will take an unusual course. He is born not to wealthy royalty in a palace but to poor peasants in a stable. His birth is acclaimed not by princes but by lowly shepherds. Ominously, Simeon announces that the child will cause division in Israel and will be "a sign that will be spoken against" (2:34). Already Luke's narrative casts its lot with the outsiders and the oppressed.

Coin of Caesar Augustus. According to Luke, Joseph and Mary came to Bethlehem because of a census decreed by Caesar Augustus.

The last episode in chapter 2 is not part of the birth narrative *per se*, since it concerns Jesus' Passover visit to Jerusalem as a twelve-year-old boy (2:41–52). This is the only account from Jesus' childhood found in our Gospels. The purpose of this story is to transition to Jesus' ministry by demonstrating his exceptional spiritual and physical growth. The account has two themes. The first is Jesus' growing awareness of his unique *father-son* relationship with God. This theme climaxes in verse 49 when Jesus announces that he stayed in Jerusalem because he had to be about his Father's business (or, "in my Father's house"). Though Jesus continues in submission to his human parents (v. 51), his obedience to his heavenly Father surpasses all earthly commitments.

The second theme is Jesus' growth in *wisdom*, as revealed in his dialog with the Jewish teachers in the temple. The narrator's editorial comments in 2:40 and 2:52 "frame" (an *inclusio*) the account with this wisdom motif. Luke's readers would have recognized the motif of a hero who shows unusual intelligence as a child (see fig. 9.3). More significant,

View of Bethlehem, from Shepherds' Field Church west to the city

the Old Testament background is Isaiah's description of the coming Messiah endowed with wisdom from God:

> The Spirit of the LORD will rest on him—
> > the Spirit of wisdom and of understanding,
> > the Spirit of counsel and of power,
> > the Spirit of knowledge and of the fear of the LORD.
>
> —Isaiah 11:2

At an early age, Jesus demonstrates his messianic credentials through an awareness of a unique father-son relationship with God and through his extraordinary God-given wisdom.

The Preparation of the Savior (3:1–4:13)

Like the other Gospels, Luke sets the stage for Jesus' ministry with the coming of John the Baptist. Three features unique to Luke reveal his special interests. First, he provides a detailed dating for the ministries of Jesus and John, setting them in the context of the vast Roman Empire and the religious and political milieu of first-century Palestine (3:1–2). His purpose is both historical and theological: to ground the Jesus-event in space and time and to stress its worldwide significance. The coming of the Messiah is not just a minor Jewish affair in the tiny Roman province of Judea but an epoch-turning event affecting all of humanity.

> The coming of the Spirit is for Luke the key sign of the dawn of eschatological salvation.

Second, while all three Synoptics cite Isaiah 40:3 with reference to John the Baptist, Luke lengthens the quote to Isaiah 40:5, confirming the worldwide significance of these events: "And all mankind will see God's salvation" (Luke 3:4–6). As Simeon predicted earlier, the Messiah will be both glory for Israel and "a light for revelation to the Gentiles" (2:32; see Isa. 42:6; 49:6).

Third, only Luke recounts John's ethical preaching (3:10–14). The Baptist's warning of impending judgment ("The ax is already at the root of the trees") is accompanied by a call for social justice ("Those who have two coats, let them share with those who have none"). Submission to John's "baptism of repentance" produces not an otherworldly pie-in-the-sky spirituality but a radical transformation of individuals and society, bringing them in line with God's justice and righteousness — the ethics of the kingdom of God.

Following the account of John's ministry, Jesus' baptism marks the beginning of his public ministry. Luke downplays the role of John by narrating his arrest and imprisonment before the baptism (3:19–20). This places the emphasis on the descent of the Spirit and the Father's acclamation from heaven. The coming of the Spirit is for Luke the key sign of the dawn of eschatological salvation. Just as the renewal of the Spirit of prophecy in the birth narrative sounded the overture for the kingdom age, so now Jesus is filled with and empowered by the Spirit to inaugurate that age. For Luke, the descent of the Spirit represents Jesus' "anointing" as Messiah ("Anointed One"; see 4:1, 14, 18), and the Father's voice from heaven confirms this identity. "You are my son" alludes to Psalm 2:7, confirming that Jesus is the Messiah from David's line; "with you I am well pleased" alludes to Isaiah 42:1, revealing that he is the Spirit-endowed Servant of the LORD.

Dove

> Luke's genealogy, which culminates with Adam, reflects Luke's interest in the salvation available to all humanity.

The genealogy provides further confirmation that Jesus is the Messiah (3:23–37). As in Matthew, Jesus' ancestry is traced back through David and Abraham, confirming that he is the fulfillment of God's covenants. He is the descendant of Abraham, through whom "all nations on earth will be blessed" (Gen. 22:17–18; Luke 1:54–55, 72–73), and the descendant of David, who will reign forever on Israel's throne (2 Sam. 7:12–16; Luke 1:32–33). Yet while Matthew's genealogy begins with Abraham, Luke's goes back to Adam. This fits his emphasis on the universal application of the Gospel. Jesus is not just Israel's Messiah; he is the Savior of all humanity. The conclusion of the genealogy, which identifies Adam as "the son of God," sets up the temptation narrative, where Jesus' obedient sonship is tested. (For other differences in the genealogies, see "The Ancestry of Jesus" in chap. 14.)

The temptation is the last stage in Jesus' preparation (4:1–13). Its theme is the obedience of the Son to the Father. The narrative develops two analogies, contrasting Jesus with both *Adam* and the nation *Israel*. While Adam, the first son of God, failed in his test of obedi-

Modern east wall of the old city of Jerusalem, looking up at the southeast pinnacle, perhaps the "winglet" of the temple, where Satan tempted Jesus.

ence, Jesus the true Son resists temptation and so succeeds. Similarly, while God's son Israel (Exod. 4:22–23) failed when tested in the wilderness (Ps. 95:8–11), Jesus the true Son succeeds. Jesus' forty days in the wilderness are analogous to Israel's forty years, and the three Old Testament passages Jesus cites all relate to Israel's failure (Deut. 8:3; 6:13, 16).

While Matthew and Luke record the same three temptations, the order of the last two is reversed. Matthew ends with Jesus on the mountain, probably to coincide with his emphasis on mountain revelations (cf. Matt. 5:1). Luke ends in Jerusalem, in line with his emphasis on the city as the focal point of God's saving actions. (See "Theological Themes: Jerusalem and the Temple" later in this chapter.)

For Luke, the temptation is more than mere testing. It is the beginning of a cosmic struggle with Satan that will rage throughout Jesus' ministry, both directly (8:12; 10:18; 11:14–22; 13:11–17) and through demonic opposition (4:31–37; 9:38–42; 10:17; 11:14–22). Jesus is the "stronger one" who has arrived to overpower the strong one (11:21–22).

The Galilean Ministry of the Savior (4:14–9:50)

Jesus' ministry in Galilee, often identified as his "period of popularity," is covered in Luke 4:14–9:50. Throughout this section, Jesus proclaims the message of the kingdom of God, calls disciples, and performs miracles demonstrating his kingdom authority. His popularity grows and grows. As in the other Synoptics, opposition begins here, with the religious leaders challenging Jesus' claim to forgive sins (5:21–26), his association with sinners (5:27–32; 7:36–50), his failure to fast (5:33–39), and his apparent Sabbath violations (6:1–11).

The curtain opens on the Galilean ministry with Jesus' **Nazareth sermon** (4:14–30), given in the town where he was raised. Luke moves this important episode forward from its later position in Mark (6:1–6) to serve as a summarizing introduction for Jesus'

Gospel events in Galilee

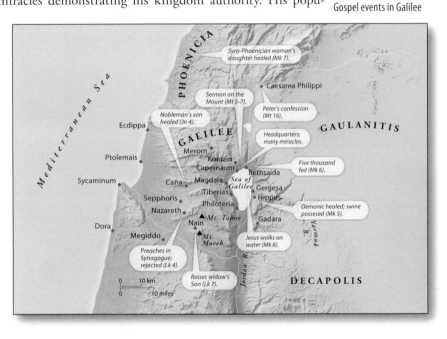

ministry. Jesus participates in the synagogue service, reading Isaiah 61 and applying it to himself, essentially declaring himself to be God's Messiah:

> The Spirit of the Lord is on me, because he has anointed me to preach good news to the poor. He has sent me to proclaim freedom for the prisoners and recovery of sight for the blind, to release the oppressed, to proclaim the year of the Lord's favor.
>
> —4:18–19, citing Isaiah 61:1–2; 58:6

Z. Radovan, Jerusalem

A cliff near Nazareth

This message of freedom and hope would have struck a chord with the citizens of Nazareth, who saw themselves as the poor and oppressed whose deliverance Jesus announced. Yet Jesus shocks his audience by pointing out that in the past, God favored Gentiles like the widow of Zarephath and Naaman the Syrian. They, not Israel, were the recipients of God's grace. Enraged, the townspeople drive Jesus out of town and attempt to throw him off a cliff. Jesus walks through the crowd and escapes.

The sermon is significant because it plays out in miniature the story which will unfold in the Gospel. Jesus' rejection in Nazareth foreshadows his coming rejection by his own people Israel. His announcement that "no prophet is accepted in his hometown" (v. 24) becomes a prediction of his death in Jerusalem. Yet through his resurrection, he will provide spiritual deliverance for Jew and Gentile alike.

Following the sermon, the narrator recounts stories showing how Jesus fulfills this ministry. As predicted in Isaiah 61, Jesus preaches the good news to the poor (4:31–32, 43–44), frees prisoners oppressed by Satan (4:31–37, 41), and heals the sick (4:38–39, 40; 5:12–14, 17–26).

During the Galilean ministry, Jesus also calls and trains disciples. While all three Synoptics describe Jesus' calling of Peter and his fishing companions, only Luke links this to a dramatic nature miracle (5:1–11). Peter, exhausted after an unsuccessful night of fishing, is reluctant to take his boat out again at Jesus' request. Finally conceding, he is awed and humbled when the net comes back overflowing. Jesus then calls Peter to catch people instead of fish. Jesus' extraordinary authority provokes authentic discipleship. The true disciple approaches Jesus in awe and humility and gives up all to follow him (5:8, 11). The call of Levi (5:27–32), a despised tax collector, similarly demonstrates that Jesus came to call not the "righteous" — that is, the *self*-righteous — but sinners who recognize their need of him.

> Luke's account of Jesus' inaugural sermon at his hometown synagogue of Nazareth sets the stage for the events which play out in the rest of the Gospel.

Jesus has been proclaiming the kingdom of God. Now, in his Great Sermon (6:17–49), he defines the radical values of that kingdom for his disciples. (See fig. 8.8, p. 228, for the relationship to Matthew's Sermon on the Mount.) Like Matthew, Luke begins with Beatitudes. Yet his are more concrete, omitting the spiritual qualifications found in Matthew. "Blessed are the poor *in spirit*" becomes "blessed are you who are poor." This does not mean that Luke rejects a spiritual significance. The poor are oppressed because of their allegiance to the Son of Man (6:22). But as with elsewhere in this Gospel, social and economic realities go hand in hand with spiritual ones. This is brought home by Luke's four "woes," which balance the blessings. The rich and powerful are castigated for their independence from God and their oppression of the poor. The kingdom of God brings a radical reversal of fortunes and a reordering of society's values.

Central to this new order is a radical new ethic of love, directed even toward one's enemies. God's people are to respond with good deeds to those who hate them, to bless those who curse them, and to pray for those who mistreat them (6:28). Such actions are summed up in the "Golden Rule": "Do to others as you would have them do to you" (6:31). The demand for this kind of love arises from the identity of the people of God. To love only those who love you would reflect no more than the standards of the people of the world (6:32–34). God's children must live to a higher standard, reflecting the nature of their Father, who loves even those who are ungrateful and wicked (6:35).

How will people respond to this radical kingdom preaching? Following the sermon, Luke narrates a series of episodes illustrating various responses to Jesus. The repeated theme is that outsiders, outcasts, and the lowly receive forgiveness and healing, while the proud and self-righteous miss out. A Roman centurion expresses such faith in Jesus' ability to heal his servant that Jesus ironically exclaims, "I have not found such great faith even in Israel!" (7:1–10). A poor widow's son is raised from the dead to the astonishment of the crowd (7:11–17). Jesus commends a sinful woman—probably a prostitute—for anointing his feet with costly perfume, while rebuking the pious Pharisee Simon for not even showing him common hospitality (7:36–50). Jesus' pronouncement summarizes this section: Those who have been forgiven much, love much; those who think they need no forgiveness, love little (7:47). The narrator explicitly states this theme in the midst of Jesus' accolades for

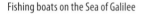

Fishing boats on the Sea of Galilee

Richard Strauss

John the Baptist (7:24–35). While the people, even sinful tax collectors, accepted John's baptism of repentance, the Pharisees and scribes in self-righteousness "rejected God's purpose for themselves" (7:29–30). The parable of the soils (8:1–15) illustrates these various responses to the gospel. Good soil—those receptive to the words of Jesus—persevere and produce a great harvest. The other soils do not.

Another key theme of this section is the identity of Jesus. Three times the question is raised by characters in the narrative. First, John the Baptist sends his disciples to ask whether Jesus is "the one who was to come" (the Messiah; 7:19). Second, when Jesus calms the storm, the disciples ask in amazement, "Who is this? He commands even the winds and the water, and they obey him" (8:25). Finally, Herod Antipas hears of Jesus' actions and wonders, "Who, then, is this I hear such things about?" (9:9). The answer unfolds through Jesus' words and deeds. His actions reveal his messianic authority, healing the sick, casting out demons, raising the dead, and performing nature miracles like feeding the five thousand and calming the storm. Jesus then explains these actions with reference to the fulfillment of Scripture (especially Isaiah): "Go back and report to John what you have seen and heard: The blind receive sight, the lame walk, those who have leprosy are cured, the deaf hear, the dead are raised, and the good news is preached to the poor" (7:22; cf. Isa. 26:19; 29:18–19; 35:5–6; 61:1–2). This saying has special significance for Luke's readers since Jesus defined his ministry this way in the Nazareth sermon (4:18–19). His messiahship is revealed not through a war of conquest with the Romans but by inaugurating the signs of the kingdom age predicted by Isaiah the prophet.

> As in Mark and Matthew, the confession of Peter in Luke marks a key turning point, as Jesus radically clarifies the role of the Messiah.

The question "Who is this?" finds its explicit answer in the confession of Peter, who declares that Jesus is "the Christ of God" (9:18–27). The confession is the climax of the first stage of Jesus' self-revelation (chaps. 4–9). What the angel Gabriel had prophesied about Jesus (1:33–35) and what his miracles have revealed is now proclaimed by Peter, the representative of the disciples. As in Mark and Matthew, the confession also marks a key turning point in the narrative, as Jesus now radically clarifies the role of the Messiah. In the first of three "passion predictions," he confirms that the role of the Messiah is to suffer and die, rising again on the third day (9:21–22; cf. 9:43–45; 18:31–34). His disciples must follow him in cross-bearing discipleship (9:23–26).

At the transfiguration which follows, the veil over Jesus' person is lifted and his closest disciples, Peter, James, and John, are given a glimpse of his true glory (9:28–36). In Matthew and Mark, the transfiguration is usually seen as a preview of the glory of Jesus' second coming. Luke's presentation suggests instead the heavenly glory of Jesus' resurrection and exaltation. Only Luke mentions that the topic

Mount Tabor, the traditional site of the transfiguration

© Neal Bierling/Zondervan Image Archives

of Jesus' conversation with Moses and Elijah is his "departure" (*exodos*), which he was going to fulfill in Jerusalem (9:31). The term "departure" probably refers to the whole event of Jesus' death, resurrection, and ascension, and calls to mind the exodus from Egypt, God's great act of deliverance in the Old Testament. Through suffering, Jesus the Messiah will lead God's people to salvation through a new and greater "exodus."

The Mission of the Savior: The Journey to Jerusalem (9:51 – 19:27)

The events following Peter's confession (9:20) form a transition into the next phase of Jesus' ministry. At Luke 9:51, Jesus "resolutely set out for Jerusalem." As noted earlier, what follows is called the travel narrative, or the journey to Jerusalem, since for the next ten chapters Jesus is heading for Jerusalem to accomplish his messianic role. What is unusual about this "journey" is that Jesus does not head straight for Jerusalem but wanders from place to place. Though notices in the text occasionally remind the reader that Jesus is traveling (9:57; 10:1, 38; 18:35; 19:1), or that he is heading for Jerusalem (9:51 – 56; 13:22, 33; 17:11; 18:31; 19:11, 28, 41; cf. 19:45), the bulk of the material is not a travel itinerary at all but the teaching of Jesus together with a few miracle stories. In short, the journey is not a straight-line trip to Jerusalem but *a period of Jesus' heightened resolve* to reach his Jerusalem goal. It expresses a changed emphasis in his ministry as he "resolves" to go to Jerusalem to fulfill the role of the suffering Messiah. Here we see the key symbolic and theological role of Jerusalem in Luke's work. It is in Jerusalem the prophets were killed, and there God will accomplish his salvation (13:32 – 35).

> The travel narrative in Luke is not a straight-line journey to Jerusalem but a period of Jesus' heightened resolve to reach his Jerusalem goal.

The road from Jerusalem to Jericho followed this gorge, known as the Wadi Kelt.

While much of the material in these ten chapters appears in Matthew in different contexts, much else is unique to Luke. Many stories and parables are concerned with God's special care for the poor and outcast. For this reason, this section has sometimes been called the **Gospel for the Outcast** (9:51–19:27). Well-known parables include the good Samaritan (10:29–37), the rich fool (12:13–21), the great banquet (14:16–24), things lost (sheep, coin, and son; 15:1–32), the rich man and Lazarus (16:19–31), the persistent widow (18:1–8), and the Pharisee and the tax collector (18:9–14). All of these in some way carry the theme of *reversal*: humble "outsiders" receive blessings or commendation, while prideful "insiders" suffer rebuke or loss (see fig. 9.4).

Figure 9.4—Parables of Luke's "Gospel for the Outcast" (chaps. 9–18)
Scenes of Reversal and Surprise

The Good Samaritan (10:29–37). An assaulted man's true neighbor turns out to be not his fellow Jews but a despised Samaritan who offers him comfort and aid. The parable teaches that authentic spiritual life is defined not by ethnic heritage but by love for God and for others.

The Rich Fool (12:13–21). When a rich man's farm produces a bumper crop, he chooses to store it all for a life of luxury. God rebukes him as a "fool" and predicts his impending death. The parable teaches the danger of greed. All of our resources are merely gifts from God to be used for his service.

The Great Banquet (14:16–24). When a man throws a great banquet, his invited guests all make excuses and refuse to come. In response, he sends his servants to bring in the town's most despised members—the poor, handicapped, and outcast. The parable reflects Jesus' ministry, in which Israel's religious elite refuse Jesus' kingdom invitation, while spiritual outsiders—the poor, sinners, Samaritans, and Gentiles—respond with faith and repentance.

Lost Coin, Lost Sheep, Lost Son (15:1–32). While the loss of something valuable—whether a coin, a sheep, or a prodigal son—results in sadness and grief, finding the lost brings joy and celebration. While the religious leaders turned their backs on sinners, the Father rejoiced when even one was found.

The Rich Man and Lazarus (16:19–31). A rich man and a penniless beggar both die, experiencing a dramatic reversal in the afterlife. The parable teaches that our attitudes and actions—particularly those toward the less fortunate—carry eternal consequences. In the parable's conclusion, Abraham says that the rich man's brothers would not respond even if Lazarus rose from the dead to warn them. The veiled message is that even Jesus' resurrection will not be enough to convince Israel's obdurate leadership.

The Persistent Widow (18:1–8). A poor widow facing an unjust and uncaring judge finds justice by wearing the man down with her persistence. Jesus here uses a "lesser to greater" argument to show that if this is the case with an evil judge, how much more will our loving heavenly Father meet the needs of his children who are persistent in prayer?

The Pharisee and the Tax Collector (18:9–14). Jesus shocks his audience by telling a parable about two men praying in the temple. While a despised but repentant tax collector receives forgiveness from God, a pious but hypocritical Pharisee does not. God requires not an outward show of religiosity but an inward heart of humility.

The journey is also marked by Jesus' training of the disciples and the theme of the cost of discipleship. In an opening passage, three people approach Jesus, all with aspirations of discipleship. For each, Jesus sets out the radical cost of following him (9:57 – 62). This is followed by many accounts about discipleship: the commissioning of the seventy (10:1 – 24), the unique revelation to the disciples through the Son (10:21 – 24), the story of Mary and Martha, where Mary represents a true disciple (10:38 – 42), instruction on the cost of discipleship (14:25 – 35), the parable of the shrewd manager (16:1 – 13), and teaching on righteous living (e.g., prayer, 11:1 – 13; worry, 12:22 – 31; watchfulness, 12:35 – 48, 17:20 – 37; faith, 17:5 – 10; humility, 18:9 – 17; the dangers of wealth, 12:13 – 21, 16:19 – 31, 18:18 – 30; etc.).

The journey climaxes with the **episode of Zacchaeus** (19:1 – 10) and the parable of the ten minas (19:12 – 27). Zacchaeus is the ultimate of Israel's outcasts — not just a tax collector but a *chief* tax collector, the worst among the worst. Yet Jesus reaches out and offers salvation even to him. The "today" of salvation announced in Nazareth (4:21) now arrives in Zacchaeus's home: "Today salvation has come to this house, because this man, too, is a son of Abraham" (19:9). Luke 19:10 provides a fitting summary not only for the Zacchaeus account but for Luke's whole Gospel: "For the Son of Man came to seek and to save what was lost."

Luke's parable of the ten minas is similar to Matthew's parable of the talents (Matt. 25:14 – 30), since both concern the need for good stewardship during Jesus' absence. Yet Luke's version has a second theme which relates to Jesus' Jerusalem "departure." The narrator says that Jesus told the parable "because he was near Jerusalem and the people thought that the kingdom of God was going to appear at once" (19:11). The landowner of Matthew becomes in Luke a royal prince who goes away to receive a kingdom.[4] At the end, the citizens who have rejected his reign are brought forward and executed. The implication is that Jesus will receive his throne not when he enters Jerusalem but at his ascension to God's right hand, and that his reign will be consummated when he returns in judgment (see Luke 9:31, 51; 22:69; Acts 2:30 – 36; 3:19 – 23). Jesus' heavenly reign again is a key theme in Luke's narrative.

> The Zacchaeus episode represents the climax to Luke's travel narrative as a chief tax collector responds to Jesus' message of God's love for the lost.

A sycamore tree in Jericho

© Neal Bierling/Zondervan Image Archives

The Savior in Jerusalem: Conflict and Controversy (19:28 – 21:38)

Jesus' approach to Jerusalem (19:28 – 44) sets the stage for the climax of the narrative. Descending from the Mount of Olives — the place where the Messiah was expected to arrive (Zech. 14:4) — Jesus comes to Jerusalem riding on a donkey, fulfilling the prophecy of the humble, peace-bringing king of Zechariah 9:9. Whereas in Matthew the crowds

---

4. The parable may have its background in the story of Herod's son Archelaus, who violently put down protests after his father's death. In response, the Jews sent a delegation to Rome to petition against his kingship.

View of the Mount of Olives from the Temple Mount

cried out, "Blessed is he who comes in the name of the Lord" (see Ps. 118:26), in Luke it is *the disciples* who recognize the event's significance and herald Jesus even more explicitly as the Messiah: "Blessed is *the king* who comes in the name of the Lord" (19:38). When the Pharisees call on Jesus to rebuke his disciples, he responds that if they are silenced, the stones themselves will cry out. All of creation should now rejoice, for the time of God's redemption has arrived.

Again we see the paradox of Jerusalem, representing both God's salvation and Israel's rejection. Jesus weeps over the city and predicts her destruction (19:41–44). She will be judged for refusing to acknowledge her Messiah. In the beginning of Luke's Gospel, Zechariah announced that God was about to "visit" his people with salvation (1:68). Now at the end, Jesus laments that Jerusalem has missed the time of God's "visitation" (19:44). Jesus then enters the temple and drives out the sellers, symbolically acting out the judgment just predicted (19:45–47).

In chapter 20, the narrator records a series of debates pitting Jesus against the religious leaders in Jerusalem (see fig. 7.6). As the boy Jesus once impressed Israel's teachers with his Spirit-endowed wisdom (2:46–47), so now that same wisdom reveals his messianic authority and exposes the deceit of Israel's leaders. In the midst of these controversies, Jesus tells the parable of the wicked tenant farmers. As in Mark and Matthew, the parable is an allegory drawing images from Isaiah's parable of the vineyard (Isaiah 5) to indict Israel's leaders for their opposition to God's prophets in the past and for their murder of God's Son. The leaders recognize that Jesus has spoken the parable against them and plot his arrest (20:19). Ironically, their rage causes them to act out the role Jesus has just predicted.

The episode of the widow's offering which follows stands in contrast to the greed and hypocrisy of the scribes. While they exploit others for gain (20:45–47), she gives self-sacrificially from her poverty (21:1–4). The theme of reversal appears again: the humble, the poor, and the oppressed are exalted, while the mighty are brought down.

With the time of his departure rapidly approaching, Jesus now instructs his disciples on the catastrophic events to come for Jerusalem and the signs which will accompany his return (Luke 21:5–36). Luke's version of Jesus' end-times Olivet Discourse follows the same basic structure as the other Synoptics but places greater stress on the soon-to-come siege and destruction of Jerusalem. The discourse is open to various interpretations but is perhaps best divided into two periods: (1) signs of the present age, including the appearance of false messiahs, catastrophic (but common) events like wars, famines, and earthquakes, widespread persecution of believers, and the destruction of Jerusalem (AD 70) (vv. 8–24); (2) events which will herald the end of the age: signs in the heavens and chaos on the earth, culminating in the glorious return of the Son of Man (vv. 25–28). The discourse concludes with the parable of the fig tree to encourage believers to watchfulness and readiness (vv. 29–36).

The Passion of the Savior in Jerusalem (22:1–23:56)

The climax of the Gospel is now reached with Jesus' passion (chaps. 22–23). It begins with Judas's agreement to betray Jesus, and includes the Last Supper, the arrest on the Mount of Olives, Peter's denial, Jesus' subsequent hearings (before the Sanhedrin, Pilate, Herod, and Pilate again), and his crucifixion and burial. The primary theme of the passion narrative is the fulfillment of Scripture, as Jesus the righteous and innocent suffering Servant remains faithful to God's purpose and calling. The central *christological theme*, repeated throughout the trial and crucifixion, is Jesus' *innocence*. This theme confirms his identification as the righteous suffering Servant of Isaiah 53.

> The central christological theme of Luke's passion narrative is Jesus' innocence, portraying him as the righteous Servant of Isaiah 53.

While in general Luke does not stress the saving significance of the cross, the Last Supper narrative is an exception, as Jesus interprets his coming death as the sacrifice which will establish the new covenant (22:20; cf. Jer. 31:31–34). The ritual of the bread and the cup will serve as a reminder to the disciples of his sacrifice for them. Jesus again predicts his betrayal and death, placing them in the context of fulfilled prophecy (22:22, 36–37): "Yes, what is written about me is reaching its fulfillment" (v. 37).

In the narrative which follows, the failures of the disciples contrast with Jesus' faithful endurance. They argue about who is the greatest, so he teaches again about servant leadership (22:24–29). He continues to encourage and train them: affirming that they have stood with him in his trials (v. 28), declaring their leadership role in his coming kingdom (vv. 29–30), predicting Simon's denial but also his subsequent restoration (vv. 31–34). He also calls them to a new level of readiness for mission, modifying the instructions that he gave when he first sent them out to preach (9:3–5). They are now to take purse, bag, and even sword. The coming crisis will be far more challenging than anything before. In this way, Luke prepares his readers for the apostles' missionary outreach in Acts.

Following the meal, Jesus and his disciples proceed to the Mount of Olives, where Jesus agonizes in prayer over his coming ordeal (22:39–46). Jesus' true humanity and his willing obedience are evident as he prays, "Father, if you are willing, take this cup from me; yet not my will, but yours be done." In contrast, the weakness of the disciples is shown as they fall asleep, failing to obey Jesus' call to watchfulness and prayer.

Judas the betrayer suddenly appears with a crowd to arrest him (22:47–53). In a brief attempt to defend Jesus, one of the disciples strikes the servant of the high priest with a sword, cutting off his ear. Luke alone recounts that Jesus heals the man—a sign of his compassion and divine control of the situation. Jesus prohibits further resistance but then rebukes the leaders for coming after him at night like a criminal.

Jesus is arrested and taken to the house of the high priest (22:54–65). Peter follows at a distance and, in the outer courtyard, three times denies that he is Jesus' disciple. With dramatic flair, Luke describes how at the moment of betrayal, Jesus turns and looks directly at Peter. Peter flees and weeps bitterly, having failed his Lord.

At daybreak, Jesus is brought before the Sanhedrin (22:66–71). When they ask if he is the Messiah, Jesus refuses to answer, for two reasons: they will not believe him nor will they answer a question he would pose. The point is that they have repeatedly refused to "answer" God's call through his ministry. Jesus then indirectly affirms his messianic identity with an allusion to Psalm 110: the Son of Man will be vindicated and enthroned at God's right hand. Both Matthew and Mark include an allusion to Daniel 7 ("and coming on the clouds of heaven"), but Luke again stresses Jesus' present heavenly reign over his future return in glory. Jesus' messianic response calls forth another question from the Sanhedrin: "Are you then the Son of God?" Jesus' ambiguous response, "you say that I am," essentially means, "By asking that question you know that I am making that claim." They accept this as an affirmation and call for his conviction.

The Church of All Nations, rock and altar remembering when Jesus left his disciples and prayed alone

The Sanhedrin next brings Jesus before the Roman governor, Pilate (23:1–25), where—hoping for a conviction of treason—they present charges that become more political: misleading the nation, opposing Roman taxes (a false accusation: 20:20–26), and claiming to be Christ, a king. Although Pilate concludes that Jesus is not a political threat, he does not want to displease the Sanhedrin. An apparent solution arises when he learns that Jesus is from Galilee, the jurisdiction of Herod Antipas (see 3:1). Herod is in Jerusalem for the Passover, so Pilate sends Jesus to him. From a narrative perspective, Pilate may want to avoid personal liability for a difficult decision, or perhaps he is seeking expert Jewish advice from Herod. In any case, Herod is delighted, hoping to see Jesus perform a miracle. Jesus remains silent under questioning, so Herod mocks his claim to kingship and returns him to Pilate. Only Luke records this appearance before Herod. In a third phase of the

Roman trial, Pilate reconvenes the Sanhedrin and announces his intention to release Jesus. Under the vehement objections of the leaders and the people (who for the first time in Luke now turn against Jesus), he capitulates, releasing the insurrectionist Barabbas and turning Jesus over to be crucified.

Luke's crucifixion scene shows Jesus faithfully fulfilling his call to suffer as God's Servant (23:26–49). Though a victim of injustice, he is in charge of his fate. He continues to act as a prophet, calling on the grieving women to weep for themselves, not for him, because of the coming destruction of Jerusalem (23:28–31; cf. 13:34–35; 19:41–44; 21:20–21). He continues to dispense God's grace, forgiving his enemies and offering salvation to the repentant criminal (23:34, 43). There is great irony in the crucifixion scene. The rulers, the soldiers, and even one of the criminals mock Jesus because he claimed to save others but cannot save himself. Jesus stays faithful to his calling by refusing to save himself, and so brings salvation to others. Jesus dies after entrusting himself to the Father's care.

Coin of Herod Antipas

While in Mark the centurion sees Jesus' death and declares him to be "the Son of God," in Luke he announces that Jesus is "innocent" (*dikaios*). As noted above, this theme is central to Luke's passion narrative, appearing repeatedly throughout the trials and crucifixion. Pilate, Herod, the repentant criminal, and the centurion all declare Jesus to be innocent (23:4, 14–15, 22, 41, 47). There is a play on words here in Greek, since *dikaios* can mean "innocent" or "righteous." The same word is used in the Greek Old Testament of Isaiah's suffering Servant, who gives himself for the sins of the people (Isa. 53:11 LXX). Jesus dies as the Servant of the LORD, faithfully fulfilling the Scripture-ordained role of the Messiah.

As in the other Gospels, Joseph of Arimathea requests the body of Jesus and buries it in his own tomb (23:50–54). The narrative receives a dramatic pause as the women prepare spices and then rest on the Sabbath.

The Resurrection and Ascension of the Savior (24:1–53)

Luke provides three accounts of resurrection appearances: the women at the tomb (24:1–12), the appearance to two disciples on the road to Emmaus (24:13–35), and the appearance to the eleven disciples in Jerusalem (24:36–49). The episode of the **Emmaus disciples** occurs only in Luke and represents his most theologically significant contribution to the resurrection narratives. Cleopas and his companion represent the discouragement and unbelief of Jesus' followers. When they meet Jesus on the road (his identity is hidden from them), they express profound disappointment at the tragic events in Jerusalem. While Jesus of Nazareth was a great prophet, they had hoped that he might be more—the Messiah

The account of the Emmaus disciples is Luke's most important contribution to the Gospel resurrection narratives, confirming that the death and resurrection of the Christ is the fulfillment of God's purpose in salvation history.

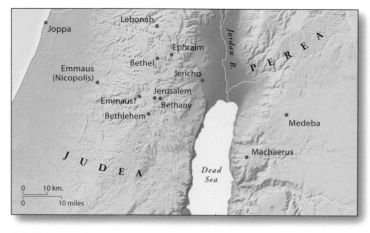

Probable location of Emmaus

who would redeem Israel. Yet his crucifixion dashed their hopes. Jesus responds by rebuking them for their hardness of heart. Did not the Scriptures predict the suffering of the Messiah? School is in session as Jesus takes them through the Hebrew Scriptures, showing how they all point to the Christ. He is the centerpoint of salvation history.

Though equipped with the truth of Scripture, the two do not recognize Jesus until he breaks bread with them. As is the case elsewhere in Luke, Jesus meets people in personal fellowship and communion. When Jesus disappears, they joyfully rush back to Jerusalem, where they find the apostles already announcing the same message: Jesus is risen indeed! Jesus suddenly appears to them all. The true bodily resurrection is affirmed as the disciples touch Jesus and he eats in their presence. His teaching affirms two important themes of Luke-Acts (24:45 – 49): (1) Jesus' death and resurrection, prophesied in Scripture, bring forgiveness of sins to all who repent and believe; (2) the disciples are to be his witnesses, going forth in the power of the Spirit to preach the good news of salvation to all nations, from Jerusalem to the ends of the earth.

The Gospel ends with a brief account of Jesus' ascension, described in more detail in Acts 1:1 – 11. The ascension gives closure to the Gospel and sets the stage for Jesus' guidance of his church from his authoritative position at the right hand of God (cf. Acts 2:33 – 36).

Latrun monastery traditionally associated with Luke 24 and the two disciples going to Emmaus

© Neal Bierling/Zondervan Image Archives

Canada Park, Latrun in the Emmaus area

LUKE'S PORTRAIT OF JESUS: THE SAVIOR FOR ALL PEOPLE

Like the many sides of a diamond, Luke's portrait of Jesus is multifaceted, and many titles are used for him. Since the overall theme of Luke-Acts is the arrival of God's end-times salvation (see "Theological Themes" below), the best summarizing description for Jesus is *the Savior for all people.* Two titles which are especially important for Luke, helping to explain Jesus' saving role, are *prophet* and *Christ* (Messiah).

Prophet Like Moses, Mighty in Word and Deed

More than the other Gospels, Luke presents Jesus as a great prophet. When Jesus raises the widow's son from the dead, the people cry out, "A great prophet has appeared among us" (7:16). The disciples on the Emmaus road identify him as "a prophet, powerful in word and deed" (24:19). While the people link Jesus' prophetic office to his miracles and teaching, Jesus connects it especially to his suffering. At Nazareth, he affirms that "no prophet is accepted in his hometown" (4:24) and later accuses Israel of murdering her own prophets (11:47–52). As he journeys to Jerusalem, he affirms that "no prophet can die outside Jerusalem!" (13:33).

> Luke presents Jesus as the Savior for all people.

In Acts this portrait is further clarified as Peter identifies Jesus as the **prophet like Moses** predicted in Deuteronomy 18:15 (see Acts 3:22–23; 7:37). Like Moses, Jesus proclaims God's word and performs miracles. And as Moses warned, those who do not heed God's prophet will be "cut from among his people."

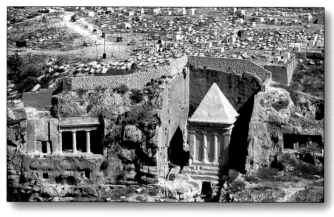

Zechariah's tomb in the Kidron Valley. Jesus identified himself as one who would suffer like the prophets of old.

Luke's prophetic portrait thus has three key components: (1) Jesus performs miracles and proclaims God's word like the great prophets of old; (2) like the prophets, Jesus will suffer for his faithfulness; (3) if Israel does not heed God's prophet, divine judgment will follow. Luke's readers know that this will come to fulfillment in the destruction of Jerusalem.

Christ the Lord

Though Jesus' status as a prophet is important, it is exceeded by his role as Messiah. This is evident already in the birth narrative. While John the Baptist is a great prophet, Jesus is the Messiah and the Son of God (1:32–33). He is the "Savior ... Christ the Lord" (2:11). These four important titles—Messiah (Christ), Son of God, Savior, and Lord—are closely linked, all portraying Jesus as God's agent of deliverance, the fulfillment of God's saving purpose.

The startling revelation to which Luke's narrative builds is that God's salvation is accomplished not only through a suffering prophet but through the suffering Messiah. This is the main theme of the Emmaus resurrection account. Though the two disciples already recognize Jesus as a great prophet (24:19), Jesus opens their eyes to Scripture, showing them that *the Christ had to suffer* (24:25–27). This is repeated to all of the disciples in the following episode (24:46) and serves as a repeated refrain in Acts (3:18; 17:3; 26:23). The Messiah fulfills the role of the suffering Servant of Isaiah 53, bringing salvation to his people.

> The startling revelation to which Luke's narrative builds is that God's salvation is accomplished not just through a suffering prophet but through the suffering Messiah.

The connection between Jesus' messiahship and God's saving purpose appears at the climax of Peter's Pentecost speech (Acts 2:29–39). God's promise to David to place one of his descendants on his throne is fulfilled through Jesus' resurrection and exaltation to God's right hand as "Lord and Christ" (Pss. 132:11; 16:8–11; 110:1). Salvation is now available to all who repent and believe. As reigning Messiah and Lord, Jesus pours out God's Spirit to empower his followers to take this message of salvation to the ends of the earth.

OTHER CHARACTERS IN LUKE'S GOSPEL

Apostles in Training

As we have seen, the disciples in Mark appear as failures, and in Matthew as having little faith. Luke provides a more positive slant. We might say they are "apostles in training." The narrator clearly has his eyes on Acts, where the apostles will play a decisive leadership role in the expansion of the church. Six times in the Gospel, the Twelve are already called "apostles" (in Matthew once, in Mark twice).

This is not to say the picture is all rosy. The disciples still have many failings. They argue over who is the greatest (9:46; 22:24), jealously exclude others from Jesus' ministry (9:49; 18:15–16), and are rebuked by Jesus for vindictiveness against a Samaritan village (9:53–55). Their faith is weak (8:22–25; 9:12–13, 40–41), they sleep when they should be alert (9:32; 22:45–46), and they fail to comprehend the meaning of Jesus' passion (9:45; 18:34). Peter still denies Jesus (22:54–62), and the disciples cowardly watch Jesus die from a distance (23:49).

> Luke's portrait of the disciples, presenting them as "apostles in training," is more positive than Matthew's and especially Mark's.

Yet negative scenes are softened. In the healing of the boy with seizures, Luke omits the statement about the disciples' lack of faith (9:41–43; Matt. 17:20). Twice the narrator excuses their failure to understand the passion by noting that "its meaning was concealed from them" (9:45; 18:34). After the first passion prediction, Luke omits all reference to Peter's challenge and Jesus' rebuke "Get behind me Satan!" (9:21–22; Mark 8:32–33). He omits Mark's statement that the disciples scattered in fear at Jesus' arrest (9:53; Mark 14:50).

Positive statements are also made. Through the Son, the disciples have received unique divine revelation hidden from others (10:21–24). They have left all to follow Jesus, and so will be rewarded many times over (18:28–30). Jesus confers on them a kingdom—they will reign on thrones judging the twelve tribes—because they have remained through his trials (22:28–30). Though predicting Peter's denial, Jesus prays for his restoration. Peter's horrific denial now becomes a growth-producing ordeal after which he will "turn back" and strengthen his brothers (22:32).

These are no longer the "antidisciples" of Mark's Gospel but immature disciples on the road to becoming authoritative leaders in the church.

The Religious Leaders

The religious leaders are portrayed somewhat differently in Luke than in the other Gospels. In Matthew, they are evil to the core, with no hope of redemption. In Luke, their primary trait is *self-righteousness*, resulting in foolish rejection of God's invitation to salvation.[5] This theme is epitomized by the call of Levi. When the Pharisees and scribes criticize Jesus for eating with sinners, Jesus responds that he has come not for the "righteous" but sinners (5:27–32). The leaders are not righteous but *self*-righteous. They "pretend to be righteous" (20:20), seeking self-justification (10:29). They "justify themselves in the eyes of people" (16:15) and are "confident of their own righteousness, looking down on everybody else" (18:9–12).

The theme is summed up in 7:30, where the self-righteous leaders "reject God's purpose for themselves," and so lose out on salvation. They are "foolish people" (11:40, 52)

---

5. See M. A. Powell, "The Religious Leaders in Luke: A Literary-Critical Study," *JBL* 109 (1990): 103–20; idem., *What Is Narrative Criticism?* 63.

who out of ignorance refuse to repent and so miss God's coming (19:42, 44). Jesus' parables drive this theme home. In the great banquet, the invited guests refuse the host's invitation and so miss the celebration (14:15–24). In the parable of the lost sheep, Jesus concludes with "there will be more rejoicing in heaven over one sinner who repents than over ninety-nine righteous persons *who do not need to repent*" (15:7, emphasis added). In the parable of the prodigal son, the older brother refuses to join the celebration for his brother's safe return (15:29–31).

> The primary characteristic of the religious leaders in Luke is that they are "self-righteous," rejecting God's invitation to salvation.

This pride and self-righteousness results in little gratitude toward God or love for other human beings. Jesus tells Simon the Pharisee that he loves little because he has been forgiven little (7:40–47). While the good Samaritan stops to help an injured Jew, Israel's religious leaders pass by on the other side out of contempt for human life (10:31–32).

Though Matthew views the religious leaders as intractably lost, in Luke there is still hope. Because their failure comes from foolishness and ignorance, they have a second chance to repent and receive salvation. The stage is set for Acts, in which Peter preaches in Jerusalem that "I know that you acted in ignorance, as did your leaders.... Repent, then, and turn to God" (3:17–19). Throughout Acts, Paul goes from synagogue to synagogue, calling out a faithful remnant. Israel need only repent to receive "times of refreshing" from the Lord (3:19).

We have treated all of the religious leaders together as antagonistic to the gospel, but Luke sometimes draws a distinction between various groups: Pharisees, Sadducees, scribes, chief priests, elders, and rulers. Some scholars have concluded that Luke views the Pharisees more favorably than either the Sadducees or the chief priests, treating them almost as "quasi-Christians" (especially in Acts). While it is true that Luke shares more theological affinity with the Pharisees than the Sadducees, especially with reference to the resurrection (Luke 20:27; Acts 23:8), the Pharisees must still be viewed as antagonists in Luke's narrative. The distinctions Luke draws arise primarily because he recognizes that the chief priests, elders, and Sadducees had their power base in Jerusalem, and so were the primary conspirators in Jesus' arrest and, later, the main opponents of the Jerusalem church. While certain religious leaders receive commendation for spiritual discernment (Zechariah the priest, Jairus the synagogue ruler, Joseph of Arimathea [a Sanhedrin member]), these characters represent a variety of groups and are part of Luke's broader theme that God is calling out a faithful remnant from within Israel.

THEOLOGICAL THEMES

As we noted in chapter 1, Luke is the most thematic of the four Gospels, with certain key themes resurfacing again and again in the narrative.

Promise-Fulfillment: The Salvation of God

The central theme of Luke-Acts is *the arrival of God's salvation, available now to people everywhere*. As predicted in the prophets, God has acted through Jesus the Messiah to save his people Israel, and this salvation is now going forth to the whole world. Though the author slants his Gospel to a Gentile audience, he grounds it firmly in its Jewish roots. The key for Luke is the *continuity* between the history of Israel, the person and work of Jesus, and the establishment of the church.

While this theme reaches its climax in Acts, there are many examples of universality already in Luke's Gospel: the dating of Jesus' career in secular history (1:5; 2:1; 3:1–2), the genealogy descending to Adam (3:23–38), the extended quote of Isaiah 40:5 ("all mankind will see God's salvation" [3:6]), and the reference to God's blessings for Gentiles in the Nazareth sermon (4:25–27). Various stories point forward to the Gentile mission. Jesus commends the centurion, saying, "I have not found such great faith even in Israel" (7:9). Though all of the Synoptics describe the mission of the Twelve (9:1–6), only Luke records a second mission involving seventy[6] of his disciples (10:1–20). The number seventy probably represents the nations of the world, since seventy names are listed in the "table of nations" in Genesis 10.

> The central theme of Luke-Acts is the arrival of God's salvation, available now to all people everywhere.

This theme of universal salvation has both agreements and differences with Matthew. For Matthew, the commission to go to all nations is given only after Jesus' resurrection (Matt. 28:18–20; contrast Jesus' command in 10:5–6). In Luke, already in the birth narrative Simeon prophesies that salvation will extend to the Gentiles (2:32). All along it was God's plan to bring salvation to all peoples. By fulfilling the promises to Israel, Jesus becomes Savior of the whole world.

While both Matthew and Luke have a strong emphasis on promise and fulfillment, their approaches are very different here as well. Matthew repeatedly identifies individual Old Testament texts as fulfilled in Jesus' life. Luke takes a more holistic approach: the whole of Jesus' life and ministry is a fulfillment of prophecy. As Jesus tells the Emmaus disciples, Scripture finds its culmination and fulfillment in the Messiah (24:27).

The Dawn of Salvation and the Coming of the Spirit

The theme of universal end-times salvation is closely linked by Luke to the coming of the Holy Spirit. In his Pentecost sermon in Acts, Peter cites the prophet Joel to show that "in the last days, God says, I will pour out my Spirit on all people" (Acts 2:17; Joel 2:28–32). A key theme for Luke is that *the coming of the Spirit heralds the dawn of the new age.* The activity of the Spirit appears in three distinct periods in Luke-Acts: in preview in the birth narrative, in empowerment for Jesus' ministry, and in the abiding presence of Jesus in his church:

> A key theme for Luke is that the coming of the Spirit heralds the dawn of the new age.

1. In the birth narrative, the angel Gabriel prophesies that John will be filled with the Holy Spirit from his mother's womb (1:15; cf. 1:41–44), and Elizabeth and Zechariah are filled with the Spirit when they break into prophetic utterance (1:41, 67). The Spirit also rests on righteous Simeon,

---

6. Some manuscripts identify the number as seventy-two, probably because the Septuagint lists seventy-two nations in Genesis 10.

granting guidance and revelation (2:25–27). There was a widespread tradition in Judaism that the gift of prophecy had been withdrawn from Israel with the last of the prophets and would reappear in the end times. The renewal of the prophetic gift confirms that God's salvation is about to arrive.

2. The Spirit also plays a prominent role in Jesus' ministry. In fulfillment of Isaiah's prophecies (42:1; 61:1–2), the Messiah is "anointed" by the Spirit at his baptism and "filled with the Spirit" to accomplish his task (Luke 3:22; 4:1, 14, 18; 10:21).

3. Following his ascension to God's right hand, Jesus pours out the Spirit to empower his followers to accomplish their commission: taking the message of salvation to the ends of the earth (Acts 2:17–41). Jesus, endowed with God's Spirit during his earthly ministry, now mediates the Spirit to his church. Luke reveals a remarkably high Christology, as the Spirit of God becomes the Spirit of Jesus (Acts 16:6–7) — God's empowering presence among his people.

Divine Sovereignty and the Purpose of God

The theme of *divine sovereignty and purpose* permeates Luke's narrative. The Greek term *dei* ("it is necessary") occurs forty times in Luke-Acts, confirming that all that is happening is part of God's plan of salvation. While some scholars have linked this to the Greek conception of unchangeable fate, Luke speaks rather of God's purpose accomplished. Human free will is not obliterated; God works through human actions — both positive and negative — to achieve his purpose. Though wicked men put Jesus to death, this was God's plan, accomplishing salvation by raising him from the dead (Acts 2:23–24; cf. Luke 24:7, 26–27, 44–47; Acts 3:18; 4:28).

Salvation for Outsiders: A New Age of Reversals

In her birth-narrative hymn, Mary praises God for exalting the humble and bringing down the mighty (1:51–53). This theme of reversal becomes a critical one for Luke. Salvation comes not to the rich, powerful, and influential but to those who humble themselves before God. Jesus mingles with people from all positions in life — the poor, social outcasts, sinners, and tax collectors — offering salvation to all. This, in turn, serves as a preview for the Gentile mission in Acts, where the gospel will break out of its Jewish exclusiveness to become a message for all people everywhere.

> In Luke's Gospel, salvation comes not to the rich, powerful, and influential but to "outsiders" — those who humble themselves before God.

The Poor and Oppressed. In his inaugural sermon at Nazareth, Jesus preaches "good news to the poor" (4:16–22). His Beatitudes are more concrete than Matthew's (6:20–21), and he balances these with woes against the rich (6:24–25). Jesus calls the Pharisees "lovers of money" (16:14) and tells his hearers to invite the poor and handicapped to their banquets (14:12–13). He tells parables of radical reversal of fortunes like the rich fool (12:13–21) and the rich man and Lazarus (16:19–31). Is Luke speaking here of physical poverty, or only of spiritual poverty? The answer must be both, since those with few resources are more apt to trust in God.

Sinners and Tax Collectors. The theme of Jesus' association with sinners—common in the Synoptics—is even more prevalent in Luke. Only Luke describes Jesus' anointing by an immoral woman who "loves much" because she has been forgiven much (7:36–50). Luke alone recounts the stories of Zacchaeus (19:1–10) and the repentant criminal on the cross (23:39–43). The parables of the prodigal son (15:11–32) and the Pharisee and the tax collector (18:9–14) are also unique to Luke. In all of these stories, it is not the "religious" but the repentant who find salvation.

Samaritans. Luke speaks more of Samaritans than the other Gospels do. Jesus tells the parable of the good Samaritan (10:29–37), James and John are rebuked for wanting to call down fire from heaven on a Samaritan village (9:51–56), and the one leper who returns to thank Jesus is a Samaritan (17:11–19). This not only continues the theme of the gospel for the outcast (Samaritans were despised by Jews) but also sets the stage for Acts, where the gospel will pass through Samaria on its way to the Gentile world (Acts 1:8; 8:4–25).

Women. While women were generally relegated to positions of little status in the ancient world, Luke emphasizes the value Jesus placed on them as disciples and partners in ministry. No other Gospel gives so much emphasis to the women who played a part in Jesus' ministry. Luke refers to thirteen women not mentioned elsewhere in the Gospels. The first two chapters deal especially with women (Mary, Elizabeth, and Anna). Other passages include the widow of Nain (7:12–15), the woman who anointed Jesus' feet (7:36–50), the women who supported Jesus (8:1–3), the woman with a blood disease (8:43–48), Mary and Martha (10:38–42), the "daughter of Abraham" (13:10–17), the poor widow (21:1–4), the "daughters of Jerusalem" who lament Jesus (23:27–31), those who watched the crucifixion (23:49), and those who report the resurrection (23:55–24:11).

A Samaritan priest with an ancient Samaritan Pentateuch dating from the seventeenth century, in a Samaritan synagogue in Nablus. Luke shows a special interest in the Samaritans.

Jerusalem and the Temple: Settings of Rejection and Salvation

Jerusalem plays a symbolic as well as geographical role in Luke-Acts. The Gospel begins and ends in the temple in Jerusalem (1:9; 24:53). Jerusalem is the place where God's presence dwells and from which his salvation will be achieved (9:31). Yet it is also a symbol of God's stubborn and rebellious people, where the prophets are murdered (13:33–34). The whole of Luke-Acts can be viewed symbolically as a journey to and from Jerusalem. Through much of the Gospel, Jesus journeys toward the city, arriving at the story's climax (9:51–56; 13:22, 33; 17:11; 18:31; 19:11, 28). He weeps over the city for her rejection of him and for the judgment which will follow (19:41–44). Yet through Jesus'

Jerusalem plays an ambivalent role in Luke-Acts, representing both the glorious place of God's salvation and the nation which rejects that salvation.

Left: Inscription forbidding entry to Gentiles into the Court of Israel in the temple of Jerusalem. *Right:* A view of the temple from the northwest, from the model of Jerusalem at the Holy Land Hotel in Jerusalem. Jerusalem and the temple are important settings for Luke, symbolizing both the place of salvation and the rejection of Jesus by Israel.

death, resurrection, and ascension, salvation is achieved. The message of salvation now goes forth from Jerusalem to the ends of the earth (24:47; Acts 1:8).

Joy, Praise, and Celebration

The dawn of God's end-times salvation is marked by joy and praise to God. Words relating to joy, rejoicing, and praise are common throughout Luke-Acts. Gospel stories often end with the recipients of God's benefits praising God (5:25–26; 7:16; 13:13; 17:15, 18; 18:43). This theme continues in Acts (2:47), where praise accompanies both healings (3:8–9; 4:21) and the salvation of the Gentiles (11:18; 13:48; 21:20). Luke's message is clear: *God is to be praised, for the joyful time of redemption has arrived.*

This theme of celebration is also seen in the unusual number of banquet and meal scenes in Luke. Throughout the Gospel, Jesus is often seen at meals or telling stories with banquet settings.[7] This theme may be related to the importance of table fellowship in the church of Luke's day, especially with reference to Jew-Gentile relationships. It is certainly also related to the biblical metaphor of the messianic banquet, in which God's final salvation is described as a great banquet when "the LORD Almighty will prepare a feast of rich food for all peoples" (Isa. 25:6–8). Jesus dines with people of all kinds, sinners and tax collectors on the one hand, and even Pharisees on the other. The invitation to the salvation celebration is offered to all. Yet as the parable of the great banquet reveals, the religious

---

7. Luke 5:29; 7:33–34, 36; 9:10–17; 10:38–40; 11:37; 12:36; 13:29; 14:7–14, 15–24; 15:23; 16:19–21; 20:46; 22:16, 18, 30; 24:41–43.

leaders decline Jesus' call to the feast and miss out, while outsiders respond with joy and are saved (14:15 – 24).

Prayer and Intimate Fellowship with the Father

Luke lays special emphasis on Jesus' prayer life. He records nine prayers of Jesus, of which only two appear in the other Gospels. Jesus prays at his baptism (3:21), after healing a man with leprosy (5:16), before calling the Twelve (6:12), at a private time with his disciples (9:18), at the transfiguration (9:28), before teaching the disciples to pray (11:1), for Peter before his denial (22:32), for his murderers from the cross (23:34), and with his last breath (23:46). Jesus also teaches his disciples how to pray (11:1 – 4) and encourages them to diligent prayer during trials (18:1; 21:36; 22:40). Two of Luke's parables deal with the need for persistent prayer (11:5 – 13; 18:1 – 8). Prayer is also a prominent theme in the birth narrative (1:10, 13; 2:38) and in Acts.[8]

Luke's purpose in all of this is to show Jesus' unique relationship with God. To do his Father's will, he must stay in intimate fellowship with him. The church of Luke's day would be encouraged to do the same.

THE HISTORICAL SETTING OF LUKE'S GOSPEL: AUTHOR AND LIFE SETTING

Authorship

There is near universal agreement that the Third Gospel and Acts were written by the same author, since they share common style, theology, and addressees (Theophilus). Acts 1:1 explicitly refers to "my former book." Early church tradition unanimously ascribes these works to Luke, a physician and part-time companion of the apostle Paul. This external evidence can be supplemented with internal evidence. Several times in Acts, the author uses the first-person plural "we," indicating that he traveled with Paul during his second and third missionary journeys and eventually went with him to Rome (16:10 – 17; 20:5 – 21; 21:1 – 18; 27:1 – 28:16). From the Pauline Letters, we know that Luke was both a companion of Paul and was with him in Rome (Col. 4:7 – 17; Philem. 23 – 24; cf. 2 Tim. 4:10 – 11).

Some have doubted that the author was a companion of Paul, claiming that their theologies are different and that the portrait of Paul in Acts is different from the historical Paul of the Epistles. In Acts Paul is conciliatory toward the Judaizers, while in Galatians he condemns them for preaching a different gospel (Acts 16:4; 21:20 – 26; Gal. 1:6). Yet while there are different theological emphases (owing to different purposes in writing), there is nothing contradictory in either theology or portraiture. The Paul of the Epistles can also be conciliatory, living like a Jew to win the Jews (1 Cor. 9:20).

The author claims not to have been an eyewitness of what he wrote in the Gospel but rather to have thoroughly investigated the events before composing his work. Tradition tells us that Luke was a converted Gentile. This agrees with Colossians 4:11 – 14, where Paul distinguishes Luke from his Jewish companions. This would help to explain the author's keen interest in the Gentile reception of the gospel. Luke's exceptional knowledge of Juda-

---

8. Acts 1:14, 24; 2:42; 3:1; 4:24 – 31; 7:59 – 60; 9:11; 10:4, 9; 12:5, 12; 13:3; 14:23; 16:25; 20:36; 21:5.

ism and the Hebrew scriptures (in Greek translation) suggests that before following Christ, he may have been a "God-fearer," a Gentile worshiper of the God of Israel.

Date

The date of the Gospel is closely tied to its companion volume Acts. Since Paul is in prison in Rome at the end of Acts (about AD 62), Luke may have finished Acts before Paul's release and later martyrdom. This would place Acts around AD 62 and the Gospel a few years earlier.

> Before following Christ, Luke may have been a "God-fearer," a Gentile worshiper of the God of Israel.

On the other hand, if Mark was the first Gospel written and was composed shortly before the destruction of Jerusalem (mid to late 60s; see Mark 13:14), Luke and Acts would have come later, from the late 60s onward. In this case, Luke could have a different reason for ending Luke-Acts with Paul in Rome, perhaps to show that the Gospel had reached "the ends of the earth" (Acts 1:8).

Some have said the book must be dated after AD 70, since Luke's description of the siege and destruction of Jerusalem is more detailed than Mark's, and so must have been written after the fact (Luke 21:20–24). This conclusion begins with the invalid assumption that Jesus could not have predicted the future. Even for those seeking a natural explanation it is unsatisfactory, since Luke's description of the destruction is quite general and could apply to almost any Roman siege. Without more evidence, the date of Luke-Acts remains an open question.

Occasion and Narrative Purpose

Who was this Theophilus to whom Luke and Acts are addressed? The name means "one who loves God," and some claim Luke is writing generally to believers. More likely, Theophilus is an individual, probably the patron who sponsored Luke's project. The writing of a book of this length was an expensive endeavor in the ancient world, and it was common to dedicate such a work to an influential patron (see fig. 9.1). The address "most excellent" indicates Theophilus's high social or political status. Luke's claim to be providing "certainty" concerning "the things you have been taught" may suggest that Theophilus is a new Christian needing instruction or an interested unbeliever. Apart from these observations, his identity remains a mystery.

Though dedicated to Theophilus, the Gospel and Acts are almost certainly intended for a wider audience, perhaps the church or churches with which Luke and Theophilus are associated. Yet the specific provenance (place of origin) and destination remain a mystery. Many suggestions have been made (Rome, Philippi, Achaia, Antioch, etc.), but little evidence can be marshaled for any of them.

We are on firmer ground concerning the general purpose for which Luke wrote. He states that, having investigated everything carefully, he is confirming for Theophilus "the certainty of the things you have been taught" (Luke 1:1–4). Luke writes to confirm the gospel; that is, to demonstrate the authenticity of the claims of Christianity. This confirmation certainly relates to accusations made by the church's Jewish opponents. The author takes pains to show that Jesus is the Jewish Messiah, that it was God's purpose for him to suffer, die, and rise again, that the mission to the Gentiles was ordained and instigated by God, and that Paul is not a renegade Jew but a faithful servant of the Lord. There are also indications that Luke seeks to deflect Roman criticism. Both Jesus (in the Gospel) and Paul (in Acts) are repeatedly confirmed as innocent of Roman charges. Christianity is not a dangerous new religion but the fulfillment of Judaism (a legal religion in Roman eyes), the consummation of God's plan of salvation.

> Theophilus was probably the patron who sponsored Luke's writing of the Gospel and Acts.

The diversity of Luke's work suggests that he is writing for a variety of reasons: to teach believers about the origin of their faith, to defend Christianity against its opponents, and to establish a firm historical foundation for the gospel now advancing around the world.

READING LUKE TODAY

The generator chugs in the background as the young missionary, a wiry man with dark-rimmed glasses, shorts, and sandals sets up the portable video machine. A white sheet hung between two trees serves as a screen. Around the glowing embers of a fire, thirty or so natives from the remote tribe sit on rocks and logs. As the video begins, they become mesmerized by the story unfolding before them. A child is born in poverty and grows to manhood. He begins an extraordinary career as a wandering teacher. The tribespeople nod and chatter among themselves as he tells parables and stories from everyday life. They watch in awe as he heals the sick, calms the raging sea, and raises the dead. Yet tragedy looms. The man is seized by his enemies, tortured, and hung on a wooden cross. He dies in agony and despair. The natives shout protests, sobbing and shouting as the tragedy plays out. But this is not the end. Their sorrow turns to joy as the man rises in victory from the dead. They cheer and weep as he ascends to heaven, announcing to his followers that salvation has been achieved.

Similar showings of this film have occurred countless times around the world, in remote jungle tribes, in rural villages, and in teeming metropolises. In fact, it is the most widely viewed movie in human history. No, it is not *Star Wars* or *Titanic* but *The Jesus Film* produced by Campus Crusade for Christ. It has been translated into over seven hundred languages and has been seen by more than five billion people worldwide.[9]

While movies about Jesus have traditionally drawn scenes from all four Gospels, *The Jesus Film* follows the narrative of one Gospel: Luke. It seems somehow appropriate that a film which has been dubbed into more languages and seen by more diverse people groups than any other is based on the Gospel which most clearly announces that salvation is for all people everywhere—from every tribe, nation, and language. I think Dr. Luke would be pleased.

---

9. See www.jesusfilm.org for information on *The Jesus Film*.

1. Luke and Acts form a theological and narrative unity (Luke-Acts), sharing a common purpose and common theological themes.

2. The central theme of Luke-Acts is *the arrival of God's end-times salvation.* As predicted in the prophets, God has acted through Jesus the Messiah to save his people Israel, and this salvation is now going forth to the whole world.

3. Important subthemes include (a) the Spirit as a sign of God's end-times salvation, (b) the sovereign purpose of God, (c) salvation for outsiders, (d) joy and praise in response to God's salvation, (e) Jerusalem and the temple as settings of rejection and salvation, and (f) Jesus' prayer life and intimacy with the Father.

4. Luke's portrait of Jesus — the Savior for all people — focuses especially on his roles as (a) prophet like Moses, mighty in word and deed, and (b) Messiah and Lord, who brings in the age of salvation through his life, death, resurrection, and ascension.

5. Luke-Acts contains some of the finest literary Greek in the New Testament.

6. Luke writes with a greater historical interest than the other Gospel writers.

7. Luke's most distinctive structural feature is the travel narrative (Luke 9–19), an extended account of Jesus' journey to Jerusalem.

8. Luke's birth narrative (Luke 1–2) presents Jesus as the promised Messiah from the line of David, anxiously awaited by the righteous remnant of Israel. Key features include the parallels between the births of John and Jesus, and the hymns, or praise songs, which carry the story forward.

9. In the only account from Jesus' childhood recorded in the four Gospels, Luke describes Jesus' extraordinary wisdom and obedient relationship with his heavenly Father (2:41–52).

10. Luke's genealogy traces Jesus' ancestry to Adam, emphasizing that the message of salvation is for all of humanity.

11. Jesus' Nazareth sermon (4:14–30) sets the stage for the rest of the Gospel by demonstrating God's concern for Gentiles and foreshadowing Israel's rejection of her Messiah.

12. Jesus' Galilean ministry in Luke reveals the reception of the gospel by outsiders, outcasts, and the lowly, while the proud and self-righteous miss out.

13. The question of Jesus' identity, posed throughout the Galilean ministry, is answered in Peter's confession that he is "the Christ of God" (9:18–27). As in Matthew and Mark, this episode marks a key turning point as Jesus begins teaching about his suffering fate in Jerusalem.

14. In Luke 9:51, Jesus "resolves" to go to Jerusalem. The travel narrative which follows has been called the Gospel for the Outcast, because many of the stories and parables concern God's love for the lost.

15. The journey to Jerusalem (travel narrative) climaxes with the story of Zacchaeus and the parable of the minas, which reaffirm God's love for the lost (Luke 19:10) and the need for faithful stewardship after Jesus' departure.

16. As in Matthew and Mark, Jesus' time in Jerusalem is marked by debates and controversies with the religious leaders, climaxing in his passion. The primary theme is the fulfillment of Scripture through the Messiah's death, resurrection, and ascension.

17. Jesus' trial and crucifixion are marked by the recurrent christological theme of Jesus' innocence. He is the righteous and innocent Servant of the LORD (Isaiah 53).

18. The account of the Emmaus disciples is Luke's most important contribution to the resurrection narratives. Its theme is the fulfillment of Scripture through the death and resurrection of the Messiah.

19. The authorship of Luke-Acts by Luke, a physician and missionary companion of the apostle Paul, is well supported by both external and internal evidence. Luke was a second generation Christian (Luke 1:1 – 4) and probably a Gentile (Col. 4:11 – 14). The date of writing is unknown and may be anytime from the late 50s to the 80s of the first century.

20. Theophilus was likely an influential patron who sponsored the writing of the Gospel. He may have been a recent convert to Christianity. Luke must also be writing to a broader audience, seeking to confirm the truth of the gospel message and the gospel messengers.

» KEY TERMS «

Luke-Acts	Theophilus	Zacchaeus episode
prologue of Luke	birth narrative hymns	Emmaus disciples
historiography	Nazareth sermon	prophet like Moses
travel narrative	Gospel for the Outcast	

1. What do we mean by the "unity" of Luke-Acts?

2. How does Luke's literary style compare with the other Gospels?

3. What is the narrator's purpose in introducing such a strong Jewish emphasis in the birth narrative?

4. What is the central theme of the birth narrative? What two structural features carry this theme forward?

5. What are the two themes of the episode of the boy Jesus' visit to Jerusalem?

6. What is unique about Luke's presentation of the ministry of John the Baptist?

7. What is the main emphasis of Luke's genealogy? How does it compare with Matthew's?

8. What is the theme of the temptation account? With whom is Jesus contrasted?

9. How is Jesus' Nazareth sermon (Luke 4) important for Luke's narrative purpose?

10. What are the main features of Jesus' Galilean ministry?

11. In what way is Peter's confession a key turning point in the narrative?

12. How does the transfiguration in Luke prepare for Jesus' journey to Jerusalem? How is Luke's description of this event unique?

13. What role does the travel narrative play in Luke's Gospel?

14. Why is the travel narrative also called "the Gospel for the Outcast"? Name some of the stories and parables that carry forward this theme.

15. What role does Jerusalem play in Luke's Gospel?

16. What role does the story of Zacchaeus play at the climax of this journey?

17. What is the central theme of Luke's passion narrative? What christological theme appears repeatedly throughout the trial and crucifixion narrative?

18. What does Jesus reveal to the Emmaus disciples about the role of the Christ?

19. Summarize two main features of Luke's Christology.

20. What is the central theme of Luke-Acts?

21. Identify some of the important subthemes and state how they relate to this central theme.

22. Note some of the evidence for the universal application of salvation in Luke's Gospel.

23. What is the significance for Luke of Jesus' sending out of the seventy (seventy-two)?

24. What do the "we" passages tell us about the author of Luke-Acts?

25. What do we know about Luke from Acts and from Paul's Epistles? What do we know about him from church tradition?

26. Who might Theophilus have been? Why did Luke write his two-volume work?

Digging Deeper

Commentaries

Beginning and Intermediate

Bock, Darrell L. *Luke*. NIV Application Commentary. Grand Rapids: Zondervan, 1996.

Danker, Frederick W. *Jesus and the New Age: A Commentary on St. Luke's Gospel*. Rev. ed. Philadelphia: Fortress, 1988.

Ellis, E. Earle. *The Gospel of Luke*. New Century Bible. Grand Rapids: Eerdmans, 1981.

Evans, Craig A. *Luke*. New International Biblical Commentary. Peabody, MA: Hendrickson, 1990.

Evans, C. F. *Saint Luke*. Philadelphia: Trinity Press International, 1990.

Green, Joel. *The Gospel of Luke*. New International Commentary on the New Testament. Grand Rapids: Eerdmans, 1997.

Johnson, Luke Timothy. *The Gospel of Luke*. Sacra Pagina. Collegeville, MN: Liturgical Press, 1992.

Stein, Robert H. *Luke*. New American Commentary. Nashville: Broadman, 1992.

Tannehill, Robert C. *Luke*. Abingdon New Testament Commentaries. Nashville: Abingdon, 1996.

Advanced and Greek/Technical

Bock, Darrell L. *Luke*. 2 vols. Baker Exegetical Commentary. Grand Rapids: Baker, 1994–96.

Bovon, François. *Luke 1: A Commentary on the Gospel of Luke 1:1–9:50*. Hermeneia. Minneapolis: Fortress, 2002.

Fitzmyer, Joseph A. *The Gospel according to Luke*. 2 vols. Anchor Bible. Garden City, NY: Doubleday, 1981–85.

Marshall, I. Howard. *The Gospel of Luke*. New International Greek Testament Commentary. Grand Rapids: Eerdmans, 1978.

Nolland, John. *Luke*. 3 vols. Word Biblical Commentary. Dallas: Word, 1989–93.

Themes and Theology of Luke

Bovon, François. *Luke the Theologian: The Interpretation of Luke and Acts, 1950–2005*. Waco, TX: Baylor Univ. Press, 2006.

Cadbury, Henry J. *The Making of Luke-Acts*. 2nd ed., with a new introduction by Paul N. Anderson. Peabody, MA: Hendrickson, 1999.

Conzelmann, Hans. *The Theology of St. Luke*. New York: Harper and Row; London: Faber and Faber, 1960.

Esler, Philip F. *Community and Gospel in Luke-Acts: The Social and Political Motivations of Lucan Theology.* Society for New Testament Monograph Series 57. Cambridge: Cambridge Univ. Press, 1987.

Fitzmyer, Joseph A. *Luke the Theologian: Aspects of His Teaching.* Eugene, OR: Wipf and Stock, 2004.

Green, Joel B. *The Theology of the Gospel of Luke.* Cambridge: Cambridge Univ. Press, 1995.

Jervell, Jacob. *Luke and the People of God: A New Look at Luke-Acts.* Minneapolis: Augsburg, 1972.

Juel, Donald. *Luke-Acts: The Promise of History.* Atlanta: John Knox, 1983.

Keck, Leander E., and J. Louis Martyn, eds. *Studies in Luke-Acts.* Nashville: Abingdon, 1966.

Maddox, Robert. *The Purpose of Luke-Acts.* Edinburgh: T. and T. Clark, 1982.

Marshall, I. Howard. *Luke: Historian and Theologian.* 2nd ed. Downers Grove, IL: Intervarsity, 1998.

O'Toole, Robert F. *The Unity of Luke's Theology.* Wilmington, DE: Glazier, 1984.

Powell, Mark Allan, *What Are They Saying about Luke?* New York: Paulist, 1989.

Strauss, Mark L. *The Davidic Messiah in Luke-Acts: The Promise and Its Fulfillment in Lukan Christology.* Sheffield: Sheffield Academic, 1995.

Talbert, Charles H. *Reading Luke.* Rev. ed. Macon, GA: Smyth and Helwys, 2002.

Talbert, C. H., ed. *Perspectives on Luke-Acts.* Edinburgh: T. and T. Clark, 1978.

Wilson, Stephen G. *The Gentiles and the Gentile Mission in Luke-Acts* Cambridge: Cambridge Univ. Press, 1973.

Newer Approaches and Methods

Kingsbury, Jack Dean. *Conflict in Luke: Jesus, Authorities, Disciples.* Minneapolis: Fortress, 1991.

Kurz, William S. *Reading Luke-Acts: Dynamics of Biblical Narrative.* Louisville: Westminster/John Knox, 1993.

Levine, Amy-Jill, ed. *A Feminist Companion to Luke.* With Marianne Blickenstaff. Cleveland, OH: Pilgrim, 2004.

Neyrey, Jerome H., ed. *The Social World of Luke-Acts: Models for Interpretation.* Peabody, MA: Hendrickson, 1991.

Shellard, Barbara. *New Light on Luke: Its Purpose, Sources and Literary Context.* London: Sheffield Academic, 2002.

Tannehill, Robert C. *The Narrative Unity of Luke-Acts: A Literary Interpretation.* Vol. 1, *The Gospel according to Luke,* 1986. Vol. 2, *The Acts of the Apostles,* 1990. Philadelphia: Fortress.

Bibliography

Mills, Watson E. *The Gospel of Luke.* Lewiston and Lampeter: Mellen, 1994.

CHAPTER 10

John
THE GOSPEL OF THE SON WHO REVEALS THE FATHER

» **CHAPTER OVERVIEW** «

1. Literary Features
2. The Plot of John's Gospel
3. John's Portrait of Jesus: The Son Who Reveals the Father
4. Other Characters in John's Gospel
5. Theological Themes
6. Narrative Purpose
7. The Historical Setting of John's Gospel: Author and Life Setting
8. Reading John Today

» **OBJECTIVES** «

After reading this chapter, you should be able to:

- Identify the main literary features of John's Gospel, especially its differences from the Synoptics.
- Describe the main features of John's portrait of Jesus.
- Identify the central theme and narrative purpose of John's Gospel.
- Identify the fourfold structure of John, including the significance of the book of "signs" and the book of "glory."
- Identify and explain the significance of the "I am" statements made by Jesus in John.
- Summarize the main theme of John's prologue.
- Explain the narrative and theological significance of Jesus' interviews with Nicodemus and the Samaritan woman.
- Summarize the nature of Jesus' dialogues and debates with the religious leaders.
- Describe the narrative and theological significance of the raising of Lazarus.
- Summarize the main themes of Jesus' Farewell Discourse, including the role of the Spirit after Jesus' departure.
- Explain the nature of John's theological dualism and the distinct Johannine teaching about salvation.
- Provide evidence for the authorship and likely provenance of the Fourth Gospel.

The Gospel of John is unique among the Gospels. Though written in a simple style and with simple vocabulary, below this simplicity lies profound theological truth. As early as the third century, Clement of Alexandria was referring to this as a "spiritual Gospel." Paradoxically, new believers love John because even a child can understand it, while brilliant scholars continue to mine its depths for theological riches.

LITERARY FEATURES

Unique Content

The reader approaching John's Gospel immediately notices a picture strikingly different from the Synoptic Gospels. While the Synoptics share many common features, about 90 percent of John is unique. Key features of Jesus' ministry are absent. There are no exorcisms or parables (but see 12:24), no table fellowship with sinners. The key Synoptic phrase "kingdom of God" occurs only twice. Most of Jesus' teaching is unique, and five of John's eight miracles do not occur in the Synoptics. Many key Synoptic events are absent, including Jesus' baptism, his temptation, the transfiguration, and the institution of the Lord's Supper.

John also includes many stories not found in the Synoptics: the miracle of changing water to wine, Jesus' conversations with Nicodemus and the Samaritan woman, the raising

» CENTRAL THEME «

Jesus is the divine Son of God who reveals the Father, providing eternal life to all who believe in him.

» KEY VERSE «

John 3:16 (cf. 1:14; 20:30 – 31)

» BASIC OUTLINE OF JOHN «

1. Prologue (1:1 – 18)
2. The Book of Signs (1:19 – 12:50)
3. The Book of Glory (13:1 – 20:31)
4. Epilogue (21:1 – 25)

of Lazarus, Jesus' washing of the disciple's feet, Jesus' high priestly prayer, the account of doubting Thomas, and many others.

Only John reports Jesus' extensive Judean ministry, as he travels back and forth between Galilee and Judea. The Synoptics are more linear, with a single movement from Galilee to Jerusalem. They provide little information concerning the length of Jesus' ministry, mentioning only the Passover associated with Jesus' crucifixion. John refers to three Passovers (2:13; 6:4; 11:55) and possibly a fourth (5:1), suggesting a ministry between 2½ and 3½ years long.

Jesus also speaks more openly about himself in John than in the other Gospels. In the Synoptics, Jesus' teaching focuses on the kingdom of God and his role as its inaugurator. In John, he speaks much more about himself and his unique relationship to the Father. Jesus makes seven **"I am" statements** (see fig. 10.3)—metaphorical descriptions of himself and his role as the Son who reveals the Father. There is no "messianic secret" in John.

Unique Literary Style

John's literary style is also unique. It is characterized by simplicity, with short sentences connected by coordinate conjunctions ("and"). The style is repetitious, with parallelism used for emphasis (e.g., John 14:27: "Peace I leave with you; my peace I give you."). There

Church of St. John in Ephesus

are also many contrasts: light and darkness, truth and falsehood, life and death, above and below. While John's vocabulary is basic, seemingly "simple" words like *know, abide, believe, witness, truth, life, light, glory,* and *the world* carry profound theological significance.

This unique style relates not only to the narrator's comments but also to Jesus' words. Jesus speaks not in parables and short wisdom sayings, as in the Synoptics, but in long discourses and dialogues with his opponents. The Synoptics relate Jesus' teaching on the kingdom of God, repentance, and right behavior toward God and others. In John, Jesus speaks more on philosophical issues of truth, life, and knowing God. Jesus' style of speaking so resembles the narrator's that sometimes it is difficult to tell when Jesus stops speaking and the narrator starts. For example, in Jesus' dialogue with Nicodemus in John 3, most "red letter" Bibles continue Jesus' words through verse 21. But it is not clear in the text whether he is still speaking. Jesus speaks in the first person ("I") in verses 3–12, then switches to the third person with reference to the "Son of Man" in verses 13–15. Verses 16–21 continue in the third person but now speak of Jesus as the "Son" sent by the Father: "For God so loved the world that he gave his one and only Son." Are these Jesus' words or John's? It is difficult to tell.

This raises the difficult issue of how much this Gospel records the actual words of Jesus, and how much of it is the author's interpretation of Jesus' life and teaching. This question does not challenge the authority of the text, since inspiration applies to everything the author wrote — speech, actions, narration, interpretation. But it does affect how we view the literary genre of the Fourth Gospel. Is this Gospel meant to be a historical record of Jesus' life, or a theological meditation on its significance? Or both? We will discuss these issues in greater detail in chapter 12.

The Relationship of John to the Synoptics

The many differences between John and the Synoptics also raise the question of their literary relationship. Did the author of the Fourth Gospel know and use the Synoptics, or is he writing independently of them? Until the twentieth century, it was generally believed that John wrote to supplement and interpret the other Gospels. The tide turned in the mid-twentieth century when P. Gardner-Smith and others argued for John's literary independence. The stories which John and the Synoptics share come not from direct borrowing, it was argued, but from the use of common traditions.[1] Today scholars are divided. A minority still hold to John's direct dependence on the Synoptics.[2] Others, like Gardner-Smith, reject any link apart from the use of common traditions. A mediating position denies direct borrowing but thinks John may know one or more of the Synoptics and assumes his readers will be familiar with their content.[3] This third perspective is perhaps the most appealing, since it recognizes both John's dependence and independence. He is interacting within the world of early Christianity, yet writes to accomplish his own unique purpose.

Two Historical Settings, Two Levels of Meaning

As we have seen, narrative always has two historical settings, the setting of the events portrayed and the later setting of the author. The events of the Gospels occurred during Jesus' ministry in Palestine about AD 30. But the Gospels themselves were written much later (twenty-five to sixty years) and in various contexts throughout the Roman Empire.

The Gospel of John is unique in that the boundary between its two settings is often blurred. At times the narrator seems to be speaking not only of the conflict between Jesus and his opponents but also of the late-first-century conflict between the author's Christian community (the **Johannine community**) and its Jewish opponents. This blurring is evident in many ways but is most striking in the author's frequent use of the term *Ioudaioi* ("Jews" or "Jewish leaders") for Jesus' opponents. This is odd, since Jesus and his disciples were also Jews. Historically, the conflict between Jesus and the religious leaders was *Jew versus Jew*. The author's use of this term for Jesus' opponents suggests that the conflict is now *Christian versus Jew* and that he is writing at a time when the church has broken with the synagogue. Scholars find further evidence for this break in John's repeated references to expulsion from the synagogue (9:22; 12:42; 16:2). The possibility of two settings and two levels of meaning should be kept in mind when reading John.

Structure

The Gospel has a relatively simple structure. It begins with a **prologue** (1:1–18) identifying Jesus as the preexistent "Word" (*Logos*)—God's self-revelation—who became a human being to bring grace and truth to humankind. It ends with an epilogue (chap. 21) describing a

---

1. P. Gardner-Smith, *Saint John and the Synoptic Gospels* (Cambridge: Cambridge Univ. Press, 1938); C. H. Dodd, *Historical Tradition in the Fourth Gospel* (Cambridge: Cambridge Univ. Press, 1963).

2. See, for example, C. K. Barrett, *The Gospel according to John*, 2nd ed. (Philadelphia: Westminster, 1978), 15–26.

3. See Richard Bauckham, "John for Readers of Mark," in *The Gospel for All Christians*, ed. R. Bauckham (Grand Rapids: Eerdmans, 1998), 147–71.

postresurrection appearance to the disciples, Jesus' commissioning of Peter to "feed my sheep," and the identification of the **Beloved Disciple** as the author.

The main body of the Gospel has two parts, sometimes called the **Book of Signs** (1:19 – 12:50) and the **Book of Glory** (13:1 – 20:31). The former contains seven miracles, or "signs," which reveal Jesus' identity and call people to faith in him (see fig. 10.1). The Book of Glory is so called because Jesus' passion is repeatedly described as his glorification (7:39; 12:23; 13:31 – 32; 17:1, 4; cf. 21:19). This section contains the Last Supper, the Farewell Discourse, and the passion and resurrection narratives.

Teaching Types: Personal Interviews, Public Debate, and Private Teaching

Jesus' teaching falls into three types: interviews with individuals (3:1 – 21; 4:1 – 38), dialogue and debates with the Jewish leaders (5:19 – 47; 6:25 – 59; 7:14 – 44; 8:12 – 59; 9:40 – 10:21; 10:22 – 42; 12:23 – 36), and private teaching of his disciples (14:1 – 16:33). All of these — and the Gospel as a whole — are implicit calls to faith and decision. Those who encounter Jesus cannot help but be changed by his overwhelming presence.

(1) Personal Interviews. Twice John describes Jesus' extended conversations with individuals: with **Nicodemus** and the Samaritan woman. Both follow a similar pattern (see fig. 10.2): Jesus introduces a spiritual metaphor (new birth, 3:3; living water, 4:7, 10) which provokes interest but also misunderstanding (3:4; 4:9, 11). Jesus clarifies the spiritual significance (3:5; 4:13 – 14, 21 – 24). The episodes climax as Jesus identifies himself (3:13 – 21; 4:26), an implicit call to faith.

(2) Public Debate. The main part of the Gospel contains extended dialogue and debate between Jesus and his opponents. These debates, too, follow a similar pattern. Jesus performs a miracle or teaches. This provokes a response or challenge from his hearers, followed by further teaching from Jesus. This to-and-fro eventually concludes with a response toward Jesus — often mixed — from the hearers. The debate in chapter 7 ends with some claiming that Jesus is a prophet, others that he is the Christ, and still others denying that the Christ could come from Galilee. The narrator concludes, "Thus the people were divided because of Jesus" (7:43). The division is between those moving toward faith in Jesus and those moving away from it.

(3) Private Teaching. Jesus' Farewell Discourse in chapters 14 – 16 makes up the third type of extended teaching. In this long section, Jesus describes the coming role of the Holy Spirit, identifies himself as the true vine in whom the disciples must abide, instructs them on aspects of community life, and warns them of coming persecution. The message throughout is encouragement to faithfulness and assurance of his abiding presence. In chapter 17, the "high-priestly prayer," Jesus prays that the disciples be kept safe and remain faithful.

Figure 10.2—Personal Interviews	
Parallels in John 3 and 4	
Nicodemus *John 3*	**The Samaritan Woman** *John 4*
(1) Jesus sparks interest with a spiritual metaphor: new birth (3:3).	(1) Jesus sparks interest with a spiritual metaphor: living water (4:10).
(2) Nicodemus is confused (3:4).	(2) The woman is confused (4:11 – 12).
(3) Jesus clarifies the spiritual significance (3:5).	(3) Jesus clarifies the spiritual significance (4:13, 21 – 24).
(4) More confusion by Nicodemus (3:9).	(4) More confusion by the woman (4:15).
(5) More clarification and a mild rebuke from Jesus (3:10 – 12).	(5) More clarification and a mild rebuke from Jesus (4:21 – 24).
(6) Jesus identifies himself as the Son of Man, the Son of God, and the light (3:13 – 21).	(6) Jesus identifies himself as the Messiah (v. 26).
(7) No response recorded.	(7) The woman reports to the town; many Samaritans believe.

The "Signs" of the Gospel

While the Gospel records only eight miracles, these "**signs**" (*sēmeia*) play a key role in Jesus' self-revelation. Seven appear in the Gospel proper, and one (the miraculous catch of fish) in the epilogue (fig. 10.1). The signs are often interpreted by Jesus' teaching. Jesus feeds the five thousand and then gives a discourse on the bread of life (chap. 6). Similarly, he raises Lazarus from the dead after identifying himself as the resurrection and the life (11:25 – 26).

Each sign reveals Jesus' identity and mission and calls forth a decision from the hearers. After the first sign, changing water to wine at the wedding in Cana, the narrator notes that "this, the first of his miraculous signs, Jesus performed at Cana in Galilee. He thus revealed his glory, and his disciples put their faith in him" (2:11). The sign reveals Jesus' glory, which provokes faith in him as the self-revelation of God. This is somewhat different from the Synoptic miracles, which point to the in-breaking of the kingdom of God and Jesus' authority as its inaugurator (Matt. 12:28; Luke 11:20).

Metaphor and Symbol

John's "spiritual" Gospel often operates at the level of metaphor and symbol. Jesus is identified at the outset as the "Word," a metaphor for God's communicative presence. John the

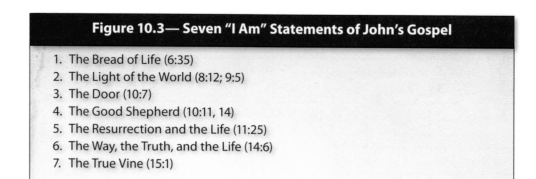

Figure 10.3— Seven "I Am" Statements of John's Gospel

1. The Bread of Life (6:35)
2. The Light of the World (8:12; 9:5)
3. The Door (10:7)
4. The Good Shepherd (10:11, 14)
5. The Resurrection and the Life (11:25)
6. The Way, the Truth, and the Life (14:6)
7. The True Vine (15:1)

Baptist calls him the "Lamb of God," a symbol for sacrificial death (1:29). The seven "I am" statements are also metaphorical (see fig. 10.3). Jesus is the bread of life, the light of the world, the door, the good shepherd, the resurrection and the life, the one true path to life, and the true vine. Like so much else in this Gospel, simple and everyday images reveal profound theological truth.

For those without faith, however, the symbols mask the truth, creating confusion and misunderstanding. Nicodemus cannot comprehend the metaphor of new birth. The woman at the well is at first confused by Jesus' reference to living water. His Jewish opponents are baffled when Jesus—referring to his own body—says, "Destroy this temple, and I will raise it again in three days" (2:19). Like the Synoptic parables, the metaphors and symbols of the Fourth Gospel both reveal and conceal.

Metaphors and symbols in John: Jesus is the bread of life.

Irony

Since misunderstanding is a common theme in John, irony plays a major role as characters deny or question things that, ironically, are true. Nathanael asks if anything good can come from Nazareth (1:46). The Samaritan woman asks sarcastically, "Are you greater than our father Jacob?" (4:12). The religious leaders reject Jesus since they know he came from Galilee and the Messiah's origin is supposed to be unknown (7:27). But in fact, they do not know where he is from, since his true origin is from heaven (3:13, 31; 6:32–33, 38, 50–51).

Irony also appears in double meanings given to words. Jesus tells Nicodemus that he must be "born again." The Greek *anōthen* can mean either "again" or "from above." While Nicodemus misunderstands this as physical rebirth, Jesus means spiritual or heavenly birth through the Spirit. Jesus offers the Samaritan woman "living water" (4:10). She misunderstands "living" to mean bubbling spring water, but Jesus means spiritual water which gives eternal life (4:13–14).

In a greater sense, the whole Gospel is ironic, since God's great salvation is accomplished through the death of his Son. In a play on words, Jesus repeatedly refers to his crucifixion as a "lifting up" (3:14; 8:28; 12:32–34). The physical lifting of the cross—a

www.FreeStockPhotos.com

symbol of horrific death—points to Jesus' glorious victory and exaltation following his resurrection.

THE PLOT OF JOHN'S GOSPEL

Prologue (1:1–18)

The prologue is the most profound statement of Jesus' identity (Christology) in the New Testament, identifying Jesus as the "Word" (*Logos*), the preexistent creator of the universe, distinct from the Father yet fully divine. The term *Logos* had a conceptual background both in Judaism and in Greek philosophical thought.[4] In the Old Testament, God's word is the dynamic force of his will. The psalmist declares, "By the word [LXX: *logos*] of the LORD were the heavens made" (Ps. 33:6). God speaks, and it is done (Isa. 55:11). In Greek philosophy, *logos* was used of the divine reason which brought unity and order to the cosmos. Jewish and Greek ideas come together in the Hellenistic Jewish philosopher Philo, who identified the *Logos* as the messenger of God, mediator between God and creation.[5] Similar imagery appears in the personification of Wisdom found in the book of Proverbs and later Jewish wisdom literature (Sir. 1:1–10; Wisdom of Solomon). Wisdom was present with God before creation and comes to earth to teach human beings. The author of the prologue probably chose the term because of its rich conceptual background, drawing from both its Greek and Jewish background. Yet in the prologue itself, he gave the term new and deeper theological significance by applying it to the profound mystery of the incarnation of the Son of God.

> The prologue of John (1:1–18) is a literary masterpiece and statement of high Christology summarizing the Gospel's main theme: Jesus as the self-revelation of God.

Some have suggested that the prologue is an early Christian hymn which the author has incorporated into the Gospel. This is possible, but in its present form, the prologue serves as a fitting introduction, sharing the Gospel's central theme: *Jesus the one and only Son is the self-revelation of God, who through his incarnation brought life and light to humanity.* The *Logos* title (God's self-revelation) becomes John's shorthand way of summarizing this theme.

The prologue appears to be structured as a **chiasm** (inverse parallelism), with an A-B-C-D-C-B-A pattern (see fig. 10.4). Verses 1–5 (A) and 16–18 (A′) summarize the identity and mission of the Word. Verses 6–8 (B) and 15 (B′) describe the testimony of John the Baptist to the Word. Verses 9–10a (C) and 14 (C′) introduce the incarnation of the Word. Verses 10–13, the middle point (D), present humanity's response to the Word.

The prologue begins with an allusion to Genesis 1:1 ("In the beginning"), identifying Jesus with the creator God. The Word was "with God" from the beginning but also "was God." This carefully crafted Greek sentence confirms that the Son is distinct from the Father but fully divine. His deity is confirmed in that he is the preexistent creator of

---

4. See Craig A. Evans, *Word and Glory: On the Exegetical and Theological Background of John's Prologue*, JSNTSup 89 (Sheffield: Sheffield Academic, 1993); Elizabeth Harris, *Prologue and Gospel: The Theology of the Fourth Evangelist*, JSNTSup 107 (Sheffield: Sheffield Academic, 1994).

5. Philo, *Who Is the Heir of Divine Things?* 205–6 (M. E. Boring, K. Berger, C. Colpe, eds., Hellenistic Commentary to the New Testament [Nashville: Abingdon, 1995], 241).

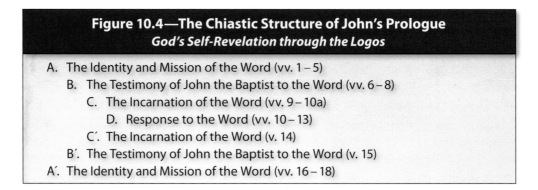

Figure 10.4—The Chiastic Structure of John's Prologue
God's Self-Revelation through the Logos

A. The Identity and Mission of the Word (vv. 1 – 5)
  B. The Testimony of John the Baptist to the Word (vv. 6 – 8)
    C. The Incarnation of the Word (vv. 9 – 10a)
      D. Response to the Word (vv. 10 – 13)
    C′. The Incarnation of the Word (v. 14)
  B′. The Testimony of John the Baptist to the Word (v. 15)
A′. The Identity and Mission of the Word (vv. 16 – 18)

all things (v. 3), bringing life and light to humanity (v. 4). The references to life and light transition from the Word's work at creation to his work of redemption. Just as God spoke light and life into existence, so the Word through his incarnation brings revelation "light" and eternal "life" to humanity. Scholars debate whether verse 5b should be translated "the darkness has not *understood* it," or "has not *overcome* it." The Greek can mean either, and both fit John's theology. The latter seems most likely, however, since the whole of John's Gospel plays out the struggle between light and darkness.

The allusion to the incarnation leads to the description of John the Baptist (vv. 6 – 8, 15). John is emphatically said to be "not the light" but to bear testimony to the light (v. 8). As in the Synoptics, John's role is subordinate, to prepare the way for the Messiah and to point others to him (v. 15). The Fourth Gospel emphasizes this even more than the Synoptics, causing scholars to speculate that the author may be responding to later followers of the Baptist who claimed that John, not Jesus, was the Messiah (cf. Acts 18:25; 19:1 – 7). John's description of Jesus as superior (v. 15) is followed by a contrast between the law given through Moses and the grace and truth which came through Jesus Christ (v. 16 – 17). The law, like John, was merely preparation for the fullness of revelation through the Son.

Moving inward in the chiasm, verses 10 – 11 describe the negative response to the Word. The world which he created did not recognize him. He came to "his own" (neuter plural = the things which were his), but "his own" (masculine plural = his own people) did not receive him. While his own people must be the Jews, the parallelism with "the world" in verse 10 confirms a broader reference as well. The rejection by Israel mirrors rejection by the world—all those in rebellion against God.

Figure 10.5—John 1:18
"God the One and Only"?

Students familiar with the traditional "only begotten Son" in the King James version are surprised to read the NIV's "God the One and Only" in John 1:18. (Cf. TNIV: "The one and only Son, who is himself God.") This is both a translation issue and a textual one. The Greek word *monogenēs* most likely means "unique" or "one of a kind" rather than "only begotten," and so is appropriately translated "the one and only." Furthermore, the earliest and most reliable manuscripts of John 1:18 read *monogenēs theos* ("unique God") instead of *monogenēs huios* ("unique Son").

The positive response to the Word comes in verses 12–13. Those who received him by faith are adopted as God's children through spiritual rebirth. Verse 14 summarizes the incarnation, when the *Logos* took on true human form: "The Word became flesh and made his dwelling among us." The verb translated "made his dwelling" is from the same root as the word used in the Greek Old Testament for the tabernacle (*skēnē*), the portable temple Israel carried in the wilderness (Exodus 25–30). The author indicates that God's presence has again come to "tabernacle" with his people: "We have seen his glory, the glory of the One and Only, who came from the Father" (v. 14).

The prologue concludes with a summary of its theme: "No one has ever seen God, but God the One and Only, who is at the Father's side, has made him known" (v. 18; see fig. 10.5). The invisible God who is pure spirit is revealed through Jesus the incarnate Word.

The Book of Signs (1:19–12:50)

Testimonies to Jesus (1:19–51). The Gospel proper begins with a series of "testimonies" (1:19, 32, 34) concerning Jesus' identity. As in the Synoptics, Jesus' ministry begins with John the Baptist. John's role, summarized in the prologue, is now affirmed by the Baptist himself. When questioned by the Jerusalem authorities, John denies that he is the Christ, or Elijah, or the Prophet (1:19–21). Jewish end-times speculation viewed Elijah as the forerunner of the Messiah (Mal. 3:1; 4:5–6). "The Prophet" is probably the "prophet like Moses" of Deuteronomy 18:15 (see Acts 3:22; 7:37), another figure of end-times speculation. As in the Synoptics, John identifies himself from Isaiah 40:3: "I am the voice of one calling in the desert, 'Make straight the way for the Lord.'" His role is to prepare the way for the Messiah, whose sandals he is unworthy to untie (1:23, 27). When Jesus enters the scene, John again

Tel Salim, a possible location of John's baptism ministry

Gordon Franz/ZIBBC

points to him as superior (1:30) and calls him the **Lamb of God** who takes away the sin of the world. The title indicates sacrificial death, recalling the Passover lamb (Exodus 12), the daily sacrifices in the temple, and Isaiah's suffering Servant, who is led like a lamb to the slaughter (Isa. 53:7).

Unlike the Synoptics, the Fourth Gospel does not recount Jesus' baptism by John, perhaps to avoid any suggestion that John is superior. But the baptism is implied when John describes his vision of the Spirit's descent upon Jesus (1:32). Like the voice from heaven at Jesus' baptism (Mark 1:11), John's own testimony confirms that Jesus is the Son of God (1:34).

> The Fourth Gospel's model for discipleship is that individuals are invited to "come and see," to experience Jesus' transforming presence.

The next day, John the Baptist again points to Jesus as the Lamb of God, and two of his disciples leave to follow Jesus (1:35–39). This is proper, since John's role is to point others to Jesus. These, in turn, bring still others. Andrew finds his brother Simon and brings him to Jesus, announcing that he has found the Messiah. Philip, called by Jesus the next day, brings Nathanael, announcing that he has found the one predicted by Moses and the prophets. While Nathanael is skeptical of Jesus' Nazareth origin, Jesus astounds him with his omniscience and Nathanael confesses, "Rabbi, you are the Son of God; you are the King of Israel!" These scenes represent the Fourth Gospel's model for discipleship. Individuals are invited to "come and see" (1:39, 46), to experience Jesus' transforming presence. These in turn invite others, who themselves are changed through a personal encounter with Jesus.

These passages also serve a role similar to the early episodes in the Synoptics, bearing testimony that Jesus is the Messiah. Jesus is identified with a variety of messianic titles: Christ (Messiah), the Lamb of God, the Son of God, the one predicted by Moses and the prophets, and the king of Israel.

The First Sign: Changing Water into Wine at Cana (2:1–12). John relates that Jesus' first sign occurs during a wedding in Cana, a small village in Galilee. First-century Jewish weddings were extravagant affairs, lasting an entire week or more (Judg. 14:17; Tob. 8:20; 10:7). The whole village would have been invited, and Jesus came with his mother and his disciples. When the wine runs out—a major social embarrassment for the host and the bridegroom—Jesus' mother approaches him for help. Jesus responds with a mild rebuke, saying "My time has not yet come," but then relents by changing water into wine. The **miracle at Cana** has the intended result. Jesus' glory is revealed and his disciples believe in him (2:11).

Large terra-cotta storage jars for oil or wine (Dor excavations, third century BC)

There is more to this first miracle than meets the eye. In Mark 2:18–22, Jesus compares his ministry to a wedding banquet, with himself as the bridegroom. This in turn alludes to Old Testament passages where God's end-times salvation is described as a messianic banquet. Isaiah 25:6 predicts that "the LORD Almighty will prepare a feast of rich food for all peoples, a banquet of aged wine—the best of meats and the finest of wines." Jesus' ministry is "new wine" which cannot be placed in old wineskins (Mark 2:22). Similar

New Testament Cana of Galilee. View looking southwest from the Beth Netofa ridge down at Khirbet Qana.

symbolism appears in John, where Jesus appears as the bridegroom of the wedding feast (3:28–30). The jars of water used for ceremonial washing (2:6) represent the old Jewish ritual, now replaced by the new wine of the messianic banquet. By changing water to wine, Jesus symbolically announces that God's end-times salvation has arrived.

The reader may wonder what Jesus means that his "hour" had not yet arrived, and why he performed the miracle anyway. In John's narrative, Jesus' "hour" is his death and resurrection, when he will be "lifted up" and glorified (7:6, 8, 30; 8:20; 12:23; 13:1; 17:1). The narrator indicates in this way that the miracles of the Gospel are merely previews pointing forward to the true and final sign, Jesus' death and resurrection.

Clearing the Temple (2:13–25). This point is driven home in the account which follows. Jesus goes up to Jerusalem for the first Passover of the Gospel and is appalled to find sellers of sacrificial animals and money changers turning the temple into a marketplace (2:13). When he makes a whip out of cords and drives them out, the religious leaders demand a sign from him to prove his authority. Jesus responds, "Destroy this temple, and I will raise it again in three days" (2:19). While his opponents think Jesus means the Jerusalem temple, the narrator clarifies that he was speaking of the temple of his body. Jesus points to his passion, death, and resurrection as the ultimate sign.

Depiction of Jesus' turning the water into wine. This painting is in a Franciscan church in Cana, the site where Jesus performed the miracle.

The clearing of the temple, like the prior episode, has symbolic significance. Just as changing water to wine shows that the old is giving way to the new, so Jesus' actions against the temple signify the end of its sacrificial system (and coming destruction in AD 70). In the new age of fulfillment, Jesus' once-for-all Passover sacrifice will make atonement for sins. (For the Synoptic placement of the temple cleansing at the *end* of Jesus' ministry, see chap. 12, p. 391.)

Interview with Nicodemus (3:1–21). Jesus' miracles and actions in the temple create curiosity as well as concern among the Jewish leadership, and one of them seeks a private audience. While expressing interest (3:2; cf. 7:50–51), Nicodemus demonstrates spiritual blindness and so represents the religious leaders of Jerusalem. Jesus' reference to being born "again" or "from above" (*anōthen*) is misunderstood by Nicodemus as physical rebirth. Jesus clarifies that a person must be born "of water and of the Spirit." The water here has been interpreted in various ways: as (1) physical birth, (2) spiritual cleansing, or (3) baptism. The first is unlikely, since Jesus would hardly stress the necessity of physical birth. The third is possible, but how could Nicodemus be expected to know anything about Christian baptism at this point in the story? (Unless *John's* baptism of repentance is in mind.) The second interpretation is most likely, fitting well the Old Testament and Jewish background of eschatological renewal. Ezekiel 36:25–27 links water cleansing with the end-times coming of the Spirit:

> I will sprinkle clean water on you, and you will be clean; . . . I will give you a new heart and put a new spirit in you; . . . And I will put my Spirit in you and move you to follow my decrees and be careful to keep my laws.

Jesus rebukes Nicodemus, a teacher of Israel, for failing to understand spiritual realities (3:10). Such heavenly truths are available only through the Son of Man, who has come down from heaven. He must be "lifted up"—like the serpent that Moses lifted up in the wilderness (Num. 21:8–9)—so that those who believe in him may receive eternal life (3:13–15). Whether Jesus or the narrator is speaking in 3:16–21, these verses summarize the theme of John's Gospel. God loved the world so much that he sent his Son. Those who believe in him receive eternal life, a present possession and a future inheritance. John's theological **dualism** is evident here. There are two kinds of people in the world, those who believe in the Son, live in the light, and have eternal life, and those who reject the Son, live in darkness, and are already condemned (see fig. 10.6).

Figure 10.6—Dualism in John's Gospel	
Children of Light	**Children of Darkness**
Believe on the Son.	Reject the Son.
Walk in the light.	Walk in darkness.
Live by the truth.	Follow the lie.
Have eternal life now.	Are condemned already.
Will never perish.	Abide in God's wrath.
Are from above.	Are from the earth.

Following the Nicodemus episode, John the Baptist gives his final testimony to Jesus. Again he stresses Jesus' superiority. Jesus is the bridegroom, while John is merely the "best man." John's joy comes from seeing the arrival of the bridegroom. "He must become greater; I must become less" (3:30).

Interview with the Samaritan Woman at the Well (4:1–38). When Jesus learns that the Pharisees are investigating his activities, he returns north to Galilee, passing through Samaria. While it is not true that Jews always went around Samaria, relations between Samaritans and Jews were always tense and often hostile, and contact was generally avoided. The narrator's comment that Jesus "had" to go through Samaria suggests divine necessity. God had ordained this special appointment.

When the disciples enter the Samaritan village of Sychar to purchase provisions, Jesus waits beside the well of Jacob, striking up a conversation with a woman who comes to draw water. The confrontation itself is startling, since a Jewish man, particularly a respected rabbi, would never speak with an unknown woman, and especially not a Samaritan woman.

The conversation follows a pattern similar to the Nicodemus story. In both, Jesus sparks interest with a spiritual analogy ("born again," 3:3; "living water," 4:10), his statement is misunderstood, and he elaborates, eventually revealing his identity as the Messiah (see fig. 10.2). The two stories also present striking contrasts. Nicodemus is among the spiritual elite of Israel, the religious "insiders." The woman is at the opposite end of the social spectrum: she is a woman, a despised Samaritan, and a social outcast. Yet, shockingly, she responds to Jesus' message while Nicodemus remains spiritually blind.

The episode has several themes: (1) salvation arises from Judaism, not Samaritan religion, (2) Judaism is fulfilled with the coming of the Messiah, (3) salvation is now available to all who believe, and (4) disciples of Jesus bring others to him. When the woman asks Jesus why

> In his nighttime interview with Jesus, Nicodemus represents the spiritual blindness of Israel's leaders.

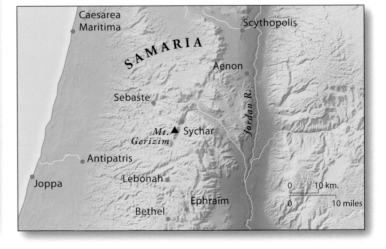

Left: A Middle Eastern well. *Below:* Map of Samaria.

Mount Gerizim, where the Samaritans worshiped

Jews worship at the Jerusalem temple while Samaritans worship on Mount Gerizim, Jesus confirms that "salvation is from the Jews" (4:22). Yet in the new age of salvation, neither temple nor mountain will be sacred, since true worshipers will worship in spirit and in truth (4:21, 23–24). True spiritual life comes not from Jewish ritual but from a relationship with the Father through the Son.

> The Samaritan woman represents the ultimate outsider—a woman, a despised Samaritan, and a social outcast—yet she demonstrates more spiritual responsiveness than Nicodemus.

The woman returns to her village and tells the townspeople, "Come, see a man who told me everything I did. Could this be the Christ?" She thus demonstrates the "come and see" attitude of a true disciple (see 1:36, 39, 41, 46).

Meanwhile, the disciples encourage Jesus to eat, but he speaks of his spiritual "food"—doing the will of the Father. In context, this means harvesting the spiritual fields which are "ripe for harvest" (4:35). As Jesus speaks, the Samaritans are making their way through the fields toward him, dramatically illustrating the ongoing harvest. As the Samaritans affirm, Jesus is indeed the "Savior of the world" (4:42).

Second and Third Signs: Healings in Cana and Jerusalem (4:43–5:45). After two days with the Samaritans, Jesus returns to Galilee, where the second sign of the Gospel takes place. In an account similar to the healing of the centurion's servant in Matthew 8:5–13 and Luke 7:1–10, Jesus heals from afar the son of a royal official (perhaps an officer in Herod Antipas's court). The story forms an *inclusio* (bookend) with the account of changing water into wine, since both occur in Cana, both are identified as signs (the first and second), and both produce faith ("So he and all his household believed," v. 53). What is interesting here is that Jesus first rebukes the man for seeking a sign (v. 48) but then announces his son is healed. The man believes Jesus (v. 50) even before seeing the sign and so demonstrates the kind of faith Jesus is seeking. In 20:29, Jesus will say to Thomas, "Blessed are those who have not seen and yet have believed."

The third sign is the healing of a disabled man at the Pool of Bethesda while Jesus is attending a Jewish festival in Jerusalem (5:1–15). This is the beginning of the back-and-forth debate between Jesus and the Jewish leaders which characterizes much of the Book of Signs (chaps. 5–10). These chapters

A model of the Pool of Bethesda

are also marked by a "replacement" motif, which shows Jesus to be the fulfillment of the various festivals of Judaism (see fig. 10.7 and fig. 10.8). This particular healing occurs on the Sabbath, which serves as the model for all of the other Jewish festivals (Exod. 31:12–13). Jews were commanded not to work on the Sabbath (Exod. 31:14–17), but Jesus justifies his actions by noting, "My Father is always at his work to this very day, and I, too, am working" (v. 17). The only one who must work on the Sabbath is God, since he always sustains the universe. Shockingly, Jesus gives himself the same status as God, above the Sabbath law. Jesus' opponents recognize this exalted claim and seek to kill him, because "not only

Figure 10.7—Jewish Calendar and Festivals

Festival	New Year (Rosh Hashanah) Tishri 1		Day of Atonement (Yom Kippur) Tishri 10	Tabernacles (Booths, In-gathering) Tishri 15–22		Hanukkah (Dedication) Kislev 25

Month	Hebrew: Ab	Elul	Tishri	Heshvan	Kislev	Tebet
	English: **July**	**Aug.**	**Sept.**	**Oct.**	**Nov.**	**Dec.**

Festival	Purim Adar 13–14	Passover and Unleavened Bread Nisan 14, 15–21	Pentecost Sivan 6	

Month	Hebrew: Shebet	Adar	Nisan	Iyar	Sivan	Tammuz
	English: **Jan.**	**Feb.**	**March**	**April**	**May**	**June**

Figure 10.8—Jesus and the Fulfillment of the Jewish Festivals	
Sabbath	John 5
Passover	John 6
Tabernacles	John 7–8
Hanukkah	John 10

was he breaking the Sabbath, but he was even calling God his own Father, making himself equal with God" (v. 18). Jesus responds by describing his relationship with the Father (5:19–30). Though the Son submits to the Father's will in all things, he shares the Father's attributes as the giver of life and the final judge of all things. Jesus concludes by pointing to three "testimonies" which confirm his identity: the testimony of John the Baptist (5:33–35), the testimony of the signs which he performs (5:36–38), and the testimony of the Scriptures (5:39–47). Jesus' opponents are rejecting him because they do not believe what Moses wrote concerning him (v. 46).

Fourth and Fifth Signs: Feeding the Five Thousand, Walking on Water, the Bread of Life (6:1–71). As Jesus' actions in chapter 5 revealed a replacement motif with reference to the Sabbath festival, so chapter 6 reveals a Passover motif (see fig. 10.9). The episodes here—feeding the five thousand, rescue through water, bread from heaven—all recall the Passover deliverance and Exodus from Egypt.

> Chapters 5–10 of John are marked by a "replacement" motif, which shows Jesus to be the fulfillment of the various festivals of Judaism.

The feeding of the five thousand—the fourth sign of the Gospel—is the only miracle which appears in all four Gospels. When Jesus withdraws to a mountainside with his disciples, a large crowd follows him. There Jesus feeds over five thousand men (plus women and children?) with five barley loaves and two fishes. The feeding has several Old Testament parallels. Like the changing of water into wine at Cana, the miracle typifies the messianic banquet, God's eschatological promise to feed and shepherd his people (Isa. 25:6–8; 65:13–14). By feeding the people with God's abundant provision, Jesus symbolically serves as the host of God's end-times salvation.

Left: Tabgha, traditional site of the miracle of loaves and fishes. *Right:* Large reed basket for storing or transporting agricultural products.

© Neal Bierling/Zondervan Image Archives

Z. Radovan, Jerusalem

Another parallel appears in 2 Kings 4:42–44, where the LORD miraculously multiplies bread so that the prophet Elisha can feed a hundred men with twenty barley loaves, with "more left over" (cf. John 6:12–13).

Most important, the miracle recalls Israel's manna in the wilderness (Exodus 16; Numbers 11). The people respond to the sign by saying, "Surely this is the Prophet who is to come into the world" (6:14). As in 1:21, this is probably the prophet like Moses of Deuteronomy 18:15. The people recognize Jesus' Moses-like ability to miraculously feed them and assume he is God's end-times agent. When they attempt to make him their king, he withdraws by himself (6:15). His hour has not yet come.

As in Matthew and Mark, the feeding miracle is followed by the account of Jesus walking on water (6:16–24; Matt. 14:22–33; Mark 6:47–51). This fifth sign recalls the Passover-Exodus scene of Moses leading Israel through the water (Exodus 13–15). As Yahweh demonstrated his mighty power over the sea, so Jesus reveals divine authority over nature. When Jesus walks toward the storm-tossed boat, he calls out, "It is I. Don't be afraid." The phrase "It is I" (Greek: *egō eimi*, "I am") appears often in John and recalls God's self-description in the Exodus account as the "I AM"—the self-existent LORD of all (Exod. 3:14). This self-identification by Jesus will be made even more explicit in 8:58.

Top: Fish from Galilee. *Bottom:* A Byzantine-era mosaic depicting the miracle of the loaves and fishes at Tabgha on the Sea of Galilee.

Figure 10.9—Passover and the Feast of Unleavened Bread

Passover was one of three pilgrim feasts which Jewish males were expected to attend (Exod. 23:14–17; Deut. 16:16; cf. *m. Ḥag.* 1:1, which provides exceptions). The other two were Pentecost and the Feast of Tabernacles. Passover was the Jewish festival commemorating the deliverance of the Hebrews from slavery in Egypt. The angel of death spared the firstborn sons of the Hebrews, "passing over" those households which sacrificed a lamb and placed its blood on the doorframes (Exodus 12). It was celebrated on the 15th of Nisan (March/April), the first month in the Jewish calendar. Lambs were sacrificed in the temple on the afternoon of Nisan 14 and were roasted and eaten with unleavened bread that evening (Nisan 15 began after sunset). Family or larger units celebrated Passover together. Unleavened bread was then eaten for seven days during the Feast of Unleavened Bread, which immediately followed Passover (Lev. 23:6; Exod. 12:17–20; 34:18). The term Passover was sometimes used for both festivals. Extensive traditions and liturgy eventually became attached to Passover, though how much of this was practiced in Jesus' day is unknown.

John further links the feeding miracle to the wilderness manna by recounting Jesus' discourse on the bread of life on the following day (6:22–59). The true bread from heaven was not the manna in the wilderness or the loaves the people ate but God's gift of his Son. As is often the case in John, Jesus' hearers misunderstand his words, wondering how he, the son of Joseph, can be bread from heaven. This allows Jesus to explain the bread's spiritual significance. The bread of eternal life comes to whoever "eats my flesh and drinks my blood" (6:54). Jesus' words, which are similar to those he speaks at the institution of the Lord's Supper, refer to receiving salvation through his sacrificial death on the cross.

> The feeding of the five thousand recalls Israel's manna in the wilderness, and Jesus then teaches that he is the "bread of life" which comes down from heaven.

Jesus' puzzling discourse on bread from heaven and eating his flesh provokes a crisis among his disciples, and some stop following him (6:60, 66). When Jesus asks the Twelve whether they too will go, Peter responds, "Lord, to whom shall we go? You have the words of eternal life. We believe and know that you are the Holy One of God" (6:68–69). Jesus then affirms that he has chosen the Twelve but that one of them — Judas — will betray him (6:70–71). Like Peter's confession in the Synoptics (Mark 8:29, par.), this episode confirms the loyalty of the eleven disciples and begins the narrative's turn toward its climax in Jerusalem.

Teaching at the Feast of Tabernacles, the Light of the World (Chaps. 7–8). Chapter 7 begins with Jesus' brothers encouraging him to go to Jerusalem for the Feast of Tabernacles to perform miraculous signs and so prove to the world that he is the Messiah. The narrator points out that Jesus' brothers did not believe in him (7:5), so their quest for signs, like that of the religious leaders' (2:18, 6:30), is a negative thing, evidence of their unbelief. Jesus refuses to go to Jerusalem with them but later goes privately. The point seems to be that opposition is mounting and Jesus is avoiding confrontation, since his hour has not arrived. There are repeated references throughout chapters 7 and 8 that his opponents are seeking to kill him (7:19, 20, 25; 8:37, 40).

Chapters 7 and 8 record Jesus' teaching at the Feast of Tabernacles, also called the Feast of Booths. Tabernacles was one of three great festivals during which Jewish pilgrims would come to Jerusalem (Pentecost and Passover were the other two). Originally a harvest festival, Tabernacles came to be a commemoration of Israel's wilderness wanderings (Lev. 23:33–43). As they do elsewhere in John, Jesus' actions and teaching draw on traditional symbols associated with the festival. The seventh day of Tabernacles was marked by water-pouring and lamp-lighting ceremonies (*m. Sukkah* 4:1, 9–10; 5:2–4). Jesus alludes to these when he announces that *he* will provide streams of living water for the thirsty

A first-century oil lamp. Jesus teaches in John that he is the light of the world.

(7:37–39) and that he is the "light of the world" (8:12). Jesus is the fulfillment of Israel's history and traditions.

Despite Jesus' private arrival, while in Jerusalem he engages in further debate. The pattern is now familiar to the reader. Jesus makes a statement about himself, to which his opponents respond with a challenge or accusation. Jesus refutes their claims and provides further teaching. The debates are full of misunderstanding and characteristic Johannine irony. Jesus' opponents accuse him of being demon-possessed and deluded for thinking his life is threatened (7:20; 8:48, 52). They insist that they are children of Abraham and children of God (8:39, 41). But in fact, it is his opponents who have the devil as their father (8:44), and they are indeed plotting his death (7:25, 32). Irony is also evident as some deny that Jesus is the Messiah, since they know where he came from—Nazareth (7:27). According to some Jewish traditions, the Messiah would have an unknown origin. The reader recognizes that Jesus' true origin is indeed unknown, since he is from heaven (3:13, 31; 6:32–33,

> Jesus' use of the absolute "I am" (*egō eimi*) in 8:57–59 recalls Yahweh's self-identification in Exodus 3:14.

38, 50–51). When Jesus says he will go to a place they cannot come (heaven), they misunderstand and wonder whether he is going to the Jewish communities of the Diaspora to teach the Greeks (7:35). The irony is that in John's day, Jesus' message is indeed going to the Gentile world. The irony continues when others reject him, since Scripture says that "the Christ will come from David's family and from Bethlehem, the town where David lived" (7:41–42). There seems to be double irony here. While Jesus' true origin is "from above," his earthly origin is just as Scripture predicted: from Bethlehem and the line of David.

Jesus' discourse ends with another astonishing claim (8:57–59). When the Jewish leaders ironically ask if Jesus is greater than their father Abraham, he responds that Abraham rejoiced to see his day. The religious leaders wonder how he could have seen Abraham, since he is less than fifty years old. Jesus replies, "Before Abraham was born, I am!" Jesus' use of the absolute "I am" (*egō eimi*) again suggests God's self-identification in Exodus 3:14. Jesus' opponents apparently understand this claim, since they pick up stones to kill him. Jesus escapes and hides, since his hour has not yet come.

Figure 10.10—The Woman Caught in Adultery (John 7:53–8:11)
An Authentic Tradition?

The story of the woman caught in adultery, which appears in our Bible at John 7:53–8:11, does not seem to have been an original part of John's Gospel. Its style and vocabulary are unlike the rest of the Gospel, it breaks the flow of the narrative, and it does not appear in the oldest and most reliable manuscripts. In some others, it appears at a different place (after John 7:36; 7:44; or 21:25) and even in a different Gospel (after Luke 21:38).

What can we say about the story? While probably not an original part of John, the story has the ring of authenticity and sounds very much like what we know of the historical Jesus. Many scholars consider it to be an authentic historical episode, a "floating tradition" which was passed down by word of mouth and eventually found its way into different places in the New Testament.

www.FreeStockPhotos.com

© Neal Bierling/Zondervan Image Archives

Above: An artist's reconstruction of the Pool of Siloam. *Left:* The remains of the Pool of Siloam.

Sixth Sign: Healing a Man Born Blind (Chap. 9). The sixth sign of the Gospel continues events at the festival of Tabernacles and plays off the imagery of light (and sight) associated with the festival. The story begins when the disciples ask if a man's blindness was caused by his own sins or the sins of his parents. Jesus rejects both explanations, saying the purpose was to reveal God's work. He then heals the man by placing mud and saliva on his eyes and telling him to wash in the Pool of Siloam. The washing recalls Elijah's healing of Naaman the Syrian by having him wash in the Jordan River (2 Kings 5:10–14). The rest of the episode concerns the aftermath of the healing, with dialogues between Jesus, the man, his parents, and the Jewish authorities. The miracle of sight symbolizes the progress of the narrative. As the man progressively gains greater spiritual in*sight*, the religious leaders decline toward greater blindness. The man first identifies Jesus as "the man they call Jesus" (v. 11), then "a prophet" (v. 17), then "from God" (v. 33), and finally worships him with the confession "Lord, I believe" (v. 38). The religious leaders are at first divided about Jesus (v. 16), then call him "a sinner." Johannine irony climaxes the encounter as they ask sarcastically, "What? Are we blind too?" In fact they are!

As is the case elsewhere in John, behind the conflict between Jesus and the religious leaders appears to be the conflict between the Johannine community and its Jewish opponents. The repeated references to expulsion from the synagogue in this passage (9:22, 34, 35; cf. 12:42; 16:2) probably mirror what is happening in the author's day.

The Good Shepherd and Teaching at the Feast of Dedication (10:1–42). Another Jewish festival, the Feast of Dedication or Hanukkah (also called the Festival of Lights), is the context for Jesus' teaching in chapter 10. Hanukkah celebrated the rededication of the temple by Judas Maccabee (164 BC) after its desecration by Antiochus IV Epiphanes (see chap. 4, p. 102). Though the festival is not mentioned until verse 22, Jesus' teaching on the Good Shepherd in verses 1–21 already recalls Hanukkah and the events leading up to the Maccabean revolt, when false shepherds led the people astray. John's readers would likely make this connection, since the description of false shepherds in Ezekiel 34:2–10 had become part of the Hanukkah liturgy of Judaism.[6]

In two of his "I am" statements, Jesus identifies himself as the good shepherd, who willingly gives his life for his sheep, and as the gate of the sheepfold, allowing access to eternal life. The religious leaders, in contrast, are mere hired hands who care little for the sheep, or worse yet, robbers who break in to steal the sheep. Like the false shepherds who allowed the corruption of Judaism during the days of Antiochus, so they have led Israel astray. Again, Jesus' teaching provokes a mixed response. Some say he is demon-possessed and a lunatic, while others wonder how a demon-possessed man could heal or teach this way (10:19–21).

Coming to him in the temple during the festival, the religious leaders finally demand from Jesus, "If you are the Christ, tell us plainly." Jesus responds that he has already told them and that his works have confirmed his identity. When Jesus concludes, "I and my Father are one," his opponents take up stones again to kill him, accusing him of blasphemy by claiming to be God (10:24–33). Jesus' response points to Psalm 82:6, where Israel's judges (or perhaps angelic powers) were called "gods" because of the authority God gave

---

6. See A. Guilding, *The Fourth Gospel and Jewish Worship: A Study of the Relation of St. John's Gospel to the Ancient Jewish Lectionary System* (Oxford: Clarendon, 1960), 129–32.

View of a typical sheepfold in the hill country of Benjamin.

them. Jesus here uses a rabbinic style of "lesser to greater" argument. If the word *gods* is used even of lesser mediators, how can they accuse him — the One and Only Son sent by the Father — of blasphemy for claiming to be the Son of God?

> The raising of Lazarus is the climax of the seven signs of the Gospel of John, serving as a preview of Jesus' own resurrection. The episode also prompts the religious leaders to act against him.

In the face of growing opposition, Jesus withdraws from Jerusalem to the other side of the Jordan River, setting the stage for his final approach to Jerusalem.

Seventh Sign: The Raising of Lazarus (Chap. 11). Chapters 11 and 12 serve as a transition from the Book of Signs to the Book of Glory, turning the narrative toward its Jerusalem climax. The **raising of Lazarus** is the climax and the greatest of the seven Gospel signs, serving as a preview for the ultimate sign — Jesus' own resurrection. It also carries the plot forward by prompting the religious leaders to act decisively against him.

All of the signs are intended to bring glory to the Father and to provoke faith in the Son. This one is no exception. When Jesus hears of Lazarus's illness, he delays going to see him for two days, saying, "This sickness will not end in death. No, it is for God's glory so that God's Son may be glorified through it." There is irony here. Though Lazarus will die, physical death is mere "sleep" (11:11) for those who believe in Jesus. Jesus' apparent complacency in helping Lazarus is for a greater purpose: to bring glory to God and draw forth faith from the disciples (11:4, 15).

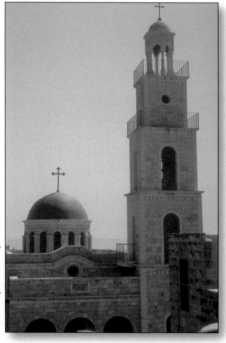

Bethany, home of Mary, Martha, and Lazarus

© Neal Bierling/Zondervan Image Archives

Jesus' conversation with Lazarus's sisters, Martha and Mary, provides the context for Jesus' self-revelation (11:17–37). Both have faith in Jesus' healing power, saying Lazarus would not have died if Jesus had arrived sooner (11:21, 32). When Jesus confirms to Martha that Lazarus will live, she assumes he means the traditional Jewish understanding of resurrection at the end of time. Jesus corrects her by saying, "I am the resurrection and the life." This statement has profound significance for the Gospel's theology. Jesus himself is the source of resurrection life, bestowing eternal life in the present on all who believe that he is "the Christ, the Son of God, who was to come into the world" (11:25–27).

Lazarus's resurrection has the intended result, bringing glory to God and provoking faith (11:40, 41, 45). Another result, however, is to galvanize the opposition of the religious leaders, who plot to take Jesus' life. The passage is full of irony. Because Jesus gives life to Lazarus, the religious leaders plot to take his life. Yet through his death, he will bestow eternal life on all who believe. The justification of the religious leaders is also ironic. "If we let him go on like this, everyone will believe in him, and then the Romans will come and take away both our place and our nation" (11:48). The irony is that the Gospel will go forth to all people, and the Romans will come to destroy the temple and the nation (in AD 70). The irony continues as the high priest Caiaphas justifies the action against Jesus: "It is better for you that one man die for the people than that the whole nation perish." The narrator notes that the high priest inadvertently prophesies that Jesus will die for the Jewish nation (and for all of the children of God) (11:49–51).

Coming to Jerusalem (Chap. 12). Because of this opposition, Jesus withdraws for a short time but then returns to Bethany shortly before Passover. Back at Lazarus's home, Jesus attends a dinner at which Mary anoints his feet with expensive perfume (12:1–11). The anointing, like the Lazarus episode, prepares the reader for Jesus' death and resurrection. When Judas objects to the waste of costly perfume, Jesus affirms that Mary's

Doorway of the traditional site of the tomb of Lazarus in Bethany

act is an anointing for burial. While Judas represents the evil schemes of Jesus' opponents, Mary models the faithful and devoted disciple. (On the relationship of this anointing to those in the Synoptics, see chap. 12, p. 391.)

The triumphal entry in John has many similarities with the Synoptics, representing Jesus' public declaration of his messiahship (12:12–19). The difference is that similar claims have already appeared throughout John. His messiahship is no secret for those with faith. Jesus enters the town on a donkey, with the crowd shouting "Hosanna!" and reciting the traditional pilgrim psalm: "Blessed is he who comes in the name of the LORD!" (Ps. 118:26). As in Matthew, the episode is identified as the fulfillment of Zechariah 9:9: "See, your king is coming, seated on a donkey's colt" (John 12:15; Matt. 21:5). The event provokes anger and jealousy from the Pharisees, who exaggerate its significance: "Look how the whole world has gone after him!" (John 12:19; cf. Luke 19:39). Ironically, in John's day the message of salvation is indeed going to the whole world.

Roman and Phoenician glass juglets used for perfume

Jesus indicates that the passion narrative is beginning by announcing, "The hour has come for the Son of Man to be glorified" (12:23). In language reminiscent of Gethsemane in the Synoptics, Jesus agonizes over his coming death. Yet unlike in the Synoptics, Jesus does not ask God to change his plan (Mark 14:36, par.), since he has come for this very purpose, to glorify the Father's name (12:27–28). As in the Synoptic baptism and transfiguration accounts, the Father speaks from heaven, confirming Jesus' mission (12:28).

In the last section of the Book of Signs, the narrator explains why so many Jews have rejected Jesus despite the many signs (12:37–43) and provides a summary of Jesus' teaching (12:44–50). As with elsewhere in the New Testament, Isaiah 6:1–4 is cited to show

Tradition locates the Last Supper in the Cenacle on Mount Zion. This present structure was reconstructed by Franciscans in 1335. *Left:* The Cenacle exterior view. *Above:* Interior view of the Upper Room.

that Israel's blindness was in fulfillment of Scripture and was part of Israel's rebellious history (12:40; Mark 4:12; Matt. 13:14 – 15; Luke 8:10; Acts 28:26 – 27). Verses 44 – 50 summarize Jesus' teaching in this first half of the Gospel. He has come to reveal the Father who sent him and to bring light to the world. Those who reject him are condemned, but those who believe receive eternal life.

The Book of Glory (13:1 – 20:31)

Story time slows dramatically at this point, and the next five chapters contain Jesus' teaching during the Last Supper. While the Book of Signs (chaps. 1 – 12) concerned Jesus' self-revelation to the world, the Book of Glory begins with private teaching for his disciples.

The Last Supper (Chap. 13). The account starts with the evening meal — probably the Passover[7] — during which Jesus washes the disciples' feet (13:1 – 17). When Peter, appalled that Jesus would act like a lowly servant, at first refuses to let Jesus wash his feet, Jesus teaches that all who follow him must imitate his model of self-sacrificial love and service (13:12 – 17). Two negative examples of discipleship follow, as Jesus predicts Judas's betrayal and Peter's denial (13:18 – 30, 36 – 38). Johannine symbolism is apparent as Judas departs and the narrator adds, "And it was night" (13:30). Between these two failures of discipleship (in a kind of *inclusio*) Jesus gives the disciples a new command: to love one another. By this love, all people will know they are his disciples (13:35). Though not wholly original (see Lev. 19:18), the command to love is new in that it sums up and epitomizes the whole law (cf. Matt. 22:37 – 40). Love is the hallmark of Christian discipleship throughout the Johan-

---

7. See the discussion of this passage in chapter 12, (pp. 393 – 94).

nine literature. This scene introduces the first reference to the Beloved Disciple (13:23), the enigmatic figure whose testimony gave rise to the Gospel (21:24).

Farewell Discourse (Chaps. 14–16). The **Farewell Discourse** which follows appears to be modeled after Moses' in Deuteronomy 31–33 and similar "testaments" in the Old Testament and Judaism. A testament represents the last words of a great leader, summarizing his life, making predictions about the future, appointing successors or heirs, and calling them to live by certain standards.

Jesus describes his departure and promises to send the Spirit to take his place. While the Fourth Gospel usually speaks of salvation as a present possession, here Jesus speaks of it also in the future, when he will return to take his followers to his Father's home (14:3, 28). They can trust him for this since he is "the way and the truth and the life" (14:6). This phrase is probably a *hendiadys* (two or more words expressing a single idea): "the one true way to life." The Son provides the only way to the Father and to eternal life.

> In the Farewell Discourse, Jesus' final great teaching episode in John (chaps. 14–16), he warns the disciples of dangers to come and promises them the presence of the Spirit to guide and protect them.

During his absence, Jesus promises to send the Spirit as a **paraclete** (Greek: *paraklētos*), meaning "counselor" or "advocate." The Spirit will mediate the presence of the Father and the Son to the disciples, teaching, guiding, and comforting them (14:16–20, 26–27; 15:26–27; 16:5–16). But the disciples can be successful only if they "abide" in him. Just as a branch gains sustenance from the vine, so they will bear fruit only by staying close to him (15:1–8). Abiding means especially abiding in "love"—love which the Father has for the Son, and which the Son has given to them (15:9–17). The greatest love of all is giving your life for a friend (15:13), the very thing Jesus is about to do for them.

Abiding in Jesus is essential because of the hostile environment in which the disciples will live. The world alienated from the Father and the Son will hate and persecute them, throwing them out of the synagogues and even killing them (15:18–16:4). Yet the Spirit has a role with reference to the world as well, convicting it of sin, righteousness, and judgment (16:5–11). Like a prosecuting attorney, the Spirit will reveal the guilt and coming judgment of the world. To the disciples, however, the Spirit will reveal all truth (16:12–16). This probably refers not only to the apostles' writing of Scripture but also to divine guidance for all believers.

In the conclusion of the discourse, the disciples express their faith in Jesus and show increased understanding of his mission and identity (16:29–30). Jesus affirms this growing faith but points out its instability by predicting that they will all abandon him (16:31–32). While this is a rebuke of the disciples' weakness, it is even more an affirmation of Jesus' strength. Though they will have trouble in this world, they can take heart because "I have overcome the world" (16:33).

Jesus' Prayer for the Disciples (Chap. 17). The Last Supper narrative concludes with Jesus' **high-priestly prayer**, so called because Jesus acts as a priestly mediator for his disciples. While the central theme is protection and unity for them, Jesus begins by praying for himself (17:1–5). Announcing again that "the time has come," he prays that the Father would glorify the Son so that the Son may glorify the Father. In this way, he will bestow eternal life on all those the Father has given him. Eternal life is defined as a relationship with the Father through the Son: knowing "you, the only true God, and Jesus Christ, whom you have sent" (17:3).

Jesus then turns to pray for his disciples, not only those present (17:6–19) but all who will believe in the future (17:20–26). Jesus affirms the authenticity of their belief—except for Judas, the "one doomed to destruction"—and prays for their unity and protection. Unity is essential to maintain their connection to the Father and the Son. Protection is necessary since they are in the world but not of the world—that is, they are not part of the world system controlled by the evil one. Jesus prays that they would be "sanctified" in truth—set apart from the world and set apart to God. The prayer ends as it began, with a request that Jesus' coming glorification would reveal the Father.

Arrest and Trial (18:1–19:16). After praying, Jesus crosses the Kidron Valley with his disciples to a garden (Gethsemane in Matthew and Mark). Story time picks up again and events move rapidly toward the arrest and crucifixion. The central theme is that *Jesus is in control of his destiny and is acting according to God's plan.* When Judas shows up with soldiers and representatives from the high priest to arrest Jesus, the narrator notes that he knew "all that was going to happen to him" (18:4). Jesus takes the initiative, asking the crowd whom they are seeking and then responding *egō eimi* ("I am [he]").

> A strong kingship motif carries through John's passion narrative. Yet Jesus' kingdom is "not of this world."

As with elsewhere in John, the phrase recalls the divine name of God (Exod. 3:14; John 8:58). The context suggests that this is the meaning here and that John presents the scene as a **theophany**—an appearance of God before human beings, producing awe and fear. Evidence for this is the crowd's response. Overwhelmed, they pull back and fall to the ground (18:6). Though the prisoner, Jesus reveals sovereign authority. He gives the orders, telling the crowd to let the disciples alone and commanding Peter to put away his sword (18:8–9, 11). Everything is happening according to plan. Jesus says, "Shall I not drink the cup the Father has given me?" (18:11). The narrator repeatedly notes that Jesus' own prophecies are coming true (18:9, 32).

Only the Fourth Gospel describes Jesus' appearance before the high priest Annas (18:19–24). Though Caiaphas was the official high priest, his father-in-law, Annas (who had been deposed by the Romans in AD 15), still wielded much influence (cf. Luke 3:2). Yet Jesus stands unflinchingly before him, rebuking the high priest for this secret interrogation (18:20–21). When an official strikes Jesus for this seemingly impudent comment, Jesus remains defiant, since he is only speaking the truth (18:23). The narrator emphasizes these

Z. Radovan, Jerusalem

A Jewish ossuary with the name Caiaphas carved in Hebrew on the side. An ossuary is the box into which the bones of the deceased were placed after the flesh had decomposed.

themes of boldness and truth by sandwiching (intercalation) Jesus' testimony between the accounts of Peter's denial. The faithful Son of God speaks truly (18:19–23), while the cowardly disciple tells lies (18:15–18, 25–27).

Annas sends Jesus to Caiaphas, who takes him before the Roman governor Pilate. During his interview with Pilate, Jesus demonstrates the same confidence and control. Although Jesus is on trial, he interrogates Pilate (18:34). He openly speaks of his kingship—though it is "not of this world"—and boldly claims his words are true (18:36–37). This is the beginning of a strong kingship-royalty motif which will carry through the passion narrative. When Pilate warns Jesus that he has the power to crucify him, Jesus replies that Pilate has no authority except from God (19:11). In contrast to Jesus' faithfulness, Pilate is cynical, wavering, and fearful. While Jesus testifies to the truth, Pilate sarcastically responds, "What is truth?" While repeatedly declaring Jesus innocent (18:38; 19:4, 6) and wishing to release him (18:31, 39; 19:10, 12), Pilate is fearful of the religious leaders (19:8) and eventually gives in to their wishes (19:16).

The religious leaders are portrayed as flat characters, vehemently opposed to Jesus and seeking his death. Hypocritically, they refuse to enter Pilate's palace to avoid ceremonial uncleanness (18:28) yet seek the execution of an innocent man (18:31; 19:6, 7, 15). In their blindness, they claim the pagan Caesar as their king over God's own Messiah (19:12, 15), confirming that they are indeed "of the world." Ironically, throughout the trial Jesus is mocked by Pilate, soldiers, and religious leaders as "king of the Jews" (18:33, 37, 39; 19:3, 12, 14, 15, 19, 21); the reader knows that Jesus is indeed the king (1:49; 12:13, 15; 18:36–37).

The Crucifixion (19:16–42). The crucifixion scene reveals the same theme of God's sovereign purpose and control. The narrator repeatedly stresses that what is happening is in fulfillment of Scripture: the dividing of Jesus' garments (19:24; Ps. 22:18), his thirst on the cross (19:28; perhaps from Ps. 69:21), his unbroken bones (19:36; Exod. 12:46; Ps. 34:20), the piercing of his side (19:37; Zech. 12:10). Jesus has the presence of mind from the cross to entrust his mother to the care of the Beloved Disciple (19:25–27). He chooses to end his life "knowing that all was now completed" (19:28) and with his last words cries out, "It is finished" (19:30). Salvation has been accomplished. In the end, Jesus releases his spirit (19:30). No one takes his life; he willingly gives it up (cf. 10:11, 15, 17–18; 15:13).

As in the Synoptics, Jesus' body is taken by Joseph of Arimathea and buried in a new tomb. Only John notes that Joseph was a secret disciple and that he was aided in the burial by Nicodemus. The description of the soldiers' discovery that Jesus was already dead (19:33), the water and blood from his side (19:34), the testimony of the Beloved Disciple (19:35), and the burial ritual (19:40–42) all confirm for the reader that Jesus is indeed dead, preparing for the miracle of the resurrection. These events also carry theological significance. Jesus' unbroken bones recall the Passover lamb (19:36; Exod. 12:46), and the blood and water represent the cleansing power of his sacrificial death (see John 3:5; 4:10–24; 7:37–39).

The Resurrection (Chap. 20). John's resurrection narrative consists of five scenes with three resurrection appearances: Mary Magdalene discovers the empty tomb (20:1–2), Peter and the Beloved Disciple run to the tomb (20:3–9), Jesus appears to Mary (20:10–18), then to all of the disciples except Thomas (20:19–23), and finally to Thomas (20:24–29). A fourth resurrection appearance in Galilee occurs in the epilogue (21:1–23).

A Roman spearhead. John describes how a Roman soldier pierced Jesus' side with a spear and blood and water came out.

Figure 10.11—The Myths about Mary Magdalene

Who was Mary Magdalene? We can actually say more about who she was not. She was not a prostitute, she did not anoint Jesus' feet and wipe them with her tears, and she certainly did not marry Jesus or bear children by him (as has been claimed in sensationalistic books like *The Da Vinci Code*). There is not a shred of evidence for any of these claims. The myth about Mary as a prostitute arose because of confusion in the church between various women: Mary Magdalene, Mary of Bethany (Luke 10, John 11), the sinful woman who anointed Jesus' feet in Luke 7:36–50, and the woman caught in adultery (John 7:53–8:11). In the late sixth century, Pope Gregory the Great delivered a homily in which he pronounced all of these different women to be one and the same. The confusion has persisted ever since. Indeed, Mary Magdalene is perhaps the most misrepresented woman in the Bible. From the Gospels, all we know about Mary are four facts:

1. She was one of the women disciples who supported Jesus financially (Luke 8:2–3).
2. She had seven demons cast out of her (Luke 8:2).
3. She was with other women at the crucifixion (Mark 15:40; Matt. 27:56; John 19:25), at the burial (Mark 16:1; Matt. 27:61), and at the empty tomb (Mark 15:47; Matt. 28:1; Luke 24:10).
4. According to John, Mary went to the tomb alone and was the first witness to the resurrected Jesus (John 20:1–2, 10–18).

Yet we should not understate who Mary was either. She must have been a significant follower of Jesus, since she is always listed first among the women disciples (except in John 19:25), just as Peter is among the Twelve. She was also granted the high privilege of being the first to witness the resurrection. While we should resist the temptation to speculate much beyond this, there is clearly much more we would like to know about this remarkable woman.

For details see Mark L. Strauss, *Truth and Error in "The Da Vinci Code": The Facts about Jesus and Christian Origins* (San Diego: Alethinos Books, 2005), 61–87.

While the Synoptics describe a group of women visiting the tomb on Easter morning, John mentions only Mary Magdalene. When Mary discovers the stone rolled away, she assumes Jesus' body has been stolen and runs to inform Peter and "the other disciple" (presumably the Beloved Disciple). Running to the tomb, they discover it empty except for Jesus' grave clothes. The Beloved Disciple becomes the model for resurrection faith when "he saw and believed" (20:8).

The first resurrection appearance comes to Mary. Weeping outside the tomb, she first sees two angels and then Jesus, who she assumes is the gardener. Only when he speaks her name does she recognize him. Jesus' puzzling words, "Do not hold on to me, for I have not yet returned to the Father" (20:17) probably mean that she must stop depending on his physical presence, since he will soon ascend to the Father. The disciples' relationship with Jesus is changing and will now be mediated through the Spirit he is sending.

The second resurrection appearance is to all of the disciples except Thomas while they are meeting in secret for fear of their Jewish opponents. Jesus appears suddenly, confirming the truth of his resurrection with his nail-scarred hands and spear-punctured side. He then gives the Johannine equivalent of the Great Commission, "As the Father has sent me, I am sending you" (20:21), and bestows the Holy Spirit by breathing on the disciples (20:22).

From a narrative perspective, this latter is John's equivalent of Pentecost, when Jesus gives the Holy Spirit he has promised. From a historical perspective, it may be viewed as an interim filling to hold the disciples over till Pentecost seven weeks later (Acts 2:1–4).

The third appearance is again to the disciples, this time with Thomas present. Thomas's initial doubts are turned to faith as he sees Jesus and touches his scars. His acclamation, "My Lord and my God!" (20:28) may be seen as an *inclusio* with John 1:1, "framing" the entire Gospel around the theme of Jesus as the self-revelation of God. The Gospel which began with "the Word was God" climaxes with "my Lord and my God!" Jesus then pronounces a blessing on those who, unlike Thomas, have believed even though they have not seen. This comment applies to believers of every age but was especially directed toward the struggling believers of John's community.

The Gospel proper concludes with its statement of purpose: "that you may believe [or "continue to believe"; see the section "Narrative Purpose" later in this chapter] that Jesus is the Christ, the Son of God, and that by believing you may have life in his name" (20:31). The Gospel as a whole is a call to decision.

> The Gospel proper concludes with its statement of purpose: "that you may believe that Jesus is the Christ" (20:31). The whole Gospel is a call to decision.

Epilogue (21:1–25)

Chapter 21 is often called an epilogue or an appendix, since the Gospel seems to reach a conclusion in chapter 20, and since this chapter reflects on the Gospel and ties up loose ends. The epilogue relates a fourth resurrection appearance (the third to the disciples): a miraculous catch of fish (21:1–14), followed by Jesus' conversation with Peter (21:15–23). The miracle is similar to that described in Luke 5:4–7. Both stories concern Peter's call, Luke's to initial discipleship and this one to church leadership, to shepherd Jesus' flock. The key significance here is the restoration of Peter. Peter's three affirmations to Jesus' repeated question, "Do you love me?" (21:15, 16, 17) balance and correct Peter's three denials (18:17, 25, 27). Jesus uses one word for love in his first two questions (*agapaō*), to which Peter responds with a different word (*phileō*). Jesus' third question and Peter's third answer both use *phileō*. Some scholars think this lexical shift is meaningful and that Jesus is condescending to Peter's inability to express ultimate God-like love (*agapē*). More likely, the change is merely stylistic. Two different Greek words are also used for "sheep" (*arnia, probata*), "feed" (*boskō, poimainō*), and "know" (*oida, ginōsko*) with no difference in meaning. Furthermore, elsewhere in John no distinction is made between *agapaō* and *phileō*. The narrative purpose of the episode is not to distinguish different kinds of love but to affirm Peter's restoration and his position as shepherd in Jesus' new community.

The epilogue closes with two statements which seem intended to clear up confusion about the Beloved Disciple. First, when Jesus predicts Peter's martyrdom (21:18–19), Peter asks about the fate of the Beloved Disciple. The narrator clarifies that Jesus' response was not that this disciple would not die but only that his fate was in Jesus' hands (and so none of Peter's business). The implication seems to be that the Beloved Disciple was nearing death, or perhaps had recently died, and some were claiming this would contradict Jesus' words.

Second, the narrator affirms that the testimony of the Fourth Gospel came from this Beloved Disciple and that "we know that his testimony is true" (21:24). This is the closest any Gospel comes to naming its author. It also suggests that while the Beloved Disciple put these traditions in writing, his followers edited them into this final form. The book concludes with a statement similar to 20:30, that Jesus' words and deeds far exceed anything that a book or books could contain (21:25).

JOHN'S PORTRAIT OF JESUS: THE SON WHO REVEALS THE FATHER

Jesus' identity is on center stage throughout the Fourth Gospel, which presents the most exalted Christology in the New Testament. Jesus is the unique Son of God who has come from the Father. He is God's Word (*Logos*), his self-revelation (1:1, 14, 18). Whoever has seen him has seen the Father (14:9). While distinct from the Father ("with God," 1:1), he is fully God ("was God," 1:1; 20:28), the "I AM" who existed before Abraham (8:24, 28, 58). He shares God's attributes. He is the creator of all things (1:3, 10), the giver and sustainer of life (5:16 – 18, 26; 6:27, 35, 50 – 58), who will raise the dead (5:21, 25; 4:53; 6:39 – 40, 44, 54; 10:28; 11:25 – 26) and serve as final judge (5:22, 27). He is omniscient (1:48; 2:24 – 25; 6:15; 8:14; 13:1, 11; 21:17). As the Son sent from above, he provides the only access to the Father and to eternal life: "No one comes to the Father except through me" (14:6; cf. 3:16, 36; 4:14; 5:21 – 26; 6:33, 35, 51 – 58, 68; 8:12; 10:10, 17 – 18; 11:25; 17:2 – 3). The Father and Son operate in complete unity (10:30; 14:10) and know one another perfectly (10:15).

> Jesus' identity is on center stage throughout the Fourth Gospel, which presents the most exalted Christology in the New Testament.

While the Gospel speaks of Jesus as equal with God (5:18; sometimes called **ontological equality**), there is also a strong **functional subordination**. By this we mean that while Jesus is fully divine, he lives in complete dependence on the Father. The Son does nothing by himself but only what the Father directs him to do (5:19; 8:29). He has come to do the will of the Father who sent him (3:16, 34; 4:34; 6:38; 7:28; 8:26, 42; 12:49) and to bring glory to him (8:29; 14:13; 17:4). This functional subordination is in line with the central theme of the Gospel: *The role of the Son is to reveal the Father and bring others into a relationship with him.*

While John's exalted Christology exceeds traditional Jewish expectations for the Messiah, the author does not avoid messianic categories. As in the Synoptics, Jesus is the Messiah (John 1:41; 4:25 – 26), the king of Israel (1:49; 12:13), and the fulfillment of Old Testament prophecies. In some ways, John has a stronger Jewish accent than the other Gospels, charting Jesus' ministry according to Jewish festivals and building images and allusions which echo Old Testament themes. Only John uses the transliterated form *messias*, from the Hebrew *mashiach* ("Messiah" = "Anointed One," 1:41; 4:25). Elsewhere in the New Testament (and nineteen times in John), the Greek translation *christos* is used ("Christ" = "Anointed One"). The author is clearly concerned to show that the community which worships Jesus the Messiah is the true people of God, the heirs of the promises made to Israel.

OTHER CHARACTERS IN JOHN'S GOSPEL

The Disciples

The Synoptics place great emphasis on Jesus' calling and training the Twelve, sending them out as apostles to preach and to heal. In John, the disciples remain a more amorphous group of followers. John speaks of a disciple or the disciples seventy-nine times, but the Twelve only four times (eleven times in Mark). Three of these references are in chapter 6, where the Twelve represent those few who remain with Jesus after his teaching on the bread of life. From a narrative perspective, the disciples represent all those who follow Jesus, both in Jesus' ministry and in the Johannine community. They respond positively to his signs and teaching but also frequently misunderstand his words. Their questions and misunderstandings, like those of Jesus' opponents, provide the context in which Jesus clarifies his identity and mission.

> From a narrative perspective, the Beloved Disciple represents the model disciple, a faithful and informed follower of Jesus.

The two most prominent disciples are Peter and the enigmatic Beloved Disciple ("the disciple whom Jesus loved"). As in the Synoptics, Peter is bold yet erratic. He confidently confesses his faith in Jesus (6:69) and in loyalty lashes out against Jesus' enemies (18:10). Yet a few verses later, he denies he even knows Jesus (18:15–18, 25–27). Peter's character is formed through humility, first at Jesus' washing of the disciples' feet and then through his restoration. With Peter's three confessions, he is finally ready to assume the roles of a shepherd over Jesus' flock and a martyr for his Lord (21:15–19).

We will discuss the historical identity of the Beloved Disciple later. From a narrative perspective, he represents the model disciple, a faithful and informed follower of Jesus. First appearing at the Last Supper, he is a close confidant of Jesus, sitting at the privileged position by his side (13:23–25). He follows Jesus after his arrest and provides Peter access to the high priest's courtyard (18:15–16). He is present at the crucifixion, and Jesus places Mary in his care (19:26–27), indicating a relationship closer even than physical family. He outruns Peter to the tomb of Jesus and is the first to believe in the resurrection (20:4). In Galilee, he is the first to recognize the resurrected Lord on the lakeshore (21:7). Finally, he is identified as the reliable source for the Gospel, providing faithful testimony to Jesus' ministry (21:24). All true disciples—those whom Jesus loves—should aspire to this kind of faith and devotion.

> John's theological dualism is most evident in his portrayal of Jesus' opponents: the religious leaders, the world, and Satan.

The Antagonists: The Religious Leaders, "the World," and Satan

John's theological dualism is most evident in his portrayal of Jesus' opponents. There is little gray or middle ground. You are either for God or for Satan, of light or of darkness, from above or from below. Jesus' primary opponents are the religious leaders, **the world**, and Satan.

The Greek term *Ioudaioi* ("Jews," "Judeans," or "Jewish leaders") occurs only rarely in the Synoptics but appears sixty-three times in John. While occasionally carrying a neutral sense of ethnic descent (2:6; 4:9), it is usually negative, referring to the Jewish religious leaders who oppose Jesus. As we have seen, the best explanation is that John is writing at a time when the church has broken with the synagogue. The debate between Jewish Christianity and Judaism is no longer an inter-Jewish debate but one between Christians and Jews.

John's portrayal of the Jewish religious leaders is not wholly negative. While most reject Jesus, others believe (2:23; 7:31; 8:31; 11:45; 12:42), and the narrator often refers to their divisions (7:12, 43; 9:16; 10:19). Yet as the narrative progresses, hostility increases as they resolve to kill Jesus (5:18; 7:1, 19, 25; 8:37, 40; 10:31; 11:53). They do not believe their own Scriptures, which testify to him (5:39, 47), and so God's word does not dwell in them (5:38). They do not know the Father or the Son (8:19, 47, 55). They are "of this world" (8:23) and "from below" (8:23). Judas, who himself is called "a devil" (6:70), is prompted by Satan to betray Jesus into the hands of the religious leaders (13:2, 27), who are themselves children of the devil (8:44).

These connections between the religious leaders, the world, and Satan reflect John's dualistic perspective. By opposing Jesus, these leaders have allied themselves with the evil world system (1:10; 7:7; 14:17, 22) and with Satan, "the prince of this world" (12:31; 14:30; 16:11). The "world" (*kosmos*), like *Ioudaioi*, can be used neutrally of the place where people dwell (1:10; 9:39; 13:1; 16:21, 28; 17:5, 24; 18:37) or the people whom God sent Jesus to save (1:10; 3:16, 17; 4:42; 6:33, 51; 8:12; 9:5; 17:21). More often, it carries connotations of the evil world system ruled by Satan (1:10; 7:7; 12:31; 14:17, 22, 30; 15:18–19; 16:8, 11, 20, 33; 17:16). Like the religious leaders, the world does not know Jesus (1:10; 17:25) and so hates him (7:7; 15:18) and his followers (17:14).

Minor Characters

A host of minor characters appear in a scene or two in the Fourth Gospel: Nicodemus, the woman at the well, the royal official, the man born blind, Mary, Martha, Lazarus. Disciples also appear in minor roles: Andrew, Philip, Nathanael, and Thomas. These characters often provide the context in which Jesus' self-revelation takes place, asking often ignorant questions which prompt Jesus' teaching. They also function as models of discipleship, particularly when they introduce others to Jesus. John the Baptist points his disciples to Jesus (1:36), Andrew brings Peter (1:40), Philip brings Nathanael (1:45), the Samaritan woman brings the townspeople (4:29). The faithful disciple is one who, after encountering Jesus, brings others to him.

> The central theme of the Fourth Gospel is the revelation of the Father through the Son.

THEOLOGICAL THEMES

The Revelation of the Father through the Son

The central theme of the Gospel is the revelation of the Father through the Son. God loved the world so much that he sent his Son to save it. Those who believe in him have eternal life. Those who reject him are condemned already (3:16–17). As God's "Word" made flesh, Jesus has perfect knowledge of the Father and now offers this knowledge and relationship to all who believe. Images of light, life, and sight characterize those who come to know the Father through Jesus the Son.

Over against the themes of knowledge and sight are Jesus' opponents, who remain in darkness and are blind to the truth. The themes of misunderstanding and spiritual blindness permeate the Gospel. Jesus' opponents are ignorant of spiritual realities because they do not know the Father or the Son (7:28; 8:19, 55; 15:21; 17:25).

Salvation as Knowing God, Eternal Life in the Present

In the Synoptic Gospels, salvation is identified especially with entrance into the kingdom of God. In John, it is usually described as **eternal life**. John does occasionally speak of the kingdom of God (see John 3:3, 5) and the Synoptics of eternal life (see Mark 10:17, 30, par.), but these references are exceptional. Both John and the Synoptics describe salvation as both "already" and "not yet," having both present and future dimensions. (For future eschatology in John, see 3:16; 6:39; 10:28; 14:3, 28; 21:23.) But the greater emphasis in the Fourth Gospel is on the present. The Son came to bring eternal life, and this is now available to all who believe (5:24–26). Jesus says, "I have come that they may have life, and have it to the full" (10:10). While Jesus will raise the dead on the last day (6:39, 40, 44, 54), he is already the resurrection and the life, bestowing eternal life on those who believe (11:25). This is called **realized eschatology**; God's end-times salvation is already present in the life of the believer.

Salvation is a present possession because eternal life is equivalent to *knowing God*, a relationship with the Father through the Son. "Now this is eternal life: that they may know you, the only true God, and Jesus Christ, whom you have sent" (17:3). This relationship with God happens through regeneration, being "born again" (3:3), when the Father and the Son come to live in the believer (14:23). When this happens, they come to know the truth and are set free (8:32, 36). They now walk in the "light" (3:21; 8:12; 12:36, 46).

The Paraclete

Since the Son brings life and light, how will the disciples manage after he leaves? The answer is that he will send another "counselor" or "advocate" (*paraklētos*), the Holy Spirit who will mediate his presence to them (14:16–26; 15:26–27; 16:7–15). It is in fact better that he is leaving, since the indwelling presence of the Father and the Son will enable them to do even greater works than his (14:12; 16:7).

> While Luke presents the Spirit primarily as the sign of the new age, in John the Spirit is another paraclete, who will act in Jesus' place to mediate the presence of the Father.

John shares with Luke-Acts a special interest in the work of the Spirit. In both, the Spirit represents the continuing presence of Jesus in his church, empowering, guiding, and directing the disciples on their mission. Yet there are important differences. For Luke, the coming of the Spirit is especially the fulfillment of prophecy, the evidence of the dawning of the new age of salvation and proof that the last days have begun (Acts 2). In John, the greater emphasis is on the Spirit's role as *another* paraclete, who will act in Jesus' place to mediate the presence of the Father. As Jesus imparted life, light, and knowledge of the Father to the disciples, so now the Spirit will do the same thing.

He will guide them into all truth, testifying about Jesus and reminding them of all he taught them (14:26; 15:26).

NARRATIVE PURPOSE

The Fourth Gospel states its purpose clearly: "Jesus did many other miraculous signs in the presence of his disciples, which are not recorded in this book. But these are written that you may believe that Jesus is the Christ, the Son of God, and that by believing you may have life in his name" (20:30–31).

The author writes to call forth faith in Jesus. While this suggests an evangelistic purpose, the Gospel seems intended to bring confidence for believers as well. The reading "that you might believe" (*hina pisteusēte*, an aorist subjunctive) is disputed, and some early manuscripts could be translated "that you might continue to believe" (*hina pisteuēte*, a present subjunctive). These two purposes — to provoke belief and perseverance — are not mutually exclusive, and both are probably aspects of the author's purpose. The bottom line is that John's Gospel is a call to decision. Readers are not only introduced to the story of Jesus Christ, the Son of God; they are called to respond in faith to him.

THE HISTORICAL SETTING OF JOHN'S GOSPEL: AUTHOR AND LIFE SETTING

Authorship

Like the Synoptics, the Fourth Gospel does not name its author. It comes close, however, by identifying the author with "the disciple whom Jesus loved": "This is the disciple who testifies to these things and who wrote them down. We know that his testimony is true" (21:24).

This identification finds support in the narrative. The author claims to be an eyewitness (1:14; 19:35; 21:24, 25) and demonstrates firsthand knowledge of the events portrayed,

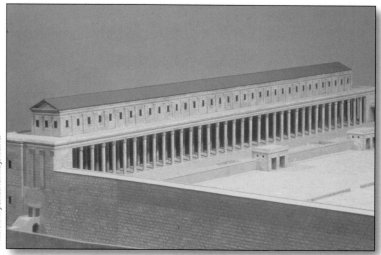

A model of Solomon's Colonnade, the magnificent portico that surrounded the outermost court of the temple

© Neal Bierling/Zondervan Image Archives

often noting incidental details, like the number of jars at Cana ("six," 2:6), the number of years of illness ("thirty-eight," 5:5), the name of the slave whose ear Peter sliced off ("Malchus," 18:10), and the number of fish caught in Galilee ("153," 21:11). This last is particularly striking, since no symbolic significance seems to be attached to the number. The author also shows good knowledge of Palestine (Samaria between Judea and Galilee, 4:3–4; Jacob's well at Sychar, 4:5), and particularly the city of Jerusalem (the Pool of Bethesda; the Pool of Siloam, 9:7; Solomon's Colonnade, 10:23). These last three are particularly significant since they were destroyed by the Romans in AD 70.

The author also has good knowledge of Jewish festivals and traditions (2:6, 23; 6:4; 7:2, 37–39; 10:22; 19:14, 31) and introduces Hebrew and Aramaic words like *Rabbi* and *Rabboni* ("teacher," 1:38; 20:16), *Messias* ("Messiah," 1:41; 4:25), and *Kēphas* ("Rock," Peter, 1:42). While many scholars once believed that the Fourth Gospel was the most Greek of the Gospels, today it is often viewed as the most Jewish. The discovery of the Dead Sea Scrolls, which reveal the same sort of dualism between light and darkness, and the children of God and the children of Satan suggests that the Fourth Gospel's traditions arose in a Palestinian rather than a strictly Hellenistic context.

Who, then, was this Beloved Disciple? Some have suggested that he is a literary fiction representing the model of a faithful follower. This is unlikely considering the explicit identification in 21:24. Others have pointed to Lazarus, since he first appears near the time the Beloved Disciple shows up (11:1; 13:23)

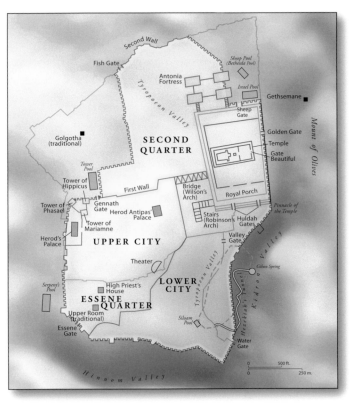

The author of John's Gospel demonstrates detailed awareness of the geography of Jerusalem, suggesting he has firsthand knowledge of the city before its destruction in AD 70.

and since he is explicitly said to be loved by Jesus (11:36). Most recently, Thomas has been suggested, since his story concludes the Gospel proper and since he asks to see Jesus' side (20:24–29; only the Beloved Disciple saw the spear-piercing, 19:35).[8] The weight of evidence, however, favors the church's traditional identification with the apostle John, son of Zebedee and one of the Twelve. Irenaeus, writing in the late second century, claims that "afterwards, John, the disciple of the Lord, who also had leaned upon His breast, did himself publish a Gospel during his residence at Ephesus in Asia."[9] Irenaeus says he received this tradition from Polycarp, a disciple of John himself.

This identification finds support in the narrative itself. The Beloved Disciple appears as a close associate of Peter (13:24; 20:2–10; 21:2, 7, 20–24), suggesting he was one of the "inner circle" of disciples (Peter, James, and John). Since

> The author of the Fourth Gospel shows good knowledge of Palestinian geography as well as Jewish festivals and traditions.

8. See J. H. Charlesworth, *The Beloved Disciple: Whose Witness Validates the Gospel of John?* (Valley Forge, PA: Trinity, 1995). Charlesworth also points to the community which arose around the traditions of Thomas with its own literature (*Gospel of Thomas*, etc.) and a special interest in the Fourth Gospel.

9. Irenaeus, *Against Heresies* 3.1.1 in *The Ante-Nicene Fathers*, ed. Alexander Roberts and James Donaldson, vol. 1 (New York: Charles Scribner's Sons, 1899), 414.

James was martyred at an early date (Acts 12:1 – 5), John remains the most likely candidate. Further evidence for this is that John is never mentioned by name in the book. This is an unusual omission for so prominent a disciple, unless he is indeed "the disciple whom Jesus loved."

But questions have also been raised. Eusebius, the fourth-century church historian, quotes the early church father Papias (c. AD 130) and concludes that there were two different men named John who ministered in Ephesus — John the apostle and a later individual called **John the Elder**. Some scholars conclude that the Johannine literature should be associated with this other John. Papias's statement is unclear, however, and both of his references may be to John the apostle. The first reference is to the apostles generally, and the latter to the living witnesses. As the sole surviving apostle, John appears in both lists. The title "elder" (*presbyteros*) does not necessarily distinguish this figure from the apostle John since all of the apostles are called elders in the previous statement.

Challenges to Johannine authorship are also made from the narrative itself. Why doesn't the Fourth Gospel record any of the key Synoptic events in which Peter, James, and John were present (the raising of Jairus' daughter, the transfiguration, the prayer in Gethsemane)? Furthermore, although John followed Jesus from his early Galilean ministry (Mark 1:19), the Beloved Disciple appears first in the Last Supper narrative (John 13:23). Others have argued that John was likely martyred too early to write the Gospel, since Jesus predicted that James and John would both experience the "baptism" (martyrdom?) which he will undergo (Mark 10:38).

None of these objections is conclusive. Because the Fourth Gospel utilizes so little of the Synoptics it is precarious to draw conclusions based on the absence of certain passages. Since John does not list the Twelve by name nor recount their appointment by Jesus, we cannot determine with any certainty when the Beloved Disciple began to follow Jesus. (It may be as early as 1:35.) Jesus' words in Mark 10:38 are open to various interpretations and cannot be forced to mean early martyrdom. The most likely candidate for authorship remains the apostle John.

The Composition of the Gospel: A Johannine Community?

Complicating the question of authorship is the claim that the Gospel was produced in stages. The last few verses (and perhaps the whole epilogue) were clearly added after the Gospel was written, since it refers to the author's writing in the past (21:25). The prologue may also have been an early Christian hymn which was integrated into the Gospel. Nowhere else in the Fourth Gospel is Jesus called the *Logos*, and words like "tabernacled"

(1:14), "fullness" (1:16), and "grace" (1:16) appear only here. There are also some awkward transitions in the Gospel which may indicate editorial activity. For example, at the end of chapter 14, Jesus says, "Come now; let us leave," but then keeps talking for three more chapters (chaps. 15–17).

Because of these complications, many scholars prefer to speak not of a single author but of a Johannine community from which the Gospel arose. This community, it is supposed, was founded by the Beloved Disciple and followed his distinctive teachings. While he was responsible for many of the stories and perhaps even the first draft of the Gospel, the rest emerged gradually and in stages over the course of time. The three Johannine letters (1–3 John), which share common vocabulary, style, and theology with the Gospel, probably also arose within this community.

> Many scholars prefer to speak not of a single author for the Fourth Gospel but of a Johannine community from which the Gospel arose.

While there is little doubt that the Fourth Gospel arose within a distinct community with it own beliefs and concerns, attempts to specify stages of composition are hypothetical and raise more questions than they answer. Whether or not the prologue was composed separately, it forms a fitting introduction to the Gospel. It seems best to treat the Gospel as a literary unity rather than to draw speculative conclusions based on compositional theories.

Place, Occasion, and Date

Since the eighteenth century, it was common among critical scholars to date the Fourth Gospel to the late second century, assuming its exalted view of Jesus was a late development in the church. The discovery of the **John Rylands manuscript (p⁵²)**, a small fragment of

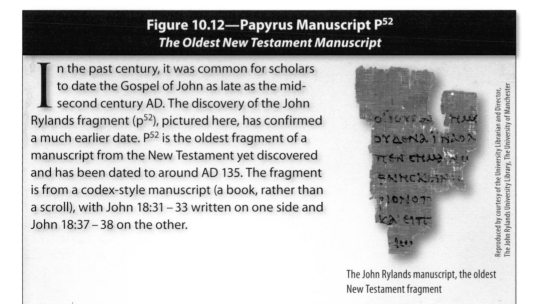

Figure 10.12—Papyrus Manuscript P⁵²
The Oldest New Testament Manuscript

In the past century, it was common for scholars to date the Gospel of John as late as the mid-second century AD. The discovery of the John Rylands fragment (p⁵²), pictured here, has confirmed a much earlier date. P⁵² is the oldest fragment of a manuscript from the New Testament yet discovered and has been dated to around AD 135. The fragment is from a codex-style manuscript (a book, rather than a scroll), with John 18:31–33 written on one side and John 18:37–38 on the other.

The John Rylands manuscript, the oldest New Testament fragment

John dated to the first half of the second century, has refuted this claim, and most scholars today date the Gospel to the late first century (see fig. 10.12).

Church tradition claims that the apostle John ministered in Ephesus in the latter part of the first century and that it was there he wrote the Gospel. While such traditions are not infallible, this setting fits well the Gospel's content. Ephesus was a major crossroads of the Roman world and had a large Jewish population. In the late first century, Christians had broken with the Jewish synagogue and were increasingly viewed with suspicion by the secular authorities. This alienation would account for the Gospel's strong polemic against both the "Jews" and the "world." The church that was in the world but not of the world found itself more and more in conflict with its opponents. John writes both to encourage believers to remain faithful to the Son and to call unbelievers to faith in him.

> Church tradition claims that the apostle John ministered in Ephesus in the latter part of the first century and that it was there he wrote the Gospel.

The Epistles of John may also help us locate the time and place of the Gospel. First John indicates strong opposition to the growing influence of **Docetism** and Gnosticism in the church. Docetism was the belief that Christ only appeared to be human. According to church tradition, a Docetist named Cerinthus was John's primary opponent in Ephesus. If the Epistles came from Ephesus in Asia minor, it is likely that the Gospel too arose about that time and place. The Gospel's strong affirmation of both Jesus' true deity and real humanity also fits well with the church's early clashes with Gnosticism, which denied the incarnation of the Son of God.

Ephesus, traditional site of John's writing

Gordon Franz/ZIBBC

A few scholars have argued for a very early date for John, even in the 50s or 60s of the first century. The best evidence for this are certain present-tense verbs related to places in Jerusalem. John 5:2 reads, "Now there is in Jerusalem near the Sheep Gate a pool, which in Aramaic is called Bethesda." Such a statement seems odd if the book was written after the destruction of Jerusalem in AD 70, when the pool no longer existed. While this evidence is intriguing, it could be related to John's style of writing or his use of a source. It does not seem enough to overrule the strong church tradition for a late-first-century date. Yet it should caution us against overconfidence concerning the date and specific life setting of the Gospel.

READING JOHN TODAY

With its elegant simplicity and deep spiritual insight, John's Gospel is perhaps the most loved of the four Gospels. It is also the most widely distributed, sometimes being printed as a separate pamphlet, an evangelistic "tract" to lead people to Christ. I have one of these on my shelf with an introduction in many different languages and a conclusion explaining how to receive Jesus as savior. The author of the Fourth Gospel would surely be pleased with such a publication, fitting as it does his narrative purpose: "that you may believe that Jesus is the Christ, the Son of God, and that by believing you may have life in his name" (John 20:31). John's Gospel is fundamentally a call to decision. Like the characters in the story—Nicodemus, the Samaritan woman, Peter, and others—each reader encounters the claims of Jesus and must respond with acceptance or rejection.

Nor is there any middle ground in this decision. Though a beautiful literary work, John's Gospel does not espouse a spiritual sentimentality or religious pluralism. John draws a stark contrast between those who believe in Jesus and those who reject him, the children of God and the children of Satan, those in the light and those in darkness. Jesus preaches an exclusive gospel: the Son is the only way to the Father. All others stand condemned. Forged in the heat of competing religious claims, the Gospel is both a call for faith leading to life, and a warning against disbelief leading to death. To be sure, this is an unpopular message in today's society, in which claims to absolute truth are dismissed as naive and relativism is the order of the day. But it is a message the Fourth Evangelist passionately believed the world needed to hear.

1. John's Gospel is unique among the Gospels, with a distinct literary style and much unique content.

2. John often refers to Jesus' opponents as *Ioudaioi* ("Jews" or "Jewish leaders"), suggesting that he is writing to a community that has broken away from the larger Jewish community.

3. The Gospel has four sections: (a) Prologue, (b) Book of Signs (seven miracles together with teaching and dialogue), (c) Book of Glory (the Last Supper and passion narratives), (d) Epilogue.

4. Jesus' teaching falls into three main types: interviews with individuals, dialogue and debate with the religious leaders, and private teaching for the disciples.

5. The Gospel is full of metaphors and symbols, with much verbal and situational irony.

6. The prologue describes Jesus as the incarnate Word (*Logos*) of God, the one and only Son who reveals the Father and brings life and light to humanity.

7. As in the Synoptics, John the Baptist is the forerunner who prepares the way for Jesus the Messiah. John identifies Jesus as the Lamb of God who takes away the sin of the world.

8. Jesus' first miracle at Cana in Galilee (chap. 2) reveals his glory, and his disciples believe in him. The wedding miracle is symbolic of the messianic banquet, a picture of God's final salvation.

9. Jesus' clearing of the temple symbolically indicates the end of the sacrificial system and the coming of salvation through the destruction of the new "temple" (Jesus' body).

10. Nicodemus (chap. 3) represents the spiritual blindness of Israel's religious leaders, who fail to comprehend the spiritual reality of new birth through the Spirit.

11. The account of the Samaritan woman (chap. 4) demonstrates that Jesus is the promised Messiah who brings living water (eternal life) to all who believe.

12. Jesus' healing of the lame man at the Pool of Bethesda (chap. 5) is the beginning of the back-and-forth debate between Jesus and the religious leaders in the context of the Jewish festivals. By healing on the Sabbath, Jesus identifies himself with the Father, who works even on the Sabbath to sustain the universe.

13. The feeding of the five thousand (chap. 6) is the only miracle to appear in all four Gospels. Jesus is the bread of life who provides true spiritual manna, recalling the Passover festival.

14. Though many disciples desert Jesus, Peter (representing the Twelve) confesses that he is the Holy One of God who brings words of eternal life (6:68).

15. In his teaching at the Feast of Tabernacles (chaps. 7 – 8), Jesus draws on festival symbols to identify himself as living water and the light of the world. He also identifies himself as the "I am" — the divine name of God from Exodus 3:14.

16. The healing of the man born blind (chap. 9) contrasts the spiritual blindness of Israel's leaders with the spiritual insight of those who believe in Jesus.

17. Recalling the Hanukkah festival, Jesus contrasts himself as the good shepherd with the religious leaders, who are thieves or mere hired hands (chap. 10).

18. The raising of Lazarus (chap. 11), the greatest of the seven "signs," reveals Jesus' authority as bringer of resurrection life and provokes the religious leaders to act against him.

19. As in the Synoptics, Jesus' triumphal entry serves as a public announcement of his messiahship (Zech. 9:9).

20. The Book of Glory (chaps. 13–20) begins with the Last Supper narrative. Jesus washes the disciples feet, teaches on servanthood and love, and gives his Farewell Discourse (chaps. 14–16). He promises to send the Spirit as teacher, comforter, and guide during his absence. The disciples are called to "abide" in him.

21. In his "high-priestly prayer" (chap. 17), Jesus asks the Father for protection and unity for his disciples.

22. The main theme of the trial and crucifixion in John is that Jesus is in control of his destiny and is acting according to God's plan (chaps. 18–19).

23. John's resurrection narrative is unique in Jesus' appearance to Mary Magdalene alone and in appearances to the disciples first without, and then with, Thomas present. Thomas's confession, "My Lord and my God!" frames (an *inclusio*) the entire Gospel between two acclamations of Jesus' deity (1:1; 20:28).

24. The epilogue (chap. 21) includes the miraculous catch of fish, the restoration and commissioning of Peter, and the role of the Beloved Disciple in the composition of the Gospel.

25. John's Gospel presents the most exalted Christology in the New Testament. Jesus is the preexistent *Logos*, the Son of God who perfectly reveals the Father and brings people into relationship with him.

26. The two most prominent disciples in the Gospel are Peter and the enigmatic Beloved Disciple.

27. John provides a dualistic perspective in which Jesus represents light, truth, and life and stands over against Satan and the evil world system representing darkness, deceit, and death.

28. The central theme of John's Gospel is the revelation of the Father through the Son. God loved the world so much that he sent his Son to save it, so that those who believe in him gain eternal life.

29. Salvation in John is identified especially as eternal life, which is defined both as a present possession and a future inheritance.

30. John's primary narrative purpose is to call people to faith in Jesus the Christ and Son of God so that they might have eternal life in his name (20:30 – 31).

31. The identification of the Beloved Disciple with the apostle John has been the historical position of the church. Though it's not without some problems, it fits well with both internal and external evidence.

32. Though John's Gospel likely arose within a unique and distinct "Johannine" community (or communities) within early Christianity, attempts to identify the exact beliefs and life situation of this community, or to trace a composition history of the Gospel, remain problematic.

33. John's Gospel was likely written in the late first century and was likely composed by the apostle John while he was ministering in Ephesus.

» KEY TERMS «

"I am" statements	chiasm	ontological equality
Johannine community	Lamb of God	functional subordination
prologue of John	miracle at Cana	the world
Logos	dualism	eternal life
Beloved Disciple	raising of Lazarus	realized eschatology
Book of Signs	Farewell Discourse	John the Elder
Book of Glory	paraclete	John Rylands manuscript (p[52])
Nicodemus	high-priestly prayer	Docetism
"signs"	theophany	

1. How is John unique among the Gospels? What kinds of Synoptic material does John not include in his Gospel?

2. How is John's style unique?

3. What does John's Gospel tell us about the length of Jesus' public ministry?

4. Identify the basic fourfold structure of John.

5. What three main types of teaching appear in John's Gospel?

6. What are the purpose and significance of the "signs" of John's Gospel?

7. What is the main theme of the prologue of John's Gospel?

8. How do the interviews with Nicodemus and the Samaritan woman contribute to John's purpose?

9. Which miracle appears in all four Gospels? What is its significance in John?

10. What is the significance of Jesus' "I am" statement in John 8:58?

11. What key role does the raising of Lazarus play in John's narrative?

12. What will be the Spirit's role after Jesus' departure? What does *paraclete* mean?

13. What does Jesus ask for in his "high-priestly prayer"?

14. What is the main theme of John's trial and crucifixion narrative?

15. How is Thomas' declaration in 20:28 significant for John's narrative progression?

16. Summarize the Christology of John's Gospel.

17. What do we mean by John's theological dualism?

18. What is the central theme of John's Gospel?

19. How is the theme of salvation presented in John's Gospel and how is this different from the Synoptics?

20. What is the narrative purpose of John's Gospel?

21. Summarize the evidence suggesting that John the apostle wrote the Fourth Gospel. What problems exist with this identification?

22. When and where does the early church tradition claim John wrote his Gospel?

23. How did the discovery of the John Rylands fragment influence the dating of John?

Digging Deeper

Commentaries

Beginning and Intermediate

Barrett, C. K. *The Gospel according to John*. 2nd ed. Philadelphia: Westminster, 1978.

Beasley-Murray, George R. *John*. Word Biblical Commentary. Waco, TX: Word, 1987.

Bruce, F. F. *The Gospel of John*. Grand Rapids: Eerdmans, 1983.

Burge, Gary M. *John*. NIV Application Commentary. Grand Rapids: Zondervan, 2000.

Carson, D. A. *The Gospel according to John*. Pillar New Testament Commentary. Grand Rapids: Eerdmans, 1991.

Köstenberger, Andreas. *John*. Baker Exegetical Commentary. Grand Rapids: Baker, 2004.

Kruse, Colin. *The Gospel according to John*. Tyndale New Testament Commentary. Grand Rapids: Eerdmans, 2004.

Kysar, Robert. *John*. Augsburg Commentary on the New Testament. Minneapolis: Augsburg, 1986.

Lincoln, Andrew T. *The Gospel according to Saint John*. Black's New Testament Commentary. Peabody, MA: Hendrickson, 2005.

Lindars, Barnabas. *The Gospel of John*. New Century Bible. Grand Rapids: Eerdmans, 1981.

Morris, Leon. *The Gospel according to John*. New International Commentary. Rev. ed. Grand Rapids: Eerdmans, 1995.

Witherington, Ben, III. *John's Wisdom: A Commentary on the Fourth Gospel*. Louisville: Westminster John Knox, 1995.

Advanced and Greek/Technical

Brown, Raymond E. *The Gospel according to John*. 2 vols. Anchor Bible. Garden City, NY: Doubleday, 1966–70.

Bultmann, Rudolf. *The Gospel of John*. Edited by G. R. Beasley-Murray. Oxford: Blackwell, 1971.

Haenchen, Ernst. *John*. 2 vols. Hermeneia. Philadelphia: Fortress, 1984.

Keener, Craig S. *The Gospel of John: A Commentary*. 2 vols. Peabody, MA: Hendrickson, 2003.

Schnackenburg, Rudolf. *The Gospel according to St. John*. 3 vols. New York: Herder and Herder, 1968–82.

Themes and Theology of John

Ashton, J. *Understanding the Fourth Gospel*. New York: Oxford Univ. Press, 1991.

Beasley-Murray, George R. *Gospel of Life: Theology in the Fourth Gospel*. Peabody, MA: Hendrickson, 1991.

Brown, Raymond E. *The Community of the Beloved Disciple*. New York: Paulist, 1979.

Brown, Raymond E., and Francis J. Moloney. *An Introduction to the Gospel of John*. Anchor Bible Reference. New York: Doubleday, 2003.

Burge, Gary M. *The Anointed Community: The Holy Spirit in the Johannine Tradition*. Grand Rapids: Eerdmans, 1987.

———. *Interpreting the Fourth Gospel*. Grand Rapids: Baker, 1992.

Cassidy, Richard J. *John's Gospel in New Perspective: Christology and the Realities of Roman Power.* Maryknoll, NY: Orbis, 1992.

Dodd, C. H. *The Interpretation of the Fourth Gospel.* Cambridge: Cambridge Univ. Press, 1968.

Harrington, Daniel J. *John's Thought and Theology: An Introduction.* Wilmington, DE: Michael Glazier, 1990.

———. *John the Son of Zebedee: The Life of a Legend.* Columbia, SC: Univ. of South Carolina Press, 1994; Minneapolis: Fortress, 2000.

Köstenberger, Andreas. *Encountering John: The Gospel in Historical, Literary and Theological Perspective.* Grand Rapids: Baker, 1999.

Kysar, Robert. *The Fourth Evangelist and His Gospel: An Examination of Contemporary Scholarship.* Minneapolis: Augsburg, 1975.

Morris, Leon. *Jesus Is the Christ: Studies in the Theology of John.* Grand Rapids: Eerdmans; Leicester: Intervarsity, 1989.

Painter, John. *The Quest for the Messiah: The History, Literature, and Theology of the Johannine Community.* Rev. ed. Nashville: Abingdon, 1993.

Pryor, John W. *John: Evangelist of the Covenant People.* Downers Grove, IL: InterVarsity, 1992.

Sloyan, Gerald. *What Are They Saying about John?* New York: Paulist, 1991.

Smalley, Stephen S. *John: Evangelist and Interpreter.* 2nd ed. Downers Grove, IL: Intervarsity, 1998.

Smith, D. Moody. *John among the Gospels: The Relationship in Twentieth-Century Research* Minneapolis: Fortress, 1992.

———. *The Theology of the Gospel of John.* Cambridge: Cambridge Univ. Press, 1995.

Talbert, Charles H. *Reading John.* Rev. ed. Macon, GA: Smyth and Helwys, 1999.

Van Tilborg, Sjef. *Reading John in Ephesus.* Leiden: Brill, 1996.

Newer Methods and Approaches

Culpepper, R. Alan. *Anatomy of the Fourth Gospel: A Study in Literary Design.* Philadelphia: Fortress, 1983.

Levine, Amy-Jill, ed. *A Feminist Companion to John.* With Marianne Blickenstaff. New York: Sheffield Academic, 2003.

Malina, Bruce J., and Richard L. Rohrbaugh. *Social-Science Commentary on the Gospel of John.* Minneapolis: Fortress, 1998.

Newheart, Michael Willett. *Word and Soul: A Psychological, Literary, and Cultural Reading of the Fourth Gospel.* Collegeville, MN: Liturgical Press, 2001.

Stibbe, M. W. G. *John as Storyteller: Narrative Criticism and the Fourth Gospel.* SNTSMS 73. Cambridge: Cambridge Univ. Press, 1993.

Bibliography

Mills, Watson E. *The Gospel of John.* Lewiston and Lampeter: Mellen, 1995.

PART FOUR

The Historical Jesus

CHAPTER 11

Searching for the Real Jesus

» CHAPTER OVERVIEW «

1. The Historical Quests for Jesus

   The First Quest
   No Quest
   The New (Second) Quest

2. The Contemporary Scene: A Third Quest?

   Questions of Method and Context
   The Results: Contemporary Portraits of Jesus

3. Conclusion

» OBJECTIVES «

After reading this chapter, you should be able to:

- Summarize the nature and characteristics of the three "quests" for the historical Jesus, including some of the scholars associated with each.
- Describe historical and philosophical factors which led to the rejection of the historicity of the Gospels.
- Explain the perspective of Rudolf Bultmann and especially his dichotomy between the historical Jesus and the Christ of faith.
- Discuss the main methodological issues related to contemporary Jesus studies.
- Summarize the main contemporary portraits of Jesus.

Students are often surprised and disturbed to learn that many biblical scholars reject the notion that Jesus was anything more than a mere man. How can this be, they ask, if Jesus himself claimed to be the Son of God and even God himself? Were not the Gospels written by eyewitnesses or close associates of the eyewitnesses?

The answer to these questions is that many critical scholars do not consider the Gospels to be eyewitness accounts. They are rather the result of a long process of creative storytelling and mythmaking by communities far removed in place and time from the historical Jesus. The Jesus of the Gospels is not the "historical Jesus" but the "Christ of faith," exalted and deified by later Christians.

To understand how this perspective came to be, we must briefly survey the modern quests for the historical Jesus. It is sometimes said that where we are is determined by where we have been, and this is certainly true in Gospel studies. Ideas do not arise in a vacuum but develop over time in social and intellectual climates. Since the books on the historical Jesus could fill a library, we will survey only a few of the writers and movements which marked key milestones in the quest for the historical Jesus.

It should be noted that we are here surveying the movements that led to the radical rejection of the historical Jesus. During this period, there were many significant works produced by moderate and conservative scholars which reached more positive conclusions.[1] Our interest here is primarily in the trends leading to skepticism and rejection of the historicity of the Gospels.

THE HISTORICAL QUESTS FOR JESUS

The First Quest: The Nineteenth-Century Quest for the Historical Jesus

The traditional approach of the church through the ages has been to treat the Bible as the inspired Word of God and the Gospels as historically accurate and reliable. This perspective began to be seriously challenged during the period of European history known as the Enlightenment (seventeenth and eighteenth centuries), when the philosophy of **rationalism** dominated the intellectual scene. Rationalism claimed that reason—what can be logically understood by the mind—was the sole test of truth. Anything that could not be rationally explained was not true. Supernatural elements in the Bible were viewed with skepticism or disbelief. Historical criticism began to be applied to the biblical texts to study them like any other historical documents.

> Historical criticism was first applied to the Bible during the Enlightenment (seventeenth and eighteenth centuries), when the philosophy of rationalism dominated the intellectual scene.

Over the next century, many books on the life of Jesus were written which sought to explain away the supernatural elements of the Gospels. The **First Quest for the Historical Jesus** is usually traced to **Herman Samuel Reimarus** (1694–1768), a professor of oriental languages in Hamburg, Germany. Reimarus wrote a

---

1. See especially the works of conservatives like H. P. Liddon, A. Edersheim, J. B. Lightfoot, B. F. Wescott, F. W. Farrar, A. E. J. Rawlinson, and moderates like V. Taylor, O. Cullmann, J. Jeremias.

controversial article which he chose not to publish during his lifetime. After his death, the article was discovered and published by Gotthold Lessing under the title "On the Intention of Jesus and His Disciples."[2] In it Reimarus challenged the traditional understanding of Jesus and his mission. He claimed that Jesus had no grand aspirations to establish a new religion but considered himself a human messiah who would free his people from the Romans and establish a political kingdom on earth. When Jesus' hopes were dashed at his arrest and crucifixion, his disciples stole his body and began proclaiming his resurrection.

Reimarus's view that the Christian faith began through fraud and deceit has been almost universally rejected by scholars. But his work set off a flurry of rationalistic research on the historical Jesus. While the works which followed did not usually attribute such deceptive motives to the disciples, most tried to explain Jesus in nonsupernatural terms. H. E. G. Paulus (1761 – 1851), for example, claimed that most of Jesus' miracles could be explained from unrecognized causes or mistaken observations. The feeding of the five thousand occurred when rich people present were encouraged by the little boy's unselfish example to share their own lunches. Jesus only appeared to walk on water, when in fact he was walking near shore with a mist covering his feet. The raising of Lazarus was actually Jesus' rescue of his friend from a premature burial in a comatose state. Paulus proposed a similar "swoon theory" for Jesus' resurrection. Jesus only appeared to be dead on the cross and was revived in the coolness of the tomb. While such explanations seem absurd today (more unbelievable than the miracles themselves), they were commonplace in nineteenth-century reconstructions of Jesus'

> The First Quest for the historical Jesus was a nineteenth-century movement which sought to explain the events of Jesus' life from a rationalistic perspective.

Left: One of the most popular "lives" of Jesus written during the First Quest was by Ernst Renan. *Right:* Adolf von Harnack's book *What Is Christianity?* epitomized the results of the First Quest.

life. Perhaps the most famous of these biographies of Jesus was that of the Frenchman Ernest Renan, whose romanticized *Life of Jesus* (*Vie de Jésus*, 1863) was a popular success, selling sixty thousand copies during its first six months in print.

The common thread running through these works was that Jesus was a mere man, an ethical teacher proclaiming the love of God and the brotherhood of all human beings. The classic description of this so-called liberal Christ was Adolf von Harnack's *What Is Christianity?* published in 1901. Harnack argued that Jesus' self-identification as the Son of God was no more than his awareness that God was the father of all humanity. He concluded

---

2. Herman Samuel Reimarus, "On the Intention of Jesus and His Disciples," in Charles H. Talbert, ed., Ralph S. Fraser, trans., *Reimarus: Fragments* (Philadelphia: Fortress, 1970).

that the message of Jesus could be summed up as the fatherhood of God and the infinite value of the human soul.

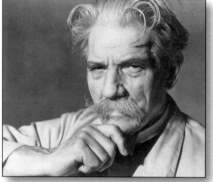

The multi-talented Albert Schweitzer — scholar, medical doctor, musician, philanthropist—wrote a devastating critique of the First Quest in his book *The Quest for the Historical Jesus.*

No Quest: Rudolf Bultmann and the End of the First Quest

When Harnack wrote his classic book on the liberal Jesus, the movement it epitomized was already in decline. Scholars had begun to recognize that far-fetched rationalistic explanations could not adequately account for the miracle stories which permeated all layers of the Gospel tradition. Furthermore, the Jesus that emerged was almost completely detached from his first-century context. The First Quest was chronicled and critiqued by **Albert Schweitzer** in *The Quest for the Historical Jesus*, published in 1910.[3] Schweitzer demonstrated that these nineteenth-century researchers re-created Jesus in their own image, transforming the historical Jesus into a modern philanthropist preaching an inoffensive message of love and brotherhood.

With the decline of the First Quest, a more pessimistic attitude toward Jesus studies developed, with many scholars claiming that almost nothing could be known about the historical Jesus. Gospel studies entered what is sometimes called the period of **No Quest**, when radical skepticism dominated the discussion. The key figure of this period was **Rudolf Bultmann**, the most influential New Testament scholar of the twentieth century. Bultmann influenced a whole generation of scholars, including members of the Jesus Seminar and other recent critics of the Gospels. Like all writers before and since, Bultmann was a product of his times. A survey of those who influenced him will put this period in perspective.

Ernst Troeltsch: Foundations of the Historical-Critical Method. In 1898, **Ernst Troeltsch** published an article titled "On Historical and Dogmatic Method in Theology."[4] Drawing on the rationalistic philosophy of Immanuel Kant, Troeltsch set out three principles which have guided historical-critical research ever since:

1. *The principle of methodological doubt* states that all historical judgments are statements of probability and relative truth, open to later correction or revision. This principle denies the existence of universal or absolute statements of religious dogma.
2. *The principle of analogy* asserts that all historical events are similar in quality and should be understood with reference to our common experience. If loaves and fishes do not multiply today, then they did not do so in ancient times.
3. *The principle of correlation* affirms that all historical phenomena exist in a chain of cause and effect. There is no effect without an adequate and sufficient cause.

---

3. Albert Schweitzer, *The Quest for the Historical Jesus: A Critical Study of Its Progress from Reimarus to Wrede*, trans. W. Montgomery (New York: Macmillan, 1954).

4. Ernst Troeltsch, "Historical and Dogmatic Method in Theology (1898)," in *Religion in History*, trans. J. L. Adams and W. F. Bense (Minneapolis: Fortress, 1991), 11–32. The German title was "*Über historische und dogmatische Methode in der Theologie.*"

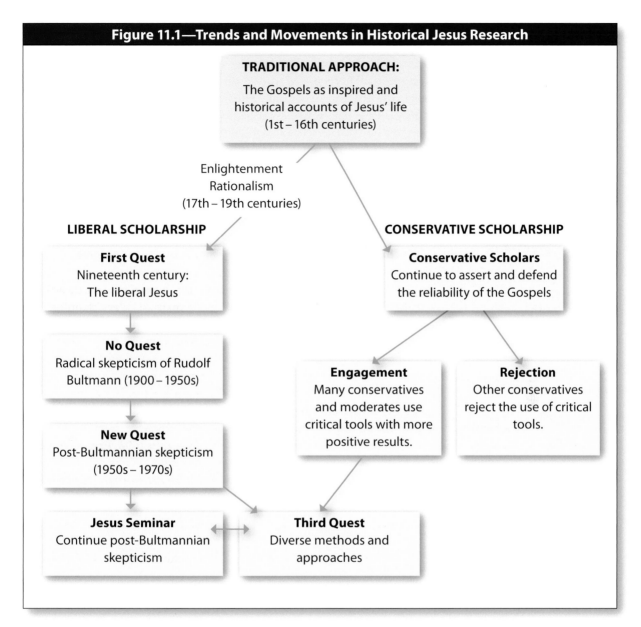

Figure 11.1—Trends and Movements in Historical Jesus Research

TRADITIONAL APPROACH:
The Gospels as inspired and historical accounts of Jesus' life
(1st – 16th centuries)

Enlightenment Rationalism
(17th – 19th centuries)

LIBERAL SCHOLARSHIP

CONSERVATIVE SCHOLARSHIP

First Quest
Nineteenth century:
The liberal Jesus

Conservative Scholars
Continue to assert and defend the reliability of the Gospels

No Quest
Radical skepticism of Rudolf Bultmann (1900 – 1950s)

Engagement
Many conservatives and moderates use critical tools with more positive results.

Rejection
Other conservatives reject the use of critical tools.

New Quest
Post-Bultmannian skepticism
(1950s – 1970s)

Jesus Seminar
Continue post-Bultmannian skepticism

Third Quest
Diverse methods and approaches

Together, these principles denied the uniqueness of Christianity and effectively ruled out supernatural intervention in human events.

David Friedrich Strauss: The Gospels as Myth. In 1835, early in the days of the First Quest, **D. F. Strauss** (at only twenty-seven years old) published a work called *The Life of Jesus Critically Examined.*[5] The work shocked the academic community and resulted in Strauss's removal from his teaching position at the University of Tübingen. In the book,

5. David Friedrich Strauss, *The Life of Jesus Critically Examined*, trans. G. Elliot (Philadelphia: Fortress, 1972).

Strauss introduced the notion of myth as the best explanation for the Gospel miracles. While agreeing with the antisupernatural assumptions of other critics, he considered it absurd that the miracles were natural events misperceived by eyewitnesses. He suggested instead that they were myths which had developed over the course of time. This was possible, he argued, because the Gospels were not eyewitness accounts but anonymous documents written in the mid- to late-second century AD, far removed from the historical events. The profound influence of Strauss was that later writers did not try to explain away the Gospel miracles rationalistically but considered their genre to be myth and legend created by the early church.

David Friedrich Strauss's work *The Life of Christ Critically Examined* claimed the Gospels were full of myths created by the early church.

William Wrede: The Gospels as Theological Propaganda. If Strauss claimed the Gospels were overlaid with myths, **William Wrede** sought to show that they were theologically rather than historically motivated. In 1901, Wrede published a groundbreaking work called *The Messianic Secret*.[6] Up to this point, even most liberals considered Mark's Gospel to be an early and mostly reliable account of the framework of Jesus' ministry. Wrede countered that from the start Mark had theological interests that overruled his historical ones. Noting that in the earliest Gospel tradition there was little evidence that Jesus claimed to be the Messiah, Wrede concluded that the historical Jesus lived an essentially unmessianic life. After the resurrection, when Jesus' followers came to believe that he was in fact the Messiah, the church had to deal with the unmessianic nature of the tradition. According to Wrede, Mark provided the answer with a creative rewriting of the Gospel story, introducing a motif Wrede called the "messianic secret." In Mark's Gospel, Jesus repeatedly silences demons (1:24, 34; 3:11–12; 5:7), insists that miracles be kept quiet (1:44; 5:43; 7:36; 8:26), and warns his disciples to tell no one that he is the Messiah (8:30; 9:9). Wrede concluded that these passages were created by Mark to explain away Jesus' unmessianic life. (For a response to Wrede, see fig. 7.3 in chap. 7.) The significance of Wrede's work was that the Gospels were now increasingly viewed not as historical documents but as apologetically motivated propaganda, intended to promote the theological perspectives of the communities which produced them. A modern scholar who has followed in Wrede's shoes is Burton Mack, who claims in his book *A Myth of Innocence* (1988) that Mark's Gospel is almost entirely fiction, created to provide the early church with a "foundation myth."[7]

Johannes Weiss: Jesus as Apocalyptic Prophet. If Strauss and Wrede questioned the historicity of the Gospel genre, **Johannes Weiss** (1863–1914) challenged the nineteenth-century view of Jesus as an enlightened, liberal social reformer preaching the kingdom of God as an ethical and spiritual ideal. Weiss sought to place Jesus' kingdom preaching in its first-century context—a Judaism ripe with apocalyptic fervor. In this context, the kingdom of God was understood as God's end-times intervention to judge the wicked and deliver the righteous. According to Weiss, Jesus was a wild-eyed eschatological prophet calling people to repent in preparation for the imminent end of the world. When Jesus' message was rejected, he came

---

6. William Wrede, *The Messianic Secret*, trans. J. C. G. Greig (Cambridge: James Clarke, 1971). The German title was *Das Messiasgeheimnis in den Evangelien.*

7. Burton L. Mack, *A Myth of Innocence: Mark and Christian Origins* (Philadelphia: Fortress, 1988).

Part Four:
The Historical Jesus

to believe he had to suffer vicariously for the people in order to bring in the kingdom. Jesus thus made his way to Jerusalem and sacrificed himself for the nation. Weiss's view has been termed "consistent eschatology," since for him Jesus was expecting the cataclysmic end of the world in the near future, consistent with the apocalyptic Judaism of his time.

Albert Schweitzer was greatly influenced by Weiss's view and popularized it in *The Quest for the Historical Jesus*. Schweitzer concluded that at his baptism, Jesus came to believe he was the Messiah who would bring in the kingdom of God. When the kingdom failed to arrive, Jesus attempted to force it by going to Jerusalem, where he was arrested and crucified. Ironically, Schweitzer has been accused of doing exactly what he criticized the nineteenth-century liberals for doing — developing a psychological and historical profile of Jesus through a selective use of the sources.

The History of Religions School. Another key influence on Bultmann and his followers was a movement which grew up in the nineteenth and early twentieth centuries known as the **history of religions school** (*die religionsgeschichtliche Schule*). The premise of this movement was that religious growth is evolutionary and that all religions develop from simple to complex. Scholars thus sought Christianity's roots in earlier traditions, especially in Babylonian and Persian religions. Particularly significant for Gospel studies was the work of Wilhelm Bousset, who in his book *Kyrios Christos* (1913) claimed that the earliest Aramaic-speaking church expected Jesus to return as the Son of Man but did not worship him as Lord (*kyrios*).[8] It was only in the Greek-speaking church of Antioch, under the influence of Hellenistic religions (which used the title *kyrios* for their gods), that Jesus came to be identified as Lord. According to Bousset, these pagan influences explain how a mere man — a Jewish peasant teacher — could very quickly be worshiped as a god.

Martin Kähler: The Historical Jesus and the Christ of Faith. In 1892, **Martin Kähler** wrote a short book titled *The So-Called Historical Jesus and the Historic Biblical Christ*.[9] The work was a scathing attack on the rationalistic nineteenth-century attempts to reconstruct an antisupernatural Jesus. Kähler's main point was that the so-called historical Jesus reconstructed by the rationalists was not the real Jesus at all but a figment of scholarly imagination. The real Jesus is the Christ of faith, proclaimed by the apostles and now worshiped in the church. Fundamental to Kähler's view is the claim that it is impossible, through historical means, to reconstruct a biography of Jesus. This is because the *kerygma*, the Christian preaching about the exalted Christ, is so interwoven into the Gospel narratives that there is no nonsupernatural "Jesus of history." For Kähler this was not a problem or loss, since what is ultimately important for the church is not *Historie* (a German word meaning "what actually happened") but *Geschichte* (the interpretation or significance of what happened). For believers, the Jesus of history and the Christ of faith are one and the same. Ironically, while Kähler's work was meant to recover the significance of Jesus for the church, it was used by Bultmann and others to draw a strict dichotomy between the **Jesus of history** and the **Christ of faith**, and so to cut off Christianity from its historical roots.

---

8. Wilhelm Bousset, *Kyrios Christos*, trans. John E. Steely (Nashville: Abingdon, 1970).

9. Martin Kähler, *The So-Called Historical Jesus and the Historic Biblical Christ*, trans. Carl E. Braaten (Philadelphia: Fortress, 1964). The German title was *Die sogennante historische Jesus und die geschichtliche biblische Christus*.

Figure 11.2—Key Influences on Rudolf Bultmann

Bultmann's Perspective

J. Weiss: *Jesus as Apocalyptic Prophet*

- Almost nothing can be known about the historical Jesus, except that he was an apocalyptic prophet who proclaimed the kingdom of God.

Martin Kähler: *Distinguishing the Jesus of History from the Christ of Faith*

- The early church was interested not in the *Jesus of history* but in the *Christ of faith*, speaking through the prophets.

D. F. Strauss: *The Gospels as Myth, not History*

- In the early communities, the Gospel stories were created and embellished with legend and myth.

W. Wrede: *The Messianic Secret in Mark*

- The Gospels are not historical biographies but theological propaganda created to reflect the community's beliefs.

W. Bousset and the History of Religions School

- As the stories passed from a Jewish to a Hellenistic environment, Jesus' status was slowly exalted from a Jewish Messiah to a Hellenistic Lord and Son of God.

Form criticism was developed by H. Gunkel for the Old Testament and applied to the New Testament by Bultmann, Schmidt, and Dibelius.

- Form criticism is used to analyze the communitys' creative activity and "demythologize" the New Testament.

Existentialist Philosophy of M. Heidegger

- New Testament truth found not in the Jesus of history but in an existentialist encounter with the Christ of faith.

Kähler's work has an interesting modern parallel in the writings of Luke Timothy Johnson, a Roman Catholic scholar who offers a scathing critique of the radical conclusions of the Jesus Seminar (see fig. 11.3) while rejecting altogether the legitimacy of a historical quest for Jesus.[10]

---

10. Luke Timothy Johnson, *The Real Jesus: The Misguided Quest for the Historical Jesus and the Truth of the Traditional Gospels* (San Francisco: HarperSanFrancisco, 1996).

Rudolf Bultmann: Extreme Skepticism and Demythologizing the Gospels. Rudolf Bultmann served as professor of New Testament at the University of Marburg in Germany from 1921–51. Like his predecessors, Bultmann began with the rationalistic assumption that it is impossible for modern man to accept the prescientific worldview of the biblical writers, a worldview which presupposed the reality of miracles, spirit beings, and a three-storied universe (earth, heaven, and hell).

Like Strauss, Bultmann claimed that the Gospels were filled with myths which arose in the context of the preaching of the early church. How could the disciples have allowed such myths to propagate? Bultmann responded that the earliest church had little interest in the historical Jesus. They were concerned only with the Christ of faith whom they worshiped in the present, rather than with the Jesus of history shrouded in the mysteries of the past (a takeoff from Kähler's view). Since the Christ of faith was still speaking to the church through his prophets, the church felt there was no inconsistency in placing the words of these prophets and teachers on the lips of Jesus. Bultmann assumed that eyewitnesses played almost no role in passing down the traditions about Jesus.

> Rudolf Bultmann claimed that the early church had little interest in the historical Jesus; they were more concerned with the Christ of faith whom they worshiped in the present.

It followed that the origin of the Gospel traditions must be found in the theological concerns of the early church rather than in the life of the historical Jesus. Like Wrede, Bultmann claimed that the creative activity of the community is the starting point for Gospel studies. Bultmann utilized form criticism to study this period of oral transmission. As we have seen in chapter 2, the early form critics assumed that as the early church communities preached the stories about Jesus, they created, embellished, and expanded them to meet their needs. Each story had a particular life setting in the church (*Sitz im Leben*) in which it was created and used.

If the Gospels bear witness to the life of the church rather than to the historical Jesus, then little can be known about the real Jesus. Bultmann wrote, "I do indeed think that we can know almost nothing concerning the life and personality of Jesus."[11] In general, Bultmann followed the view of Weiss that Jesus was an apocalyptic prophet expecting the imminent end of the world. He suffered and died tragically when his expectations failed to materialize. For Bultmann, however, these historical events were of little consequence, since the Christian faith is not about the Jesus of history but is about the Christ of faith. He went so far as to say that to depend on historical evidence for faith is theologically perverse and equivalent to trying to be justified by works (an echo from his Lutheran roots).

If the Gospels do not bear witness to the historical Jesus, is there any truth in the Christian faith? Bultmann answered yes and claimed the key was in an existentialist worldview. Following the existentialist philosophy of Martin Heidegger, he claimed that human beings continually live with the dreadful prospect of death and nothingness. They seek to escape

---

11. Rudolf Bultmann, *Jesus and the Word*, trans. L. P. Smith and E. H. Lantero (New York: Scribner's, 1958), 8.

this dread by living "inauthentically" — that is, by becoming absorbed in life's pursuits. The goal of existentialism is to recognize the dilemma of nothingness, yet live authentically, open and honest toward the future.

Bultmann claimed that Heidegger and the New Testament had the same basic understanding of humanity's plight, except that the New Testament provided the answer. Unfortunately, this solution was obscured by the mythological worldview of the first century. By "demythologizing" the New Testament — removing the layers of myth — we can reach the true existentialist message of Jesus. Bultmann concluded that Jesus' essential message was an existential "call to decision," to live a life of "authentic existence."

The New (Second) Quest and the Post-Bultmannians (1953–1970s)

While some of Bultmann's students continued to express his high level of skepticism, others questioned whether he had gone too far. By separating the Jesus of history from the Christ of faith, Bultmann severed Christianity from its historical roots. Could the existentialist message of the New Testament be linked to the historical Jesus? In an attempt to answer this question, a second quest was launched. Its beginning is usually dated to a lecture by **Ernst Käsemann** called "The Problem of the Historical Jesus," delivered on October 20, 1953, to a reunion of Bultmann's students.[12] Käsemann's call for a new quest resulted in a resurgence of research on the historical Jesus.[13] Important contributors to this **New (Second) Quest** include Ernst Füchs, Gerhard Ebeling, and Günther Bornkamm. Bornkamm's classic volume *Jesus of Nazareth* is perhaps the most influential work of this period.[14]

> The New (Second) Quest for the historical Jesus (1950s–1970s) was instigated by Bultmann's former students, who followed the same basic methods and worldview as their mentor.

While rejecting Bultmann's extreme skepticism, these scholars started with the same basic premises: (1) an existentialist worldview; (2) rejection of the supernatural; (3) a strict dichotomy between the Jesus of history and the Christ of faith; (4) the Gospels as theological rather than historical documents; (5) the far removal in place and time of the Gospel writers from the eyewitnesses; and (6) the form-critical assumption that most of the Gospel tradition was created and embellished by the early Christian communities.

Since they started with these assumptions, it is not surprising that the New Quest did not get very far beyond Bultmann's skepticism. What can be known about Jesus can be summarized in a few short statements: he came from Nazareth; he was baptized by John; he preached and told parables about the kingdom of God; he viewed this kingdom as com-

---

12. Ernst Käsemann, "The Problem of the Historical Jesus," in *Essays on New Testament Themes*, trans. W. J. Montague (London: SCM, 1964), 15–47.

13. The New Quest was chronicled by James M. Robinson in *A New Quest of the Historical Jesus* (London: SCM, 1959). The movement got its name from this book.

14. Günther Bornkamm, *Jesus of Nazareth*, trans. Irene McLuskey and Fraser McLuskey (New York: Harper and Row, 1960), published in German in 1956.

ing in the near future and (perhaps) as already present in some sense; he performed, or was believed to have performed, exorcisms and healings; he gathered a group of disciples around him; he associated with outcasts and sinners; he challenged the Jewish leaders of his day; he was arrested and charged with blasphemy and sedition; and he was crucified by the Romans. It was generally denied that Jesus claimed to be the Messiah, that he predicted his own death, or that he rose from the dead.

Figure 11.3—The Jesus Seminar

The Jesus Seminar, founded by Robert Funk and John Dominic Crossan in 1985, has been a lightening rod for controversy over the past two decades. The Seminar's seemingly innocuous goal was "to renew the quest for the historical Jesus and to report the results of its research to more than a handful of gospel specialists."* Yet beyond this, the Seminar contended that the church had been duped by fundamentalists who were glossing over what scholars really knew about the historical Jesus. This provocative claim has attracted much media attention, with the Seminar actively promoting its views through newspapers, magazines, radio, television, and the internet.

Meeting twice yearly for over ten years, the Seminar examined and voted on the words and actions of Jesus. Their unusual voting procedure was a parody of "red letter" editions of the Bible (in which the words of Jesus are printed in red): each Gospel episode was deemed to be either red (authentic), pink (something like Jesus), gray (inauthentic, but ideas close to Jesus), or black (inauthentic). In the end, only a little over 15 percent of the sayings and deeds of Jesus were deemed to be authentic (red or pink). The Seminar's results were published in two volumes: *The Five Gospels: The Search for the Authentic Words of Jesus* (1993) and *The Acts of Jesus: The Search for the Authentic Deeds of Jesus* (1998).

Many scholars—conservatives and liberals alike—have criticized the Jesus Seminar on a variety of fronts. The following are some of the more important criticisms:

1. Unconventional voting procedure often resulting in idiosyncratic results.
2. Tendency to disconnect Jesus from both his Jewish context and the church which followed him.
3. Hypercritical approach to the Gospels, while more positive toward noncanonical sources (especially "Q," the Gnostic *Gospel of Thomas*, *Secret Gospel of Mark*, etc.).
4. Circular reasoning, beginning with a preconceived idea about Jesus—as an itinerant Cynic sage—and rejecting even solid evidence contrary to this portrait.
5. Overstressing the words of Jesus at the expense of his actions.
6. Selective and inconsistent use of criteria, especially the criterion of dissimilarity.
7. Unwarranted claims to scholarly objectivity (while functioning as polemicists).
8. Unwarranted claims of representing the consensus of New Testament scholarship.

While evangelicals have often dismissed the Seminar as hopelessly biased and hostile toward orthodox Christianity, this is not entirely fair. A number of Seminar members have made significant contributions toward biblical scholarship, and it is important to weigh the Seminar's claims on a case-by-case, argument-by-argument basis. See the bibliography for important scholarly responses to the Seminar.

*Robert W. Funk, Roy W. Hoover, and the Jesus Seminar, *The Five Gospels: The Search for the Authentic Words of Jesus*, new translation and commentary by Robert W. Funk, Roy W. Hoover, and the Jesus Seminar (New York: Polebridge, 1993), 34.

Those who distinguish the Third Quest from the Jesus Seminar point to the following general tendencies of each.

Jesus Seminar	Third Quest
• Greco-Roman influences stressed. • Jesus' ministry interpreted noneschatologically. • Gospels have little historical value. Approximately 15 percent of the Gospel material is authentic. Almost nothing in John. • Priority of noncanonical and hypothetical sources: *Gospel of Thomas*, Q, *Gospel of Peter*, *Secret Gospel of Mark*. • Two criteria of authenticity, *dissimilarity* and *multiple attestation*, produce minimalist results. • Primary focus on short aphorisms and parables of Jesus.	• Jewishness of Jesus stressed. • Eschatology a key focus of Jesus' teaching and actions. • Much of the Synoptic material is authentic, though John is still viewed with caution and reservations. • Priority of canonical Gospels as sources; insights drawn from other sources. • More diverse methodologies and approaches tend to produce more comprehensive and integrative results. • Focus on both words and deeds of Jesus.

Some key representatives:
  • Robert Funk
  • Burton Mack
  • John Dominic Crossan
  • Marcus Borg (also treated with Third Quest)
	Some key representatives:
	  • Ben Meyer
	  • A. E. Harvey
	  • Geza Vermes
	  • E. P. Sanders
	  • John P. Meier
	  • N. T. Wright
	  • Ben Witherington III

THE CONTEMPORARY SCENE: A THIRD QUEST?

With only meager results to show for its work, by the 1970s the so-called New Quest had mostly died down. From the 1980s onward, however, a flurry of research has emerged reviving the search for the real Jesus. This new work has been dubbed by some to be a **Third Quest** for the historical Jesus. It has been sparked by advances in biblical and archeological studies, the deployment of new methodologies (sociocultural, anthropological, feminist, etc.), and in part, at least, by the controversial work of a group of scholars known as the **Jesus Seminar** (see fig. 11.3). Some chroniclers identify the Jesus Seminar as part of this Third Quest. Others treat the Seminar as a separate and idiosyncratic movement (see fig. 11.4). Since the Third Quest is a highly diverse movement encompassing scholars of all stripes, and since some Jesus Seminar members are also identified with the Third Quest (e.g., Marcus Borg), we will treat these two together as part of the broad movement of recent Jesus studies. We will first summarize key methodological questions in contemporary research, and then survey some of the portraits of Jesus which have emerged in recent years.

Questions of Method and Context

Is the Quest Legitimate? Historical Pessimism versus Historical Optimism. The foundational methodological question is whether a "scientific" historical enquiry into Jesus is possible or even desirable. Scholars like Luke Timothy Johnson, echoing the work of Martin Kähler, reject any study of the historical Jesus which isolates him from the Christ of faith. The "real Jesus" is discovered not through criteria of authenticity or historical methodology but through an existential faith-encounter with the risen Lord.[15] On the other side, most scholars consider it both possible and necessary to investigate the historical Jesus using a rigorous historical method. On this side are scholars who reach more conservative conclusions, like N. T. Wright and Ben Witherington, as well as those who reach more liberal ones, like John Dominic Crossan and Marcus Borg.

While it is certainly true that the "real Jesus" cannot be known completely through historical investigation, this does not render historical-Jesus research misguided or invalid. The historical Jesus—defined as knowledge about Jesus which can be attained through historical research—is a subset of truth about the real Jesus. It is not a complete picture, since many questions remain unanswered about who Jesus was as a complex human being. Nor can historical research account for faith-encounters with the living Lord. In short, while conclusions about the historical Jesus are always partial and incomplete, this does not mean they are invalid or false. We can know much about the person of Jesus without knowing everything.

> Some scholars, like Luke Timothy Johnson, reject any study of the historical Jesus which isolates him from the Christ of faith.

What Is Our Data? The Scope and Reliability of Sources. If the historical Jesus is a legitimate object of study, what sources bring us closest to him? Most Jesus scholars assume Markan priority—that Mark was the first Gospel written and was used as a source by both Matthew and Luke. Most also assume that Matthew and Luke used another common source or sources, designated Q, or the Synoptic Sayings Source. Whether Q was a single source or a body of written and oral material is debated, but it is widely recognized as a valuable source for traditions about the historical Jesus.

Within this consensus, there is great diversity concerning the historical value of these Gospel traditions. Some view the Synoptic Gospels as generally reliable unless there is good evidence to the contrary. Others function from the perspective of methodological doubt, assuming a story is inauthentic unless it can be proven otherwise. The Jesus Seminar, for example, adopted the slogan "when in doubt, leave it out."[16] Another matter concerns the historical value of John. Many scholars either generally ignore the Fourth Gospel or treat it with great skepticism. Others see John as containing early and valuable traditions which followed a different trajectory of transmission than the Synoptics.

The value of noncanonical and hypothetical sources is also debated. Most controversial are claims that certain apocryphal gospels, like the second-century *Gospel of Thomas*, con-

---

15. Johnson, *The Real Jesus*.

16. Robert W. Funk and the Jesus Seminar, *The Acts of Jesus: The Search for the Authentic Deeds of Jesus* (San Francisco: HarperSanFrancisco, 1998), 37.

tain traditions older and more reliable than the New Testament Gospels themselves. John Dominic Crossan builds his controversial portrait of Jesus in part from the sayings of Jesus in the *Gospel of Thomas*, a hypothetical early edition of Q, and a supposed "Cross Gospel" which he reconstructs from the apocryphal *Gospel of Peter*.[17] The Jesus Seminar, too, considers the *Gospel of Thomas* to be an important early source. The title of their book on the sayings of Jesus, *The Five Gospels*, refers to the four canonical Gospels plus the *Gospel of Thomas*.[18] The Seminar has been criticized for elevating late apocryphal works and reconstructed sources above the earliest first-century sources available to us: Matthew, Mark, Luke, and John.

Jesus scholars debate the value of noncanonical sources, like the *Gospel of Thomas* and the hypothetical Q document.

What Criteria Do We Use? Once sources are established, how does one judge the authenticity of individual sayings and events? With the claim by the New Quest that it was indeed possible to know something about the historical Jesus, scholars developed and refined various criteria, known as the **criteria of authenticity**, to judge the historicity of the sayings of Jesus. Since these criteria are widely used by scholars today, it is worthwhile to briefly examine them.

(1) The *criterion of dissimilarity* is the most basic of the criterion. It claims that a saying or an action of Jesus is authentic if it is dissimilar to the characteristic emphases both of ancient Judaism and of the early church. For example, Jesus' identification of himself as the Son of Man may be deemed authentic since it was not a common messianic title in first-century Judaism, nor was it used by the early church in its confessions of Jesus.

One problem with this criterion is that while it may tell us what was *unique* about Jesus, it does not tell us what was *characteristic* about him. Jesus grew up as a Jew in the first-century world of Judaism. To divorce him from this background and context will inevitably result in a distorted picture of his mission and message. Further, it is beyond dispute that the early church was greatly influenced by the teaching of their Lord. To suggest that none of the issues critical to the life of the church arose out of Jesus' teaching borders on the ridiculous. Another serious problem with this criterion is that it presupposes we know a great deal about both Judaism and early Christianity. Who is to say that what we consider to be unique to Jesus was not actually a part of Jewish thought of his day?

(2) The *criterion of coherence* is used in conjunction with the criterion of dissimilarity. Once characteristics of the teaching of Jesus are established by the criterion of dissimilarity, these can be used to substantiate other similar sayings which could not themselves meet that test.

(3) A third test, the *criterion of multiple attestation*, claims that a saying or story is authentic if it appears in most or all of the sources behind the Gospels. Results here depend on one's conclusion concerning the synoptic problem. A scholar who accepts the four-source theory would say that a teaching which appears in Mark, Q, and L or M is likely to be

---

17. John Dominic Crossan, *The Historical Jesus: The Life of a Mediterranean Jewish Peasant* (San Francisco: HarperSanFrancisco, 1991).

18. Robert W. Funk, Roy W. Hoover, and the Jesus Seminar, *The Five Gospels: The Search for the Authentic Words of Jesus*, new translation and commentary by Robert W. Funk, Roy W. Hoover, and the Jesus Seminar (New York: Polebridge, 1993).

authentic. For example, Jesus' practice of eating with sinners appears in all strands of Gospel tradition (Mark 2:15–17; Q: Matt. 11:18–19; L: Luke 15:1–2; M: Matt. 21:28–32). Similarly, sayings predicting the destruction of the temple appear in various layers of the Gospel tradition (Mark 13:1–2 [= Matt. 24:2; Luke 21:5–6]; Mark 14:58 [= Matt. 26:61]; Mark 15:29 [= Matt. 27:40]; John 2:19–21; Acts 6:14; Jerusalem: Luke 19:41–44; 21:24).

(4) A fourth criterion, the *criterion of embarrassment*, claims that statements that would have produced theological difficulties or embarrassment in the church are likely to be authentic. For example, Jesus' statement that no one knows the day or the hour of the coming of the Son of Man (Mark 13:32) is likely to be authentic since the church would hardly have created a saying which attributed ignorance to the Son. One problem with this criterion is that what seems embarrassing to us may not have seemed so to the early church. There also may be reasons we cannot immediately recognize for the creation of such a saying.

(5) The *criterion of Semitic flavor* states that if a tradition has a pronounced Jewish or Palestinian flavor, then it is more likely to be authentic. This would include sayings which contain Aramaic words or which envisage Palestinian social conditions. For example, Jesus' use of the Aramaic term *abba* (father) in Mark 14:36 would be viewed as most likely authentic. This criterion also has limited validity. While an Aramaic word suggests that a saying came from a Semitic context, an authentic saying could have lost its Semitic flavor through idiomatic translation into Greek. Nor can this criterion prove authenticity, since the saying could be traced to the Aramaic-speaking church, rather than to Jesus himself.

> The criteria of authenticity were developed to test the authenticity of the words and actions of Jesus. The most widely utilized are the criteria of dissimilarity and multiple attestation.

(6) The *criterion of divergent traditions* says that when an author preserves traditions which do not serve his purpose, they are more than likely to be authentic. For example, Jesus' statement "Do not go to the Gentiles" in Matthew 10:5–6 appears to be at odds with the Great Commission to go to all nations in Matthew 28:16–20. To some this would suggest it is pre-Matthean, and so probably authentic. While this criterion has some validity, it must be applied cautiously, since it assumes certainty concerning an author's purpose. Matthew 10:5–6 would not contradict Matthew's theology if it is part of his purpose to show that Jesus' first mission was to the Jews and only after they rejected the message to turn to the Gentiles. Events which seem at first to be at odds with the narrative may on closer examination be found to be integral to it.

In addition to these specific problems, the criteria are often used subjectively and in a circular manner to prove whatever the investigator wishes. For example, in the Synoptics there are three kinds of Son of Man sayings, concerning (1) Jesus' earthly ministry, (2) his suffering, and (3) his return in glory. Using the criterion of dissimilarity, one could conclude that the suffering usage is certainly authentic, since the early church did not take up the title Son of Man in its confession of Jesus and since there is no evidence that first-century Jews used the title to describe a suffering messiah. Bultmann, however, argued that only the apocalyptic Son of Man sayings were authentic. This is because he believed Jesus was expecting the return of the Son of Man but could not have anticipated his own suffering role.[19] He ignored his own criterion when it contradicted his notion about what Jesus could or could not have said.

This kind of subjectivity is common in the use of the criteria, especially since they can be used to contradict each other. The criterion of Semitic influence can be used to support things which agree with first-century Judaism, while the criterion of dissimilarity can rule out the same material. Too often the criteria are used selectively and arbitrarily to "prove" whatever the investigator wants to prove. While the criteria thus have some validity, they must be used with great caution and humility, since a scholar's preconceptions concerning the historical Jesus can easily bias the results.

> Some scholars build a portrait of Jesus from the ground up, evaluating individual pericopae using the criteria of authenticity. Others take a top-down approach, starting with a broad hypothesis and testing it against the data.

N. T. Wright seeks to overcome some of the problems associated with this criterion by proposing what he calls a "double criterion of similarity and dissimilarity." By this he means that "when something can be seen to be credible (though perhaps deeply subversive) within first-century Judaism, *and* credible as the implied starting point (though not the exact replica) of something in later Christianity, there is a strong possibility of our being in touch with the genuine history of Jesus."[20]

This method has also been dubbed the *criterion of explanation*, since it seeks to provide a plausible explanation for the rise of Christianity within its first-century Jewish context. This criterion is used not so much to analyze the authenticity of individual pericopae but rather to explain Jesus' message and mission as a whole in relation to its antecedents (first-century Palestinian Judaism) and successors (the early Christians). This raises our next methodological question: whether to utilize a case-by-case or a broad-brush approach to the Jesus tradition.

How Do We Proceed? Inductive versus Deductive Methodologies. A fourth methodological question beyond sources and criteria concerns the nature of analysis, whether to proceed inductively or deductively. Some methodologies are primarily inductive, seeking to move from individual facts to conclusions. Scholars like John P. Meier and the members of the Jesus Seminar seek to build a portrait of Jesus from the ground up, comprehensively evaluating the authenticity of each individual pericope using the criteria of authenticity. The story of Jesus becomes a jigsaw puzzle which the historian must put together from a myriad of pieces. One problem with this approach is its subjectivity, as investigators must weigh many bits of evidence for every episode. With so much conflicting data, the investigator's preconceptions concerning the historical Jesus — whether positive or negative — will almost inevitably steer the data toward certain results. A more neutral enquirer would likely conclude that the historicity of most Gospel stories cannot be proven one way or the other.

Other scholars take a more deductive top-down approach, starting with a broad hypothesis and then testing it against the data. The goal here is not to make every bit of data fit the

---

19. See Rudolf Bultmann, *Theology of the New Testament*, trans. K. Grobel (New York: Scribner's, 1951), 1:30–32.

20. N. T. Wright, *Jesus and the Victory of God* (Minneapolis: Fortress, 1996), 132.

hypothesis but rather to find a hypothesis which fits the preponderance of the evidence. N. T. Wright utilizes this kind of broad-brush approach, proposing a hypothesis based on a general understanding of Jesus in his historical context, and then testing this hypothesis against the data. He is less concerned with establishing the historicity of individual events or sayings, instead seeking a portrait of Jesus which fulfills the requirement of a good hypothesis. A good hypothesis, he argues, must do three things: (1) explain the greatest part of the data, (2) be simple and coherent, and (3) make sense of other areas outside of the immediate area of study (in this case, the nature of first-century Judaism and the shape of the church which followed).[21] Wright draws from the important work of Ben Meyer, who in *The Aims of Jesus* proposed the method of critical realism as a more balanced approach for studying Jesus.[22] In contrast to either extreme skepticism or naive realism, critical realism seeks a hypothesis which explains the greatest part of the data through careful historical-critical investigation.

Marcus Borg, though a member of the Jesus Seminar, also takes a more global approach. He writes, "Though we cannot ever be certain that we have direct and exact quotation from Jesus, we can be relatively sure of the *kinds* of things he said, and of the main themes and thrusts of his teaching."[23] A somewhat similar method is adopted by E. P. Sanders, who starts with a core of almost certainly authentic material and then fashions a hypothesis which can then be tested against other evidence.[24] One danger of this approach is that investigators may adopt strained interpretations of the data in order to make it fit their hypothesis. No one likes to abandon their cherished hypothesis — even when confronted by contrary facts!

Worldview Considerations: Natural or Supernatural Presuppositions? Perhaps the most controversial of methodological questions is how to deal with supernatural elements in the Gospels. We have seen that the First Quest sought to explain Jesus' miracles as natural events that were either misunderstood or misperceived. D. F. Strauss responded that this is ludicrous and that the miracles must instead be viewed as myths which developed long after the fact. Bultmann adopted the mythological explanation, claiming that it is impossible for modern man to accept a supernatural worldview.

> Perhaps the most controversial of methodological questions is how to deal with supernatural elements in the Gospels.

How do contemporary Jesus scholars treat the supernatural? Some attempt to take a neutral hands-off approach. John P. Meier, for example, claims that miracles are outside the realm of historical enquiry, since they cannot be judged by empirical evidence. While a historian may confirm that Jesus did things that were considered by his contemporaries to be supernatural acts, the historian cannot render a verdict on whether a miracle actually occurred.[25] One problem with this perspective is that it runs contrary to the task of the historian, which is to

21. N. T. Wright, *The New Testament and the People of God* (Minneapolis: Fortress, 1996), 98 – 109; idem., *Jesus and the Victory of God*, 133.

22. Ben F. Meyer, *The Aims of Jesus* (London: SCM, 1979).

23. Marcus J. Borg, *Jesus: A New Vision* (San Francisco: Harper and Row, 1987), 25 – 26.

24. E. P. Sanders, *Jesus and Judaism* (Philadelphia: Fortress, 1985), 11; *The Historical Figure of Jesus* (New York: Penguin, 1993), 10 – 11.

25. John P. Meier, *A Marginal Jew: Rethinking the Historical Jesus*, 3 vols. (New York: Doubleday, 1991, 1994, 2001), 2:511 – 14.

determine cause-and-effect relationships between historical events. The report of a miracle cries out for an explanation, whether it be a natural or supernatural one.

Many scholars opt for the former, assuming a naturalistic worldview. Most members of the Jesus Seminar take this perspective. According to the promotional blurb on the cover of the Seminar's *The Acts of Jesus*, "Jesus practiced healing . . . relieving afflictions we now consider psychosomatic." Paula Fredriksen similarly concludes that the diseases Jesus healed were probably psychosomatic in nature: "Did Jesus of Nazareth, then, perform miracles? Here I as a historian have to weigh the testimony of tradition against what I think is possible in principle. I do not believe that God occasionally suspends the operation of what Hume called 'natural law.' What I think Jesus might possibly have done, in other words, must conform to what I think is possible in any case."[26]

John Dominic Crossan also rejects a supernatural explanation, drawing on the work of medical anthropologists to distinguish between disease and illness.[27] Disease is the physical condition, involving bacteria, viruses, or other physical causes. Illness is the broader social meaning attributed to this condition. The leper who met Jesus had both a disease (like psoriasis) and an illness, "the personal and social stigma of uncleanness, isolation, and rejec-

Marcus Borg

tion." According to Crossan, Jesus did not cure diseases but rather healed illnesses. He writes, "I presume that Jesus, who did not and could not cure that disease or any other one, healed the poor man's illness by refusing to accept the disease's ritual uncleanness and social ostracization. Jesus thereby forced others either to reject him from this community or to accept the leper within it as well."[28]

Marcus Borg takes a somewhat more open perspective. While rejecting a supernatural interventionist model of God, he also rejects purely psychosomatic explanations, preferring to speak of "paranormal healings." "Inexplicable and remarkable things do happen," he writes, "involving processes that we do not understand. I do not need to know the explanatory mechanism in order to affirm that paranormal healings happen."[29] In other words, Borg accepts that Jesus' healings may be outside the "laws of nature" as we understand them, but he refuses to call them supernatural acts of God.

Other scholars, like Ben Witherington and N. T. Wright, are more willing to entertain supernatural explanations if these best account for the evidence. Wright argues for an open but cautious approach: "It is prudent, methodologically, to hold back from too hasty a judgment on what is actually possible and what is not within the space-time universe. There are more things in heaven and earth than are dreamed of in post-Enlightenment philosophy, as those who have lived and worked in areas of the world less affected by Hume, Lessing and Troeltsch know quite well."[30]

26. Paula Fredriksen, *Jesus of Nazareth, King of the Jews* (New York: Vintage, 1999), 114–15.

27. Crossan, *Historical Jesus*, 319–20; idem., *Jesus: A Revolutionary Biography* (San Francisco: HarperSanFrancisco, 1994), 80–82.

28. Crossan, *Jesus: A Revolutionary Biography*, 82.

29. Marcus Borg, in M. J. Borg and N. T. Wright, *The Meaning of Jesus: Two Visions* (San Francisco: HarperSanFrancisco, 1999), 67.

30. Wright, *Jesus and the Victory of God*, 187.

We will discuss the philosophical foundations as well as the nature and significance of Jesus' miracles in more detail in chapter 17.

What Was Jesus' Context? The nature of Jesus' context is another issue of considerable controversy and debate, especially the ethnic, social, and political diversity of Galilee, the center of his early ministry. One key issue is the extent of hellenization in the region. How much would Jesus have come in contact with Greek philosophical and religious traditions? Some contemporary portraits of Jesus rely heavily on a context in which Jesus would have had extensive encounters with non-Jewish ideas. A second issue concerns the socioeconomic climate of Galilee. Was there a dramatic contrast between rich and poor, the haves and the have-nots? Did wealthy estate owners exploit and oppress poor peasant farmers, or was there relative stability between common people and the aristocracy? These economic factors also relate to the nature of Jesus' following. Did Jesus interact with the wealthier, more hellenized populations of the urban centers of Galilee, like Sepphoris and Tiberias, or did he mostly work in the villages among the rural poor? Should Jesus himself be classified as a peasant, or was he something else? A third, closely related issue is the political climate of Galilee. Was this region a hotbed of dissension and revolt, or was there relative calm during Jesus' career? Were Zealots active in the Galilee, or did they arise only later, shortly before the revolt of AD 66–73? Where scholars come down on these issues of context significantly impacts their interpretation of the life and times of Jesus.

What Was Jesus' Message? An Eschatological or Non-Eschatological Kingdom? All scholars accept that the kingdom of God was at the center of Jesus' message. But what did he mean by this? As we have seen, the nineteenth-century First Quest saw the kingdom as essentially non-eschatological, concerning spiritual and social renewal. J. Weiss and A. Schweitzer challenged this notion, claiming that in its first-century context, the kingdom must refer to the apocalyptic intervention of God to save and to judge. This historical debate continues today in a modified form, with disagreement over whether Jesus' kingdom was primarily eschatological or non-eschatological. John Dominic Crossan, Marcus Borg, and most members of the Jesus Seminar interpret Jesus' teaching as non-eschatological, concerning a transformation of society through spiritual and social renewal.[31] Other scholars, like E. P. Sanders, N. T. Wright, John P. Meier, Bart Ehrman, Dale Allison, and Paula Fredriksen see Jesus as an eschatological prophet announcing the arrival of God's final salvation. As we shall see, one's view of the nature and significance of Jesus' kingdom preaching to a great extent determines one's assessment of his life and ministry.

N. T. Wright

The Results: Contemporary Portraits of Jesus

While there are as many interpretations of Jesus as there are Jesus scholars today, we can group these diverse perspectives into various categories. We will survey five main portraits of Jesus: a Cynic-like philosopher, a spirit-endowed holy man, a social revolutionary, an eschatological prophet, and the Messiah.

---

31. Crossan, *Historical Jesus*, 238, calls Jesus' kingdom preaching "eschatological" but defines this as "a generic term for world-negation extending from apocalyptic eschatology ... through mystical or utopian modes, and on to ascetical, libertarian, or anarchistic possibilities." He then contrasts Jesus' "ethical eschatology" with John the Baptist's "apocalyptic eschatology."

A Wandering Cynic-like Philosopher. Perhaps the most controversial recent portrait of Jesus is that he was an itinerant **Cynic-like philosopher**, a poet-peasant whose clever sayings and parables challenged the social and religious conventions of his day. This hypothesis was first developed in detail by F. Gerald Downing[32] and has been adopted and expanded by Burton Mack[33] and especially **John Dominic Crossan**.[34] It is also the portrait most widely espoused by members of the Jesus Seminar. Jesus, it is said, had much in common with the Greek philosophical movement known as Cynicism. **Cynics** were countercultural philosophers and preachers who intentionally rejected the social conventions of their day. They were typically wandering itinerants, dressed as beggars with a cloak, a bag, and a staff, wearing their hair long and their beards unkempt. Crossan refers to them as "hippies in a world of Augustan yuppies."[35] The Cynic movement is usually traced to Diogenes of Sinope (400–325 BC), who was known for his witty and iconoclastic sayings and outrageous behavior which shocked the cultural sensibilities of his day. The word cynic comes from the Greek word for dog and refers to Diogenes' shameless public behavior, like using abusive language, defecating in public, and performing sexual acts in the open. The Cynics' goal was not primarily to offend (though they often relished doing just that) but to get back to nature, to demonstrate a simple, unencumbered and unpretentious lifestyle apart from social and cultural restraints.

> The portrait of Jesus as a Cynic-like philosopher identifies him as a wandering countercultural peasant espousing egalitarian ideals.

According to Crossan, Jesus was similar to the Cynics in that he challenged the social and religious conventions of his day and sought to inaugurate the "brokerless kingdom of God." As we have seen, in the Greco-Roman world, everything depended on strict social and religious boundaries and brokered relationships between clients and patrons. Institutions like government and temple were established to protect these boundaries and so maintain the divinely established order. According to Crossan, Jesus challenged these authorities and claimed that all people could have an unbrokered relationship with God, apart from any mediators or religious institutions. He ignored the purity laws and religious boundaries of Judaism, eating with religiously defiled sinners and tax collectors and touching ceremonially unclean people like lepers, a menstruating woman, and even dead bodies. Jesus envisioned a radical social and spiritual revolution—the inauguration of an egalitarian kingdom of God.

According to this perspective, Jesus had no messianic ambitions and no intentions to establish a movement. He did not connect his mission to Israel's history or to her promised salvation, and he saw no sacrificial or saving significance in his death. In fact, his death was merely an accident of history: Jesus' attacks on the social and religious hierarchy made him unpopular with those in power. When he went too far, challenging the temple leadership by

---

32. Gerald F. Downing, *Christ and the Cynics: Jesus and Other Radical Preachers in First-Century Tradition* (Sheffield: Sheffield Academic, 1988); idem., *Cynics and Christian Origins* (Edinburgh: T. and T. Clark, 1992).
33. Mack, *A Myth of Innocence.*
34. Crossan, *Historical Jesus*; idem., *Jesus: A Revolutionary Biography.*
35. Crossan, *Historical Jesus*, 421.

overturning the money changers' tables, he was summarily arrested and crucified. Crossan denies that there even was a trial. Rather, the Roman soldiers probably had standing orders to arrest anyone who created trouble during Passover. Jesus was seized, beaten, and crucified; his followers fled; his body was probably discarded and eaten by dogs.[36] End of story.

In light of this radical revision of the Gospel story, it is not surprising that Crossan's thesis has provoked such ire among traditional Christians. But is there any legitimacy in the Cynic hypothesis? The primary strength of this view is its attempts to account for Jesus' radical message of love and acceptance for all people, and his equally radical actions in dining with sinners and social outcasts and condemning the pretensions of the religious leaders of his day.

The weaknesses of this view, however, are many. While some of Jesus' teaching and behavior bears superficial similarities to the Cynics, there are far more differences than similarities. The greatest problem with the Cynic hypothesis is its failure to account for so much of the Gospel tradition, even data which passes strict criteria of authenticity. For example, Crossan and the Jesus Seminar deny that Jesus appointed twelve disciples, since this would imply a hierarchical structure of leadership and would also connect his movement to Israel's history (12 = the twelve tribes of Israel).[37] Yet the choice and number of disciples easily passes the criterion of multiple attestation, appearing in multiple sources and layers of the Gospel tradition.

Arriving at a Cynic-like Jesus also requires a selective use of sources and a kind of circular reasoning. The assumption is made that Jesus was a peasant-sage who spoke only in short aphorisms and parables, who did not view himself as the Messiah, and who had no intention of starting a movement. Any evidence contrary to this portrait is subsequently rejected. Since the hypothetical Q document and the apocryphal *Gospel of Thomas* are both collections of sayings, their material is considered to be most reliable. Furthermore, since neither Q nor Thomas contain a passion narrative, Jesus' death is said to have had little importance for the earliest Christians. In contrast, the canonical Gospels—which clearly portray Jesus as the Messiah acting intentionally to accomplish God's salvation—are assumed to be late and secondary. In a circular manner, the assumptions determine the conclusions.

Related to this, proponents of the Cynic hypothesis reject an eschatological interpretation of Jesus' kingdom preaching. They claim the kingdom of God is not about God's intervention to bring end-times salvation but rather is about spiritual transformation through social renewal. Passages are subsequently deemed inauthentic whenever Jesus speaks of the future coming of the Son of Man. Yet this theme fits both the criterion of multiple attestation and the criterion of dissimilarity: the coming Son of Man appears in multiple sources, and Jesus' use of it is unique within both Judaism and the early church. Similarly, although the Q material contains eschatological teaching, the Seminar excludes this material since it assumes that Jesus could not have spoken this way. They go so far as to propose that there must have been an earlier edition of Q which did not contain this eschatological material. (A hypothesis built on a hypothesis!) Again, assumptions about a non-eschatological Jesus determine the results.

---

36. Crossan, *Jesus: A Revolutionary Biography*, 123–58.

37. Funk writes, "there was general agreement among the Fellows that the number 'twelve' in connection with an inner circle of disciples is a fiction" (*The Acts of Jesus*, 71).

The Cynic hypothesis has also been accused of focusing on the sayings of Jesus at the expense of his actions. Scholars have increasingly recognized that Jesus' actions also tell us a great deal about his beliefs and intentions. Jesus' entrance into Jerusalem riding on a colt, for example, or his clearing of the money changers from the temple, have important significance concerning how he viewed himself.

Finally, identifying Jesus as an itinerant Cynic philosopher tends to sever him both from his Jewish background and from the church which arose after him. While the Jesus Seminar denies that Jesus announced the future coming of the kingdom, they acknowledge that both Judaism and John the Baptist before Jesus, and the early church after him, held strong expectations for the coming kingdom. Such a disconnection from both antecedents and successors flies in the face of good historical research, which attempts to understand persons and events within their historical context, seeking cause-and-effect relationships to explain historical events.

> The non-eschatological Cynic hypothesis tends to sever Jesus from both his Jewish background and from the church which arose after him.

A Jewish Mystic or Spirit Person. A second contemporary portrait of Jesus is that he was a mystic or **spirit person** whose intimacy with God enabled him to accomplish extraordinary things. This view has ancient roots but is often linked today to Geza Vermes, whose groundbreaking book *Jesus the Jew* sought to reestablish the Jewishness of Jesus.[38] Vermes compared Jesus' miracles to those of **charismatic** Jewish holy men whose prayers were answered because of their piety and intimacy with God. The two most important of these holy men, Honi the Rainmaker and Hanina ben Dosa, performed miracles which bear some similarities to those of Jesus (see chap. 17, pp. 460–61).

The most influential recent portrait of Jesus as a mystic and holy man is that of **Marcus Borg**, who, like Crossan, was an influential member of the Jesus Seminar.[39] For Borg, Jesus was a "spirit person" or a charismatic uniquely in touch with God. A spirit person is defined as someone for whom the sacred (God or any transcendent reality) is an experiential reality. Jesus would spend many hours—sometimes entire nights—in meditation and prayer. He had visions and other ecstatic experiences. He called God his Father and experienced unique intimacy with him. He tapped into the power of the divine to perform exorcisms and heal illnesses. Borg compares Jesus to other historical figures who had special spiritual insight, like the Buddha, Lao Tzu, Saint Francis of Assisi, and Jewish holy men like Honi the Rainmaker and Hanina ben Dosa.

According to Borg, Jesus sought to reform the social world of Judaism with a new vision of holiness. Israel's religion was based on purity laws which separated and excluded. This system was hierarchical and centered on the boundaries set forth by the temple system and Torah observance. Israel's holiness laws separated Jews from Gentiles, priests from laity, men from women, the unclean from the clean. Jesus declared a new paradigm based on the love

---

38. Geza Vermes, *Jesus the Jew* (London: Collins, 1973).

39. Borg, *Jesus, A New Vision*; Borg, *Meeting Jesus Again for the First Time: The Historical Jesus and the Heart of Contemporary Faith* (San Francisco: HarperSanFrancisco, 1994).

and graciousness of God toward all people. He and his disciples ate with all kinds of people and proclaimed an egalitarian society of compassion and shared resources. He taught that holiness came not through the purity laws of temple and Torah but through an existential encounter with the divine.

Jesus met his fate because of this opposition to authoritarian structures. His radical call for the elimination of religious and social barriers and distinctions challenged Israel's elite, who maintained their power through these boundaries. Borg suggests that when Jesus confronted the priestly leadership by overturning the tables in the temple, he was arrested by the religious authorities and turned over to the Romans, who crucified him under a charge of insurrection.

The strength of Borg's thesis is that it locates Jesus within his Jewish context more clearly than the Cynic hypothesis does. As a holy man and a social prophet, Jesus fits within the tradition of Israel's prophets, who called for social justice and reform. One weakness is that Borg, like Crossan and the Jesus Seminar, rejects an eschatological dimension to Jesus' kingdom preach-

> The identification of Jesus as a spirit person portrays him as a Jewish mystic uniquely in touch with God.

ing. As noted above, this cuts Jesus off from both his Jewish antecedents and the early Christians. Another problem is Borg's rejection of any messianic self-consciousness on Jesus' part. This is surprising since Borg accepts as historically reliable a number of events which appear to have strong messianic implications (choosing twelve disciples, entering Jerusalem on a donkey, clearing the temple, etc.). Finally, Borg seems to establish a false dichotomy between God's gracious acceptance of sinners and his demand for purity and holiness. The evidence suggests that Jesus preached both God's free forgiveness of sinners and a high standard of righteousness—one that must exceed even that of the scribes and Pharisees (Matthew 5–7). Purity is not the antithesis of God's grace but the natural result of a life restored and renewed by God.

A Social Revolutionary. A few scholars have suggested over the years that Jesus should be viewed as a political or **social revolutionary**, sympathetic with the Zealots and advocating the violent overthrow of the Romans.[40] This view is not widely held today, since so much of Jesus' teaching runs strongly counter to it (see Mark 12:17, par.; Matt. 5:38–48; Luke 6:27–36). A more influential thesis is that of Richard Horsley, who claims Jesus was not a political but a social revolutionary.[41] Horsley defines a political revolution as top down, the violent overthrow of political leadership. Jesus, he argues, advocated not a political revolution but a social one, a transformation of community life from the bottom up.

According to Horsley, the context of Jesus' ministry was a Galilee dominated by a colonial-like class struggle, with tension and conflict between the urban ruling elite and the economically oppressed peasants. This created a "spiral of violence," with oppression leading to protest, leading to greater repression, and finally to revolt. In this context, Jesus functioned as a social prophet, moving among the rural poor and preaching a radical

---

40. See S. G. F. Brandon, *Jesus and the Zealots: A Study of the Political Factor in Primitive Christianity* (New York: Charles Scribner's Sons, 1967).
41. Richard A. Horsley, *Jesus and the Spiral of Violence* (San Francisco: HarperSanFrancisco, 1987).

reorganization of village life and a new social order. He called for the establishment of an egalitarian society, without hierarchy or patriarchy. He blessed the poor and condemned the rich. He taught that people should love their neighbors as themselves; they should turn the other cheek when injured; they should forgive debts and return land which had been taken away. Families should be reorganized without earthly fathers or teachers, calling only God their father.

The portrait of Jesus as a social revolutionary, advocated especially by Richard Horsley, views him as working for a social transformation of community life.

Horsley downplays the spiritual dimensions of Jesus' preaching. The kingdom of God was not a spiritual or religious entity but a political and social one. Jesus taught little about spiritual salvation or the afterlife. He was not an **eschatological prophet**, proclaiming God's final intervention to save and to judge. Nor was he a messiah proclaiming himself to be king. He was rather a social prophet, calling for a new social and political order. Horsley acknowledges that Jesus probably expected God would soon come to complete the social revolution and overthrow the oppressive governing power. Yet this would be accomplished by God alone; Jesus' role was not to foment rebellion but to bring about a social reformation.

Though Jesus did not advocate military revolt, he nevertheless represented a major threat to the ruling elite, challenging the hierarchical and authoritarian foundations of society. He repudiated the temple and its ruling class as instruments of power and coercion among the people. This challenge inevitably resulted in Jesus' arrest and crucifixion.

The strength of Horsley's theory is that he takes seriously the social and political dimensions of Jesus' context. Socioeconomic issues surely played an important role in Jesus' ministry, as indicated by Jesus' frequent references to poverty and wealth. These powerful factors have been too often neglected in studies of the historical Jesus. The weakness of Horsley's view is its failure to account satisfactorily for the spiritual and eschatological dimensions of Jesus' preaching and actions. The evidence is strong that Jesus called for repentance and spiritual renewal, a new heart oriented toward God. Furthermore, as we have noted before, it is impossible to draw a strict dichotomy between politics and religion in first-century Israel. Jesus' proclamation of a new social order would surely have contained spiritual and eschatological significance for his hearers. Finally, in defending his theory of a class struggle, Horsley downplays the role and influence of religious groups like the Pharisees, who would have played a mediating role between the peasantry and the ruling elite.[42]

R. David Kaylor draws on Horsley's work, affirming Jesus' social and political agenda, but emphasizes more strongly that Jesus was a social prophet calling Israel back to her covenant traditions. For Kaylor, Jesus fits into the classic tradition of the Jewish prophets, who called for a society of peace and justice. He writes that "Jesus was political in the same way the preexilic prophets in general were political: He believed that God's blessing of the people depended on their manifesting in the political sphere the justice God required

---

42. This point is made by Ben Witherington III, *The Jesus Quest: The Third Search for the Jew of Nazareth*, 2nd ed. (Downers Grove, IL: InterVarsity, 1997), 148–50.

Figure 11.5—Some Key Historical Jesus Scholars

The last quarter-century has seen a flurry of research on the historical Jesus, utilizing a variety of methods and coming to diverse conclusions. Below are some of the more provocative and influential portraits of Jesus proposed by recent Jesus scholars.

Author	Portrait of Jesus	Key Works
Morton Smith	A first century **magician** performing deeds through the power of a spirit	*Jesus the Magician* (1978)
F. Gerald Downing	A **countercultural Cynic philosopher**	*Cynics and Christian Origins* (1988)
Burton Mack	A **Cynic-like teacher**, transformed into a god by Mark and the later church	*The Myth of Innocence* (1988)
John Dominic Crossan	A **Cynic-like Jewish peasant** preaching egalitarian values and challenging social norms	*The Historical Jesus* (1991) *Jesus: A Revolutionary Biography* (1994)
Geza Vermes	A **charismatic Jewish miracle worker**, much like other Jewish Hasidim (holy men) of his day	*Jesus the Jew* (1973) *The Religion of Jesus the Jew* (1993)
Marcus Borg	A charismatic Jewish **mystic and "spirit person,"** uniquely in touch with the divine	*Jesus: A New Vision* (1988) *Meeting Jesus Again for the First Time* (1994)
Richard Horsley	A Jewish **social prophet**, promoting a peasant social revolution	*Jesus and the Spiral of Violence* (1987)
E. P. Sanders	A Jewish **eschatological prophet**, expecting God's imminent intervention in history to restore Israel, establish the kingdom, judge, and reward	*Jesus and Judaism* (1985) *The Historical Figure of Jesus* (1993)
John Meier	A Jewish **eschatological prophet**, preaching both a present and future kingdom	*A Marginal Jew* (3 vols.: 1991, 1994, 2001)
Ben Witherington III	A Jewish **sage and eschatological prophet**, embodying the wisdom of God	*The Christology of Jesus* (1990) *Jesus the Sage* (1994) *Jesus the Seer* (1999)
N. T. Wright	A Jewish **eschatological prophet**, announcing Israel's restoration and return from spiritual exile	*Who Was Jesus?* (1992) *Jesus and the Victory of God* (1996)

of covenant people."[43] As in Horsley's scheme, Jesus' challenge to the ruling powers was viewed as subversive, resulting in his execution.

An Eschatological Prophet. A widely held view among scholars today is that Jesus was an eschatological prophet, announcing the imminent coming of God's end-times salvation. The perspective can be traced back to the pioneering work of J. Weiss, made popular by A. Schweitzer in his *Quest for the Historical Jesus.* As we have seen, Schweitzer's influential book was an important factor in the demise of the First Quest. This perspective continues to hold strong appeal in the world of scholarship and, in its various manifestations, probably represents the majority view among Jesus scholars today.

> The portrait of Jesus as an eschatological or apocalyptic prophet claims he was a herald announcing the imminent coming of God's end-times salvation.

This view's prominence in recent years may be traced especially to the work of **E. P. Sanders**, whose 1985 book *Jesus and Judaism* made a significant impact on Jesus studies.[44] Sanders, an expert on first-century Judaism, began with the premise that there are certain "almost indisputable facts" about Jesus and his followers. In *Jesus and Judaism*, Sanders lists eight of these.[45] In his subsequent work, *The Historical Figure of Jesus*, he modifies and expands this to fifteen: (1) Jesus was born about 4 BC near the time of the death of Herod the Great; (2) he spent his childhood and early adult years in Nazareth, a Galilean village; (3) he was baptized by John the Baptist; (4) he called disciples; (5) he taught in the towns, villages, and countryside (but apparently not in the cities) of Galilee; (6) he preached "the kingdom of God"; (7) about the year 30 he went to Jerusalem for Passover; (8) he created a disturbance in the temple area; (9) he had a final meal with the disciples; (10) he was arrested and interrogated by Jewish authorities, specifically the high priest; (11) he was executed on the orders of the Roman prefect, Pontius Pilate; (12) his disciples at first fled; (13) they saw him (in what sense is not certain) after his death; (14) as a consequence, they believed he would return to found the kingdom; (15) they formed a community to await his return and sought to win others to faith in him as God's Messiah.[46]

From these foundational points, Sanders builds a portrait of Jesus within the context of first-century Judaism. He concludes that Jesus' ministry must be understood with reference to Israel's restoration theology, the pervasive hope in first-century Judaism that God would soon intervene to bring salvation to Israel, to judge the wicked, and to establish his kingdom of justice and righteousness. According to Sanders, Jesus should be seen as an eschatological prophet announcing the imminent arrival of the kingdom of God. Two of Jesus' actions are of particular significance: his choice of twelve disciples and his actions against the temple. The number twelve clearly implies that Jesus had in mind the eschatological restoration of

---

43. R. David Kaylor, *Jesus the Prophet: His Vision of the Kingdom on Earth* (Louisville: Westminster/John Knox, 1994).

44. Sanders, *Jesus and Judaism.*

45. Ibid., 11: he was a Galilean who preached and healed; he called disciples and spoke of there being twelve; he confined his actions to Israel; he engaged in a controversy about the temple; he was crucified by Roman authorities; after his death, his followers continued as an identifiable movement; and at least some Jews persecuted parts of the new movement.

46. E. P. Sanders, *The Historical Figure of Jesus* (New York: Penguin, 1993), 10–11.

Israel's twelve tribes. Jesus' statements about the temple's destruction—widely attested in various layers of the tradition—together with his action in driving out the money changers strongly suggest that Jesus expected the destruction of the temple and its replacement with a new eschatological temple.

While Crossan, Borg, and Horsley emphasize present dimensions of the kingdom, Sanders stresses its future coming. Jesus taught that the Son of Man would soon come in judgment (though Sanders does not think Jesus viewed himself as this figure). Jesus' exorcisms and healing miracles were meant to show that he was God's spokesman for the end times, and that the new age was at hand. His entrance into Jerusalem was likely an intentional fulfillment of Zechariah 9:9, symbolically announcing the coming kingdom. His last meal with his disciples anticipated the messianic banquet in the kingdom of God.

Sanders downplays Jesus' conflicts with the Pharisees, claiming that these episodes were mostly created by the church as a result of its later conflicts with the Jews. This perspective arises from Sanders' understanding of first-century Judaism, espoused earlier in his work *Paul and Palestinian Judaism*.[47] There Sanders argued that the common view of first-century Judaism as a legalistic religion of works salvation is false, a caricature created by Paul and the early Christians in their debates with the Jews and then propagated through centuries of anti-Semitism. According to Sanders, Judaism was a religion not of legalism but of grace. Sanders coined the term **covenantal nomism** to describe the Jewish perspective on the law. This means that God chose Israel and made a covenant with the nation, giving it the law as a gift of grace. Obedience to the law was not a means of salvation but rather was the means for maintaining the covenant relationship with God established through grace. Those who maintained this covenant relationship with God through obedience, atonement, and God's mercy belonged to the group who would be saved.

But if Judaism was not a legalistic religion of works, what brought Jesus into conflict with its leaders? According to Sanders, Jesus did not seek to abolish the law nor did he oppose laws related to Sabbath, diet, or purity. In fact, he had few theological differences with his Jewish contemporaries. Like many other Jesus scholars, Sanders sees the temple incident as the likely cause of his death. While Caiaphas and Pilate probably did not consider Jesus to be a real threat, they viewed him as a religious fanatic and a troublemaker. Caiaphas arrested him, gave him a hearing, and turned him over to Pilate to be crucified. Like Schweitzer, therefore, Sanders considers Jesus to have been a failed eschatological prophet who was wrong about his prediction of the imminent end of the world.

The strength of Sanders' view of Jesus is that it positions him squarely within his first-century context. The Judaism of Jesus' day was characterized by strong eschatological expectations, as evidenced in the preaching of Jesus' immediate predecessor, John the Baptist. Furthermore, the earliest church communities also held strong eschatological hopes, as Paul's early letters confirm.[48] This strength, however, also leads to a weakness, as Sanders assumes too quickly that Jesus would have been in near total agreement with his contemporaries. This lack of uniqueness makes it difficult to explain Jesus' profound impact on his

---

47. E. P. Sanders, *Paul and Palestinian Judaism: A Comparison of Patterns of Religion* (Philadelphia: Fortress, 1977). Cf. *Judaism: Practice and Belief, 63 B.C.E.–66 C.E.*

48. See 1 Thess. 1:10; 2:19; 3:13; 4:13–18; 5:1–11.

followers and the continuation of his movement after his death. It also makes it difficult to explain the reason for his arrest and crucifixion. Sanders' dismissal of the Gospel controversy stories as unhistorical seems unwarranted, especially since these episodes have strong and diverse attestation in the Gospel tradition.

The most unusual part of Sanders' thesis, and one which has received the most criticism, is his claim that Jesus did not require repentance of those he invited into the kingdom. Sanders says that the "sinners" of the Gospel tradition were not merely nonobservant Jews but truly wicked people who flouted God's law. Yet Jesus freely offered them a place in his kingdom without requiring repentance. This part of Sanders' argument is particularly odd in light of his repeated claims of continuity between Jesus and Judaism, since the necessity of repentance was an important theme in Jewish restoration theology. It also runs counter to Sanders' denial of any real conflict between Jesus and the Pharisees. Surely Jesus' acceptance of sinners without repentance would have provoked hostility among the scrupulous Pharisees.

Other scholars who view Jesus as an apocalyptic or eschatological prophet include Bart Ehrman,[49] Dale Allison,[50] and Paula Fredriksen.[51] Ehrman revives the view of Albert Schweitzer that Jesus was a Jewish apocalypticist who expected the cataclysmic end of the world in the very near future. Jesus got it wrong, however, and the end did not occur. Fredriksen too identifies Jesus as an eschatological prophet who thought the kingdom was soon to arrive—perhaps even coming at the Passover of his crucifixion. She follows many aspects of Sanders' work, stressing the continuity between Jesus and Judaism, especially in the area of Jewish purity teaching. Fredriksen raises an intriguing question also discussed by Sanders: What can account for the fact that Jesus was arrested and crucified as a messianic pretender but his disciples were not subsequently rounded up and destroyed? She concludes that while neither Pilate nor the Jewish authorities saw Jesus as much of a threat, some Jewish pilgrims began proclaiming his kingship at his entrance to Jerusalem. Pilate, always wary of popular revolt during the tumultuous Passover period, had Jesus summarily arrested and executed. The crucifixion was more of a preemptive warning against the political aspiration of others than a recognition of Jesus' messianic ambitions.

A more complex portrait of Jesus as an eschatological prophet is presented by **John P. Meier**, whose massive *A Marginal Jew: Rethinking the Historical Jesus*[52] is the most ambitious Jesus study to date. Three large volumes have been completed in a projected four-volume series. Meier's method is somewhat similar to the Jesus Seminar, methodically examining each saying and event in the Gospels using the criteria of authenticity.[53] His conclusions, however, are very different, finding much more of historical value in the Gospels.

---

49. Bart Ehrman, *Jesus: Apocalyptic Prophet of the New Millennium* (New York: Oxford Univ. Press, 1999).

50. Dale Allison, *Jesus of Nazareth: Millenarian Prophet* (Minneapolis: Fortress, 1998).

51. Fredriksen, *Jesus of Nazareth, King of the Jews.*

52. Meier, *Marginal Jew.*

53. The five main criteria he uses are embarrassment, discontinuity, multiple attestation, coherence, and what he calls "the criterion of Jesus' rejection and execution." This last is something like the criterion of explanation but with an emphasis on the reasons for Jesus' crucifixion. Unlike Crossan and the Jesus Seminar, Meier generally rejects the value of the apocryphal gospels like the *Gospel of Thomas* and gives more credibility to the traditions in John. For example, he affirms John's chronology over that of the Synoptics, arguing that Jesus' ministry likely lasted longer than one year.

Meier's description of Jesus as a "marginal Jew" is meant not to minimize Jesus' importance or historical impact but rather to provoke interest in his enigmatic identity. Jesus was "marginal" in a variety of ways: he was a mere blip on the radar screen of the Greco-Roman world; he marginalized himself by leaving his trade and family to become an itinerant preacher; his controversial teachings placed him outside the mainstream of the religious teachers of his day; and his teachings and actions provoked the hostility of everyone "from pious Pharisees, to political high priests, to an ever vigilant Pilate."[54]

In his second volume, Meier describes Jesus' ministry under three headings: mentor, message, and miracles. *Mentor* refers to John the Baptist, who baptized Jesus (suggesting a discipleship relationship) and whose eschatological preaching of the need for repentance in light of coming judgment Jesus adopted. Jesus' *message* was built on this eschatological foundation. While Crossan, Borg, and Horsley focus on present dimensions of the kingdom, and Sanders on its future coming, Meier sees the kingdom as both present and future, a multifaceted symbol for both God's universal rule over creation and the consummation of that reign in the future. Jesus was not primarily a social or political prophet calling for the reformation of society but rather an eschatological prophet announcing the imminent coming of the kingdom of God. Concerning the third feature, *miracles*, Meier strongly asserts that Jesus performed deeds—healings, exorcisms, even raising the dead—which were considered by his contemporaries to be miracles. But Meier refuses to conclude that these were actually supernatural acts, since he considers such claims to be outside the realm of historical inquiry.

While Meier's portrait of Jesus as an eschatological prophet has much in common with Sanders', he differs sharply in his conclusions about Jesus and the law. While Sanders sees Jesus as little different than the Pharisees, essentially affirming the continuing validity of the Mosaic law, Meier sees Jesus as a charismatic (Spirit inspired) figure who claimed the authority to alter or even revoke aspects of the law. This brought him into conflict with the religious leaders of his day, eventually resulting in his crucifixion.

The strength of Meier's work is its systematic and methodical analysis, which provides greater objectivity than most contemporary Jesus studies. A weakness is the lack of an overarching synthesis to explain the aims and intentions of Jesus. Meier holds so many diverse traditions about Jesus in tension that it is sometimes difficult to see the forest for the trees.

A different slant on Jesus as an eschatological prophet is provided by **N. T. Wright**, whose multivolume study (three of five are completed) rivals the length and depth of Meier's.[55] As noted earlier, Wright approaches his study much differently than Meier or the Jesus Seminar. Rather than examining each individual pericope, he establishes an overarching hypothesis, which he then tests against the data.[56] Using his "double criterion of similarity and dissimilarity," Wright seeks to construct a portrait of Jesus which fits credibly within first-century Judaism but which also explains the rise of early Christianity, in which Jesus was worshiped as God and viewed as the savior of the world.

---

54. Meier, *Marginal Jew*, 1:9.

55. The whole endeavor is called *Christian Origins and the Question of God* and consists (so far) of three volumes: N. T. Wright, *The New Testament People of God* (Minneapolis: Fortress, 1992); idem., *Jesus and the Victory of God* (Minneapolis: Fortress, 1996); and idem., *The Resurrection of the Son of God* (Minneapolis: Fortress, 2003).

56. Wright, *New Testament People of God*, esp. 31–46, 80–120. Wright draws this methodology from the important work of Ben Meyer, *The Aims of Jesus* (London: SCM, 1979).

Wright's most unique contribution may be his claim that many first-century Jews viewed themselves as still in exile, suffering under Roman oppression as God's judgment for the nation's sin. In this climate, Jesus identified himself as an eschatological prophet, announcing that Yahweh—Israel's God—was about to return in triumph to Zion to restore Israel and bring her out of exile. Jesus called for repentance and faith, which meant more than an individual moral response. It was, rather, a rejection of the old way of being Israel, and identification with Jesus and the new community of restored Israel. This new Israel was a community not of separation and exclusion but of welcome and inclusion, loving instead of hating, forgiving enemies and turning the other cheek. In this way, Jesus interpreted Israel's exile in a shocking way: the real enemy was not Roman oppression but rather Satan and his forces, who had deceived Israel into believing that the way to victory was through power and conquest.

Unlike Sanders, Wright accepts the authenticity of Jesus' conflict with the Pharisees. But these conflicts were not about legalistic works-righteousness. Rather, Jesus criticized those laws which symbolized Jewish exclusivity: Sabbath observance, purity codes, and the sacrificial system of the temple. The new age of salvation meant the end of this system of exclusion and the creation of a new community which would be a light to all people.

Wright interprets Jesus' words and actions through this matrix of Jewish restoration theology. Jesus' parables are interpreted to symbolize the new exodus deliverance of the people of God. His miracles are signs that the promised restoration is about to take place. The healings show that those who have previously been excluded are now being restored. The exorcisms reveal that Satan and his forces are being defeated. Jesus' association with sinners and outcasts symbolizes the new community of inclusion.

And what about the crucifixion? Wright claims that the crucifixion was not a tragic accident of history but was viewed by Jesus as part of God's purpose and plan. Jesus believed that he was acting as Israel's representative, dying for her sins and so opening the way for her spiritual return from exile. Salvation would come not through physical conquest of the Romans but through his sacrifice for others. Jesus, then, was not a failed eschatological prophet (as Sanders, Ehrman, Fredriksen, and others claim) but rather accomplished the task he set out to achieve. Just as he predicted, Jerusalem and the temple were destroyed (ending the sacrificial system), and the church emerged as the community of faith in the new age of salvation.

These points make it clear that Wright understands eschatology differently than these other scholars. It is not the end of the world (the space-time universe) but the end of the present age and the beginning of a new world order. Wright reinterprets passages which have been traditionally viewed as future eschatology. The Olivet Discourse concerns only the destruction of AD 70, not a future consummation. Passages about the coming Son of Man are not about Jesus' returning to earth at the second coming but about his exaltation to the right hand of God.

It should also be clear from all of this that for Wright, Jesus is more than an eschatological prophet. He not only announces God's salvation but also accomplishes it, leading God's people to salvation. Indeed, Wright goes so far as to say that Jesus viewed himself as the embodiment of Yahweh himself, returning to Zion to bring his people out of exile. This identification helps to explain how the early church—though holding fast to a monotheistic worldview—came to worship Jesus as divine.

The Messiah. N. T. Wright's identification of Jesus as more than an eschatological prophet raises a fifth portrait of Jesus which must be noted: the traditional (and biblical!) view that Jesus was the Messiah. As we have seen, the term Messiah, or Anointed One, can mean many different things. At a minimum, it means one who not only *announces* God's salvation (a prophetic role) but also *accomplishes* it (a messianic role). While cautious, E. P. Sanders acknowledges that Jesus "thought that God was about to bring in his kingdom, and that he, Jesus, was God's last emissary. He thought therefore that he was in some sense 'king.'"[57] Similarly, Meier sees Jesus as not only the proclaimer of the kingdom but also in some sense its enactor. Jesus "makes the kingdom already present for at least some Israelites by his exorcisms and miracles of healing" and "mediates an experience of the joyful time of salvation."[58]

Other scholars also attribute some kind of a messianic self-consciousness to Jesus. Peter Stuhlmacher argues for the general reliability of the Gospel tradition, especially Mark, and claims that Jesus' actions from the baptism onward indicate a clear messianic consciousness.[59] Marinus de Jonge concludes that "Jesus not only announced the kingdom of God; he inaugurated it … It is probable that he regarded himself as the Messiah and Son of David inspired and empowered by the Spirit."[60] James D. G. Dunn claims that while Jesus rejected some kinds of messianic acclamations, especially those with strong political connotations, he did not reject the idea outright. Jesus' identification of himself with texts such as Isaiah 61:1–2 suggests that he saw himself and his mission as messianic in nature.[61] Ben Witherington considers the most comprehensive description of Jesus to be as "sage," the embodiment of God's wisdom. Yet he also acknowledges that Jesus functioned both as a prophetic and a messianic figure.[62] Other scholars who affirm that Jesus viewed himself as in some sense the Messiah include I. H. Marshall and Markus Bockmuehl.[63] These studies confirm that the use of a rigorous historical methodology does not necessarily negate a portrait of Jesus in fundamental agreement with the Gospel presentations of him.

James D. G. Dunn

---

57. Sanders, *Historical Figure of Jesus*, 248.

58. Meier, *Marginal Jew*, 2:454.

59. Peter Stuhlmacher, *Jesus of Nazareth—Christ of Faith* (Peabody, MA: Hendrickson, 1993).

60. Marinus de Jonge, *God's Final Envoy: Early Christology and Jesus' Own View of His Mission* (Grand Rapids: Eerdmans, 1998), 109; cf. idem., *Jesus, the Servant Messiah* (New Haven, CT: Yale Univ. Press, 1991).

61. James D. G. Dunn, "Messianic Ideas and Their Influence on the Jesus of History," in *The Messiah,* ed. James H. Charlesworth (Minneapolis: Augsburg Fortress, 1992), 365–81; idem., *Jesus Remembered* (Grand Rapids: Eerdmans, 2003), 889–90.

62. See Ben Witherington III, *The Christology of Jesus* (Philadelphia: Fortress, 1984); *Jesus the Sage: The Pilgrimage of Wisdom* (Minneapolis: Augsburg Fortress, 1994); *Jesus the Seer: The Progress of Prophecy* (Peabody, MA: Hendrickson, 1999).

63. Markus Bockmuehl, *This Jesus: Martyr, Lord, Messiah* (Edinburgh: T. and T. Clark, 1994), 77–102, 165; I. H. Marshall, *The Origins of New Testament Christology* (Downers Grove, IL: InterVarsity, 1976), 56–57. Cf. the survey in Witherington, *The Jesus Quest*, 214–18.

CONCLUSION

This chapter has confirmed that one's assessment of the historical Jesus depends on many factors: the sources examined, the criteria utilized, the methods employed, the historical context presumed, and the worldview of the investigator. The most decisive factor, however, is the reliability or unreliability attributed to the Gospels as historical accounts. Those who take the Gospels as generally reliable come up with a Jesus very much like the one portrayed in the Gospels. Those who doubt the reliability of the Gospels base their conclusions on one small slice of the pie—that part of the evidence which they consider historical. They treat the rest as theological polemic and mythmaking by the early church. This raises the critical question of just how reliable the Gospel tradition is. In the next chapter, we will address this question.

» CHAPTER SUMMARY «

1. Controlled by Enlightenment-era rationalism, the nineteenth-century Quest for the Historical Jesus (the First Quest) sought to establish Jesus as a nonsupernatural teacher of love and humanistic philosophy.

2. Albert Schweitzer's classic book *The Quest for the Historical Jesus* undermined the First Quest by showing that the authors created a Jesus in their own image.

3. Ernst Troeltsch set out principles which have guided the antisupernatural tendencies of the historical-critical method.

4. D. F. Strauss treated the Gospel stories as mostly myths invented by the early church.

5. William Wrede challenged the First Quest's assumption concerning the historicity of Mark's Gospel, claiming that Mark was a creative theologian who invented much of his story around the motif of the "messianic secret."

6. Johannes Weiss sought to place Jesus in the context of first-century Judaism, portraying him as an apocalyptic prophet announcing the imminent end of the world.

7. Martin Kähler argued against the First Quest by claiming that it is impossible to discover a nonsupernatural historical Jesus in the Gospels. What is important is the risen and exalted Christ of faith, who is worshiped by the church.

8. Building on the work of Schweitzer, Wrede, Weiss, Kähler, and others, Rudolf Bultmann's radical skepticism led to a period of No Quest, when many scholars considered the historical Jesus both unattainable and irrelevant.

9. The New (Second) Quest was launched by Ernst Käsemann and other students of Bultmann. Yet by adopting much of their teacher's skepticism, the New Quest produced only a minimalist portrait of Jesus.

10. The Third Quest is a name given to the spate of recent Jesus scholarship, which utilizes a variety of new methodologies.

11. Sometimes viewed as part of the Third Quest, sometimes viewed as distinct, the Jesus Seminar is a group of scholars who have met to vote on the sayings and deeds of Jesus. The Seminar rejects as unhistorical most of the sayings and stories in the Gospels.

12. Conclusions about Jesus are determined by many factors: the sources examined, the criteria utilized, the method employed, the historical context presumed, and the worldview of the investigator.

13. The "criteria of authenticity" are used by scholars to test the historicity of the words and deeds of Jesus. The most basic criterion is the criterion of dissimilarity, which claims sayings of Jesus are authentic if they are unique from Judaism and early Christianity.

14. While potentially effective tools, the criteria are open to subjectivity and abuse. Researchers often find only the Jesus they are looking for.

15. Five main portraits of Jesus are developed by contemporary Jesus scholars: Cynic-sage, spirit person, social revolutionary, eschatological prophet, and Messiah.

» KEY TERMS «

rationalism
First Quest for the Historical
    Jesus
Herman Samuel Reimarus
Albert Schweitzer
No Quest
Rudolf Bultmann
Ernst Troeltsch
D. F. Strauss
William Wrede
Johannes Weiss

history of religions school
Martin Kähler
Jesus of history versus Christ of
    faith
Ernst Käsemann
New (Second) Quest
Third Quest
Jesus Seminar
criteria of authenticity
Cynics, Cynic-like philosopher
John Dominic Crossan

spirit person
charismatic
Marcus Borg
social revolutionary
eschatological prophet
E. P. Sanders
covenantal nomism
John P. Meier
N. T. Wright

1. What role did Herman Samuel Reimarus play in launching the First Quest for the historical Jesus?

2. What were the characteristics of the First Quest?

3. What impact did Albert Schweitzer's book *The Quest for the Historical Jesus* have on the First Quest?

4. Summarize the significance of Ernst Troeltsch, D. F. Strauss, Johannes Weiss, William Wrede, Martin Kähler, and the history of religions school for historical Jesus studies.

5. Summarize the perspective of Rudolf Bultmann. Why is Bultmann's era known as the period of No Quest?

6. What is the difference between the historical Jesus and the Christ of faith, according to Bultmann and others?

7. How was the New (Second) Quest started? What are its characteristics?

8. What is the Third Quest? What is the Jesus Seminar? What were its goals? What were its conclusions?

9. What are the "criteria of authenticity"? Summarize the criteria of dissimiliarity, coherence, multiple attestation, embarrassment, and divergent traditions.

10. What is the difference between an inductive and a deductive approach to the historical Jesus?

11. Summarize the five main portraits of Jesus: Cynic-like philosopher, spirit-endowed holy man, social revolutionary, eschatological prophet, and Messiah.

12. Match the following Jesus scholars with the portraits of Jesus noted in question 11: John Dominic Crossan, Marcus Borg, Richard Horsley, E. P. Sanders, John P. Meier, and N. T. Wright.

Digging Deeper

Surveying the Historical Quests

Borg, Marcus. *Jesus in Contemporary Scholarship.* Valley Forge, PA: Trinity Press International, 1994.

Dunn, James D. G. *New Perspectives on Jesus: What the Quest for the Historical Jesus Missed.* Grand Rapids: Baker, 2005.

Powell, Mark Allan. *Jesus as a Figure of History: How Modern Historians View the Man from Galilee.* Westminster: John Knox, 1998.

Schweitzer, Albert. *The Quest for the Historical Jesus: A Critical Study of Its Progress from Reimarus to Wrede.* Translated by W. Montgomery. New York: Macmillan, 1954.

Strimple, Robert. *The Modern Search for the Real Jesus: An Introductory Survey of the Historical Roots of Gospels Criticism.* Phillipsburg, NJ: P and R Publishing, 1995.

Witherington III, Ben. *The Jesus Quest: The Third Search for the Jew of Nazareth.* Downers Grove, IL: InterVarsity, 1995.

Criteria of Authenticity

Calvert, D. G. A. "An Examination of the Criteria for Distinguishing the Authentic Words of Jesus." *New Testament Studies* 18 (January 1972): 209–19.

Evans, Craig A. *Jesus.* IBR Bibliographies 5. Grand Rapids: Baker, 1992. See pp. 52–67.

France, R. T. "The Authenticity of the Sayings of Jesus." In *History, Criticism and Faith.* Edited by Colin Brown. Downers Grove, IL: InterVarsity, 1976.

Hooker, Morna D. "Christology and Methodology." *New Testament Studies* 17 (July 1971): 480–87.

———. "On Using the Wrong Tool." *Theology* 75 (November 1972), 570–81.

McKnight, Scot. *Interpreting the Synoptic Gospels.* Grand Rapids: Baker, 1988. See pp. 58–69.

Perrin, Norman. *Rediscovering the Teaching of Jesus.* New York: Harper and Row, 1967.

Porter, Stanley E. *The Criteria for Authenticity in Historical-Jesus Research: Previous Discussions and New Proposals.* JSNTSup 191. Sheffield: Sheffield Academic, 2000.

Stein, R. H. "The 'Criteria' for Authenticity." In *Studies of History and Tradition in the Four Gospels.* Edited by R. T. France and D. Wenham. Gospel Perspectives 2. Sheffield: JSOT Press, 1980.

Theissen, Gerd, and Dagmar Winter. *The Quest for the Plausible Jesus: The Question of Criteria.* Translated by M. Eugene Boring. Louisville: Westminster John Knox, 2002.

The Third Quest and Contemporary Jesus Studies

Allison, Dale. *Jesus of Nazareth: Millenarian Prophet.* Minneapolis: Fortress, 1998.

Bock, Darrell L. *Studying the Historical Jesus: A Guide to Sources and Methods.* Grand Rapids: Baker, 2002.

———. *Jesus according to Scripture: Restoring the Portrait from the Gospels.* Grand Rapids: Baker, 2002.

Bockmuehl, Markus. *This Jesus: Martyr, Lord, Messiah.* Edinburgh: T. and T. Clark, 1994.

Bockmuehl, Markus, ed. *The Cambridge Companion to Jesus.* Cambridge: Cambridge Univ. Press, 2001.

Borg, Marcus J. *Jesus: A New Vision.* San Francisco: Harper and Row, 1987.

———. *Meeting Jesus Again for the First Time: The Historical Jesus and the Heart of Contemporary Faith.* San Francisco: HarperSanFrancisco, 1994.

Crossan, John Dominic. *The Historical Jesus: The Life of a Mediterranean Jewish Peasant.* San Francisco: HarperSanFrancisco, 1991.

———. *Jesus: A Revolutionary Biography.* San Francisco: HarperSanFrancisco, 1994.

Dunn, James D. G. *Jesus Remembered.* Grand Rapids: Eerdmans, 2003.

Ehrman, Bart. *Jesus: Apocalyptic Prophet of the New Millennium.* New York: Oxford Univ. Press, 1999.

Fredriksen, Paula. *Jesus of Nazareth, King of the Jews.* New York: Vintage, 1999.

Harvey, A. E. *Jesus and the Constraints of History.* Philadelphia: Westminster, 1982.

Horsley, Richard A. *Jesus and the Spiral of Violence.* San Francisco: HarperSanFrancisco, 1987.

De Jonge, Marinus. *God's Final Envoy: Early Christology and Jesus' Own View of His Mission.* Grand Rapids: Eerdmans, 1998.

———. *Jesus, the Servant Messiah.* New Haven: Yale Univ. Press, 1991.

Kaylor, R. David. *Jesus the Prophet: His Vision of the Kingdom on Earth.* Louisville: Westminster/John Knox, 1994.

Mack, Burton L. *The Lost Gospel: The Book of Q and Christian Origins.* San Francisco: HarperSanFrancisco, 1993.

———. *Who Wrote the New Testament? The Making of the Christian Myth.* San Francisco: HarperSanFrancisco, 1995.

McClymond, Michael J. *Familiar Stranger: An Introduction to Jesus of Nazareth.* Grand Rapids: Eerdmans, 2004.

Meier, John P. *A Marginal Jew: Rethinking the Historical Jesus.* 3 vols. New York: Doubleday, 1991, 1994, 2001.

Meyer, Ben F. *The Aims of Jesus.* London: SCM, 1979.

Sanders. E. P. *The Historical Figure of Jesus.* New York: Penguin, 1993.

———. *Jesus and Judaism.* Philadelphia: Fortress, 1985.

Theissen, Gerd, and Annette Merz. *The Historical Jesus: A Comprehensive Guide.* Minneapolis: Fortress, 1996.

Vermes, Geza. *Jesus the Jew.* London: Collins, 1973.

Witherington III, Ben. *The Christology of Jesus.* Minneapolis: Fortress, 1990.

———. *Jesus the Sage: The Pilgrimage of Wisdom.* Minneapolis: Fortress, 1994.

———. *Jesus the Seer: The Progress of Prophecy.* Peabody, MA: Hendrickson, 1999.

Wright, N. T. *Jesus and the Victory of God.* Minneapolis: Fortress, 1996.

———. *Who Was Jesus?* Grand Rapids: Eerdmans, 1993.

Jesus Seminar Works

Funk, Robert W., Roy W. Hoover, and the Jesus Seminar. *The Five Gospels: The Search for the Authentic Words of Jesus.* New York: Macmillan, 1993.

Funk, Robert W., and the Jesus Seminar. *The Acts of Jesus: The Search for the Authentic Deeds of Jesus.* New York: HarperCollins, 1998.

———. *The Gospel of Jesus according to the Jesus Seminar.* Santa Rosa, CA: Polebridge, 1999.

Funk, Robert W. *The Gospel of Mark: Red Letter Edition.* With Mahlon H. Smith. Sonoma, CA: Polebridge, 1991.

Some Responses to the Jesus Seminar

Boyd, Gregory A. *Cynic Sage or Son of God? Recovering the Real Jesus in an Age of Revisionist Replies.* Wheaton: Victor, 1995.

Johnson, Luke Timothy. *The Real Jesus: The Misguided Quest for the Historical Jesus and the Truth of the Traditional Gospels.* San Francisco: HarperSanFrancisco, 1996.

Wilkins, Michael J., and J. P. Moreland, gen. eds. *Jesus Under Fire: Modern Scholarship Reinvents the Historical Jesus.* Grand Rapids: Zondervan, 1995.

Wright, N. T. "Five Gospels but No Gospel: Jesus and the Seminar." In *Crisis in Christology: Essays in Quest of Resolution.* Edited by W. R. Farmer. Livonia, MI: Dove Booksellers, 1995.

CHAPTER 12

The Historical Reliability of the Gospels

» CHAPTER OVERVIEW «

1. The Role of Presuppositions in Historical Research
2. Were the Gospel Writers Biased?
3. The Burden of Proof
4. Luke-Acts and Ancient History Writing
5. A Generally Reliable Gospel Tradition
6. Contradictions between the Gospels?
7. The Historical Reliability of John
8. Conclusion: The Gospels as History *and* Theology

» OBJECTIVES «

After reading this chapter, you should be able to:

- Discuss the role of presuppositions in historical research.
- Summarize the main evidence for the general reliability of the Gospel tradition.
- Provide suggested solutions for apparent contradictions among the Gospels.
- Explain some of the reasons for differences between John and the Synoptics.

Controversy erupted in early 2004 with the promotion leading up to the release of Mel Gibson's film *The Passion of the Christ*, a graphic portrayal of the last twelve hours of Jesus' life. Opposition came especially from those who said the movie was anti-Semitic, portraying the Jews as murderers of Christ. Some scholars claimed that the movie was meticulously accurate. Others said it was historically inaccurate, a distorted view of history. How could two such different judgments be made concerning the same film?

The answer lies in the different views of the historicity of the Gospels. While the *Passion* generally follows the Gospel narratives, skeptics argue that these accounts are inaccurate, portraying the Jews in a worse light, and the Romans in a better one, than is historically justified. The Gospels are not straightforward history, they claim, but theological propaganda written during a time of intense religious and political turmoil. In the context of the early church's conflict with the synagogue, the Gospel writers sought to show that Christianity was the true successor to Judaism and that the Jews stood under judgment for rejecting their Messiah. Living in the shadow of the powerful Roman Empire, they also affirm Jesus' innocence by Roman standards, that his crucifixion was a judicial mistake made under pressure. These needs, it is argued, shaped the tone of the passion narratives.

So which is correct? Are the Gospels unbiased history or theological propaganda? The truth lies between these two extremes. First, no one writes unbiased history. The Gospels certainly contain theological polemic written to defend the church's claims to be the authentic people of God. They are not anti-Semitic, but they are pro-Christian, defending the claim that Jesus is the Jewish Messiah. Assuming this theological motivation, we must still ask the historical question: Are the Gospels reliable history? This is the issue we turn to in this and the following chapters.

THE ROLE OF PRESUPPOSITIONS IN HISTORICAL RESEARCH

One's assessment of the historical value of the Gospels inevitably depends on one's philosophical and theological presuppositions. If you start with an antisupernatural worldview, you will discount reports of miracles. If you assume Jesus was nothing more than a disillusioned Jewish preacher, you will explain away the church's deification of him. On the other hand, if you accept the supernatural as a possibility and take the Gospel writers at their word, you will find much in them of historical value. It is impossible to set aside presuppositions when approaching these texts (or any texts!) — to approach them with a "blank slate."

> While acknowledging that all reading is to a certain degree subjective, we must not despair of all claims to objectivity.

While acknowledging that all reading is to a certain degree subjective, we must not despair of all claims to objectivity. Even postmoderns who reject absolute truth acknowledge the value of evidence to determine historical reliability. Without such judgments, no court of law could render a decision of guilt or innocence, no newspaper could report anything as factual, no history could be written and believed. Even those who reject the objectivity of truth live as though historical truth is attainable and demonstrable. Although we can never claim to have the last word on the historical reliability of the Gospels, it is possible to weigh the evidence for their trustworthiness.

WERE THE GOSPEL WRITERS BIASED?

A common accusation against the Gospels is that the beliefs of the Evangelists colored and therefore distorted their presentation of Jesus. Were the Gospel writers biased historians? If we mean by biased "holding certain convictions," then the answer is yes, since there is no such thing as an unbiased historian. Everyone has a worldview and a belief system through which they process reality, whether that worldview is theistic, atheistic, or agnostic. The Gospel writers passionately believed in the message they proclaimed and desired for others to believe it. Did this distort their conclusions? An analogy is appropriate here. If an American wrote a history of the United States, would that history necessarily be unreliable and distorted? Or more pointedly, some of the most important accounts of the Nazi Holocaust have been composed by Jews. Does this fact render the accounts inaccurate? On the contrary, those passionately interested in the events are often the most meticulous in recording them. To claim that the Gospels cannot be historical because they were written by believers is fallacious. The important question is not whether the Gospel writers were biased but whether they were credible historians.

> Those passionately interested in particular events are often the most meticulous in recording them.

THE BURDEN OF PROOF

Critics of the Gospels often assume that a saying or an action attributed to Jesus is inauthentic unless proven otherwise. The **burden of proof**, they say, is on those who claim authenticity. But this is an unfair bias against the Gospels. The burden of proof should lie with whomever is making a claim. If I say the Gospels contain reliable information, the burden is on me to provide supporting evidence. Similarly, those who deny the historicity of the Gospels must supply corroborating evidence. Neither historicity nor nonhistoricity can be merely assumed.

What happens when there is not enough evidence to confirm or disprove an event or a saying of Jesus? Here the principle of general trustworthiness must be taken into account. If a writer or historian can be demonstrated to be generally reliable, then the benefit of the doubt may be given to that writer in disputed cases.

LUKE-ACTS AND ANCIENT HISTORY WRITING

Did the Gospel writers write accurate history? Luke indicates this was his intent:

> Many have undertaken to draw up an account of the things that have been fulfilled among us, just as they were handed down to us by those who from the first were eyewitnesses and servants of the word. Therefore, since I myself have carefully investigated everything from the beginning, it seemed good also to me to write an orderly account for you, most excellent Theophilus, so that you may know the certainty of the things you have been taught.
>
> —Luke 1:1–4

Notice the piling up of historical terms: "eyewitnesses," "carefully investigated," "orderly account," "certainty." Luke clearly claims to be writing accurate history. Critics respond that these claims are of little value, since history writing in a modern sense was unknown in the ancient world. While it is certainly true that some ancient historians were

Not only is Luke a man of historical detail, but he also has a keen sense of the Zeitgeist, or "spirit of the times."

better than others, it is wrong to deny that good history existed in the ancient world. The Hellenistic historian Polybius criticizes other writers for making up dramatic scenes and calls on them to "simply record what really happened and what really was said" (*Histories* 2.56.10). This shows not only that there were good and bad historians but that intelligent writers and readers in the first century distinguished fact from fiction. It is not so different from today, when careful readers must discern between accurate news and tabloid journalism. Luke's reliability as a historian must be judged from the evidence, not from sweeping generalizations about ancient history.

Was Luke a reliable historian? In *The Book of Acts in the Setting of Hellenistic History*, Colin Hemer conducted a detailed critical study of Luke's historical references in Acts, concluding that Luke was a meticulous and reliable historian.[1] Others have come to similar conclusions.[2] Particularly striking is Luke's attention to historical detail, providing names of cities and titles of government officials which are accurate for both time and place. This is especially significant since such names changed frequently. For example, Luke accurately identifies Sergius Paulus as *anthypatos* ("proconsul") of Cyprus (Acts 13:7) and Publius as the *prōtos* (something like "the first man" = governor) of Melita (Acts 28:7). City officials are *stratēgoi* in Philippi (Acts 16:20), *politarchai* in Thessalonica (Acts 17:6), and *asiarchai* in Ephesus (Acts 19:31), all historically accurate designations. This would be like someone accurately distinguishing titles like supervisor, councilor, mayor, governor, senator, representative, speaker of the house, vice president, and president. We would expect those who knew the meaning of such titles to have firsthand knowledge of American government. If Luke was so meticulous with these kinds of details in Acts, he was surely also careful in research and writing about the Jesus tradition.

Not only is Luke a man of historical detail, but he also has a keen sense of the **Zeitgeist**, or "spirit of the times." In Luke 3:2, he identifies both Annas and Caiaphas as high priests in Israel. This is not technically correct, since Israel had only one high priest. Yet Luke knows that while Caiaphas was the official high priest appointed by the Romans, his father-in-law, Annas, the former high priest, was the real power of the priesthood (cf. Acts 4:6; John 18:13, 24). Luke understands not only the official terms and titles but also the political intrigue behind the scenes.

John McRay

An inscription identifying the office of politarch, a title which Luke accurately gives to city officials in Thessalonica (Acts 17:6, 8). Findings like this indicate Luke's reliability as a historian.

A GENERALLY RELIABLE GOSPEL TRADITION

We may speak of Luke's value as a historian, but were the traditions he received historically reliable? We turn next to some evidence that the church carefully passed down the traditions about Jesus.

---

1. Colin J. Hemer, *The Book of Acts in the Setting of Hellenistic History*, ed. Conrad Gempf (Tübingen: Mohr, 1989).
2. See especially Martin Hengel, *Acts and the History of Earliest Christianity*, trans. John Bowden (London: SCM, 1979). Both of these scholars are respected historians, not merely apologists for their perspective.

The Testimony of the Eyewitnesses. Some critics claim that the eyewitnesses to the events of Jesus had little to do with passing down the tradition. But this contradicts the strong evidence that the apostles were the primary guardians and transmitters of the story of Jesus (Luke 1:2; Acts 1:21–22; 2:42; 6:2, 4; 1 Cor. 9:1; Gal. 2:2–10). Throughout the New Testament, the testimony of eyewitnesses is highly esteemed (John 19:35; 21:24; Acts 1:21–22; 10:39, 41; 1 Cor. 15:6; 1 Peter 5:1; 2 Peter 1:16; 1 John 1:1–3). A high view of the tradition is seen in Romans 6:17 and 1 Corinthians 7:10, 12.

A grandfather teaches his grandson Torah. Judaism has a history of the careful transmission of authoritative tradition. It is likely the disciples carefully passed on Jesus' words and deeds.

Z. Radovan, Jerusalem

The Faithful Transmission of the Gospel Tradition. The evidence suggests that the early church carefully transmitted the words and deeds of Jesus. The closest analogy to the transmission process of the early church is that of the rabbis of Palestinian Judaism, who revered and carefully transmitted their oral traditions.[3] It seems likely that the early disciples of Jesus were similarly careful to pass on the authentic words of their Lord. Evidence for this is Paul's use of terms like "received" (*paralambanō*) and "passed on" (*paradidōmi*), technical terms in Judaism for the careful handing down of tradition (1 Cor. 11:23; 15:1–2).

The Church's Willingness to Preserve Difficult Sayings. Further evidence of the church's accurate transmission is their faithfulness in preserving difficult sayings of Jesus. For example, in Mark 13:32 Jesus admits that even he doesn't know the day or the hour of his return. It seems unlikely that the church would create a saying that attributed ignorance to Jesus. If stories and sayings were constantly being created and altered, why not simply eliminate those which presented theological difficulties? (See also Matt. 10:5–6; Mark 9:1.)

> There is little evidence that the sayings of Christian prophets were confused with the sayings of the historical Jesus.

The Distinction between the Words of Jesus and of Christian Prophets. Bultmann and others argued that the early church freely created words and deeds of Jesus because the Christ of faith was still speaking through his prophets and apostles. But there is little evidence that the sayings of Christian prophets were confused with the sayings of Jesus. Paul clearly distinguishes between the teachings of Jesus and his own inspired instructions (1 Cor. 7:8, 10, 12, 25, 40). It is unlikely that the apostles and other eyewitnesses would have allowed such free creation by prophets claiming to speak for Jesus.

The Absence of Discussion on Key Issues in the Later Church. If the later church created words of Jesus to meet its present needs, why are there no sayings for many topics

3. See B. Gerhardsson, *The Reliability of the Gospel Tradition* (Peabody, MA: Hendrickson, 2001); *Memory and Manuscript: Oral Tradition and Written Transmission in Rabbinic Judaism and Early Christianity; with Tradition and Transmission in Early Christianity* (Grand Rapids: Eerdmans, 1998).

that were burning issues in the early church? There is nothing about circumcision and the charismatic gifts, and very little on baptism, the Gentile mission, food laws, and church-state relations.

The Ethical Argument: Were the Disciples Deceivers? But did the eyewitnesses tell the truth? As we saw in the last chapter, Reimarus argued that the disciples propagated a great fraud in order to keep the Jesus story alive. But it pushes the limits of credulity to argue that the same early Christians who taught the greatest ethical system in the world, passionately proclaimed the truth of their message, and suffered and died for their faith were at the same time dishonest schemers and propagators of a great fraud.

New Testament scholars have long recognized that in most cases we have not the exact words (*ipsissima verba*) of Jesus but rather his authentic voice (*ipsissima vox*).

These points indicate, at the least, the general reliability of the Gospel tradition. The church seems to have taken special care in accurately passing down the accounts of Jesus' words and deeds. This makes the presupposition of nonhistoricity inappropriate and places the burden of proof on those who would question the authenticity of particular Gospel stories and sayings.

CONTRADICTIONS BETWEEN THE GOSPELS?

With so much common material in the Gospels, it is not surprising that there are apparent contradictions between them. How do we account for these? In reality, most claims of contradictions result from demanding more historical precision than the Gospels intend to provide. The Gospels were never meant to be videotapes of events or word-for-word transcripts. It is the normal method of history writing—both ancient and modern—to summarize accounts, paraphrase speeches, omit extraneous details, and report events from a particular vantage point. Most supposed contradictions in the Gospels can be readily explained from common practices in history writing.

Paraphrasing and Interpretation

New Testament scholars have long recognized that in most cases we have not the *exact words* (***ipsissima verba***) of Jesus but rather his *authentic voice* (***ipsissima vox***). The essential meaning is communicated using different words. In one sense this is obvious, since Jesus normally spoke Aramaic but the Gospels are in Greek. Almost all of his words are translations, hence interpretations. (All translation involves interpretation, since a translator must determine what the Aramaic means in order to provide an equivalent word or phrase in Greek.) Many differences in wording or idiom may be attributed to differences in translation and style.

As authoritative interpreters, the Gospel writers sometimes move beyond simple translation or paraphrase to bring out the theological significance of Jesus' words. For example, Jesus' Beatitude in Luke "blessed are the poor" (Luke 6:20) becomes in Matthew "blessed are the poor in spirit" (Matt. 5:3). While it is possible that Matthew's phrase is original or that Jesus said both on different occasions, more likely Matthew is clarifying the spiritual significance of Jesus' words. Similarly, in Matthew 7:11 Jesus says, "How much more will your Father in heaven give *good gifts* to those who ask him!" In Luke, Jesus says "give *the*

Holy Spirit." Again, it is impossible to be certain which is original, or whether Jesus said both. But since the coming of the Holy Spirit is a leading theme in Luke-Acts, the author may be preparing for his later narrative by clarifying that the greatest thing which God gives is the Holy Spirit.

Another example is the centurion's statement from the foot of the cross. While in Matthew and Mark, the centurion says, "Surely this man was *the Son of God!*" (Mark 15:39; Matt. 27:54), in Luke he says, "Surely this was a *righteous* [or 'innocent'] man" (Luke 23:47). Both statements are important climaxes in their respective Gospels. Son of God is a key title for both Matthew and Mark, and Jesus' innocence is a major theme in Luke's passion narrative. The centurion may have said both, or Luke may be emphasizing that Jesus' status as Son of God means he is the innocent and righteous Servant of the LORD (Isa. 53:11). He would thus be citing not the exact words but the theological implication of the centurion's statement.

The point is that we cannot always be sure what is verbatim citation and what is the author's authoritative explanation. But to label these as errors or contradictions is to treat the Gospels as something they were never intended to be.

Abbreviation and Omission

The Gospel writers are clearly selective, omitting many extraneous details and including features important to their narrative purposes. Sometimes abbreviation or omission leaves readers with the impression of contradiction.

Matthew is famous for abbreviating accounts. While in Mark, Jesus curses the fig tree on one day and the disciples discover it withered the next, in Matthew the cursing and withering appear together, apparently on the second day (Mark 11:12–14, 20–25; Matt. 21:18–22). We may conclude that Matthew is interested not in providing a strict chronology but rather in emphasizing the fact of the miracle. Similarly, the raising of Jairus's daughter is greatly abbreviated in Matthew, leaving the incorrect impression that the daughter was already dead when Jairus first spoke with Jesus (Matt. 9:18–26; Mark 2:21–43; Luke 8:40–56).

> The Gospel writers are clearly selective, omitting many details and including features important for their narrative purposes.

A shortened version of events also appears in the healing of the centurion's servant. In Matthew, the centurion himself comes to Jesus, while in Luke he sends a group of Jewish elders (Matt. 8:5–13; Luke 7:1–10). What seems like a contradiction is simply an abbreviated way of speaking. If I left a message for our dean with his secretary, and someone later asked him, "Did Mark Strauss tell you so and so?" he would certainly say yes, even though I did not speak with him directly. The centurion spoke with Jesus through the elders. Something similar occurs when James and John request the chief seats in the kingdom (Matt. 20:20–21; Mark 10:35–37). While in Mark the request is their own, in Matthew it comes from their mother. Historically, the two brothers probably approached Jesus through their mother in order to sound less presumptuous. Mark, who portrays the disciples in a more negative light, does not mention the mother and so clarifies that this is *their* prideful request.

Another example of omission is when one Gospel speaks of two individuals while another reports only one. There are two demon-possessed men in Matthew 8:28 but only one in Mark 5:2, two blind men in Matthew 20:30 and one in Mark 10:46, two angels at the tomb in Luke 24:4 and one in Mark 16:5. While we must not simply gloss over these difficulties, two comments are in order. First, none of the writers insist there was only one individual. Mark may identify the main figure or spokesperson and ignore the other. Second, such a minor discrepancy is not enough to undermine the general reliability of the account. Indeed, it points to the credibility of the process of Gospel transmission that the church did not suppress such minor difficulties.

Reordering of Events and Sayings

As we have seen, the Gospel writers do not necessarily follow a chronological order and often rearrange events for topical or theological reasons. A classic example is the temptation account in Matthew and Luke, where the last two temptations are in reverse order (Matt. 4:1 – 11; Luke 4:1 – 13). It is difficult to tell which is original, since both climax at locations appropriate to their respective Gospels. Luke, who stresses the importance of Jerusalem and the temple, ends with Jesus on the pinnacle of the temple. Matthew, who portrays mountains as places of revelation, ends with Jesus on a high mountain surveying the kingdoms of the world. Whichever is original, the changed order does not negate the historicity of the event. Another important example of reordering is Luke's account of Jesus' Nazareth sermon, which Luke apparently moved forward from a later position in Mark to serve as an introduction to Jesus' ministry (Luke 4:16 – 30; Mark 6:1 – 6; Matt. 13:3 – 58).

Not only events but also sayings and sermons are sometimes arranged for topical or theological reasons. As we have seen, scholars debate whether Matthew's Sermon on the Mount was a single sermon delivered by Jesus or Matthew's compilation of Jesus' teaching.

Luke's temptation account climaxes in Jerusalem, while Matthew's climaxes on a high mountain, indicating each Evangelist's unique perspective.

The latter is suggested by the material which appears elsewhere in Luke. But of course Jesus may have taught the same or similar things on many occasions. (What preacher doesn't!) The point is that rearranging Jesus' teaching material does not nullify its historicity.

Reporting Similar Events and Sayings

Related to reordering is the question of similar events or sayings. Did Jesus clear the temple once or twice? While the Synoptic Gospels place the event at the end of Jesus' ministry (Matt. 21:12–13; Mark 11:15–17; Luke 19:45–46), John places it at the beginning (John 2:13–17). It is not far-fetched to think that after three years Jesus would have lashed out again at the marketplace atmosphere of the temple. The earlier event would have been long since forgotten, allowing Jesus to catch the temple authorities off guard. On the other hand, it was also within the Evangelists' authority to rearrange events to emphasize their significance. It is possible that Mark, followed by Luke and Matthew, moved this episode to the end of Jesus' ministry to make it a final pronouncement of judgment against Israel, or that John moved the event to the beginning to serve as an introduction to the Book of Signs (John 1:19–11:57).

In some cases, the episodes are different enough that they should be treated as separate events. The Gospels recount at least three callings of the disciples. John recounts that Andrew, a disciple of John the Baptist, brought his brother Simon to Jesus, who nicknamed him Cephas ("Peter"; John 1:35–42). Matthew and Mark narrate the call of the two sets of fishermen brothers—Andrew and Peter; James and John—beside the Sea of Galilee (Mark 1:16–20; Matt. 4:18–22). Finally, Luke describes Jesus' miraculous catch of fish, when Peter, James, and John drop everything to follow him (Luke 5:1–11). While these could be different versions of the same event, it is more likely that the disciples' decision to follow Jesus came gradually and in stages. Luke suggests as much by narrating the healing of Peter's mother-in-law before the account of the miraculous catch (Luke 4:38–39). The disciples obviously knew Jesus and his ministry prior to their decision to suspend their careers and follow him full time.

Another example of this phenomenon are three scenes in which Jesus is anointed with expensive perfume. Matthew and Mark describe the anointing of Jesus' head by a woman at the home of Simon the leper during the last week of his life (Matt. 26:6–13; Mark 14:3–9). A similar episode appears in John, six days before Passover, and the woman is identified as Mary the sister of Lazarus (John 12:1–8). While these are probably descriptions of the same event, Luke describes another anointing much earlier in Jesus' ministry (Luke 7:36–50). In this case, Jesus is dining with a Pharisee named Simon and the woman is a notorious sinner. While both anointings occur at the home of a man named Simon, this was a common name in first-century Palestine. Other details in the accounts are so different that we should probably think of two separate events. Jesus' respect toward women produced great loyalty and love, and anointing was a common sign of honor and hospitality. It is not far-fetched to propose that a similar event occurred on two different occasions.

This passage raises the difficult question of **doublets**. Doublets are two episodes, often in the same Gospel, which critics claim arose from the same story. Examples are the two feeding miracles, of the five thousand and of the four thousand (Mark 6:32–44; 8:1–10;

Matt. 14:13–21; 15:32–39), and Matthew's two separate accounts of the healing of two blind men (Matt. 9:27–31; 20:29–34). Have the Gospel writers mistakenly treated two versions of the same story as different historical events? Since Jesus often ministered to the multitudes (who were often hungry!) and since he healed many people, there is no reason to conclude that these accounts must have come from the same original. It is just as likely that Jesus fed the multitudes at least twice and on more than one occasion healed two or more blind men.

Certain parables are also treated as doublets: Matthew's parable of the marriage feast and Luke's parable of the great banquet (Matt. 22:1–14; Luke 14:16–24), and Matthew's parable of the talents and Luke's parable of the minas (Matt. 25:14–30; Luke 19:11–27). But again, these stories are different enough to be treated as distinct events. Jesus probably told similar stories and sayings on many occasions.

THE HISTORICAL RELIABILITY OF JOHN

While historical difficulties in the Synoptics generally relate to their similarities, in John the problem is the differences. How can this Gospel portray such a different perspective on the life of the same Jesus? Why are so many episodes unique and so much Synoptic material left out? Why does Jesus speak so differently? Some scholars find these questions so daunting they construct their portrait of the historical Jesus almost exclusively from the Synoptics. This is to a certain extent understandable, since John is admittedly a more interpretive Gospel and seems to operate on a different plane than the Synoptics. Yet over the last few decades, there has been an increased interest in and respect for the historicity of John.

> Over the last few decades, there has been an increased interest in and respect for the historicity of the Gospel of John.

The Author as Eyewitness

In chapter 10, we surveyed the compelling evidence that the traditions of the Fourth Gospel go back to the eyewitness testimony of the Beloved Disciple, and that this individual was most likely the apostle John. The author claims to be an eyewitness (1:14; 19:35; 21:24–25), provides many incidental details one would expect only from an eyewitness (2:6; 5:5; 18:10, 15–16; 21:11), is familiar with predestruction Jerusalem (5:3; 9:7; 10:23; 18:28; cf. 4:5–6), and knows the traditions and customs of Palestinian Judaism (2:6, 23; 6:4; 7:2, 37–39; 10:22; 19:14, 31). The Jewishness of the Gospel is confirmed by the use of Aramaic and Hebrew terms (1:38, 41–42; 4:25; 20:16), and parallels with the vocabulary and theological concepts of the Dead Sea Scrolls.

This concern for detail also appears in John's chronology, which indicates three Passovers and a ministry of approximately three years (2:13; 6:4; 11:55). Most scholars accept that this chronology is more precise than the Synoptics, which refer to only one Passover. It would be surprising if Jesus, as a faithful Jew, did not attend a number of Jewish festivals in Jerusalem. This should not be viewed as a contradiction of the Synoptics, since they provide little information concerning the length of Jesus' ministry and never say that Jesus' ministry lasted only one year. In fact, they imply at various points that Jesus was in Jerusalem on occasions prior to passion week (Matt. 23:37; Luke 13:34; Mark 6:3–6; 14:12–16; Luke 6:17; 10:38–42).

While it is uncertain whether John used the Synoptics as sources, the author was certainly aware of their traditions and may have intentionally supplemented them to address the concerns of his readers. This is suggested by John 20:30 and 21:25, where the author acknowledges that Jesus did much more than could be included in his work and that the episodes he has chosen were for the purpose of calling others to faith.

Alleged Contradictions with the Synoptics

Most of the alleged contradictions between John and the Synoptics are quite easily explained by recognizing that John, like the other Gospel writers, included, omitted, abbreviated, arranged, edited, and interpreted his material in such a way as to emphasize particular themes. This editing process means we have different and complementary presentations but not necessarily contradictory ones.

For example, John describes *Mary's* anointing of Jesus' *feet* with perfume *six days* before Passover (John 12:1–8), while Mark describes the anointing of his *head* by an *unnamed woman*, apparently *two days* before Passover (Mark 14:1–9; cf. Matt. 26:6–13).

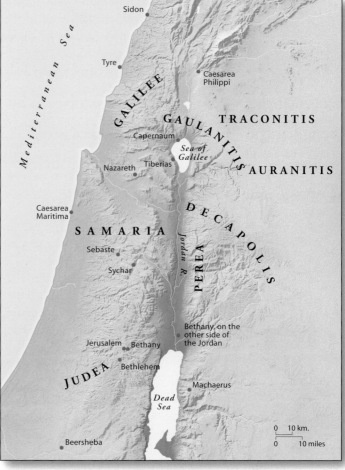

John reveals a detailed awareness of Palestinian geography and Jewish customs.

While we could propose two anointings (three counting Luke 7:36–50), the better conclusion is that Mark has rearranged the chronology for theological reasons, to place the episode beside the plot against Jesus in Mark 14:1–2. As the religious leaders wickedly plot Jesus' death, a faithful follower reverently prepares his body for burial. The two days before Passover would then be a reference to the plot against Jesus, not the anointing. The other differences are insignificant. Mark never refers to this Mary (the sister of Martha) elsewhere, and so her name is not important for him here. The anointing of both feet and head would have been a common practice. Mark seems to allow for this when he refers to the anointing of Jesus' "body" for burial (Mark 14:8).

While most differences may be explained by the author's minor editing, others seem to be more obvious contradictions. While the Synoptics identify the Last Supper as a Passover meal (Mark 14:16, par.), John seems to treat it as an ordinary meal before Passover (John 13:2; 18:28). This, it is argued, is so that John can portray Jesus as the Lamb of God crucified on the eve of Passover, precisely when the Passover lambs were sacrificed in Jerusalem ("the day of preparation of Passover Week," John 19:14, 31, 42). While Jesus certainly dies as the Passover lamb in John (John 1:29, 36), there is no necessary contradiction with the Synoptics. Some scholars resolve the difficulty by pointing to evidence that the Passover was celebrated on different days by different groups of Jews, Galileans and Judeans, or Sadducees and Pharisees. Another possibility is that the Greek phrase *paraskeuētou pascha* ("preparation for Passover") used in John means not the preparation day for the Passover meal but the preparation day for the Sabbath of Passover week (that is, Friday). This is the most common meaning for the word *paraskeuē* (see Mark 15:42). In this case, in both John and the Synoptics, Jesus eats the Passover meal on Thursday evening (the beginning of Passover, which continues until Friday afternoon) and was crucified on Friday, the day of Passover and the eve of the Sabbath of Passover week. While none of these options is without some difficulties, each presents a plausible solution.[4]

> Most of the alleged contradictions between John and the Synoptics are quite easily explained by recognizing that John, like the other Gospel writers, . . . interpreted his material in such a way as to emphasize particular themes.

Other examples could be cited, but these are sufficient to show that most apparent contradictions have reasonable explanations when the Evangelists are given appropriate freedom to tell their stories and are unshackled from unreasonable expectations for historical precision.

John's Style and the Words of Jesus

But what about Jesus' unique style of speaking in John? As we noted in chapter 10, it is often difficult to tell when Jesus stops speaking and the narrator begins. Did the author compose these discourses and place them on the lips of Jesus?

It is certainly true that John is the most interpretive of the Gospels and that the author feels free to explain and elaborate on Jesus' words. Yet it is going beyond the evidence to claim that the discourses are fiction. First, we have to remember that the author may use his own style, rather than Jesus' exact words, to provide Jesus' essential message. Since John is not literarily dependant on the Synoptics, his translation of Jesus' Aramaic teachings would naturally reflect his own style. Second, Jesus tells the disciples that the Spirit would guide them in remembering and understanding his words (John 14:25–26; 15:26–27; 16:14). John's Gospel may at times reflect this Spirit-inspired interpretation.

But third, we must not overstate the differences between Jesus' speech in the Synoptics and in John. A striking passage in Matthew 11:25–27 (cf. Luke 10:21–22) confirms that Jesus did speak in the manner represented in John:

> At that time Jesus said, "I praise you, Father, Lord of heaven and earth, because you have hidden these things from the wise and learned, and revealed them to little children. Yes, Father, for this was your good pleasure. All things have been committed to me by my

---

4. For further details, see Craig Blomberg, *The Historical Reliability of the Gospels* (Downers Grove, IL: InterVarsity, 1987), 175–78.

Father. No one knows the Son except the Father, and no one knows the Father except the Son and those to whom the Son chooses to reveal him."

These words recall passages like John 3:35; 7:29; 10:14–15; 13:3; 17:2, 25. Similarly, in Mark 9:37, Jesus says "whoever welcomes me does not welcome me but *the one who sent me*" (cf. Luke 9:48; 10:16; Matt. 10:40). The language echoes John 12:44 and 13:20, and the phrase "the one who sent me" occurs twenty-three times in John. These passages indicate that John's style may not be imposed on Jesus so much as influenced by the way Jesus actually spoke.

The Christology of John

Finally, we must deal with the exalted Christology of John's Gospel. How do we account for John's explicit affirmations of Jesus' deity (John 1:1; 20:28) when the Synoptics are so much more reserved in this regard? Again, these differences should not be overstated. There is little in John which cannot be found implicitly in the Synoptics, where Jesus exercises the attributes of God: forgiving sins (Mark 2:5, par.), reading minds (Mark 2:8, par.; Matt. 12:25), and receiving worship (Matt. 2:11; 14:33; 28:9, 17; Luke 24:52). He is the judge of all humanity, determining people's eternal destiny (Matt. 7:21–23; 25:31–46). Following the resurrection, he mediates the Holy Spirit—the presence of God—to his people (Luke 24:49; Acts 1:5, 8; 2:33) and promises his divine presence among them (Matt. 18:20; 28:20; Acts 16:7).

Nor can it be said that the Synoptic emphasis on Jesus' messiahship is absent in John. As in the Synoptics, Jesus is the Messiah (John 1:41; 4:25), the king of Israel (John 1:49; 12:13), and the fulfillment of Old Testament prophecies. As in the Synoptics, he is wholly dependent on the Father and committed to doing his will (John 5:19, 30; 6:38; 8:28; Mark 14:36, par.).

Although Jesus speaks more readily about himself in John than in the Synoptics, this, too, must not be overdrawn. Jesus still speaks with reserve, using symbolism and metaphor. His "I am" statements are often misunderstood by his hearers (John 6:42, 52; 10:19–20; 14:5, 8). The people and the religious leaders express confusion and wonder about his identity (John 5:12; 6:14; 7:5, 12, 15, 25, 27, 31, 35, 40–44; 8:25, 48, 52; 10:25; 12:34). John stresses that the disciples did not understand many aspects of Jesus' teaching until after the resurrection (John 2:22; 12:16). This is not much different from the Synoptics, in which speculation surrounds Jesus' identity (Mark 8:28, par.; Luke 9:9; Mark 14:61, par.; 15:2, par.). In both John and the Synoptics, there is a defining moment in Jesus' ministry when the disciples recognize him as Messiah and commit to follow him (Mark 8:29; Matt. 16:16; Luke 9:20; John 6:68–69).

CONCLUSION: THE GOSPELS AS HISTORY *AND* THEOLOGY

Much of the rejection of the historicity of the Gospels arose from the recognition that these are documents written for a theological purpose. Beginning with the work of William Wrede, the Gospels were viewed as first and foremost theological works intended to promote the perspective of the author and his community.

In our study of each of the four Gospels, we have emphasized this theological dimension. Yet it is unjustified to assume that theological documents cannot also be historical ones. While the Gospels arose in the context of the needs and concerns of the early church communities and were written to address those needs, the writers also believed that the good news of Jesus Christ was firmly grounded in history. The evidence suggests that the Gospel writers were passionate about preserving the words and deeds of Jesus and that their historical reliability was an essential part of their theological significance. A close examination reveals that good history can also be good theology.

» CHAPTER SUMMARY «

1. While no one reads the Gospels without presuppositions, this does not mean all truth is relative. Historical events can be judged by carefully weighing the evidence.

2. The fact that the Gospel writers have strong faith commitments does not negate the historical reliability of their Gospels. All historians have a worldview and a belief system which motivates their writing.

3. Luke's skill as a historian has been demonstrated especially in Acts, where he is a meticulous researcher with reference to names, places, and titles. Luke also demonstrates a keen sense of the Zeitgeist, or "spirit of the times," in which he writes.

4. Evidence for the general reliability of the Gospel tradition includes (a) the value given to eyewitness testimony, (b) the pattern of careful oral transmission in Palestinian Judaism, (c) the church's willingness to preserve difficult sayings, (d) the distinction made between the words of Jesus and of Christian prophets, (e) the absence of created sayings on issues of later concern to the church, and (f) the high ethical standards of the disciples.

5. Apparent contradictions in the Gospels often disappear when it is recognized that the Evangelists were not producing verbatim accounts but had the freedom to paraphrase, interpret, abbreviate, and reorder events and sayings to fit their theological purposes. They were not just reporters but inspired interpreters of the Jesus event.

6. Though the reliability of John's Gospel has been questioned even more than the Synoptics, recent research has produced greater respect for its historicity.

7. Jesus' unique style of speaking in John is not as different from the Synoptics as is sometimes supposed and may be explained by a combination of John's paraphrase of Jesus' teaching and his Spirit-inspired interpretation of Jesus' words.

8. John's high Christology is not as unique as is sometimes supposed. The Synoptics also reveal an implicit high Christology, while John shares with them an emphasis on Jesus' messiahship and the mystery which surrounds his identity.

9. It is a false dichotomy to contrast the historical and theological features of the Gospels. Good history can also be good theology.

burden of proof

Zeitgeist ("spirit of the times")

ipsissima verba ("exact words")

ipsissima vox ("authentic voice")

doublets

1. Is it possible to write or read history without being influenced by presuppositions and a world-view?

2. Do the faith commitments of the Gospel writers negate their claim to write accurate history? Why or why not?

3. What do we mean by the "burden of proof" in Gospel studies? On whom does the burden lie?

4. What is some of the evidence that Luke was an accurate historian?

5. What is the evidence for a generally reliable Gospel tradition?

6. How might we explain some of the apparent contradictions among the Gospels?

7. What is the evidence for the historical reliability of John?

8. How do we explain the different way Jesus speaks in John's Gospel?

9. Can good theology also be good history? Explain.

Digging Deeper

General Reliability of the Gospels

Barnett, Paul. *Is the New Testament Reliable?* 2nd ed. Downers Grove, IL: Intervarsity, 2005.

Blomberg, Craig. *The Historical Reliability of the Gospels.* Downers Grove, IL: InterVarsity, 1987.

Bruce, F. F. *The New Testament Documents: Are They Reliable?* 6th ed. Downers Grove, IL: InterVarsity, 1981.

Gerhardsson, Birger. *The Reliability of the Gospel Tradition.* Peabody, MA: Hendrickson, 2001.

Marshall, I. H. *I Believe in the Historical Jesus.* Grand Rapids: Eerdmans, 1977.

Thomas, Robert L., and Stanley N. Gundry. *A Harmony of the Gospels with Explanations and Essays: Using the New American Standard Bible.* San Francisco: HarperSanFrancisco, 1986.

Wilkins, Michael J., and J. P. Moreland, eds. *Jesus Under Fire.* Grand Rapids: Zondervan, 1995.

Historical Sources for Jesus

Dunn, James D. G. *The Evidence for Jesus.* Philadelphia: Westminster, 1985.

France, R. T. *The Evidence for Jesus.* London: Hodder and Stoughton, 1986.

Difficult Sayings of Jesus

Bruce, F. F. *Hard Sayings of Jesus.* Downers Grove, IL: InterVarsity, 1983.

Stein, Robert H. *Difficult Passages in the Gospels.* Grand Rapids: Baker, 1984.

Historicity of Luke-Acts

Hemer, C. J. *The Book of Acts in the Setting of Hellenistic History.* Edited by C. H. Gempf. WUNT 2.49. Tübingen: Mohr, 1989.

Hengel, Martin. *Acts and the History of Earliest Christianity.* Philadelphia: Fortress, 1979.

Mosley, A. W. "Historical Reporting in the Ancient World." *NTS* 12 (1965–66): 10–26.

Historicity of John

Blomberg, Craig. *The Historical Reliability of John's Gospel: Issues and Commentary.* Downers Grove, IL: InterVarsity, 2001.

Dodd, C. H. *Historical Tradition in the Fourth Gospel.* Cambridge: Cambridge Univ. Press, 1963.

Robinson, John A. T. *The Priority of John.* Edited by J. F. Coakley. London: SCM, 1985.

CHAPTER 13

The Contours and Chronology of Jesus' Ministry

» CHAPTER OVERVIEW «

1. Basic Contours of Jesus' Ministry
2. A Chronology of Jesus' Life

» OBJECTIVES «

After reading this chapter, you should be able to:
- Summarize the key events in Jesus' ministry (agreed on by most scholars).
- Identify the likely chronology of Jesus' birth and public ministry.

BASIC CONTOURS OF JESUS' MINISTRY

What can we know about the historical Jesus? Chapter 11 indicated the bewildering array of interpretations scholars have given to Jesus. While these differences are great, there are a number of core features about Jesus' life and ministry on which almost everyone would agree. To explore these, let us imagine a resident of Palestine two thousand years ago. We will call him Simeon, a Jewish merchant of moderate means living in Galilee in the early decades of the first century. Simeon might appear in our Gospels as an occasional member of the crowd who sees Jesus from afar and wonders about his identity and fate. What would he have known about Jesus of Nazareth?[1]

A Portrait of Jesus from Afar

First, Simeon would certainly have heard about the movement surrounding the man called John "the Baptizer." John, a fierce-eyed prophet dressed in a camel-hair cloak and a leather belt reminiscent of the prophet Elijah's, emerged from the Judean desert to begin an itinerant preaching ministry along the Jordan River. He called people to repent of their sins and to prepare for God's coming judgment, a fiery ordeal which would purge Israel of sinners and establish God's just and righteous rule. John was much like the prophets of the Hebrew Scriptures, a lone figure warning God's people to submit to God's rule or face judgment. They must turn from wickedness and live lives of righteousness and social justice, providing for those in need. The common people of the land, hungry for hope of relief from their poverty and oppression, flocked to the

The Judean desert, site of John the Baptist's ministry

desert by the hundreds—perhaps even the thousands—to hear John's powerful preaching and to heed his call for baptism. This baptism, or dunking, in the Jordan River was a symbol of God's cleansing of their hearts, and their identification with God's kingdom. Simeon may have even journeyed to the desert himself to see this remarkable man and hear his provocative message.

John the Baptist's actions were viewed with suspicion by both the political authorities and the religious leaders in Israel. The former were wary that his preaching could provoke a popular revolt. The latter feared that such a revolt would bring the Roman legions and spell disaster for the temple and their religious authority. Simeon may have wondered whether John's ministry was ultimately a good thing or a bad thing. He despised the Roman authorities—especially their crushing taxes—and longed for a return to the glorious days

---

1. My inspiration for this method is Gerd Theissen's fascinating historical novel *The Shadow of the Galilean: The Quest of the Historical Jesus in Narrative Form* (Philadelphia: Fortress, 1987).

of the kingdoms of David and Solomon, or even of the limited independence achieved by the Maccabean freedom fighters. He knew that the prophets had spoken of a time when Israel would once again live with secure borders in peace and independence, and when God's justice would be the rule of the land. But he also feared the horrific consequences of war. Too often in the past, "prophets" and "messiahs" had arisen with bold claims of deliverance, only to be rejected by the religious authorities and crushed by the might of Rome.

Simeon would have first heard about Jesus from reports of his teaching and healing in the towns and villages around Galilee. He knew that there was some connection between Jesus and John, but the exact relationship was unclear. Some said Jesus had been one of John's disciples. At the very least, Jesus affirmed John's mission by submitting to his baptism. Though not a formally trained rabbi, Jesus was called Rabbi by the people because of his exceptional teaching gifts. He taught differently than other Jewish teachers and scribes, who generally repeated the traditions passed on by the elders. Jesus instead preached with unique personal authority, often invoking the phrase "In truth [amēn] I say to you ..." His central message concerned the coming of God's kingdom and the need for people to repent of their sins and submit to God's rule. His message was not unlike John's, though apparently with less fire and brimstone. It also had a stronger ethical dimension. Like John, he spoke of a radical transformation which the kingdom of God would bring, but this transformation was less about apocalyptic judgment and more about a radical new orientation toward God and others. The essence of the law, Jesus said, was love for God and love for one's neighbor. Unlike the Zealots, he spoke of loving not just friends but even enemies, doing good to those who persecute you, and turning the other cheek instead of lashing back in revenge. Such an attitude did not win him friends among the revolutionaries set on overthrowing the Roman authorities. Jesus also spoke to God as his father and encouraged his followers to do the same.

Jesus' early ministry centered on the villages and towns around Galilee.

Simeon heard Jesus speak on several occasions and found his words inspiring and fascinating but also perplexing and disturbing. Some of it he did not understand, since Jesus often spoke in enigmatic parables. Simeon once heard him speak of the kingdom as a very small seed which would grow into a large plant. Another time, Jesus described the kingdom as a pearl for which one should sell everything to possess. This sounded good to Simeon, although he was not sure what it meant.

Jesus had also gained a reputation as a healer and an exorcist. People began bringing their sick to him from all over Galilee to be healed and to have demons cast out. Simeon himself saw one such exorcism. A young man was brought before Jesus screaming and writhing on the ground. Jesus took hold of him and commanded the evil spirit to come out. Immediately the man calmed down and his parents took him home in peace. Simeon

Traditional site of Jesus' Sermon on the Mount. The sea of Galilee is in the background.

marveled at the rabbi's healing touch. There were many similar reports of healings, and a rumor circulated that Jesus had actually raised a young girl from the dead. Simeon was unsure about such reports but recognized that Jesus was a powerful teacher, healer, and exorcist—certainly a prophet sent from God. Some other reports he found incredible, such as the claim that Jesus fed huge numbers of people in the desert with only meager rations. The story reminded Simeon of Israel's manna in the wilderness and of Isaiah's prophecies of a great messianic banquet. Simeon wondered whether perhaps Jesus was producing parables with his actions as well as his words.

Jesus' behavior raised questions about his identity, and there was no shortage of opinions. After John the Baptist was arrested by Herod Antipas and executed as a political threat, some said that Jesus was actually John risen from the dead. More sober minds called him a great prophet, perhaps even Elijah, whom the prophet Malachi said would return before the day of final judgment. Others wondered whether he might be the Son of David, who would restore the glories of the United Kingdom of Israel. This last seemed unlikely to Simeon, since Jesus did not appear to be a David-like military ruler, leading Israel's armies to victory.

While Jesus had many followers, he chose a small group of twelve to be his special disciples. That number was surely significant, Simeon thought. It must mean that Jesus viewed his followers as representative of the righteous remnant of Israel and that his goal was the reformation of Israel.

Yet if Jesus was to restore Israel, he did not seem to have the political clout or religious influence to do so. In fact, he made even more enemies than John the Baptist. Though generally avoiding conflict with political authorities, Jesus' teaching and actions antagonized the religious leaders, especially the Pharisees and scribes whose spheres of influence overlapped with his own. He publicly criticized them for their hypocrisy and warned them of coming judgment. He also took a casual attitude to the law, which they so carefully observed. He apparently healed people and allowed his disciples to pick grain on the Sabbath day, when work was forbidden. He also ignored the Pharisees' strict rules concerning ceremonial cleansing, not requiring his disciples to wash their hands in the prescribed manner before meals. Worst of all, he practiced table fellowship with sinners, tax collectors, and various other riffraff. While such behavior was to be expected of commoners—the uncouth people of the land—Jesus' reputation as a rabbi made his behavior scandalous among the religious leaders.

While Simeon admired many Pharisees for their piety and spiritual devotion, he had also seen their pride and hypocrisy. Like others in positions of power, the Pharisees loved the honor they were shown in the marketplace and jockeyed for the best seats at banquets. Simeon admired Jesus' courage for challenging their ostentation but thought it reckless to make enemies of those he might someday need. Mediterranean culture was one of reciprocity, in which a favor given was eventually returned, and yet Jesus seemed constantly to be burning his bridges.

Unlike John the Baptist, Jesus was not an ascetic. He did not encourage his disciples to fast and seemed to enjoy a good party. Some Pharisees even called him a drunkard, but these accusations seemed groundless to Simeon. Everything he had heard about Jesus pointed to a man of personal conviction and integrity, even if he was an enigma in many other respects.

Though Jesus visited Jerusalem periodically for the Jewish festivals, he seemed to give special significance to the last Passover of his life. In fact, some said he brought the crisis onto himself by intentionally provoking the authorities. First, he created a disturbance with his arrival, approaching Jerusalem riding a donkey, descending from the Mount of Olives with his followers accompanying him. Some regarded this as an enactment of Zechariah's prophecy, with Jesus portraying himself as the peace-loving, Solomon-like king who enters Jerusalem in a regal procession, bringing peace. Those who knew the Scriptures could not help but wonder whether Jesus was making a claim to be the Son of David, the Anointed One.

Map of Israel showing location of Galilee, Samaria, and Judea.

What Jesus did next was even more disturbing. Claims had been made that Jesus predicted the destruction of the temple (and even that he himself would destroy it!). Now Jesus entered the temple and drove some money changers from the premises with a whip. Though the incident was relatively minor, it seemed to some an act of occupation, or even of symbolic judgment. Such desecration and defiance of the authorities could hardly be ignored, and the high priest and his advisors decided they must act. Learning of Jesus' whereabouts by bribing one of his disciples (a certain Judas), they arrested Jesus on the eve of Passover and brought him before the Sanhedrin for questioning. What Jesus confessed to during this trial is uncertain, but charges of blasphemy, temple desecration, and leading the people astray were certainly made. The Sanhedrin next delivered Jesus to the Roman governor Pilate, where a charge of sedition—claiming to be a king in opposition to Caesar—was brought forward. Pilate, a pragmatic and unscrupulous leader always quick to enforce Roman "justice" and prevent revolt, had Jesus flogged and then crucified. A *titulus* was placed over Jesus' cross identifying him (ironically) as the "King of the Jews."

Simeon was deeply grieved when he heard of these events. While unconvinced that Jesus was a savior who would bring freedom to his people, he had hoped that this reform movement might come to something. Unfortunately, Jesus suffered the horrific fate of so many before him who had challenged the powers that be.

The crucifixion of Jesus would have been the end of the matter, except that after his death, Jesus' followers began announcing that they had seen him alive, risen from the dead. They proclaimed that Jesus was the Messiah, God's anointed one, and that his resurrection was vindication by God of his messianic status. The movement which he had begun did not die but grew and flourished in the years which followed. While a relatively small number of Jews came to believe that Jesus was the Messiah, the movement soon spread to the Gentile world, where it gained large numbers of adherents across the Mediterranean region.

The General Progress of Jesus' Ministry

By viewing Jesus' ministry from a distance through the eyes of our imaginary character, Simeon, we have drawn a minimalist portrait of the Gospel story which most scholars would affirm. These basic parameters of Jesus' ministry are reflected in summaries of the Jesus story in the book of Acts:

> You know what has happened throughout Judea, beginning in Galilee after the baptism that John preached—how God anointed Jesus of Nazareth with the Holy Spirit and power, and how he went around doing good and healing all who were under the power of the devil, because God was with him.
>
> We are witnesses of everything he did in the country of the Jews and in Jerusalem. They killed him by hanging him on a tree, but God raised him from the dead on the third day and caused him to be seen. He was not seen by all the people, but by witnesses whom God had already chosen—by us who ate and drank with him after he rose from the dead.
>
> —Acts 10:37–40 (cf. 2:22–24; 3:13–15; 13:24–31)

Notice the following core elements:

- The preaching of John the Baptist
- The baptism of Jesus and the beginning of his ministry
- Galilean ministry of healing and exorcism
- Judean ministry climaxing in Jerusalem and conflict with the religious leaders

- Crucifixion: Arrest and execution in Jerusalem
- Resurrection appearances

Of course, the problems come when we try to fill in the gaps, raising questions like, How did Jesus view his own life and mission? Did he identify himself as a prophet, a messiah, the Son of God? Did he consider himself divine? If so, what did he mean by this? What did Jesus mean by the "kingdom of God," and how did he view his relationship to it? (Announcer? Inaugurator? The king himself?) Did Jesus perform miracles? His contemporaries certainly viewed him as a healer and an exorcist, but what was the nature of these actions? Were they supernatural cures or something else? Did Jesus perform "nature miracles" like feeding the multitudes and calming the sea? Concerning his death, did Jesus intentionally provoke his own crucifixion? If so, how did he view his death? As a martyr? As an attempt to bring in the kingdom of God? As a sacrifice for sins? Finally, what happened after Jesus' death? What was the nature and significance of the resurrection appearances? What did his disciples believe about their resurrected Lord? These questions and more represent the fundamental debate concerning the historical Jesus. In the chapters that follow, we will try to answer them.

A CHRONOLOGY OF JESUS' LIFE

The Date of Jesus' Birth

According to both Matthew and Luke, Jesus was born during the reign of Herod the Great (Matt. 2:1; Luke 1:5). The Jewish historian Josephus confirms that Herod died in the thirty-fourth year of his reign, the equivalent of 4 BC on our calendar (the year 750 on the Roman calendar).[2] This means that our calendar, which was developed by the sixth-century monk Dionysius Exiguus, has the birth of Jesus miscalculated by at least four years. Most scholars place Jesus' birth sometime between 7 and 4 BC. There is little other evidence to establish a more precise date. The census to which Luke refers cannot be dated with certainty (Luke 2:1; see chap. 14 for details), and we do not know how long Joseph and Mary were in Egypt before Herod died (Matt. 2:14–15). Attempts have also been made to identify the star of Bethlehem with a particular astral phenomenon. As early as 1606, the astronomer Johannes Kepler suggested that the star may have been a nova or supernova, the explosion of a star. There are records of such a nova seen by Chinese astronomers in 5 or 4 BC.[3] Kepler also noted a conjunction of the planets Jupiter and Saturn, which occurred in the constellation Pisces in the year 7 BC. This latter event is intriguing since Pisces was sometimes associated with the Hebrews and with the end times, Saturn with the Syria-Palestinian region, and Jupiter with a world ruler.[4] This could explain

> Most scholars place Jesus' birth near the end of Herod the Great's reign, sometime between 7 and 4 BC.

Coin of Caesar Augustus, Roman emperor at the time of Jesus' birth.

Z. Radovan, Jerusalem

---

2. Josephus, *Ant.* 17.8.1 §191; *J.W.* 1.33.8 §167.
3. R. T. France, "Scripture, Tradition and History in the Infancy Narratives of Matthew," *Gospel Perspectives* (Eugene, OR: Wipf and Stock, 2003), 2:243.
4. Raymond E. Brown, *The Birth of the Messiah* (New York: Doubleday, 1977), 171–73.

Johannes Kepler suggested that the star of Bethlehem may have been a nova or supernova, the explosion of a star.

why the magi came to Israel looking for a king. But all of these proposals remain speculative and hypothetical, and the star could have been any number of natural or supernatural phenomena.

The month, or even the season, of Jesus' birth is also uncertain. The traditional date of the Western church is December 25th, and in some eastern churches January 6th. The former seems to have arisen in the time of Constantine (AD 306 – 337), perhaps to replace the pagan feast of Saturnalia. The only clue from the text is Luke's reference to shepherds living outside (Luke 2:8), which would normally occur during the warmer months, perhaps March through November. On the other hand, there is some rabbinic evidence for year-round grazing, so a December date is not impossible (*m. Šeqal.* 7:4).

The Date of Jesus' Ministry

While Jesus' ministry began sometime around AD 30, the precise year is uncertain. Luke says that the ministry of John the Baptist began in the fifteenth year of Tiberius Caesar (Luke 3:1). Tiberius became emperor in AD 14, at the death of his stepfather, Augustus, and reigned until AD 37. John's ministry would then have begun about AD 29 and Jesus' shortly after, perhaps AD 30. A difficulty arises, however, since Tiberius became co-regent

	Figure 13.1—Chronology in John's Gospel	
2:13	"When it was almost time for the Jewish Passover, Jesus went up to Jerusalem."	First Passover, spring AD 27 (or 30)
4:35	"Do you not say, 'Four months more and then the harvest'? I tell you, open your eyes and look at the fields! They are ripe for harvest."	If a literal reference, could be late AD 27 or early 28 (or AD 30 – 31). The barley harvest was in March, the wheat in April-May.
5:1	"Some time later, Jesus went up to Jerusalem for a feast of the Jews."	An unnamed feast, perhaps Tabernacles in fall of AD 28 (or AD 31)
6:4	"The Jewish Passover Feast was near."	Third Passover (second named), spring AD 29 (or AD 32). Jesus remains in Galilee.
7:2	"But when the Jewish Feast of Tabernacles was near …"	Tabernacles, fall AD 29 (or AD 32)
10:22	"Then came the Feast of Dedication at Jerusalem. It was winter."	Hanukkah, winter AD 29 (or AD 32)
11:55	"When it was almost time for the Jewish Passover, many went up from the country to Jerusalem for their ceremonial cleansing before the Passover."	Final Passover, spring AD 30 (or 33)

Part Four:
The Historical Jesus

Figure 13.2—Possible Chronology of Jesus' Ministry

Following early dates (AD 27 – 30) and four Passovers (add three years for later dates [AD 30 – 33])

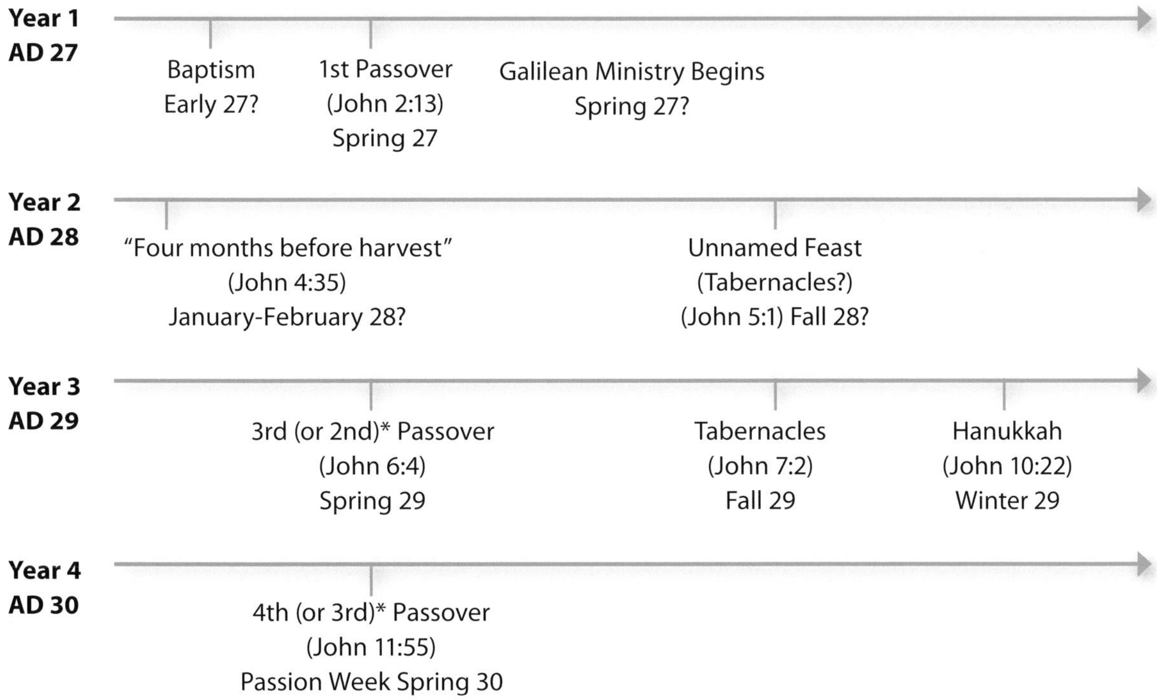

Year 1
AD 27

Baptism
Early 27?

1st Passover
(John 2:13)
Spring 27

Galilean Ministry Begins
Spring 27?

Year 2
AD 28

"Four months before harvest"
(John 4:35)
January-February 28?

Unnamed Feast
(Tabernacles?)
(John 5:1) Fall 28?

Year 3
AD 29

3rd (or 2nd)* Passover
(John 6:4)
Spring 29

Tabernacles
(John 7:2)
Fall 29

Hanukkah
(John 10:22)
Winter 29

Year 4
AD 30

4th (or 3rd)* Passover
(John 11:55)
Passion Week Spring 30

*Jesus' ministry would be reduced by one year (from AD 28 – 30) if the reference in John 4:35 is merely proverbial and if the unnamed feast of John 5:1 occurred in the fall or winter of the first year, rather than the second.

with Augustus in AD 11 or 12. Following this earlier date, Jesus' ministry may have begun around AD 26 or 27. Possible support for this earlier date comes from John 2:20, where on Jesus' first Passover visit to Jerusalem, the Jews claim that "it has taken forty-six years to build this temple." According to Josephus, Herod began rebuilding the temple in the eighteenth year of his reign (*Ant.* 15.11.1), about 20 or 19 BC. Forty-six years from this comes to about AD 27 or 28 (there is no year zero).

Luke identifies Jesus' age at the beginning of his ministry as "about thirty years old" (3:23), an approximation which would fit either earlier or later dates. If Jesus was born between 7 and 4 BC, he would have been from 33 – 36 years old in AD 30, or 30 – 33 years old in AD 27. While either date works, a slight edge may be given to the latter, with a public ministry beginning about AD 27.

The length of Jesus' ministry is also uncertain. As we have seen, the Synoptic Gospels mention only one Passover, but John refers to three (John 2:13; 6:4; 11:55). This would make the length of Jesus' ministry between 2½ and 3½ years (see figs. 13.1 and 13.2). We must be cautious here, however, since John's chronology may not be precise. If John moved

Tiberius Caesar, Roman emperor during Jesus' public ministry

the cleansing of the temple from the end of Jesus' ministry to the beginning, the Passover mentioned there would be an anachronistic reference to Jesus' last Passover. This would produce a ministry of 1½ to 2½ years. Since we have favored two separate temple clearings, we will follow the longer chronology.

The Date of Jesus' Crucifixion

The Gospels suggest that Jesus ate the Last Supper with his disciples on Thursday evening of Passover week and was crucified on Friday. He was buried shortly before the Sabbath on Friday evening. The actual date of the crucifixion is more difficult to determine and depends on our conclusion concerning the day Passover occurred in that year. This in turn is complicated by the differences between the Synoptics and John, which seem to present Jesus and the religious leaders celebrating Passover on different days (Thursday evening or Friday evening respectively; see chap. 12, pp. 393–94, for possible solutions).

Passover takes place on the fifteenth of Nisan (March-April). Since the Jewish day begins at dusk, Passover begins in the evening of Nisan 14 with the Passover meal and concludes the next afternoon, Nisan 15. The issue is still more complicated since Jews figured their calendar with reference to the new moon, which was not always a precise reading. Astronomers have concluded that Passover (Nisan 14–15) probably came on Friday in both AD 30 and 33. This again makes both the early and late dates for Jesus' ministry possible. The earlier date has Jesus' ministry beginning in AD 26 or 27 and his crucifixion at Passover of AD 30. The later date has the ministry beginning in AD 29 or 30 and the crucifixion in AD 33.

» CHAPTER SUMMARY «

1. Core features of Jesus' ministry (agreed on by almost everyone) include the prophetic ministry of John the Baptist, the baptism of Jesus by John, Jesus' preaching about the kingdom of God and healing ministry in Galilee, growing opposition by Jewish religious authorities, Jerusalem ministry during which there was an incident in the temple, arrest by Jewish and/or Roman authorities, trial of some sort by Jewish and Roman authorities, execution by the Romans ordered by Pontius Pilate, followed by reports of his resurrection by his disciples.

2. Jesus was born sometime between 7 and 4 BC during the reign of Herod the Great.

3. Jesus' public ministry probably occurred either from AD 27 to 30 or AD 30 to 33. Both dates have supporting evidence, though the earlier one is perhaps more likely.

4. Jesus was likely crucified on Friday, Nisan 15 (Passover), in either AD 30 or 33.

1. Identify the key features of Jesus' ministry which are agreed on by almost everyone.

2. Between what years was Jesus born? Who was reigning in Israel at the time?

3. About how old was Jesus when his public ministry began? How do we know this?

4. What are the most likely dates for Jesus' public ministry and for his crucifixion? During what Jewish festival was Jesus crucified?

Digging Deeper

Making Sense of the Historical Jesus

See bibliography in chapter 11.

Chronological Questions

Brown, Raymond E. *The Birth of the Messiah.* Updated ed. New York: Doubleday, 1993.

Caird, George B. "Chronology of the NT," in *Interpreter's Dictionary of the Bible*, 1:599–607. New York: Abingdon, 1962, 1:599–607.

Donfried, Karl P. "Chronology," in *Anchor Bible Dictionary*. New York: Doubleday, 1992, 1:1012–16.

Finegan, Jack. *Handbook of Biblical Chronology.* Rev. ed. Peabody, MA: Hendrickson, 1998.

Hoehner, Harold W. *Chronological Aspects of the Life of Christ.* Grand Rapids: Zondervan, 1977.

CHAPTER 14

Jesus' Birth and Childhood

» CHAPTER OVERVIEW «

1. The Genre of the Birth Narratives: History or Fiction?
2. The Ancestry of Jesus
3. The Virginal Conception
4. Bethlehem Birthplace
5. The Census
6. The Birth of Jesus
7. Jesus' Family Life

» OBJECTIVES «

After reading this chapter, you should be able to:

- Describe the nature of the birth narratives as either midrash or historical narrative.
- Note key differences between the genealogies of Matthew and Luke and the possible reasons for these differences.
- Summarize the historical evidence for events surrounding Jesus' birth, including the virginal conception, the census, the Bethlehem birth, and the visit of the magi.
- Describe Jesus' family life in terms of parents' social status, siblings, occupational and religious training, and languages spoken.

THE GENRE OF THE BIRTH NARRATIVES: HISTORY OR FICTION?

The **birth narratives** of Matthew and Luke are sometimes left out of the discussion of the historical Jesus because of skepticism concerning their historicity. Are these later legends created by Christians, or are they reliable traditions? Some have argued that the birth stories are to be identified with the Jewish interpretive procedure known as **midrash** (a Hebrew term meaning "inquiry" or "commentary"). While midrash may refer broadly to rabbinic-style interpretation of the biblical text, it is used here more specifically of fictional expansions on the Old Testament narrative. Yet while Matthew and Luke clearly utilize Old Testament themes and motifs and have theological goals in crafting their narratives, there is no evidence of wholesale creation of material. As we have seen with reference to the Gospels as a whole, theological motives do not rule out accurate historical reporting.

(1) Luke explicitly states his careful method of historical investigation immediately before presenting his birth narrative (Luke 1:1–4). It is unlikely he expects the birth stories to be read as anything other than historical narrative. Further, the nature of the birth narratives is not significantly different from the rest of the Gospels. It is difficult to believe that the Evangelists expected them to be read as a completely different genre (like midrash).

(2) While the two narratives tell different stories and are presumably independent of one another, they share common features: Jesus is born during the reign of Herod the Great; Joseph, his father, is a descendant of David; Joseph and Mary are legally engaged but have not yet had sexual relations when she becomes pregnant; the pregnancy is said to come through the supernatural intervention of the Holy Spirit; angels announce the approaching birth and that the child is to be named Jesus; the child will be the Messiah from the line of David and savior of his people; Jesus is born in Bethlehem in Judea but is raised in Nazareth in Galilee. These common features confirm that there were stories of Jesus' origin circulating in the early church from which both Matthew and Luke drew their material.

(3) Most scholars see significant evidence for sources in the birth narratives. For Luke, this is apparent in the Semitic-style of the birth narrative, which contrasts quite sharply with the rest of the Gospel and especially with Acts. Similarly, while Matthew frequently cites Old Testament fulfillment formulas, he seems not to be composing his narrative around these citations but rather to be inserting them at appropriate points in the traditions he has received. For example, the account of Herod's murder of the children in Bethelem is unlikely to have been created by Matthew around Jeremiah 31:15, since there is no reference to Bethlehem or to a ruler's murderous schemes in the Jeremiah text. More likely, the tradition of mourning associated with the Bethlehem massacre recalled for Matthew the Jeremiah text, which he then inserted into his narrative (Matt. 2:17–18).

Since Matthew's story is told from the perspective of Joseph and Luke's from the perspective of Mary, it is not unlikely that the traditions were passed down from these two sides of Jesus' family. The presence of Mary and of Jesus' brothers in the early church provides a possible avenue for their transmission (see Acts 1:14; 1 Cor. 9:5).

THE ANCESTRY OF JESUS

The Old Testament predicted that a messianic king would one day arise to reestablish the Davidic dynasty (2 Sam. 7:11–16; Isa. 9:1–7; 11:1–9; Jer. 23:5–6; Ezek. 34:23–24;

Figure 14.1—The Genealogies of Matthew and Luke
From David to Jesus

Matthew	Luke (reverse order)
David	David
Solomon	Nathan
Rehoboam	Mattatha
Abijah	Menna
Asa	Melea
Jehoshaphat	Eliakim
Joram	Jonam
Uzziah	Joseph
Jotham	Judah
Ahaz	Simeon
Hezekiah	Levi
Manasseh	Matthat
Amon	Jorim
Josiah	Eliezer
Jeconiah	Joshua
Shealtiel	Er
Zerubbabel	Elmadam
Abiud	Cosam
Eliakim	Addi
Azor	Melchi
Zadok	Neri
Achim	Shealtiel
Eliud	Zerubbabel
Eleazer	Rhesa
Matthan	Joanan
Jacob	Joda
Joseph	Josech
Jesus	Semein
	Mattathias
	Maath
	Naggai
	Hesli
	Nahum
	Amos
	Mattathias
	Joseph
	Jannai
	Melchi
	Levi
	Matthat
	Heli
	Joseph
	Jesus

37:24–25), and both Matthew and Luke affirm Jesus' Davidic ancestry. In addition to repeatedly identifying Jesus' father, Joseph, as a descendant of David (Matt. 1:20; Luke 1:27; 2:4), both provide **genealogies** linking Jesus to David's line (Matt. 1:1–17; Luke 3:23–38). The genealogies have a number of important differences. Matthew's proceeds temporally from Abraham to Jesus, while Luke's moves backward from Jesus all the way to Adam. This descent to Adam is likely related to Luke's desire to identify Jesus with salvation for all humanity. While the genealogies are essentially the same from Abraham to David, from David to Jesus they are different. First, Luke's list is much longer, containing forty names between David and Joseph, compared with Matthew's twenty-six. This can be explained by the common practice of abbreviating genealogies. Matthew seems to skip generations in order to structure his genealogy around groups of fourteen generations (Matt. 1:17; the Hebrew and Greek words for "son" can also mean "descendant"). Much more problematic are the different names. Matthew follows the line of David's son Solomon, while Luke follows the line of Nathan, another son of David (see fig. 14.1). This discrepancy has been explained in a variety of ways.

(1) Some consider one or both genealogies to be unhistorical, created by Christians to provide Jesus with a Davidic lineage and legitimate messianic credentials. This conclusion is unnecessary, since independent confirmation of Jesus' Davidic ancestry is provided by Mark (Mark 10:47–48), Paul (Rom. 1:3; 2 Tim. 2:8), the author of Hebrews (Heb. 7:14), and the book of Revelation (Rev. 5:5; 22:16). There is also an interesting story from the early church historian Eusebius. He cites Hegesippus as claiming that the Roman Emperor Domitian (AD 81–96) once summoned to Rome the grandsons of Jude, Jesus' half brother, fearing that as members of the royal line of David they might be politically dangerous. Finding them to be merely poor farmers, Domitian let them go.[1] This quaint story provides evidence that Jesus' family had an awareness that they were descendants of David.

(2) The traditional solution to the two genealogies is that Luke provides Mary's while Matthew gives Joseph's. Evidence for this is Luke's emphasis on Mary throughout the birth narrative. This proposal is sometimes linked to the judgment pronounced against the line of Solomon by Jeremiah, who prophesied that no descendant of Jehoiakim (Jer. 36:30) or of his son Jechoniah (Jer. 22:24–30) would sit on the throne of David. Jesus avoided this judgment because he was the legal rather than physical descendant of Joseph. One problem with this view is that Luke's list begins with Joseph, who seems to be identified as the son of Heli. Another is that throughout Luke's birth narrative, it is Joseph's, not Mary's, Davidic descent which is stressed (Luke 1:27; 2:4).

(3) Another common solution is that both genealogies are related to Joseph, but while Matthew presents a royal or legal genealogy (the official line of Davidic kings), Luke lists Joseph's actual physical descendants.

(4) A whole range of ingenious proposals explain how Joseph could have two genealogies. Some say Mary had no brothers to carry on her father Heli's name, so at her marriage, Heli adopted Joseph as his own son and heir. Joseph could then rightly be identified as heir to both lines. Others trace one line through Joseph's father (Heli) and the other through his maternal grandfather (Jacob). More complex solutions appeal to the Old Testament laws

---

1. Eusebius, *Ecclesiastical History* 3.19.1–20.8

of **levirate marriage**, whereby the brother of a man who died childless would marry his widow to produce heirs for him (Deut. 25:5–10). In this case, Heli and Jacob were either brothers or half brothers. When one died, the other married his widow, producing Joseph as his offspring. This would leave Joseph with two fathers, a natural one and a legal one, and therefore two genealogies.

With such a plethora of possibilities, it is impossible to be dogmatic about any one solution or to confidently reject or confirm its historicity. What can be affirmed is that there was widespread recognition of Jesus' legitimate Davidic ancestry within the early church.

THE VIRGINAL CONCEPTION

Both Matthew and Luke claim that Mary became pregnant during the period of her engagement to Joseph and that this was accomplished through the Holy Spirit (Matt. 1:18–25; Luke 1:26–38). Traditionally called the virgin birth, the event is better termed a **virginal conception**, since the conception was miraculous and the birth was apparently normal.[2] The historicity of the virginal conception was a major issue of scholarly debate in the nineteenth and twentieth centuries. Skeptics claimed that the story arose through syncretism with pagan stories related to gods impregnating human women, or that it was created by later Christians to provide a "fulfillment" of Isaiah 7:14.

Yet the biblical account is very different from pagan myths, with no hint of a sexual union between Mary and the Holy Spirit. Most scholars have abandoned such appeals to pagan parallels. Nor is it likely that the early Christians created the story to fulfill Isaiah 7:14, since this passage was not interpreted with reference to the Messiah by the Jews of Jesus' day. It is more likely that Christians, aware of the traditions of Jesus' unusual birth, discovered in Isaiah 7:14 a typological prophecy which found its final fulfillment in Jesus. Jesus was the ultimate Immanuel—truly "God with us." That the virginal conception is not a late addition to the Gospel story is suggested by its independent attestation in Matthew and Luke and by possible allusions to it elsewhere in the New Testament (see Mark 6:3 [where Jesus is called "Mary's son" rather than "Joseph's son"]; John 8:41 [where Jesus' opponents hint that he was an illegitimate child]; Gal. 4:4).

What is the theological significance of the virginal conception? Some have argued it was necessary to protect Jesus' sinless nature, but the narratives themselves do not indicate this purpose. The Messiah could have entered human life free from sin with or without a virginal conception. Nor is Scripture explicit on the details of the conception. Did God create the sperm for Mary's egg? Did he create a fertilized embryo? This latter question raises questions about how Jesus could have been fully human if he had no physical connection to Mary or Joseph. The former raises the question of how Jesus could have avoided Mary's sinful nature. The Roman Catholic answer is the immaculate conception, whereby Mary herself was born free from sin. But this doctrine has no basis in Scripture. In the final analysis, the details remain a mystery. What is certain from the text is that the conception of Jesus was a supernatural act of God, confirming that God himself was about to accomplish the salvation which no human being could achieve. Luke links Jesus' virginal conception

---

2. In some Roman Catholic theology, the birth is also considered virginal and supernatural, and Mary is said to have remained a virgin through the process of birth and afterward.

The present Church of the Nativity was built in the fourth century over a cave site in Bethlehem traditionally thought to be the site of Christ's birth. The statue is of Jerome, early church father and translator of the Vulgate.

to his status as Son of God (1:35), showing that in some mysterious way the event brought together the human and the divine in the person of Jesus.

BETHLEHEM BIRTHPLACE

Though Jesus was raised in **Nazareth**, Matthew and Luke identify Jesus' birthplace as **Bethlehem** (Matt. 2:1; Luke 2:4–7). Bethlehem's theological significance is as the birthplace and hometown of David, Israel's greatest king and the prototype of the Messiah (1 Samuel 16; 2 Samuel 7). Micah 5:2–5 predicts that a great ruler will come from Bethlehem, a new David who will shepherd God's people and bring peace and security to the nation. Matthew links Jesus' Bethlehem birth to the fulfillment of the prophecy of Micah 5:2, while Luke connects it more generally with Jesus' Davidic lineage and his role as the Davidic Messiah, the king who will bring salvation to Israel.

Critics often deny that Bethlehem was Jesus' birthplace, claiming that the title Jesus of Nazareth is evidence that Jesus was really from Nazareth in Galilee and that the Bethlehem story was created to "fulfill" Micah 5:2. Against this is the fact that both Matthew and Luke attest to the birthplace independently. (See also the ironic reference in John 7:42.) Luke does not even link Bethlehem to the Micah passage, suggesting that it was a part of the tradition distinct from this fulfillment motif.

THE CENSUS

According to Luke, the event which brought Jesus' family to Bethlehem was a **census** conducted by the emperor Caesar Augustus (Luke 2:1). While censuses for tax purposes were common in the Roman Empire, there are several historical problems with this one.

(1) First, we have no other evidence of a single empire-wide census under Augustus. Would not such a major event have left a record in Roman history? In fact, this is not a

major difficulty. We know that Augustus reorganized the administration of the empire and conducted numerous local censuses. Luke is probably treating a local Palestinian census as part of Augustus's empire-wide reorganization of the provinces.

(2) A second problem is that Luke says this was the first census while Quirinius was governor of Syria (2:2). According to Josephus, Quirinius's governorship began in AD 6, ten years too late for Jesus' birth. Various solutions are possible here. There is some evidence that Quirinius may have held a prior governorship or at least a broad administrative position over Syria at the time of Jesus' birth. Others have suggested that Luke is referring to a census completed by Quirinius but begun by an earlier governor. Still others note that the Greek word for "first" (*prōtē*) may be translated "before," so that Luke is saying this census took place *before* Quirinius's governorship of Syria.

(3) A third problem is Luke's statement that "everyone went to his own town to register," since there is no evidence that the Romans required a return to ancestral homes for tax purposes. While this is generally true, Judea was a client kingdom of **Herod the Great**, and so a census may have been conducted in a Jewish, rather than in a Roman, manner. There is also evidence that in some areas, property owners had to return to the district where they owned land. Perhaps Joseph owned property in Bethlehem.

In summary, while there are problems related to the census, there is not enough evidence either to refute or confirm Luke's claim. Considering his historical accuracy elsewhere, his statement should be given the benefit of the doubt.

THE BIRTH OF JESUS

A careful reading of the birth narrative produces a picture quite different from the traditional Christmas pageant, in which shepherds, wise men, angels, and farm animals all crowd in a stable around the holy family. The text does not say that Jesus was born on the night Mary and Joseph arrived in Bethlehem; rather, it indicates he was born sometime during their stay there (Luke 2:6). The "**inn**" (*katalyma*) was probably not an ancient hotel with an innkeeper, since a small village like Bethlehem would not have had such accommodations. Luke uses a different Greek word in Luke 10:34 for a roadside inn (*pandocheion*). The word *katalyma* normally means either a guest room in a private residence or a caravansary, an informal public shelter where travelers would gather for the night. The most likely scenario is that Joseph and Mary were staying with relatives or friends and, because of crowded conditions, were forced to a place reserved for animals. This could have been a lower-level stall attached to the living

A stone feeding or watering manger, found at Megiddo

quarters of the home or, as some ancient traditions suggest, a cave used as a shelter for animals.[3] The "manger" where Jesus was laid was a feeding trough for animals, and the traditional "swaddling clothes" were strips of cloth intended to keep the limbs straight, a sign of motherly care and affection (Ezek. 16:4).

---

3. This tradition appears in the *Protevangelium of James* 18–19; Justin Martyr, *Dialogue with Trypho* 78.4; and Origin, *Against Celsus* 1.15.

Left: Matthew recounts that Joseph, warned in a dream of Herod's evil intentions, took Mary and Joseph to Egypt. *Right:* A typical caravansary, a stopping place for caravans. This one is located in Nuweiba in Egypt.

While Luke recounts the angelic announcement to humble shepherds in the hills around Bethlehem, Matthew tells of **magi**, or wise men, who came from the east. Contrary to the traditional manger scene, Matthew does not say there were three magi (the number three comes from the three gifts) or that they arrived with the shepherds on the night of Jesus' birth. Mary and Joseph are living in a house in Bethlehem when they come (2:11), and Herod the Great tries to kill the children in Bethlehem two years of age and under (2:16), indicating that Jesus may have been as old as two. The magi were probably Persian or Arabian astrologers (not kings, as is sometimes supposed) who charted the stars and attached religious significance to their movements. While some have doubted the historicity of this visit, it bears the marks of credibility. It was widely believed in the ancient world that the stars heralded the birth of great people, and the Roman historians Suetonius and Tacitus even speak of an expectation that a world ruler would come from Judea.[4] It is not surprising that Eastern astrologers would see in a particular astral phenomenon the sign of the birth of a Jewish king.

Warned in a dream of Herod's evil intention to kill the child, Joseph escapes with the family to Egypt, where he remains until the death of Herod. While the historian Josephus does not mention Herod's massacre of the infants of Bethlehem, this is not surprising since Bethlehem was a small village and the number of children could not have been large. Considering Herod's many ruthless actions in murdering sons, wives, and all manner of political opponents, this event was of little historical consequence. At the same time, Matthew's account fits well what we know of Herod's paranoia and ruthless cruelty. The irony of the magi's visit is that while even pagan astrologers come to worship the Jewish Messiah, the illegitimate king of the Jews seeks to destroy him.

When Joseph is informed in a dream that Herod has died, he returns to Israel. Hearing that Herod's cruel and incompetent son **Archelaus** is ruling in Judea, he moves to Nazareth in Galilee, where Jesus grows up. Luke, too, confirms that Jesus' family returned to Nazareth

---

4. Suetonius, *Vespasian* 4; Tacitus, *Histories* 5.13.

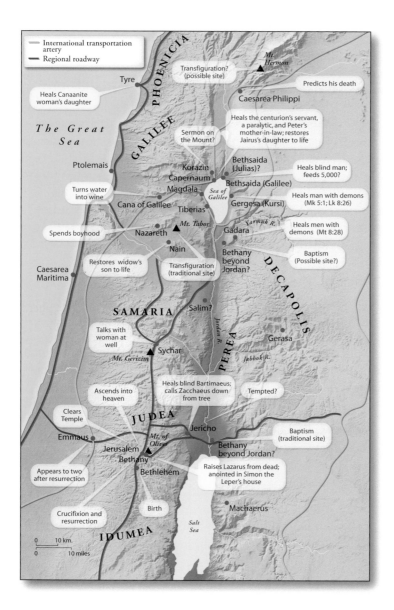

International transportation artery
Regional roadway

PHOENICIA

Transfiguration? (possible site)

Mt. Herman

Tyre

Predicts his death

Heals Canaanite woman's daughter

Caesarea Philippi

The Great Sea

GALILEE

Heals the centurion's servant, a paralytic, and Peter's mother-in-law; restores Jairus's daughter to life

Sermon on the Mount?

Ptolemais

Korazin
Capernaum
Magdala

Bethsaida (Julias)?

Heals blind man; feeds 5,000?

Turns water into wine

Cana of Galilee

Sea of Galilee

Bethsaida (Galilee)

Tiberias

Gergesa (Kursi)

Heals man with demons (Mk 5:1; Lk 8:26)

Mt. Tabor

Yarmuk R.

Nazareth

Gadara

Heals men with demons (Mt 8:28)

Spends boyhood

Nain

Bethany beyond Jordan?

DECAPOLIS

Baptism (Possible site?)

Caesarea Maritima

Restores widow's son to life

Transfiguration (traditional site)

SAMARIA

Salim?

Jordan R.

PEREA

Talks with woman at well

Gerasa

Mt. Gerizim

Sychar

Jabbok R.

Heals blind Bartimaeus; calls Zacchaeus down from tree

Tempted?

Ascends into heaven

Clears Temple

JUDEA

Emmaus

Jericho

Jerusalem

Mt. of Olives

Baptism (traditional site)

Bethany

Bethany beyond Jordan?

Appears to two after resurrection

Bethlehem

Raises Lazarus from dead; anointed in Simon the Leper's house

Crucifixion and resurrection

Birth

Machaerus

Salt Sea

IDUMEA

0   10 km.
0   10 miles

Map of Israel showing significant events in Jesus' life

after his birth, though he does not mention an extended stay in Bethlehem or the sojourn in Egypt (Luke 2:39). As we have seen, it is common for the Gospel writers to abbreviate, condense, or skip over events which were not important to their theological purpose.

JESUS' FAMILY LIFE

According to the Gospels, Jesus had four brothers — James, Joseph, Judas, and Simon — and at least two sisters (Mark 6:3; Matt. 13:55 – 56). There is a lively debate concerning the actual relationship of these siblings. Roman Catholic theologians have traditionally followed the interpretation of Jerome that these are not true brothers and sisters but cousins.

The world of New Testament scholarship was rocked on October 21, 2002, by the announcement by the *Biblical Archaeological Review* of the discovery of an ossuary bearing the remarkable inscription in Aramaic, "James, son of Joseph, brother of Jesus." An ossuary is a bone box used by first-century Jews to store the bones of the dead after the body has decomposed in a tomb (see p. 324). Many scholars concluded that the box once contained the bones of Jesus' half brother James.

Unfortunately, the box was discovered in the collection of an antiquities dealer, rather than at an archeological site, and its origin was viewed with suspicion. The Israel Antiquities Authority eventually declared it to be a forgery, though other scholars continue to affirm its authenticity.

What is the importance of the box? Though no credible scholar doubts the fact that Jesus existed, this box would be the first physical object directly connected to him. From a historical perspective, however, it provides no new information about the historical Jesus.

This is usually suggested to protect the perpetual virginity of Mary. But Greek has a distinct word for cousin (*anepsios*, Col. 4:10), making this view unlikely. A second view is that these are children from a previous marriage of Joseph, who was a widower. This is possible, and there are some indications that Joseph may have been somewhat older than Mary. He never appears during Jesus' public ministry, and so likely died before Jesus began to preach. This scenario may also be suggested when Jesus from the cross commends his mother to the care of the Beloved Disciple, not to his own brothers (John 19:26–27). Could Mary have had a more distant relationship with them? But if these are children from a previous marriage,

> According to the Gospels, Jesus had four brothers— James, Joseph, Judas, and Simon—and at least two sisters.

it is odd that no mention is made of them in the birth narrative. The story seems to imply that Jesus is the firstborn of *both* Mary and Joseph. The most likely explanation is that these are the brothers of Jesus born to Mary and Joseph after the birth of Jesus. Matthew 1:25 implies that Mary and Joseph had normal sexual relations after Jesus was born.

The Gospels portray Mary and Joseph as faithful and pious Jews (Matt. 1:19; Luke 1:28–30, 38). At Jesus' birth, they fulfill the law's requirements concerning circumcision, purification, and the dedication of their firstborn to the Lord (Luke 2:21–24). Jesus' father was a carpenter (Matt. 13:55), and like most children of his day, Jesus followed in his father's career (Mark 6:3). The Greek term translated "carpenter" (*tektōn*) is a general one, referring to someone who built with materials like stone, wood, or metal. Joseph and his sons may have been primarily stonemasons, building homes and public buildings. Or they may have made farm tools (plows, yokes, wheels, carts), household items (windows, doors, locks), or furniture (chairs, tables, cabinets, chests). The family's social status would have been among the working poor, though there is no evidence that they were destitute. This relative poverty is indirectly confirmed by the sacrifice offered for Mary's purification in Luke 2:24 ("a pair of doves or two young pigeons")—a sacrifice prescribed for the poor in Leviticus 12:8. While the Greeks generally looked down on such craftsmen as uneducated and unsophisticated, in Judaism they were considered necessary and important professions, though not as noble as the scribe who studied the law (Sir. 38:24–32).

Nazareth, while only a small village, was located just a few miles from the major Hellenistic-Jewish city of **Sepphoris**. It is possible that Joseph and his sons found work in this commercial center. This would have given Jesus some exposure to Greek-speaking people and Greco-Roman city life. Like most Jewish boys, Jesus would have been educated in the local synagogue, where he learned the Scriptures and the Hebrew language. We know from his Nazareth sermon that he could read Hebrew (Luke 4:16–20). This means Jesus was probably trilingual, speaking Aramaic in the home and with friends, using Hebrew in religious contexts, and conversing in Greek in business and governmental contexts.

Display of tools used by the ancients in the construction of their buildings. Joseph's occupation as a *tektōn* meant he was a craftsman working with wood, stone, or metal.

Apart from these generalities, we know almost nothing about Jesus' early life. To be sure, later Christians composed **infancy gospels**, fanciful accounts of Jesus' boyhood which turned him into a child prodigy and miracle worker. As we have seen ("Addendum" in chap. 1), the late second-century *Infancy Gospel of Thomas* has the boy Jesus making clay pigeons fly and lengthening beams in Joseph's carpentry shop. Such stories have no historical foundation. Jesus no doubt had a rather ordinary childhood as a Jewish boy growing up in a conservative Israelite household.

The only biblical account from Jesus' childhood comes from Luke, who describes his growth toward physical and spiritual maturity and illustrates this with a Passover visit to Jerusalem when Jesus was twelve years old (Luke 2:40–52, see p. 266). Jewish tradition held that a boy became responsible to observe the law when he was thirteen years old

Modern Nazareth. Though he was born in Bethlehem, the Gospels agree that Jesus was raised in Nazareth in Galilee. The black-roofed building is the Basilica of the Annunciation, traditional site of Gabriel's appearance to Mary.

The only biblical account from Jesus' childhood comes from Luke, who describes a Passover visit to Jerusalem when Jesus was twelve years old.

(though the bar mitzvah ceremony is of later origin).[5] By taking Jesus to Jerusalem to celebrate Passover, his parents are preparing him for his covenant responsibilities. The family would have traveled from Nazareth to Jerusalem—a journey of four or five days—in a caravan of relatives and friends for protection. This explains how Jesus' parents could have left him behind in Jerusalem, assuming he was with friends elsewhere in the caravan. When his anxious parents finally discover him in the temple, he is sitting at the feet of the Jewish teachers, who marvel at his wisdom. His question, "Didn't you know I had to be in my Father's house?" confirms a growing awareness of his special father-son relationship with God. Though conclusions about Jesus' childhood self-consciousness are speculative, Luke claims that by puberty he had a growing awareness of the special role he would play in God's plan.

---

5. *m. Niddah* 5:6; *m. Avot* 5:21; *Genesis Rabbah* 63:10.

» CHAPTER SUMMARY «

1. Though the birth narratives serve as theological introductions to the Gospels of Matthew and Luke, they also contain reliable traditions concerning the birth and childhood of Jesus.

2. The differences between the two genealogies can be plausibly explained in various ways. They may represent, respectively, the genealogies of Joseph and Mary, a royal genealogy versus a physical genealogy, or Joseph's natural genealogy versus a legal one (through adoption or levirate marriage).

3. There is little evidence to suggest that Jesus' virginal conception was a myth created by the church to fulfill prophecy. Matthew and Luke independently attest to it, and Luke does not explicitly link it to Isaiah 7:14. The event confirms that Jesus' conception was a supernatural act of God, bringing together the human and divine in one person.

4. While some scholars claim Jesus was born in Nazareth, Matthew and Luke independently attest to Jesus' Bethlehem birth. Since Luke does not mention Micah 5:2, it is unlikely that the tradition was created around this prophecy.

5. While the census described in Luke 2 does not have clear corroboration in Roman records, it fits Caesar Augustus's pattern of provincial restructuring. Considering Luke's record elsewhere as a reliable historian, it would be imprudent to reject the event as unhistorical.

6. The "inn" from which Jesus' parents were turned away was probably not an ancient hotel but the sleeping quarters of a private residence. Because of crowded conditions, Jesus was born in a humble place reserved for animals.

7.   The magi, probably court astrologers from Persia or Arabia, arrived as much as two years after Jesus' birth, while his family was living in a house in Bethlehem.

8.   Herod's attempt to kill the infants of Bethlehem fits well his character as a cruel and despotic ruler. Considering Herod's many atrocities, it is not surprising that this minor event is not recorded by Josephus or other historians.

9.   Because Archelaus, Herod's cruel and incompetent son, was ruling in Judea after his father's death, Joseph and Mary returned to Nazareth after their residence in Egypt.

10. Jesus likely had an ordinary childhood growing up in a conservative Jewish home. He had four brothers and some sisters and would have learned carpentry from his father. Luke's account of his childhood visit to Jerusalem confirms Jesus' growing awareness of a unique father-son relationship with God.

» KEY TERMS «

birth narratives	Nazareth	magi
midrash	Bethlehem	Archelaus
genealogies	census	*tektōn*
levirate marriage	Herod the Great	Sepphoris
virginal conception	"inn" (*katalyma*)	infancy gospels

» DISCUSSION AND STUDY QUESTIONS «

1.   What is the evidence that Matthew and Luke are using historical traditions in their birth narratives, rather than merely creating stories to fit their theological agendas?

2.   What are the main differences between the genealogies of Matthew and Luke?

3.   Identify some possible solutions to the problem of two different genealogies for Jesus.

4.   What is the theological significance of Jesus' virginal conception? (What has been proposed and what is clear from the text?)

5.   What is the theological significance of Jesus' birth in Bethlehem?

6.   What are some of the problems and possible solutions concerning the census associated with Jesus' birth?

7. Identify some common misconceptions related to the birth of Jesus, such as the nature of the inn, the number of magi, and the time of their arrival.

8. How does the massacre of the infants in Bethlehem fit the known character of Herod the Great?

9. Who were Jesus' brothers? What was their actual relationship to Jesus? (Identify the various views.)

10. What does it mean that Jesus was a "carpenter"? Where might he have worked?

11. What are the infancy gospels?

12. What does the account of Jesus' Passover visit to Jerusalem suggest about his growing awareness of his relationship to God?

Digging Deeper

The Birth Narratives Generally

Brown, Raymond E. *The Birth of the Messiah.* 2nd ed. New York: Doubleday, 1993.

France, R. T. "Scripture, Tradition and History in the Infancy Narratives of Matthew." In *Gospel Perspectives* 2:239 – 66.

Laurentin, René. *The Truth of Christmas beyond the Myths: The Gospels of the Infancy of Christ.* Translated by Michael J. Wrenn et al. Petersham, MA: St. Bede's, 1986.

Witherington III, Ben. "Birth of Jesus." In *DJG*, 60 – 74.

Genealogy of Jesus

Huffman, Douglas S. "Genealogy." In *DJG*, 253 – 59.

Johnson, M. D. *The Purpose of Biblical Genealogies.* SNTSMS 8. 2nd ed. Cambridge: Cambridge Univ. Press, 1988.

Overstreet, R. L. "Difficulties of New Testament Genealogies." *Grace Theological Journal* 2 (1981): 303 – 26.

The Virgin Birth

Cranfield, C. E. B. "Some Reflections on the Virgin Birth." *Scottish Journal of Theology* 41 (1988): 177 – 89.

Machen, J. Gresham. *The Virgin Birth of Christ.* New York: Harper, 1930.

The Family of Jesus

Bauckham, R. J. *Jude and the Relatives of Jesus in the Early Church.* Edinburgh: T. and T. Clark, 1990.

CHAPTER 15

The Beginning of Jesus' Ministry

» CHAPTER OVERVIEW «

1. John the Baptist, Herald of Messianic Salvation
2. The Baptism of Jesus
3. The Temptation of Jesus

» OBJECTIVES «

After reading this chapter, you should be able to:

- Summarize the role and ministry of John the Baptist according to the Gospels.
- Discuss the likely background and purpose of John's "baptism of repentance."
- Explain the significance of Jesus' baptism, including the Old Testament allusions from God's voice from heaven.
- Identify the main theme of the temptation account, and explain the significance of the implicit analogies to Israel in the wilderness and Adam in the garden.

JOHN THE BAPTIST, HERALD OF MESSIANIC SALVATION

As we have seen, all four Gospels link the beginning of Jesus' ministry with the appearance of **John the Baptist** (Matt. 3:1–12; Mark 1:1–8; Luke 3:1–20; John 1:6–8, 15, 19–36). John's role is explained with prophecies from Isaiah 40 and Malachi 3 and 4. He is the "voice of one calling in the desert" preparing the way for the Lord (Isa. 40:3) and the Elijah-like messenger who will prepare God's people for the Day of the Lord (Mal. 3:1; 4:5–6; Matt. 11:14; 17:12). Though Josephus speaks of a variety of prophets and doomsayers who arose during the first century, John's message of the Coming One who would soon follow was unprecedented.

Only Luke's Gospel provides information concerning John's early life. He is born to Zechariah and Elizabeth, pious Jews of priestly descent living in the hill country of Judea (Luke 1:5–6, 39). Zechariah served as priest in the Jerusalem temple, and Elizabeth was a relative of Jesus' mother, Mary (1:36). Elizabeth was old and childless until God miraculously intervened and she became pregnant. John's special prophetic role is presaged when Mary visited Elizabeth and the baby "leaped for joy" in Elizabeth's womb (1:44). What, if any, contact John and Jesus had before their public ministries is unknown, since Jesus was raised in Galilee and John in Judea.

After the account of John's birth, Luke mentions only that John "grew and became strong in spirit; and he lived in the desert until he appeared publicly to Israel" (1:80). Some have speculated from this desert lifestyle that John may have had contact with the monastic community at Qumran near the Dead Sea. In an intriguing comment, Josephus writes that the Essenes "neglect wedlock, but choose out other persons' children, while they are pliable, and fit for learning, and esteem them to be of their kindred, and form them according to their own manners" (*J.W.* 2.8.2 §§120–21). If John's elderly parents died before he reached adulthood, it is possible that he was raised by this community. John's message has interesting points in common with the Qumran sect. Both shared a strong expectation for the imminent arrival of God's final salvation; both used the prophecy of Isaiah 40:3 (1QS 8:14); both identified themselves with the righteous remnant called out from apostate Israel; and both practiced ritual washings of some sort. Unfortunately, there is not nearly enough evidence to confirm this fascinating hypothesis.

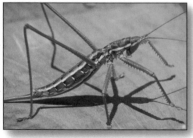

John lived off the land, with a diet consisting of locusts and wild honey.

Since he was born shortly before Jesus (Luke 1), John was probably about thirty when his ministry began. He is portrayed as carrying on an itinerant preaching ministry in the Judean wilderness and baptizing people in the Jordan River. The Fourth Gospel speaks of John's ministry along the Jordan at Aenon near Salim (John 3:23), across the Jordan from Samaria. Since he faced opposition from Herod Antipas, tetrarch of Galilee and Perea, John's ministry may have extended the length of the Jordan, from the Dead Sea in the south to Galilee in the north.

John must have been a striking figure, emerging from the wilderness dressed in camel skin and a leather belt (Mark 1:6), garb reminiscent of the prophet Elijah (2 Kings 1:8). His diet of locusts and wild honey, though strange today, was typical of ascetics who lived off the land. The Dead Sea Scrolls even provide instructions on how to eat locusts (CD 12:13).

John preached a "baptism of repentance for the forgiveness of sins," warning people to repent in light of the coming fiery judgment of God (Mark 1:4, 7–8; Luke 3:3, 15–18). Josephus describes John's baptism as a symbolic purification of the body which followed the purification of the soul by righteousness (*Ant.* 18.5.2 §117). The background to this baptism has been a matter of much debate. Some have seen parallels to the ceremonial washings practiced by the Essenes and other Jewish groups. As an act of ceremonial cleansing, individuals would dip themselves into a **mikveh**, or immersion pool. At Qumran, such washings, like John's, represented a turning from sin to participate in the eschatological community of God (1QS 5:13–14). Yet John's baptism is different in that it appears to be a one-time event rather than a repeated ritual. Others have pointed to the Jewish practice of **proselyte** (new convert) **baptism**, in which case John may be calling the apostate nation to become true Jews once again. While this fits the message of John, it is unclear whether proselyte baptism was practiced by Jews in the first century. John's baptism is perhaps best viewed as his unique eschatological application of cleansing and initiatory rituals found in first-century Judaism.

> John preached a "baptism of repentance for the forgiveness of sins," warning people to repent in light of the coming fiery judgment of God.

According to the Gospels, John explicitly denied messianic claims and announced that one "more powerful" was coming after him (Mark 1:7–8; Matt. 3:11–12; Luke 3:15–18; John 1:24–28; 3:23–36). While John baptized with water, this messianic figure would baptize with the Holy Spirit and with fire. Some argue this "baptism" refers to two distinct events, a Spirit baptism for the righteous and a fire baptism for the wicked. More likely, John refers to one Spirit-and-fire baptism which purifies the righteous and judges the wicked. Isaiah 4:4 speaks in an eschatological context of a "spirit of judgment and a spirit of fire" which will "cleanse the bloodstains from Jerusalem" (cf. Mal. 3:2).

A pitchfork and sifting basket for winnowing grain. John the Baptist warned of coming judgment, when God would separate the wheat (the righteous) from the chaff (the wicked).

Some scholars have claimed that historically John's ministry had nothing to do with Jesus but that John was expecting God himself to come and bring in the Day of the Lord. It was later Christians who transformed John into the forerunner of the Messiah. Yet the evidence suggests otherwise. John's statement about being unworthy to untie the sandals of the Coming One (attested independently in the Fourth Gospel and the Synoptics: Mark 1:7, par.; John 1:27) suggests that John was expecting a human successor. Similarly, John's later doubts about Jesus are inexplicable unless he already had some messianic expectations concerning him (Luke 7:18–35; Matt. 11:2–19). It is unlikely that the church would create an episode in which John raised doubts about Jesus' messianic status.

A mikveh, or pool for Jewish ritual purity washings.

Jesus identifies John as the last and greatest of the Old Testament prophets, indeed the greatest person ever born. Yet, paradoxically, "the one who is least in the kingdom of God is greater than he" (Luke 7:28; Matt. 11:11; cf. Luke 16:16). The meaning of this paradox may be that while John announced the age of salvation, he did not see its establishment. The "least in the kingdom" are those who are blessed to live in the age of fulfillment, with the new life imparted through Jesus' resurrection and the indwelling power of the Holy Spirit. While John was the herald of the new age of salvation, Jesus was its inaugurator.

John's challenge to the status quo eventually led to his death. According to Mark, Herod Antipas imprisoned John when he spoke out against Herod's divorce and subsequent marriage to Herodias, his brother Philip's wife. Such a marriage was viewed as incestuous by pious Jews (Lev. 18:16; 20:21). While Herod was reluctant to execute John, he was coerced into doing so by Herodias. During Herod's birthday celebration, Herodias's daughter Salome pleased him with her dancing, and Herod offered the girl anything, up to half his kingdom. Prompted by her mother, Salome requested the head of John the Baptist on a platter. Fearing a loss of face before his guests, Herod ordered John's execution (Mark 6:17–29; Matt. 14:1–12). Josephus also refers to John's arrest and execution but attributes it more generally to Herod's fear that John would provoke an uprising *(Ant.* 18.5.2 §§116–19; see fig. 15.1).

Figure 15.1—Josephus on the Death of John the Baptist

Now, some of the Jews thought that the destruction of Herod's army came from God, and that very justly, as a punishment of what he did against John, that was called the Baptist; for Herod slew him, who was a good man, and commanded the Jews to exercise virtue, both as to righteousness towards one another, and piety towards God, and so to come to baptism; for that the washing [with water] would be acceptable to him, if they made use of it, not in order to the putting away [or the remission] of some sins [only], but for the purification of the body; supposing still that the soul was thoroughly purified beforehand by righteousness. Now, when [many] others came in crowds about him, for they were greatly moved [or pleased] by hearing his words, Herod, who feared lest the great influence John had over the people might put it into his power and inclination to raise a rebellion (for they seemed ready to do anything he should advise), thought it best, by putting him to death, to prevent any mischief he might cause, and not bring himself into difficulties, by sparing a man who might make him repent of it when it should be too late. Accordingly he was sent a prisoner, out of Herod's suspicious temper, to Macherus, the castle I before mentioned, and was there put to death. Now the Jews had an opinion that the destruction of this army was sent as a punishment upon Herod, and a mark of God's displeasure against him.

— Josephus, *Jewish Antiquities* 18.5.2 §§116–19

428 Part Four:
The Historical Jesus

Machaerus, Herod the Great's fortress, where Herod's son Antipas imprisioned and eventually killed John the Baptist

There is no contradiction here, since Josephus gives the political reason for the arrest while Mark provides the specific occasion of the execution. Mark's account fits well the power struggles and political intrigue common to the Herodian dynasty.

The movement begun by John continued after his death, and followers of the Baptist appear later in the book of Acts (Acts 18:25; 19:1–7).

THE BAPTISM OF JESUS

The **baptism of Jesus** marks the beginning of his public ministry. Apart from the crucifixion, it is perhaps the least disputed historical event of Jesus' life. Even radical skeptics accept that Jesus was baptized by John, since the church would hardly have invented a story in which Jesus appears to submit to the authority of John. The baptism and descent of the Spirit is narrated in the three Synoptics (Matt. 3:13–17; Mark 1:9–11; Luke 3:21–22) and alluded to in John (John 1:29–34).

> Jesus' baptism by John is one of the least disputed historical events of his life.

Why did Jesus submit to John's baptism of repentance? Only Matthew suggests a reason. When John resists Jesus' request for baptism, Jesus responds that it should be done "to fulfill all righteousness" (Matt. 3:15). Righteousness here probably means faithful submission to God's purpose. In this way, Jesus connects his ministry with John's and associates himself with those who are responding in repentance to John's preaching.

The Spirit's descent and the voice from heaven have sometimes been described as a vision experienced by Jesus alone, although John 1:32 indicates that John the Baptist also witnessed it. If Jesus' willingness to be baptized represented his identification with repentant

Jordan River, site of John's ministry. View looking east at a portion of the river between the south end of the Sea of Galilee and Beth Shan.

Israel, the descent of the Spirit provided the empowerment to accomplish his messianic task. Luke in particular identifies the Spirit's descent as Jesus' "anointing" as Messiah (Luke 3:21–22; 4:1, 14, 18).

The descent of the Spirit "as a dove" may mean that the Spirit looked like a dove or merely that the descent was similar to a bird's flight. The symbolism has been widely discussed. Some see an allusion to Genesis 1:2, where the Spirit "hovers" over the waters at creation. Jesus could here be identified with the new creation. Others suggest an allusion to Genesis 8:8–12, where Noah's dove represents God's gracious deliverance after judgment.

The voice from heaven signifies the Father's affirmation of Jesus' person and mission. We have discussed its significance in our study of the individual Synoptics (see pp. 225, 268). "You are my son" comes from Psalm 2:7, where God announces the Messiah's divine sonship and legitimate rule from Mount Zion. "With you I am well pleased" echoes Isaiah 42:1, where the faithful and suffering Servant of the LORD is identified as God's chosen one. Finally, "whom I love" may perhaps represent an Isaac-Jesus typology from Genesis 22:2, where Isaac is Abraham's only son "whom you love." Abraham's willingness to offer his beloved son would be analogous to God's offering of his Son. If all three allusions are present, this single announcement makes the extraordinary claim that Jesus is the promised Messiah who will offer himself as a sacrifice for his people.

THE TEMPTATION OF JESUS

All three Synoptics connect Jesus' baptism with the **temptation of Jesus** in the wilderness (Matt. 4:1–11; Mark 1:12–13; Luke 4:1–13). This is a common pattern in the Old Testament and in Judaism, in which commissioning by God is often followed by a period of testing (cf. Sir. 2:1). Empowered by the Spirit as Messiah at his baptism, Jesus is led into the wilderness to be tempted by Satan. The main theme of the temptation is the obedience of the Son to the will of the Father. Will Jesus submit to the purpose of the Father, or will he pursue the path of personal glory? Satan repeatedly tempts Jesus to exploit his position as the Son of God for his own gain.

While Mark merely states that the temptation took place, Matthew and Luke detail three incidents (see pp. 226, 268). As we have seen, these are analogous to the experience of Israel in the wilderness. While God's "son" Israel (Exod. 4:22–23) failed when tested in the wilderness, Jesus the true Son remains obedient and emerges victorious. Jesus' forty days are analogous to Israel's forty years, and the three Old Testament passages Jesus cites all relate to Israel's failures in the desert. Israel was tested with hunger so that she would learn dependence on God, but she constantly complained. Jesus depends wholly on God for his sustenance, quoting Deuteronomy 8:3: "Man does not live on bread alone." Israel doubted God's power and put him to the test at Meribah. Jesus refuses to throw himself from the temple and so test the LORD God, citing Deuteronomy 6:16: "Do not put the Lord your God to the test." Finally, Israel was commanded to worship God alone but turned to idolatry (Deut. 9:12; Judg. 3:5–7). Jesus rejects the devil's offer of the kingdoms of the world in exchange for his worship, quoting Deuteronomy 6:13: "Worship the Lord your God, and serve him only." As the Messiah and Son of God, Jesus represents the nation Israel and succeeds where she failed. He will now fulfill Israel's Old Testament mandate, revealing God's glory and taking the message of salvation to the ends of the earth.

> As the Messiah and Son of God, Jesus represents the nation Israel and succeeds where she failed.

An Adam-Jesus typology may also be present in the temptation account, with Jesus resisting the temptation to which Adam and Eve succumbed (see pp. 268–69). The presence of Satan as the personal tempter would be analogous to the serpent's temptation of Eve. In this case, Jesus is the second Adam who will reverse the results of the fall. Mark's reference to the wild beasts may play on this Eden theme (Mark 1:13). Luke's genealogy, which

---

Figure 15.2—Jesus' Temptations ... and Ours

Is the temptation account meant to provide an example for all believers? Some have compared the three temptations to 1 John 2:16, linking them respectively with the lust of the flesh (stones to bread), the lust of the eyes (offer of world kingdoms), and the pride of life (jump from the temple pinnacle). While there are some parallels here, the three do not match up exactly. It is going too far, on the other hand, to argue that Jesus' temptations were wholly unique to him as the Messiah. Certainly believers today are tempted to act independently from God, to worship other gods, and to test God's faithfulness. Jesus' response of obedience to scriptural guidelines and of trust in and dependence on God are surely meant as examples for believers to follow (Heb. 2:18; 4:15).

©Neal Bierling/Zondervan Image Archives

Mount of Temptation near Jericho, traditional site of Jesus' temptation

appears just before his temptation account, identifies Adam as the "son of God." Where Adam the first son of God was tested and failed, Jesus the true Son of God succeeds.

The historicity of the temptation has been doubted by some, but there are good reasons for accepting that the story originated with Jesus himself. There are no clear parallels to such an encounter with Satan in the Old Testament or Judaism, and no good reason why the early church would create such an account. The kind of messianic temptations Jesus experienced were unique to his mission, not the common experience of believers. The criterion of dissimilarity would thus favor the story's authenticity. The criterion of multiple attestation also applies, since the scene appears in both Mark and Q.

Concerning its nature, the temptation may have been at least partly visionary, an experience which Jesus later recounted to his disciples. Luke suggests a visionary dimension when he says that Satan showed Jesus all of the kingdoms of the world "in an instant" (Luke 4:5). Whether visionary or not, the Gospels present them as real temptations from a personal Satan, part of Jesus' preparation for his messianic ministry.

1. John the Baptist is presented in all four Gospels as the precursor for Jesus, the prophetic herald of messianic salvation.

2. John's water baptism has antecedents in Jewish ceremonial cleansings and proselyte baptism but is best viewed as a unique application symbolizing a person's repentance and preparation for the kingdom of God.

3. Jesus identified John as the last and greatest of the Old Testament prophets.

4. John was imprisoned and eventually executed by Herod Antipas after criticizing Herod for his divorce and remarriage to Herodias, his brother Philip's wife.

5. Jesus' baptism by John is one of the most undisputed events in his life. It marks Jesus' "anointing" as Messiah and his empowering for ministry. The voice from heaven, echoing Psalm 2:7, Isaiah 42:1, and perhaps Genesis 22:2, implicitly identifies Jesus as the Messiah, who will offer himself as a sacrifice for sins.

6. Jesus' temptation concludes his preparation and commissioning for ministry. The account is analogous to Israel's testing in the wilderness and Adam's testing in the garden. Where Adam and Israel failed, Jesus succeeds, confirming that he is the true Son of God, able to accomplish God's final salvation.

» KEY TERMS «

John the Baptist	proselyte baptism	temptation of Jesus
mikveh	baptism of Jesus	

» DISCUSSION AND STUDY QUESTIONS «

1. What role does John the Baptist play in the Gospel tradition? What Old Testament verses are used to describe him? How did Jesus describe him?

2. What is the possible background to John's "baptism of repentance"?

3. What were the circumstances leading to John's death?

4. Why is the historicity of Jesus' baptism by John assured?

5. Why might Jesus have submitted to John's baptism?

6. What might be the significance of the dove? Of the Old Testament allusions in the voice from heaven?

7. What is the main theme of the temptation account?

8. What two analogies appear to be present? Explain their significance.

Digging Deeper

John the Baptist

Scobie, Charles H. H. *John the Baptist*. Philadelphia: Fortress, 1964.

Taylor, Joan E. *The Immerser: John the Baptist within Second Temple Judaism*. Grand Rapids: Eerdmans, 1997.

Webb, Robert. "John the Baptist and His Relationship to Jesus." In *Studying the Historical Jesus*. Edited by Bruce Chilton and Craig A. Evans. Leiden: Brill, 1994.

———. *John the Baptizer and Prophet: A Socio-Historical Study*. Sheffield: JSOT Press, 1991.

Wink, W. *John the Baptist in the Gospel Tradition*. Cambridge: Cambridge Univ. Press, 1968.

Witherington III, Ben. "John the Baptist" In *DJG*, 383–91.

The Baptism of Jesus

Beasley-Murray, G. R. *Baptism in the New Testament*. Grand Rapids: Eerdmans, 1962.

Dockery, David S. "Baptism." In *DJG*, 55–58.

The Temptation of Jesus

Gerhardsson, Birger. *The Testing of God's Son*. Lund: Gleerup, 1966.

Gibson, Jeffrey B. *The Temptations of Jesus in Early Christianity*. Sheffield: Sheffield Academic, 1995.

Twelftree, Graham H. "Temptation of Jesus." In *DJG*, 821–27.

CHAPTER 16

The Message of Jesus

» CHAPTER OVERVIEW «

1. Jesus the Teacher
2. Jesus' Central Message: The Kingdom of God
3. Jesus and the Law: The Ethics of the Kingdom
4. The Greatest Commandment and the Character of God
5. Grace and Works: The Free Gift and the Cost of Discipleship
6. Social Justice: The Rich and the Poor
7. The Parables of the Kingdom

» OBJECTIVES «

After reading this chapter, you should be able to:

- Describe the nature and uniqueness of Jesus' teaching.
- Explain the background and meaning of the kingdom of God in Jesus' teaching.
- Summarize Jesus' teaching concerning the law of Moses and its fulfillment.
- Relate Jesus' teaching about God's free grace to his teaching on the high cost of discipleship.
- Discuss the significance of Jesus' teaching about poverty and wealth.
- Explain the nature and purpose of Jesus' parables and suggest principles for their accurate interpretation.

JESUS THE TEACHER

The Gospels confirm that Jesus was a teacher with extraordinary gifts. Mark notes that "the people were amazed at his teaching, because he taught them as one who had authority, not as the teachers of the law" (Mark 1:22). The scribes of Jesus' day taught with constant appeal to the traditions of the past, referring to legal precedents set by the rabbis before them. They would say, "Rabbi Akiba said …" In contrast, Jesus taught with a sense of originality and personal authority, predicating his statements with "truly [*amēn*] I say to you …" (Matt. 5:18, 26, etc.). Jesus' teaching attracted people because they sensed that the words he spoke were truly the words of God. (For more on Jesus' use of *amēn*, see chap. 18, p. 471).

> Jesus taught with a sense of originality and personal authority, predicating his statements with "truly [*amēn*] I say to you …"

In addition to this sense of personal authority, Jesus' teaching style also captivated his audience. He spoke in a clear and concrete manner, using down-to-earth language and stories drawn from everyday life. He avoided the philosophical jargon and esoteric language of many of the philosophers and religious leaders of his day. Jesus also used a range of literary devices, including proverbs, metaphors, similes, riddles, puns, hyperbole, paradox, and irony (see fig. 16.1). Who can forget Jesus' striking hyperbole of a camel trying to squeeze its enormous snout through the tiny eye of a needle (Mark 10:25, par.), or the bizarre scene of a person trying to take a tiny splinter from a friend's eye while ignoring the enormous beam sticking out of their own eye (Matt. 7:3–5)? Such imagery caught the imagination of the people, causing them to hang on to his every word.

Z. Radovan, Jerusalem

These needles were excavated in Jerusalem and date to the Roman era. Jesus said it is easier for a camel to get through the eye of a needle than for a rich man to enter the kingdom of God.

Much of Jesus' teaching was in poetic form, making it easy to memorize. Hebrew poetry did not usually rhyme but used parallel lines to produce its rhythmic effect. **Synonymous parallelism** may be seen in Matthew 7:7, where three parallel lines repeat similar thoughts:

Ask and it will be given to you;
Seek and you will find;
Knock and the door will be opened to you.

— Matthew 7:7

Antithetical parallelism appears a few verses later, where consecutive lines represent contrasting thoughts:

A good tree cannot bear bad fruit,
and a bad tree cannot bear good fruit.

— Matthew 7:18

In addition to being captivated by his sense of authority and his engaging style, Jesus' hearers were also captivated by the content of the message itself: *the proclamation of the*

Figure 16.1—Common Figures of Speech Used by Jesus		
Name	**Description**	**Examples**
Proverbs and Aphorisms	Short, memorable statements of wisdom or truth	• "Do not judge, or you too will be judged" (Matt. 7:1). • "No one who puts his hand to the plow and looks back is fit for service in the kingdom of God" (Luke 9:62).
Metaphor	An implicit comparison between two unlike things	• "You are the light of the world" (Matt. 5:14). • "I am the good shepherd. The good shepherd lays down his life for the sheep" (John 10:11).
Simile	An explicit comparison between two things, usually with the words "as" or "like"	• "Go! I am sending you out like lambs among wolves" (Luke 10:3). • "To what can I compare this generation? They are like children sitting in the marketplaces and calling out to others" (Matt. 11:16).
Paradox	A seemingly contradictory statement that is nonetheless true	• "For whoever wants to save his life will lose it, but whoever loses his life for me will save it" (Luke 9:24). • "For even the Son of Man did not come to be served, but to serve, and to give his life as a ransom for many" (Mark 10:45).
Hyperbole	An exaggeration used for emphasis or effect	• "If anyone comes to me and does not hate his father and mother, his wife and children, his brothers and sisters—yes, even his own life—he cannot be my disciple" (Luke 14:26). • "It is easier for a camel to go through the eye of a needle than for a rich man to enter the kingdom of God" (Mark 10:25).
Pun	A play on words using terms that sound or look alike	• "And I tell you that you are Peter [*petros*], and on this rock [*petra*] I will build my church" (Matt. 16:18). • "You blind guides! You strain out a gnat [Aramaic: *galma*] but swallow a camel [Aramaic: *gamla*]" (Matt. 23:24).
Riddle	A question or statement requiring thought to answer or understand	• "Jesus answered them, 'Destroy this temple, and I will raise it again in three days'" (John 2:19, referring to his own body). • "How can Satan drive out Satan? If a kingdom is divided against itself, that kingdom cannot stand" (Mark 3:23–24).
Irony	(1) An expression marked by a deliberate contrast between apparent and intended meaning (2) Also, incongruity between what might be expected and what actually occurs	(1) "Jesus said to them, 'I have shown you many great miracles from the Father. For which of these do you stone me?'" (John 10:32). (2) "Many will come from the east and the west, and will take their places at the feast with Abraham, Isaac and Jacob in the kingdom of heaven. But the subjects of the kingdom will be thrown outside, into the darkness, where there will be weeping and gnashing of teeth" (Matt. 8:11–12).

kingdom of God. Jesus claimed that through his words and actions, God's end-times salvation was breaking in on human history. Many of Jesus' sayings and parables concern the nature and significance of the kingdom of God.

JESUS' CENTRAL MESSAGE: THE KINGDOM OF GOD

When Jesus began preaching in Galilee, his message concerned the coming of the kingdom of God. Mark writes that Jesus came into Galilee preaching, "The time has come … The kingdom of God is near. Repent and believe the good news!" (Mark 1:15; cf. Matt. 4:17; Luke 4:43). What *is* the kingdom of God, and what did Jesus mean by saying that it was "near" or "at hand"?

The Jewish Background

Two ideas about God's kingdom existed side by side in Judaism. The first was God's everpresent reign as king over all the earth. In Isaiah 43:15, God announces, "I am the LORD, your Holy One, Israel's Creator, your King." Psalm 99:1 proclaims, "The LORD reigns, let the nations tremble; he sits enthroned between the cherubim, let the earth shake." God's kingdom has no boundaries. It is universal and eternal: "Your kingdom is an everlasting kingdom, and your dominion endures through all generations" (Ps. 145:13). In this sense, God's kingdom is not so much a realm as a reign. It is his sovereign dominion over all things.

Though God is now king, other passages speak of a day when he will establish his kingdom on earth. Isaiah 24:23 describes a time when "the LORD Almighty will reign on Mount Zion and in Jerusalem, and before its elders, gloriously" (cf. Zech. 14:9). Both ideas—the universal and the future reigns of God—appear in the Old Testament and in the Jewish literature of Jesus' day. Sometimes the universal reign is predominant, with God portrayed as the sovereign king of the universe. Other times, the future or eschatological hope is in view. In much of the apocalyptic literature, the persecuted people of God long for the day when he will intervene to defeat their enemies and establish his reign on earth. The present evil age will then pass into the age to come, a time of glory, justice, and righteousness for Israel.

Jesus and the Kingdom

Jesus' preaching acknowledged both senses of the kingdom of God. In the present, God is the sovereign Lord of the universe, who feeds the birds of the air and clothes the lilies of the field (Matt. 6:26–30). People are to "seek first his kingdom" by submitting to his sovereign authority (Matt. 6:33). The Lord's Prayer in Matthew places the phrases "your kingdom come" and "your will be done" in synonymous parallelism (Matt. 6:10). For God's kingdom to come means for all people to submit to his authority, so that his will may be done "on earth as it is in heaven."

Yet Jesus also taught that the kingdom of God was a future state believers would one day enter (Mark 9:47; Matt. 7:21; 25:34). He referred to a time when his disciples would know that the kingdom was near (Luke 21:31). The coming of the kingdom would mean the judgment of the wicked (Matt. 25:41), the establishment of a redeemed community founded on righteousness and justice (Matt. 13:36–43), and perfect fellowship with God at the messianic banquet (Luke 13:28–29; Matt. 8:11). Jesus looks forward to eating and drinking with his disciples in the kingdom of God (Mark 14:25; Luke 22:16, 18; Matt. 26:29). God's instrument in the establishment of this future kingdom is the Son of Man, who will return and gather God's chosen people from the ends of the earth (Mark 13:26–27, par.; cf. Luke 17; Matt. 16:27–28). In these contexts, the kingdom of God is synonymous with the age to come, when God will judge the wicked and vindicate his people.

What was radically unique about Jesus' teaching was his claim that this end-times kingdom of God was even now arriving through his own words and actions. The eschatological kingdom was not merely future but also in some sense already present. People receive it and enter it in the present (Mark 10:15; Luke 12:32; 16:16; Matt. 11:11–12; 21:31; 23:13). Jesus announces that the kingdom of God is "at hand" (Mark 1:14–15). While this Greek expression could mean either "near" (soon to arrive) or "at hand" (already present), the latter seems most likely. Jesus saw the Old Testament promises already coming to fulfillment. In the synagogue of Nazareth, he cites the prophecy of Isaiah 61:1–2:

> The Spirit of the Lord is on me,
>   because he has anointed me
>   to preach good news to the poor.
> He has sent me to proclaim freedom for the prisoners
>   and recovery of sight for the blind,
> to release the oppressed,
>   to proclaim the year of the Lord's favor.
>
> —Luke 4:18–19

The "year of the Lord's favor" is language associated with the Old Testament Year of Jubilee (Leviticus 25) and functions in Isaiah 61 as a metaphor for God's end-times salvation—the establishment of his kingdom. In verse 21, Jesus concludes, "*Today* this scripture is fulfilled in your hearing." Jesus viewed his ministry as establishing God's rule and kingdom.

While Judaism saw the eschatological kingdom coming at the end of the age, when God would defeat Satan and usher in the age to come, Jesus proclaimed that God was acting now to reveal his kingdom and defeat Satan. When accused by the Pharisees of casting out demons by Satan's power, Jesus refutes the charge and then points to the real source of his authority: "But if I drive out demons by the finger of God, *then the kingdom of God has come to you*" (Luke 11:20; cf. Matt. 12:28). Jesus' exorcisms manifest the kingdom by asserting God's reign over the reign of Satan. Similarly, in Luke 17:21, when the Pharisees ask Jesus when the kingdom of God is coming, he responds, "The kingdom of God is in your midst." Some have translated this "within you," in the sense of "in your hearts," but this is unlikely. Jesus would not have said that the kingdom was in the hearts of the Pharisees. The expression probably means "among you" or "in your midst," referring to the presence of Jesus himself. Through Jesus' presence, God is establishing his reign.

We must therefore acknowledge both present and future dimensions in Jesus' kingdom preaching. The kingdom is both already and not yet. In the present, people are called to submit to God's authority and so "enter" his kingdom (Mark 10:15, 23–25; Matt. 21:31;

> What was radically unique about Jesus' teaching was his claim that the end-times kingdom of God was even now arriving through his words and actions.

23:13; Luke 11:52; 18:16–17). When they do, they freely receive God's salvation benefits available through Jesus Christ and become heirs of the kingdom (Matt. 25:34). The kingdom is frequently viewed as the salvation gift itself (Mark 10:15; Luke 12:32; Matt. 5:3, 10). Yet while Jesus inaugurated the kingdom at his first coming, he will consummate it at his return (Mark 13:26–27, par.). Satan was defeated in the ministry of Jesus and at the cross, but his final destruction awaits the end.

The New Testament Epistles, looking back on what Jesus accomplished, reflect this same perspective. While the present evil age continues, the new age has broken into history through the coming of Jesus Christ (Gal. 1:4). Believers now experience God's eschatological salvation "in Christ," through their relationship with him. Paul reminds the Colossians that God "has rescued us from the dominion of darkness and brought us into the kingdom of the Son he loves" (Col. 1:13). When Jesus defeated death and rose again, he became the "firstfruits" of the resurrection (1 Cor. 15:23) and so entered the new age of salvation, the kingdom of God. Believers enter the kingdom through their identification with Jesus in his life, death, and resurrection (Romans 6; Col. 3:1–3). Paul writes, "If anyone is in Christ, the new creation has come: The old has gone, the new is here!" (2 Cor. 5:17 TNIV). Yet complete salvation and full inheritance of the kingdom awaits the future (Eph. 1:18; 5:5; Rom. 13:11; 1 Cor. 6:9–10; 15:50; 2 Tim. 4:18). The church lives simultaneously in both ages, when salvation has been accomplished but not yet consummated.

JESUS AND THE LAW: THE ETHICS OF THE KINGDOM

Jesus called people not only to acknowledge God's kingdom but also to submit to it in their daily lives. The inauguration of the kingdom creates a new way of life and a radical new kingdom ethic. How does this new ethic relate to the Mosaic law which governed Israel's national life?

We have seen that the study of Torah, the law of Moses, represented a core value in first-century Judaism (chap. 6). What was Jesus' attitude toward the law, and how does it relate to his kingdom preaching? We have examined this question in chapter 8 from the perspective of Matthew's theology. Here we will expand on that discussion with reference to Jesus' kingdom program. On the one hand, Jesus affirmed the eternal validity of the law, stating that not the smallest letter would disappear from it until everything was fulfilled (Matt. 5:18–20). On the other hand, Jesus seemed to ignore and even alter aspects of the law. In Mark 7:18–19, Jesus apparently cancels the dietary laws of the Old Testament: "Don't you see that nothing that enters a man from the outside can make him 'unclean'?" The narrator adds that "in saying this, Jesus declared all foods 'clean.'" Similarly, in six antitheses in the Sermon on the Mount, Jesus reinterprets, intensifies, and apparently alters Old Testament commands (Matt. 5:17–48). Jesus also seems to neutralize the Sabbath command by healing on the Sabbath (Mark 3:1–6, par.), defending his disciples' picking of grain on the Sabbath (Mark 2:25–26, par.), and claiming to be "Lord of the Sabbath" (Mark 2:28, par.). In John, Jesus claims that just as the Father works on the Sabbath, so he can work (John 5:17–18). How do we harmonize these seemingly contradictory statements? Did Jesus abolish the law or affirm it? Two points should be kept in mind: (1) Jesus' emphasis on the true essence and purpose of the law, and (2) his role as the fulfillment of the law.

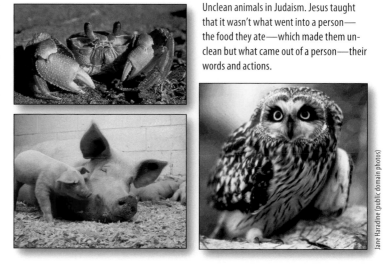

Unclean animals in Judaism. Jesus taught that it wasn't what went into a person—the food they ate—which made them unclean but what came out of a person—their words and actions.

Jane Haradine (public domain photos)

The True Essence of the Law

Much of Jesus' teaching challenges the legalistic and sometimes hypocritical manner in which the law was applied. He castigates the Pharisees and scribes for tithing the smallest of spices yet neglecting the fundamental aspects of the law, like justice, mercy, and faithfulness (Matt. 23:23; Luke 11:42). When challenged because his disciples did not practice the ceremonial washings prescribed in the "tradition of the elders" (the oral law later transcribed in the rabbinic writings), Jesus responds by quoting Isaiah 29:13: "These people honor me with their lips, but their hearts are far from me. They worship me in vain; their teachings are merely human rules" (Mark 7:6–7 TNIV; cf. Matt. 15:1–9). Jesus is not here condemning the oral traditions of the Pharisees simply because they were a human invention. The purpose of their oral law was a noble one: to apply God's commandments to the new and changing circumstances of everyday life. Jesus condemns them rather for practicing their traditions without regard for the true spirit and purpose of the law.

This is seen in Jesus' apparent disregard for Sabbath traditions. When challenged by the Pharisees, Jesus reminds them that the Sabbath was created to benefit people: "The Sabbath was made for people, not people for the Sabbath" (Mark 2:27 TNIV). God does not arbitrarily put burdens on his people. Yet the scribes and Pharisees had turned the Sabbath into a burden to bear rather than a gift to enjoy (cf. Luke 11:46; Matt. 23:4). There is heavy irony in Mark 3:1–6 (par.), where the religious leaders are seeking to catch Jesus working on the Sabbath when he heals a man with a shriveled hand. Jesus first asks, "Which is lawful on the Sabbath: to do good or to do evil, to save life or to kill?" and then he heals the man. In Matthew, Jesus points out the hypocrisy of the Pharisees, who will happily rescue their sheep from a pit on the Sabbath but will not help a man. Are not people more valuable than sheep? (Matt. 12:11–12). Jesus' point is that doing good on the Sabbath is acceptable since it celebrates the true meaning of the Sabbath, a good gift from God. Jesus does not overrule the Sabbath; he brings out its true meaning. Ironically, immediately afterward, the Pharisees do evil on the Sabbath by plotting Jesus' death (Mark 3:6, par.).

The true essence of the law is also the key to the six antitheses of the Sermon on the Mount (Matt. 5:21–48), in which Jesus contrasts what was said to the ancients with his own authoritative teaching. Jesus pushes beyond the external requirements to the true intention of God. It is not just murder that is a sin (Exod. 20:13) but anger—murder of the heart (Matt. 5:21–26). The command against adultery (Exod. 20:14) extends to lust—adultery of the heart (Matt. 5:27–30). While divorce was allowed by Moses (Deut. 24:1), this was merely a concession to human sinfulness; it was never part of God's will or desire for the lifelong covenant of marriage (Matt. 5:31–32). The Old Testament commanded that oaths must be kept (Num. 30:2). But Jesus says oaths are unnecessary when people act and speak with integrity and truthfulness (Matt. 5:33–37). God's command for justice, "eye for eye, and tooth for tooth" (Exod. 21:24), was often used as justification for personal retribution. While not denying the need for social justice or judicial punishment, Jesus calls for a response of good when confronted by evil (Matt. 5:38–42). Love should be shown not only to your neighbor (Lev. 19:18) but even to your enemies. This reflects the heart of God, who shows kindness even to sinners (Matt. 5:43–48). This radical new ethic is ultimately neither radical nor new but wholly in line with the character of God, whose kingdom Jesus is announcing.

> Jesus pushes beyond the external requirements of the law to the true intention of God.

Jesus as Fulfillment of the Law

While much of Jesus' teaching brings out the true meaning of the law, other teaching suggests a radical new orientation to the law for God's people. How do we account for the fact that the early church did not feel compelled to worship on the Sabbath (Saturday) or to observe the Old Testament dietary laws? The answer must be found in Jesus' role not just as the interpreter of the law but also as its fulfillment. The authority with which Jesus speaks already points in this direction. With his refrain, "You have heard that it was said ... but I tell you ..." (Matt. 5:21–48), Jesus affirms that he is more than an interpreter of the law. He speaks for God in the kingdom age. He does not just explain the Sabbath command. He is "Lord of the Sabbath" (Mark 2:28).

Jesus' attitude toward the law must be understood in the context of his proclamation of the kingdom of God. Jesus announced that in his own words and deeds, the kingdom of God was breaking into human history. To understand the implications of this for the law of Moses, we must look to the Old Testament background. While Israel repeatedly broke God's law and demonstrated covenant unfaithfulness, God remained faithful to his promises. In Jeremiah 31, he promised a new covenant with his people which would provide forgiveness of sins, knowledge of God, and the writing of the law on their hearts (Jer. 31:31–34). This new covenant cannot be separated from Jesus' announcement of the kingdom. At the Last Supper, Jesus explicitly links his death to the establishment of the new covenant and the coming of the kingdom (Mark 14:24–25; Matt. 26:28–29; Luke 22:20; 1 Cor. 11:25).

The transformation of the law under the new covenant provides a framework for Jesus' teaching. Jesus announces that he came not to abolish the law but to fulfill it (Matt. 5:17). Though various interpretations have been suggested for the word "fulfill" (*plēroō*), it seems best to view it in the sense of "bring to its culmination." How did Jesus fulfill the law? To answer this, we must understand the purpose of the law. The law was never intended as a means of attaining salvation or entering a covenant relationship with God. The covenant came through God's gracious initiative. Keeping the law was Israel's grateful response to God and her means of receiving the benefits and fellowship promised in the covenant. As discussed in chapter 11, this perspective is known today as covenantal nomism, a term popularized by E. P. Sanders (see p. 373). The purpose of the Mosaic law was twofold: (1) to reveal God's righteous standards and (2) to provide the means of forgiveness when Israel failed to meet those standards. God's people were to be holy because God was holy. When they failed, forgiveness was possible through repentance and the sacrificial system established in the law.

> Jesus announces that he came not to abolish the law but to fulfill it, to bring it to its intended culmination.

Jesus fulfilled the first purpose of the law in two ways: in his teaching, he interpreted the true meaning of the law, and in his conduct, he lived a life of perfect righteousness. He fulfilled the second purpose by becoming "a ransom for many" through his sacrificial death—the blood of the covenant (Mark 10:45; 14:22–24). While this second purpose is only briefly discussed in the Gospels (see chap. 19), it finds fuller exposition in the Epistles. Because humanity is unable to achieve perfect obedience, the law condemns (Rom. 3:20; 4:15; 5:20). Through his sacrificial death, Jesus received the condemnation of the law and paid the penalty for humanity's sins (Rom. 3:25; 8:3–4; 2 Cor. 5:21; Heb. 10:10; 1 Peter 3:18; 1 John 2:2).

If the law is fulfilled or culminated in Christ, is any aspect of it still binding on believers? Some have answered by appealing to the difference between civil, ceremonial, and moral commands in the Old Testament. While the civil laws related only to ethnic Israel, and the ceremonial were fulfilled in Jesus' death, the moral commands are still binding on believers. The problem with this is that no such distinction is made in Scripture, and it is often impossible to tell which commands are moral. For example, is the Sabbath command (one of the Ten Commandments) moral or ceremonial? If moral, how can Paul apparently deny its obligation on believers? (See Rom. 14:5–6; Col. 2:16.) It seems better to say that the whole law is fulfilled in Christ.

What, then, did Jesus mean when he said that no part of the law would disappear until all was accomplished (Matt. 5:17)? The answer is that the law is not abolished, but its purpose and function are transformed (fulfilled) with the coming of Jesus and the in-breaking of the kingdom of God. The law continues to reveal God's righteous character and to play a prophetic role in pointing to Christ (Luke 24:25–27, 45–47). But the individual regulations of the law are not binding on believers, because they live no longer under the Mosaic covenant but under the new covenant. God's righteous standards are now written on their hearts, not on tablets of stone. Their relationship with God is mediated not through the written law but through the one who fulfilled the law, Jesus the Messiah, and through the Spirit which he gives.

How, then, do we explain Jesus' statement that "whoever breaks the least of these commandments will be called least in the kingdom of God" (Matt. 5:19)? Does this mean that believers are to keep every commandment of the Old Testament law? This is unlikely, since Jesus himself teaches the contrary (Matt. 5:21–48; 15:1–20; Mark 7:19). It must mean that those new-covenant believers who have the law written on their hearts are not less obedient to God's standards than old-covenant believers but are more obedient. Their righteousness must exceed that of the scribes and Pharisees (Matt. 5:20), who practiced an outward righteousness, because kingdom ethics require an inward "heart" righteousness, based not on written regulations but on the character of God, whose presence now dwells in believers through his Spirit.

THE GREATEST COMMANDMENT AND THE CHARACTER OF GOD

This perspective helps to explain much of Jesus' ethical teaching. Jesus' appeal to the spirit of the law over mere outward conformity (Matthew 5) looks beyond the written law given at Sinai to the moral character of God, who gave these laws. For new-covenant believers living in the kingdom age, God's standards are discerned through the Spirit, who reveals God's character and mediates his will, and through the life of Jesus, who lived in full submission to God's purpose. Jesus' affirmation of the spirit of the Sabbath over rigid rules for its observance is an appeal to the nature of God, who rested on the seventh day and created a Sabbath rest for the benefit of his creatures (Mark 2:27, par.). The Lord of the Sabbath came to provide God's eschatological rest, not new rules to burden his people. (See Matt. 11:28–30: "Come to me, all you who are weary and burdened, and I will give you rest.... For my yoke is easy and my burden light.")

> Love for God and love for others fulfills the law because these imperatives reflect the essential nature of God, whose love motivates his behavior toward all of creation.

This focus on God's character is also evident in Jesus' teaching on love. When a scribe asks about the greatest commandment, Jesus responds that the greatest is to "love the Lord your God with all your heart and with all your soul and with all your mind" (quoting Deut. 6:4–5), and the second to "love your neighbor as yourself" (quoting Lev. 19:18). "All the Law and the Prophets hang on these two commandments" (Matt. 22:34–40; cf. Mark 12:28–31; Luke 10:25–28; Rom. 13:8, 10; Gal. 5:14). Love for God and love for others fulfills the whole law because these imperatives reflect the essential nature of God, whose love motivates his behavior toward all of creation. Because believers are "children of your Father in heaven" (TNIV), they are to love their enemies, just as their Father does (Matt. 5:44–45). Jesus can sum up the law by saying, "Be perfect, therefore, as your heavenly Father is perfect" (Matt. 5:48). This is not the imposition of an impossible and ultimately frustrating standard of perfection on believers. It is rather the insistence that the nature of God—in all its perfection—is the guide for behavior in the new age of salvation.

GRACE AND WORKS: THE FREE GIFT AND THE COST OF DISCIPLESHIP

The age of the Spirit is the age of grace, and God's free gift of salvation to sinners is a leading theme in Jesus' teaching. Jesus dines with sinners, a symbol of God's gracious acceptance. People enter the kingdom not through works of righteousness but through repentance and faith. Jesus often commends the faith of those around him (Mark 2:5, par.; Matt. 8:10; 7:9; 9:22, 29; 15:28; Luke 7:9) and heals by saying, "Your faith has made you well" (Mark 5:34, par.; Mark 10:52, par.; Luke 7:50; 17:19). He calls for faith like a child, humble dependence on God (Mark 10:14–15, par.; Matt. 11:25, par.; 18:3). The sinful woman who anoints Jesus' feet is forgiven much, and so loves much (Luke 7:36–50). The prodigal son is received back by the loving father without working off his debt (Luke 15:11–32). The tax collector in the temple is forgiven through humble repentance, while the prideful Pharisee leaves unforgiven (Luke 18:9–14). The repentant criminal on the cross is offered a place in paradise despite having no opportunity for good works (Luke 23:43). The gospel of Jesus is a gospel of grace offered to sinners.

An Egyptian farmer plowing a field. Jesus called his disciples to unwavering discipleship. Those who put their hand to the plow must not look back (Luke 9:62).

© Neal Bierling/Zondervan Image Archives

Yet beside these statements of God's free forgiveness are those about the high cost of discipleship. Jesus calls for his disciples to leave everything and follow him. They are to deny themselves, take up their crosses, and follow him (Mark 8:34–38, par.; Luke 14:27; Matt. 10:38). No one can serve two masters, so devotion to God must be absolute (Matt. 6:24; Luke 16:13). Intensity of love for God should make other relationships look like hate (Luke 14:26; cf. Matt. 10:37). No one who puts his hand to the plow and then looks back is fit for the kingdom of God (Luke 9:62). God's people are to be perfect, as he is perfect (Matt. 5:48).

How do we reconcile statements of salvation as a free gift and of the high cost of discipleship? The answer must lie in the difference between entrance into the kingdom—a free gift offered to sinners—and the standards expected of those whose lives have been transformed by the kingdom's power. Righteous actions arise out of a life made new. Those who have become children of God through faith gain a new outlook on life, and devotion to the kingdom becomes their passion and motivation. The radical self-sacrificial lifestyle to which Jesus calls his disciples is the consequence of, not the condition for, a life transformed by the Spirit of God.

SOCIAL JUSTICE: THE RICH AND THE POOR

Hand in hand with God's attribute of love are attributes of mercy and justice. Like that of the Old Testament prophets, Jesus' teaching is full of admonitions for a just and merciful society. He preaches good news to the poor and reaches out to the outcasts of society, sinners, lepers, Samaritans, Gentiles, women, and children. He strongly warns of the destructive power of riches. The Beatitudes in Luke pronounce not only blessings on the poor and oppressed but woes against the rich and self-sufficient (Luke 6:20–26; cf. Matt. 5:3–12). It is impossible to serve God and mammon (Matt. 6:24). The rich young man cannot enter the kingdom unless he gives up his dependence on riches. "It is easier for a camel to go through the eye of a needle than for a rich man to enter the kingdom of God" (Mark 10:25, par.). Jesus often speaks of the reversal of fortunes which the kingdom brings. Many parables and stories in Luke drive this point home. The rich fool stores up treasure for a comfortable retirement only to face the loss of everything at death (Luke 12:15–21). The rich man who ignored the poor beggar Lazarus in life faces greater suffering in the afterlife (Luke 16:19–31).

> Like that of the Old Testament prophets, Jesus' teaching is full of admonitions for a just and merciful society.

A hoard of gold coins. Jesus warned of the danger of the love of mammon, or worldly wealth.

Is Jesus speaking in these contexts of physical poverty, or is this language metaphorical, referring to those who are spiritually poor? By the first century, the term "the poor" (*anawim*) was sometimes used in Judaism to designate the righteous remnant of God's people, who lived in humble dependence on him. Matthew's Beatitudes speak of those who are "poor in spirit" (Matt. 5:3). Yet while there are certainly spiritual dimensions in Jesus' teaching on poverty, it is impossible to exclude the physical from Jesus' concrete illustrations. Those who are physically poor and oppressed are naturally driven to greater trust in and dependence on God. Conversely, those who treat riches as their own, rather than as entrusted resources for God's service, live in defiance of his sovereignty. It *is* impossible for a rich man to enter the kingdom of God (this is the point of Jesus' shocking statement in Mark 10:25, par., and it must not be softened), since by definition a rich man is one who views his riches as his own. Yet while it is impossible for people, Jesus adds, "All things are possible with God" (Mark 10:27, par.). Salvation comes through renunciation of all human effort and achievement—including wealth—and through humble dependence on God.

The same principle applies to leadership in the community of faith. Those who seek power and control over others cannot be disciples of the Son of Man, who came to serve, not to be served, and to give his life as a ransom for many (Mark 10:45). Leadership in the kingdom is achieved not through power or coercion but through service and self-sacrifice. The first must become last. While the rulers of this world lord their power over their subjects, those who would lead in the messianic community of faith do so as servants, empowering others to be all that God has called them to be.

THE PARABLES OF THE KINGDOM

Jesus' most important teaching device was the parable, using vivid and memorable scenes from everyday life to teach profound spiritual truths. While other rabbis and teachers of Jesus' day used parables to illustrate their teachings, none used them as often or as effectively as Jesus did.

The Nature of Parables

The Greek term *parabolē* has a broader range of meaning than the English term parable and may refer to a variety of figures of speech, including proverbs, metaphors, analogies, and parables. For our purposes, a **parable** proper may be defined as "a story from daily life illustrating a moral or spiritual lesson." Throughout the history of the church, Jesus' parables have been interpreted in a variety of ways.

For much of church history, the parables were seen as theological allegories. An allegory is a story in which the characters and events stand for something else, so that the literal sense suggests a deeper spiritual or symbolic meaning. The most famous examples of such allegorizing come from St. Augustine, the fourth-century church father. He claimed that in the parable of the good Samaritan, for example, the man who is beaten represents Adam, the robbers are the devil and his angels, the priest signifies the Old Testament priesthood, the good Samaritan is Christ, the animal who carries the man represents the incarnation of Christ, the inn is the church, and the innkeeper is the apostle Paul![1] Other church writers similarly found allegorical elements in almost every detail of Jesus' parables. It should be obvious that this kind of allegorizing is not only highly subjective but ignores the meaning of the parable in Jesus' context.

In response to this history of allegorizing, in the late nineteenth century, **Adolf Jülicher** claimed that such interpretations were completely misguided.[2] The parables were not allegories but similitudes (extended similes), stories intended to convey only one main point. Individual characters and events must not be allegorized. For example, the parable of the good Samaritan is not an allegory of the history of salvation. It rather makes just one

---

1. Augustine, *Quaestiones Evangeliorum* 2.19.
2. Adolf Jülicher, *Die Gleichnisreden Jesu*, 2 vols. (Tübingen: Mohr, 1899).

Sower's Cove, traditional site of Jesus' teaching in parables (Mark 4; Matthew 13; Luke 8)

point: what it means to be a neighbor. Jülicher went so far as to reject as inauthentic any allegorical elements which he found in the parables. These were not original to Jesus, he claimed, but were added later by the early church. Jülicher's distinction between parables and allegories had a major impact on New Testament scholarship and transformed the way Jesus' parables were understood.

Many scholars today, while acknowledging the importance of Jülicher's work, insist that he went too far. While rejecting the outlandish allegorization that characterized much of church history, they recognize that parables often contain allegorical elements and that sometimes a parable may make more than one point. For example, the parable of the prodigal son (Luke 15:11 – 32) is not just about God's love for the lost but is also an indictment against those who, like the older brother, don't share that concern. Furthermore, there are allegorical elements in this parable. The father represents God, the younger son represents the sinners to whom Jesus is ministering, and the older brother represents the religious leaders who show only disdain for these sinners.

The parable of the wicked tenant farmers (Mark 12:1 – 12, par.) is the most allegorical of Jesus' parables, with all of the main features carrying symbolic significance (see pp. 187–89). While most parables are not allegories, there are allegorical elements in many parables, especially those related to Jesus' preaching about the kingdom of God.

The Purpose of the Parables: To Reveal and to Conceal

One of the reasons Jesus taught in parables was to communicate truth in a vivid, powerful, and memorable manner. But another reason relates to the enigmatic nature of the parables themselves. When Jesus' disciples asked him the meaning of the parable of the sower (Mark 4:1–9, par.), he first explained why he spoke in parables, citing Isaiah 6:9–10:

> The secret of the kingdom of God has been given to you. But to those on the outside everything is said in parables so that,
> "they may be ever seeing but never perceiving,
> and ever hearing but never understanding;
> otherwise they might turn and be forgiven!"
>
> —Mark 4:11–12 (cf. Matt. 13:11–15; Luke 8:10)

The term "secret" (*mystērion*) refers to a mystery hidden in the past, now revealed to those who are responding in faith. The secret in this case is that the kingdom of God — God's final salvation — is now breaking into human history through Jesus the Messiah. The passage is difficult because it seems to suggest that the parables intentionally hide the truth from some people. The solution is in Jesus' quotation from Isaiah 6:9–10, a passage which in its Old Testament context refers to Israel's unwillingness to respond to the prophets' message (cf. Deut. 29:4; Jer. 5:21; Ezek. 12:2). When Israel rejected God, God hardened her heart, choosing to accomplish his purpose not just despite her unbelief but by means of her unbelief. Just as God hardened Pharaoh's heart to accomplish his sovereign purpose in the exodus (Exod. 8:15, 32; 9:12; 10:1), so he hardened the heart of rebellious Israel in Isaiah's day. Her fate was sealed. Her judgment was inevitable. Yet God would accomplish his purpose through that hardening. Similarly, when Israel's leaders rejected Jesus' kingdom announcement, God hardened their hearts so that "they may be ever seeing but never perceiving." God would then use that rejection to accomplish his sovereign purpose, the salvation of humanity through the sacrificial death of Jesus.

This confirms that Jesus spoke in parables both *to reveal* and *to conceal* (see p. 182). To those responsive to his kingdom message, the parables illuminate the meaning of the kingdom. But to those who because of their hard-heartedness reject the message, the parables hide the truth.

Interpreting the Parables

Various principles should be kept in mind when reading the parables.

(1) First, always interpret the parable in the context of Jesus' ministry. The parable of the sower (Mark 4:1–9, par.) is often interpreted with reference to different responses to present-day preaching of the Gospel. While this may be a valid application of the text, its original meaning must be seen in the responses of Jesus' hearers to his preaching of the kingdom.

The parables have become so familiar to Christians that we often miss the powerful impact they would have had to a first-century Jewish hearer. For example, the parable of the good Samaritan would have been shocking and scandalous to Jesus' Jewish audience, who could not imagine that a hated Samaritan would care more for an injured Jew than would a priest or a Levite, Israel's religious elite (Luke 10:25–37). Contrary to our retrospective understanding, in the parable of the Pharisee and the tax collector (Luke 18:9–14), the prayer of the Pharisee would have sounded to a first-century Jew not hypocritical but high-minded and holy. On the other hand, the very presence of a tax collector in the temple would have been viewed as offensive. Jesus surely shocked his audience when he concluded, "I tell you that this man [the tax collector], rather than the other, went home justified before God" (v. 14).

(2) Second, always keep in mind Jesus' central message of the kingdom of God. Jesus' teaching in parables is closely associated with his proclamation of the kingdom, and most parables illustrate or illuminate aspects of the kingdom. This is especially true of the parables of Mark 4, Matthew 13, and Luke 8, which frequently begin something like "the kingdom of God [or heaven] is like . . ." The parable of the sower reveals various kinds of responses to Jesus' kingdom preaching (Mark 4:1 – 9, 13 – 20, par.). The parables of the mustard seed and of the leaven confirm that the kingdom will start small but grow to fill the whole earth (Matt. 13:31 – 33, par.). The parable of the wheat and the tares reveals that in its present phase, the kingdom will exist alongside the evil world system, but at the end, evil will be rooted out (Matt. 13:24 – 30, 36 – 43). The parable of the strong man demonstrates that through exorcisms Jesus' kingdom authority is defeating and binding the kingdom of Satan (Mark 3:22 – 27, par.). The parables of the new wine and unshrunk cloth teach that the kingdom is a whole new age of salvation which completes and fulfills the old (Mark 2:21 – 22, par.).

Cheryl Dunn/ZIBBC

Wineskin

Many parables, especially those in Luke, reveal God's love for the lost and his free offer of grace to sinners. This is true of the parables of the lost sheep, the lost coin, and the prodigal son (Luke 15), the two debtors (Luke 7:41 – 43), the Pharisee and the tax collector (18:9 – 14), the unmerciful servant (Matt. 18:23 – 35), and the laborers in the vineyard (Matt. 20:1 – 16). The parable of the great banquet shows that God's offer of salvation goes out to all people, but also that it is rejected by many in Israel (Luke 14:15 – 24). This theme of Israel's rejection and coming judgment also appears in the parables of the wicked tenants (Mark 12:1 – 12, par.) and the barren fig tree (Luke 13:6 – 9). The need for good stewardship during the present age is another major theme of the parables, appearing in the parables of the talents (Matt. 25:14 – 30), the minas (Luke 19:11 – 27), the ten virgins (Matt. 25:1 – 13), and the faithful and unfaithful servants (Matt. 24:45 – 51).

This small sampling reveals how the parables must be understood first and foremost in the context of Jesus' kingdom preaching, and how, in turn, they illuminate the nature of that kingdom.

(3) A third key to interpreting the parables is to be aware of cultural, historical, and literary allusions. Jesus often borrowed imagery or allusions from the Old Testament or from his own cultural and historical contexts. Recognizing this imagery is often crucial to the parable's interpretation. The parable of the wicked tenant farmers in Mark (Mark 12:1 – 12) begins with language reminiscent of the song of the vineyard in Isaiah 5, and so

should be interpreted in light of this Old Testament passage. Jesus' hearers would surely have recognized this allusion.

(4) Fourth, seek the primary point of the parable. While a parable may teach several related truths, all of these will normally relate to one central point. The primary message of the parable will often come at the end, or in a concluding remark made by Jesus. For example, at the end of the parable of the Pharisee and the tax collector, Jesus says, "For everyone who exalts himself will be humbled, and whoever humbles himself will be exalted" (Luke 18:14). The point of the parable is the danger of pride and self-righteousness, and the need for humility and repentance.

(5) Fifth, be cautious concerning allegorical elements. If allegorical elements are present, they should relate directly to Jesus' historical context, his intention in telling the parable, and his proclamation of the kingdom of God.

(6) Finally, examine the context of the parable in the Gospel in which it appears. The Evangelists often rearranged their material for thematic purposes, and sometimes a parable is intended to bring out a particular point in its narrative context. A good example of this is the parable of the ten minas in Luke 19:11–27. The parable is similar to Matthew's parable of the talents (Matt. 25:14–30), and both teach the need for good stewardship by Jesus' disciples. Luke, however, uses the parable to make another point—namely, the reason the kingdom did not appear on earth when Jesus first entered Jerusalem. Luke introduces the parable with the clarification, "He went on to tell them a parable, because he was near Jerusalem and the people thought that the kingdom of God was going to appear at once." In the parable, a nobleman goes away to receive a kingdom, eventually returning to reward his servants and punish his enemies. Luke's purpose in placing the parable here is to dispel Jewish criticism that as the Messiah, Jesus should have established his kingdom on earth at his triumphal entry into Jerusalem. Luke counters that from the beginning, Jesus taught that he would depart and receive his royal authority in heaven (cf. Acts 2:29–36), from whence he would return one day to reward those who were faithful and to judge those who rejected him. While the parable teaches an important lesson on stewardship, it also serves Luke's purpose by revealing the nature of Jesus' messianic reign.

» CHAPTER SUMMARY «

1. Jesus taught with extraordinary personal authority and engaged his audiences with captivating stories and vivid figures of speech.

2. His central message concerned the coming of the kingdom of God. The kingdom is both a present reality and a future hope. God's end-times salvation has been inaugurated in the present through Jesus' words and deeds and will be consummated in the future when the Son of Man returns in glory. It is both "already" and "not yet."

3. Concerning the law of Moses, Jesus (a) emphasizes the true meaning and spirit of the law, a reflection of God's righteous character, and (b) identifies himself as the fulfillment of the law, establishing a new covenant through his righteous life and death on the cross.

4. Jesus' teaching about the law looks past the law given at Mount Sinai to the very character of God, who gave the law. The whole law can be summed up in the love commandment, because this reflects the fundamental nature of God, who is absolute love.

5. Jesus' teaching emphasizes both God's free grace offered to sinners and the high cost of discipleship. Radical commitment to Jesus Christ is the natural consequence of a life freely transformed by God's Spirit.

6. Jesus' teaching on poverty and wealth must be seen as both literal and spiritual. Entering the kingdom of God requires the repudiation of self-sufficiency and humble dependence on God.

7. Jesus' parables used vivid and memorable scenes from everyday life to teach profound spiritual truth. While not all of the features of the parables can be allegorized, many parables do contain allegorical elements.

8. To understand the parables, it is important (a) to interpret them first and foremost in the context of Jesus' ministry, (b) to relate them to his preaching of the kingdom of God, (c) to recognize their cultural and literary background in the Old Testament and Judaism, (d) to seek the primary point of the parable, (e) to exercise caution concerning allegorical elements, and (f) to determine the narrative function of the parable in the Gospel in which it appears.

» KEY TERMS «

synonymous parallelism	simile	irony
antithetical parallelism	paradox	parable
figures of speech used by Jesus:	hyperbole	Adolf Jülicher
proverbs and aphorisms	pun	
metaphor	riddle	

1. What distinguished Jesus' teaching from that of the scribes of his day? What were Jesus' favorite teaching techniques?

2. What was Jesus' central message? What is the Old Testament and Jewish background to the kingdom of God? What did Jesus mean by the "kingdom of God"? How do the present and future dimensions of the kingdom relate to one another?

3. Did Jesus affirm the validity of the Old Testament law, or did he overrule it? What is the solution to this paradox?

4. How did Jesus bring out the true meaning of the law? In what ways is Jesus the fulfillment of the law?

5. How can we reconcile Jesus' teaching on God's free grace offered to sinners and the high cost of discipleship?

6. Is Jesus' teaching about poverty and wealth meant to be taken spiritually or literally? How do these two relate to one another?

7. Summarize the history of research on parables, especially in relation to whether they should be interpreted allegorically.

8. According to Mark 4:11 – 12, why did Jesus teach in parables?

9. Identify key principles for interpreting the parables.

Digging Deeper

General

Hengel, Martin. *The Charismatic Leader and His Followers.* New York: Crossroad, 1981.

Riesner, Rainer. "Teacher." In *DJG*, 807 – 11.

Stein, Robert H. *The Method and Message of Jesus' Teachings.* Louisville: Westminster John Knox, 1994.

Jesus and the Kingdom

Beasley-Murray, G. R. *Jesus and the Kingdom of God.* Grand Rapids: Eerdmans, 1986.

Chilton, Bruce D. *God in Strength.* Sheffield: JSOT, 1987.

Kümmel, W. G. *Promise and Fulfillment: The Eschatological Message of Jesus.* Translated by Dorothea M. Barton. London: SCM, 1957.

Ladd, G. E. *The Presence of the Future.* Grand Rapids: Eerdmans, 1974.

Jesus and the Law

Banks, Robert. *Jesus and the Law in the Synoptic Tradition.* SNTSMS 28. Cambridge: Cambridge Univ. Press, 1975.

Moo, Douglas. "Law." In *DJG,* 450–61.

Sanders, E. P. *Jesus and Judaism.* Philadelphia: Fortress, 1985.

———. *Jewish Law from Jesus to the Mishnah: Five Studies.* Philadelphia: Trinity, 1990.

Westerholm, S. *Jesus and Scribal Authority.* ConBNT 10. Lund: Gleerup, 1978.

Ethics of the Kingdom/Love Command/Social Concerns

Chilton, Bruce, and J. I. H. McDonald. *Jesus and the Ethics of the Kingdom.* Grand Rapids: Eerdmans, 1987.

Davids, P. H. "Rich and Poor." In *DJG,* 701–10.

Furnish, V. P. *The Love Command in the New Testament.* Nashville: Abingdon, 1972.

Harvey, A. E. *Strenuous Commands: The Ethics of Jesus.* Philadelphia: Trinity, 1990.

Houlden, J. L. *Ethics in the New Testament.* New York: Oxford, 1977.

Hurst, L. D. "Ethics of Jesus." In *DJG,* 210–22.

Perkins, Pheme. *Love Commands in the New Testament.* New York: Paulist, 1982.

Schmidt, T. E. *Hostility to Wealth in the Synoptic Gospels.* JSNTSup 15. Sheffield: JSOT, 1987.

The Parables

Blomberg, Craig L. *Interpreting the Parables.* Downers Grove, IL: InterVarsity, 1990.

Crossan, John Dominic. *In Parables.* New York: Harper and Row, 1990.

Dodd, C. H. *The Parables of the Kingdom.* London: Nisbet, 1936.

Hedrick, Charles W. *Parables as Poetic Fictions: The Creative Voice of Jesus.* Peabody, MA: Hendrickson, 1994.

Jeremias, J. *The Parables of Jesus.* New York: Scribner's, 1963.

Jülicher, A. *Die Gleichnisreden Jesu.* 2 vols. Tübingen: Mohr [Paul Siebeck], 1888–89.

Snodgrass, Klyne R. "Parable." In *DJG,* 591–601.

Stein, Robert H. *An Introduction to the Parables of Jesus.* Philadelphia: Westminster, 1981.

Young, Brad H. *The Parables: Jewish Tradition and Christian Interpretation.* Peabody, MA: Hendrickson, 1998.

CHAPTER 17

The Miracles of Jesus

» CHAPTER OVERVIEW «

1. The Question of Miracles
2. Did Jesus Perform Miracles?
3. Ancient Parallels to Jesus' Miracles
4. The Significance of Jesus' Miracles: The Power and Presence of the Kingdom
5. Conclusion

» OBJECTIVES «

After reading this chapter, you should be able to:
- Discuss and respond to objections to the possibility of miracles.
- Provide evidence that Jesus was renowned as an exorcist and a healer.
- Compare Jesus' healings with other first-century miracle workers' healings.
- Discuss the significance of Jesus' exorcisms, healings, revivications, and nature miracles.

THE QUESTION OF MIRACLES

As we have seen, many of the negative conclusions concerning the historical Jesus can be traced back to the rationalistic worldview of the Enlightenment. The scientific method which developed in the seventeenth and eighteenth centuries sought cause-and-effect relationships for all that occurred in the natural world. Alongside this method arose the philosophies of **deism** and **materialism**. Deists claimed that God created the ordered world and then left it to run by natural laws—as a clock is wound up by its maker and then allowed to run on its own. Philosophical materialism asserts that the world is a closed system of cause and effect without outside intervention. In this mechanistic worldview, miracles are treated as contrary to the laws of nature and therefore impossible.

The problem with this claim is that it assumes its own conclusion—a closed system in which miracles cannot occur—and confuses the scientific method with the philosophical worldview of materialism. As a philosophy, materialism asserts that all of reality can be explained through the natural laws of matter and energy. The scientific method, in contrast, examines cause-and-effect relationships through experimentation, drawing conclusions through observation and repeatability. Science operates under the assumption that the world of matter and energy behaves in a consistent manner, but it does not address the philosophical question of whether any reality lies outside of this material world or whether normal patterns of nature are ever interrupted by a new causal agent, a supernatural force or being.

Miracles are, therefore, outside the realm of strict scientific investigation (which entails experimentation, observation, and repeatability). The question of miracles must be addressed first philosophically, as to their possibility, and then historically, as to their actual occurrence.

Philosophical Objections to Miracles

Perhaps the most influential philosophical opposition to the miraculous came from the pen of the eighteenth-century Scottish philosopher **David Hume**.[1] Hume's primary argument was that human experience confirms the certainty and inviolability of the laws of nature. Since miracles are by definition violations of these laws, it would take an overwhelming amount of evidence—an impossibly high standard of proof—to confirm any miracle. Belief in miracles is therefore irrational.

A serious problem with Hume's argument is that it assumes *a priori* that the laws of nature are inviolable and absolute. But these so-called laws are really observations and hypotheses, human perceptions of how energy and matter work. As science has advanced, many supposedly inviolable laws have been radically modified and revised. Much that happens in the universe is beyond our expectations or present understanding. Furthermore, nothing in Hume's argument rules out the intervention of a god to alter the expected pattern of nature.

Hume advanced four additional arguments to support his claim: (1) No miracle has ever been attested by a sufficient number of educated and rational

David Hume (1711–76)

The Granger Collection, New York

---

1. David Hume, *Enquiries Concerning the Human Understanding and Concerning the Principles of Morals*, ed. L. A. Selby-Bigge, 2nd ed. (Oxford: Clarendon, 1902).

456 Part Four:
The Historical Jesus

witnesses to be proven true; (2) there is a human tendency to believe the spectacular, things that cause wonder and surprise; (3) most reports of miracles occur among ignorant and barbarous people; and (4) claims of miracles occur in all religious traditions, thus nullifying one another.

None of these arguments is conclusive. The first and the third are simply false. There is a wealth of information from reliable and rational witnesses attesting to miracles throughout history. The apostle Paul speaks of over five hundred witnesses who saw Jesus alive after his death (1 Cor. 15:6). Certainly not all of these were irrational or delusional. Nor can it be said that in a prescientific age people were so gullible that they were willing to believe anything. We have many statements from ancient writers and historians expressing the kind of caution and skepticism toward the miraculous that is expressed today.[2] On the other hand, even in the rationalistic West, the majority of people still believe in the possibility of miracles and the supernatural. Indeed, the postmodern worldview has shown greater openness to experience outside of the realm of naturalistic explanation.

While Hume's second argument — human tendency to crave the spectacular — is certainly true, it says nothing about whether miracles are possible. We could present an equally true counterargument that people are in general quite skeptical of supernatural claims. All sides affirm that caution must be exercised when judging a miraculous claim. Nor does the fourth claim prove that miracles are impossible. No one is suggesting that all claims of the miraculous are true, or that misperceptions, trickery, or fraud are never involved. Furthermore, not every supernatural act need be attributed to God. The Bible speaks of Satanic and demonic supernatural activity. Reports of miracles in other religious traditions neither prove nor disprove the miracles of Christianity.

Miracles and the Historical Method

While the study of miracles is outside the realm of strict scientific investigation, it is not outside the realm of historical research, which depends on the written and oral reports of those who witnessed such events. The historian's role is to find out what happened, not to assume what could or could not have happened. Which is more historically objective, to assume miracles cannot occur, or to keep an open but cautious perspective? Based on personal experience, we might say miracles are uncommon and outside the realm of normal experience, but we cannot rule in advance that they are impossible. A miracle should be believed if there is enough historical evidence to confirm it with a high degree of probability. Noted New Testament scholar Raymond Brown writes, "Historicity ... should be determined not by

> While the study of miracles is outside the realm of strict scientific investigation, it is not outside the realm of historical research, which depends on the written and oral reports of those who witnessed such events.

2. See A. E. Harvey, *Jesus and the Constraints of History* (Philadelphia: Fortress, 1982), 102. Harvey points to examples in Josephus, *Ant.* 1.104–8; 4.158; 17.354; Philostratus, *Life of Apollonius* 4.45; 5.13–16; Herodotus, *Historiae* 2.55–7, 73, 156; 4.95–6, 105; Thucydides, *History of the Peloponessian War* 5.26, 3–4; 1.126.4–6; Polybius, *Histories* 2.17.6; 2.56.10; 16.12.6f.; 3.47.6ff.; Plutarch, *Camillus* 6.14; *Marcus Coriolanus* 37.3ff.; *Marius* 36.5f.; *Pericles* 35.2; Dionysius of Halicarnassus, *Antiquitates romanae* 2.56.2–3.

what we think possible or likely, but by the antiquity and reliability of the evidence.... As far back as we can trace, Jesus was known and remembered as one who had extraordinary powers."[3]

To determine the historicity of a miracle, we must ask questions like, Is the event contextually plausible? What circumstances might have prompted the creation of such a story? Who witnessed the event? Were these reliable and credible witnesses? How was the event recorded and passed down to later generations?

DID JESUS PERFORM MIRACLES?

There is nearly universal agreement today—among liberals and conservatives alike—that Jesus was viewed by his contemporaries as a healer and an exorcist. The Gospel tradition is permeated with the miraculous. Rationalistic quests for the historical Jesus sometimes claimed that the miracle stories were developed by the church as they gradually deified Jesus, transforming him from a human teacher to the powerful Son of God. Yet peeling away the supernatural to find a nonmiraculous core of Gospel tradition is like peeling an onion. When the last peel is removed, nothing is left to study. Miracles appear in all strata of the Gospel tradition, isolated by source critics: Mark, Q, M, L, John. References to Jesus' miracles also appear in a variety of Gospel genres, including miracle stories, pronouncement stories, controversy stories, sayings, parables, commissioning accounts, passion narratives, and summaries of Jesus' activities.[4]

> There is nearly universal agreement today that Jesus was viewed by his contemporaries as a healer and an exorcist.

Jewish sources outside of the New Testament also refer to Jesus' miracles. Josephus states that Jesus was "a doer of startling deeds" (*Ant.* 18.3.3 §63), a probable reference to his miracles. The Babylonian Talmud claims Jesus was executed because he practiced magic and led Israel astray (*b. Sanh.* 43a). While this passage is a strong polemic against Jesus and Christianity, it admits as reliable the tradition that Jesus performed supernatural acts. The early church leader Origen quotes his second-century pagan opponent Celsus as claiming that Jesus worked certain magical powers which he had learned in Egypt.[5]

While this data does not prove that Jesus actually performed miracles, it confirms that he was widely acclaimed as a miracle-worker—even among his enemies. As we noted, this cannot be dismissed as merely the ignorant superstition of antiquity. The people of Jesus' day could be as skeptical as people today. The Gospels treat Jesus' miracles not as commonplace or as the expected norm for charismatic leaders but as surprising and astonishing to those who witnessed them. Jesus' powerful teaching and healing produced a profound impact among his followers, convincing them that he was the Messiah and the Son of God.

The question of whether Jesus performed specific miracles recorded in the Gospels must be judged on a case-by-case basis. In most episodes, there is little information out-

---

3. Raymond Brown, *An Introduction to New Testament Christology* (New York: Paulist, 1994), 25n. 24.

4. Graham H. Twelftree, *Jesus the Miracle Worker: A Historical and Theological Study* (Downers Grove, IL: InterVarsity, 1999), 256; Barry L. Blackburn, "Miracles," in *DJG*, 556.

5. Origen, *Contra Celsus* 1.38.

side of the account itself by which to judge it. Much therefore depends on the attitude and approach one takes to the Gospels. If we assume miracles are impossible, then the account will, of course, be rejected. If we affirm that miracles are possible and that Jesus was an exceptional person viewed by his contemporaries as a miracle-worker, then it is reasonable to conclude that the event took place. In chapter 12, we pointed to evidence of a generally reliable Gospel tradition drawn from eyewitness accounts. The burden of proof may therefore be placed on those who would deny the historicity of individual miracles.

> Jesus uses no incantations or magical objects in his miracles, and there is no sense that his power is in the technique or that he must impel God to act on his behalf.

The historicity of Jesus' miracles is also suggested by the lack of convincing parallels from the Hellenistic world of his day. Before examining the significance of Jesus' miracles, we will turn briefly to the question of Greek and Jewish parallels.

ANCIENT PARALLELS TO JESUS' MIRACLES

Those who believe that the miracle stories were created by the early church often cite parallels in the ancient world. It is said that stories of miracle-working Greek and Jewish heroes encouraged the church to attribute similar miracles to their hero, Jesus. Three parallels are most commonly cited.

(1) First-Century Magic. Various scholars have argued that Jesus' miracle-working should be identified as a kind of first-century magic.[6] Yet while Jesus was derogatorily called a "magician" and "sorcerer" in later Jewish and pagan propaganda, his exorcisms and healings show little affinity with ancient magical arts or the occult. Magicians and exorcists sought to coerce a deity to act on their behalf by using a variety of techniques, including rituals, incantations, spells, potions, herbs, and magical objects.[7] Jesus uses no incantations or magical objects, and there is no sense that the power is in the technique or that Jesus must impel God to act on his behalf. Rather, he commands demons from his own authority, and they immediately submit. He heals with his own authoritative words because of his compassion and in response to the faith of the recipient. These are not showy demonstrations of the magical arts but confirmation of the in-breaking power of the kingdom of God.

(2) Hellenistic "Divine Men." Parallels to Jesus' miracles have also been noted in accounts of various Hellenistic miracle-workers and wise men believed to be divine or semidivine—sometimes known as **divine men**

Magic bowl. While in later anti-Christian propaganda Jesus was accused of being a magician, his miracles have little in common with ancient magical arts. This is a bowl with Aramaic incantations meant to protect a person from evil spirits (from Babylonia, fifth to sixth century AD).

---

6. See Morton Smith, *Jesus the Magician* (New York: Harper and Row, 1973); John M. Hull, *Hellenistic Magic and the Synoptic Tradition* (London: SCM, 1974).

7. For examples, see H. D. Betz, ed., *The Greek Magical Papyri in Translation* (Chicago: Univ. of Chicago Press, 1986).

> Now there was one, whose name was Onias,
> a righteous man he was, and beloved of God,
> who, in a certain drought, had prayed to God
> to put an end to the intense heat, and whose
> prayers God had heard, and had sent them rain.
>
> —Josephus, on Onias (Honi) the Rainmaker,
> *Ant.* 14.2.1 §22

(*theoi andres*).[8] There are certainly at least superficial similarities between Hellenistic miracle stories and those in the Gospels. The most striking appear in the widely cited account of **Apollonius**, a first-century teacher and wonder-worker from Tyana in Cappadocia. His biography was composed by the third-century author Philostratus. Parallels include Apollonius's extraordinary wisdom demonstrated as a child, his healings and exorcisms, his purported mastery over storms, and his apparent resuscitation of a young woman who had died on her wedding day.[9] While these are impressive, there are far more differences than similarities, and most scholars deny any direct dependence between the story of Apollonius and the Gospels.[10] If there was borrowing, it was most likely Philostratus who embellished his account from the Gospels, rather than vice versa, since he wrote a hundred and fifty years after Apollonius's death and more than a hundred years after the Gospels were written.

While individual accounts of healings or miracles may bear incidental similarity to Gospel miracles, Jesus' ministry as a whole has a very different focus. The Gospel miracles lack the magical features and arbitrary character of Hellenistic stories. Their background and inspiration is better seen in the Old Testament themes of the restoration and renewal of creation, and of the powerful presence of the kingdom of God.

(3) Jewish Charismatic Rabbis. Finally, parallels to Jesus' miracles have been drawn to **charismatic** (spiritually gifted) Jewish **holy men**, rabbis known for their powerful prayers for healing and rainfall. As we noted in chapter 11 (p. 368), the two most widely cited examples of these are Honi the Rainmaker and Hanina ben Dosa.[11] Honi (or Onias), also known as the Circle Drawer, lived in the first century BC and is reputed to have prayed to God for rainfall during a drought. When it did not rain, he drew a circle on the ground and stood in it, telling God that he would not leave it until it rained. Rain subsequently fell (*m. Taᶜan.* 3:8; cf. Josephus, *Ant.* 14.2.1 §22). Hanina ben Dosa, a first-century-AD rabbi, was known for his healings and exorcisms and is said to have once healed a boy from a distance (*b. Ber.* 34b), reminiscent of Jesus' healing of the centurion's servant (Matt. 8:5–13; Luke 7:1–10).

---

8. See especially Hans Dieter Betz, "Jesus as Divine Man," in *Jesus and the Historian*, ed. F. Trotter (Philadelphia: Westminster, 1968). The designation itself is problematic since the term divine man (*theos anēr*) occurs only rarely in the literature. The Hellenistic world had a variety of figures—kings, philosophers, prophets, wise men, healers, priests, and magicians—considered to possess special and even supernatural gifts.

9. Philostratos, *Life of Apollonius of Tyana*, trans. F. C. Conybeare, Loeb Classical Library (London: Heinemann; Cambridge, MA: Harvard Univ., 1912).

10. For criticism of the divine-man motif, see Barry L. Blackburn, "'Miracle Working ΘΕΟΙ ΑΝΔΡΕΣ' in Hellenism (and Hellenistic Judaism)," in *Gospel Perspectives* 6:185–218; David Tiede, *The Charismatic Figure as Miracle Worker* (Missoula: Scholars, 1972); Carl Holladay, *Theos Anēr in Hellenistic Judaism* (Missoula: Scholars, 1977); Gerd Thiessen, *Miracle Stories of the Early Christian Tradition* (Philadelphia: Fortress, 1983).

11. See especially Geza Vermes, *Jesus the Jew* (London: Collins, 1973), 69–79; William S. Green, "Palestinian Holy Men: Charismatic Leadership and Rabbinic Tradition," *ANRW* 2.19.2 (1979): 626–47.

One problem with comparing these Jewish holy men to Jesus is the lateness of the sources which describe them. The closest parallels to Jesus' miracles appear in the Talmud, which was written hundreds of years after the Gospels themselves. It seems more likely that the miracles of Jesus influenced the traditions about these holy men, rather than vice versa. Furthermore, while there are some superficial parallels to Jesus' individual miracles, his ministry as a whole is very different. These rabbis were known as pious men of God whose devotion and prayer prompted God to act on their behalf. Jesus, on the other hand, claimed not only intimacy with God but also personal authority to perform miracles, linking them to the presence of the kingdom of God in his words and deeds.

Contrary to the view that miracle-workers and magicians were a dime a dozen in the Greco-Roman world and that Jesus' followers would have naturally attributed such actions to him, it is remarkable how few real parallels to Jesus' miracles appear in the ancient world. Jesus' miracles find their background not in Hellenistic magical spells, nor in proofs of authority of divine men, nor even in the pious prayers of God's people, but in his role as agent and inaugurator of the kingdom of God.

THE SIGNIFICANCE OF JESUS' MIRACLES: THE POWER AND PRESENCE OF THE KINGDOM

The Synoptic Gospels draw a close connection between Jesus' proclamation of the kingdom of God and his miracles. The exorcisms and healings are intended to reveal the presence and power of the kingdom in Jesus' ministry.

Exorcisms

As we've noted, it is widely accepted that Jesus was recognized by his contemporaries as an exorcist. Not only do the **exorcisms** appear in various layers of the Gospel tradition, but they appear in sayings which almost certainly come from the historical Jesus (Mark 3:22–27; 9:39; Luke 13:32). What significance, then, did Jesus give to his exorcisms? The evidence suggests that he viewed them as a spiritual assault on the dominion of Satan by the kingdom of God. In the first exorcism in Mark, Jesus enters the synagogue at Capernaum and encounters a man possessed by an evil spirit. The demon cries out, "What do you want with us, Jesus of Nazareth? Have you come to destroy us? I know who you are — the Holy One of God!" Jesus silences the demon and then casts him out (Mark 1:21–28; Luke 4:31–37). The authenticity of this episode is rendered more likely by the appearance of the title Holy One of God, which was not a title for the Messiah in Judaism or a common title for Jesus in the early church. The criterion of dissimilarity would suggest a historical recollection here. The demon recognizes Jesus as God's agent and reacts with terror, knowing his power to destroy him. Only one demon is mentioned, but the reference to "us" indicates that the whole realm of demonic hordes is aware of Jesus' coming and shudders in fear. This is not an isolated encounter. Rather, through his exorcisms, Jesus is invading and breaking down the demonic ramparts of Satan's kingdom.

> Jesus' exorcisms and healings are intended to reveal the presence and power of the kingdom in his ministry.

This theme appears most clearly in the Beelzebub controversy (Mark 3:22–27; Matt. 12:22–30; Luke 11:14–15, 17–23). Again we have good reason to accept the historicity of the episode. It would pass the test of multiple attestation, since the episode appears in both Mark and Q. Furthermore, Jesus' reference to the exorcisms of the Pharisees (Matt. 12:27; Luke 11:19) would have been an embarrassment to the early church, and so it is unlikely to have been created. When the Pharisees accuse Jesus of casting out demons by the power of Beelzebub (Satan), Jesus first refutes the charge by noting how foolish it would be for Satan to cast out his own demons. He then offers an alternative explanation: "But if I drive out demons by the Spirit of God, then the kingdom of God has come upon you" (Matt. 12:28). Luke has "the finger of God" for Matthew's "the Spirit of God" (Luke 11:20), both expressions indicating God's active agency in the exorcisms. The kingdom of God is manifested through the defeat of Satan in Jesus' exorcisms. Jesus then offers an analogy: Satan is like a strong man trying to protect his estate, but Jesus is a stronger man who attacks and plunders Satan's property. Through his exorcisms, Jesus is attacking and taking back Satan's "possessions," those people over whom Satan has gained control. The exorcisms are proof that the kingdom of God is engaging and overwhelming the kingdom of Satan.

> The evidence suggests that Jesus viewed his exorcisms as a spiritual assault on the dominion of Satan by the kingdom of God.

Healings

Like the exorcisms, Jesus' **healings** are closely associated with his kingdom proclamation. This comes out most clearly in the question of John the Baptist (Luke 7:18–23; Matt. 11:2–6). John, imprisoned by Herod Antipas, sends his disciples to ask whether Jesus is indeed the "Coming One" (the Messiah). The passage has a ring of authenticity since the church is unlikely to have created a story in which John, elsewhere a key witness to Jesus, expresses doubts about his identity. The story thus fits the criterion of embarrassment.

Jesus' response to John's disciples illuminates the significance he gave to his healing miracles: "Go back and report to John what you have seen and heard: The blind receive sight, the lame walk, those who have leprosy are cured, the deaf hear, the dead are raised, and the good news is preached to the poor" (Luke 7:22; Matt. 11:4–5). Jesus is here alluding to passages from Isaiah which predict God's final salvation — the messianic age — when evil will be defeated and the effects of sin and the fall of humanity will be reversed (Isa. 26:19; 29:18–19; 35:5–6; 61:1–2). Isaiah 35:5–6 reads, "Then will the eyes of the blind be opened and the ears of the deaf unstopped. Then will the lame leap like a deer, and the mute tongue shout for joy. Water will gush forth in the wilderness and streams in the desert." Jesus' healing miracles are evidence of the coming of the kingdom, a foretaste of the restoration of creation promised in Isaiah and the prophets. Just as Adam's fall brought sickness and death, so Jesus' coming will bring healing and life.

The aggressive stance Jesus takes against demons also appears in his healing ministry. The kingdom is not defensive but offensive, actively transforming the world. This is evident in Jesus' approach to those who are healed. In Judaism, touching a dead body, a person with leprosy, or a woman in her menstrual period would render a person unclean. Yet the

Gospel writers take special note that Jesus reached out and touched the man with leprosy (Mark 1:41, par.), the dead body of Jairus's daughter (Mark 5:41, par.), and the coffin of a widow's son (Luke 7:14). He was also touched by the bleeding woman (Mark 5:27, par.). In each case, Jesus was not rendered unclean; rather he "cleansed" or healed the person. The kingdom of God is not defiled by the world but brings transformation to it.

Raising the Dead

The most dramatic of Jesus' healings are the three occasions he raises people from the dead: Jairus's daughter (Mark 5:21–43, par.), the widow's son (Luke 7:11–17), and Lazarus (John 11). There is also the allusion to Isaiah 26:19 in Jesus' response to John: "the dead are raised" (Luke 7:22; Matt. 11:5). While sometimes called "resurrections," these are better termed **resuscitations** or **revivications**, since they restore normal mortal life rather than immortal resurrection life. In Jewish and Christian thought, resurrection occurs at the end of time, when believers receive glorified and immortal bodies. According to Paul, Jesus' own resurrection was the "firstfruits"—the beginning and guarantee—of this end-times resurrection (1 Cor. 15:20; cf. Col. 1:18).

While many scholars have been willing to accept that Jesus was an exorcist and a healer—sometimes attributing his cures to psychological or psychosomatic healing—there is greater skepticism toward accounts of raising the dead and the so-called nature miracles. Yet the same criteria apply to these more dramatic miracles as to the "lesser" healings and exorcisms. If we grant that miracles are theoretically possible, and if there is a God who intervenes in the world, then there is no reason to rule out such feats. Like the others, these miracles should be accepted if they pass the normal tests of historical veracity.

Jesus' healing miracles are a foretaste of the restoration of creation promised in Isaiah and the prophets.

Though there are only three accounts of actual revivications and two additional references in the teaching of Jesus, these five occur in five different strata of Gospel sources, including Mark (Mark 5:21–43), Q (Luke 7:22; Matt. 11:4–5), L (Luke 7:11–17), M (Matt. 10:8), and John (John 11). Raising the dead—as an authentic feature of Jesus' ministry—thus fits the criterion of multiple attestation. There are also individual details in these accounts which suggest their historicity. We have noted the likely authenticity of the question of John the Baptist in Luke 7 and Matthew 11. The raising of Jairus's daughter also has marks of authenticity: (1) The identification of Jairus by name is unusual for a healing account; (2) Jairus's position as a "synagogue ruler" is unlikely to have been created by the early church, which was in active opposition to the synagogue; (3) there seems no reason Mark would introduce Jesus' Aramaic words *Talitha koum* ("child, arise," Mark 5:41) unless this was an actual reminiscence of an eyewitness profoundly moved by a life-changing event. Similar evidence of authenticity can be found in the accounts of the raising of the widow's son (Luke 7:11–17) and of Lazarus (John 11).[12]

---

12. See Murray J. Harris, "'The Dead Are Restored to Life': Miracles of Revivification in the Gospels," in *Gospel Perspectives* 6:295–326; John Meier, *A Marginal Jew: Rethinking the Historical Jesus*, 3 vols. (New York: Doubleday, 1991, 1994), 2:773–75.

Jesus' answer to John, with its allusion to Isaiah 26:19 ("the dead are raised"), indicates that the significance of these resuscitations is the same as the other healings, symbolically inaugurating the kingdom of God and the new creation. Jesus claims to be God's agent of restoration not only for Israel but for the whole world, bringing the life-giving power of the new age. Though not the final resurrection, the revivications provide a preview and foretaste of the consummation of the kingdom.

Nature Miracles

Perhaps the most difficult miracles for modern critics to accept as authentic are those in which Jesus demonstrates authority over the powers of nature — turning water into wine, multiplying loaves and fishes, withering a fig tree with a command, walking on the water, and calming the storm. For many, these feats seem more like the arbitrary actions of the Greek gods than the in-breaking power of the kingdom of God. Yet as Craig Blomberg points out, these **nature miracles** have striking parallels with Jesus' parables and function like enacted parables.[13] As the parables reveal the mystery of the kingdom to those with ears to hear, so the nature miracles demonstrate the in-breaking power of the kingdom to those with eyes to see. Since the parables are among the sayings of Jesus most widely accepted as authentic, there is no reason to reject the nature miracles out of hand. The criterion of coherence — that sayings and actions of Jesus are likely authentic when they cohere with other authentic sayings — favors their authenticity. The main obstacle to accepting them is an antisupernatural bias, judging in advance that such things cannot happen. Yet if God can heal the sick and raise the dead, why can he not calm the sea?

> The nature miracles function like enacted parables, demonstrating the in-breaking power of the kingdom to those with eyes to see.

An example of the symbolic significance of these nature miracles is the withering of the fig tree at Jesus' entrance to Jerusalem (Mark 11:12–14, 20–25; Matt. 21:18–22). The story is not a petty outburst of temper by Jesus, as some have supposed, but an enacted parable. In the Old Testament, Israel is often compared to a fig tree or an unfruitful vineyard which God will judge.[14] This imagery is taken up elsewhere by Jesus in a parable of an unfruitful fig tree (Luke 13:6–9). The fig tree in the parable and the fig tree which Jesus withers outside Jerusalem both represent the leaders of Israel, who face God's judgment if they fail to repent at Jesus' kingdom proclamation.

Another example of an enacted parable is Jesus' turning water to wine at the wedding in Cana of Galilee (John 2:1–11). While at first sight the miracle seems like a kind gesture to avoid embarrassment for the bridal party, in fact it carries rich symbolic significance. Elsewhere, Jesus tells a parable about the danger of putting new wine in old wineskins. When the new wine ferments and expands, it will burst the old wineskin (Mark 2:18–22). The meaning of the parable is that the "new wine" of the kingdom of God is a radical new

---

13. Craig Blomberg, "The Miracles as Parables," in *Gospel Perspectives* 6:327–59.
14. Hos. 9:10–16; Mic. 7:1; Jer. 8:13; 24:1–10; Isa. 5:1–7; 28:3–4; Joel 1:6–12.

thing which God is accomplishing. It cannot simply be poured into the old wineskins of legalistic Judaism. It is noteworthy that the jars at Cana are said to be "the kind used by the Jews for ceremonial washing" (John 2:6). The "water" of Jewish legalism is transformed into the new "wine" of the kingdom. This symbolism is further reinforced by the frequent identification of the kingdom with feasting and banquet imagery in the Gospels (Matt. 22:1–10; 25:1–13; Luke 12:35–40; 13:24–30; 14:15–24) and the Old Testament portrait of salvation as a "messianic banquet," when "the LORD Almighty will prepare a feast of rich

Water jars

food for all peoples, a banquet of aged wine" (Isa. 25:6). Jesus repeatedly identifies himself as the bridegroom at a wedding banquet (Mark 2:19–20, par.; Matt. 25:1–13; John 3:29). Together, this rich imagery suggests that the miracle of changing water to wine is not an arbitrary show of power but an enacted parable meant to teach Jesus' disciples about the nature of salvation and the kingdom of God.

Messianic banquet imagery is also present in the feeding miracles (Mark 6:32–44, par.; 8:1–10, par.). Just as God through Moses supplied manna in the wilderness to the Israelites, so Jesus, the bread of life, provides the blessings of food to the crowds in the desert. The symbolism of bounty—everyone filled, and twelve baskets and seven baskets left over—reflects the bountiful gift of salvation which God pours out on his people. In blessing the bread and distributing it to the people, Jesus symbolically presides over the messianic banquet, offering God's sustenance to all who will receive it.

Gathering storm clouds over the Sea of Galilee. Jesus' nature miracles include events like calming the sea and turning water to wine.

The miracles of calming the storm and walking on water move in a different but related direction, revealing Jesus' divine authority over the forces of nature. In the Old Testament, the LORD God is celebrated as the master of the storm and sea (2 Sam. 22:16; Pss. 18:15; 65:7; 89:9; 104:6–7; 106:9; 107:23–32; Isa. 50:2; Nah. 1:4). Psalm 89:9 reads, "You rule over the surging sea; when its waves mount up, you still them." In Psalm 107:25, the LORD "spoke and stirred up a tempest that lifted high the waves." Yet when his people cry out to him, "He stilled the storm to a whisper; the waves of the sea were hushed" (v. 29). The coming of the kingdom means peace and protection for God's people from spiritual and natural dangers. As the agent of the kingdom of God, Jesus represents God's powerful presence with his people (Mark 1:3; Luke 1:68; 7:16).

CONCLUSION

The question of Jesus' miracles is first of all a philosophical one (Are miracles possible?) and second a historical one (Is there sufficient evidence to accept as reliable specific miracle stories?). If miracles are not ruled out in advance, the accounts of Jesus' miracles fare well under critical scrutiny. They are widely attested to in a range of Gospel sources and forms, and they cohere well with the almost certainly authentic preaching of Jesus about the kingdom.

For Jesus, the miracles are not showy demonstrations of power or even proof of his identity. They are rather manifestations of the in-breaking power of the kingdom of God, a foretaste and preview of the restoration of creation promised by God through the prophets of old, now coming to fulfillment through Jesus the Messiah.

The question of Jesus' miracles raises the deeper question of his own self-consciousness. How did he view himself and his purpose in relation to God and Israel? It is to this question we turn in the next chapter.

» CHAPTER SUMMARY «

1. The question of miracles must be examined first philosophically, concerning their logical possibility, and then historically, concerning their actual occurrence.

2. Contrary to the claims of David Hume, no valid philosophical argument mitigates against the possibility of supernatural intervention in the so-called laws of nature.

3. Historically, a miracle should be accepted or rejected if there is enough historical evidence to confirm it with a high degree of probability.

4. There is near universal agreement that Jesus was viewed by his contemporaries as a healer and an exorcist.

5.   Parallels between Jesus' miracles and those of first-century magicians, Hellenistic divine men, or charismatic holy men are unconvincing, making it unlikely that the church created the Gospel miracle tradition in imitation of these.

6.   Jesus' miracles reveal the power and presence of the kingdom in his actions. The healings and exorcisms symbolize the reversal of the curse and the defeat of sin and Satan. The resuscitations reveal the power of the final resurrection with the coming of the kingdom.

7.   The so-called nature miracles function as enacted parables, revealing the in-breaking power of the kingdom and the dawn of the new age of salvation.

» KEY TERMS «

deism	Apollonius	resuscitations, revivications
materialism	charismatic holy men	nature miracles
David Hume	exorcisms	
divine men	healings	

» DISCUSSION AND STUDY QUESTIONS «

1.   In what ways is the question of miracles both a philosophical one and a historical one?

2.   How would you answer David Hume's objections to miracles?

3.   Why do most historians accept that Jesus had a reputation as a healer and an exorcist? What is the evidence for this?

4.   To what ancient parallels have Jesus' miracles been compared? What similarities and differences were there between Jesus and so-called divine men? What similarities and differences were there between Jesus and charismatic holy men?

5.   According to Jesus' teaching, what was the significance of his exorcisms? His healings? The revivications? The nature miracles?

Digging Deeper

Blackburn, Barry L. "Miracles and Miracle Stories." In *DJG*, 549–60.

———. "The Miracles of Jesus." In *Studying the Historical Jesus: Evaluations of the State of Current Research*. Edited by B. Chilton and C. A. Evans. Leiden: Brill, 1994, 353–94.

Blomberg, Craig. *The Historical Reliability of the Gospels*. Downers Grove, IL: InterVarsity, 1987. See chap. 3, "Miracles."

Brown, Colin. *Miracles and the Critical Mind*. Grand Rapids: Eerdmans, 1984.

Craig, William Lane. "The Problem of Miracles: A Historical and Philosophical Perspective." In *Gospel Perspectives: The Miracles of Jesus*. Vol. 6. Eugene, OR: Wipf and Stock, 2003.

Kee, Howard Clark. *Miracles in the Early Christian World*. New Haven, CT: Yale Univ., 1983.

Latourelle, Rene. *The Miracles of Jesus and the Theology of Miracles*. Translated by Matthew J. O'Connell (New York : Paulist, 1988).

Lewis, C. S. *Miracles: A Preliminary Study*. New York: Macmillan, 1947.

Theissen, Gerd. *The Miracle Stories of the Early Christian Tradition*. Philadelphia: Fortress, 1983.

Twelftree, Graham H. *Jesus the Exorcist: A Contribution to the Study of the Historical Jesus*. Peabody, MA: Hendrickson, 1993.

———. *Jesus the Miracle Worker: A Historical and Theological Study*. Downers Grove, IL: InterVarsity, 1999.

van der Loos, H. *The Miracles of Jesus*. NovTSup. Leiden: Brill, 1968.

Wenham, David, and Craig Blomberg, eds. *The Miracles of Jesus*. Gospel Perspectives. Vol. 6; Sheffield: JSOT, 1986.

CHAPTER 18

The Messianic Words and Actions of Jesus

» CHAPTER OVERVIEW «

1. The Authority of Jesus
2. The Aims of Jesus
3. The Messianic Titles

» OBJECTIVES «

After reading this chapter, you should be able to:

- Summarize the authoritative claims of Jesus and their significance with reference to his self-understanding.
- Identify key events and features of Jesus' ministry which provide insight into his aims or intentions.
- Describe the Jewish background for various messianic titles attributed to Jesus (Messiah, Son of Man, Son of God, Lord) and discuss their meaning in the context of his ministry.

Jesus' preaching about the kingdom and his reputation as a miracle-worker raise the critical question of how he understood his identity and purpose. While building a psychological profile is beyond the bounds of historical research, Jesus' words and deeds can tell us a great deal about how he viewed himself in relation to the nation Israel and her scriptural heritage.

In the twentieth century, most research on the historical Jesus focused on two areas: (1) the so-called messianic titles used of Jesus, like Messiah (Christ), Lord, Son of Man, Son of God, and Son of David, and (2) testing the sayings of Jesus using the criteria of authenticity. More recently, interest has shifted to a broader, more contextual, and comprehensive approach, viewing Jesus' whole ministry within the context of first-century Judaism and the Greco-Roman world. Particularly important is the connotative significance of both the words and actions of Jesus. The questions become not simply, Did Jesus claim to be the Messiah? but more broadly, What options were open to Jesus in his historical context? How would his actions have been understood within the world of first-century Judaism? What aims might he have hoped to achieve? How do we account for the unique beliefs and teachings of the movement which arose after his death?

Examining both Jesus' words and deeds in the context of first-century Judaism can tell us a great deal about his self-identity and his aims. In this chapter, we will survey significant events and titles in the Gospels which can be traced with a high degree of certainty to the historical Jesus.

THE AUTHORITY OF JESUS

Announcing and Inaugurating the Kingdom

As we have seen, one of the most undisputed features of Jesus' ministry is his announcement of the kingdom of God. The significance of this message in the context of Israel's history must not be underestimated. Jesus claimed to be the agent of God's final salvation, bringing restoration to Israel, and healing and wholeness to the world. The coming of the kingdom and the renewal of creation are inseparable themes in the prophets, especially Isaiah. Even if we leave off the question of whether Jesus considered himself in any sense divine, his claim of authority to announce and establish the kingdom of God was truly an audacious one.

> Jesus claimed to be the agent of God's final salvation, bringing restoration to Israel and healing and wholeness to the world.

Authority over Demons and Disease

The significance Jesus gave to his healings and exorcisms reinforced this claim to be the inaugurator of God's kingdom. As we saw in the last chapter, while healers and exorcists were not unknown in the ancient world, Jesus was unique in connecting his healings and exorcisms to the in-breaking power of God's reign. If his exorcisms were the work of God, "then the kingdom of God has come upon you" (Matt. 12:28; Luke 11:20). The healings were evidence that Isaiah's signs of the new age were being fulfilled in Jesus' ministry (Luke 7:22–23; Matt. 11:4–5). He was acting as God's final agent of salvation for Israel and for the world.

Authority to Speak for God: Jesus' Use of *Amēn* ("Truly I Say to You")

The Greek term **amēn**, "in truth" or "truly," appears over one hundred times in the Gospels, always on the lips of Jesus: "Truly I say to you …" (Matt. 5:18, 26; 6:2, 5; etc.). In John's Gospel, this introductory phrase is doubled for emphasis: "Truly, truly I say to you …" (John 1:51; 3:3, 5; etc.). The word is a transliteration of the Hebrew ʾāmēn, which comes from a verb meaning "confirmed" or "verified." In the Old Testament, it was used at the end of a saying to confirm its validity, much as we might say "Amen!" (Deut. 27:15; Ps. 41:13; etc.). The authenticity of Jesus' use of the term is confirmed by at least three criteria of authenticity:

1. *The Criterion of Semitic Flavor.* The Hebrew origin of the term confirms that its use goes back to the early Aramaic-speaking church and almost certainly to Jesus himself.
2. *The Criterion of Dissimilarity.* Jesus uses it in a unique and unprecedented manner at the *beginning* of his sayings to demonstrate the authority with which he spoke. Yet the term was not taken up after Jesus by the early church, and so could not have originated with them.
3. *The Criterion of Multiple Attestation.* The term appears in all strata of the Gospel tradition.

Jesus' use of *amēn* is another indication of his extraordinary sense of divine authority.[1] Rather than appealing to the authority of his predecessors, as the rabbis did, Jesus appeals to his own authority. The closest Old Testament parallel is the solemn declaration of the prophets, "Thus says the Lord …" Jesus appears to be saying that his words must be heeded because they are the very words of God.

Authority over the Law and the Sabbath

This sense of personal authority comes through especially in Jesus' attitude toward the law and his declarations about the Sabbath. We have already seen that Jesus spoke of the fulfillment of the law in his ministry and expressed unprecedented authority to expand and reinterpret the law for the new age of salvation. With his repeated assertion, "You have heard that it was said … but I tell you …" (Matt. 5:21–48), Jesus affirms that he now speaks for God in the kingdom age (see chap. 16, pp. 442–44).

This same sense of authority may be seen in the Sabbath controversies, in which Jesus clashes with the Pharisees concerning his apparent violation of the Sabbath command (Mark 2:23–28, par.; Mark 3:1–6, par.; Luke 13:10–17; 14:1–6; John 5:2–18; 9:1–41). The multiple attestation of this theme indicates its historicity. In the

Jesus' disciples were accused of breaking the Sabbath when they "gleaned" a snack from the wheat fields they were passing through.

---

1. For overview and bibliography see G. F. Hawthorne, "Amen," in *DJG*, 7–8; B. Chilton, "Amen," in *ABD* 1:184–86.

Gleaners in a field in Jordan near the Dead Sea

first episode, Jesus' disciples begin picking and eating kernels of grain as they are walking through a grain field (Mark 2:23–28, par.). The Pharisees accuse them of breaking the law—not because they are stealing (the law allowed such snacking; Deut. 23:25) but because they are violating the Sabbath command prohibiting work (Exod. 20:8–11; 34:21; Deut. 5:12–14). Jesus responds by pointing to the Old Testament precedent of David, who technically broke the law by eating the consecrated bread set aside only for the priests (1 Samuel 21). David was justified because the meeting of human needs—the true spirit of the law—takes priority over an individual regulation. The law was instituted not to restrict people but to guide and enrich their lives. As Jesus says, "The Sabbath was made for people, not people for the Sabbath." He then concludes that "the Son of Man is Lord even of the Sabbath" (Mark 2:27–28). This statement is probably a play on words. Since the Hebrew idiom *ben ʾādām* ("son of man") means a "human being," it could mean that the Sabbath was made for people, and so people have authority over it. Yet in the context of Jesus' ministry, Son of Man must also carry its full sense as an exalted title for the Messiah (see discussion of this title later in this chapter). If human beings have authority over the Sabbath, how much more does the Son of Man, the Lord of the Sabbath?

Jesus' most exalted claim related to the Sabbath appears in John's Gospel. When Jesus heals a lame man at the Pool of Bethesda, he is accused by the Jewish leaders of breaking the Sabbath (John 5:16). Jesus responds by comparing his actions to God's ("my Father"), who also works on the Sabbath to sustain creation (5:17). The analogy infuriates his opponents, who plot to kill Jesus because "he was even calling God his own Father, making himself equal with God" (5:18). As in the Synoptics, Jesus makes the extraordinary claim that his personal authority overrides that of the Sabbath command. While some doubt the historicity of any story in John in which Jesus refers to himself, the claim here is not much different than the Synoptics, where Jesus is Lord of the Sabbath.

> Unlike other rabbis or prophets, Jesus placed himself in authority over the law and the Sabbath.

Again, the significance of Jesus' claims about the law and the Sabbath must not be understated. They go beyond the words and actions of a prophet who merely speaks for God. Unlike other rabbis or prophets, Jesus places himself in authority over these two foundations of Judaism. He judges the law, rather than vice versa, and does so on the basis of his role in salvation history. He is not just the law's interpreter but its fulfillment.

Authority to Forgive Sins

Another extraordinary claim by Jesus was his authority to forgive sins. In the account of the healing of the paralytic, Jesus demonstrates not only healing power and divine knowledge of his opponents' thoughts but also the authority to forgive the man's sins (Mark 2:1–12;

Matt. 9:1–8; Luke 5:17–26). Elsewhere, when Jesus is anointed by a sinful woman, he announces, "Your sins are forgiven" (Luke 7:36–50).

Some have argued that this claim is not so profound, since Jesus is merely acting as God's agent. He is offering God's forgiveness, not his own. It should first be noted that this is not how the Gospel writers understood it, since they present Jesus' audience as shocked and indignant at Jesus' claims. In the healing of the paralytic, the religious leaders reason, "He's blaspheming! Who can forgive sins but God alone?" (Mark 2:7). In the account of the sinful woman, the other guests wonder, "Who is this who even forgives sins?" (Luke 7:49). From the perspective of his hearers, Jesus is claiming a prerogative of God alone.

> Just as Jesus' healings confirm that Isaiah's signs of final salvation are now being fulfilled, so his offer of forgiveness is evidence that he is inaugurating the new covenant between God and his people.

Even if we suppose that Jesus is acting merely as God's agent, the claim to forgive sins is extraordinary when placed in the context of Jesus' kingdom preaching. The prophet Jeremiah promised free forgiveness of sins as part of the eschatological new covenant which God would make with his people (Jer. 31:31–34). This new covenant is inextricably connected to the coming of the kingdom of God, as Jesus will confirm in the Last Supper narrative (Luke 22:20, 29–30). Just as Jesus' healing of the paralytic confirms that Isaiah's signs of final salvation are now being fulfilled ("The blind receive sight, the lame walk," Luke 7:22; Isa. 35:5–6), so his offer of forgiveness is evidence that he is inaugurating the new covenant between God and his people ("I will forgive their wickedness and will remember their sins no more," Jer. 31:34). The two kinds of healings—spiritual and physical—are two sides of the same coin, both evidence of the in-breaking power of the kingdom of God in Jesus' words and actions.

Authority at the Final Judgment

One of the most astonishing claims made by Jesus was that the destiny of human beings depended on their response to him. In Mark 8:35–38, par., Jesus says, "For whoever wants to save his life will lose it, but whoever loses his life for me and for the gospel will save it.... If anyone is ashamed of me and my words in this adulterous and sinful generation, the Son of Man will be ashamed of him when he comes in his Father's glory with the holy angels."

In Matthew 10:32–33 and Luke 12:8–9, Jesus says, "Whoever publicly acknowledges me I will also acknowledge before my Father in heaven. But whoever publicly disowns me I will disown before my Father in heaven" (TNIV; cf. Mark 9:37; Matt. 10:40). The Old Testament portrays God alone as the judge of the whole world (Pss. 9:8; 50:6; 82:8; 94:2; 96:13; 98:9; Isa. 2:4). Yet Jesus claims the prerogative to act as final judge of the righteous and the wicked (cf. Matt. 25:31–46).

THE AIMS OF JESUS

Closely related to Jesus' authority is the question of what he was trying to accomplish. We have touched on this in previous discussions. It seems impossible to deny that Jesus saw his ministry as integral to the establishment of the kingdom of God. Here we will deal with evidence that Jesus intended to establish a new community of faith, a restored Israel. In the next chapter, we will examine how this aim was related to his predictions concerning his death.

Calling Disciples: A New Community of Faith

One of the most undisputed aspects of Jesus' ministry was his call of disciples. In Matthew and Mark, Jesus is walking beside the Sea of Galilee when he sees two pairs of brothers, Simon and Andrew, and James and John, mending their nets beside the lake. He calls them, and they immediately leave their nets and follow him (Matt. 4:18 – 22; Mark 1:16 – 20). Jesus' sense of authority is on center stage. When he calls, these men leave everything—family, career, and possessions—and follow him. This pattern of calling others to follow him

---

Figure 18.1—The Twelve
Matthew 10:1 – 16; Mark 3:13 – 19; Luke 6:12 – 16; Acts 1:13

Simon Peter

The most prominent of the Twelve, Simon Peter is always named first in the lists of disciples. Jesus gave him the nickname Peter (Greek: *Petros*; Aramaic *Cephas*; John 1:42), meaning "rock," and entrusted him with the "keys" of the kingdom after Peter proclaimed Jesus to be the Christ (Matt. 16:13 – 20). Though he denied Jesus, he was afterward restored to leadership (John 21:15 – 19) and appears as representative and spokesperson of the Twelve throughout the Gospels and Acts.

Andrew, Brother of Simon Peter

Previously a follower of John the Baptist, Andrew brought his brother Simon to meet Jesus (John 1:40 – 44). Andrew also brought the boy with the loaves and fishes to Jesus (John 6:8 – 9) and, together with Philip, brought a group of Greeks who sought to meet Jesus (John 12:20 – 22). Andrew and Peter were from Bethsaida (John 1:44) but operated their fishing business from Capernaum (Mark 1:29).

James, Son of Zebedee

Like Peter and Andrew, James and his brother John were fishermen who followed the call of Jesus (Mark 1:19). Jesus gave them the nickname *Boanerges*, meaning "sons of thunder" (Mark 3:17), perhaps because of their volatile temperaments. James was the first of the apostles martyred for his faith (Acts 12:1 – 2).

John, Brother of James

Traditionally believed to be the youngest of the Twelve, John, his brother James, and Peter are viewed as the "inner circle," Jesus' closest disciples who accompanied him when he raised Jairus's daughter (Mark 5:37) and on the Mount of Transfiguration (Mark 9:2). John is also recognized in the tradition as the Beloved Disciple, the author of the Fourth Gospel and the three Epistles which bear his name.

Philip

Philip, who like Peter and Andrew was from Bethsaida, introduced Nathanael to Jesus (John 1:45). Outside of the lists of disciples, he appears only in a few scenes in John (John 6:5 – 7; 12:21 – 22; 14:8 – 9), most famously asking Jesus to show the disciples the Father, to which Jesus replies, "Anyone who has seen me has seen the Father" (John 14:9).

---

appears throughout the Gospel tradition (Mark 2:14, par.; 8:34, par.; 10:21, par.; Matt. 8:22; Luke 5:11; 9:59; 14:27; John 1:43; 10:27; 12:26).

Discipleship was common in Jesus' day, both in Judaism and in the broader Hellenistic world, and students would often seek out and attach themselves to a respected rabbi or philosopher. Jesus appears to have been unique in actively seeking out and calling his disciples. Also unique was the commitment he demanded of them. In our culture, it is difficult to comprehend the social price these disciples would have paid for their action. In first-century Judaism, maintaining one's social position and loyalty to the family estate were among the highest of values. To leave one's parents and the family business for a wandering lifestyle would have brought shame to these men and their families. When James and John "left their father Zebedee in the boat ... and followed him" (Mark 1:20), they were making a radical break with the past and a costly commitment to Jesus.

Figure 18.1—The Twelve CONTINUED

Bartholomew

Bartholomew means "son of Tolmai," and it has often been speculated that he is the same as the man named Nathanael in John 1:45 (cf. John 21:2, where Nathanael appears with others who are apostles).

Matthew the Tax Collector

The First Gospel identifies this disciple as the tax collector called Levi by Mark and Luke (Matt. 9:9; Mark 2:14; Luke 5:27). He is traditionally believed to be the author of the First Gospel.

Thomas

Also known as Didymus, a name meaning "twin" (John 11:16; 20:24; 21:2), Thomas is best known as the disciple who doubted Jesus' resurrection until he saw and touched Jesus himself. Church tradition claims Thomas later evangelized eastward into India.

James the Son of Alphaeus

Sometimes identified as James the Lesser (or younger) of Mark 15:40, it is also possible he is the brother of Matthew-Levi, since both of their fathers are named Alphaeus (Mark 2:14).

Thaddaeus, Lebbaeus, or Judas the Son of James

This name is the most disputed. Matthew and Mark refer to Thaddaeus (though some manuscripts in Matthew refer to Lebbaeus). Luke refers to Judas the son of James. These may be different names or nicknames for the same person. John 14:22 distinguishes this Judas from Judas Iscariot.

Simon the Cananaean (Zealot)

In Luke, this Simon is called the Zealot; in Mark and Matthew, he is the Cananaean, from an Aramaic term meaning "zealous one." It is unclear if Simon was merely zealous for Judaism or whether he was previously part of the Zealot movement advocating the violent overthrow of the Romans.

Judas Iscariot, Who Betrayed Him

Iscariot probably means "man from Kerioth" (a region of Judea) and was probably a family name (John 6:71). The Fourth Gospel asserts that Judas, as treasurer, used to pilfer the group's money even before he betrayed Jesus (12:6).

The Gospels are full of Jesus' teaching concerning the radical cost of discipleship. Those who wish to be his disciples must deny themselves, take up their cross, and follow him—an image of sacrificial death (Mark 8:34; Matt. 16:24; Luke 9:23). Those who love family more than Jesus are not worthy of him (Matt. 10:37–38; Luke 14:26–27). Though the cost is high, the rewards are great. Whoever loses his life for Jesus will ultimately save it (Mark 8:35, Matt. 16:25, and Luke 9:24; also Matt. 10:39, Luke 17:33, and John 12:25). Those who leave all to follow him will receive more blessings in return, both in this age and in the age to come (Mark 10:28–30; Matt. 19:29; Luke 18:28–30).

While Jesus had many followers, the Gospels agree that he chose twelve to form a unique group (Mark 3:13–19; Matt. 10:1–4; Luke 6:12–16; cf. 1 Cor. 15:5). The term **disciple** (*mathētēs*) means "a follower" and is sometimes used of all who followed Jesus (John 19:38; Matt. 27:57; Luke 6:13, 17). More often, it refers to the twelve apostles (*apostoloi*) whom Jesus chose from among his larger group of followers (Luke 6:13; Matt. 10:2). The term **apostle** means "a messenger, one sent with a particular message or task." Jesus first called **the Twelve** to "be with him" and later sent them out to preach and to heal (Mark 3:14–15; 6:7–13, par.).

> Jesus almost certainly viewed this new community of the Twelve as the righteous remnant of Israel, the reconstituted people of God.

In its Jewish context, the number twelve was profoundly significant. A first-century Jew would have certainly connected this number to the twelve tribes of Israel. Jesus himself made this connection at the Last Supper, when he told the Twelve that in his kingdom, they would sit on twelve thrones judging the tribes of Israel (Luke 22:30; Matt. 19:28). Jesus almost certainly viewed this new community of followers as the righteous remnant of Israel, the reconstituted people of God.

This conclusion fits well the context of first-century Judaism, in which other groups—like the sectarians at Qumran—viewed themselves as the authentic remnant of Israel. It also fits well with Jesus' preaching of the kingdom. The twelve tribes had not existed as a united kingdom since the glorious days of King David and his son Solomon. The civil war which followed Solomon's reign resulted first in two separate kingdoms, Israel and Judah, and then in defeat and exile for both. The Assyrian and Babylonian exiles left deep scars in the nation's consciousness. While many Jews had returned from Babylonian exile, the motley band of returnees under Persian rule did not fit the glorious and triumphant restoration—led by Yahweh himself!—which was predicted in the prophets (Isaiah 40). N. T. Wright argues that there was a widespread belief in Judaism that Israel was still in exile, both spiritually and physically.[1] Many Jews longed for the day when God would bring about a new exodus, a true return from exile to reunify and restore the tribes of Israel (Isa. 11:10–16; 49:6; Ezek. 45:8; 47:13; Mic. 2:12; Sir. 48:10; *Pss. Sol.* 17:28). This hope was often linked to the coming reign of the LORD's anointed, the Messiah from the line of David (Isa. 11:1–16; Jer. 23:5–8; Hos. 3:5; *Psalms of Solomon* 17–18; 4 Ezra 13). Jesus' choice of the Twelve together with his preaching about the kingdom confirm that he saw his mission as in some sense the restoration of Israel. It is also important to note that Jesus

---

1. N. T. Wright, *Jesus and the Victory of God* (Philadelphia: Fortress, 1996).

did not count himself as one of the Twelve. This indicates that he viewed himself as their unique leader—the LORD's anointed—appointed to accomplish the great restoration.

While some scholars have doubted that Jesus could have viewed himself as the Messiah, it seems hard to imagine how—in light of his extraordinary claims about the kingdom of God and his calling of the Twelve as the restored remnant of Israel—he could have conceived of himself in any other way.

Dining with Sinners: The Universal Offer of the Kingdom

Another aspect of Jesus' ministry which is both unique and undisputed historically is his frequent association with sinners and other outcasts of society. This behavior, which particularly offended his religious opponents, is a major theme in the Gospel tradition. Jesus had a reputation for being "a friend of tax collectors and 'sinners'" (Luke 7:34; Matt. 11:19).

The call of Levi illustrates Jesus' behavior (Mark 2:13–17; Luke 5:27–32; cf. Matt. 9:9–13). Jesus shocks the religious leaders by calling a despised tax collector to be his disciple. He then doubly shocks them by accepting an invitation to a banquet in Levi's home. This was probably a banquet in Jesus' honor to celebrate Levi's conversion and to introduce Jesus to Levi's friends and associates. Appalled, the Pharisees and scribes demand from Jesus' disciples, "Why does he eat with tax collectors and sinners?" Table fellowship had great significance in the ancient world and meant social acceptance of those with whom one dined. In Judaism, a scrupulous Pharisee would not eat at the home of a common Israelite since he

Model of a Roman-period table arrangement. At a banquet, guests would be seated according to their social status. Yet Jesus dined with sinners and the most despised members of society, a demonstration of God's offer of free grace.

could not be sure that the food was ceremonially clean or that it had been properly tithed (*m. Demai* 2:2). He especially would not dine with a known sinner or a despised tax collector. The Pharisees expect Jesus, a rabbi, to act in this same exclusive manner. Instead, Jesus goes out of his way to associate with sinners. To the Pharisees' question, he responds with a proverb and its explanation: "It is not the healthy who need a doctor, but the sick. I have not come to call the righteous, but sinners to repentance." The great physician came to heal not the self-righteous but sinners who recognize their need of repentance and spiritual healing.

Jesus' words and actions demonstrate something new and revolutionary about the kingdom of God. No longer is fellowship with God the exclusive right of priests and the religious elite, or of a single nation. The new age of salvation means free forgiveness of sins to all who respond in faith. Throughout the Gospels, Jesus' teaching and

> No longer is fellowship with God the exclusive right of priests and the religious elite, or of a single nation. The new age of salvation means free forgiveness of sins to all who respond in faith.

parables reflect this great paradox and reversal. The proud and self-righteous reject the kingdom and are rejected. Sinners and outcasts joyfully repent and so receive the kingdom.

Jesus and the Gentiles: Salvation for All Humanity

Most remarkable is Jesus' attitude toward the Gentiles — the ultimate outsiders from Israel's perspective. It seems clear that Jesus sought at first to direct his ministry only to the Jews. When he commissions the Twelve, he tells them to go only to "the lost sheep of Israel" (Matt. 10:6) and at first refuses to exorcize a Gentile woman's daughter, saying, "I was sent only to the lost sheep of Israel" (Matt. 15:24). These sayings are unlikely to have been created by a church actively proclaiming the gospel to Gentiles. Jesus clearly viewed the gospel message as first for the Jews, God's chosen people (like Paul did, Rom. 1:16). This fits Jesus' proclamation of the kingdom of God, which in the Old Testament would be inseparable from Israel's history as a nation. It also fits Jesus' appointment of the Twelve. Jesus was calling out a righteous remnant from within Israel.

Yet Jesus repeatedly hints that his message of salvation is a universal one which will ultimately go to all people everywhere. When he heals the servant of a Roman centurion, Jesus marvels at the man's faith and remarks, "I have not found such great faith even in Israel!" (Luke 7:1 – 10; Matt. 8:5 – 13). He then predicts that many outsiders will come from east, west, north, and south for the feast in the kingdom of God, while many in Israel will be rejected and cast out (Matt. 8:11 – 12; cf. Luke 13:28 – 29). The messianic banquet will not be for Israel alone, but for all those who submit in faith to God's call.

This theme, too, fits both Jesus' kingdom preaching and the Old Testament background. The age of salvation is portrayed by the prophets as a time when all nations will stream to Jerusalem to worship the Lord:

> In the last days
> the mountain of the Lord's temple will be established . . .
> and all nations will stream to it.
> Many peoples will come and say,
> "Come, let us go to the mountain of the Lord,
>   to the house of the God of Jacob.
> He will teach us his ways,
>   so that we may walk in his paths."
> The law will go out from Zion,
>   the word of the Lord from Jerusalem.
>
> —Isaiah 2:2 – 3

This theme took two distinct tracks in Judaism. In one stream of tradition, the Gentiles are depicted as subject to Israel, coming to Jerusalem as vassals to pay tribute and to recognize the Lord's sovereignty. This stream is prominent in the literature of Second Temple Judaism, in which the nations which have ruled Israel now become her servants. The other stream — and the one with which Jesus identified — affirms not the subjection of the nations but their salvation. Israel's glorious restoration will bring a "light of revelation" to the Gentiles. All humanity will experience God's salvation (Isa. 42:6; 49:6; Luke 2:32;

Acts 13:47). In the Old Testament, Israel was called to be a light for the Gentiles and to reveal his glory to the nations (Isa. 49:6). In fulfillment of Israel's mission, Jesus now calls out a righteous remnant from within Israel to proclaim the arrival of God's salvation to the nations (Luke 24:46–48; Acts 1:8; Matt. 28:16–20).

Jesus' association with a variety of outsiders—sinners, tax collectors, Samaritans, lepers, women, and Gentiles—thus points to a larger issue with reference to the kingdom of God. God's salvation reaches beyond ethnic, social, and gender boundaries, breaking down walls of separation. The restoration of Israel is the inauguration of a greater plan to defeat Satan, sin, and death, and to bring restoration and reconciliation to a fallen creation.

> The restoration of Israel is the inauguration of a greater plan to defeat Satan, sin, and death, and to bring restoration and reconciliation to a fallen creation.

The Triumphal Entry

As Jesus' general actions of calling disciples and dining with sinners have symbolic significance with reference to his aims and intentions, so also do specific actions like entering Jerusalem on a colt and clearing the temple of money changers. Jesus' entrance into Jerusalem on "Palm Sunday," an event recorded in all four Gospels, is widely regarded as based on an authentic event (Mark 11:1–10; Matt. 21:1–9; Luke 19:28–40; John 12:12–19). Its significance is that Jesus seems to be deliberately acting out the prophecy of Zechariah 9:9, and so presenting himself as the messianic king.

The triumphal entry on Palm Sunday depicted in a painting inside the church in Bethphage

Pilgrims coming to Jerusalem for one of the festivals would normally approach the city on foot. Yet Jesus intentionally sends his disciples to procure a young donkey, one which has never been ridden before. If they are questioned, they are to reply, "The Lord has need of it." The scene recalls the Middle Eastern practice of impressment, whereby subjects of a king would be expected to make resources available to him for his use (see 1 Sam. 8:16). The fact that the young donkey is unridden suggests its purity and appropriateness for a king. The scene is particularly striking since Jesus is never depicted elsewhere in the Gospels as riding an animal. Why at this point? The most likely answer is that Jesus intentionally imitated Zechariah 9:9: "Rejoice greatly, O Daughter of Zion! Shout, Daughter of Jerusalem! See, your king comes to you, righteous and having salvation, gentle and riding on a donkey, on a colt, the foal of a donkey."

Some scholars have claimed that the Gospel story is a legend created by the early church to portray Jesus as the Messiah. This is unlikely for various reasons. First, Mark's version, presumably the earliest, does not explicitly refer to Zechariah 9:9. If the story was created around this prophecy, we might expect Mark (and Luke) to quote it. Second, the cry of the crowd, "Hosanna! Blessed is he who comes in the name of the Lord!" has the mark of authenticity. As we have noted before, these words allude to Psalm 118 (v. 26), a common psalm of pilgrims coming to Jerusalem for the feasts of Tabernacles and Passover. Hosanna is a Hebrew word meaning "save now." It is unlikely that the Greek-speaking church would have invented a saying which uses a Hebrew term and which only opaquely refers to Jesus' messianic identity. Finally, the independent attestation of the event in John's Gospel suggests it is an early tradition, probably going back to an event in Jesus' life.

> With his entry into Jerusalem on a donkey, Jesus is symbolically announcing a messianic claim and challenging Israel's leaders to respond.

If the episode was intentionally enacted by Jesus, what does it mean? Like the cursing of the fig tree and the cleansing of the temple, it seems to be both an act of self-revelation and a provocation. Jesus is symbolically announcing his messianic claim and challenging Israel's leaders to respond. His identification with Zechariah 9:9 also tells us something about his messianic consciousness. Jesus does not enter the city riding a war horse, ready for battle against the Romans, but rather as the humble peace-bringing king. He will bring salvation not through physical conquest but through self-sacrificial service.

Cleansing the Temple

A second episode even more widely accepted as authentic among scholars is Jesus' "cleansing" of the temple (Mark 11:11–17; Matt. 21:12–21:12–17; Luke 19:45–46; cf. John 2:13–17). Jesus enters the temple, driving out those who are selling animals for sacrifices and overturning the tables of the money changers. These money changers exchanged various currencies for Tyrian shekels, which were used to pay the temple tax. Jesus objects that the money changers and sellers are changing God's house from a house of prayer into "a den of robbers." Almost all scholars today agree (1) that Jesus performed some kind of symbolic action in the temple, and (2) that it was this action which prompted Jesus' opponents to act against him (see Mark 11:18; Luke 19:47).

Jesus' actions are often identified as a cleansing to remove defilement. This would follow the model of the Maccabees, who purified and rededicated the temple after it was defiled by the pagan sacrifices of Antiochus Epiphanes. Jesus restores the temple once again to "a house of prayer for all nations" (Mark 11:17).

While Jesus' actions were certainly a purging, there seems more to the event than this. In both Matthew and Mark, the incident is closely related to Jesus' cursing of the fig tree. As we have seen, this latter event is almost certainly a symbolic act of judgment against Israel. Elsewhere, Jesus repeatedly predicts the coming judgment and destruction of Jerusalem and the temple (Mark 13:2, par.;

Tyrian shekels, which were used to pay the temple tax

Luke 13:34–35; 19:41–44). At his trial and crucifixion, he is accused of claiming that *he* would destroy the temple (Mark 14:58, par.; Mark 15:29, par.; cf. Acts 6:14). This accusation may be a distortion of his earlier predictions about its destruction and his teaching about "the body of his temple" (John 2:19–21). It seems likely, therefore, that Jesus' actions in the temple were not only a cleansing but a symbolic act of judgment, an enacted parable of its destruction.

Some scholars, like E. P. Sanders, claim that Jesus envisioned not only the destruction of the temple but also its restoration.[2] There is a tradition in Judaism that the coming Messiah would restore and rebuild the temple to be more glorious than ever (2 Sam. 7:13; Zech. 6:13; Mal. 3:1). While this interpretation is possible, more likely Jesus saw the temple's permanent replacement as a part of the dawning of the new age, the arrival of the kingdom of God. In the new age of salvation, forgiveness of sins would no longer come through the temple and its sacrificial system but through Jesus' sacrifice on the cross, "the temple of his body" destroyed and rebuilt through death and resurrection (John 2:19, 21). As Jesus tells the Samaritan woman, in the days to come, God's people would worship him "neither on this mountain [Mount Gerizim] nor in Jerusalem" but "in spirit and in truth" (John 4:21–24). We will examine Jesus' perspective on his death in the next chapter.

> It seems likely that Jesus' actions in the temple were not only a cleansing but a symbolic act of judgment, an enacted parable of its destruction.

THE MESSIANIC TITLES

We have seen that the actions of Jesus reveal a great deal about his aims. We turn finally to the messianic titles, and the constellation of ideas which surround them, in order to provide further insight into Jesus' self-perception and ministry goals.

Christ (Messiah)

Central to the early church's understanding of the identity of Jesus was the claim that he was the **Messiah**, or Christ. The English term messiah comes from the Hebrew *mashiach*,

---

2. E. P. Sanders, *Jesus and Judaism* (Philadelphia: Fortress, 1985), 73, 75, 77, 227, 233.

meaning "anointed one." The term Christ comes from the Greek translation of the Hebrew term (*christos*, from *chriō*, "to anoint").

Background. Anointing with oil symbolized being set apart to God's service. Israel's kings and priests were anointed, as also were ritual objects used in worship (the altar of burnt offering, the ark of the covenant, etc.). The term thus came to be used metaphorically of people whom God had set apart for special service. In the Old Testament, the phrase "the LORD's anointed" is most commonly used of Israel's king but was also assigned to priests, prophets, and even the Persian king Cyrus, God's agent to return the Jews from exile (Isa. 45:1). By further extension, the term Messiah eventually came to be used of God's end-times agent of salvation. This use does not yet appear in the Old Testament but seems to have been coming into common parlance by the first century. As we noted in chapter 5, expectations for God's end-times salvation took various forms at different places and times. In some literature, God himself is viewed as savior; other times, he uses a messiah or other divine agent. The most common messianic expectation of Jesus' day was for the Davidic Messiah — the ideal king from the line of David. It is usually this figure who is intended when we speak of the Jewish Messiah.

Jesus the Messiah. Did Jesus claim to be the Messiah? Critics have long doubted that Jesus viewed himself in this way. It is certainly true that he used great reserve with reference to the title. In the Synoptics, he almost never explicitly claims it. When Jesus is identified as the Messiah, it is usually by demons, whom Jesus silences (Mark 1:24–25, 34; 3:11–12), or by his accusers (Mark 14:61; 15:32). As we have seen, William Wrede treated this paucity of evidence as Mark's strategy to cover up Jesus' unmessianic life. Mark created a "messianic secret" in which Jesus silenced others about his messiahship.[3] The two key Synoptic passages in which Jesus appears to accept the title are themselves disputed. In Mark's version of Peter's confession (Mark 8:29), Jesus does not explicitly affirm Peter's claim that "you are the Christ" but instead goes on to speak of the suffering of the Son of Man. Later, Jesus is asked by the high priest Caiaphas at his trial, "Are you the Christ, the Son of the Blessed One?" While in Mark, Jesus answers explicitly, "I am" (Mark 14:62), in Matthew he uses the more enigmatic, "You have said so" (Matt. 26:64 TNIV). Some argue this means something like, "That is what you say, not me."

While it is true that Jesus makes few explicit statements, there is a large body of evidence that he viewed himself as Israel's end-times Savior. We have already seen his extraordinary claims to authority as the inaugurator of the kingdom, as victor over Satan and over disease, as fulfillment of the law, and as final judge of the world. His actions in entering Jerusalem in imitation of Zechariah 9:9 and his clearing of the temple also have strong messianic implications. One wonders how Jesus could have made such audacious claims and performed such actions and not have considered himself to be the Messiah.

The confession of Peter and Jesus' answer to Caiaphas are also likely to be positive affirmations. Messianic claims were not uncommon in first-century Palestine, arising from a variety of prophetic and revolutionary figures. It would be incredible — considering Jesus' words and deeds — if his disciples had not wondered whether he might be the Messiah.

Messiah means "anointed one." Kings, priests, and prophets were anointed for service. This horn-shaped vessel may have been used for anointing.

---

3. See chapter 11, p. 352, and fig. 7.3, p. 180.

Jesus' question and Peter's confession are credible in this context. Also significant is the church's universal affirmation after the resurrection that God had vindicated his Messiah. If there was no speculation concerning Jesus before his death, why did the church so quickly exalt him to Messiah afterward? The more likely scenario is that the disciples' hopes and expectations about Jesus were confirmed by their experience of the resurrection.

The same conclusions can be drawn from Jesus' confession before Caiaphas. While the details of Jesus' trial before the Sanhedrin have been doubted by some, it seems certain that the Jewish authorities were involved in some way in Jesus' arrest. Jesus' actions in the temple—a direct challenge to the priestly authority of the high priest and his associates—would certainly have prompted such a response. During his hearing, Jesus would certainly have been asked in what role he was playing or by what authority he was acting. If he had denied messianic claims, it is unlikely he would have been crucified. In fact, the evidence is overwhelming that Jesus was crucified as a messianic pretender. Few would doubt the historicity of the *titulus*, or nameplate, placed on the cross announcing his offence as "king of the Jews" (Mark 15:26; Matt. 27:37; Luke 23:38; John 19:19–22). The criterion of dissimilarity points to its authenticity since king was not a common title used of Jesus in the early church. The whole crucifixion scene (the crown of thorns, the purple robe, the soldiers' mocking him as a king) reinforces this view that Jesus was executed as "king of the Jews" and that this charge was based on his messianic actions and claims.

> It would be incredible— considering Jesus' words and deeds—if his disciples had not wondered whether he might be the Messiah.

Why then was Jesus so reticent about using the title Messiah? The most likely reason was its political and militaristic connotations. While the Messiah was never a purely political figure, he was widely expected to destroy Israel's enemies and to secure her physical borders. The *Psalms of Solomon*, a Jewish work produced in the mid-first century BC, portrays the coming "son of David" as one who will "destroy the unrighteous rulers" and "purge Jerusalem from Gentiles who trample her to destruction" (*Pss. Sol.* 17:21–23). Jesus probably avoided the title because it risked communicating an inadequate understanding of the kingdom and his messianic role. Jesus came not to defeat the Roman legions but to bring victory over Satan, sin, and death.

Another reason scholars have suggested for Jesus' avoidance of the title is a Jewish belief that no person could be declared the Messiah until *after* he had accomplished the messianic task. It was God who would ultimately reveal and vindicate his anointed one.[4] While this explanation is intriguing, it is difficult to determine how widespread this Jewish tradition was or even whether it goes back to the time of Jesus.

Son of Man

While showing great reserve with reference to the title Messiah, Jesus' favorite self-designation was **Son of Man**. The Greek phrase *ho huios tou anthrōpou* is a literal (and somewhat

---

4. For references, see R. N. Longenecker, *The Christology of Early Jewish Christianity,* reprint ed. (Grand Rapids: Baker, 1981), 71–74. Cf. *b. Sanhedrin* 98a; Justin Martyr, *Dialogue* 8.4.

Figure 18.2—The Coming Son of Man

In my vision at night I looked, and there before me was one like a son of man, coming with the clouds of heaven. He approached the Ancient of Days and was led into his presence. He was given authority, glory and sovereign power; all peoples, nations and men of every language worshiped him. His dominion is an everlasting dominion that will not pass away, and his kingdom is one that will never be destroyed.

—Daniel 7:13–14

awkward) translation of the Hebrew *ben ʾādām* ("son of man"), which means a "person" or a "human being." Jesus probably used the Aramaic equivalent *bar ʾenash*.

Background. The phrase is often used in the Old Testament to contrast the lowliness of humanity with the transcendence of God. In the book of Ezekiel, the prophet is called "son of man" ninety-three times. A special use of the phrase appears in Daniel 7:13–14, where an exalted messianic figure—one "like a son of man" (that is, having human form)—comes with the clouds of heaven into the presence of the Ancient of Days (God) and is given authority, glory, and an eternal kingdom. In the context of Daniel, this Son of Man appears to be identified not only with the "saints of the Most High" (7:18, 27) but also as an individual figure (7:13–14). This is similar to the Servant of the Lord in Isaiah 40–55, who is identified with corporate Israel (Isa. 44:1; 49:3) and as an individual (Isa. 42:1). The key to interpreting this dual image may be that the Messiah functions as representative head of his people Israel.

Was Son of Man a title for the Messiah in Judaism? The Jewish apocalyptic work *1 Enoch* uses the title for a messianic heavenly deliverer who saves his people and judges the wicked (*1 Enoch* 37–71; cf. *4 Ezra* 13). The portrait is clearly drawn from Daniel 7, but it is debated by scholars whether this section of *1 Enoch* is pre- or post-Christian, and so whether Jesus' hearers would have understood Son of Man to be a messianic title.

Jesus the Son of Man. It seems beyond dispute that Jesus used the title, since it appears exclusively on his lips in the Gospels and since the later church did not adopt it as a messianic title (and so did not create it). But there is enormous scholarly debate concerning which kinds of sayings are authentic and what Jesus meant by the title. There are three main types of sayings:

1. *Sayings about the earthly work of the Son of Man*, such as Mark 2:10, "The Son of Man has authority on earth to forgive sins."
2. *Sayings about the suffering Son of Man*, such as Mark 8:31, "the Son of Man must suffer many things and be rejected by the elders, chief priests and teachers of the law."
3. *Sayings about the apocalyptic Son of Man*, such as Mark 14:62, "And you will see the Son of Man sitting at the right hand of the Mighty One and coming on the clouds of heaven."

These last "apocalyptic" sayings are clearly related to the exalted messianic figure described in Daniel 7:13–14.

Some scholars consider only the sayings in the first group to be authentic, treating the title as nothing more than a self-designation ("I, who speak to you"). Others treat only the third—the apocalyptic sayings—as authentic, but claim that Jesus was referring not to himself but to a messianic figure he expected in the future. As evidence, they point to Luke 12:8, where Jesus speaks both of "me" and "the Son of Man" in the same sentence (but see the parallel in Matt. 10:32).

While it is impossible in this short space to deal sufficiently with so complex a topic, it is not unreasonable to treat all three types of sayings as authentic. The three are closely interrelated and fit well with aspects of Jesus' ministry which can be confirmed as authentic on other grounds. We have argued that Jesus saw himself as a unique messianic figure whose role was to announce and inaugurate God's kingdom. There is no evidence in the Gospels that he was looking for a successor—another Son of Man. His mission was not to conquer the Romans but to act as a humble servant, suffering for the sake of others. As we shall see in the next chapter, there is strong evidence that Jesus anticipated his death and that he interpreted it as a sacrifice of atonement for others. He also expected to be vindicated by God after suffering. The three types of sayings all fit this broader portrait of Jesus derived from his authentic words and deeds.

We conclude that Jesus likely adopted the title Son of Man for three related reasons:

1. It stressed his humanity and so his identification with the people of God.
2. It alluded to Daniel 7:13 in a veiled way, revealing his messianic identity and the glory he would receive after he had suffered.
3. At the same time, it did not carry the political dynamite of titles like Messiah or Son of David. Jesus could define his messiahship on his own terms, rather than on the basis of popular expectations.

Son of God

Another title closely related to Jesus' messiahship is **Son of God**. Like Christ, this designation became a key confessional title in the early church. The early Christian hymn cited by Paul in Romans 1:3–4 identifies Jesus as God's Son, now resurrected from the dead. We will first summarize the background to this title and then ask whether Jesus applied it to himself.

Background. In the past, it was common to seek parallels to the Son of God title in pagan religions, in which rulers, heroes, and deities were sometimes referred to as children of God. Today these parallels are generally rejected since closer parallels can be found in the Old Testament and Judaism.[5] While angels are occasionally referred to as "sons of God" in the Old Testament (Job 1:6; 2:1; 38:7; Pss. 82:6; 89:6), more important parallels are to the nation Israel and the king from David's line. Israel was God's son by virtue of God's unique calling, deliverance, and protection. Hosea 11:1 reads, "When Israel was a child, I loved him, and out of Egypt I called my son." Similar references to God as the father of his people

---

5. See especially Martin Hengel, *The Son of God: The Origin of Christology and the History of Jewish-Hellenistic Religion*, trans. John Bowden (Philadelphia: Fortress, 1975).

appear throughout the Old Testament.[6] The Davidic king is referred to as the son of God by virtue of his special relationship to God and his representative role among the people. In the Davidic covenant, the LORD promises David concerning his descendant that "I will be his father and he will be my son" (2 Sam. 7:14; cf. Pss. 2:7; 89:26). By extension, later Judaism seems to have identified the coming Messiah as the son of God. Though the evidence is sketchy, three texts from Qumran appear to apply this Davidic promise tradition to the coming Messiah (4QFlor 1:11 [= 4Q174]; 1QSa 2:11–12 [= 1Q28a]; 4Q Aramaic Apocalypse [=4Q246]).

Jesus as the Son of God. While some scholars reject that Jesus could have considered himself the Son of God in any unique sense, several pieces of evidence point to the title's authenticity.

(1) First, as just noted, by the first century, Son of God seems to have been coming into use as a title for the Messiah. If Jesus was acclaimed by some as the Messiah, it is not surprising that he would also be called Son of God. In a number of New Testament passages, Son of God is almost synonymous with Christ. The angel Gabriel links Jesus' identification as "Son of the Most High" with his reception of the throne of David (Luke 1:32). Peter confesses that Jesus is the "Christ, the Son of the living God" (Matt. 16:16), and the high priest questions whether Jesus is "the Christ, the Son of the Blessed One" (Mark 14:61; Matt. 26:63). In these and other texts, Son of God essentially means "the Messiah from David's line" (cf. Mark 1:1; Luke 4:41; 22:70; John 11:27; 20:31; Acts 9:20, 22).

> Jesus' use of the Aramaic term *Abba* ("Father") in prayer suggests that he considered himself to have a unique relationship with God.

(2) Second, Jesus' use of the Aramaic term *Abba* ("Father") in prayer suggests that he considered himself to have a unique relationship with God. The fact that the Greek-speaking church preserved this Aramaic term renders it likely that it goes back to Jesus himself (Mark 14:36; cf. Rom. 8:15–16; Gal. 4:6). While it is not quite right to say that the term means "daddy" (Jewish adults addressed their parents in this way), *Abba* does express considerably more intimacy than was common for Jews in prayer. While sometimes referring to God as "our heavenly Father," they rarely if ever addressed him directly as "father" (*Abba*). Jesus' use of the term appears to be unprecedented, expressing unique intimacy with the Father.[7]

Furthermore, while Jesus encouraged his disciples to pray to God as their Father, their sonship appears to have been dependent on his. No saying of Jesus links the disciples to Jesus so that together they would say "our Father." The Lord's Prayer is designed specifically for the disciples. Jesus seems rather to have viewed his divine sonship as unique, mediating a special father-son relationship to his disciples.

(3) Three key Synoptic passages provide evidence that Jesus spoke of himself as the unique Son of God. The first is the parable of the tenants, in which Jesus refers to the son who is murdered by the farmers overseeing the father's vineyard (Mark 12:1–11, par.). The

---

6. Exod. 4:22; Num. 11:12; Deut. 14:1; 32:5, 19; Isa. 43:6; 45:11; Jer. 3:4, 19; 31:9, 20; Hos. 2:1.

7. See Joachim Jeremias, *The Prayers of Jesus* (Philadelphia: Fortress, 1978); idem., *New Testament Theology* (New York: Scribner, 1971), 63–68.

parable is sometimes dismissed as inauthentic since it refers allegorically to Jesus' mission and death. But there is good evidence for its authenticity. First, the setting of the parable fits well with the situation of Galilee in Jesus' day, with its great landed estates and the inevitable tension between absentee owners and the dispossessed peasantry. Second, the absence of any reference to the vindication or resurrection of the son suggests that the parable was not created by the early church. Only if we assume that Jesus could not have spoken about his own mission or predicted his own death must the parable be judged inauthentic.

A second text is Mark 13:32 (Matt. 24:36), where Jesus speaks concerning the time of the end, "No one knows about that day or hour, not even the angels in heaven, nor the Son, but only the Father." It seems unlikely that the church would create a saying which attributes ignorance to the Son. The text is significant since Jesus refers to himself in an absolute sense as the Son in relation to the Father.

A similar conclusion can be drawn from Matthew 11:27 (Luke 10:22), where Jesus speaks of the intimacy of the relationship between the Father and the Son: "All things have been committed to me by my Father. No one knows the Son except the Father, and no one knows the Father except the Son and those to whom the Son chooses to reveal him." This verse has sometimes been dismissed as inauthentic, since it uses language of esoteric knowledge similar to Jesus' words in the Gospel of John. Three responses can be made to this. First, it is inappropriate to assume that anything resembling Jesus' teaching in John is inauthentic. As we have seen, the value given to John as a historical source is increasing among scholars. Second, the absolute language of the Son and the Father here is little different than in Mark 13:32, which is probably authentic. Third, as Joachim Jeremias has demonstrated, the idea that Jesus is the recipient and mediator of the knowledge of God appears elsewhere in the Synoptics.[8] The se three texts provide strong evidence that Jesus considered his relationship with God to be one of special intimacy and that he viewed himself as a unique mediator between God and his people.

Lord

Perhaps the most exalted title given to Jesus in the early church was Lord (Greek: *kyrios*). To confess Jesus as **Lord** was to attribute to him authority and allegiance above all other authorities, rulers, or gods (Rom. 10:9; 1 Cor. 12:3; Phil. 2:11). One difficulty in determining the meaning of *kyrios* in the Gospels is its wide range of senses both in Judaism and in the Greco-Roman world. It could be a simple term of respect (like "sir"), a term of ownership or authority ("owner," "master"), or a designation for an exalted deity ("lord" or "god"). The Septuagint (LXX) uses *kyrios* over six thousand times as a translation of the Hebrew *Yahweh* (translated, "the LORD"), the proper name for the God of Israel (See fig. 5.1, p. 124).

The difficult question is how the early church came to call Jesus Lord while still maintaining monotheism, belief in the one true God. Wilhelm Bousset argued in his classic work *Kyrios Christos* that the use of *kyrios* for Jesus arose in the Greek-speaking church under the influence of pagan religions, which referred to their deities as lords.[9] Only in

---

8. Mark 4:11; Matt. 5:17; Luke 15:1–7, 8–10, 11–31, etc.; Jeremias, *Prayers*, 49–51.

9. Wilhelm Bousset, *Kyrios Christos: A History of the Belief in Christ from the Beginnings of Christianity to Irenaeus*, trans. John E. Steely (Nashville: Abingdon, 1970).

this Greek context, it is argued, could a Jewish teacher be transformed into a divine being. There is evidence, however, that the Aramaic-speaking church of Palestine had already begun addressing Jesus as Lord. In 1 Corinthians 16:22, Paul preserves the Aramaic expression *maranatha*, meaning "Our Lord come!" The same term appears in the *Didache*, a church manual from the early second century AD (*Didache* 10:6; cf. Rev. 22:20). Not only does this confirm that the earliest church identified Jesus as Lord, but it also shows that they viewed him as their transcendent master who would one day return.

Larry Hurtado and others have shown that identifying Jesus as a divine being was not beyond the scope of Jewish monotheism, since first-century Jewish writings depicted a variety of heavenly agents acting on God's behalf, including angels and exalted patriarchs like Enoch and Moses.[10] The personification of wisdom in Judaism, as well as descriptions of the divine *Logos*—the efficacious Word of God—also opened the way to speak of Jesus as God's self-revelation.

So in what sense does the title Lord go back to the historical Jesus? On the one hand, it is likely that Jesus' disciples referred to him as Master, using the Aramaic term *mārî*. But does Lord ever carry a more exalted or even a divine sense in the Gospels? A key passage in this regard is Mark 12:35–37, where Jesus asks the riddle about how the Christ can be the "son of David" if in Psalm 110:1 David calls him "my Lord": "The Lord said to my Lord: 'Sit at my right hand until I put your enemies under your feet'" (Mark 12:36, citing Ps. 110:1). The first Lord in the Hebrew text of Psalm 110:1 is *Yahweh*; the second is *adonai*, referring to the Messiah. The point Jesus makes is that since David addresses the Messiah as his superior, "my Lord," the Messiah must be more than simply the earthly son of David. In favor of the historicity of this saying is the cryptic way Jesus refers to his messiahship, which is characteristic of his reserve elsewhere. If the saying is authentic, it indicates that Jesus viewed traditional messianic expectations as inadequate to describe the exalted status of the Christ. While the saying does not explicitly identify the Messiah as a preexistent or divine figure, it certainly comes close.

Jesus as God?

Can we go farther and say that Jesus identified himself with Yahweh, the God of Israel? If we take into account the Gospel of John, the answer would seem to be yes, since Jesus apparently identifies himself with the "I AM" of the Exodus account (John 8:58). Yet many scholars are unwilling to accept this as an authentic saying of Jesus.

While the Synoptic Gospels stop short of identifying Jesus as the Second Person of the Trinity in the manner of the later christological creeds of the church, they exhibit a very high implicit Christology. In his important work *Jesus and the Victory of God*, N. T. Wright points to convincing evidence that Jesus viewed himself as the embodiment of Yahweh, returning to Zion to bring his people out of exile. Jesus' actions in inaugurating a new exodus (Isaiah 40), his self-designations as "the bridegroom" and "the shepherd" (titles for Yahweh in the Old Testament), his calling of the Twelve (just as Yahweh called

---

10. Larry W. Hurtado, *One God, One Lord: Early Christian Devotion and Ancient Jewish Monotheism*, 2nd ed. (Edinburgh: T. and T. Clark, 1998); *Lord Jesus Christ: Devotion to Jesus in Earliest Christianity* (Grand Rapids: Eerdmans, 2003).

Israel into existence), his words as the expression of divine Wisdom (Matt. 11:25–30; Luke 10:21–22), his supremacy over law and temple, and his unique father-son relationship with God—all of these point to a very high (one could even say a divine) Christology.[11]

With these conclusions, we approach the limits of what a historian can say about the historical Jesus. Going beyond this takes us into the realm of faith confessions arising from the believer's experience of the risen Christ, rather than past events capable of historical verification. Yet with these results, we can conclude that the later christological creeds of the church, in which Jesus is confessed as God the Son and as the Second Person of the Trinity, need not be viewed as distortions or evolutionary transmutations of a Jewish rabbi into a divine Lord. They can rather be seen as a natural development arising from the church's reflection on and contemplation of the words and deeds of the historical Jesus.

---

11. N. T. Wright, *Jesus and the Victory of God*, 612–53.

» CHAPTER SUMMARY «

1. The actions as well as the words of Jesus can tell us a great deal about his self-understanding and his aims.

2. Jesus' extraordinary authority is evident in many ways: his claim to be the inaugurator of the kingdom of God, his authority over demons and disease, his claim to speak for God, his authority over the law, his forgiveness of sins, and his claim to be the final judge of all people.

3. Jesus' aims or intentions are seen in various ways:

   a. He appoints the Twelve, representing the remnant of Israel and the end-times people of God.

   b. He associates with sinners and outcasts, offering them free forgiveness of sins in the new age of salvation.

   c. He repeatedly hints that his message will go to the Gentiles, evidence that Isaiah's promise of light to the Gentiles is now being fulfilled (Isa. 42:6; 49:6).

   d. Jesus' entry into Jerusalem on a donkey was an intentional enactment of Zechariah 9:9, indicating that Jesus is the peace-bringing king of Israel.

   e. Jesus' clearing of the temple was likely a symbolic act of judgment, indicating that the age of temple worship was giving way to the new covenant age of salvation.

4. The messianic titles attributed to Jesus tell us a great deal about his identity and purpose:

   a. Jesus' words and actions suggest he believed himself to be the Messiah, God's end-times agent of salvation.

b. Son of Man, Jesus' favorite self-designation, emphasizes his true humanity and identifies him with the exalted messianic figure in Daniel 7:13 – 14, but avoids the political preconceptions associated with other titles like Messiah and Son of David.

c. The evidence is strong that Jesus considered himself the unique Son of God: the title is closely linked to Jesus' messiahship; the Aramaic term *Abba* ("Father"), which Jesus used to address God, is almost certainly authentic; several Synoptic passages where Jesus identifies himself as the Son have a good claim to authenticity (Mark 12:1 – 11, par.; Mark 13:32 and Matt. 24:36; and Matt. 11:27 and Luke 10:22).

d. Passages like Mark 12:35 – 37 suggest that Jesus viewed himself as the exalted Lord, greater even than David.

e. While Jesus does not explicitly identify himself as divine in the Synoptics, his claims to speak and act with the authority of Yahweh come close and suggest that the church's later christological confessions are a natural development of meditation on the significance of Jesus' person and work.

» KEY TERMS «

amēn	the Twelve	Son of God
disciple	Messiah	Lord
apostle	Son of Man	*maranatha*

» DISCUSSION AND STUDY QUESTIONS «

1. What claims did Jesus make which exhibit his extraordinary sense of authority?

2. What do the following features of Jesus' ministry indicate about his aims or purpose?

   a. His appointment of the Twelve

   b. His association with sinners and outcasts

   c. His attitude toward the Gentiles

   d. His entrance into Jerusalem on a donkey

   e. His clearing of the temple

3. Summarize the Jewish background of the following messianic titles: Messiah, Son of Man, Son of God, Lord.

4. Summarize the evidence that Jesus identified himself with each of these titles. What did he mean by them?

5. What does *maranatha* mean, and what is its significance for the early church?

Digging Deeper

General Works

Chilton, Bruce, and Craig A. Evans, eds. *Authenticating the Activities of Jesus.* Leiden: Brill, 1999.

Crossan, John Dominic. *The Historical Jesus: The Life of a Mediterranean Jewish Peasant.* San Francisco: HarperSanFrancisco, 1991.

Harvey, A. E., *Jesus and the Constraints of History.* Philadelphia: Westminster, 1982.

Hurtado, Larry W. *Lord Jesus Christ: Devotion to Jesus in Earliest Christianity.* Grand Rapids: Eerdmans, 2003.

Jeremiahs, J. *The Prayers of Jesus.* Philadelphia: Fortress, 1978.

Marshall, I. Howard. *Jesus the Saviour: Studies in New Testament Theology.* London: SPCK, 1990.

Meier, John P. *A Marginal Jew: Rethinking the Historical Jesus.* 3 vols. New York: Doubleday, 1991, 1994, 2001.

Meyer, Ben F. *The Aims of Jesus.* London: SCM, 1979.

Sanders. E. P. *Jesus and Judaism.* Philadelphia: Fortress, 1985.

Stein, Robert H. *Jesus the Messiah: A Survey of the Life of Christ.* Downers Grove, IL: InterVarsity, 1996.

Witherington III, Ben. *The Christology of Jesus.* Minneapolis: Fortress, 1990.

Wright, N. T. *Jesus and the Victory of God.* Minneapolis: Fortress, 1996.

Messianic Titles and Their Significance

Cullmann, Oscar. *The Christology of the New Testament.* Translated by Shirley C. Guthrie and Charles A. M. Hall. Philadelphia: Westminster, 1959.

Dunn, James D. G. *Christology in the Making: A New Testament Inquiry into the Origins of the Doctrine of the Incarnation.* 2nd ed. Grand Rapids: Eerdmans, 1996.

Hahn, Ferdinand. *The Titles of Jesus in Christology: Their History in Early Christianity.* Translated by Harold Knight and George Ogg. New York: World, 1969.

Hengel, Martin. *The Son of God: The Origin of Christology and the History of Jewish-Hellenistic Religion.* Translated by John Bowden. Philadelphia: Fortress, 1975.

Hurtado, Larry W. *One God, One Lord: Early Christian Devotion and Ancient Jewish Monotheism.* 2nd ed. Edinburgh: T. and T. Clark, 1998.

Marshall, I. H. *The Origins of New Testament Christology* (Downers Grove, IL: InterVarsity, 1976).

Moule, C. F. D. *The Origin of Christology.* Cambridge: Cambridge Univ. Press, 1977.

CHAPTER 19

The Death of Jesus

» CHAPTER OVERVIEW «

1. Historical Circumstances of the Death of Jesus
2. Jesus' Perspective on His Coming Death

» OBJECTIVES «

After reading this chapter, you should be able to:

- Discuss the likelihood of Roman and Jewish participation in the arrest, trial, and crucifixion of Jesus.
- Summarize the historical situation of, and likely causes for, the opposition to and execution of Jesus.
- Provide evidence that Jesus predicted his suffering and death.
- Discuss the significance Jesus gave to his approaching death.

HISTORICAL CIRCUMSTANCES OF THE DEATH OF JESUS

Much of the scholarly discussion about the circumstances of Jesus' death relates to the question of who was responsible for his arrest and crucifixion. Historically, the primary responsibility has been placed on the Jewish leadership and the Jews in Jerusalem. Throughout the centuries, this has sometimes had tragic consequences, resulting in anti-Semitism and violence against Jews. More recent trends in scholarship have shifted the blame to the Romans. The tendency to blame the Jews, it is said, arose in the decades after the crucifixion with the church's growing conflict with the synagogue and its desire to convince Rome that Christianity was no threat to the empire.

> Most contemporary scholars recognize that both Jewish and Roman authorities must have played some role in Jesus' death.

Most contemporary scholars recognize that there is not an either-or solution to this question, but that both Jewish and Roman authorities must have played some role in Jesus' death. First, Jesus was crucified—a Roman rather than a Jewish means of execution. (Stoning was the more common Jewish method.) There is good evidence that at this time the Jewish Sanhedrin did not have authority to carry out capital punishment (John 18:31; *y. Sanh.* 1:1; 7:2).[1] The Roman governor **Pontius Pilate** no doubt gave the orders for Jesus' crucifixion, and Roman soldiers carried it out. At the same time, all that we know about Jesus' teachings and actions suggest that he was more apt to offend and provoke the Jewish religious leaders than the Roman authorities. It is unlikely that the Romans would have initiated action against him without prompting from the Jewish authorities.

So was Jesus crucified for political reasons or religious reasons? Raising the question this way actually misrepresents first-century Judaism, in which religion and politics were inseparable. Jesus' death was no doubt motivated by the perceived threat felt by the religio-political powers of his day. We will look in turn at the motivations, tendencies, and actions of these authorities.

Pilate and the Romans

The evidence points to the conclusion that Jesus was executed by the Romans for sedition—rebellion against the government. First, he was crucified as "king of the Jews." As noted in the last chapter, the *titulus* on the cross announcing this is almost certainly historical. Second, he was crucified between two "robbers" or "criminals"—Roman terms used of insurrectionists (Mark 15:27; Matt. 27:38; Luke 23:33; John 19:18). Another insurrectionist, Barabbas, was released in his place (Mark 15:7; Matt. 27:16; Luke 23:19; John 18:40). Finally, the account of charges brought to Pilate by the Sanhedrin in Luke's Gospel are related to sedition: "And they began to accuse him, saying, 'We have found this man subverting our nation. He opposes payment of taxes to Caesar and claims to be Christ, a

---

1. The stoning of Stephen in Acts 7 was probably a mob action rather than a judicial proceeding, and Josephus relates that the stoning of Jesus' brother James in AD 62 was an illegal action, for which the high priest Ananus was deposed (*Ant.* 20.9.1 §§200–203).

	Figure 19.1—A Chronology of Passion Week	
Sunday	Triumphal Entry	Mark 11:1–11; Matt. 21:1–11; Luke 19:29–44; John 12:12ff.
Monday	Cursing the fig tree	Mark 11:12–14; Matt. 21:18–19
	Cleansing the temple	Mark 11:15–18; Matt. 21:12–13; Luke 19:45–48
Tuesday	Withered fig tree seen by disciples	Mark 11:19–25; Matt. 21:19–22
	Temple controversies (Wednesday?)	Mark 11:27–12:44; Matt. 21:23–23:39; Luke 20:1–21:4
	Olivet Discourse (Wednesday?)	Mark 13:1–37; Matt. 24:1–25:46; Luke 21:5–36
Wednesday	No mention of events on Wednesday	See Mark 14:1 and John 12:1 for evidence of this day
Thursday	Last Supper	Mark 14:17–26; Matt. 26:20–30; Luke 22:14–30
	Betrayal and arrest	Mark 14:43–52; Matt. 26:47–56; Luke 22:47–53; John 18:2–12
	Trial before Annas and Caiphas	Mark 14:53–72; Matt. 26:57–75; Luke 22:54–65; John 18:13–27
Friday	Morning trial by the Sanhedrin	Mark 15:1; Matt. 27:1; Luke 22:66
	Trial before Pilate and Herod	Mark 15:2–19; Matt. 27:2–30; Luke 23:1–25; John 18:28–19:16
	Crucifixion and burial	Mark 15:20–46; Matt. 27:31–60; Luke 23:26–54; John 19:16–42
Saturday	Dead in tomb	
Sunday	Resurrection and ascension	Mark 16:1–8; Matt. 28:1–20; Luke 24:1–53; John 20:1–21:25

king.... He stirs up the people all over Judea by his teaching. He started in Galilee and has come all the way here'" (Luke 23:2, 5).

While this evidence confirms the charge against Jesus, it raises the mystifying question of why Jesus was crucified, since he had almost nothing in common with other rebels and insurrectionists of his day. He advocated love for enemies and commanded his followers to respond to persecution with acts of kindness (Matt. 5:38–48; Luke 6:27–36). He affirmed the legitimacy of paying taxes to Caesar (Mark 12:14, 17; Matt. 22:17, 21; Luke 20:22, 25). At his arrest, he ordered his disciples not to fight but to put away their swords (Matt. 26:52; Luke 22:49–51). His few enigmatic sayings about taking up the sword probably carry spiri-

A model of a Roman-period cross with a nameplate on top

tual rather than military significance (Matt. 10:34; Luke 22:36, 38).[2] Jesus' kingdom preaching would hardly be viewed by Pilate as instigating a military coup. Furthermore, the fact that Jesus' followers were not rounded up and executed after his death, and were even allowed to form a faith community in Jerusalem, confirms that Jesus was not viewed as inciting a violent insurrection. The early church was surely following the teaching of its master when it advocated a life of love, unity, and self-sacrifice (Acts 2:42–47; 4:32–35).

Why, then, did Pilate have Jesus crucified? While it is unlikely that Pilate viewed Jesus as a significant threat, he also had little interest in justice or compassion. We know from other sources that Pilate's governorship was characterized by a general disdain toward his Jewish subjects and brutal suppression of opposition. At the same time, his support from Rome was shaky at best, and he feared antagonizing the Jewish leadership lest they complain to the emperor. Pilate had originally been appointed governor of Judea in AD 26 by Sejanus, an advisor to Emperor Tiberius. When Sejanus was caught conspiring against Tiberius and was executed in AD 31, Pilate too came under suspicion. Pilate's tenuous position is well illustrated by the Jewish philosopher Philo, who writes about an incident when the Jews protested against Pilate's actions in placing golden shields in Herod's palace in Jerusalem:

> The evidence points to the conclusion that Jesus was executed by the Romans for sedition — rebellion against the government.

> He feared that if they actually sent an embassy [to Rome] they would also expose the rest of his conduct as governor by stating in full the briberies, the insults, the robberies, the outrages and wanton injustices, the executions without trial constantly repeated, the ceaseless and supremely grievous cruelty. So with all his vindictiveness and furious temper, he was in a difficult position.[3]

While Philo may be exaggerating Pilate's faults, the picture here is remarkably similar to that of the Gospels — an unscrupulous and self-seeking leader who loathed the Jewish leadership but feared antagonizing them. When the Jewish leaders warn Pilate, "If you let this man go, you are no friend of Caesar" (John 19:12), he would surely have felt both anger and fear. Most likely, Pilate ordered Jesus' execution because (1) it placated the Jewish leaders and so headed off accusations against him to Rome; (2) it preemptively eliminated any threat Jesus might pose if the people actually tried to make him a king; and (3) as in similar

2. See Martin Hengel, *Was Jesus a Revolutionist?* (Philadelphia: Fortress, 1971); Ernst Bammel and C. F. D. Moule, eds., *Jesus and the Politics of His Day* (Cambridge: Cambridge Univ. Press, 1984). For the contrary view that Jesus was a revolutionary, see S. G. F. Brandon, *Jesus and the Zealots: A Study of the Political Factor in Primitive Christianity* (Manchester: Manchester Univ. Press, 1967).

3. Philo, *Legum allegoriae* 302f. (Colson, LCL). Pilate was eventually recalled to Rome in AD 36 after a typically ruthless military action against the Samaritans (Josephus, *Ant.* 18.4.2 §§85–87).

Figure 19.2—Crucifixion

Crucifixion was used both as a means of execution and for exposing an executed body to shame and humiliation. It was also meant to send a message of fear to other would-be rebels. The Romans practiced a variety of forms. The main stake or *palus* generally remained at the place of execution, while the victim would be forced to carry the crossbeam or *patibulum* (Luke 23:26). The crossbeam was placed either on top of the *palus* (like a "T") or in the more traditional cross shape (†). The victim would be affixed to the cross with ropes or, as in the case of Jesus, with nails (John 20:25). Sometimes various positions were used to maximize torture and humiliation. Seneca wrote that "some hang their victims with head toward the ground, some impale their private parts, others stretch out their arms on a fork-shaped gibbet" (Seneca, *Dialogue 6* [*To Marcia on Consolation*] 20.3). Death was caused by loss of blood, exposure, exhaustion, and/or suffocation, as the victim tried to lift himself to breathe. Victims sometimes lingered for days in agony. Crucifixion was viewed by ancient writers as the cruelest and most barbaric of punishments.

The bones of a crucified man named Jehohanan were discovered in 1968 at *Givʾat ha Mivtar* in the Kidron Valley northeast of the Old City of Jerusalem and have been dated between AD 7 and 70. He was probably crucified for taking part in one of the various insurrectionist movements of the first century.

See Martin Hengel, *Crucifixion in the Ancient World and the Folly of the Message of the Cross*, trans. J. Bowden (Philadelphia: Fortress, 1977).

cases, it ruthlessly warned other would-be prophets and messiahs that Rome would stand for no dissent.

Jewish Opposition

We have discussed previously the nature of Jewish opposition to Jesus. During his Galilean ministry, he faced opposition primarily from the Pharisees and their scribes. In his last week in Jerusalem, the opposition came especially from the priestly leadership under the authority of the high priest and the Sanhedrin, which was dominated by the Sadducees. In chapter 6, we pointed out that Torah (the law) and temple were the two great institutions of Judaism. Jesus apparently challenged the authority and continuing validity of both, posing a significant threat to Israel's leadership.

The Pharisees and Scribes. The opposition Jesus faced from the Pharisees and scribes centered especially on his teaching and actions relating to the law and the Sabbath. He claimed authority over the law, treated the Sabbath command as secondary to human needs, and accused the Pharisees of elevating their oral law—mere human traditions—over the commands of God. He also accused them of pride, hypocrisy, and greed, warning the people to do as they say but not as they do (Matt. 23:3). These actions certainly did not win him friends among the religious leaders.

Jesus' proclamation of the kingdom of God and his calling of twelve disciples would have also provoked anger among the Pharisees, who considered themselves the rightful guardians of Israel's traditions. Jesus' call for them to repent, his warning of coming judgment, and his actions in creating a new community of faith all sent the message that

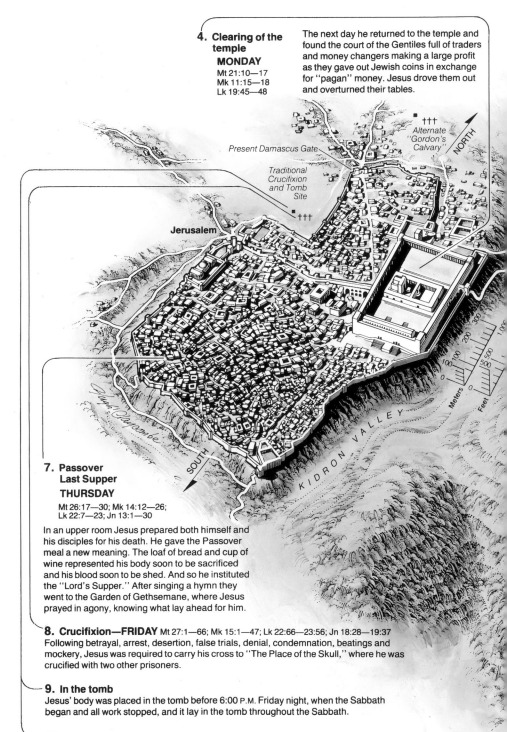

4. Clearing of the temple
MONDAY
Mt 21:10—17
Mk 11:15—18
Lk 19:45—48

The next day he returned to the temple and found the court of the Gentiles full of traders and money changers making a large profit as they gave out Jewish coins in exchange for "pagan" money. Jesus drove them out and overturned their tables.

Alternate "Gordon's Calvary"

NORTH

Present Damascus Gate

Traditional Crucifixion and Tomb Site

Jerusalem

KIDRON VALLEY

SOUTH

7. Passover Last Supper
THURSDAY

Mt 26:17—30; Mk 14:12—26;
Lk 22:7—23; Jn 13:1—30

In an upper room Jesus prepared both himself and his disciples for his death. He gave the Passover meal a new meaning. The loaf of bread and cup of wine represented his body soon to be sacrificed and his blood soon to be shed. And so he instituted the "Lord's Supper." After singing a hymn they went to the Garden of Gethsemane, where Jesus prayed in agony, knowing what lay ahead for him.

8. Crucifixion—FRIDAY Mt 27:1—66; Mk 15:1—47; Lk 22:66—23:56; Jn 18:28—19:37
Following betrayal, arrest, desertion, false trials, denial, condemnation, beatings and mockery, Jesus was required to carry his cross to "The Place of the Skull," where he was crucified with two other prisoners.

9. In the tomb
Jesus' body was placed in the tomb before 6:00 P.M. Friday night, when the Sabbath began and all work stopped, and it lay in the tomb throughout the Sabbath.

10. Resurrection—SUNDAY Mt 28:1—13; Mk 16:1—20; Lk 24:1—49; Jn 20:1—31
Early in the morning, women went to the tomb and found that the stone closing the tomb's entrance had been rolled back. An angel told them Jesus was alive and gave them a message. Jesus appeared to Mary Magdalene in the garden, to Peter, to two disciples on the road to Emmaus, and later that day to all the disciples but Thomas. His resurrection was established as a fact.

5. Day of controversy and parables

TUESDAY Mt 21:23—24:51;
Mk 11:27—13:37; Lk 20:1—21:36

IN JERUSALEM

Jesus evaded the traps set by the priests.

ON THE MOUNT OF OLIVES
OVERLOOKING JERUSALEM
(Tuesday afternoon,
exact location unknown)

He taught in parables and warned the people against the Pharisees. He predicted the destruction of Herod's great temple and told his disciples about future events, including his own return.

6. Day of rest

WEDNESDAY
Not mentioned in the Gospels

The Scriptures do not mention this day, but the counting of the days (Mk 14:1; Jn 12:1) seems to indicate that there was another day concerning which the Gospels record nothing.

M O U N T   O F   O L I V E S

To the "Wilderness of Judea"

To the "Wilderness of Judea"

Bethphage

The Roman road climbed steeply to the crest of the Mount of Olives, affording a spectacular view of the Desert of Judea to the east and Jerusalem across the Kidron valley to the west.

1. Arrival in Bethany

FRIDAY Jn 12:1

Jesus arrived in Bethany six days before the Passover to spend some time with his friends, Mary, Martha and Lazarus. While here, Mary anointed his feet with costly perfume as an act of humility. This tender expression indicated Mary's devotion to Jesus and her willingness to serve him.

3. The Triumphal Entry
SUNDAY

Mt 21:1—11; Mk 11:1—11;
Lk 19:28—44; Jn 12:12—19

On the first day of the week Jesus rode into Jerusalem on a donkey, fulfilling an ancient prophecy (Zec 9:9). The crowd welcomed him with "Hosanna" and the words of Ps 118:25-26, thus ascribing to him a Messianic title as the agent of the Lord, the coming King of Israel.

2. Sabbath — day of rest
SATURDAY
Not mentioned in the Gospels

Since the next day was the Sabbath, the Lord spent the day in traditional fashion with his friends.

Bethany

To Jericho and the Dead Sea

Israel needed restoration and that her leaders were illegitimate and corrupt. In the boiling cauldron of religion and politics that was first-century Palestine, Jesus' words would have provoked strong opposition.

The Priestly Leadership, the Sanhedrin, and the Sadducees. While Jesus certainly made enemies before his final journey to Jerusalem, it was the events of the final week which resulted in his crucifixion. As we noted in the last chapter, Jesus' clearing of the temple is widely recognized as the key episode which provoked the Jewish authorities to act against him.

> Jesus' clearing of the temple is widely recognized as the key episode which provoked the Jewish authorities to act against him.

In Mark's account of Jesus' Jewish trial, "false witnesses" are brought forward who testify, "We heard him say, 'I will destroy this man-made temple and in three days will build another, not made by man.'" The high priest then questions him, "Are you the Christ, the Son of the Blessed One?" to which Jesus' replies, "I am ... and you will see the Son of Man sitting at the right hand of the Mighty One and coming on the clouds of heaven." The high priest responds with rage and accuses Jesus of blasphemy. The whole assembly calls for his death (Mark 14:58–65; cf. Matt. 26:55–68; Luke 22:66–71).

Gordon's Calvary, a traditional, though unlikely, site for the crucifixion. Note the skull-like outcropping.

Some have questioned the historicity of this scene, claiming it violates Jewish trial procedures. The Mishnah states that it is illegal for the Sanhedrin to meet at night, on the eve of Passover, or in the high priest's home. A second hearing would also have been necessary for a death sentence, and a charge of blasphemy could be sustained only if Jesus had uttered the divine name of God (*m. Sanh.* 4:1; 5:5; 7:5; 11:2). This argument is not decisive for four reasons. First, the procedures set out in the Mishnah were codified in AD 200 and may not all go back to the time of Jesus. Second, even if they do go back to the first century, they represent an ideal situation which may or may not have been followed in Jesus' case. The existence of guidelines suggests abuses in the past. They may have arisen as correctives to illegitimate trials like this one. Third, the Mishnah represents predominantly Pharisaic traditions, but the Sadducees were dominant in the Sanhedrin of Jesus' day. Finally, there is good evidence that blasphemy was sometimes used in Judaism in a broader sense than uttering the divine name, including actions like idolatry, arrogant disrespect for God, or insulting his chosen leaders.[4]

On closer inspection, Mark's trial account makes good sense when viewed in the context of Jesus' ministry. Jesus' temple action would naturally have prompted the high priest to ask if he was making a messianic claim. Jesus' response combines two key Old Testament

---

4. See Darrell Bock, *Blasphemy and Exaltation in Judaism* (Grand Rapids: Baker, 2000), 30–112.

passages, Psalm 110:1 and Daniel 7:13. The first indicates that Jesus will be vindicated by God and exalted to a position at his right hand. The latter suggests Jesus will receive sovereign authority to judge the enemies of God. By combining these verses, Jesus asserts that the Sanhedrin is acting against the Lord's anointed, that they will face judgment for this, and that Jesus himself will be their judge! Such an outrageous claim was blasphemous to the body, which viewed itself as God's appointed leadership, the guardians of his holy temple. Jesus was challenging not only their actions but also their authority and legitimacy. Such a challenge demanded a response.

> By combining Psalm 110:1 and Daniel 7:13, Jesus asserts that the Sanhedrin is acting against the Lord's anointed and so will face judgment. Such a challenge demanded a response.

There were also political and social consequences to consider. Jesus' actions in the temple—probably viewed by the Sanhedrin as an act of sacrilege—together with his popularity among the people, made it imperative to act against him quickly and decisively. A disturbance of the peace might bring Roman retribution and disaster to the nation and its leaders. The earlier words of the Pharisees and chief priests in John are plausible in this scenario: "If we let him go on like this, everyone will believe in him, and then the Romans will come and take away both our place and our nation" (John 11:48).

The Sanhedrin therefore turned Jesus over to Pilate, modifying their religious charges to political ones—sedition and claiming to be a king in opposition to Caesar—and gaining from Pilate a capital sentence.

The likely location of Golgotha, in the model of first-century Jerusalem at the Holy Land Hotel.

© Neal Bierling/Zondervan Image Archives

Figure 19.3—A Harmonistic Overview of Jesus' Trials		
Phase	**Authority/Time/Place**	**Events/Judgment**
THE JEWISH TRIAL		
1. First Jewish Phase (John 18:13–24)	Annas Thursday evening, Annas's courtyard	Only John tells us that Jesus was originally sent to Annas, the former high priest and father-in-law of Caiaphas, for his initial questioning.
2. Second Jewish Phase (Mark 14:53–65; Matt. 26:57–68; Luke 22:54)	Caiaphas and part of the Sanhedrin Thursday night, Caiaphas's courtyard (Peter's denial begins here)	False witnesses are brought against Jesus. When asked if he is the Christ, the Son of God, he responds positively but defines his role as that of the Son of Man. He is accused of blasphemy, mocked, and beaten.
3. Third Jewish Phase (Mark 15:1a; Matt. 27:1; Luke 22:66–71)	The full Sanhedrin Friday, early morning	While all three Synoptics mention this phase of the trial, Luke alone describes Jesus' confession in terms similar to those recorded by Mark and Matthew the evening before.
THE ROMAN TRIAL		
1. First Roman Phase (Mark 15:1b–5; Matt. 27:2, 11–14; Luke 23:1–5; John 18:28–38)	Pilate Friday, early morning at the Praetorium	The Sanhedrin leads Jesus away to the governor Pilate, who asks him if he is the king of the Jews. Jesus responds positively. In John's account, Jesus explains that his kingdom is not of this world.
2. Second Roman Phase (Luke 23:6–12)	Herod Antipas Friday morning at Herod's palace	Luke alone records that when Pilate learned Jesus was from Galilee, he sent him to Herod, who was visiting Jerusalem. Herod questions Jesus without success, abuses him, and returns him to Pilate.
3. Third Roman Phase (Mark 15:6–15; Matt. 27:15–26; Luke 23:13–25)	Pilate Friday morning at the Praetorium	Holding to his custom to release a prisoner at Passover, Pilate attempts to free Jesus. Prompted by the chief priests, the crowds call for Barabbas's release and Jesus' crucifixion. Pilate scourges Jesus and turns him over for crucifixion.

JESUS' PERSPECTIVE ON HIS COMING DEATH

We turn from the external factors which provoked Jesus' death to his own perspective and intention. Did Jesus expect to die? Did he intend to? If so, how did he view his death?

Did Jesus Foresee His Death?

According to the Synoptics, from Peter's confession at Caesarea Philippi onward, Jesus warned his disciples of his impending fate. Three times he predicts that the Son of Man will suffer and die and then rise again (Mark 8:31–32, par.; 9:31, par.; 10:33, par.). Some have argued that these **passion predictions** are prophecies created after the fact by the church, since Jesus could not have predicted his own death. Yet there is good evidence for their historicity: (1) Jesus uses the title Son of Man, which is characteristic of the historical Jesus rather than the later church; (2) there is no reference to the cross in these sayings; (3) there is no atonement theology expressed in them. Surely if the church invented these sayings, they would have included the significance of Jesus' death.[5] Even from a merely human perspective, Jesus could have foreseen his likely fate. He faced constant opposition from the Pharisees and scribes, who considered him to be working by the power of Beelzebub (Mark 3:22–27) and to be a blasphemer (Mark 2:7), a false prophet (Mark 14:65), and a Sabbath breaker (Mark 2:23–28; 3:1–6; Luke 13:10–17; 14:1–6; John 5:1–18; 7:19–24). He must have known that they wished to get rid of him. He also surely knew that entering Jerusalem as he did and clearing the temple would have been viewed as a dangerous provocation by the temple authorities.

> There is much historical evidence that Jesus foresaw and even predicted his impending death.

Jesus the Suffering Prophet. In the same vein, Jesus often spoke of the persecution and murder of the Old Testament prophets and identified himself with them (Mark 6:4, Matt. 13:57, and Luke 4:24; Mark 12:1–11, par.; Matt. 5:12; 13:57; 23:29–39; Luke 6:23, 26; 11:47–50; 13:33–35). In the Nazareth synagogue, he said that "no prophet is accepted in his hometown" (Luke 4:24, par.) and later affirmed that he was heading to Jerusalem to die: "I must keep going today and tomorrow and the next day—for surely no prophet can die outside Jerusalem!" (Luke 13:33). The early church is unlikely to have created these "prophet" sayings, preferring exalted titles for Jesus, like Christ, Son of God, and Lord. It is safe to conclude that Jesus viewed himself as a prophet and expected the fate which befell the prophets—persecution and even death.

Expectations of Coming Crisis. There are also a number of Jesus' sayings which point cryptically to a coming crisis. At the Last Supper, he calls for his disciples to sell their cloak and buy a sword (Luke 22:35–38). Such a saying would hardly have been created by the later church. In Mark 14:27, Jesus quotes Zechariah 13:7: "I will strike the shepherd, and the sheep will be scattered." Jesus also speaks of bringing fire to the earth and of the cup he must drink and the "baptism" he must undergo (Luke 12:49–50; Mark 10:38)—Old

---

5. Ben Witherington III, *The Gospel of Mark: A Socio-Rhetorical Commentary* (Grand Rapids: Eerdmans, 2001), 242–43.

Testament images of coming calamity.[6] All of these have a strong claim to authenticity and speak of a dangerous crisis which Jesus expected to face.

The Significance of Jesus' Death

If Jesus expected his own death, what significance did he give to it? The most important evidence for this comes from two key passages: the words and actions of Jesus at the Last Supper, and the ransom saying in Mark 10:45.

The Last Supper: Passover, Exodus, Sacrifice, and New Covenant (Mark 14:23–24; Matt. 26:26–29; Luke 22:15–20; 1 Cor. 11:23–26). The **eucharistic words** of Jesus at the Last Supper have a strong claim to authenticity. In about AD 55, Paul wrote to the church in Corinth:

> For I received from the Lord what I also passed on to you: The Lord Jesus, on the night he was betrayed, took bread, and when he had given thanks, he broke it and said, "This is my body, which is for you; do this in remembrance of me." In the same way, after supper he took the cup, saying, "This cup is the new covenant in my blood; do this, whenever you drink it, in remembrance of me."
>
> —1 Corinthians 11:23–26

Paul claims to have received this tradition from those who were believers before him. Since Paul's conversion occurred just a few years after Jesus' death, about AD 35, this eucharistic tradition must be very early. Further evidence that these words go back to the historical Jesus is their independent attestation in Mark and Luke, and an Aramaic substratum which has been identified beneath the Greek.[7] The significance of Jesus' words are to be found in four closely related Jewish symbols: Passover, exodus, sacrifice, and covenant. The Synoptics explicitly identify the Last Supper as a Passover meal, and there is strong evidence to support this. Like the Passover, the Last Supper was eaten at night (the normal daily meal was in the late afternoon), while reclining (ordinary meals were eaten sitting), and in the city of Jerusalem. Though Jesus was staying in Bethany, he came to Jerusalem since the Passover had to be eaten within the city limits. The meal ended with a hymn, presumably the *Hallel* psalms sung at the end of the Passover meal (Psalms 115–18; Mark 14:26; Matt. 26:30). Jesus acts as the traditional head of the household in explaining the meaning of the Passover. Yet Jesus' words confirm that this is no ordinary Passover but the establishment of a new Passover for the new age of salvation—the kingdom of God.

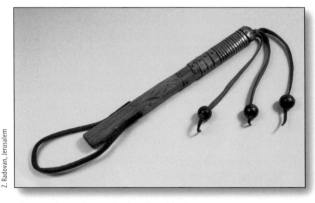

A Roman whip with a wooden handle and leather straps

The original Passover represented God's greatest act of deliverance in the Hebrew scriptures and the creation of Israel as a nation. With his mighty power, Yahweh defeated

---

6. The cup of suffering: Ps. 75:8; Isa. 51:17, 22; Jer. 25:15, 28; 49:12. An overwhelming flood or deluge: Ps. 18:4; 42:7; 69:1–2; Isa. 8:7–8; 30:28; Jonah 2:5.

7. See Joachim Jeremias, *The Eucharistic Words of Jesus* (London: SCM, 1966).

Pharaoh with ten plagues, delivered his people through the sacrificial blood of the Passover lamb, and brought them out of slavery in Egypt. Giving them his law at Mount Sinai, he established a covenant relationship with them. When Israel was later oppressed and defeated by her enemies, the prophets would predict the day when Yahweh would return to Zion to accomplish a new and greater exodus (Isa. 11:11–16; 35:1–10; 40:1–5; Jer. 23:5–8; Hos. 2:14–15; etc.).

Jesus' eucharistic words recall and transform the rich symbols of Passover, announcing the arrival of the new exodus and a new covenant. The unleavened bread of the Passover meal represents Jesus' body, given for his disciples. The implication is that he is the new Passover lamb (cf. 1 Cor. 5:7). The Passover wine represents the blood of the new covenant. Jesus' words in Mark 14:24, "This is my blood of the covenant," echo Exodus 24:8, where Moses sprinkles the blood of the sacrifice on the people and says, "This is the blood of the covenant that the LORD has made with you." In Luke 22 and 1 Corinthians 11, Jesus speaks explicitly of the *new* covenant, a clear allusion to Jeremiah 31 and the eschatological new covenant which will bring forgiveness of sins and personal knowledge of God (Jer. 31:31–34; cf. Zech. 9:9–11).

> Jesus' eucharistic words at the Last Supper suggest that he viewed his death as a sacrifice of atonement, leading his people into a new covenant relationship with God.

Jesus' words at the Last Supper thus fit well his preaching about the kingdom of God and the dawn of the new age. They also provide important clues as to how he viewed his approaching death. Drawing symbolism from the Passover meal, the covenant at Sinai, and the new exodus and new covenant imagery in the prophets, Jesus inaugurates a new Passover meal celebrating the new covenant and the arrival of the kingdom of God. While the first covenant was instituted with the blood of sacrificial animals, this new covenant will be established through his own blood. It seems likely, therefore, that Jesus viewed his death as a sacrifice of atonement, leading his people in a new exodus from bondage to sin and death.

Another Old Testament allusion in Jesus' eucharistic words takes us further toward Jesus' understanding of his death. Jesus speaks of "my blood of the covenant, which is poured out for many" (Mark 14:24; Matt. 26:28 adds "for the forgiveness of sins"). The phrase "poured out for many" probably alludes to Isaiah 53:11–12, where the Servant of the LORD "will justify many" and "bore the sin of many." With these words, Jesus identifies himself as Isaiah's suffering Servant and interprets his coming death as a sacrifice of atonement for the sins of his people.

The Ransom Saying (Mark 10:45). This self-understanding finds support in Jesus' words in Mark 10:45. After calling his disciples to a life of servant leadership (Mark 10:42–44), Jesus concludes, "For even the Son of Man did not come to be served, but to serve, and to give his life as a ransom for many" (10:45). The term "ransom" or "redemption" (*lytron*) means a price paid to free someone, like a slave or a prisoner of war. The preposition *for* is the Greek *anti*, which normally carries the sense "instead of" or "in the place of." Jesus thus interprets his death as a substitutionary payment or sacrifice for his people. The term

The Good Friday processional on the Via Dolorosa (way of sorrow).

"many" does not mean "some but not all" but contrasts the "one" who dies with the "many" who will be saved.

The authenticity of the saying has been challenged by some scholars. It is argued that Jesus could not have spoken of his death in this forthright manner and that the saying reflects the church's later atonement theology. Yet the words have an Aramaic background which argues for their authenticity. Furthermore, we have pointed to strong evidence that Jesus not only viewed himself as the Messiah inaugurating the kingdom of God (chap. 18) but also expected to suffer and die (see above). Since everything else in Jesus' words and deeds pointed to his role as the culmination of Israel's history and scriptures, we would expect him to understand his death in the same way.

What, then, is the most likely background to Jesus' words in Mark 10:45? The idea of a righteous man dying a martyr's death for the sins of others appears in some Jewish writings of Jesus' day. In 4 Maccabees 6:27–29, the martyr Eleazar prays that God would be merciful to his people, who have broken the law, and identifies his death as a sacrifice for them. A much closer parallel, however, is found in the description of the **suffering Servant** in Isaiah 53:10–12:

> Yet it was the LORD's will to crush him and cause him to suffer,
>   and though the LORD makes his life a guilt offering,
> he will see his offspring and prolong his days,
>   and the will of the LORD will prosper in his hand.
> After the suffering of his soul,
>   he will see the light [of life] and be satisfied;

by his knowledge my righteous servant will justify many,
   and he will bear their iniquities.
Therefore I will give him a portion among the great,
   and he will divide the spoils with the strong,
because he poured out his life unto death,
   and was numbered with the transgressors.
For he bore the sin of many,
and made intercession for the transgressors.

Jesus' identification of himself as a servant who offers himself as a "ransom" for "the many" (Mark 10:45) strongly echoes Isaiah 53:10–12, suggesting that he saw his role as Isaiah's Servant of the LORD (cf. Mark 1:11; 9:7; 14:24; Matt. 8:17; 12:15–21; Luke 4:16–21; 22:37 [= Isaiah 53:12]; John 1:29, 36; 12:38).

We may conclude that it is likely that Jesus not only foresaw his death but moved to make it happen, interpreting it in light of the suffering Servant of Isaiah 53—a sacrificial act of atonement for the sins of his people.

» CHAPTER SUMMARY «

1. The evidence suggests that both Roman and Jewish authorities were active participants in the arrest and trial of Jesus. The crucifixion was ordered by Pilate and carried out by Roman soldiers.

2. Pilate probably acted against Jesus to placate the temple leadership, to prevent a popular revolt, and to serve as a grim warning to other troublemakers.

3. The Jewish authorities probably acted against Jesus because he threatened their influence among the people and because he directly challenged their legitimacy as guardians of Torah and temple.

4. Even apart from Jesus' explicit passion predictions, there is good evidence that he foresaw and predicted his coming death. He faced strong opposition from the religious leaders and frequently compared himself to the suffering prophets of old.

5. The significance Jesus gave to his coming death can be discerned through his eucharistic words at the Last Supper and the ransom saying of Mark 10:45, both of which have strong claims to authenticity. Together these indicate that Jesus saw his death as a sacrificial death for the sins of his people, bringing spiritual freedom through a new exodus and establishing a new covenant relationship with God.

» DISCUSSION AND STUDY QUESTIONS «

1. What role did the Roman authorities and the Jewish religious leaders likely play in the arrest, trial, and crucifixion of Jesus?

2. Why did Pilate act against Jesus?

3. What brought Jesus into conflict with the scribes and Pharisees? With the high priest and the Sanhedrin?

4. What is the evidence that Jesus foresaw and predicted his death?

5. What significance did Jesus give to his death? What evidence is there for the historicity of Jesus' eucharistic words and of the ransom saying of Mark 10:45?

Digging Deeper

The Death of Jesus

Allison, D. C., Jr. *The End of the Ages Has Come: An Early Interpretation of the Passion and Resurrection of Jesus*. Philadelphia: Fortress, 1985.

Brown, Raymond. *The Death of the Messiah: From Gethsemane to the Grave: A Commentary on the Passion Narratives in the Four Gospels*. New York: Doubleday, 1994.

Green, Joel B. *The Death of Jesus: Tradition and Interpretation in the Passion Narrative*. WUNT 2:33. Tübingen: Mohr (Paul Siebeck), 1988.

———. "Death of Jesus." In *DJG*, 146–63.

Hengel, Martin. *The Atonement: The Origins of the Doctrine in the New Testament*. Philadelphia: Fortress, 1981.

McKnight, Scot. *Jesus and His Death: Historiography, the Historical Jesus, and Atonement Theory*. Waco, TX: Baylor Univ. Press, 2005.

The Trial of Jesus

Blinzler, J. *The Trial of Jesus.* 3rd ed. Cork: Mercier, 1961.

Bock, Darrell. *Blasphemy and Exaltation in Judaism: The Charge against Jesus in Mark 14:53–65.* Grand Rapids: Baker, 2000.

Catchpole, D. R. *The Trial of Jesus.* Studia Post-Biblica 18. Leiden: Brill, 1971.

Corley, Bruce. "Trial of Jesus." In *DJG*, 841–54.

The Last Supper

Barth, M. *Rediscovering the Lord's Supper.* Atlanta: John Knox, 1988.

Jeremias, Joachim. *The Eucharistic Words of Jesus.* New Testament Library. London: SCM, 1966.

Klappert, B. "Lord's Supper." In *NIDNTT* 2:520–38.

Léon-Dufour, Xavier. *Sharing the Eucharistic Bread: The Witness of the New Testament.* Mahwah, N.J.: Paulist, 1987.

Marshall, I. H. *Last Supper and Lord's Supper.* Grand Rapids: Eerdmans, 1980.

Marxsen, W. *The Lord's Supper as a Christological Problem.* Philadelphia: Fortress, 1970.

Reumann, J. *The Supper of the Lord.* Philadelphia: Fortress, 1985.

Stein, Robert. "Lord's Supper." In *DJG*, 444–50.

The Ransom Saying

Barrett, C. K. "The Background of Mark 10:45." In *New Testament Essays: Studies in Memory of T. W. Manson.* Edited by A. J. B. Higgins. Manchester: Manchester Univ. Press, 1959. See pp. 1–18.

Brown, Colin, "Redemption, λυτρον." In *NIDNTT* 3:189–200.

Marshall, I. H. "The Development of the Concept of Redemption in the New Testament." In *Reconciliation and Hope: New Testament Essays on Atonement and Eschatology Presented to L. L. Morris.* Edited by R. Banks. Exeter: Paternoster, 1974. See pp. 153–69.

Page, Sydney, "Ransom Saying." In *DJG*, 660–62.

———. "The Authenticity of the Ransom *Logion* (Mark 10:45b)." In *Gospel Perspectives.* Edited by R. T. France and David Wenham. Eugene, OR: Wipf and Stock 2003. 1:137–61.

Stuhlmacher, P. "Vicariously Giving His Life for Many, Mark 10:45 (Matt. 20:28)." In *Reconciliation, Law and Righteousness: Essays in Biblical Theology.* Philadelphia: Fortress, 1986. See pp. 16–29.

CHAPTER 20

The Resurrection of Jesus

» CHAPTER OVERVIEW «

1. Rationalistic Explanations for the Resurrection
2. Historical Evidence for the Resurrection
3. The Significance of the Resurrection

» OBJECTIVES «

After reading this chapter, you should be able to:

- Summarize the rationalistic explanations for the resurrection, especially the claim that the resurrection stories are legendary tales arising out of the visionary experiences of the disciples.
- Present the most historically reliable evidence in support of the resurrection.
- Describe the meaning of resurrection in its first-century Jewish context.
- Explain the theological significance of Jesus' resurrection, as viewed within this first-century context of meaning.

Throughout the New Testament, the resurrection is viewed as *the vindication of the message and mission of Jesus.* If God raised Jesus from the dead, then his claims are true and the salvation he announced has been achieved. The apostle Paul affirmed that if the resurrection did not take place, Christianity is a false religion and should be abandoned:

> And if Christ has not been raised, our preaching is useless and so is your faith. More than that, we are then found to be false witnesses about God.... And if Christ has not been raised, your faith is futile; you are still in your sins. Then those also who have fallen asleep in Christ are lost. If only for this life we have hope in Christ, we are to be pitied more than all others.
>
> —1 Corinthians 15:14–19 TNIV

> Throughout the New Testament, the resurrection is viewed as the vindication of the message and mission of Jesus.

For Paul, the death and resurrection of Jesus was the turning point in human history, the transition from the age of promise to the age of fulfillment. If the resurrection took place, Christianity is true; if it didn't, Christianity is folly and Christians are only to be pitied. No event in human history has more riding on it than the resurrection.

RATIONALISTIC EXPLANATIONS FOR THE RESURRECTION

As with the other Gospel miracles, critics have sought to discount the resurrection through rationalistic explanations. Four main alternatives to the physical resurrection of Jesus have been proposed.

The Swoon Theory

The **swoon theory** is the view that Jesus never really died on the cross. He simply swooned or fainted and the soldiers assumed he was dead. He was placed in the tomb alive, perhaps in a comatose state, where the cool air revived him. He escaped from the tomb, appeared to his disciples, and subsequently died of his injuries.

This explanation stretches the limits of the imagination and has been rightly rejected by almost all critical scholars. The Romans were experts at crucifixion, and it is inconceivable

Left: A rolling stone tomb located nineteen miles southwest of Jerusalem in the Shephelah. *Right:* View inside the second (interior) room of the tomb, looking at one of the arcosolia and an ossuary. The arcosolium is the indentation in the wall, with the flat shelf and the arch above it.

www.HolyLandPhotos.org

www.HolyLandPhotos.org

Figure 20.1—A Harmonistic Overview of the Resurrection Narratives	
THE EMPTY TOMB	
1. The visit of the women (Mark 16:1 – 8; Matt. 28:1 – 8; Luke 24:1 – 11; John 20:1)	All four Gospels report that women were the first to discover the empty tomb. John mentions only Mary Magdalene. Mark names three women: Salome, Mary Magdalene, and another Mary; Matthew mentions two, the two Marys. Luke refers to the two Marys, Joanna, and "other women" and says that they reported these things to the Eleven.
2. The visit of Peter and John (John 20:2 – 10)	John says Mary Magdalene informed Peter and the Beloved Disciple, who ran to examine the empty tomb.
THE RESURRECTION APPEARANCES	
1. To Mary Magdalene (John 20:11 – 18)	John describes Jesus' appearance to Mary. At first she supposes he is the gardener but recognizes him when he says her name. She reports to the disciples that she has seen the Lord.
2. To the other women (Matt. 28:9 – 10)	Matthew alone relates Jesus' appearance to the other women. They are told to tell the disciples to go to Galilee, where they will see Jesus.
3. To the Emmaus disciples (Luke 24:13 – 35)	Luke alone recounts Jesus' appearance to two disciples (one named Cleopas) as they are traveling to Emmaus. Their eyes are opened to recognize him when he breaks bread.
4. To the Eleven, except Thomas (Luke 24:36 – 43; John 20:19 – 25)	The Emmaus disciples report to the apostles; Jesus suddenly appears in their midst. John describes the same event and reports that Thomas was not present on this occasion.
5. To the Eleven with Thomas (John 20:26 – 31)	John reports that eight days later, Jesus appears again to the disciples, this time with Thomas present. Thomas responds by addressing Jesus as "my Lord and my God!"
6. To seven disciples while fishing (John 21:1 – 25)	John alone reports that Jesus appears to seven disciples while they are fishing on the sea of Galilee. They experience a miraculous catch of fish (cf. Luke 5:1–11), and Jesus eats with them.
7. To the Eleven in Galilee (Matt. 28:16 – 20)	Matthew reports that following Jesus' command (Matt. 28:10), the disciples go to a designated mountain in Galilee, where they see Jesus. He gives them the Great Commission.
8. To the disciples in Jerusalem (Luke 24:44 – 49; Acts 1:3 – 8)	All of Luke's appearances occur in or around Jerusalem. While Luke 24:44 – 49 appears to be the same account as the appearance to the Eleven without Thomas, Acts 1:3 says Jesus appeared to the disciples over a forty-day period. Since Luke follows with an account of the ascension (Luke 24:50 – 53; Acts 1:9 – 12), this may be a separate event after the Galilean appearances.
9. Special appearances to Peter, James (Jesus' brother), five hundred others, and Paul (1 Cor. 15:5 – 7)	Paul relates that Jesus appeared to Peter (corroborated by the Emmaus disciples in Luke 24:34), to his brother James, to more than five hundred others, and finally to Paul himself.

This tomb is located west of the Old City and just east of (below) the King David Hotel. One of the best-preserved rolling-stone tombs in the country.

that they would have botched the job. The incidental references to the soldiers leaving Jesus' legs unbroken and blood and water coming from the spear wound in his side provide additional evidence of his death (John 19:32–37). Even if Jesus were still alive when laid in the tomb, the chances are practically nil that he could recover from the severe trauma of flagellation, crucifixion, bleeding, and exposure, and that he could then single-handedly roll back the large stone at the tomb's entrance (uphill from the inside!), overpower the guards, and escape. Even if the guards at the tomb are viewed as a later invention, the scenario is unbelievable.

A rolling tombstone

Most damaging of all, it is inconceivable that a barely alive Jesus staggering into Jerusalem could have convinced his disciples that he had risen victoriously from the dead. Such a Jesus would have prompted pity, but certainly not worship and adoration as the glorified Lord and Savior. We must remember that these same disciples were willing to die for the truth that Jesus had risen from the dead.

The Wrong Tomb Theory

The **wrong tomb theory** is the theory that on Easter morning, the women got confused concerning where Jesus was buried and came across an empty tomb. Excited by their discovery, they began proclaiming the resurrection.

This explanation is also highly unlikely. The tomb of Joseph of Arimathea was a private one in a garden setting, not one plot identical to many others in a cemetery (John 19:41). The Synoptics report that the women carefully noted the location of the tomb in order to return later to anoint the body (Matt. 27:61; Mark 15:47; Luke 23:55). Would they all have forgotten so quickly where their beloved teacher was buried? We then have to suppose that everyone else also went to the wrong tomb. According to John, Peter and the Beloved Disciple ran directly to the tomb after hearing the report from Mary Magdalene (John 20:2–10). Could they have independently made the same mistake? Why did Jesus' opponents not go to the right tomb and set everyone straight? Even if the women, the disciples, and the religious leaders all went to the wrong tomb, surely Joseph of Arimathea would have been able to find his own tomb.

The Theft Theory

The **theft theory**, the oldest rationalistic explanation of the resurrection (dating to the first century), holds that the disciples stole the body. Matthew reports that this story was widely circulated in his day (Matt. 28:11–15). This theory creates enormous problems both historically and ethically. Historically, all the evidence indicates that the disciples were emotionally devastated and discouraged following the crucifixion. There is little to indicate they expected a resurrection, much less plotted to fake one. Ethically, are we to believe that the same disciples who developed the greatest ethical system in the world and proclaimed the gospel as God's ultimate truth in fact propagated a great hoax and a lie?

This view, like the previous two, is discounted by almost all scholars. Even those who reject the historicity of the resurrection acknowledge that Jesus' disciples believed he was alive. David Friedrich Strauss, the radical critic who treated the entire Gospel miracle tradition as myth, claimed that it was virtually certain "that the Apostles themselves had the conviction that they had seen the risen Jesus."[1]

---

1. David Friedrick Strauss, *The Life of Jesus Critically Examined*, ed. Peter C. Hodgson, trans. George Eliot (Philadelphia: Fortress, 1972), 739.

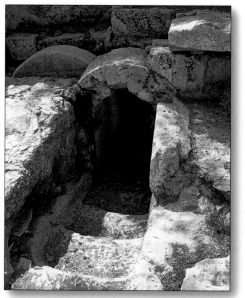

Other examples of rolling-stone tombs

Visionary and Legendary Development Theories

Few modern critical scholars hold to any of the previous three views. Almost all who deny the resurrection today hold to the **legendary development theory**, which claims that the Gospel narratives arose as legendary developments of early visionary experiences. It is said that in the days, weeks, months, and even years after the death of Jesus, Peter and the other disciples began having visions and dreams in which they saw Jesus alive. These visions were probably first understood spiritually as the church came to believe that Jesus had been vindicated and exalted by God in the heavenly realm. In time, however, this spiritual resurrection took on concrete form with the belief that Jesus had risen bodily from the grave. Resurrection legends subsequently arose in which an empty tomb was discovered and Jesus' disciples saw him alive.

This view is the most difficult to refute since it claims that none of the resurrection narratives can be trusted as reliable. There was no guard posted at the tomb, the women did not discover an empty tomb on Sunday morning, and no one actually saw Jesus alive. Some critics deny that Jesus was even buried or that **Joseph of Arimathea** played any role

Drawings of the reconstruction of the tomb of Christ at the Church of the Holy Sepulcher

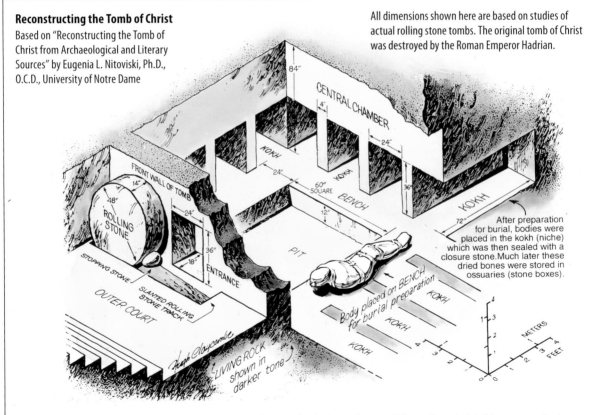

Reconstructing the Tomb of Christ

Based on "Reconstructing the Tomb of Christ from Archaeological and Literary Sources" by Eugenia L. Nitoviski, Ph.D., O.C.D., University of Notre Dame

All dimensions shown here are based on studies of actual rolling stone tombs. The original tomb of Christ was destroyed by the Roman Emperor Hadrian.

After preparation for burial, bodies were placed in the kokh (niche) which was then sealed with a closure stone. Much later these dried bones were stored in ossuaries (stone boxes).

The original tomb belonging to Joseph of Arimathea was destroyed by the Roman Emperor Habrian after a.d. 135. This reconstruction is based on 61 other "rolling stone" tombs which have remained, particulary on a classic example found in Heshbon, Jordan in 1971.

in this. John Dominic Crossan claims that, like other crucifixion victims, Jesus' body was probably discarded after the crucifixion in a place unknown to the disciples.[2] The resurrection narratives are later legends created by the church.

---

2. John Dominic Crossan, *The Historical Jesus: The Life of a Mediterranean Peasant* (San Francisco: HarperSanFrancisco, 1991), 375, 392.

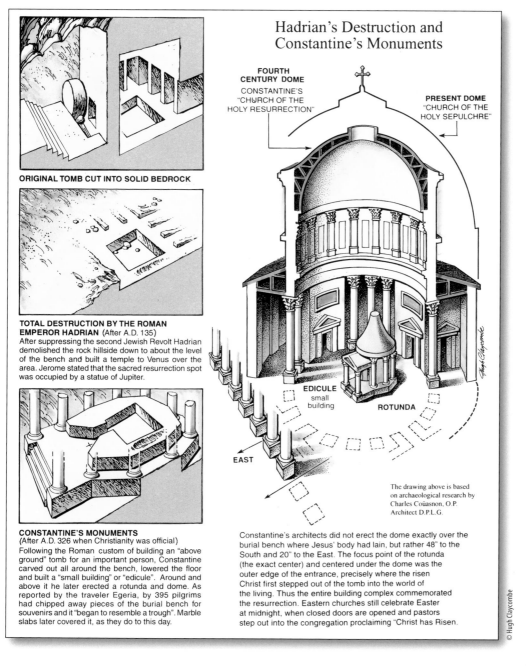

Hadrian's Destruction and Constantine's Monuments

FOURTH CENTURY DOME
CONSTANTINE'S "CHURCH OF THE HOLY RESURRECTION"

PRESENT DOME "CHURCH OF THE HOLY SEPULCHRE"

EDICULE small building

ROTUNDA

EAST

The drawing above is based on archaeological research by Charles Coüasnon, O.P. Architect D.P.L.G.

ORIGINAL TOMB CUT INTO SOLID BEDROCK

TOTAL DESTRUCTION BY THE ROMAN EMPEROR HADRIAN (After A.D. 135)
After suppressing the second Jewish Revolt Hadrian demolished the rock hillside down to about the level of the bench and built a temple to Venus over the area. Jerome stated that the sacred resurrection spot was occupied by a statue of Jupiter.

CONSTANTINE'S MONUMENTS
(After A.D. 326 when Christianity was official)
Following the Roman custom of building an "above ground" tomb for an important person, Constantine carved out all around the bench, lowered the floor and built a "small building" or "edicule". Around and above it he later erected a rotunda and dome. As reported by the traveler Egeria, by 395 pilgrims had chipped away pieces of the burial bench for souvenirs and it "began to resemble a trough". Marble slabs later covered it, as they do to this day.

Constantine's architects did not erect the dome exactly over the burial bench where Jesus' body had lain, but rather 48" to the South and 20" to the East. The focus point of the rotunda (the exact center) and centered under the dome was the outer edge of the entrance, precisely where the risen Christ first stepped out of the tomb into the world of the living. Thus the entire building complex commemorated the resurrection. Eastern churches still celebrate Easter at midnight, when closed doors are opened and pastors step out into the congregation proclaiming "Christ has Risen".

© Hugh Claycombe

To respond to this view, we must build from the ground up a body of evidence which can be viewed as having a strong claim to historical reliability.

HISTORICAL EVIDENCE FOR THE RESURRECTION

While nothing can be proven historically with absolute certainty, there are some things which have such strong evidential support that they can be affirmed beyond reasonable doubt. The following five points represent key corroborating evidence for the resurrection.

1. Jesus Was Crucified by the Romans around AD 30

No credible scholar today denies that Jesus existed or that he was crucified in Judea under orders from Pontius Pilate around AD 30. It is inconceivable, moreover, that Jesus did not die on the cross. The Romans were very good at what they did.

2. Jesus Was Buried in the Tomb of Joseph of Arimathea

All four Gospels affirm that Joseph of Arimathea, a member of the Sanhedrin, took the body of Jesus and buried it in his own tomb. There is no reason the church would create such a person or an incident unless it actually happened. Joseph's hometown of Arimathea has no symbolic significance which could explain its creation. It is particularly unlikely that the church would create a story in which a member of the Sanhedrin—the body which condemned Jesus—performed such an action (especially since Mark reports that the whole Sanhedrin voted for Jesus' condemnation; Mark 14:55, 64; 15:1). Incidental details about the burial suggest its historicity. Joseph is rich, and so has an available tomb. The tomb is an acrosolia, or a bench tomb, which is appropriate for a wealthy individual. The tomb is "new" and so is available. A convicted criminal would not be laid in a tomb in which family members were already buried.

The burial of Jesus is confirmed by the criterion of multiple attestation. It appears in independent traditions in Mark, John, Acts (2:31; 13:36–37), and most important, in a very early statement cited by Paul. Paul writes in 1 Corinthians 15:3–8:

> For what I received I passed on to you as of first importance: that Christ died for our sins according to the Scriptures, that he was buried, that he was raised on the third day according to the Scriptures, and that he appeared to Peter, and then to the Twelve. After that, he appeared to more than five hundred of the brothers at the same time, most of whom are still living, though some have fallen asleep. Then he appeared to James, then to all the apostles, and last of all he appeared to me also, as to one abnormally born.

As with the tradition of the Lord's Supper, Paul claims he received this one from believers before him. As a first-generation Christian who personally knew Peter, James, and other believers in Jerusalem, Paul's statement that Jesus "was buried" is confirmed beyond reasonable doubt.

3. The Tomb Was Discovered Empty on the Third Day

Just as the evidence is overwhelming that Jesus was buried after his death, so also is the evidence that the tomb was discovered empty shortly afterward. First, all of the Gospels testify that *women* discovered the empty tomb. This is particularly striking since in first-century Palestinian culture, women were not viewed as reliable witnesses. If the early church created stories about the empty tomb, they would surely not have introduced women as the primary witnesses.

Second, if the tomb had not been empty, the disciples could not have preached the gospel in Jerusalem. There is no historical doubt that the church began in Jerusalem shortly after Jesus' death and that the resurrection was central to the church's proclamation. Many converts were won to Christianity in Jerusalem. If the body of Jesus was still in the grave, anyone hostile to the church could have gone and presented the decaying body of Jesus. This was never done. Indeed, as far as we can tell, no objection was ever raised to Christianity that the tomb was not empty.

Top: The Garden Tomb, believed by some to be the tomb of Jesus. *Bottom:* Interior view of the Garden Tomb.

Third, and related to this, the claim that Jesus' body was stolen *presupposes* an empty tomb (Matt. 28:11–15). Matthew would have no reason to report the Jewish accusation that the disciples stole the body unless this report was actually circulating. The accusation itself assumes the empty tomb.

Finally, the very early testimony that Jesus rose on "the first day of the week" (Mark 16:2) indicates that a specific historical event—like the discovery of an empty tomb—prompted belief in the resurrection. Very early on, Christians began worshiping on the first day of the week, the Lord's Day. What could account for this change from the Sabbath (Saturday) to Sunday except the belief that Jesus arose on the Sunday after his crucifixion? Some have argued that belief in the resurrection "on the third day" arose from Hosea 6:2, a passage about Israel's restoration: "After two days he will revive us; on the third day he will restore us, that we may live in his presence." But "the third day" counting from Friday would likely have landed on Monday instead of Sunday. Only by recognizing that any part of a day is to be treated as a full day can Sunday be treated as "the third day." It seems more likely that the discovery of the empty tomb on Sunday morning prompted the Christians to read Hosea 6:2 as messianic, rather than that a messianic reading of Hosea resulted in the invention of the resurrection accounts. The Jerusalem believers were surely proclaiming the resurrection before they discovered a prediction of it in Scripture.

4. Many Credible Witnesses Saw Jesus Alive

Not only was the tomb empty, but many reliable witnesses claimed to have seen Jesus alive. Two pieces of evidence are particularly important here. First is the resurrection appearances to women. As we noted, these stories are unlikely to have been fabricated by the early church, since women were not viewed as reliable witnesses. Second, the very early primary source account of Paul in 1 Corinthians 15:3–8 (cited earlier) confirms that many people saw Jesus alive. Paul claims that Jesus appeared to Peter, to the other disciples, to James the brother of Jesus, and to more than five hundred people. He also notes that many of these were still alive, essentially challenging his critics to check out the reports for themselves. From Paul's other writings, we can see that he was not an irrational person prone to delusions but a logical and sober-minded individual dedicated to proclaiming the truth of God.

But what of the claim that these "appearances" were in fact hopeful visions that were later transformed into physical encounters? Opponents point out that Paul's experience of the resurrection cited in 1 Corinthians 15:8 was visionary, so why not these other appearances? But Paul's point in including himself in 1 Corinthians 15 is to show that he too had a commission from the resurrected Christ, not that his experience was identical with that of the other apostles. Paul himself sets his encounter apart as unique; he is "one abnormally born" (1 Cor. 15:8).

There is no evidence that the disciples first had visions or hallucinations which later developed into resurrection accounts. A vision of Christ in heaven, such as that of Stephen at his martyrdom (Acts 7:56) or of John in the book of Revelation (Rev. 1:12–16),

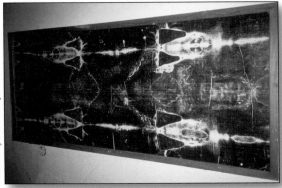

A copy of the Shroud of Turin

© Neal Bierling/Zondervan Image Archives

is qualitatively different from an earthly encounter with the resurrected Jesus. There is no reason to suppose that the former would necessarily develop into the latter. Furthermore, legendary stories generally take time to develop, yet the church was proclaiming the bodily resurrection very soon after Jesus' death.

In any case, the appearances recorded in the Gospels have little in common with religious visions or hallucinations. They appear in a variety of places, to different kinds of people in a variety of circumstances, affecting a variety of senses. Religious visions are generally personal and subjective, not communal. It is unlikely that so

Figure 20.2—The Shroud of Turin

The shroud of Turin is a centuries-old burial cloth which bears the image of a crucified man and which advocates claim is the burial shroud of Jesus. The mysterious image is often said to have been imprinted on the cloth when Jesus' body passed through it at the resurrection.

The shroud was kept in the monastery in Turin for centuries, though it is reputed to have been brought from Turkey during the Crusades. Modern scientists have spent thousands of hours investigating the shroud to determine its age and authenticity. Many have declared it to be a medieval forgery, dating it to around AD 1350. Others continue to assert its authenticity. The controversy continues today.

many different people would have had the same vision. We must also ask what could have sparked such visions? By all accounts, the disciples were not expecting Jesus to rise from the dead. When other messianic pretenders were executed by the Romans, their followers were dispersed. It would be pointless to begin proclaiming the leader's resurrection unless there was something to support it. It is also noteworthy that Jesus' brother James did not believe in him until after the resurrection (John 7:5; Mark 3:21). He did not have messianic expectations which could have sparked a vision of the resurrected Jesus.

A merely spiritual or visionary resurrection was also contrary to Jewish belief of Jesus' day. According to the Pharisees — whose beliefs on this issue both Jesus and Paul shared — the resurrection was expected at the end of time, when the bodies of the righteous and the wicked would be raised (see discussion below). Paul's whole point in 1 Corinthians 15 is the reality of bodily resurrection — that is, the close link between the corruptible body which dies and the glorified body which rises (1 Cor. 15:42). It is inconceivable that Paul, a Jew with a Pharisaic background, would speak of the resurrection and mean anything other than a bodily resurrection intimately connected with the end-times salvation of God.

5. The Transformed Lives of the Disciples

The fifth piece of verifiable evidence for the resurrection is the extraordinary change in the apostles. What else could account for the transformation of a small band of defeated disciples into a community of followers who could not be silenced by persecution or threat of martyrdom? Something happened on that Sunday morning which changed their lives, convincing them that Jesus was the risen and glorified Lord.

THE SIGNIFICANCE OF THE RESURRECTION

If the resurrection of Jesus can be verified with a high degree of probability, what did it mean in the context of Jesus' life and ministry? To understand this, we must examine the first-century Jewish context.

The Jewish Background

A theology of the resurrection is not well developed in the Old Testament. While a number of statements indicate resurrection life or continuing existence after death in God's presence,[3] only in Daniel 12 is the resurrection explicitly described:

> Multitudes who sleep in the dust of the earth will awake: some to everlasting life, others to shame and everlasting contempt. Those who are wise will shine like the brightness of the heavens, and those who lead many to righteousness, like the stars for ever and ever.
>
> —Daniel 12:2–3

The Second Temple literature reveals an expanding theology of the resurrection but also exhibits a variety of perspectives. The apocalyptic literature, with its emphasis on God's final intervention, the vindication of the righteous, and the judgment of the wicked, expands

---

3. Gen. 5:24; 1 Sam. 28:1–25; 2 Kings 2:11; Job 19:25–27; Ps. 16:10; 49:15; 73:24; Isa. 25:8; 26:19.

on Daniel's resurrection theology. At the opposite end of the spectrum, some groups, like the Sadducees, did not believe in the afterlife at all (Acts 23:8; Josephus, *Ant.* 18.1.4 §16). Others under Hellenistic influence spoke of the immortality of the soul without a clear connection to the resurrection of the body. The Pharisees, like the apocalyptists, believed in the final resurrection, when God would raise the dead, reward the righteous, and judge the wicked. Both Jesus and Paul shared this perspective (Mark 12:18–27; 1 Corinthians 15).

The Significance of the Resurrection for Jesus and the Church

What, then, would the resurrection have meant for Jesus and his followers? Placing Jesus in his first-century Jewish context suggests two key answers.

The Beginning of the Last Days and the Final Resurrection. Jesus' resurrection went hand in hand with his preaching of the kingdom of God. The arrival of God's kingdom meant that the last days had begun and that God was about to intervene in human history to judge the righteous and the wicked. If, as we have argued, Jesus viewed his death as inaugurating the new covenant and the age of salvation, his resurrection must be viewed as the beginning of the end-times resurrection of the people of God. This was not just the restoration of physical life but also glorification to a new mode of existence—the beginning of immortal, imperishable resurrection life (1 Cor. 15:50–56). As Paul puts it, Jesus is "the firstborn from among the dead" (Col. 1:18). His resurrection assures believers that they too will be raised in glorified bodies, shining "like the stars for ever and ever" (Dan. 12:3).

> In its Jewish context, Jesus' resurrection must be viewed as the beginning of the end-times resurrection of the people of God.

The Defeat of Satan, Sin, and Death. As the inaugurator of the kingdom, Jesus brings God's salvation. The resurrection confirms that Jesus' victory does not relate merely to temporal enemies but to the evil spiritual forces of the world. Jesus' exorcisms confirm that he viewed his ministry as a conflict with Satan and the forces of evil. The nature of this battle is illuminated by Jesus' other actions: his claim to forgive sins, to heal the sick, and to raise the dead. Jesus was battling not only Satan but also the power of sin, disease, and death. When we place these conflicts in the context of Jesus' preaching of the kingdom of God, a coherent picture emerges. Jesus understood his death as an atoning sacrifice for the sins of his people, reversing the effects of the fall, defeating Satan (whose tempting of Eve resulted in the fall), and restoring creation to its rightful relationship with God. In short, Jesus was restoring God's reign over creation. The resurrection demonstrated victory over death and marked the beginning of the end-times resurrection of the righteous.

To arrive at these extraordinary conclusions, we need not look centuries forward to the developed Christology of a later age, but straight into the prophetic worldview of Jesus and his contemporaries, a worldview shaped by the restoration theology of Isaiah and the prophets. Isaiah predicted the coming age of salvation, a new exodus accomplished through the Davidic Messiah and the sacrificial ministry of the Servant of the LORD. Endowed with the Spirit of God, the Messiah would make atonement for the sins of his people, ushering in the eschatological year of the LORD's favor, when the lame would walk, the blind would see, the dead would rise. Death would be swallowed up in victory, and God would create a new heaven and a new earth (Isa. 2:1–4; 11:1–16; 25:8; 26:19; 29:18–19; 35:5–6; 52:13–53:12; 61:1–2; 65:17–18).

While a modern critical scholar accustomed to dissecting Isaiah's sources might be appalled at this amalgamation of diverse traditions, we must remember that Jesus himself read Isaiah as a unity. He read it not only as a literary unity but also as a theological unity, a road map to God's purpose and plan for all of creation. He could not have read it otherwise in the first-century world in which he lived.

» CHAPTER SUMMARY «

1. Rationalistic explanations for the resurrection, like the swoon theory, the wrong tomb theory, and the stolen body theory, are generally rejected by scholars today.

2. The most widely held rationalistic explanation is that the disciples had spiritual experiences — especially through visions and dreams — that convinced them that Jesus had been vindicated and exalted by God to his right hand, and that those experiences eventually developed into resurrection legends told and retold in the church.

3. Five points of reliable historical evidence argue against this legendary development view: (a) Jesus died by crucifixion in about AD 30; (b) he was buried in a tomb owned by Joseph of Arimathea; (c) the tomb was discovered empty on the third day after his death; (d) many reliable witnesses then saw Jesus alive; (e) this event transformed the lives of his closest followers.

4. In its first-century Jewish context, the resurrection would have been understood not as a temporal event but as the end-times day of judgment, when God would raise the dead, punish the wicked, and reward the righteous.

5. Jesus' resurrection must be understood within this context. It is not simply the restoration of physical life but also the beginning of the end-times restoration of creation and the defeat of sin, Satan, and death.

» KEY TERMS «

swoon theory

wrong tomb theory

theft theory

legendary development theory

Joseph of Arimathea

» DISCUSSION AND STUDY QUESTIONS «

1. Identify various rationalistic explanations for the resurrection. What is the most widely held rationalistic explanation today?

2. Note the five pieces of highly reliable evidence which together support the historicity of the resurrection of Jesus.

3. What was the significance of the resurrection of the dead in first-century Judaism?

4. In what sense is the resurrection of Jesus the beginning of the final resurrection?

5. How would Jesus likely have understood the resurrection in light of the teaching of Isaiah and other Old Testament prophets?

Digging Deeper

Alsup, John. *The Post-Resurrection Appearances of the Gospel Tradition.* Stuttgart: Calwe Verlag, 1975.

Bode, Edward Lynn. *The First Easter Morning.* Analecta biblica 45. Rome: Biblical Institute Press, 1970.

Brown, Raymond E. *The Virginal Conception and Bodily Resurrection of Jesus.* New York: Paulist, 1973.

Craig, William Lane. *Assessing the New Testament Evidence for the Historicity of the Resurrection of Jesus.* Lewiston, NY: Edwin Mellen, 1989.

——. *The Son Rises: The Historical Evidence for the Resurrection of Jesus.* Chicago: Moody, 1981.

Craig, William Lane, and Gerd Lüdemann. *Jesus' Resurrection: Fact or Figment?* Edited by Paul Copan and Ronald K. Tacelli. Downers Grove, IL: InterVarsity, 2000.

Fuller, Daniel P. *Easter Faith and History.* London: Tyndale, 1968.

Fuller, R. H. *The Formation of the Resurrection Narratives.* London: SPCK, 1972.

Gundry, Robert H. *Sōma in Biblical Theology.* Cambridge: Cambridge Univ. Press, 1976.

Harris, Murray J. *From Grave to Glory: Resurrection in the New Testament.* Grand Rapids: Zondervan, 1990.

Ladd, G. E. *I Believe in the Resurrection of Jesus.* Grand Rapids: Eerdmans, 1975.

Moule, C. F. D., ed. *The Significance of the Message of the Resurrection for Faith in Jesus Christ.* London: SCM, 1968.

Nickelsburg, G. W. E. *Resurrection, Immortality, and Eternal Life in Intertestamental Judaism.* Harvard Theological Studies 26. Cambridge, MA: Harvard Univ. Press, 1972.

O'Collins, Gerald. *Jesus Risen: An Historical, Fundamental, and Systematic Examination of Christ's Resurrection.* New York: Paulist, 1987.

Osborne, Grant R. *The Resurrection Narratives: A Redactional Study.* Grand Rapids: Baker, 1984.

Perkins, Pheme. *Resurrection: New Testament Witness and Contemporary Reflection.* New York: Doubleday, 1984.

Sutcliffe, Edmund Felix. *The Old Testament and the Future Life.* London: Barnes, Oates, and Washborn, 1964.

Wenham, John. *Easter Enigma: Are the Resurrection Accounts in Conflict?* Grand Rapids: Zondervan, 1984.

Wright, N. T., *The Resurrection of the Son of God* (Philadelphia: Fortress, 2003).

Conclusion

We may conclude our study of the historical Jesus by drawing together some of our results. In light of the extraordinary sense of destiny and authority exhibited by Jesus throughout the Gospel tradition, it seems likely that he considered himself the center of God's unfolding purpose for Israel and the world. He claimed—whether explicitly or implicitly—to be the Messiah, God's agent to accomplish salvation and to inaugurate the kingdom of God. He viewed his coming death through the lens of the restoration theology of Isaiah and the prophets: as an atoning sacrifice for the sins of his people, accomplishing a new exodus and establishing a new covenant bringing true forgiveness of sins and an intimate knowledge of God. The evidence further suggests that Jesus did not remain in the tomb but rose alive on the third day, vindicating his claim to be the Lord's Messiah, God's agent of salvation for Israel and for the world. Reigning now at the right hand of God, he will one day return to bring salvation to his people and to judge the world.

With these last two conclusions, we are clearly crossing the always-fluid boundary between historical conclusions and faith confessions. It is impossible to read the Gospels and not play close to this line. The claims made by Jesus and by the Evangelists who interpreted him cannot be studied from a merely objective, neutral position. By its very nature, the gospel of Jesus Christ demands a response from the reader. Throughout the centuries, Christians have responded to this call for faith and have found meaning and purpose for living.

Glossary

abomination of desolation. The desecration of the temple of Jerusalem by Antiochus IV Epiphanes when he offered idolatrous sacrifices on the altar (see Dan. 11:31; 12:11). In the Olivet Discourse, Jesus used this reference to refer to a future desecration (Mark 13:14, par.).

act. A part of a narrative made up of a group of related **scenes**.

Alexander the Great. Macedonian king whose military conquests of the Eastern Mediterranean greatly advanced the process of hellenization.

amēn. The transliteration of a Hebrew term meaning "confirmed" or "verified," which Jesus used to express his unique authority as spokesman for God.

Antiochus IV "Epiphanes." The Seleucid ruler who provoked the Maccabean rebellion because of his attempts to force hellenization on the Jews.

antithetical parallelism. Common literary device in Hebrew poetry where two or more lines provide contrasting thoughts.

aphorism. A short, memorable statement of wisdom or truth.

apocalypticism. Jewish movement beginning in the second century BC which looked to God's imminent intervention in history to judge the wicked and reward the righteous.

Apocrypha. A collection of Jewish texts written after the Old Testament period which are rejected by Protestants as authoritative Scripture but accepted by Roman Catholics and Orthodox Christians.

apocryphal gospels. A broad category of books and fragments of books containing stories and sayings about Jesus which were not included in the New Testament canon. See "Addendum" in chapter 1.

Apollonius. A first-century teacher and miracle-worker from Tyana in Cappodocia who was purported to have performed healings and exorcisms somewhat similar to those of Jesus.

apostle. A term meaning "one sent with a commission" and used in the Gospels of the Twelve, Jesus' closest disciples.

Archelaus. The son of Herod the Great; his rule of Judea ended when he was deposed by the Romans.

baptism of Jesus. Inaugural event of Jesus' ministry, representing his Spirit-anointing for service.

Bar Kokhba Revolt. The second Jewish revolt (AD 132–35), led by Simon bar Koseba and resulting in the end of the Jewish state.

Beelzebub controversy. A key episode in the Synoptic Gospels (Mark 3:22–30, par.) in which Jesus is accused of casting out demons by Satan's power and responds by accusing his opponents of blaspheming the Holy Spirit.

Beloved Disciple. The figure who appears repeatedly in the Gospel of John as "the disciple whom Jesus loved," traditionally identified as John the apostle.

Bethlehem. The traditional birthplace of Jesus, confirming his fulfillment of Micah 5:2 and his legitimacy as the Messiah from David's line.

birth narrative hymns. A series of songs or hymns spoken by characters in Luke's birth narrative which bring out the theological significance of the narrative.

birth narratives. Introductory sections of Matthew and Luke which describe the events surrounding the birth of Jesus and set the stage for their theological themes.

Book of Glory. The second major section of the Gospel of John (13:1–20:31), made up of his farewell discourse and his "glorification," a designation in Johannine theology which refers to his passion, resurrection, and ascension.

Book of Signs. The first major section of the Gospel of John (1:19–12:50), which describes a series of signs which reveal Jesus' glory and call people to faith in him.

Borg, Marcus. Influential member of the Jesus Seminar and key advocate of the view that Jesus was a "spirit person" or Jewish mystic.

Bultmann, Rudolf. (1884–1976) The most influential New Testament scholar of the twentieth century. He sought to "demythologize" the New Testament in order to discern its true existential message.

burden of proof. The question of where the responsibility lies for demonstrating the authenticity of the sayings and actions of Jesus. Should one first assume historicity or nonhistoricity?

Caesar Augustus (Octavian). (63 BC–AD 14) The first true emperor of Rome; ruler of the Roman Empire at the time of Jesus' birth.

Caiaphas. Jewish high priest from AD 18–36, and so the high priest during Jesus' public ministry.

canon criticism. A type of literary criticism which studies the biblical books with reference to their historical function as the church's authoritative Scripture.

canon of Scripture. Those books viewed by the church as authoritative and so fit to be included in the Bible. Protestants, Roman Catholics, and Orthodox Christians agree on the twenty-seven books of New Testament canon, though differ on whether to include the Apocrypha in the Old Testament canon. (See discussion of the Apocrypha in chap. 5).

causation. In the analysis of a narrative, the relationship of one scene to another. A plot progresses as one event leads to another.

census. Though the census of Luke 2:1 does not appear elsewhere in Roman records, it fits the general pattern of administrative reform initiated by Caesar Augustus.

characters. Individuals or groups who function in a narrative.

charismatic. Someone considered to be filled with or to act in the power of the Spirit of God.

charismatic holy men. A class of Jewish rabbis known for their powerful prayers for healing and rainfall.

chiasm, chiasmus. Inverse parallelism, a concentric pattern in which a series of things repeats itself in reverse order.

Christology. The branch of theology concerned with the study of the nature, character, and actions of Jesus Christ.

confession of Peter. A key transitional passage in the Synoptic Gospels (Mark 8:27–31, par.), as Peter acknowledges that Jesus is the Messiah, and Jesus begins speaking about his upcoming death.

conflict. Opposition of some kind which characters in a narrative must work through to resolution.

covenant. A solemn binding agreement between two parties. The Bible is structured around God's covenant relationship with his people.

covenantal nomism. Perspective advocated by E. P. Sanders that first-century Judaism was guided not by a works salvation but by a covenant relationship with God established through grace and maintained by Torah observance.

Criteria of Authenticity. Various criteria—such as dissimilarity, coherence, and multiple attestation—developed by Jesus scholars to test the authenticity of the words and actions of Jesus.

Crossan, John Dominic. (1934–) Cofounder of the Jesus Seminar and most influential advocate of Jesus as a Cynic-like Jewish peasant.

Cynics. Countercultural Hellenistic philosophers who rejected the norms of their society and sought to live a simple, unencumbered life.

Davidic Messiah. Jewish expectation for an end-times king descended from David who would reign over Israel in righteousness and justice.

Dead Sea Scrolls. An ancient library discovered in caves near the Dead Sea in 1947 and likely associated with the first-century Jewish community at Qumran.

deconstruction. A literary approach which argues that the meaning of literary texts is unstable and relative and that meaning is ultimately imposed on texts by readers, rather than discerned from them.

deism. The philosophical perspective that God created the ordered world and then left it to run by natural laws.

Diaspora. "Dispersion"; a reference to Jews living outside Israel.

Diatessaron. An early attempt to harmonize the Gospels, produced by Tatian around AD 170.

didache. A term referring to the church's "teaching" of the Gospel traditions and stories about Jesus. Sometimes contrasted with the *kerygma*.

disciple. A term meaning "follower" (Greek: *mathētēs*), sometimes used of all who followed Jesus, sometimes of his twelve special followers.

discipleship. The role of those who follow Jesus as their Lord.

divine men. A category of Hellenistic miracle-workers claimed by some to provide parallels to the miracles of Jesus.

Docetism. An early heresy which claimed that Jesus was not a real human being but only appeared to have a physical body.

doublets. Two similar episodes, sometimes in the same Gospel, which some critics claim arose from the same original story.

dualism. The theological perspective of the Gospel of John, which envisions a strict dichotomy between opposing forces of good and evil in the world: God versus Satan, truth versus falsehood, light versus darkness. A different kind of dualism, that between the material world and the spiritual world, characterized Gnosticism.

dyadism. See **group mentality**.

dynamic characters. Characters who develop and change in the course of a narrative.

eschatology, eschatological. Referring to the end times, God's time of final salvation.

Essenes. A Jewish sect which rigorously kept the law and often lived in monastic communities. The Dead Sea scrolls were probably an Essene library.

eternal life. One of John's favorite expressions for salvation, it refers not only to immortal life that never ends but also to true spiritual life which believers possess in the present.

eucharistic words. The words used by Jesus—recorded by both Paul and the Synoptics—to establish the communal meal, or Lord's Supper, which his disciples would practice after his departure.

evaluative point of view. The values, beliefs, and worldview which the reader is expected to adopt in order to judge the events and characters of a narrative.

Evangelists. The Gospel writers are known as the Evangelists because they are proclaiming the "good news" (euangelion) about Jesus Christ and calling for faith in him.

event. Any action or saying by a character in a plot. Events are also called incidents or scene parts.

exorcism. The act of the driving or casting out of an evil spirit possessing a person. Jesus taught that his exorcisms revealed the presence and power of the kingdom of God.

Farewell Discourse. Jesus' teaching following the Last Supper in John, in which he promises his disciples his continuing presence through the Holy Spirit.

feminist and liberationist criticism. A variety of literary approaches which seek to view the text through the eyes of the oppressed, the outsider, or the minority.

First Quest for the Historical Jesus. Nineteenth-century movement which sought to interpret the life and miracles of Jesus from a rationalistic perspective.

flat characters. Simple, one-dimensional, and predictable characters in a narrative.

form criticism. A type of historical criticism which studies the oral or spoken traditions behind the written Gospel sources.

four-source theory. Builds on the **two-source theory** by adding "M" and "L" for the unique material used by Matthew and Luke.

fulfillment formulas. A common formula used by Matthew to introduce Old Testament quotations related to Jesus: "This was to fulfill what was spoken by the prophet, saying . . ."

functional subordination. The Johannine concept that while Jesus was fully equal with God in his being (ontologically), he lived in full submission to and dependence on God.

genealogies. Tables or lists which show the line of descent from earlier ancestors. Genealogies are often meant to show someone's legitimacy for a particular role or status.

genre. A distinct type of literature — like poetry, narrative, letter, gospel, or parable — which has its own "rules" of interpretation and is meant to communicate meaning in a particular manner. The Gospels are a unique literary genre, though they share features with other ancient genres.

Gentile. A person who is not a Jew.

Gnosticism. A religious movement which claimed adherents gained salvation through secret knowledge of their true heavenly origin.

Gospel for the Outcast. Another name for Luke's **travel narrative** or journey to Jerusalem (9:51–19:27), which presents the many stories and parables which stress God's love for the lost.

Gospel of Thomas. A collection of 114 sayings reputed to be from Jesus, discovered in the Nag Hammadi collection of Gnostic writings.

Great Commission. Jesus' final command to his followers after his resurrection, commissioning them to make disciples of all nations (Matt. 28:18–20).

Griesbach, or two-gospel, hypothesis. The proposal that Matthew was the first Gospel written, that Luke used Matthew as a source, and that Mark used both Matthew and Luke.

group mentality (dyadism). The perspective that essential identity comes from being a member of a family, community, or nation.

Hanukkah. The Jewish feast celebrating the victory of the Maccabees over Antiochus Epiphanes and the rededication of the temple in 164 BC.

harmony of the Gospels. A book which seeks to bring together the Gospels into a single, chronological narrative account. Most harmonies place the four Gospels in parallel columns.

Hasidim. A Hebrew term meaning "pious ones" or "holy ones"; used of those who opposed Seleucid attempts to hellenize Israel in the second century BC.

Hasmonean dynasty. The Jewish dynasty (167–63 BC) established by Judas and his brothers which ruled Israel following the victory of the Maccabees.

healings. Jesus' miracles of physical restoration, which symbolize the restoring and redemptive power of the kingdom of God.

Hellenists. Refers to those in support of hellenization (the adoption of Greek culture and language). More specifically, it can refer to those who sided with the Seleucid attempts to hellenize Israel in the second century BC.

hellenization. The spread of Greek culture and language, whether by coercion, force, or natural appeal.

Herod Antipas. The son of Herod the Great and tetrarch of Galilee and Perea between 4 BC and AD 39 during the period of Jesus' ministry.

Herod the Great. The Idumean (Edomite) ruler who gained the throne of Israel after the Roman conquest of Palestine and ruled from 37–4 BC.

high priest. The highest religious office in Judaism. The high priest oversaw temple worship and the religious life of the Jews.

high-priestly prayer. Traditional name given to Jesus' prayer for his disciples in John 17, in which he acts as a priestly mediator for them.

Hillel. (c. 60 BC–AD 20?) One of the most important rabbis of the Second Temple period. The House (or "school") of Hillel developed seven rules of interpretation which shaped the course of rabbinic interpretion after the destruction of Jerusalem. Hillel's interpretations of the law are generally less strict than the rival school of Shammai.

historiography. A term meaning "the writing of history" and referring to Luke's intention to write an accurate historical account of the origins of Christianity.

Historical Jesus research. Examines the nature and historicity of the traditions about Jesus.

History of Religions School (*Religiongeschichteschule*). A nineteenth-century German school of thought which sought to study religion in terms of its evolutionary development from simple polytheistic religions to complex monotheism.

honor and shame. Critical values in first-century Mediterranean culture, honor and shame relate to gaining or losing status and esteem from others in the community.

Hume, David. (1711–76) Influential Scottish philosopher who rejected the possibility of miracles as irrational since they contradict the inviolable laws of nature.

hyperbole. An exaggeration used for emphasis or effect.

"I am" statements. Jesus' characteristic use of metaphors to describe himself in John's Gospel. See figure 10.3.

Idumean. A Greek form of the Hebrew "Edomite," meaning a descendant of Esau, twin brother of Jacob (Israel) and son of Isaac (Genesis 25–33). Edom was located in southern Palestine and had a history of conflict with Israel. It was ruled by the Jews during the period of the Maccabees.

implied author. The literary version of the author as discerned in a narrative text. While the reader has no direct access to the real author, the implied author can be identified by discerning the beliefs, worldview, and point of view expressed in the narrative.

implied reader. An imaginary person who responds appropriately to the strategy of a narrative text.

inclusio. A "bookend" structure in which a similar statement or episode begins and ends a narrative sequence.

infancy gospels. Fanciful accounts of Jesus' boyhood which describe him as a child prodigy and miracle-worker. See "Addendum" in chapter 1.

"inn" (*katalyma*). Probably not an ancient hotel, but either a guest room in a private residence or an informal public shelter where travelers would gather for the night.

intercalation. A "sandwiching" technique, similar to ***inclusio***, where one episode is inserted ("intercalated") into the middle of another. The two episodes are generally related to a common theme.

irony. A rhetorical device where the apparent meaning is contrary to the real meaning.

Jamnia. City on the Mediterranean coast and location of the academy for the study of the law established by Rabbi Johannan ben Zakkai after the destruction of Jerusalem in AD 70.

Jerusalem temple. The central place of worship for Israel. Sacrifices were to be made only in the Jerusalem temple (Deut. 12:5 – 14).

Jesus of history versus Christ of faith. A distinction sometimes drawn between the historical figure of Jesus and the presently reigning Lord of the church, worshiped by believers today (see **Kähler, Martin**).

Jesus Seminar. A controversial group established by Robert Funk and John Dominic Crossan which met in the 1980s and 1990s and voted on the sayings of Jesus, finding very little of historical value in the Gospels.

Jewish Revolt of AD 66 – 73. (also Jewish War) The Jewish revolution against Rome, resulting in the destruction of Jerusalem and the temple (AD 70).

Johannan ben Zakkai. Famous late-first-century rabbi who established an academy for the study of the law at Jamnia on the Mediterranean coast.

Johannine community. The early Christian community which preserved the teachings of John about Jesus as represented in the Gospel of John, the three letters of John, and (perhaps) the book of Revelation.

John Rylands manuscript (p^{52}). A small papyrus fragment of the Gospel of John, dated to the early part of the second century and probably the earliest surviving manuscript of any part of the New Testament.

John the Baptist. Jesus' predecessor, who announced the coming of the Messiah.

John the Elder. An individual mentioned by the early church father Papias and considered by some to be the author of the Fourth Gospel. Others consider this another name for John the apostle.

Joseph of Arimathea. The member of the Jewish Sanhedrin whom all four Gospels identify as the one who buried Jesus' body in his own tomb.

Josephus Flavius. (37 BC–approx. AD 100) First-century Jewish historian, our most important extrabiblical source for the history and culture of first-century Judaism.

Jülicher, Adolf. (1857–1938) A pioneer in the interpretation of parables who rejected the allegorizing tendencies of earlier interpreters.

Kähler, Martin. (1835–1912) Rejected the historical Jesus quest as misguided, claiming that the only Jesus we can know is the Christ of faith.

Käsemann, Ernst. (1906–98) German professor of the New Testament and student of Bultmann whose influential 1953 essay launched the New Quest for the historical Jesus.

kerygma. A term referring to the early church's evangelistic "preaching" about the saving significance of Jesus' life, death, and resurrection.

kingdom of God. The central theme of Jesus' preaching, referring especially to God's sovereign reign and authority, but also to the consummation of the reign in an end-times (eschatological) kingdom.

kingdom of heaven. Matthew's preferred title for the kingdom of God — God's sovereign reign coming to fulfillment through the words and deeds of Jesus.

koinē **Greek.** The common language spoken for trade and diplomacy throughout the Roman Empire.

Lamb of God. Title given to Jesus by John the Baptist (John 1:29, 36), indicating his sacrificial death as the Passover lamb and suffering Servant of Isaiah 53.

legate. A ruler of a Roman imperial province.

legendary development theory. The theory—widely held among scholars—that the resurrection stories arose over time from the disciples' hopes, dreams, and visions that he was somehow still alive.

levirate marriage. The practice or requirement of marriage of a widow to the brother of her deceased husband in order to produce an heir for the dead man (Deut. 25:5–10).

Levites. Descendants of Jacob's son Levi, who were dedicated as a tribe to serve Yahweh and the temple.

literary criticism. Various methods which have in common the study of the Gospels as unified literary works. Narrative, rhetorical, and canon criticism are examples of literary approaches.

Logos. A Greek title given to Jesus in the prologue of John's Gospel which has conceptual roots in both Judaism and Hellenistic philosophy and which stresses Jesus' identity as the self-revelation of God.

Lord. Translation in the New Testament of the Greek *kyrios*, which can carry different senses, including "sir," "master," or even "God." It was used throughout the Greek Old Testament (LXX) as a translation for Yahweh, Israel's covenant name for God

Luke-Acts. The hyphenated expression used to describe Luke and Acts together as a single two-volume work, a literary and theological unity.

Maccabees, the. The name given to Judas and his brothers, who liberated Israel from Seleucid rule in the second century BC.

Maccabeus, Judas. Son of Mattathias and first great leader of the Maccabean Revolt. Maccabeus means "the hammer."

magi. Probably Persian or Arabian astrologers who charted the stars and attached religious significance to their movements.

maranatha. An Aramaic expression meaning "Our Lord come!" and revealing a very high Christology in the early Aramaic-speaking church.

Markan priority. The view that Mark was the first Gospel written and that Matthew and Luke both independently used Mark as a source.

materialism. The philosophical assumption that the world is a closed system of cause and effect without divine intervention.

Matthew, Mark, Luke, John. The four New Testament Gospels, recognized by Christians as authoritative and inspired accounts of Jesus Christ.

Meier, John P. Prolific author of multivolume work *A Marginal Jew*, which methodically examines the Jesus tradition for historicity. Meier views Jesus primarily as an eschatological prophet.

Messiah. God's end-times Savior sent to deliver his people. From a Hebrew term meaning "Anointed One" and translated into Greek as "Christ" (*christos*). See more in chapter 18.

messianic banquet. An Old Testament image of God's final salvation as a great banquet feast which God will provide for all people who worship him. (See Isa. 25:6–8.)

messianic secret. A pattern in Mark whereby Jesus repeatedly silences those who recognize him to be the Messiah or the Son of God.

metaphor. An implicit comparison between two unlike things.

midrash. A rabbinic-style interpretation of the biblical text often associated with fictional expansions of Old Testament narrative.

mikveh. An immersion pool for Jewish ceremonial washings and perhaps for the immersion of new converts.

miracle at Cana. The first miracle ("sign") of John's Gospel; Jesus turns water to wine, symbolizing the messianic banquet.

miracle story. A short narrative episode (pericope) recounting a miracle of Jesus, generally following a traditional pattern: (a) physical problem, (b) healing, (c) amazed reaction.

Mishnah. The earliest of the rabbinic writings, put into written form about AD 200, composed of the rulings of rabbis on a wide range of issues related to the application of Torah to everyday life.

monotheism. Belief in only one true God. Judaism was the first great monotheistic religion.

Nag Hammadi library. A collection of mostly Gnostic literature discovered in Egypt in 1945.

narrative criticism. A method of literary analysis which treats the Gospels as narrative or story.

narrative time. The manner in which story time is portrayed, in terms of order, speed, and duration.

narrative world. The universe created by the implied author within which a story or narrative takes place.

narrator. The "voice" that is heard telling a story.

nature miracles. A designation given to miracles which demonstrate Jesus' authority over nature, such as turning water into wine, multiplying loaves and fishes, walking on the water, and calming a storm.

Nazareth. The Galilean village where Jesus was raised.

New (Second) Quest for the Historical Jesus. A resurgence in historical Jesus research initiated by students of Rudolf Bultmann in the 1950s. Its origin is usually traced to a 1953 lecture by Ernst Käsemann.

Nicodemus. The Jewish religous leader who came to Jesus by night and later aided Joseph of Arimathea with the burial of Jesus.

No Quest. Twentieth-century period associated especially with Rudolf Bultmann and marked by extreme skepticism concerning what can be known about the historical Jesus.

Olivet Discourse. Jesus' message to the disciples given on the Mount of Olives concerning the destruction of the temple and the end of the age (Mark 13, par.).

ontological equality. A phrase meaning "equality of essence or being." While equal to God the Father in being, Jesus lived in functional subordination to him.

paganism. A general term for a polytheistic or pantheistic religion, in contrast to the great monotheistic religions of Judaism, Christianity (first century), and Islam (sixth to seventh centuries).

Palestine. The geographical region between the Jordan River and the eastern coast of the Mediterranean Sea. It is a more general term than *Israel*, which usually refers to the same region when identified as the Jewish homeland.

parable. A short fictional story or vignette illustrating a moral or spiritual lesson.

parable of the wicked tenant farmers. An important parable of Jesus that allegorized his rejection by Israel's leaders (Mark 12:1–12, par.).

parables of the kingdom. Jesus' parables which explain for the disciples the "mysteries" and nature of the kingdom of God (Mark 4; Matthew 13; Luke 8).

paraclete. A description Jesus gives to the Holy Spirit in his Farewell Discourse in John's Gospel, meaning "advocate," "counselor," or "comforter."

paradox. A seemingly contradictory statement that is nonetheless true.

passion narrative. The narrative leading up to Jesus' death, generally including the last supper, Jesus' agony in the Garden, and his arrest, trial, and crucifixion.

passion prediction. Jesus' prediction of his upcoming death.

patronage. A system common in societies with strict social distinctions, whereby a client provides honor, loyalty, and obedience to a more powerful patron or benefactor in return for favors of some kind.

Pax Romana. A Latin term meaning "Roman peace" and referring to the period of relative peace and stability established by Caesar Augustus.

pericope (*pĕríkopē*). A short, self-contained Gospel episode such as a miracle story, a parable, or a pronouncement story which may have originally circulated as an independent unit of oral tradition.

Pharisees. A religious and political party in first-century Judaism which strictly adhered to purity laws and the law of Moses, both the written law and oral traditions.

Philo. (approx. 20 BC to AD 40) First-century Jewish philosopher whose works help us understand the convergence of Judaism and Hellenism.

Pilate, Pontius. The Roman prefect or governor of the Roman province of Judea from AD 26–36, during the time of Jesus' ministry.

plot. The progress of a narrative; the sequence of events which move the story from introduction, to conflict, to climax, to conclusion.

prefect. A Roman provincial ruler of a lower rank than a proconsul or legate. Pontius Pilate was a prefect.

priests. Levites from the family of Aaron, who served as priests in the temple.

proconsul. A ruler of a Roman senatorial province.

procurator. See **prefect**.

prologue of John. The introduction to John's Gospel, which identifies Jesus as the *Logos* and provides the most exalted statement of Christology in the New Testament.

prologue of Luke. The introduction to Luke (1:1–4), written in a very fine literary style and expressing the nature and purpose of the Gospel.

pronouncement story. A short narrative episode (**pericope**) which builds to a climactic statement or pronouncement by Jesus. (See Mark 2:15–17.)

prophet like Moses. An important description of Jesus in Luke-Acts (drawn from Deut. 18:15) which is intended to warn Israel to listen to him or else face judgment (Acts 3:22–23; 7:37).

proselyte baptism. The later practice of immersion for converts to Judaism. It is uncertain when proselyte baptism was first practiced and whether it was a precursor for New Testament baptism.

proverb. A short, memorable statement of wisdom or truth.

pseudepigrapha. A large body of ancient Jewish writings—most produced during the Second Temple period—which were not included in the Apocrypha.

pseudepigraphic. Having falsely ascribed authorship.

Ptolemies. The dynasty which arose in Egypt following the division of Alexander the Great's empire. The Ptolemies controlled Palestine from about 323 to 198 BC.

pun. A play on words using terms that sound or look alike.

Qumran. A Jewish community near the Dead Sea which likely produced the Dead Sea Scrolls. Most scholars believe the Qumran community were Essenes.

rabbinic writings. Discussions and interpretations of the Jewish law produced by rabbis in the centuries after the destruction of Jerusalem.

raising of Lazarus. The climactic miracle in John's Gospel, which provokes the religious authorities.

rationalism. The philosophical perspective which claims that reason is the sole test of truth.

reader-response criticism. A variety of literary methods which find meaning not in the author's intention or in the text alone but in the response of readers.

reading horizontally. Comparing parallel Gospel accounts (especially among the Synoptics) to discern each Evangelist's unique theological perspective.

reading vertically. Reading "downward" through the story or narrative of each individual Gospel, following the progress of the narrative together with its theological themes.

real author. The actual historical author of a literary work.

realized eschatology. The theological perspective—reflected especially in John's Gospel—that God's end-times salvation is already a present possession in the life of the believer.

real reader. Any actual reader of a text, whether ancient or modern.

redaction criticism. A type of historical criticism which studies how the Gospel writers edited their sources to achieve their distinct theological goals.

Reimarus, H. S. (1694–1768) German professor whose essay "On the Intention of Jesus and His Disciples" is often viewed as launching the rationalistic **First Quest for the Historical Jesus**.

resuscitations, revivications. The restoration of mortal existence for those who have died, as in the cases of Lazarus and of Jairus's daughter. This is different than resurrection, which carries the eschatological significance of entrance into immortal and eternal life.

rhetoric. The manner in which a story is told to achieve the desired response from the reader.

rhetorical criticism. A type of literary criticism which draws on ancient categories of rhetoric to analyze how authors instruct or persuade their audiences.

riddle. A question or statement requiring thought to answer or understand.

round characters. Complex and often unpredictable narrative characters with multiple traits.

Sadducees. A religious and political party in first-century Judaism made up mostly of the priestly leadership and aristocracy.

salvation history. The story of God's actions in human history to accomplish his salvation.

Sanders, E. P. (1937–) Key advocate of the view that Jesus was an eschatological prophet in close continuity with the Judaism of his day.

Sanhedrin. The Jewish high court.

scene. A group of related **events** in a narrative. Also called episodes.

Schweitzer, Albert. (1875–1965) German theologian, musician, philosopher, and physician whose magisterial *Quest for the Historical Jesus* criticized the First Quest for the Historical Jesus for merely reimagining Jesus as a nineteenth-century rationalist.

scribes. Experts in the law of Moses.

Second Temple period. The period from the completion of the second temple (built by Zerubbabel) to its destruction, approximately 516 BC to AD 70.

Seleucids. The dynasty which arose in Syria following the division of Alexander the Great's empire. The Seleucids controlled Palestine from about 198 to 166 BC.

Sepphoris. An important Hellenistic city located a few miles from Jesus' hometown, Nazareth.

Septuagint (LXX). The Greek translation of the Hebrew Scriptures (the Old Testament). Abbreviated with Roman numerals for seventy (LXX).

Sermon on the Mount. Jesus' inaugural sermon in Matthew (chaps. 5–7), which sets out the radical values of the kingdom of God.

Servant of the Lord. A reference to Jesus as the messianic figure who appears repeatedly in Isaiah 40–55 and especially in a suffering role in Isaiah 52:13–53:12.

settings. All facets of a narrative world in which characters act and events occur. Settings can be local, temporal, or social-cultural.

Shammai. (first century BC) The house (or "school") founded by Shammai was the first major academy of Jewish sages. It generally favored a more restrictive interpretation of the law than its rival school, the House of Hillel.

signs. The term in John for miracles which reveal Jesus' glory and call forth faith in him.

simile. An explicit comparison between two things, usually with the words "as" or "like."

Sitz im Leben. A German phrase meaning "setting in life," referring to the original cultural and historical contexts in which an episode or a narrative arose.

Son of David. A traditional messianic title referring to the Messiah's descent from the line of David, Israel's greatest king.

Son of God. A title for the Messiah indicating a unique relationship with God the Father. See more in chapter 18.

Son of Man. Jesus' most common self-designation, the title is likely drawn from Daniel 7:13 and refers to Jesus' true humanity as well as his role as glorious redeemer. For more, see chapter 18.

source criticism. A type of historical criticism which seeks to identify the written sources behind each Gospel and their relationship to one another.

static characters. Characters in a narrative who remain the same throughout the story.

story time. The actual passage of time in the narrative world of a text.

Strauss, D. F. (1808–74) German scholar who claimed that Gospel events were not merely rationalistic events misconstrued by eyewitnesses (as the First Quest assumed), but rather myths which had developed over the course of time in the early churches.

structuralism. A type of literary criticism which seeks to analyze literature according to certain rules or patterns—a "grammar" of literature.

structural signals. A common phrase or expression which introduces a transition in the narrative. Matthew uses the phrases, "And it came about when Jesus finished these words …" and, "From that time Jesus began to …" to mark key transitions in his narrative.

suffering Servant. The messianic figure who appears in Isaiah 52:12 – 53:13 and offers himself as a sacrifice for the sins of God's people. New Testament writers consider Jesus to have fulfilled this role.

swoon theory. The theory that Jesus did not actually die on the cross but rather "swooned" and was then revived in the cool air of the tomb.

symbolism. A general term for one thing standing for something else.

synagogues. Local Jewish meeting places used for worship, study, assemblies, and social events.

synonymous parallelism. Common literary device in Hebrew poetry where two or more lines repeat similar thoughts.

Synoptic Gospels. The name given to Matthew, Mark, and Luke, because they present the ministry of Jesus from a similar perspective. Synoptic means "viewed together."

Synoptic Sayings Source "Q". A hypothetical source proposed to account for the material common to Matthew and Luke which does not appear in Mark. See figure 2.7.

tabernacle. The portable temple, also called "the tent of meeting," which the Israelites carried with them through the wilderness (Exodus 25 – 30).

Talmud. The complete body of Jewish oral traditions, including the Mishnah, the Tosefta, and the Gemara.

Targums. Aramaic paraphrases of and expansions on Scripture.

tektōn. Joseph and Jesus' occupation; a general term referring to someone who built with materials like stone, wood, or metal.

temptation of Jesus. Testing of Jesus by Satan in the desert; analogous to Israel's testing in the wilderness and Adam and Eve's testing in the Garden.

theft theory. The claim that Jesus' disciples stole his body and subsequently announced he had risen from the dead.

theophany. The appearance in visible form of God, or a god, to a human being.

Theophilus. The addressee in both Luke and Acts. He was probably the patron who sponsored the writing of the Gospel and Acts.

Third Quest for the Historical Jesus. A name given to the resurgence in the study of the historical Jesus from the 1980s onward, characterized by a variety of new methodologies and cross-disciplinary research.

Tiberius Caesar. The Roman emperor during the period of Jesus' public ministry. He ruled from AD 14–37.

Torah. The law given by God to Israel through Moses. The term could be used for various things: the commandments given by God, the books of the Pentateuch, the whole Old Testament, and even for the written and oral traditions.

transfiguration. The mountaintop revelation of Jesus' true glory to three disciples: Peter, James, and John (Mark 9:2–8, par.).

travel narrative. Also called the "Journey to Jerusalem," "the Central Section," and "the Gospel for the Outcast." Refers to Luke's extended and theologically-significant account of Jesus' final trip to Jerusalem (9:51 to 19:27).

triad. A pattern or group of three; a common literary device in Mark's Gospel.

triumphal entry. The traditional designation for Jesus' entrance into Jerusalem on Palm Sunday, riding on a donkey and fulfilling the prophecy of Zechariah 9:9 (Mark 11:1–10, par.).

Troeltsch, Ernst. (1865–1923) Set out highly influential philosophical principles which effectively ruled out supernatural intervention in human events.

Twelve, the. A reference to Jesus' twelve disciples—identified also as apostles—whom Jesus chose (Mark 3:13–19). This number likely represents in some sense the twelve tribes of Israel.

two-source theory. The theory that both Matthew and Luke used both Mark and "Q" as their sources. The **four-source theory** adds "M" and "L" for the unique material used by Matthew and Luke.

typology, type, antitype. A comparison or analogy made between an Old Testament person, thing, or event which serves as a precursor (a type) for a New Testament person, thing, or event (an antitype).

unity and diversity. Four unique Gospels (diversity) testify to the one Gospel of Jesus Christ (unity).

virginal conception. A more accurate description of the "virgin birth," whereby Mary conceived Jesus through the supernatural intervention of God's Spirit, rather than through sexual intercourse.

Weiss, Johannes. (1863–1914) Seeking to place Jesus in his first-century context, Weiss identified Jesus as an apocalyptic prophet expecting the imminent end of the world.

world, the. A term which in John often has the connotation of the evil world system as ruled by Satan.

Wrede, William. (1859–1906) Sought to demonstrate that the Gospels were not biographies or history but rather theologically motivated fictions.

Wright, N. T. (1948–) Innovative and influential Jesus scholar who views Jesus as an eschatological prophet restoring God's people by leading them out of spiritual exile into a new exodus deliverance.

wrong tomb theory. The theory that Jesus' followers went to the wrong tomb and so mistakenly believed he had risen from the dead.

Yahweh ("the LORD"). Israel's covenant name for God; derived from the four Hebrew consonants YHWH, the tetragrammaton ("four letters").

Zealots. Jewish insurrectionists who engaged in revolutionary activities against the Roman authorities.

Zeitgeist. The ideas prevalent in a particular time and place; in this case referring to the political and religious climate of first-century Palestine.

Index

Page numbers in italics indicate photos. Page numbers with f indicate figures.

abbreviation and omission in the Gospels, 389–90
abomination of desolation, 526
Abraham, 124, 223, 268, 317, 414
act, narrative, 71, 526
Acts, book of, 261–62
    ancient history writing and, 385–86
Acts of Jesus: The Search for the Authentic Deeds of Jesus, The (Funk), 357f, 364
adultery, 317f
Against Apion (Josephus), 117f, 263f
agriculture, 157–59, 314–15
Agrippa, Herod (Roman leader), 110, 113f
Aims of Jesus, The (Meyer), 363
aims of Jesus Christ, 473–81
Alexander the Great, 95–98, 526
Allison, D. C., 440f
Allison, Dale, 365, 374
ambiguity in language, 83–84
amen, 471, 526
Am-ha-Eretz, 138
analogy, principle of, 350
Andrew, brother of Simon Peter, 474f
Annas (high priest), 324–25, 386, 495f
anointing with oil, 482
Antigonus (Hasmonean leader), 105
Antioch, Syria, 251
Antiochus III, 100
Antiochus IV, 100–101, 132, 526
Antipater, 104–5
Antiquities of the Jews, The (Josephus), 117f
anti-Semitism, 253
antisupernatural bias, 59
antithetical parallelism, 436, 526
aphorisms and proverbs, 437f, 527, 536
Aphrodite, *151*
apocalypticism, 526
apocalyptic prophet, Jesus as, 352–53
Apocrypha, the, 141–42, 526
apocryphal gospels, 32, 40–42, 55
Apollonius (teacher), 460, 526
apologetic nature of the Gospels, 30
apostles, 476, 526
Aramaic, 97–98, 252, 488
Archelaus (Roman leader), 108, 418, 526
Arch of Titus, *115*
Aristotle, 80, 96
Arnett, Peter, 172
arrest of Jesus Christ, 35, 58, 162, 235–38, 278–79, 324–25

Aristobulus II, 104
ascension of Jesus Christ, 280, 286
assessment of form criticism, 58–60
audience criticism, 82
audiences of the Gospel writers, 31–32, 249–51
Augustine and the Synoptic Gospels, 47–48
authenticity of words and actions of Jesus, 360–62, 388–89, 470–73, 506–7
    criteria of, 360–62, 528
authority of Jesus Christ, 179–83, 188f, 229
    announcing and inaugurating the kingdom, 470
    at the final judgment, 473
    to forgive sins, 472–73, 477–78
    over demons and disease, 470
    over the law and the Sabbath, 471–72
    to speak for God, 471
    teaching style and, 436–38
authorship
    and bias of the Gospel writers, 385
    implied, 531
    of John, 332–34, 392–93
    of Luke, 289–90
    of Mark, 201–2
    of Matthew, 252–53
    real, 536
Babylonians, the, 94–95, 126, 223–24
Bacon, Benjamin, 219, 221f
banditry, social, 136–38
banquets, 153, 160, 288–89, 534
    Jesus' turning water into wine and, 308–9, 464–65
baptism of Jesus Christ, 268, 429–30, 526
Barabbas (prisoner), 137
Bar Kokhba Revolt, 119, 526
bar Koseba, Simon, 119
Bartholomew, 475f
Beardslee, William, 68
Beasley-Murray, G. R., 440f
Bedouins, *154*
Beelzebub controversy, 175, 176f, 182, 182f, 230, 462, 526
Beloved Disciple, the, 302, 327–28, 329, 333–34, 527
ben Dosa, Hanina, 368, 460
ben Zakkai, Johanan, 118, 134, 249–50, 532
Bethlehem, *224*, *266*, 416, 527
Beth Shan, *430*
betrayal of Jesus Christ, 197, 235–36, 277–78, 495f
bias, antisupernatural, 59
Biblical Archaeological Review, 420f
Birkat Ha-Minim, 250f

birth narrative of Jesus
    ancestry of Jesus and, 412–15
    Bethlehem and, *224, 266,* 416
    chronology and, 405–6
    genre of, 412
    hymns, 265–66, 286, 527
    in Luke, 264–68, 285–86, 417–19
    in Matthew, 220–25, 418
    virginal conception and, 415–16, 539
blindness, 318
Blomberg, Craig, 464
Bockmuehl, Markus, 377
bookend structure in narratives, 77
Book of Acts in the Setting of Hellenistic History, The
    (Hemer), 386
Book of Glory, 302, 322–27, 527
    crucifixion and resurrection of Jesus in, 325–27
    the Farewell Discourse in, 323
    Jesus' arrest and trial in, 324–25
    Jesus' prayer for the disciples, 323–24
    the Last Supper in, 322
Book of Signs, the, 527
    changing water into wine at Cana, 308–9
    clearing the temple, 309–10
    feeding the five thousand, walking on water, bread of
        life, 314–16
    the Good Shepherd and teaching at the Feast of Dedi-
        cation, 318–20
    healing a man born blind, 318
    healing in Cana and Jerusalem, 312–14
    interview with Nicodemus in, 302, 304, 310–11
    interview with Samaritan at the well, 311–12
    Jesus' arrival in Jerusalem, 321–22
    light of the world, 316–18
    raising of Lazarus in, 303, 320–21
    teaching at the Feast of Tabernacles, 316–18
    testimonies to Jesus in, 307–8
Borg, Marcus, 373, 375, 527
    and Jesus as a Jewish mystic, 368–69
    Jesus Seminar beliefs and, 359, 363, 364, 365
    and Jesus Seminar compared with the Third Quest,
        358f
    key works, 371f
Bornkamm, Günther, 60, 356
Bousset, Wilhelm, 353, 354f, 487
boys in New Testament times, 150–51
bread of life, Jesus as, 314–16
Brown, Raymond, 457–58
Bultmann, Rudolf, 57, 350, 353, 354f, 355–56, 527, 534
burden of proof, 385, 527
Cadbury, H. J., 261
Caesar Augustus (Roman leader), 105, 108, 110–11, 113f,
    266, 527
    census ordered by, 416–17
Caesarea Maritima, *107, 112*
Caesarea Philippi, *174, 183, 184*

Caiaphas (high priest), 128, 324–25, 373, 386, 482–83,
    495f, 527
calendar, Jewish, 313–14f, 315f, 316–18, 318–20, 333
Caligula (Roman leader), 113f
calming of the sea by Jesus Christ, 174, 180
Campus Crusade for Christ, 291
Cana
    healing at, 312–14
    water changed into wine at, 308–9, 464–65, 534
canon criticism, 80–81, 527
canon of Scripture, 32, 527
catechetical nature of the Gospels, 30
causation, 71, 527
census, Roman, 416–17, 527
central message of Jesus Christ, 438–41
central theme
    of John, 298
    of Luke, 260
    of Mark, 172
    of Matthew, 214
characterization, 73
characters, Gospel, 73–74, 527
    dynamic, 73, 529
    flat, 73, 529
    in John, 329–30
    in Luke, 282–84
    in Mark, 196–98
    in Matthew, 242–45
    round, 73, 537
    static, 73, 538
charismatic Jewish holy men, 368, 460–61, 527
chiasm, 76–77, 305–6, 527
children in New Testament times, 150–51, 163, 266–67,
    276
Childs, Brevard, 81
Christianity
    break with Judaism, 118–19, 249–50
    and the "Christian Pentateuch," 219–20, 221f
    Jesus Seminar and, 358–65
    kinship and, 163
    liberal Jesus and, 348–50
    Nero and, 205
    nineteenth-century scholarship on, 349–56
    parallels to the Qumran community, 136
    persecution of modern, 205
    post-Bultmannian skepticism and, 356–57
    radical skepticism and, 350–56
    reliability of the Gospel tradition in, 386–88
    rise after the destruction of Jerusalem, 118–19
    viewed as begun through fraud and deceit, 349–50
Christ of faith, 353, 532
Christology, 24, 528
Christology of Jesus, The (Witherington), 371f
chronology of Jesus Christ's life, 405–8
Church of All Nations, *237, 278*
Church of St. John, *300*

Church of the Holy Sepulcher, *516, 516–17*
Church of the Nativity, *224, 416*
Church of the Visitation, *265*
Cicero, 80
circumcision, 124, 151
Claudius (Roman leader), 113f
cleansing of the temple, 175, 309–10, 480–81, 495f
Clement of Alexandria, 33f, 41, 202
Cleopatra VII (queen of Egypt), 105
Clermont-Ganneau, Charles, 260
clothing and style in New Testament times, 154
CNN, 172
coherence, criterion of, 360
Combrink, H. J. B., 221f
commandment, the greatest, 188f, 444–45
commerce in New Testament times, 159–60
Commissioning of the Twelve, 219f
communication in New Testament times, 159–60
conception, virginal, 415–16, 539
confession of Peter, 183, 272, 482–83, 528
conflict, 71–72, 133, 528
      in Mark, 72, 181–83, 188–89f
consistent eschatology, 353
contemporary portrait of Jesus
      as an eschatological prophet, 372–77
      as a Jewish mystic or spirit person, 368–69
      as the Messiah, 377
      as a social revolutionary, 369–72
      as a wandering Cynic-like philosopher, 366–68
context, nature of Jesus', 365
contradictions between the Gospels
      abbreviation and omission, 389–90
      paraphrasing and interpretation, 388–89
      reordering of events and sayings, 390–91
      reporting similar events and sayings, 391–92
Conzelmann, Hans, 60
core beliefs in Judaism, 124–25
correlation, principle of, 350
courtyards of the Jerusalem temple, 126–27
covenantal nomism, 373, 528
covenant between God and Israel, 124, 528
craftsmen of New Testament times, 157
criteria of authenticity in Third Quest scholarship,
      360–62, 528
criticism, literary, 45f, 46, 68, 533
      canon, 80–81, 527
      deconstruction, 83–84
      eclectic approach to, 84–85
      feminist, 83, 529
      form, 45f, 55–60, 529
      historical, 45f, 46
      liberationist, 83, 529
      narrative, 68–79, 534
      reader-response, 82–83, 536
      redaction, 45f, 60–63, 536
      rhetorical, 79–80, 537

criticism, literary (continued)
      source, 45f, 46–55, 538
      structuralism, 81–82, 538
cross, Jesus Christ's word on the, 33–34
Crossan, John Dominic, 373, 375, 528
      characteristics of Jesus Seminar founded by, 357f, 359,
            360, 364, 365
      contrasted with the Third Quest, 358f
      on Jesus as a Cynic-like philosopher, 366–68
      key works, 371f
crucifixion of Jesus Christ. *See* death of Jesus Christ, the
Culpepper, R. Alan, 68
curtain, temple, 192, 238
Cynic-like philosopher, Jesus as a, 366–68
Cynics, 366–68, 528
Cynics and Christian Origins (Downing), 371f
Cyrus the Great, 94–95
David, King, 223–24, 268
      descendants of, 412–15, 537
Davidic Messiah, 412–15, 528
      See also Messiah, Jesus as the
Da Vinci Code, The (Brown), 326f
Day of Atonement, 127
Dead Sea Scrolls, 135, 140–41, 392, 528
death of Jesus Christ, the, 33–34, 58, 162
      date of, 408
      historical circumstances of, 494–502
      Jesus' perspective on, 503–7
      Jesus' words and, 33–34
      Jewish opposition leading to, 497, 500–501, 502f
      in John, 325
      in Luke, 279
      in Mark, 191–92
      in Matthew, 237–38
      and the Passion Week chronology, 495f
      the resurrection as defeat over, 522–23
      roles of Pilate and the Romans in, 494–97, 502f
      and the Shroud of Turin, 520f
      significance of, 504–7
deconstruction (criticism), 83–84, 528
Dedication, Feast of, 318–20
deductive versus inductive methodologies, 362–63
deism, 528
de Jonge, Marinus, 377
deliberative rhetoric, 80
Derrida, Jacques, 83
de Saussure, Ferdinand, 81
desolation, abomination of, 526
destruction of Jerusalem, 116–18, 189–91, 234, 277,
      403–4, 481
development of the Gospel tradition, 44–46
Diaspora, 99f, 100, 528
Diatessaron, 32, 528
Dibelius, Martin, 57
didache, 30, 528
Diogenes of Sinope, 366

discipleship, 528
disciples of Jesus Christ, the, 38, 528
    and the Beloved Disciple, 302, 327–28, 329, 333–34, 527
    called by Jesus, 474–77, 539
    and the cost of discipleship, 445–46
    and the Great Commission, 230, 238–39, 326, 530
    Jesus' prayer for, 323–24
    in John, 322–24, 326–28
    at the Last Supper, 235–36, 505
    in Luke, 270, 282–83
    in Mark, 197–98
    in Matthew, 242–44
    models of true, 176f, 200, 204–5
    reliability of, 388
    teaching and training of, 184–85, 275, 329
    as witnesses to the resurrection, 515–16, 520–21
discourses
    Farewell, 323, 529
    Jesus' five major, 219–20, 221f, 228–29, 231, 233–34
    Olivet, 189–91, 203, 233–34, 495f, 534
    time, 72
dissimilarity, criterion of, 360, 471
divergent traditions, criterion of, 361
divine men, Hellenistic, 459–60, 528
divine sovereignty, 286
divorce, 151–52
Docetism, 203, 336, 528
Domitian (Roman leader), 113f, *115*
doublets, 391–92, 528
Downing, F. Gerald, 366, 371f
dualism, theological, 310–11, 329, 529
Dunn, James D. G., 377
dyadism, 161, 529, 530
dynamic characters, 73, 529
early church, the
    preaching of the Gospel in, 58
    as primarily oral, 59
earthquakes, 238
Ebeling, Gerhard, 356
education in Judaism, 118, 124–25, 131, *387*
Egypt, 98, 100–101
Ehrman, Bart, 365, 374
Ein Kerem, *265*
embarrassment, criterion of, 361
Emmaus disciples, 279–80
entertainment and leisure in New Testament times, 160–61
Ephesus, *300*, 336
epideictic rhetoric, 80
Epiphanes, Antiochus (Roman leader), 100–101, 132, 526
equality, ontological, 328, 535
eschatology, 136, 529
    consistent, 353
    and Jesus as an eschatological prophet, 372–77
    and the kingdom of God, 439–40
    realized, 331, 536
    in Third Quest scholarship, 365

Essenes, 104, 135–36, 529
eternal life, 331, 529
ethos, 80
eucharistic words of Jesus, 504–5, 529
Eusebius (historian), 116, 201, 203
euthys, 175f
evaluative point of view, 69–70, 529
evangelistic nature of the Gospels, 30
    redaction criticism and, 61–62
Evangelists, the, 29, 529
events, sequence of, 71, 529
    contradictions in, 390–92
    intercalation and, 77, 174–77
    in Mark, 174
    in Matthew, 218–19
evidence for the resurrection, 518–21
exhortatory nature of the Gospels, 30
exorcisms, 174, 180, 401–2, 439, 461–62, 470, 5329
explanation, criterion of, 362
eyewitness testimonies on Jesus, 387
Ezra, 95, 130
faith
    Christ of, 353, 532
    discussed in Mark, 175, 176f
    and faithful transmission of the Gospel tradition, 387, 525
family life in New Testament times, 150–52
    group mentality and, 161
    kinship and, 163
family life of Jesus, 175, 182–83, 419–22
Farewell Discourse, 323, 529
Farmer, William R., 53
farming, 157–59
    and the parable of the wicked tenant farmers, 187, 189, 190f, 448
Feast of Dedication, 318–20
feeding the five thousand, Jesus', 314–16
feminist criticism, 83, 529
festivals, Jewish, 313–14f, 315f, 316–18, 318–20, 333, 530
fig tree, Jesus' cursing the, 464, 481, 495f
fig trees, 187
First Quest for the Historical Jesus, 348–50, 529, 536
fishing, 158, *271*
Five Gospels: The Search for the Authentic Words of Jesus, The (Funk, Hoover, and the Jesus Seminar), 357f
flat characters, 73, 529
Florus, Gessius, 115
food and meals in New Testament times, 152–53
forgiveness of sins, 472–73
form criticism, 45f, 46, 529
    assessment of, 58–60
    categories used in, 56f, 57, 58–59
    goals of, 58
    method of, 55–58
    miracle stories and, 56f, 57
    passion narratives and, 56f, 58

form criticism (continued)
    positive contributions of, 58–59
    pronouncement stories and, 56f, 57–58
    sayings and parables and, 56f
    stories about Jesus and, 56f
    weaknesses and dangers of, 59–60
Fortress of Antonia, *112*
Four Gospels: A Study of Origins, The (Streeter), 51
four-source theory of the Synoptic Gospels, 48, 50–51, 529, 539
Fredriksen, Paula, 364, 365, 374
Frei, Hans, 68
Füchs, Ernst, 356
fulfillment formulas, 529
    Jesus as fulfillment of the law and, 442–44
    in Luke, 284–85
    in Matthew, 216–18, 245, 246f
functional subordination, 328, 529
Funk, Robert, 357f, 358f
Galilee
    fishing at, 158, *271*
    Jesus' ministry in, 269–73
Galilee, Sea of, 158, *196*, *229*, *271*, *430*
    fishing in, 158
Gallio of Achaia (Roman leader), 112
Gamaliel (rabbi), 131, 250f
Garden of Gethsemane, 159, 236, *237*
Gardner-Smith, P., 301
genealogies, 529
genealogy of Jesus Christ, 220, 223–24, 268, 412–15
genre, 25–27, 28f, 530
    of the birth narratives, 412
    identification, 58–59
Gentiles, 198, 224, 288, *288*, 530
    salvation for, 286–87, 311–12, 478–79
"Gettysburg Address," 92
Gibson, Mel, 384
girls in New Testament times, 150–51
gladiators, 160
Gnosticism, 30, 32, 33f, 530
God
    character of, 444–45
    covenant with Israel, 124
    divine sovereignty and purpose of, 286
    Jesus as, 488–89
    Jesus equal with, 328
    Jesus' self-identification as, 317, 319, 349–50
    kingdom of, 29, 199–200, 438–40, 532
    the Lamb of, 303–4, 308, 393, 533
    law of, 124–25, 441–44
    "the one and only," 306f
    prayer and intimate fellowship with, 289
    presence and wisdom in Jesus, 240–41
    revealed through the Son, 330–31
    salvation as knowing, 331
    salvation through, 284–85

God (continued)
    Son of, 172, 177, 178–83, 186, 193–95, 226, 231, 241–42, 485–86, 538
    as Yahweh, 124, 317, 488, 504–5, 540
Golden Rule, the, 271
Golgotha, *501*
Good Samaritan, The, 274f, 447
Good Shepherd, the, 318–20
Gospel for the Outcast, 274, 530
Gospel of Peter, 32, 41, 360
Gospel of the Ebionites, 42
Gospel of the Hebrews, 42
Gospel of the Nazarenes, 42
Gospel of Thomas, 32, 41, 55, 357f, 359–60, 367, 530
gospels
    apocryphal, 32, 40–42, 55, 526
    doublets, 391–92, 528
    genre, 25–27, 28f
    infancy, 32, 42, 421, 531
    Synoptic, 25
    word origin, 26f
Gospels of the New Testament, the
    abbreviation and omission in, 389–90
    apologetic nature of, 30
    audiences of, 31–32
    catechetical nature of, 30
    contradictions between, 388–92
    development of, 44–46
    evangelistic nature of, 30
    exhortatory nature of, 30
    form criticism of, 45f, 55–60
    genre and, 25–27
    harmony of, 32, 35
    historical criticism of, 45f, 46
    as historical literature, 27
    as historical record, 30
    historical reliability of, 384–96
    historical setting of, 94–119
    horizontal reading of, 34, 536
    liturgical nature of, 30
    modern reading of, 32–36, 205–6, 253, 291, 337, 525
    as myth, 351–52
    as narrative literature, 28
    paraphrasing and interpretation in, 388–89
    preached in the early church, 58
    presentations by, 24–25
    purpose of, 30
    reasons for four, 32
    redaction criticism of, 45f, 60–63
    reliability of the narrators of, 84–85
    religious setting of, 123–45
    reordering of events and sayings in, 390–91
    social and cultural setting of, 149–64
    source criticism of, 45f, 46–55
    as theological literature, 29, 30

Gospels, the (continued)
    as theological propaganda, 352
    unity and diversity in, 24, 540
    vertical reading of, 32–34, 537
    See also Synoptic Gospels, the
grace and works, 445–46
grapes, 159
Great Banquet, The, 274f
Great Commission, 230, 238–39, 326, 530
greatest commandment, the, 188f, 444–45
Greco-Roman sources of information, 38–39
Greek period, the
    Alexander the Great and the hellenization of Palestine
        in, 95–98
    family life during, 151–52
    Judaism during, 96–97
    language development during, 97–98
    Ptolemaic domination of Israel during, 98–100
    Seleucid domination of Palestine during, 100–101
Griesbach, J. J., 53
Griesbach hypothesis, 53–54, 530
group mentality, 161, 530, 530
groups within Judaism, 131–38
Gulf War, 172
Gunkel, H., 354f
ha-Nasi, Judah, 143
Hanukkah, 102, 530
harmonistic overview
    of Jesus' trials, 502f
    of the resurrection narratives, 513f
harmony of the Gospels, 32, 35, 530
Harvey, A. E., 358f
Hasidim, 101, 104, 530
    Essenes and, 135
Hasmonean dynasty, the, 102–4, 530
    power of Jewish priesthood during, 128
healing by Jesus Christ, 530
    a blind man, 318
    in Cana and Jerusalem, 312–14
    significance of, 462–63, 470
heaven, kingdom of, 246–47, 532
Hebrew language, 97–98, 252
Heidegger, Martin, 354f, 355–56
Hellenists, 95–98, 530
hellenization of Palestine, the, 95–98, 530
    and Antiochus IV, 100–101
    Hasmoneans and, 103–4
Hemer, Colin, 386
Herod Antipas, 108–9, 278, *279*, 402, 530
Herodians, 138
Herodium, the, *106*
Herod the Great, 530
    and Antipater, 104
    cruelty of, 105
    death of, 107
    Judaism under, 105–7, 126, 134

Herod the Great (continued)
    patronage and, 164
    pursuit of Jesus, 224, 418–19
    sons of, 108–10
high-priestly prayer, 323–24, 530
high priests of Judaism, 128, 530
Hillel, 152, 531
historical-critical method and Ernst Troeltsch, 350–51
historical criticism of the Gospels, 45f, 46
    form, 45f, 55–60
    nineteenth-century, 348–50
    redaction, 45f, 60–63
    source, 45f, 46–55
historical evidence for the resurrection, 518–21
Historical Figure of Jesus, The (Sanders), 371f, 372
Historical Jesus, The (Crossan), 371f
historical Jesus research
    conservative, 351f
    contemporary portraits of Jesus in, 365–77
    engagement trend, 351f
    First Quest, 348–50, 351f, 530, 536
    history of religions school, 353, 531
    Jesus Seminar, 350, 351f, 357–58f, 358, 532
    key figures in, 371f
    liberal, 349–50, 351f
    miracles and, 457–58
    New Quest, 351f, 356–57, 534
    No Quest, 350–56
    rejection trend, 351f
    role of presuppositions in, 384
    Rudolf Bultmann and the end of the First Quest, 350–56
    Third Quest, 351f, 358–77, 539
historical literature, the Gospels as, 27, 30
historical reliability of the Gospels
    bias of the Gospel writers and, 385
    burden of proof and, 385
    contradictions between the Gospels and, 388–92
    the Gospel tradition and, 386–88
    John and, 392–95
    Luke-Acts and ancient history writing and, 385–86
    role of presuppositions in historical research and, 384
    scope of sources in Third Quest scholarship and, 359–60
historical setting of the Gospels, the 94–119
    Gospel of John, 301, 332–37
    Gospel of Luke, 289–91
    Gospel of Mark, 201–5
    Gospel of Matthew, 249–53
    the Greek period and, 95–101
    the Maccabees and Jewish independence and, 101–4
    the Persian period and, 94–95
    the Roman period in, 104–19
historiography of Luke, 262–63, 531
history of religions school, 353, 531
History of the Jewish People in the Age of Jesus Christ, The
    (Schürer), 250f
History of the Jewish War, The (Josephus), 117f

Holocaust, the, 253, 385
Holy of Holies, 127, 192
Holy Spirit, the
    descent on Jesus at his baptism, 62
    as inspiration for the Gospels, 54f
    Jesus and God equal with, 240
    salvation and, 285–86
homes in New Testament times, 155–56
homosexuality, 151
Honi the Rainmaker, 368, 460
honor and shame, 161–63, 531
horizontal reading of the Gospels, 34, 536
Horsley, Richard, 369–70, 371f, 373, 375
hospitality, 163–64, 271–72
Huckleberry Finn (Twain), 69
Hume, David, *456*, 531
Hurtado, Larry, 488
hymns, birth narrative, 265–66, 286, 527
hyperbole, 437f, 531
hypocrisy and the Pharisees, 133f
Hyrcanus, John, 103, 135
Hyrcanus II, 103f, 104
"I am" statements, 317, 319, 349–50, 531
identity, group, 161
Idumean, 531
implied author, 531
implied readers, 70–71, 531
inclusio, 77, 192, 227, 531
inductive versus deductive methodologies, 362–63
Infancy Gospel of Thomas, The, 42
infancy gospels, 32, 42, 421, 531
"inn," 531
intercalation, 77, 531
    in Mark, 174–77
interpretation
    of the parables, 449–51
    and paraphrasing in the Gospels, 388–89
intertestamental period, the, 94–95
interviews with individuals, Jesus', 302, 303f, 310–12
inverse parallelism, 76–77
Irenaeus, 33f, 202
irony, 77–78
    in the Gospel of John, 304–5
    in the Gospel of Mark, 177
    used by Jesus, 437f
Isaiah, 190f
Israel. *See* Jerusalem
Jairus's daughter, raising of, 175, 463, 537
James, Son of Zebedee, 474f
James (brother of John), 110
James the Son of Alphaeus, 475f
Jamnia (city), 118, 531
Jannaeus, Alexander, 103, 104
Jehohanan, 497f
Jeremias, J., 440f
Jerome, 202

Jerusalem
    covenant of God with, 124
    destruction of, 116–18, 189–91, 234, 277, 403–4
    healings in, 312–14
    Jesus as the fulfillment of, 226
    Jesus confronts, 186–87, 188–89f, 232–35, 275–77
    Levites, 128
    ministry of Jesus to, 227–30, 275–77
    rejection of Jesus by, 230–31, 287–88
    travel narrative in Luke, 263, 273–75
    triumphal entry of Jesus into, 186–87, 321–22, 479–80, 495f, 539
    See also Palestine; temple, Jerusalem
Jesus: A New Vision (Borg), 371f
Jesus: A Revolutionary Biography (Crossan), 371f
Jesus and Judaism (Sanders), 371f, 372
Jesus and the Spiral of Violence (Horsley), 371f
Jesus and the Victory of God (Wright), 371f, 488
Jesus Christ
    accepted by his disciples, 230–31
    aims of, 473–81
    ancestry of, 220, 223–24, 268, 412–15
    apocryphal gospels on, 32, 40–42
    arrest and trial of, 35, 58, 162, 191, 235–38, 278–79, 324–25, 482–83, 494–507
    ascension of, 280, 286
    authenticity of the words and actions of, 360–62, 388–89, 470–73, 506–7
    authoritative ministry of, 179–83, 188f, 229, 470–89
    on banquets, 153, 288–89
    baptism of, 268, 429–30, 526
    betrayal of, 197, 235–36, 277–78, 495f
    birth narratives, 220–25, 264–68, 405–6, 417–19
    as the bread of life, 314–16
    calming of the sea, 174, 180
    central message of, 438–41
    changing water into wine at Cana, 308–9, 464–65, 534
    childhood of, 266–67, 276
    chronology of the life of, 405–8
    cleansing of the temple, 175, 309–10, 480–81, 495f
    compared to Moses, 281
    confession before the Sanhedrin, 175, 191–92, 236, 278–79
    conflicts with the Pharisees, 133, 181, 188–89f, 402–3
    confronts Jerusalem, 186–87, 188–89f, 232–35, 275–77
    contemporary portraits of, 365–77
    crucifixion of, 33–34, 58, 162, 191–92, 237–38, 279, 325, 494–507
    cursing the fig tree, 464, 481, 495f
    as a Cynic-like philosopher, 366–68

Jesus Christ (continued)

as the Davidic Messiah, 139–40, 224, 232–33,
239–40, 272–73, 377, 522–23, 533, 537
distinction between Christian prophets and words of, 387
on the end times, 189–90
equal with God, 328
as an eschatological prophet, 372
exorcisms by, 174, 180, 401–2, 439, 461–62
expectations of coming crisis, 503–4
on family and kinship, 163
family of, 175, 182–83, 419–22
Farewell Discourse of, 323, 529
at the Feast of Dedication, 318–20
feeding the five thousand, 314–16
five major discourses of, 219–20, 221f, 228–29, 231,
233–34
Flavius Josephus on, 39–40
as fulfillment of the law, 442–44
Galilean ministry of, 269–73
as God, 488–89
God revealed through, 330–31
and the "Golden Rule," 271
on the Good Shepherd, 318–20
Gospel for the Outcast, 274
Great Commission by, 230, 238–39, 326, 530
and the greatest commandment, 188f, 444–45
Greco-Roman sources of information on, 38–39
healings by, 312–14, 318, 462–63, 530
historical information about, 27
historical quests for, 348–57
of history versus faith, 353, 532
on honor and shame, 162
on hospitality, 164, 271–72
infancy gospels on, 32, 42
interviews with individuals, 302, 303f, 310–12
irony and, 177
as a Jewish mystic or spirit person, 368–69
Jewish references to, 39–40
John's portrayal of, 328
on the kingdom of God, 199–200, 438–40
as Lamb of God, 303–4, 308, 393, 533
letters of Paul on, 38
liberal scholarship on, 349–65
as light of the world, 316–18
as Lord, 282, 487–88
Luke's portrayal of, 281–82
Mark's portrayal of, 193–95
Matthew's portrayal of, 239–42
miracle-working by, 179–81, 195, 303, 307–16, 456–66
Nazareth sermon of, 269
Old Testament language used by, 240–41
Olivet Discourse of, 189–91, 203, 219f, 233–34, 495f,
534
parable of the wicked tenant farmers, 187, 189, 190f, 535
parables of the kingdom, 219f, 231, 447–51
passion narratives on, 56f, 58, 277–79

Jesus Christ (continued)

and the passion prediction, 184–85
on the poor and oppressed, 286
prayer for the disciples, 323–24
predicts the destruction of Jerusalem, 234, 277, 403–4,
481
preparation of, 178–79, 267–69
presence and wisdom of God in, 240–41
private teaching by, 302
proclaiming and interpreting the story of, 170
as a prophet like Moses, 281, 536
public debates, 302
radical skepticism of, 350–56
raising of the dead by, 175, 180, 303, 320–21, 349,
463–64, 536
ransom saying of, 505–7
rejected by Israel, 230–31, 287–88
resurrection of, 188f, 193, 238–39, 279–80, 495f,
512–23
on Sabbath work, 75
Satan and, 196
as the Second Person of the Trinity, 488–89
secrecy motif of, 180–81
self-identification as God, 317, 319, 349–50
Sermon on the Mount, *216*, 219f, 228–29, 240, 247, 537
as Servant of the Lord, 185, 197–98, 200, 537
social-cultural settings and, 75–76
as a social revolutionary, 369–72
and social status, 164
as Son of God, 172, 177, 178–79, 193–95, 225–27,
226, 231, 241–42, 483–86, 538
as Son of Man, 483–85, 538
stories about, 56f
suffering of, 31, 183–93, 282, 484–85, 503, 506–7, 538
as a teacher, 436–38
temptation of, *226*, 268–69, 430–32, 539
testimonies to, 307–8
theology surrounding, 29
as transcendent, 249
transfiguration of, 186, 272–73, 539
triumphal entry into Jerusalem, 186–87, 321–22,
479–80, 495f, 539
typology relating Israel and, 227
walking on water, 314–16, 466
washing the disciples' feet, 154
words on the cross, 33–34
Zealot tendencies of, 137–38
See also ministry of Jesus Christ; teacher, Jesus Christ as
Jesus Film, The, 291
Jesus of history, 353, 532
Jesus of Nazareth (Bornkamm), 356
Jesus Seminar, 350, 351f, 357–58f, 358–65, 364, 532
Jesus the Jew (Vermes), 368, 371f
Jesus the Magician (Smith), 371f
Jesus the Sage (Witherington), 371f
Jesus the Seer (Witherington), 371f

Jewish Revolt of AD 66–73, 114–16, 135, 532
Johannine community, 301, 334–35, 532
John, apostle, 201, 334, 336, 474f
John, Gospel of
    arrest and trial of Jesus in, 324–25
    authorship of, 332–34, 392–93
    basic outline of, 298
    Book of Glory in, 302, 322–27, 527
    Book of Signs in, 302, 307–22, 527
    central theme of, 298
    characteristics of, 299
    characters in, 329–30
    chiasm in, 305–6
    chronology in, 406f
    clearing of the temple in, 309–10
    compared to the Synoptic Gospels, 300–301
    composition of, 334–35
    content of, 298–99
    contradictions with the Synoptics, 395
    crucifixion of Jesus in, 325
    disciples portrayed in, 329
    epilogue, 327–28
    Feast of Dedication in, 318–20
    Feast of Tabernacles in, 316–18
    feeding the five thousand in, 314–16
    the Good Shepherd in, 318–20
    healing of a blind man in, 318
    healings in Cana and Jerusalem in, 312–14
    historical reliability of, 392–95
    historical settings, 301, 332–37
    interview with Nicodemus in, 302, 304, 310–11
    irony in, 304–5
    Jesus' arrival in Jerusalem, 321–22
    Jesus as light of the world in, 316–18
    Jesus' changing water into wine in, 308–9
    Jesus' teaching in, 302
    and Johannine community, 301, 334–35
    and the John Rylands manuscript, 335–37, 532
    key verse of, 298
    the Last Supper in, 322
    literary features of, 298–305
    literary style of, 299–300
    logos, 80, 301, 305, 334–35, 488, 533
    metaphor and symbol in, 303–4
    minor characters in, 330
    as the most theological of the Gospels, 25
    narrative purpose, 332
    paracletes of, 323, 331–32
    as part of the four New Testament Gospels, 533
    place, occasion, and date, 335–37
    plot of, 305–28
    portrayal of Jesus in, 328
    presentation, 25
    prologue of, 301–2, 305–7, 535
    raising of Lazarus in, 303, 320–21
    reading today, 337

John, Gospel of (continued)
    religious leaders in, 329–30
    resurrection of Jesus in, 325–27
    revelation of the Father through the Son in, 330–31
    Samaritan woman at the well in, 311–12
    seven "signs" of, 302f, 303, 537
    structure of, 301–2
    style and words of Jesus in, 394–95
    Synoptic Gospels and, 25
    testimonies to Jesus in, 307–8
    theological dualism in, 310–11, 329
    theological themes in, 330–32
    unique perspective of, 24–25, 298–300
    walking on water in, 314–16
John Rylands manuscript, 335–36, 532
Johnson, Luke Timothy, 354
John the Baptist, 61, 271–72, 532
    baptism of Jesus by, 268, 429–30
    birth of, 264–65, 426
    and the Essenes, 136
    execution of, 175, 197, 402, 428–29
    final testimony to Jesus, 311
    Herod Antipas and, 108
    and Jesus' healings, 462
    in John, 306
    as the last and greatest Old Testament prophet,
        428
    in Luke, 267–68
    in Mark, 178–79
    in Matthew, 225, 230
    as mentor, 375
    metaphor used by, 303–4, 308
    ministry of, 426–29
    preaching style of, 400–401
John the Elder, 334, 532
Jordan River, *430*
Joseph (father of Jesus), 108, 151
    birth narratives and, 220, 223–24, 264, 412
    family life of, 419–21
Joseph of Arimathea, 514, 516, 518, 532
Josephus, Flavius, 110, 128, 140, 532
    biography, 117f
    on the death of John the Baptist, 428f
    on Epaphroditus, 263f
    on the Essenes, 135
    on Honi the Rainmaker, 460
    on the Jewish revolt of AD 66–73, 115–16
    on the Pharisees, 132f, 134
    writings on Jesus, 39–40
    on Zealots, 136
Judaism, first-century
    after the revolt of AD 66–73, 116–19
    Am-ha-Eretz, 138
    Antiochus IV and, 100–101, 132, 527
    apocalypticism in, 138–39, 527
    and the Apocrypha, 141–42, 527

Judaism, first-century (continued)
    and the Bar Kokhba Revolt, 119, 527
    break with Christianity, 118–19, 249–50
    calendar and festivals, 313–14f, 315f, 316–18, 318–20, 333, 530
    charismatic holy men of, 368, 460–61, 527
    circumcision in, 124, 151
    clothing and style in, 154
    core beliefs, 124–25
    covenant with God, 124–25
    cynics in, 366–68, 528
    Day of Atonement, 127
    and the Dead Sea Scrolls, 135, 140–41
    and the Diaspora, 99f, 100, 529
    education in, 118, 124–25, 130–31, *387*
    Essenes in, 104, 135–36
    family life in, 150–52, 163
    food and meals, 153
    Gnosticism and, 33f
    during the Greek period, 96–97
    groups within, 131–38
    Hanukkah festival in, 102
    Herodians in, 138
    under Herod the Great, 105–7, 126, 134
    high court, 128–29
    high priests, 128, 531
    historians of, 117f
    and Israel's covenantal relationship with God, 124
    and the Jerusalem temple, 125–27
    and Jesus as an eschatological prophet, 372–77
    and Jewish opposition to Jesus, 497, 500–501
    and the kingdom of God, 438
    languages used in, 97–100
    law, 124–25, 441–44, 471–72
    Levites and, 128
    literary sources for, 140–45
    Maccabean revolt, 101–2, 533
    marriage and divorce in, 151–52, 317f, 415, 533
    messianic expectation, 139–40
    as monotheistic, 124
    origins of rabbinic, 118
    Orthodox, 134
    Pharisees in, 104, 109, 117f, 131, 132–34
    priests, 128, 535
    Qumran, 135, 140–41, 426, 476, 536
    rabbinic writings, 143–45, 536
    references to Jesus in, 39–40
    as a *religio licita*, 108f
    and the resurrection of Jesus, 521–22
    and the revolt of AD 66–73, 114–16, 135, 532
    and Roman taxation, 114
    Sadducees in, 104, 131, 538
    Sanhedrin, 128–29, 175, 191–92, 236, 278–79, 500–501, 537
    scribes, 130–31, 497, 500, 537
    and the Second Temple period, 94–95

Judaism, first-century (continued)
    Shema, 130f
    social banditry and, 136–38
    study of, 118
    synagogues of, 125, 126f, 129–30, 157
    tabernacle, 125–26
    and the Talmud, 40, 143, 458, 538
    and the Targums, 145
    and the Torah, 118, 124–25, 130–31, 539
    trends in, 138–40
    Yahweh of, 124–25, 317, 488, 504–5, 540
    Zealots, 136–38, 401, 540
    See also Jerusalem; Palestine
Judas (disciple), 235–36, 278, 475f
Judas (Maccabean leader), 102
Judas the Galilean, 137
Judas the Son of James, 475f
Judea under Roman governors, 112–13
judgment, final, 473
judicial rhetoric, 80
Jülicher, Adolf, 447–48, 532
justice, social, 446–47
Kähler, Martin, 353–54, 354f, 359, 532
Kant, Immanuel, 350
Käsemann, Ernst, 356, 532, 534
katalyma, 532
Kaylor, R. David, 370
Kennedy, George A., 80
Kepler, Johannes, 405, *406*
kerygma, 30, 532
keys to the kingdom, *243*
key verses
    of John, 298
    of Luke, 260
    of Mark, 172
    of Matthew, 214
Kidron Valley, *237*
kingdom of God, the, 29, 532
    as Jesus' central message, 438–40
    Jesus' preaching on, 438–40
    Judaism and, 438
    and the Last Supper, 505
    the law and, 247–48
    in Mark, 199–200
    in Matthew, 219f, 231
    parables of, 219f, 231, 449–51
    universal offer of, 477–78
kingdom of heaven, 246–47, 532
Kingsbury, Jack Dean, 68, 219, 222f, 241
kinship and family in New Testament times, 163
koine Greek, 97, 532
Kümmel, W. G., 440f
Kyrios Christos, 353, 487, 533
Ladd, G. E., 440f
Lamb of God, the, 303–4, 308, 393, 533
languages of Palestine, 97–100, 252, 488

Last Supper, the, 58, 408
    in the chronology of Passion Week, 495f
    eucharistic words at, 504–5, 529
    Jesus' words at, 504–5
    in John, 322
    in Luke, 277–78
law, the, 124–25
    authority of Jesus over, 471–72
    Jesus and, 246–47, 441–44
    Jesus as fulfillment of, 442–44
    true essence of, 441–42
laws of transmission, 59–60
Lazarus, raising of, 303, 320–21, 349, 537
leadership, servant, 185
legates, Roman, 112, 533
legendary development theory of the resurrection, 516–17,
    533
Lessing, Gotthold, 349
levirate marriage, 415, 533
Lévi-Strauss, Claude, 81
Levites, 128, 533
liberal scholarship on Jesus
    First Quest, 349–50, 351f
    Jesus Seminar, 350, 351f, 358–65
    New Quest, 351f, 356–57
    No Quest, 350–56
liberationist criticism, 83, 529
Life of Jesus (Renan), 349
Life of Jesus Critically Examined, The (Strauss), 351–52
Life of Josephus, The (Josephus), 117f
Life of Moses (Philo), 28f
light of the world, Jesus as, 316–18
Lincoln, Abraham, 92
literary criticism. *See* criticism, literary
literary devices
    chiasm, 76–77, 305–6, 527
    inclusio, 77, 192, 227, 531
    intercalation, 77, 174–77, 531
    irony, 77–78
    metaphor, 303–4, 534
    repetition, 76
    rhetoric, 76
    symbolism, 77
literary features
    of John, 298–305
    of Luke, 261–63
    of Mark, 173–77
    of Matthew, 215–20
literary sources for first-century Judaism, 140–45
literary style
    of John, 299–300
    of Luke, 262
    of Mark, 173–74, 217f
    of Matthew, 216–20
liturgical nature of the Gospels, 30
Lives of the Caesars (Suetonius), 28f

local setting, 74
logos, 80, 301, 305, 334–35, 488, 533
Lord, Jesus as, 282, 487–88, 533
Lost Coin, Lost Sheep, Lost Son, 274f
Lucian of Samosata, 39
Luke, Gospel of
    abbreviation and omission in, 389–90
    ancient history writing and, 385–86
    authorship of, 289–90
    basic outline of, 260
    betrayal of Jesus in, 277–78
    birth narrative in, 264–68, 285–86, 412, 417–19
    calling and training of disciples in, 270, 282–83
    central theme of, 260
    characteristics of, 260
    characters in, 282–84
    conflict in, 72
    contradictions in reporting events and sayings in,
        390–92
    date of writing of, 290
    Emmaus disciples in, 279–80
    fulfillment formulas in, 442–44
    Galilean ministry of Jesus in, 269–73
    historical setting of, 289–91
    historiography of, 262–63, 531
    Holy Spirit in, 285–86
    Jesus as Lord in, 282
    Jesus compared to Moses in, 281–82
    Jesus' confrontation of Jerusalem in, 275–77
    Jesus' journey to Jerusalem in, 263, 273–75
    Jesus' rejection by Jerusalem in, 287–88
    joy, praise, and celebration in, 288–89
    literary features of, 261–63
    literary style of, 262
    as the most thematic of the Gospels, 25
    narrative purpose, 290–91
    occasion and narrative purpose of, 290–91
    paraphrasing and interpretation in, 388–89
    as part of the four New Testament Gospels, 533
    passion narrative in, 277–79
    plot of, 263–80
    portrayal of Jesus in, 281–82
    prayer and intimate fellowship with God in, 289
    preparation of Jesus in, 267–69
    presentation, 25
    prologue, 44, 263, 535
    promise-fulfillment in, 284–85
    reading today, 291
    religious leaders in, 283–84
    reordering of events and sayings in, 390–91
    similarities with the other Synoptic Gospels, 46–47,
        49f
    sources, 262
    temptation of Jesus in, 430–32
    theological themes of, 284–89
    travel narrative in, 263, 273–75, 539

Luke, Gospel of (continued)
    unique perspective of, 24–25
    unity of Acts and, 261–62
Luke-Acts, 261–62, 385–86, 533
Maccabean revolt, the, 101–2, 533
Maccabeus, Judas, 101–2, 533
Macedonians. *See* Greek period, the
Machaerus, *429*
Mack, Burton, 358f, 366, 371f
Magdalene, Mary, 325–26, 513f, 515
magi, 418, 533
magic, first-century, 459
Man, Jesus as Son of, 483–85, 538
manna, 315–16
manuscript, John Rylands, 335–36
maranatha, 488, 534
Marginal Jew, A (Meier), 371f, 374, 533
Mark, Gospel of
    abbreviation and omission in, 389–90
    authoritative ministry of the Son of God in, 179–83,
        188f
    authorship of, 201–2
    basic outline of, 172
    Beelzebub controversy in, 175, 176f, 182
    central theme, 172
    characteristics of, 173
    characters in, 196–98
    compared to Matthew, 217f
    confession of Peter in, 183
    conflict in, 72, 181–83, 188–89f
    considered to be abbreviated version of Matthew, 173
    contradictions in reporting events and sayings in,
        390–92
    date of, 203–5
    death of Jesus in, 191–92
    disciples portrayed in, 197–98, 200, 204–5
    ending of, 194f
    euthys and historical present tense in, 175f
    exorcisms in, 174
    fulfillment formulas in, 442–44
    historical setting of, 201–5
    intercalation in, 174–77
    irony in, 177
    Jesus as Servant of the Lord in, 185
    Jesus confronts Jerusalem in, 186–87
    Jesus' triumphal entry into Jerusalem in, 186–87
    John the Baptist in, 178–79
    key verse of, 172
    kingdom of God teaching in, 199–200
    literary features of, 173–77
    literary style of, 173–74, 217f
    Markan priority and, 48, 50, 533
    minor characters in, 198
    miracle-working of Jesus in, 179–81, 195
    as the most dramatic of the Gospels, 24
    narrative purpose, 201–5

Mark, Gospel of (continued)
    narrative style of, 173–74
    narrator of, 69
    the Olivet Discourse in, 189–91, 203
    parable of the wicked tenant farmers in, 187, 189, 190f
    paraphrasing and interpretation in, 389
    as part of the four New Testament Gospels, 533
    passion prediction in, 184–85
    plot of, 178–93
    portrait of Jesus in, 193–95
    preparation for the Son of God in, 178–79
    presentation, 24
    purpose of, 204–5
    reading today, 205–6
    reordering of events and sayings in, 390–91
    resurrection of Jesus in, 193
    Satan's forces and religious leaders in, 196
    setting and occasion, 202–5
    similarities with the other Synoptic Gospels, 46–47,
        49f
    suffering of Jesus in, 183–93
    temptation of Jesus in, 430–32
    theological themes in, 199–200
    topical ordering of events in, 174
    transfiguration narrative in, 186
    triads or sets of threes, 177, 539
    unique perspective of, 24–25
Markan priority, 48, 50, 534
Mark Antony (Roman leader), 105
marriage, 151, 317f
    levirate, 415, 533
Marshall, I. H., 377
Martyr, Justin, 33f
Marxsen, Willi, 60
Mary (mother of Jesus), 108, 151
    birth narratives and, 220, 223–24, 264–65, 265, 412
    family life of, 419–20
    virginal conception by, 415–16
Masada, *115*, *115–16*, 116, *154*
materialism, 533
Mattathias (priest), 101–2
Matthean priority, 53–54
Matthew, Gospel of
    abbreviation and omission in, 389–90
    appearance of the Messiah in, 225–27
    arrest and trial of Jesus in, 235–38
    audience and occasion of, 249–51
    authorship of, 252–53
    basic outline of, 214
    birth narrative in, 412, 418
    central theme of, 214
    characteristics of, 215
    characters in, 242–45
    compared to Mark, 217f
    concise style of, 216, 217f
    conflict in, 72

Matthew, Gospel of (continued)
  contradictions in reporting events and sayings in, 390–92
  crowds portrayed in, 245
  crucifixion of Jesus in, 237–38
  disciples portrayed in, 242–44
  five major discourses of, 219–20, 228–29, 231, 233–34
  fulfillment formulas in, 216–18, 245, 246f, 442–44
  genealogy and birth narrative in, 220–25
  historical setting of, 249–53
  inclusio in, 227
  and Jesus as the Son of God, 226, 231, 241–42
  Jesus rejected by Israel and accepted by the disciples in, 230–31
  Jesus the Messiah portrayed in, 239–40
  key verses, 214
  kingdom of heaven in, 246–47
  literary features of, 215–20
  literary style of, 216–20
  Mark considered an abbreviated version of, 173
  Matthean priority and, 53–54
  ministry of the Jesus to Israel in, 227–30
  as the most structured of the Gospels, 24–25
  narrative and theological purpose, 248–49
  narrative-discourse chiasm in, 221f
  narrative progression in, 222f
  narrative purpose, 248–49
  Old Testament quotations in, 216–18, 226f
  Olivet Discourse in, 233–34
  outlines of, 221–22f
  paraphrasing and interpretation in, 388–89
  as part of the four New Testament Gospels, 533
  Peter portrayed in, 243–44
  place and date, 251–52
  plot of, 220–39
  portrayal of Jesus in, 239–42
  presence of wisdom of God through Jesus in, 240–41
  presentation, 24–25
  prologue, 220–25
  promise-fulfillment theme in, 245
  reading today, 253
  religious leaders portrayed in, 245
  reordering of events and sayings in, 390–91
  resurrection and the Great Commission in, 238–39
  salvation history in, 245
  sequence of events in, 218–19
  similarities with the other Synoptic Gospels, 46–47, 49f
  structural signals and "outline" of, 219–20, 538
  temptation of Jesus in, 430–32
  on the theft theory, 515
  theological themes of, 245–48
  topical arrangement of, 218–19
  unique perspective of, 24–25

Matthew the tax collector, 475f
McKnight, Scot, 220, 222f
Meeting Jesus Again for the First Time (Borg), 371f
Meier, John P., 358f, 362, 363, 365, 533
  and Jesus as an eschatological prophet, 374–75
  key works, 371f
Messiah, Jesus as the, 139–40, 172, 177, 377, 533
  appearance of, 225–27
  contemporary portraits of, 377
  in Luke, 272–73
  in Mark, 193–95, 200
  in Matthew, 224, 225–27, 231, 232–33, 239–40
  the resurrection and, 522–23
messianic banquet, 153, 534
messianic expectation, 139–40
messianic secret, 180f, 352, 534
Messianic Secret, The (Wrede), 180f, 352
metaphor, 534
  and symbol in the Gospel of John, 303–4
  used by Jesus, 437f
methodological doubt, principle of, 350
Meyer, Ben, 358f
Michie, Donald, 68
midrash, 412, 534
mikveh, 534
Millar, Fergus, 250f
ministry of Jesus Christ
  aims and, 473–81
  authority of, 179–83, 188f, 229, 470–73
  chronology of, 406–8
  in Galilee, 269–73
  general progress of, 404–5
  Holy Spirit in, 286
  to Israel, 227–30, 275–77
  portrait of, 400–404
miracles
  ancient parallels to Jesus', 459–61
  exorcism, 174, 180, 401–2, 439, 461–62, 470, 529
  and the historical method, 457–58
  in John, 303, 307–16
  in Luke, 308–9
  in Mark, 179–81, 195
  nature, 308–9, 314–16, 464–66, 534
  philosophical objections to, 456–57
  proof that Jesus performed, 458–59
  raising of the dead, 175, 180, 303, 349, 463–64, 536
  significance of Jesus', 461–66
  stories, 56f, 57, 534
  Third Quest treatment of, 363–65
Mishnah, 143, 534
missionaries, modern, 291
monotheism, 124, 534
Mormons, 214–15
Moses, 124–25, 125, 128, 219, 228, 441
  Jesus compared to, 281, 536
  seventy elders appointed by, 128

Mount Gerizim, *312*
Mount of Beatitudes, *216*
Mount of Olives, 234, *235*, *276*, 278
Mount of Temptation, *226*, *432*
Mount Sinai, 124, *125*, 228
Mount Zion, *322*
Muilenburg, James, 80
multiple attestation, criterion of, 360–61, 471
mystic, Jesus as a Jewish, 368–69
Myth of Innocence, The (Mack), 371f
Nag Hammadi Codices, 33f, 41, 534
narratees, 70–71
narrative criticism
    assessment of, 78–79
    defined, 534
    focus of, 68
    scholars in, 68
    strengths of, 78
    weaknesses of, 78
narrative-discourse chiasm, 221f
narrative literature
    causation in, 71
    characterization in, 72
    characters in, 73–74
    chiasm in, 76–77
    conflict in, 71–72
    evaluative point of view in, 69–70
    the Gospels as, 28
    inclusio in, 77
    intercalation in, 77
    irony in, 77–78
    narrative world in, 69–70
    plot in, 71–73
    rhetoric, 76
    scenes, 71
    setting in, 74–76
    story receiver in, 70–71
    storyteller in, 69
    symbolism in, 77
narrative patterns, 76–78
narrative progression, 222f
narrative purpose, 30
    in John, 332
    in Luke, 290–91
    in Mark, 201–5
    in Matthew, 248–49
narratives, passion, 56f, 58, 277–79, 535
narrative style, 173–74
narrative time, 72, 534
narrative world, 69–70, 534
narrators, 173–74, 534
natural or supernatural presuppositions, 363–65
nature miracles, 308–9, 314–16, 464–66, 534
Nazareth, *179*, 304, 416, *421*, 534
    sermon of Jesus, 269–70
Nehemiah, 95

Nero (Roman leader), 38, 113f, 115, *204*, 205
New Quest for the Historical Jesus, 351f, 356–57, 534
Newsweek, 150
New Testament, the. *See* John, Gospel of; Luke, Gospel of;
    Mark, Gospel of; Matthew, Gospel of
Nicodemus, 302, 304, 310–11, 534
nineteenth-century scholarship on Jesus, 348–56
nomism, covenantal, 373, 528
nonhistoricity presuppositions, 59
No Quest period, the
    Bultmann, Rudolf, and, 57, 350, 353, 354f
    extreme skepticism and, 355–56, 534
    Gospels as myth in, 351–52
    Gospels as theological propaganda and, 352
    historical-critical method in, 350–51
    history of religions school and, 353
    Jesus as apocalyptic prophet in, 352–53
    Jesus of history and Christ of faith in, 353–54
    Kähler, Martin, and, 353
    Schweitzer, Albert, and, 350
    Strauss, David F., and, 351–52, 354f
    Troeltsch, Ernst, and, 350–51
    Weiss, Johannes, and, 352–53
    Wrede, William, and, 180f, 352, 354f
Octavian (Roman leader), 105, 108, 110–11, 113f, *266*,
    416–17, 527
oil, anointing with, 482
Old Testament, the
    allusions to the Last Supper, 505
    apocalyptic imagery of, 139
    on the coming Son of Man, 484, 484f
    Day of Atonement and, 127
    language used by Jesus, 240–41
    law, 124–25, 246–47
    and the Persian period, 94–95
    quotations in Matthew, 216–18, 226f
    references to the Son of God, 485–86
    references to the Son of Man, 484–85
    on salvation, 478–79
    Septuagint, 98–100, 537
    on slavery, 152
    the trial of Jesus, 500–501
    typology, 227, 539
olives, 158
Olivet Discourse, 189–91, 203, 219f, 233–34, 495f,
    534
Olympic Games, the, 161
omission and abbreviation in the Gospels, 389–90
"On Historical and Dogmatic Method in Theology"
    (Troeltsch), 350
ontological equality, 328, 535
optimism, historical, 359
Origen, 33f, 40, 202
Orthodox Judaism, 134
ossuary of James, brother of Jesus, 420f
Outcast, Gospel for the, 274, 530

outline, basic
  of John, 298
  of Luke, 260
  of Mark, 172
  of Matthew, 214
outsiders, salvation for, 286–87, 311–12, 478–79
paganism, 33f, 536
Palestine, 27, 536
  evaluative point of view and, 70
  the Greek period in, 95–101
  the hellenization of, 95–98
  Jewish Revolt of AD 66–73, 114–16
  languages of, 97–98, 488
  the Maccabean period in, 101–4
  the Persian period in, 94–95
  the Roman period in, 104–19
  Seleucid domination of, 100–101
  villages, towns, and cities of, 155–57
  See also Jerusalem
Palm Sunday, 186–87, 321–22, 479–80
Papias, 55, 201
Papyrus Egerton 2, 41–42
parables of the kingdom, 219f, 231, 447–51, 535
  interpreting, 449–51
  nature of, 447–48
  purpose of, 448–49
paracletes, 323, 331–32
paradox, 437f, 535
parallelism
  antithetical, 436, 526
  inverse, 76–77
  synonymous, 436, 538
Parallel Lives (Plutarch), 28f
paraphrasing and interpretation in the Gospels,
      388–89
passion narratives, 56f, 58, 277–79, 535
Passion of the Christ, The (motion picture), 384
passion predictions, 184–85, 503, 535
Passion Week chronology, 495f
Passover, 315f, 393–94, 404, 408
  and the Last Supper, 504–5
pathos, 80
patronage, 164, 535
Patte, Daniel, 82
patterns, narrative, 76–78
Paul, apostle, 202, 252
  authorship of Luke and, 289
  on the burial of Jesus, 518
  education of, 131
  imprisonment of, 290
  on Jesus' resurrection, 27, 512, 520
  on the Last Supper, 504
  letters of, 38
  Nero and, 113f
  time of, 204
  on witnesses to Jesus after his death, 457

Paul and Palestinian Judaism (Sanders), 373
Paulus, H. E. G., 349
Paulus, Sergius, 386
Paulus of Cyprus, Sergius (Roman leader), 112
Pax Romana, 110–14, 535
Peace Child (Richardson), 71
pederasty, 151
Pentateuch, Christian, 219–20, 221f
people of the land, 138
pericope, 55, 58, 59, 536
Persian period, the, 94–95
Persistent Widow, The, 274f
pessimism, historical, 359
Peter, apostle, 110, 474f
  confession of, 183, 272, 482–83, 528
  denial of Jesus, 191, 197, 235, 325
  fear and ignorance of, 231
  at the Last Supper, 322
  martyrdom of, 327–28
  Nero and, 113f
  and the passion prediction, 184–85
  portrayed in Matthew, 243–44
  time of, 203–4
Peterson, Norman R., 68
Pharisee and the Tax Collector, The, 274f
Pharisees, 104, 109, *117*, 535
  beliefs, 133
  characteristics of, 132–33
  conflicts with Jesus, 133, 181, 188–89f, 402–3
  Josephus on, 132f
  opposition to Jesus, 497, 500
  political influence of, 134
  as scribes, 131
Phasael (Roman leader), 104
Philip, apostle, 474f
Philip, Herod (Roman leader), 110
Philip II of Macedon, 95
Philo (scholar), 140, 496, 535
Pilate, Pontius, 38, 40, 44, *112*, 373, 535
  as governor of Juda and Samaria, 108, 113, 494–97
  in Matthew, 236–37
  and the trial of Jesus, 237, 278–79, 325, 404, 494–97,
      501
Pliny the Younger, 39
plot, 71–73, 536
  of John, 305–28
  of Luke, 263–80
  of Mark, 178–93
  of Matthew, 220–39
Poe, Edgar Allan, 69
point of view, evaluative, 69–70, 529
Polybius, 386
polygamy, 151
Pompey (Roman general), 104
Pool of Bethesda, 313, *313*, 472
Pool of Siloam, *318*

poor and oppressed, salvation for the, 286
position, social, 164
post-structuralism, 82
prayer
        high-priestly, 323–24, 530
        and intimate fellowship with God, 289
predictions, passion, 184–85, 503, 535
prefects, Roman, 112, 535
presentations by the four Gospels, 24–25
present tense, historical, 175f
presuppositions
        of nonhistoricity, 59
        role in historical research, 384
pride, 283–84
priests, Jewish, 128, 535
private teaching by Jesus Christ, 302
proclaiming and interpreting the story of Jesus, 170
proconsuls, Roman, 111, 386, 535
procurators, Roman, 112
progress of Jesus' ministry, 404–5
prologue
        of John, 301–2, 305–7, 535
        of Luke, 44, 263, 535
        of Matthew, 220–25
promise-fulfillment
        in Luke, 284–85
        in Matthew, 216–18, 245, 246f
pronouncement stories, 56f, 57–58, 536
proof, burden of, 385, 527
Propp, Vladimir, 81
proselyte baptism, 536
Protevangelium of James, 42
proverbs and aphorisms, 437f, 536
Psalms of Solomon, 139, 476, 483
pseudepigrapha, 143, 536
pseudepigraphic nature of the Gospels, 32
Ptolemaic domination of Israel, 98–100, 536
Ptolemy II Philadelphus, 99f
public buildings in New Testament times, 156
public debates, Jesus', 302
Publius (Roman leader), 386
pun, 437f, 537
purpose, narrative, 30
        in John, 332
        in Luke, 290–91
        in Mark, 201–5
        in Matthew, 248–49
purpose of God, 286
Q hypothesis, 51–53
Quest for the Historical Jesus, The (Schweitzer), 350, 353, 372
Qumran community, 135, 140–41, 426, 476, 536
rabbinic Judaism, 118
rabbinic writings, 143–45, 536
radical skepticism, 350–56
raising of the dead by Jesus, 175, 180, 303, 349, 463–64, 536

ransom saying of Jesus, 505–7
rationalism, 348, 349–50, 351f, 536
        and explanations for the resurrection, 512–18
reader-response criticism, 82–83, 536
readers
        implied, 532
        real, 70–71, 536
        story, 70–71
Reader's Digest, 220
reading the Gospels today, 32–36, 525, 536
        Gospel of John, 337
        Gospel of Luke, 291
        Gospel of Mark, 205–6
        Gospel of Matthew, 253
real author, 536
realized eschatology, 331, 536
real readers, 70–71, 536
receivers, story, 70–71
redaction criticism, 45f, 46, 536
        assessment of, 62–63
        goals of, 60, 61
        method of, 61–62
        positive contributions of, 62
        weaknesses of, 63
Reimarus, Herman Samuel, 348–49, 536
reliability, historical
        bias of the Gospel writers and, 385
        burden of proof and, 385
        contradictions between the Gospels and, 388–92
        Gospel tradition and, 386–88
        of John, 392–95
        Luke-Acts and ancient history writing and, 385–86
        role of presuppositions in historical research and, 384
        scope of sources in Third Quest scholarship and, 359–60
Religion of Jesus the Jew, The (Vermes), 371f
religious setting of the Gospels, 123–45
        core Jewish beliefs and, 124–25
        groups within Judaism, 131–38
        literary sources for first-century Jewish life and, 140–45
        synagogues, scribes, and the study of Torah, 129–31, 157
        temple, priesthood, and sacrifices, 125–29
        trends within first-century Judaism, 138–40
Renan, Ernest, 349
repetition, 76
resurrection of Jesus Christ, the
        appearances after, 513f
        as the beginning of the last days, 522
        in the chronology of Passion Week, 495f
        as the defeat of Satan, sin, and death, 522–23
        the empty tomb and, 518–19
        harmonistic overview of the narratives of, 513f
        historical evidence for, 518–21
        in John, 325–27
        legendary development theory of, 516–17, 533
        in Luke, 279–80
        in Mark, 188f, 193

resurrection of Jesus Christ, the (continued)
in Matthew, 238–39
the Old Testament and, 521–22
rationalistic explanations for, 512–18
significance of, 521–23
swoon theory of, 512–14, 538
theft theory of, 515–16, 539
as vindication of the message and mission of Jesus, 512
visionary and legendary development theories of, 516–17
witnesses to, 519, 520–21
wrong tomb theory of, 514–15, 540
resuscitations, 175, 180, 303, 349, 463–64, 537
revivications, 175, 180, 303, 349, 463–64, 537
rhetoric, 537
rhetorical criticism, 79–80, 537
Rhoads, David, 68
Rich Fool, The, 274f
Rich Man and Lazarus, The, 274f
riddles, 437f, 537
rock and foundation of the church, 244f
rolling tombstones, *514–15*
Roman empire, the
after the Jewish revolt, 116–19
and the Bar Kokhba Revolt, 119
census, 416–17, 527
clothing and style in, 154
commerce, transportation, and communication in, 159–60
and the destruction of Jerusalem, 116–18
entertainment and leisure, 160–61
family life in, 151–52
food and meals in, 152–53
government structure, 111–12
Herodian dynasty and, 108–10
Herod the Great and, 105–7, 126, 128–29
hospitality in, 163–64
and the Jewish Revolt of AD 66–73, 114–16, 135, 532
Judaism as a *religio licita* under, 108f
legates, 112, 533
patronage in, 164
and the *Pax Romana*, 110–14, 535
political stability in, 110–11
political tendencies of Jewish groups under, 137f
and the Qumran community, 135
rise of, 104–5
slavery in, 152
social status in, 164
taxation in, 113–14, 133, 188f, 198, 252, 275
treatment of Zealots, 137
villages, towns, and cities, 155–57
work, trades, and professions during, 157–59
round characters, 73, 537
Sabbath, the, 313–14, 519

Sadducees, 104, 537
beliefs and power of, 131
differences between Pharisees and, 132–33
as scribes, 131
and the trial of Jesus, 500–501
sailing, 159
salvation
eternal life and, 331, 529
and forgiveness of sins, 472–73
of God through Jesus, 284–85
grace and works in, 445–46
history, 245, 537
and the Holy Spirit, 285–86
as knowing God, 331
for outsiders, 286–87, 311–12, 478–79
and the ransom saying, 505–7
for Samaritans, 287, 311–12
of sinners and tax collectors, 287, 477–78
for women, 287, 311–12
Samaritans, 103, 287, 311–12
and parable of the good Samaritan, 274f, 447
Sanders, E. P., 358f, 363, 365, 481, 537
and Jesus as an eschatological prophet, 372–74
key works, 371f
Sanders, James A., 81
"sandwiching," 77, 532
in Mark, 174–77
Sanhedrin, the
role of, 128–29, 537
trial of Jesus before, 175, 191–92, 236, 278–79, 500–501
Satan, 70, 71, *226*
Jesus' defeat of, 246, 470, 482, 522–23
in Mark, 196
sayings and parables, 56f
scenes, 71, 527, 537
Schürer, Emil, 250f
Schweitzer, Albert, 350, 353, 365, 372, 374, 440f, 537
scribes, Jewish, 130–31, 537
opposition to Jesus, 497, 500
Seat of Moses, *234*
Second Quest for the Historical Jesus. *See* New Quest for the Historical Jesus
Second Temple period, the, 94–95, 126, 537
the Apocrypha of, 141–42
pseudepigrapha, 143
secrecy motif of Jesus, 180–81
secret, messianic, 180f, 352, 534
Secret Gospel of Mark, The, 41
Sejanus, 496
Seleucids, 98, 537
self-righteousness, 283–84
Semitic flavor, criterion of, 361, 471
Seneca, 497f
Sepphoris, 421, 537
Septuagint, 98–100, 537

Sermon on the Mount, *216*, 219f, 228–29, 240, 247, 537
Servant of the Lord, Jesus as, 185, 200, 537
setting
    defined, 537
    evaluative point of view and, 69–70
    historical. *See* historical setting of the Gospels, the
    local, 74
    social-cultural, 75–76
    temporal, 74–75
shame and honor, 161–63, 531
Shammai, 152, 537
Shaw, Bernard, 172
Shema, 130f
Shemoneh Esreh, 250f
shepherding, 157
Shroud of Turin, 520f
signals, structural, 219–20, 538
"signs" of the Gospel, 302f, 303, 537
simile, 437f, 537
Simon Peter, brother of Andrew, 32, 41
Simon the Cananaean, 475f
sin
    Jesus' authority to forgive, 472–73, 477–78
    Jesus' defeat of, 522–23
Sitz im Leben, 57, 59–60, 61, 355, 538
skepticism, extreme, 355–56, 534
slavery, 152
Smith, Joseph, 215
Smith, Morton, 41, 371f
So-Called Historical Jesus, The (Kähler), 353
social and cultural setting of the Gospels, 75–76, 79,
    149–64
    clothing and style in, 154
    commerce, transportation, and communication in,
    159–60
    entertainment and leisure in, 160–61
    family life in, 150–52, 163
    food and meals in, 152–53
    honor and shame in, 161–63
    hospitality in, 163–64
    kinship in, 163
    patronage in, 164
    social status and position in life and, 164
    social values in, 161–64
    villages, towns, and cities in, 155–57
    work, trades, and professions in, 157–59
social bandits, 136–38
social justice, 446–47
social revolutionary, Jesus as a, 369–72
social values in New Testament times, 161–64
Solomon, King, 126
Song of the Vineyard, 190f
Son of David, 412–15, 539
Son of God, Jesus as the, 172, 177, 186, 193–95, 538
    authoritative ministry of, 179–83
    identified in Matthew, 226, 231, 241–42

Son of God, Jesus as the (continued)
    Old Testament references and, 485–86
    preparation for, 178–79
Son of Man, Jesus as the, 483–85, 538
source criticism
    components of, 45f, 46
    goals of, 50, 538
    Markan priority and the two- and four-source theories,
      48, 50–51
    Matthean priority and, 53–54
    Q hypothesis and, 51–53
    and similarities between the three Synoptic Gospels,
      46–47
spirit person, Jesus as a, 368–69
St. Catherine's Monastery, *125*
static characters, 73, 538
status, social, 164
story receivers, 70–71
story time, 72, 539
Strauss, David Friedrich, 351–52, 354f, 363, 538
    on the theft theory, 515–16
Streeter, B. H., 51
structuralism, 81–82, 538
structural signals in Matthew, 219–20, 538
structure of the Gospel of John, 301–2
Stuhlmacher, Peter, 377
style, literary
    of John, 299–300
    of Luke, 262
    of Mark, 173–74
    of Matthew, 216, 217f
subordination, functional, 328, 529
Suetonius, 38–39
suffering Servant, Jesus Christ as, 31, 282, 484–85,
    506–7, 538
supernatural or natural presuppositions, 363–65
swoon theory of the resurrection, 512–14, 538
symbolism, 77, 538
    in the Gospel of John, 303–4
synagogues, 125, 126f, 129–30, 157, 538
synonymous parallelism, 436, 538
Synoptic Gospels, the, 25, 534, 538
    Augustine on, 47–48
    compared with the Gospel of John, 300–301
    contradictions between, 388–92
    contradictions with John, 395
    four-source theory, 48, 50–51, 529, 539
    harmony of, 32, 35, 530
    Jesus identified as God in, 488–89
    Jesus identified as Son of God in, 486–87
    Jesus identified as Son of Man in, 484–85
    Jesus identified as the Messiah in, 482–83
    Matthean priority and, 53–54
    observations and cautions on theories of, 54–55
    prologues, 44, 220–25, 263, 301–2, 305–7,
      535

Synoptic Gospels, the, (continued)
  sayings source "Q," 538
  similarity between, 46–47, 49f
  on the tomb of Jesus, 515
  traditional solutions to the problem of, 47–49
  two-gospel hypothesis, 53–54, 530
  two-source theory, 48, 50–51, 529, 539
  See also Gospels of the New Testament, the; Luke, Gospel of; Mark, Gospel of; Matthew, Gospel of
Syria, 98, 100
  after Herod Philip, 110
  and the Maccabees, 102
  as origin of the Gospel of Matthew, 251
  Roman legates of, 112
tabernacle, 125–26, 538
Tabernacles, Feast of, 316–18
Tacitus, 38, 111, 205
Tale of Two Cities, A (Dickens), 79
Talmud, the, 40, 143, 458, 538
Tannehill, Robert, 68
Targums, 145, 539
taxes
  collectors, 252, 275, 449–50
  under the Roman Empire, 113–14, 133, 188f, 198
  salvation for collectors of, 287
Taylor, Vincent, 57
teacher, Jesus Christ as
  on the character of God, 444–45
  of the disciples, 184–85, 275, 329
  at the Feast of Dedication, 318–20
  figures of speech and style of, 302, 436–38
  on grace and works, 445–46
  on the greatest commandment, 444–45
  on the kingdom of God, 438–40
  on the law, 441–44, 471–72
  parables of the kingdom and, 219f, 231, 447–51
  on social justice, 446–47
tekton, 420, 538
Tell-Tale Heart, A (Poe), 69
temple, Jerusalem
  as the center of Israel's religious life, 125–27
  courtyards of, 126–27
  curtain, 192, 238
  destruction of the second, 116–18, 189–91, 481
  first, 126
  Hillel and, 152, 532
  Holy of Holies, 127, 192
  Jesus' cleansing of, 175, 309–10, 480–81, 495f
  and the Second Temple period, 94–95, 126, 538
  symbolic judgment against, 176f, 287–88
  See also Jerusalem
temporal setting, 74–75
temptation of Jesus Christ, *226*, 268–69, 430–32, 539
Tertullian, 33f, 202
Testimonium Flavianum (Josephus), 39–40
theft theory of the resurrection, 515–16, 539

theme, central
  of John, 298
  of Luke, 260
  of Mark, 172
  of Matthew, 214
theological literature, the Gospels as, 29, 30
theological themes
  in John, 330–32
  in Luke, 284–89
  in Mark, 199–200
  in Matthew, 245–48
theophany, 324, 539
Theophilus, 263, 289, 290, 539
Thessalonica, *386*
Third Quest for the Historical Jesus, 351f, 358–65, 539
  contemporary portraits of Jesus in, 365–77
  criteria of authenticity in, 360–62
  eschatology and, 365
  historical pessimism versus historical optimism and, 359
  inductive versus deductive methodologies in, 362–63
  natural or supernatural presuppositions in, 363–65
  nature of Jesus' context in, 365
  questions of method and context, 359–64
  scope and reliability of sources in, 359–60
Thomas, apostle, 313, 327, 475f
Thomas, Didymus Judas, 32, 41
Tiberius Caesar, 113f, *114*, *191*, *408*, 539
time
  discourse, 72
  narrative, 72, 534
  story, 72, 538
titles, Messianic
  Christ (Messiah), 481–83
  Lord, 282, 487–88
  Son of God, 178–83, 226, 231, 241–42, 484–85, 485–86
  Son of Man, 483–85
Titus (Roman leader), 115, *116*, 117f
tombstones, rolling, *514–15*
topical ordering of events, in Mark, 174
Torah, the, 118, 124–25, 143, *387*, 441, 539
  Pharisees and, 132
  teaching by scribes, 130–31
Trajan, 39
transfiguration of Jesus Christ, 186, 272–73, 539
transmission history, 59–60
transportation in New Testament times, 159–60
travel in New Testament times, 159–60
  and Jesus' journey to Jerusalem, 263, 273–75, 539
trends in first-century Judaism
  apocalypticism, 138–39
  messianic expectation, 139–40
triads, 191, 539
  in Mark, 177

trial of Jesus Christ, the, 35, 58, 162
    in the chronology of Passion Week, 495f
    false witnesses and judges at, 500–501
    harmonistic overview of, 502f
    Jewish, 502f
    in John, 324–25
    in Luke, 278–79
    in Matthew, 235–38
    Messianic titles of Jesus and, 482–83
    Roman, 502f
Trinity, Jesus as the Second Person of the, 488–89
triumphal entry in Jerusalem, Jesus', 186–87, 321–22,
    479–80, 495f, 539
Troeltsch, Ernst, 350, 539
true essence of the law, 441–42
Twain, Mark, 69
Twelve, the, 474–77, 540
two-gospel hypothesis, 53–54, 530
two-source theory of the Synoptic Gospels, 48, 50–51,
    529, 539
typology, 227, 539
unity
    and diversity among the four Gospels, 24–25, 539
    of Luke and Acts, 261–62
values, social, 161–64
Vermes, Geza, 250f, 358f, 368
    key works, 371f
verses, key
    of John, 298
    of Luke, 260
    of Mark, 172
    of Matthew, 214
vertical reading of the Gospels, 32–34, 536
Vespasian (Roman leader), 113f, 115, *116*, 117f
Via Dolorosa, *506*
villages, towns, and cities in New Testament times, 155–57

vineyards, 159
virginal conception of Jesus Christ, 415–16, 539
von Harnack, Adolf, 349–50
Wailing Wall, the, *118*
walking on water, Jesus', 314–16, 466
Weiss, Johannes, 352–53, 354f, 365, 372, 440f, 539
Western Wall, the, *118*
What Is Christianity? (von Harnack), 349
Who Was Jesus? (Wright), 371f
wicked tenant farmers, parable of the, 187, 189, 190f, 448,
    535
Wilder, Amos, 80
Witherington, Ben, III, 358f, 359, 364, 371f
witnesses to the resurrection, 519, 520–21
women
    caught in adultery, 317f
    childbearing and, 150–51
    salvation for, 287
    as witnesses to the resurrection, 519
works and grace, 445–46
world, narrative, 69–70, 535, 540
Wrede, William, 180f, 352, 354f, 482, 540
Wright, N. T., 540
    and Jesus as an eschatological prophet, 375–77
    Jesus Seminar beliefs and, 359, 362, 363, 364,
        365
    and Jesus Seminar compared to Third Quest, 358f
    key works, 371f, 488
wrong tomb theory of the resurrection, 514–15, 540
Yahweh, 124–25, 317, 488, 504–5, 540
Yata village, *155*
YHWH, 124f
Zacchaeus (tax collector), 114
Zealots, 136–38, 401, 540
Zeitgeist, 386, 540
Zerubbabel, 95